Microsoft Office Programming: A Guide for Experienced Developers

ROD STEPHENS

Microsoft Office Programming: A Guide for Experienced Developers
Copyright © 2003 by Rod Stephens

ISBN (pbk): 1-59059-121-6

Printed and bound in the United States of America 12345678910

Trademarked names may appear in this book. Rather than use a trademark symbol with every occurrence of a trademarked name, we use the names only in an editorial fashion and to the benefit of the trademark owner, with no intention of infringement of the trademark.

Technical Reviewer: John Mueller

Editorial Board: Dan Appleman, Craig Berry, Gary Cornell, Tony Davis, Steven Rycroft, Julian Skinner, Martin Streicher, Jim Sumser, Karen Watterson, Gavin Wray, John Zukowski

Assistant Publisher: Grace Wong

Project Manager: Sofia Marchant

Copy Editor: Scott Carter

Production Editor: Janet Vail

Proofreader: Lori Bring

Compositor: Diana Van Winkle, Van Winkle Design Group

Indexer: Kevin Broccoli

Manufacturing Manager: Tom Debolski

Distributed to the book trade in the United States by Springer-Verlag New York, Inc., 175 Fifth Avenue, New York, NY 10010 and outside the United States by Springer-Verlag GmbH & Co. KG, Tiergartenstr. 17, 69112 Heidelberg, Germany.

In the United States: phone 1-800-SPRINGER, email orders@springer-ny.com, or visit http://www.springer-ny.com. Outside the United States: fax +49 6221 345229, email orders@springer.de, or visit http://www.springer.de.

For information on translations, please contact Apress directly at 2560 Ninth Street, Suite 219, Berkeley, CA 94710. Phone 510-549-5930, fax 510-549-5939, email info@apress.com, or visit http://www.apress.com.

The source code for this book is available to readers at http://www.apress.com in the Downloads section and at http://www.vb-helper.com/office.htm.

For Michelle and Ken

Contents at a Glance

Contents

About the Author

 In a previous incarnation, **Rod Stephens** was a mathematician. During his stint at MIT, he discovered the joys of algorithms and graphics, and has been programming professionally ever since. During his career he has worked on an eclectic assortment of applications spanning such topics as repair dispatch, telephone switch programming, tax processing, and training for professional football players.

Rod has written more than a dozen books that have been translated into half a dozen different languages, and more than 200 magazine articles covering Visual Basic, Visual Basic for Applications, Delphi, and Java. He is currently a columnist for *Hardcore Visual Basic* (http://w.hardcorevisualbasic.com).

Rod's popular Web site, VB Helper (http://www.vb-helper.com) receives several million hits per month and contains more than a thousand pages of tips, tricks, and example code for Visual Basic programmers. The site also contains example code for this book.

About the
Technical Reviewer

 **John Mueller** owns DataCon Services and works as a consultant to small- and medium-sized companies. He is also a freelance author and technical editor. The 61 books and more than 200 articles he has written treat topics ranging from networking to artificial intelligence, and from database management to heads-down programming. Some of his recent books include several C# developer guides, an accessible programming guide, a book on Web Matrix, and several Windows XP user guides. His technical editing skills have helped more than 33 authors refine their manuscripts. John has provided technical editing services to both *Data Based Advisor* and *Coast Compute* magazines. He has contributed articles to a number of magazines, including *InformIT, SQL Server Professional, Visual C++ Developer, Visual Basic Developer*, and *Hardcore Visual Basic*. He is currently the editor of the .NET electronic newsletter for Pinnacle Publishing (http://www.freeenewsletters.com/).

Contact John at JMueller@mwt.net or visit his Web site at http://www.mwt.net/~jmueller.

Acknowledgments

THANKS TO Sofia Marchant, John Mueller, Julian Skinner, Scott Carter, and everyone else who helped assemble this book. Special thanks to Karen Watterson, who's been both editor and friend since I started writing.

CHAPTER 1

Introduction

THE MICROSOFT OFFICE applications are powerful tools for performing everyday office chores such as formatting documents, analyzing data with spreadsheets, and making presentations to justify your salary increase, even though your current project is failing. These applications are also useful for building less work-oriented solutions such as movie databases, checkbook applications, and penny-stock price forecasters.

Although the Office applications are powerful, they have their limitations. Their features are generally applicable to a wide variety of situations, but they cannot anticipate all your specific needs. If you want to use polynomial curve fitting to predict future sales, Excel can do that. If you want to add numerology and horoscopes to your predictions, you're pretty much on your own.

Fortunately, the Microsoft Office applications include a powerful programming language for extending the applications' functionality: VBA (Visual Basic for Applications). Using VBA, you can automate simple repetitive tasks that you would otherwise need to perform manually. VBA includes a full set of looping statements (For, Do While, Loop Until) and control statements (If Then, Else, Select Case) so you can tackle much tougher problems. If you really want to use numerology in your sales forecasts, you can use VBA to do it.

As its title implies, this book is about programming the Microsoft Office XP and Microsoft Office 2003 applications. It tells how you can write everything from simple macros to full-blown applications that interact with several different Office programs, the user, and the operating system. It also explains other methods for making Office applications work together, such as OLE (Object Linking and Embedding).

The book tells when to use each of these techniques and, perhaps more importantly, when not to use them. For example, you could write a macro that capitalizes the first letter of every word in a Word document. Word already has a command for this function, however, so writing your own would be a waste of time.

This Book's Approach

If you scour the bookstores and the Web, you'll discover several books that cover Office programming for a particular application. For example, you'll find books about programming Excel, other books that tell how to program Word, and so forth. You'll even find a few books that talk about VBA programming in general without becoming bogged down in the details of any particular Office application.

Unfortunately, such books assume that you know nothing about Visual Basic (many assume you're a total moron), so they all start at the absolute beginning. They tell you what a variable is, how to declare a variable, how to build a For loop, what an If statement is, and so forth.

If you already know how to use VBA in any Office application, or if you know how to use VBScript or Visual Basic, all this material is wasted. If you already know how to program Word and you want to learn how to program Excel, you get to learn all about comments, variable declarations, subroutines, and the rest all over again. You'll probably buy a 600-page book, skip 450 pages that explain arrays and subroutine declarations, and barely get 150 pages of information out of what's left. Then, if you want to learn about PowerPoint programming, you get to do it all over again.

CAUTION *If you don't already know how to use VBA, Visual Basic, or VBScript, you may find this book a harsh introduction. Walk over an aisle or two (or start a new search if you're buying online) and pick up an introductory Visual Basic book. Even a fast read through will make this book easier to follow.*

This book is a no-nonsense guide to programming Microsoft Office XP and Microsoft Office 2003. It assumes you already know the basics of Visual Basic or VBA programming and don't want to waste time reading about variable declarations again. The goal is to provide as much information about programming each of the Microsoft Office applications as quickly as possible without rehashing the same old material.

The way you use VBA is very similar for all Office applications. Once you understand the basics, you don't need to relearn the same material for each application. The two main things you must learn about a new Office application are its features and its object model. The application's features let you know what's possible. If you don't know that an application can do something, you can't use that feature in your applications.

An application's object model is the collection of objects and methods it exposes for use in your programs. These determine what you can do programmatically with the application. Fortunately, the Microsoft developers included just about everything they could think of in the Office object models, so you can do programmatically pretty much anything you can do interactively and more.

Once you understand the application's features and object model, you are ready to program that application. The early chapters in this book describe general approaches to Office programming. Later chapters concentrate on application features and their object models.

Why You Should Learn Office Programming

Individually, the Microsoft Office applications are powerful but incomplete. Word lets you build nicely formatted documents. Excel lets you analyze data using powerful spreadsheets, formulas, and graphs. PowerPoint lets you thrill and amaze your management with presentations containing annoying animations and irritating sound effects. Access can build a database for tracking bug reports that are never cleared, and Outlook lets you schedule the thirteen weekly progress meetings where you must explain why you aren't getting any work done.

Each of these products is intended for a specific purpose; if you stray too far off course, you can get into trouble. For example, Word is designed to format documents, not to analyze data. Word's table commands let you calculate simple totals and averages, but they are much less flexible than Excel's formulas. Sure you could write some code to calculate standard deviations and hyperbolic cosines, but if you really need those types of functions, you can just use Excel.

Similarly, you could probably coerce Excel or PowerPoint into formatting a text document, but why should you? Word provides a lot more features for wrapping lines and paragraphs, controlling orphan and widow words, indexing, building tables of contents, and performing other typographic tasks. Using Excel to format a text document would be like opening a can of soup with a rock: If you beat on it long enough, it will probably work, but you may not like the result, and you probably won't be eager to repeat the experience. It's better to use the appropriate tool for each task.

The following sections describe some of the advantages Office programming offers. They explain in general terms how you can use Office applications together to build powerful integrated tools for handling common workplace scenarios. The rest of the book provides more detail.

Office Synergy

Although individual Office applications have limitations, together they can form incredibly powerful combinations. Using OLE, you can include features from one application inside another. For example, you can place an Excel spreadsheet inside a Word document or PowerPoint presentation.

You can include these objects either as links to the original file (so the linked view is updated whenever the original changes) or as copies of original files.

You can even double-click on some of these objects to open them using their original application. For example, suppose you include a copy of an Excel spreadsheet in a Word document. If you double-click on the spreadsheet, Word opens the spreadsheet using Excel. You can modify the data and close Excel to update the copy in Word.

With no programming whatsoever, you can use OLE to combine features of more than one Office application. You can consider this as programming the cheap-and-easy way.

NOTE *You can control OLE programmatically, too. You can use VBA to build and manipulate OLE objects at run time.*

Unfortunately, OLE is a rather heavy-handed solution. To use a Word document in Excel, Excel must essentially load Word and all its user interface paraphernalia. If you want to examine the document programmatically but don't need to display it to the user, you can cut out some overhead by using Office automation.

Office Automation

Microsoft has gone out of its way to make the Office applications "automation servers." An automation server is an application that lets other applications use it programmatically. It provides services for automating whatever tasks the server usually performs.

For example, a Visual Basic program can use a Word server to manipulate Word documents. Similarly, a VBA macro in Word can open an Excel spreadsheet and copy data into the spreadsheet's cells. Or a PowerPoint macro can open an Access database and extract data to use for building slides.

A single VBA program could open Access to get a customer list, open Word to print mailing labels for the customers, use Word again to print form letters, and use Outlook to send e-mail messages to the customers to say the form letters were on their way.

Macros and More

All Office applications use VBA as a macro programming language. (Before you curl your lip back in a haughty sneer, be aware that "real programmers" *do* write macros. Real programmers write in every language they can get their hands on. And today's macros are a lot more sophisticated than the original Lotus macros!)

Using VBA, you can automate simple tasks that you might normally perform manually. For example, you could write a verbosifier that translates your ordinary project status documents into manager-speak. It would replace words like *for* with phrases like *for the purpose of*, *to* with *in order to*, and *manager* with *annoyance*. You could do all this by hand but wrapping the steps into a macro would make the process easier.

Macro recorders in most Office applications make it easier to build this kind of macro that combines several simple but tedious tasks. Just turn recording on, make a few substitutions, and turn recording off. Now you can replay the recorded macro with another document to make the same set of substitutions.

 TIP *You can examine the macro's code to see how it works, then use it as a basis for your own macros.*

VBA can automate simple tasks, but it can also perform much more complex functions. VBA is a powerful programming language comparable to Visual Basic, so you can build almost any application you can describe. A VBA program can prompt the user for data, interact with the Windows operating system, upload and download files from the Internet, and even track your stock portfolio in real time.

The Bigger Picture

I once met a guy who was an Emacs Lisp programmer. Emacs is a word processor that generally runs on Unix systems, and it uses Lisp as a macro programming language. That's all this guy did. He wrote macros for Emacs. He could write a pretty fancy macro, and you can find hundreds of Emacs Lisp programs on the Web (chess, hangman, music editors, abacus, interface to French radio, astronomical calculators, you name it).

However, that's hardly enough to fill a résumé. This guy wouldn't stoop to using a "lesser" language such as C, C++, Pascal, Fortran, or even non-Emacs flavors of Lisp. A description of Visual Basic probably would have sent him into uncontrollable fits of laughter. He was happy in his tiny little universe, and that's where he wanted to stay. Since I met him, this guy has probably been dragged kicking and screaming from his lab and into the real world. Now he's probably a Java programmer trying to avoid learning too much about ASP (Active Server Pages).

Emacs Lisp and VBA are both macro languages, but VBA fits into a much larger picture. For starters, VBA is the macro language for several applications (Word, Excel, PowerPoint, and so forth). If you know how to program one, you know the basics of programming them all.

Next, VBA is a large subset of Visual Basic, so if you know VBA, you almost know Visual Basic. Similarly, VBScript (used for ASP) is a subset of VBA, so if you know VBA, you practically know VBScript and ASP programming. You'll need to pick up some details to go from being a Word programmer to an ASP Web developer, but it will be a lot easier than moving from Emacs Lisp to Java or C#. And wouldn't you prefer to have VB, VBA, VBScript, Word, Excel, Access, PowerPoint, and Outlook programming all on your résumé rather than the fact that you wrote an abacus in Lisp?

What This Book Covers (and What It Doesn't)

This book explains how to use VBA to manipulate the Microsoft Office XP and Microsoft Office 2003 applications. It does not explain everything there is to know about *using* each of the different Office applications. It explains some of the applications' more interesting features so you can see how to use them in VBA code, but it doesn't cover every last nook and cranny. Entire books have been written about using these applications, and you should look to those books for that information. For example, the *Step by Step* series published by Microsoft Press is fairly popular (that series includes *Microsoft Word Version 2002 Step by Step*, *Microsoft Excel Version 2002 Step by Step*, *Microsoft PowerPoint Version 2002 Step by Step*, *Microsoft Access Version 2002 Step by Step*, and *Microsoft Outlook Version 2002 Step by Step*).

For Word, Excel, and PowerPoint, this shouldn't be a big deal. Once you know how to display text in *italics* using VBA code (Selection.Font.Italic = True), you should be able to figure out how to display text with ~~strikethrough~~ on your own (Selection.Font.StrikeThrough = True).

On the other hand, Access and Outlook are much more than document editors in the way Word, Excel, and PowerPoint are. Access and Outlook are powerful programming environments in their own rights. Using Access, you can build forms and reports for entering, viewing, editing, and examining data in a database. Access provides its own kinds of controls, macros, and other methods for manipulating data on these forms and reports.

Similarly, Outlook provides its own tools for manipulating the objects it manages. It lets you build forms for creating specific kinds of e-mail messages (expense reports, purchase requisitions, recipes, and whatnot), calendar entries (project meetings, performance reviews), tasks, folders, and so forth.

This book touches lightly on these subjects to provide the context you need to manipulate these programs using VBA. It doesn't go into nearly the depth you would need to take full advantage of the Office applications. It explains how to use Outlook VBA to create a project meeting appointment that happens every Tuesday at 4:00, but to make Outlook do everything it possibly can, you'll need to look elsewhere.

Intended Audience

This is not a beginner's book. If you have never programmed before, you may want to pick up a more general Visual Basic or VBA programming book before you read this one. For example, you might take a look at *Programming Microsoft Visual Basic 6.0* by Francesco Balena (Microsoft Press, 1999) or *Microsoft Visual Basic 6.0 Professional Step by Step* by Michael Halvorson (Microsoft Press, 2002). You don't need to know Visual Basic in excruciating detail, however. If you know how to declare variables, write a For loop, use an If statement, and use a control's properties and methods, then you should have no trouble with this book.

 CAUTION *When you go shopping for an introductory Visual Basic book, be sure you get a book about Visual Basic 6 (or possibly Visual Basic 5). Don't buy a VB .NET book, or you'll also get a wealth of confusion at no extra cost. VBA in Microsoft Office is based on Visual Basic 6. VB .NET, the next generation in the Visual Basic evolution, is extremely different. Its version will undoubtedly be coming to VBA soon, but not in Office XP or Office 2003.*

If you have experience programming in some other language, such as C++ or Delphi, you can probably work through this book with only a little difficulty. If you understand the concepts of declaring variables, writing loops, and using If statements, then you should have no trouble following this book. Some details will be different from the language you're used to, but the ideas will be familiar.

Chapters Overview

Chapter 2, "Macros," explains fundamental concepts you should understand to program the Office applications. It explains the general structure of those applications and how they use VBA as a macro language. It shows how to use the macro recorder to quickly generate simple macros (except in Outlook, which doesn't have a macro recorder).

After you've written a macro, you need some way to execute it. Chapter 3, "Customizing Office," explains different ways you can run a macro or make it easily available to others who need to use your code. It tells how to tie macros to custom toolbar buttons and menu items.

Chapter 4, "Automatic Customization," explains how to make documents that install and remove their own customizations. Depending on your particular needs, some Office applications provide ways to do this automatically. However, the examples in this chapter demonstrate more general techniques you can use to perform actions when the user opens and closes a document.

Chapter 5, "Office Programming the Easy Way: OLE," explains how you can use OLE to avoid some possibly onerous programming chores. Briefly described earlier in this chapter, OLE lets you include the features of one Office application within another. For example, OLE lets you embed an Excel worksheet inside a Word document.

The rest of the book deals mostly with the various Office applications' object models. Chapter 6, "Introduction to Office XP Object Models," discusses features and objects shared by the different Office applications.

Chapters 7 through 10 and Chapter 12 cover the Word, Excel, PowerPoint, Access, and Outlook object models. They describe the objects, properties, and methods you will probably find most helpful in building Office applications.

Chapter 11, "Access and ADO," (ActiveX Data Objects) explains how you can use ADO to manipulate Access databases without using Access itself. ADO doesn't have the user interface that Access provides, so it is a leaner tool for when you want to manipulate a database behind the scenes.

Just as you can use ADO to work with an Access database without Access, you can use MAPI (messaging application programming interface) and CDO (Collaboration Data Objects) to perform many Outlook functions without using Outlook. Chapter 13, "Outlook, MAPI, and CDO," explains how to use MAPI and CDO to carry out several useful Outlook tasks such as sending and receiving e-mail, and working with Outlook folders.

Chapter 14, "Smart Tags," explains how you can build smart tags using Visual Basic .NET. Smart tags let you add context-sensitive features to your document text. For example, whenever the user types the word "VBA" in Word, Excel, or PowerPoint, your smart tag can provide a menu allowing the user to perform related tasks such as connecting to the Microsoft VBA Web site, checking a file server for VBA code snippets, or sending you e-mail.

Chapter 15, "Office 2003," describes developer enhancements provided by Microsoft Office 2003. These include objects for working with XML embedded in Word documents and Excel worksheets, smart tag enhancements, tools for integrating Visual Studio .NET with Office 2003, InfoPath, and smart documents, which take the context-sensitive features of smart tags one step further.

How to Use This Book

Because Chapters 2 through 5 explain fundamental concepts necessary for programming any Office application, you should read those chapters first. This book assumes that you are experienced with either Office or Visual Basic programming, so some of this material may be review for you. For example, if you are a very experienced Word programmer, you may already understand how the Word object model works, so you may not need a more general discussion of object models. Even if you have a lot of experience programming any Office application, you may want to skim these chapters to look for tidbits you don't already know.

After you have read Chapters 2 through 5, you can read the others in any order when you need them. For example, if you need to build a program that automates some task in Excel, read Chapter 8, "Excel." If you want to write a Word macro that extracts text and builds a PowerPoint presentation, read Chapter 7, "Word," and Chapter 9, "PowerPoint."

Same Play, Different Playbook

Although Office applications have much in common, they also have many differences. Certainly, a word processor (Word) and a spreadsheet application (Excel) behave differently in many ways. Even beneath the surface, the Office applications show many dissimilarities.

All Office applications provide an `Application` object that gives a VBA program access to the application's functionality. They all have a concept of a document (a manuscript in Word, a workbook in Excel, a presentation in PowerPoint, a database in Access, and "items" in Outlook). Beyond that, however, the ways you can use each application in a VBA program varies, sometimes widely.

For example, Word allows you to associate code with a document, with the global template Normal.dot, or with some other global template that you create. Excel and PowerPoint, on the other hand, only allow you to store code inside a document (a workbook in Excel or a presentation in PowerPoint). Outlook, which was the last Office application to come into the VBA fold, is undoubtedly the strangest, using Outlook forms and VBScript to build applications while still allowing you to use VBA to program the Outlook environment.

Clearly, Microsoft gave the Office applications' development teams some goals they were all supposed to meet (provide an `Application` object and an object model that gives VBA programmers access to the applications' features), but the different teams came up with slightly different solutions. It's as if they are all working on the same play, but from different playbooks.

Or, perhaps more accurately, it's like asking five artists to paint a picture of a house. Each will produce something that you can recognize as a house, but they'll differ in the details. They'll probably all have some sort of a roof, walls, doors, and windows, but they won't be the *same* house.

Even if the applications used the same approach (where they store VBA code and so forth), they would still have large, obvious differences. Word and Power-Point don't generally need the powerful financial functions and equation solvers that Excel provides. Excel and Word don't really need to record audio and timings as you step through a presentation one slide at a time.

You could probably combine the features of all of the Office applications, but the result would be a huge, bloated monster application that tried to be all things to all people. That would probably be a marketing disaster and would certainly be a maintenance nightmare.

The bottom line is that although you can learn a lot about Office programming in general from Chapters 2 through 5, you still must spend some time with each Office application to learn its foibles and idiosyncrasies. You need to learn the details of how each application supports VBA and how to use the features and tools unique to that application.

You'll see this theme repeated throughout the book, particularly in Chapters 2 through 5. The section that explains how to add custom toolbar buttons and menu items to an Office application points out the most important differences between the different Office applications.

Required Equipment and Software

This book is about Office XP and Office 2003 programming, so to get the most out of it, you will need a copy of Office XP or Office 2003. Obviously, you will need a computer capable of running Microsoft Office, but other than that, you need no special hardware or software to use this book.

Much of this book focuses on Office XP but most of the material will also work with Office 2003. Most of the code will also work with earlier versions of Microsoft Office. Some newer features may not work with older versions of Office, but most of the functionality in the Office object models has been around for quite a while. Most of the code snippets throughout this book were tested with Office 2000 and will probably work in newer and even older versions. The exceptions are Chapters 14 and 15. Chapter 14 explains smart tags, which were introduced in Office XP, so that code won't work with previous versions of Office. Because that code demonstrates new features in Office 2003, it will not run in earlier versions (although it will probably work in future versions). Similarly, Chapter 15 describes features added in Office 2003, so that code won't work in Office XP or earlier versions.

To write Visual Basic programs that manipulate Office applications, you need a copy of Visual Basic. The examples in this book were tested using Visual Basic 6, but they should work with few or no changes in Visual Basic 5.

The Book's Web Site

On the book's Web site (`www.vb-helper.com/office.htm`) you can:

- Download the examples in this book

- Download other Office programming examples

- View updates and corrections

- Read other readers' comments and suggestions

- Contribute your own VBA examples, comments, and suggestions

The book's source code, which is also available in the downloads section on the Apress Web site at `www.apress.com`, includes examples for each chapter zipped into one big WinZip archive. Download this file and unzip it into its own directory. Let WinZip extract the files into separate directories so it can create directories for each chapter.

 NOTE *You can obtain WinZip at* `www.winzip.com`*.*

 FILE *Ch04\MakeButton.doc*

Many of the book's code snippets and figures include a FILE statement similar to this one indicating the file containing the code or the file that produced the figure. For instance, the margin note here indicates that you should look in the Ch04 directory for the file MakeButton.doc.

Contacting the Author

If you have comments, suggestions, corrections, or VBA code to contribute, please e-mail them to RodStephens@vb-helper.com.

The main VB Helper Web site (www.vb-helper.com) contains more than a thousand tips, tricks, and examples, mostly for Visual Basic developers.

Summary

Separately, each Microsoft Office application is powerful but incomplete. Each provides useful tools for performing very specific tasks. VBA programming lets you break the barriers inherent in each application. It lets you extend the capabilities of each application and combine them to take full advantage of each application's strengths.

The following chapters explain how to use VBA to do with code practically anything the Office applications can do interactively. They show how to write code that performs tasks not handled directly by the Office products. They show how to invoke one Office application from code running in another application to take best advantage of both. Using these techniques, you can build solutions that do things never dreamed of by the Office product development teams.

CHAPTER 2

Macros

TRADITIONALLY, A MACRO is a relatively small piece of code that an application can execute to perform some simple task. For example, you could write a macro to build a definition list. The code could give each paragraph a hanging indentation (the lines after the first are indented) and make the words in each paragraph that appear before the first em dash bold. The result might look like this:

Macros—This chapter explains fundamental concepts you should understand to program the Office XP applications.

Customizing Office—This chapter explains different ways you can run a macro or make it easily available to others who need to use your code.

Automatic Customization—This chapter explains how to make documents that install and remove their own customizations.

Office Programming the Easy Way: OLE—This chapter explains how you can use OLE to avoid some possibly onerous programming chores.

Originally, macro languages were relatively simple. By opening up the Office applications' object models to VBA (Visual Basic for Applications), Microsoft has given VBA programmers an extremely powerful programming environment. In an Office application, you can do almost anything programmatically that you can do interactively, and lots more.

NOTE *Actually, there are some other kinds of macros. For example, Access has its own notion of what a macro is, and it's very different from a VBA macro. By making selections from dropdown menus and entering a few values, an Access user can build a sequence of commands that Access calls a macro. Even less experienced Access users can write this type of macro without any programming experience.*

This chapter explains the fundamentals of Office macro programming. It tells you how to create, record, edit, and execute macros.

CAUTION *Largely because Microsoft has integrated VBA so completely into the Office applications, VBA has become a language of choice for less skilled hackers and virus writers. This has given VBA macro programming a lot of bad press in recent years. The section "Guarding Against Macro Viruses" later in this chapter discusses some steps you can take to protect yourself from VBA macro viruses.*

First, however, this chapter explains when you should *not* write macros. In many situations, a simpler solution can save you the time and effort of writing a macro that will later require debugging and maintenance.

When *Not* to Write Macros

The *Rule of Twice* in programming is:

If you need to use a piece of code two or more times, you should put it in a separate subroutine.

For example, suppose you have a program that manages customer account information. In one part of the code, you write some code to create a new record in the account database. Later you discover another piece of code that needs to do the same thing. Rather than rewriting the code or copying and pasting it, you should move it into a separate subroutine that you can call from both places.

Placing code in a subroutine lets you maintain the code in one place rather than two or more. Later, when you find bugs (and you *will*) or you decide to make enhancements, you need to modify the code in only one place instead of hunting down all the places you've used the code, possibly in many applications.

Writing code for Microsoft Office is a bit different from writing end-user applications—in Visual Basic or C++, for example—for several reasons. Even if you will want to do something more than once, it may not be worth the effort of writing VBA code to do it for you. The following sections explain some of the reasons you may *not* want to use VBA to perform certain tasks.

NOTE *Putting the code in a separate routine also makes it easier to reuse it later. I've always found that two of something in programming is suspicious. Often, something either occurs exactly once or it might occur a lot of times. For example, I've written a lot of applications where customer records need to store customer addresses. Sometime during development, the customer says, "Oh yeah. The customer record also needs a separate Billing Address." At that point, we've gone from one address to two.*

Being the cautious type, I generalize the record to hold any number of addresses because I know that next week the customers will want to add a Shipping Address. The following week they'll add a Records Address. Then they'll decide that different shipments may go to different addresses and a single order may be split and shipped to different addresses. By the time all is said and done, they'll probably want the user to be able to define new address types on the fly.

When you see something that needs to be done twice, be suspicious. Some primitive cultures only had numbers for one, two, and many. When designing an application, you often only need one and many.

One-Time Tasks

If you're going to do something only once, it makes no sense to waste a lot of time writing macros to do it for you. Even if you're going to do something similar once or twice more, writing code may not be worth the trouble.

For example, suppose that you're composing a holiday newsletter. You bought nice stationery with evergreens, birds, and snowmen along the borders, and you want the newsletter's printed text to wobble in and out on both sides to follow the outline of the pictures. You could write a program that opened a scanned image of the stationery, scaled it to fit a printed page, determined where the blank areas on the page were, and then formatted the text the hard way by inserting carriage returns to force line breaks and using tabs to position each line on the left. While this might be an entertaining little exercise, it would probably be a huge waste of time (unless, of course, you're paid by the hour).

It would be much easier to simply insert carriage returns and tabs yourself manually. It might not be as much fun as writing an elaborate program but, unless you're planning on sending out similarly formatted newsletters weekly, you would probably be better off formatting the letter manually. You might even finish early enough to mail the letter out before the holiday season is over.

FILE *Ch02\Shaped.doc*

TIP *A relatively simple method for this kind of formatting is to create a Word AutoShape. On the Drawing toolbar (select View ➤ Toolbars ➤ Drawing), open the AutoShapes dropdown, select the Lines command, and pick the Freeform tool. Then draw a shape that covers the left side of the stationery's picture. Now select Format ➤ AutoShape. On the Layout tab, select the Tight Wrapping style. This will make the text automatically wrap around the edges of the shape. Repeat this process for the right side of the paper. Before you print, set the fill and outline colors for both shapes to white so they don't appear in the printed result.*

Even if you need to produce a similar newsletter next year, it's probably better to just do it by hand. If you write a program now, chances are you won't have the foggiest notion of how the code works in a year. If there's a bug, you'll have to spend time relearning code that you probably remember about as well as the double-angle formula from your high school trigonometry class.

Generally, if you're doing something only a couple of times, and you can do it quickly manually, you should probably just do it rather than writing a program to do it for you.

Easy Tasks

For the same reasons, easy tasks don't make particularly good candidates for Office programs. Suppose you want to begin each paragraph in your document with a hard Tab character (a practice I don't recommend). Just hit Tab when you start a new paragraph. Many touch typists do this anyway and breaking them of the habit is hard.

You could probably cook up some code to insert Tabs at the beginning of each paragraph, but it's just not that hard to type your own.

TIP *A better solution is to create a style where paragraphs are formatted to indent the first line. Then you get first-line indentation automatically. As a bonus, you can later change the style's definition to increase or decrease the indentation if necessary without needing to add or remove tabs.*

Or, just type the text without the Tabs and then later use Find and Replace to insert them. Replace the special code ^p (Paragraph) with ^p^t (Paragraph + Tab). You can replace ^p^t^t (Paragraph + Tab + Tab) with ^p^t (Paragraph + Tab) in case you accidentally type a Tab manually. You might also need to do a little cleanup for places like the last paragraph in the document, because you don't want to add a new paragraph containing only a Tab (the first replacement will put one there), but most of the work will be done for you.

Reinventing the Wheel

The Microsoft Office products have been around for a long time, and they do a lot. Each new version of Microsoft Office adds a lot of bells and whistles, and it's entirely possible that a particular whistle will do exactly what you want. It would be a big waste of your time to write a macro to do something that Office can already do for you.

For example, it would be silly to write an Excel macro to calculate the sum of the cells in row A between columns 1 and 10 because Excel's SUM command already does that (SUM(A1:A10)).

Unfortunately, the Office applications have so many features that it's hard to keep track of everything they can and cannot do. If you need to find a quadratic equation to fit some data, Excel can do that. If you want to print addresses on a sheet of Avery standard 2163 mini shipping labels, Word can do it. If you have a hankering to save your PowerPoint presentation as a series of plain HTML Web pages, PowerPoint can do that.

If you want to find a value of X for which $X^2 + 2 * X - 1 = 0$, you can use Excel's Tools ➤Goal Seek command to discover the value 0.414211263. You'll need to do some fiddling around to find the other solution –2.414183834, however. Yes, this is a somewhat esoteric calculation, but it shows how a program sometimes does almost but not exactly what you need.

 FILE *Ch02\SolveQuad.doc*

If you want to find both solutions exactly or without a bunch of guesswork, you're better off writing your own code, either as an equation in an Excel cell or as a macro that calculates the results. The quadratic formula says the two solutions to $A * X^2 + B * X + C = 0$ (where A, B, and C are constants and you want to find a value of X that satisfies the equation) are given by:

$$\frac{-B \pm \sqrt{B^2 - 4 \times A \times C}}{2 \times A}$$

For the equation $X^2 + 2 * X - 1 = 0$ (A = 1, B = 2, C = −1), this gives the values

$$\frac{2 \pm \sqrt{2^2 - 4 \times 1 \times (-1)}}{2 \times 1} = \frac{-2 \pm \sqrt{4+4}}{2} = \frac{-2 \pm 2\sqrt{2}}{2} = -1 \pm \sqrt{2}$$

This formula gives two solutions with values of approximately 0.414213562373095 and −2.41421356237309.

TIP *Before you starting writing code, you should think about whether anyone else in the world might have wanted to do the same thing at some point. If so, check the Office Help files to see if the feature you need is already there. Don't forget to consider all of the Office applications. For example, if you wanted to solve an equation in a Word document, it might be easier to solve it using Excel and then copy or link the result into the Word document rather than writing a general-purpose Word macro to do the job.*

Transferring Data

One common waste of time in Office programming is a VBA program that takes data from one Office application and inserts it into another. The Office applications already have a bunch of commands that import and export data in a variety of formats, so investing time to do this is pointless. Similarly, Word provides mail merge commands that can do things like place address information on letters (perhaps the holiday newsletter described earlier) so you don't want to reinvent that sort of feature.

For a concrete example, suppose you want to copy some data from an Excel spreadsheet into a Word table. You could write a program in Word that uses Excel to open the spreadsheet, exhumes the data, and uses it to build a Word table.

TIP *Actually, this is pretty good practice at working with an Excel server and Word tables. If you're bored, give it a try.*

If you're only going to do this once or twice, however, there's a much easier method. Simply open Word, position the cursor where you want the table, invoke the File ➤ Open command, and select the Excel spreadsheet. Word will ask you whether you want to import the entire spreadsheet or just a range of cells. After you make your selection, the program automatically loads the Excel data and stuffs it into a table.

Easier still, select the data you want in Excel and press Ctrl-C to copy it to the clipboard. Then open Word, position the cursor, and press Ctrl-V to paste the data. Word automatically figures out that this is table-like data so it shoves it into a new table.

The other Office applications also do a pretty good job of figuring out what you mean when you copy and paste. If you copy Excel data and paste it into PowerPoint, PowerPoint puts the data in a new table. Copy a table in Word and paste into a PowerPoint Text object, and PowerPoint displays the data as a run-together text string. If you don't select a Text object, however, PowerPoint puts the data in a new table.

TIP *Before you write code to copy data from one Office application to another, see if copy and paste is good enough.*

The Office applications are also good at opening files of different types. If you open an Excel spreadsheet in Word, Word creates a table to hold the spreadsheet data. Once you have the data in Word, you can copy and paste it into a more familiar format.

OLE (Object Linking and Embedding) lets you include documents from one Office application directly in another. For example, you can insert an Excel spreadsheet directly inside a PowerPoint presentation. In PowerPoint, select Insert ➤ Object. Select the Create From File option, click Browse, select the Excel document you want to insert, and click OK.

NOTE *Before you click OK, check the Link box if you want PowerPoint to link the original Excel document. Later, if the Excel document changes, the data shown in the PowerPoint presentation is automatically updated. If you leave the Link box unchecked, PowerPoint makes its own copy of the data so it is not automatically updated later.*

After you insert the OLE object into the PowerPoint presentation, double-click on it to open the data in its native application (in this case, Excel). You can then use Excel to modify the data. Chapter 5 has more to say about using OLE interactively and programmatically.

Handling Non-Native Data Formats

The Office applications provide a lot of tools for transferring data to and from other Office applications. They also provide quite a few methods for moving data in and out of non-Office applications.

If you need to export data for a non-Office application, try the File ➤ Save As command. Different Office applications can save data in many formats, including:

- Text

- Tab-delimited text

- Comma-separated value (CSV)

- Rich Text Format (RTF)

- Web pages (HTML)

- GIF, JPEG, TIF, and other graphics formats

- XML

Similarly, the different applications can read files saved in a variety of different formats. Just try opening the file and see if it works.

With all of these options available, there's a pretty good chance the Office applications can handle your data import and export needs without any programming. Spend a few minutes experimenting with Office's built-in features before you launch a major development effort. Don't waste your time if the Office developers have already done what you need.

When to Write Macros

Of course, there are many good reasons to write your own code. The most obvious of these is that you want to do something frequently, and the Office applications can't do it for you.

For instance, suppose you want to build a large sign in a comic font where every other letter is adjusted up or down a small random amount and is drawn in a randomly selected color as shown in Figure 2-1 (you can't see the color in the book, but trust me, it's there).

party Next Friday!

Figure 2-1. This text was randomly adjusted by VBA code.

You *could* do this by hand. For each character you would:

1. Select the character.

2. Select Format ➤ Font.

3. Click the Character Spacing tab.

4. Set the Position combo box to Raised or Lowered.

5. Enter the amount you want to move the character.

6. Click the Font tab.

7. Select a random color.

8. Click OK.

If you need a very short sign, this may be practical. For anything longer than a dozen or so characters, this will be mind-numbingly boring. Word doesn't have a tool to do this automatically (it would be a pretty flagrant case of feature proliferation if it did), so you'll have to build your own tool.

The RandomUpDown subroutine shown in the following code demonstrates one method for randomly moving and coloring the characters in the selected text. It begins by calling Randomize to initialize Visual Basic's random number generator.

It then loops through the Selection object's Characters array. For each character, the code uses a With statement to manipulate the character's Font object. It uses a Select Case statement to give the Font a random color, and it uses Rnd to set the Font's Position to a random value between –3 and 3. This positions the character somewhere between three points above and below the line.

 FILE *Ch02\UpDown.doc*

```
' Raise or lower the selected characters
' by a small random amount.
Sub RandomUpDown()
Dim i As Integer

    Randomize
    For i = 1 To Selection.Characters.Count
        With Selection.Characters.Item(i).Font
            Select Case Int(Rnd * 5)
                Case 0:
                    .Color = vbRed
                Case 1:
                    .Color = vbBlack
                Case 2:
                    .Color = RGB(0, 192, 0) ' Green
                Case 3:
                    .Color = RGB(0, 0, 255) 'vbBlue
                Case 4:
                    .Color = vbMagenta
            End Select
            .Position = Int(Rnd * 7 - 3)
        End With
    Next i
End Sub
```

 NOTE *The* Rnd *function returns a value between 0 (inclusive) and 1 (exclusive). That means* Int(Rnd * 5) *returns a value between 0 and 4, and* Int(Rnd * 7 - 3) *returns a value between –3 and 3.*

This code follows roughly the same steps you would take to format the characters manually. For each character, it selects a random color and position.

The objects used by the code (Selection, Selection.Characters, Selection.Characters.Item, and Selection.Characters.Item(i).Font) are part of the Word object model. Chapter 6 has more to say about the Office applications' object models in general. Chapters 7 through 10 and 12 describe individual Office applications' object models in more detail.

Complex Tasks

If a task is particularly complex, you might want to write VBA code to handle it instead of doing it manually even if you plan to do it only once. It's usually easier to debug a VBA subroutine than it is to debug a single statement entered in an Excel cell or a calculated Word field.

For example, suppose you want to calculate a complicated expression for each value in a series. In Excel, you could define the expression for the first value and then copy and paste the definition into each of the other calculated value cells. That's quick and easy, so it's probably a better solution than writing something unnecessarily elaborate.

TIP *To copy and paste a calculation from one cell to many, select the first cell and press Ctrl-C to copy its definition. Then select all of the cells where you want to place the formula and press Ctrl-V. Excel automatically adjusts the expression's parameters as necessary. For example, if you copy the formula =2*A1 from cell A2 into cells B2:H2, then Excel sets the cells' definitions to =2*B1, =2*C1, =2*D1,... =2*H1.*

But what if you need to change the formula? You'll need to type it into the first calculated cell, then copy and paste it into the other cells again. You can do that if you will need to change the formula only once, but what are the odds of that happening? There's no such thing as just one change.

Here's a way to make things easier. Define a function that performs the calculation. For example, the Nth Fibonacci number is defined by:

```
Fibonacci(0) = 0
Fibonacci(1) = 1
Fibonacci(N) = Fibonacci(N - 1) + Fibonacci(N - 2)
```

The first few values are 0, 1, 1, 2, 3, 5, 8, 13, 21, 34. The following function calculates Fibonacci numbers.

```
' Return the Nth Fibonacci number.
Function Fibonacci(ByVal N As Integer) As Double
Dim fib_i_minus_1 As Double
Dim fib_i_minus_2 As Double
Dim fib_i As Double
Dim i As Integer
```

```
    If N <= 1 Then
        Fibonacci = N
    Else
        fib_i_minus_2 = 0
        fib_i_minus_1 = 1
        For i = 2 To N
            fib_i = fib_i_minus_1 + fib_i_minus_2
            fib_i_minus_2 = fib_i_minus_1
            fib_i_minus_1 = fib_i
        Next i
        Fibonacci = fib_i
    End If
End Function
```

Now you can use this function in the calculated cells. For example, cell B2 might contain the formula =Fibonacci(B1). You can fill in many calculated cells by copying and pasting this formula just as you would copy and paste a formula that didn't invoke one of your functions.

Now if you need to change the way the function works, you simply modify the VBA code, return to the spreadsheet, and press F9 to make the spreadsheet recalculate its values. You don't need to explicitly change the calculated cells, because their definitions have not changed. They all still call the Fibonacci function, but that function's definition has changed.

Using VBA code in this manner also lets you define extremely complicated functions relatively easily. The function can use If statements, For loops, While loops, and call other functions that you have written. Doing something similar in a single Excel cell or calculated Word field would be difficult if not impossible.

Building complex functions, even those that just use plain old arithmetic, is sometimes easier in VBA code. You can use the Visual Basic editor to write the function instead of trying to type it into a tiny spreadsheet cell. You can also use the editor to step through the function as it performs its calculations to debug the code.

Throwaway Macros

Throwaway macros deserve some special attention. By their very nature, throwaway macros are used only once or twice and then thrown away. That may make you think you should just perform their task yourself and skip writing any code.

In some cases it's still easier to use VBA code to perform a one-time task. For instance, suppose you want to number the cells in a large Word table so cell (I,J) displays the text "(I, J)" as shown in Figure 2-2.

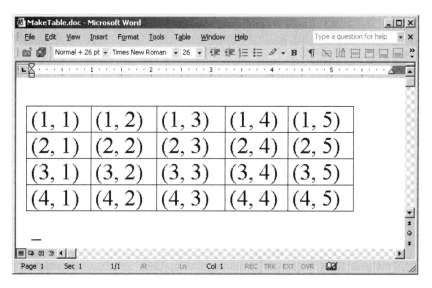

Figure 2-2. VBA code numbered the cells in this Word table.

Subroutine `MakeTableLabelCells` shown in the following VBA code generates tables like this one. The routine begins by looping through the table's rows. For each row, it uses the `Selection.TypeText` command to type the first cell's text for that row. Then for each column after the first, the routine types a `Tab` character and the next cell's value. The code ends each row with a new paragraph.

When it has added all of the table's text to the document, the subroutine moves up the same number of table lines it just created. It extends its selection as it moves, so in the end the new text is selected. The routine then uses the `Selection.ConvertToTable` command to turn the new text into a table. Finally, it uses the `AutoFormat` command to format the table using the style `wdTableFormatGrid1` (a simple grid).

FILE *Ch02\MakeTable.doc*

```
Sub MakeTableLabelCells()
Const NUM_ROWS = 4
Const NUM_COLS = 5
Dim R As Integer
Dim C As Integer
```

```
' Make the table.
For R = 1 To NUM_ROWS
    Selection.TypeText Text:="(" & Format$(R) & ", 1)"
    For C = 2 To NUM_COLS
        Selection.TypeText Text:=vbTab & _
            "(" & Format$(R) & ", " & Format$(C) & ")"
    Next C
    Selection.TypeParagraph
Next R

' Select the text and convert it into a table.
Selection.MoveUp Unit:=wdLine, Count:=NUM_ROWS, Extend:=wdExtend
Selection.ConvertToTable Separator:=wdSeparateByTabs, _
    NumColumns:=NUM_COLS, NumRows:=6, _
    Format:=wdTableFormatNone, ApplyBorders:=True, ApplyShading:= _
    True, ApplyFont:=True, ApplyColor:=True, ApplyHeadingRows:=True, _
    ApplyLastRow:=False, ApplyFirstColumn:=True, ApplyLastColumn:=False, _
    AutoFit:=True, AutoFitBehavior:=wdAutoFitFixed
Selection.Tables(1).AutoFormat Format:=wdTableFormatGrid1, ApplyBorders:= _
    True, ApplyShading:=True, ApplyFont:=True, ApplyColor:=True, _
    ApplyHeadingRows:=True, ApplyLastRow:=False, ApplyFirstColumn:=True, _
    ApplyLastColumn:=False, AutoFit:=True
End Sub
```

You could easily create the table in Figure 2-2 manually. If the table were much larger, however, it would be tedious beyond belief. Making a table with 10 columns and 1,000 rows takes practically no time using subroutine MakeTableLabelCells. Building that table by hand could take quite a while.

Coding for Other Users

One very common reason for writing VBA code is to automate a task for someone else. Although you may be able to handle the complexities of graphing cost versus quantity produced to find an optimal production level, your boss may not. In cases like that, you can build a form that simplifies data entry and generates graphical results.

You can also integrate several Office applications to give your boss a comprehensive presentation package. Your code can automatically generate a Word document reporting the results and a PowerPoint slide show for your boss to show to upper management. All this simplifies your boss's job, reduces his chances to mess things up, and makes him (and you) look good. (If you're a manager, this discussion applies to *your* boss, not to you. If you're a CEO and you don't have a boss, well, this obviously only applies to other companies and not to yours.)

TIP *Sometimes, you can find useful VBA macros on the Web. Try Microsoft's discussion groups or Office development community at* http://msdn.microsoft.com/community/office.asp.

TIP *You can also write startup macros that install buttons for the truly clueless to push to launch your tools. Chapter 4 has more to say about this.*

Writing Macros

Having decided that you want to write a macro, you can proceed a couple ways. First, you can write a macro from scratch. You may need to take this approach when writing a particularly complicated macro. However, often you can take a shortcut by recording a macro similar to the one you want to write and then modifying it.

The following sections explain how to manage macros in Office applications. They tell how to list and execute macros, record macros, set macro security levels, and how to open the Visual Basic IDE (Integrated Development Environment) to edit and debug macros.

In an Office application, if you select Tools ➤ Macro, you'll see four relevant items: Macros, Record New Macro, Security, and Visual Basic Editor. These choices are described in the following sections.

Managing Macros

The Tools ➤ Macro ➤ Macros command opens a Macros dialog that lets you create, view, edit, and execute macros. Figure 2-3 shows the dialog presented by Word. The dialogs are slightly different for other Office applications. These differences are described a little later.

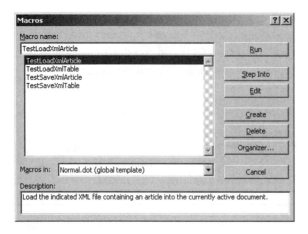

Figure 2-3. Word's Macros dialog lists available macros.

Select a macro and click Run to execute that macro. Click Step Into to start running the macro and go to its first line of code in the Visual Basic IDE. Click Edit to jump to the macro's code in the IDE. Click Delete to delete the selected macro.

While you have a macro selected, you can change its description text by typing in the Description box at the bottom.

Enter a new name in the "Macro name" text box and click Create to make a new macro. This opens the IDE with a new subroutine containing a comment indicating who made the macro and when. For instance, suppose the document's author name is set to Rod (File ➤ Properties ➤ Author field), and you create a new macro named GraphData on December 9, 2002. Then Word generates the following code. The macro's description is initially set to the barely better than useless value, "Macro created 12/9/2002 by Rod."

```
Sub GraphData()
'
' GraphData Macro
' Macro created 12/9/2002 by Rod
'


End Sub
```

In Word, you can use the "Macros in" combo box to select a group of macros. Your choices are:

- **All active templates and documents**—This lists all macros in all open documents and in Normal.dot. That's everything available to you while the current document is open.

- **Normal.dot (global template)**—This lists macros stored in Normal.dot. These macros are always available no matter what documents you have open.

- **Word commands**—This lists commands supplied by Word itself. These are only marginally useful here. For example, you could select the AllCaps macro to capitalize the selected text, but it would be just as easy to use Format ➤ Font and check the "All caps" box.

- **Document1 (document)**—This lists macros stored in the currently active document, in this case Document1.

Unfortunately, the various Office applications have a few differences in the way they handle macro code. Figure 2-4 shows the Macros dialog displayed by Excel.

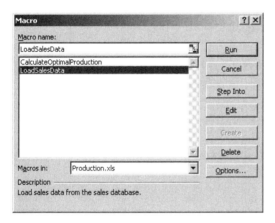

Figure 2-4. Excel's Macros dialog lists macros available in Excel.

Most of the details are the same in the Word and Excel versions of the Macros dialog, but there are two significant differences. First, Excel stores all of its macros with a specific workbook so there is no place to store global macros that corresponds to Word's Normal.dot template. This affects the choices in the "Macros in" combo box. In Excel, you have the following choices:

- **All Open Workbooks**—As you can probably guess, this displays all macros in all workbooks currently open.

- **This Workbook**—This displays macros in the active workbook.

- **Book1.xls, ...**—All loaded workbooks are listed after the This Workbook choice so you can list the macros in any single loaded workbook. Figure 2-4 lists the two macros in the workbook Production.xls.

The second difference between Word's and Excel's Macros dialog is the way in which the dialogs handle macro descriptions. You can see in Figure 2-4 that the LoadSalesData macro's description is in a label, not in a text box. That means you cannot edit it there. Instead you must click Options and enter the description in the text box on the dialog shown in Figure 2-5.

Figure 2-5. The Macro Options dialog lets you enter options for Excel macros.

Although there are differences between how the Office applications handle the details, the general ideas are the same. After you figure out one of these dialogs, you should have little trouble with the others.

Recording Macros

One of the most remarkable features of Office applications is their ability to record your actions and store them in a macro so you can play them back later. For example, you could record a macro while you select a word and make it bold and move to the beginning of the next line. By executing the recorded macro repeatedly, you could quite easily make the first word in a series of lines bold.

Macro recording not only lets you automatically save code to perform simple chores, but it also provides a useful peek into the inner workings of the Office applications. Suppose you want to build a Word macro that formats selected text so its characters are spaced farther apart than normal. You can record a macro while you select Format ➤ Font, click the Character Spacing tab, set Spacing to Expanded, and enter 30pt as the amount to adjust the characters. Now you can look at the recorded macro, shown in the following code, to see how it works.

FILE   *Ch02\SpreadLetters.doc*

```
Sub SpreadLetters()
'
' SpreadLetters Macro
' Spread the letters in the selected text
'
    With Selection.Font
        .Name = "Times New Roman"
        .Size = 12
        .Bold = False
        .Italic = False
        .Underline = wdUnderlineNone
        .UnderlineColor = wdColorAutomatic
        .StrikeThrough = False
        .DoubleStrikeThrough = False
        .Outline = False
        .Emboss = False
        .Shadow = False
        .Hidden = False
        .SmallCaps = False
        .AllCaps = False
        .Color = wdColorAutomatic
        .Engrave = False
        .Superscript = False
        .Subscript = False
        .Spacing = 30
        .Scaling = 100
        .Position = 0
        .Kerning = 0
        .Animation = wdAnimationNone
    End With
End Sub
```

Just by looking at this code, you can see that Word exposes a Selection object
to your VBA code. The Selection object has a Font property that you can use to
modify the text's font. Looking through the properties specified in the recorded
macro, you can easily learn how to modify the text's font name, size, bold, italic,
and other properties.

If you have some experience with Visual Basic or VBA programming (and this book assumes you do), then you can probably guess that you can omit any of these assignments that you do not want to change. For example, if you want to spread out the selected letters without changing the font's other properties, you can reduce the macro to the following code.

FILE *Ch02\SpreadLetters.doc*

```
' Spread the letters in the selected text
Sub ConciseSpreadLetters()
    Selection.Font.Spacing = 30
End Sub
```

If you later wanted to change the code to alter other font properties, such as the font's color or boldness, you wouldn't have too much trouble figuring out how.

Although macro recording is similar in all Office applications that allow it (Outlook does not), the details are slightly different. The following sections explain how to record macros in Word and Excel.

NOTE *This is a common theme in the Office applications. Although they follow the same general approach and provide similar macro capabilities, the details are often slightly different. Same play, different playbooks.*

Recording Word Macros

When you select Tools ➤ Macro ➤ Record New Macro, Word displays the dialog shown in Figure 2-6. Give the macro a descriptive name, select the location where Word should store the macro, and enter a description. Then click OK to start recording.

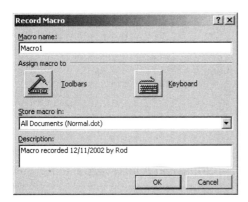

Figure 2-6. Word's Record Macro dialog lets you record actions for later playback.

Word displays the dialog shown in Figure 2-7 while it is recording a macro. Click the ‖● button on the right to pause recording and perform actions that should not be recorded. Click this button again to resume recording. Click the ■ button on the left to stop recording and finish the macro.

Figure 2-7. Word displays this tiny dialog while it records a macro.

If you look again at Figure 2-6, you'll see that the "Assign macro to" area contains two graphical buttons labeled Toolbars and Keyboard. These let you tie the new macro to a toolbar button or a keyboard shortcut. These buttons do the same thing as the Tools ➤ Customize command. You can use them now, but you may find it easier to record the macro first and assign it to a toolbar button or menu item later. Chapter 3 has a lot more to say about this.

Recording Excel Macros

Just as the various Office applications' Macros dialogs are slightly different, their Record Macro and recording dialogs are also different. Figure 2-8 shows Excel's Record Macro dialog.

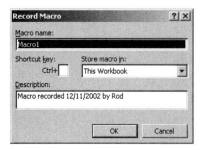

Figure 2-8. Excel's Record Macro dialog is slightly different from Word's (shown in Figure 2-6).

The different Office applications store macros in different locations, so the locations you can select in the "Store macro in" box differ. Excel's Record Macro dialog shown in Figure 2-8 also lets you assign a shortcut key directly, but Word's dialog requires additional steps. The Office applications' macro recording dialogs also vary by application. For example, PowerPoint has no Pause button.

In Excel's macro recording dialog, shown in Figure 2-9, the Pause button is replaced by a Relative Reference button (on the right). This button is unusual enough that it deserves a bit more attention. If you click this button and then record a macro, the macro is relative to the initially active cell.

Figure 2-9. Excel's macro recording dialog has a Relative Reference button instead of a Pause button.

To see how the Relative Reference button works, consider the Excel worksheet shown in Figure 2-10. Note that cell B2 is initially the active cell. Suppose you record a normal macro with the Relative Reference button *not* pressed. You click on cell F2, type "=SUM(", click and drag to select cells B2:E2, type ")", and finally press the ■ button to stop recording. When you finish, cell F2 contains the formula =SUM(B2:E2).

 FILE   *Ch02\Relative.xls*

Figure 2-10. This simple worksheet displays values by quarter and region.

Suppose you now select cell B3 and run the macro. The macro performs *exactly* the same steps as before. It moves the active cell to F2 and assigns it the formula =SUM(B2:E2). Not very useful.

Now suppose you start over with the active cell in B2 again as shown in Figure 2-10. This time you start recording and press the Relative Reference button. You perform the same steps as before, so in the end cell F2 contains the formula =SUM(B2:E2).

This time when you select cell B3 and run the macro, something very different happens. The macro moves the active cell four spaces to the right relative to its current position and lands in cell F3. It then inserts the text "=SUM(", inserts the relative range B3:E3, and closes the formula to get =SUM(B3:E3). This is much more useful than repeatedly inserting exactly the same formula into cell F2.

TIP *In this simple example, you can get the same effect with less work by filling cell F2 with the formula* =SUM(B2:E2) *and then copying and pasting it into cell F3.*

CAUTION *Note that the Relative Reference button remains pressed between macro recordings. If you use it for one macro, it will still be pressed when you record the next macro.*

Aside from the Relative Reference button, the macro recording dialogs used by the different Office applications are pretty similar. You should be able to figure out the differences without too much difficulty.

Guarding Against Macro Viruses

Microsoft has tightly integrated its Office applications by giving them a common macro language (VBA) and by exposing their object models for easy programming. That makes building powerful, comprehensive applications easy. Unfortunately, the fact that Outlook sends and receives e-mail makes writing e-mail viruses easy. The Microsoft Office applications form a powerful workplace tool, but they also form a gateway for every hacker wannabe.

Although Office does not include a hacker-proof system for stopping VBA viruses, it does include three security levels you can use to protect yourself if you know what you are doing. When you select Tools ➤ Macros ➤ Security, Word displays the dialog shown in Figure 2-11. This dialog lets you set the macro security level to High, Medium, or Low. The following sections explain what these levels mean and describe some other steps you can take to protect yourself from VBA viruses.

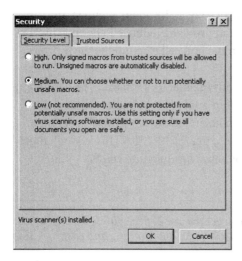

Figure 2-11. The Security dialog lets you decide whether Office applications will run macros.

High Security

When security is set at high, you can run macros only from trusted sources. If a document contains macros that are not digitally signed by a trusted source, Office opens the document and quietly disables the macros.

This is often the best setting for Office users who are not VBA programmers and who don't understand VBA well enough to know whether a macro might install a virus. To protect your naive and trusting users, set their security level at high so they can't run macros from any old Word document they find in the electronic gutters of the Internet.

You can still enable *your* macros for these users by digitally signing your code. A digital signature tells you (and Office) that the code hasn't been modified since it was signed. This means that a hacker has not opened your macros and inserted code to install a virus on the computer.

The signature also includes the name of the person who signed the code. That doesn't prevent the code from installing a virus, but it does give the name of the prime scapegoat if the code trashes someone's computer.

Digital Signatures

To digitally sign your code, you must obtain a digital signature from a *digital signature authority*, which is a responsible company such as VeriSign Inc. (not Billy Bob's Discount Cryptography Emporium). The authority will require you to identify yourself so it can vouch for your identity and include your name in the signature (so users can whine at you if something goes wrong). We wouldn't want just anyone to be able to sign documents with Microsoft's name, for example.

 NOTE *Typically, digital signature services cost a few hundred dollars. VeriSign packages start around $400, but you can add warranty features (that protect you in case your software is compromised) for up to $100,000. For more information on signing code with VeriSign's products, see* http://www.verisign.com/products/signing/code/ *or snoop around their Web site. (I'm not endorsing VeriSign in particular; it is just a well-established digital signature service.)*

Your network security administrator also may be able to generate a digital signature for you depending on how your network's security is configured. Alternatively, you can use the tool Selfcert.exe to sign documents yourself. These kinds of signatures are not as secure as those generated by an authority, because you are essentially verifying your own identity. A hacker could easily generate his own signature with Selfcert.exe using your name and attach it to a document. A self-spreading e-mail virus is unlikely to sign itself using your name, but an evildoer could conceivably forge your name.

For these reasons, you should use self-certified documents only for personal use. If you want to distribute a document widely, you should use a commercial signature authority.

Self-Certifying Code

To self-certify your VBA code, run Selfcert.exe to create a digital signature certificate. This program is probably located at C:\Program Files\Microsoft Office\ Office10\Selfcert.exe (if you installed it when you installed Office). When you run this program, you'll see the form shown in Figure 2-12. Enter the name you want to give the certificate and click OK.

Figure 2-12. Program Selfcert.exe lets you make your own digital signatures.

After you create the digital signature certificate, open the VBA code project you want to sign in the Visual Basic development environment. Select Tools ➤ Digital Signature to open the dialog shown in Figure 2-13.

Figure 2-13. The Digital Signature dialog lets you pick a digital certificate for a VBA project.

When you click the Choose button, the program displays the dialog shown in Figure 2-14.

Figure 2-14. This dialog lets you select a digital certificate for a VBA project.

FILE   *Ch02\SignedVBA.doc*

FILE   *Ch02\SignedVBA.xls*

Select the certificate you want to use to sign the code and click OK. The code's Digital Signature dialog now looks like Figure 2-15. Click the Remove button to remove the code's signature.

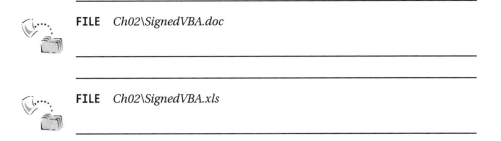

Figure 2-15. The VBA code is attached to a digital signature certificate.

Suppose you try to open a document containing VBA code that is signed with an authenticated digital signature certificate (the next section has more to say about this). If you have security set at high, then Word displays the security dialog shown in Figure 2-16.

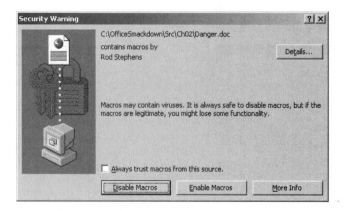

Figure 2-16. Word displays this dialog if security is high and you try to open a document containing signed VBA code.

Click the Details button to learn more about the certificate and to see a view of the certificate similar to the one shown in Figure 2-17. The red circle with the white X in the upper left and the text below it indicates that this certificate is not authenticated. The following section says more about marking your own certificates as authenticated.

If you always want to trust macros from this digital certificate source, click the check box shown in Figure 2-17. Now if you open a document containing macros signed with this certificate, Word will allow those macros to run without any warning.

Click Disable Macros to disable the macros in the document. Click Enable Macros to allow the document to run its macros.

To remove a signature from VBA code, open the Visual Basic IDE and select Tools ➤ Digital Signature to display the dialog shown in Figure 2-15. Then click the Remove button.

If you want to remove the certificate's trusted status so Word again warns you if any document contains macros even if they are signed with the certificate, open Word and select Tools ➤ Macros ➤ Security. Click the Trusted Sources tab, select the certificate as shown in Figure 2-18, and click Remove.

Figure 2-17. This dialog shows an untrusted certificate's details.

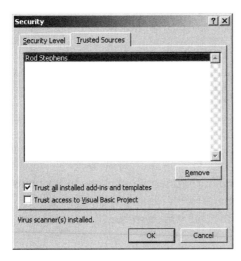

Figure 2-18. This dialog lets you revoke a certificate's trusted status.

Authenticating a Self-Made Certificate

You can mark a self-made certificate as authentic a couple ways. One of the simpler methods uses Internet Explorer. Open Internet Explorer and select Tools ➤ Internet Options. Select the Content tab and click the Certificates button. On the Certificates dialog shown in Figure 2-19, you should see your certificate listed on the Personal tab. Select the certificate, click the Export button, and save the certificate in a file.

Figure 2-19. You can use Internet Explorer to manage certificates.

Next select the Trusted Root Certification Authorities tab, click the Import button, and import the file you just made. After you finish importing the certificate onto the Trusted Root Certification Authorities tab, your system will consider the certificate authenticated.

Now back to the Visual Basic IDE. If you view the certificate again (Tools ➤ Digital Signature, click Choose, select the certificate, click View Certificate), you'll see the view shown in Figure 2-20.

Figure 2-20. This certificate is authenticated.

To remove the authentication from a self-made certificate, reopen the dialog shown in Figure 2-19 (start Internet Explorer, select Tools ➤ Internet Options, go to the Content tab, and click the Certificates button). Go to the Trusted Root Certification Authorities tab, select the certificate, and click Remove.

Signing a Document

You can use digital signature certificates not only to sign VBA code, but also to sign a Word document itself. This ensures that the document has not been modified since it was signed.

If someone modifies the document in any way and tries to save the changes, Word presents the dialog shown in Figure 2-21. If the user continues to save, Word strips off all of the document's signatures.

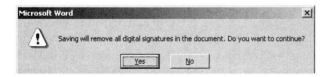

Figure 2-21. If you save changes to a signed document, Word removes the signature.

FILE   *Ch02\SignedDoc.doc*

FILE   *Ch02\SignedWorkbook.xls*

To sign a document, select Tools ➤ Options. Go to the Security tab and click the Digital Signatures button. Click the Add button, select the signature certificate you want to add, and click OK. Figure 2-22 shows the Digital Signature dialog listing the signatures attached to a document.

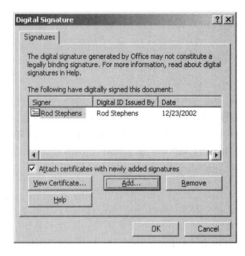

Figure 2-22. The Digital Signature dialog lists the signatures attached to a document.

Medium Security

When security is set at high, Office quietly disables macros unless they are digitally signed. When security is set at medium, Office warns you when you open a document containing macros that might be unsafe. If the macros are signed by a trusted source, they are quietly enabled. Otherwise, you must click the Enable Macros button to allow the macros to run.

Medium is undoubtedly the most useful setting for VBA developers. When you open documents containing macros that you wrote, you can click the Enable Macros button. When you open the recipe for scones that you downloaded from the Internet, you can click Disable Macros. You must use a little more intelligence about which macros you enable or disable than you would if security is set at high, but the medium setting lets you ignore the tortuous steps needed to sign code digitally.

If you download a document that may actually have a valid need to run macros, start by clicking Disable Macros. Next, open the document's VBA code and take a look. Search for `Shell` and `ShellExecute` statements, API function calls, calls to Outlook or other Office applications, anything that uses Web URLs, and any other code that looks the least bit suspicious. If you're *absolutely sure* the code is benign, close the document, reopen it, and click Enable Macros this time (you cannot run the macros if you initially clicked Disabled Macros when you first opened the document).

CAUTION *Do* not *click Enable Macros before you have examined the code! You may think, "I'll enable macros, but I won't run any of them until I look at the code." That won't work, because some Office documents have Open events that execute macros immediately before you can do anything else. As soon as you open the document, this code executes, and a virus could already be installed before you have a chance to look at the code.*

In fact, you should probably regard the presence of Document_Open (in Word) and Workbook_Open (in Excel) in the code as a bit suspicious. If these event handlers are present, take a very close look at them before you open the document with macros enabled.

If you want to be extra safe, you can use WordPad to open potentially hazardous files, such as that 1.2MB joke list your brother-in-law e-mailed to you. WordPad doesn't support macros, so it cannot run them even if you become so used to clicking the Enable Macros button that you do it by accident.

Low Security

When security is set at low, Office silently enables all macros even if they will trash your hard disk and e-mail hundreds of naughty pictures to your boss, spouse, and church group.

Because macros are integrated so deeply into Microsoft Office applications, particularly Outlook, VBA has become a panacea for hackers. Setting your security level at low is just plain suicidal. Any idiot can write a VBA virus, stick it in a document named Playmates_Tell_All.doc, and have thousands of people downloading it and infecting themselves within minutes. You may as well post your credit card numbers on a public bulletin board and get it over with.

If you are developer, it makes much more sense to set security at medium. When you open a document that contains macros, the application warns you, and you can take a look at the code yourself. If your users are inexperienced and vulnerable to macro viruses, tell them to set the security level at high. Or better still, do it for them.

About the only situation in which I can imagine setting the security level at low is on a computer completely isolated from any network that might harbor a virus and is also used by a neophyte who can't handle the complexities of clicking the Enable Macro button. Even in this case, it's only a matter of time before the user brings in a game or other "useful" tool he downloaded from the Internet on a floppy disk, and all is lost.

Application Differences

Naturally, the different Office applications handle security policy differently. For example, if a macro is in Normal.dot, Word quietly assumes it is safe to run. That's not a bad guess, because you probably put the macro in there yourself, but it does seem a bit privileged.

If a macro is in a Word document, the security settings take full effect. If security is set at high, Word refuses to run unauthenticated macros. If security is set at medium, Word warns you that the document contains macros when you open it and asks if you want to enable or disable them. If security is set at low, you get what you deserve.

Because Excel stores all macros in a particular workbook, it has no location for storing trusted macros that corresponds to Word's Normal.dot. That means Excel always behaves as Word does when a macro is stored in a document. If security is set at high, Excel refuses to run unauthenticated macros. If security is set at medium, Excel warns you when you open the document and lets you decide whether it should run macros. If security is set at low, you're just asking for a virus that sends threatening e-mails to the Internal Revenue Service.

Like Excel, PowerPoint has no location corresponding to Normal.dot, so it behaves much as Excel does. PowerPoint doesn't have an Open event that executes code when you open a presentation, so you don't need to worry about that kind of virus. Just for safety's sake, you should still review any VBA code with macros disabled before you enable them.

NOTE *The application checks security when a document is first opened. If you change the security setting, you must close and reopen the document to see any effect.*

Also keep in mind that the security check occurs only when the document is opened. If security is set at medium and you tell the application to allow macros to run, it allows all *macros in the document to run at any time without any further warning. The program won't tell you it is about to run a macro that reformats your hard drive later. It's an all-or-nothing decision when you first open the document.*

More Information on Security

VBA security can be a confusing issue. In case you don't feel you have enough information to be thoroughly confused yet, there's plenty more available on the Web. Here are a few links you can explore:

- `http://office.microsoft.com/downloads/2002/offxpsec.aspx`—The Microsoft publication *Office XP Document: Macro Security White Paper.*

- `http://office.microsoft.com/assistance/9798/virusres.aspx`—Microsoft's Web page *Anti-Virus Resources for Microsoft Office.* Some of this information doesn't apply to all versions of every Office application, but there's a lot of useful stuff here. Be sure to look at the related links section on the right.

- `http://www.sophos.com/virusinfo/whitepapers/office2000.html`—Sophos (antivirus company) article *Microsoft Office 2000 and Digital Macro Signatures.*

The Visual Basic Editor

The final item in the Tools ➤ Macro submenu is Visual Basic Editor. All Microsoft Office applications use the same macro programming language (VBA) and the same IDE. Figure 2-23 shows the Visual Basic IDE in Microsoft Word. The code shows subroutine `MakeArticle`, a function that generates an XML `Article` object. `MakeArticle` is contained in module NewMacros, which is stored in the Normal project. That project is saved with the Normal.dot template so that its modules are available to all Word documents.

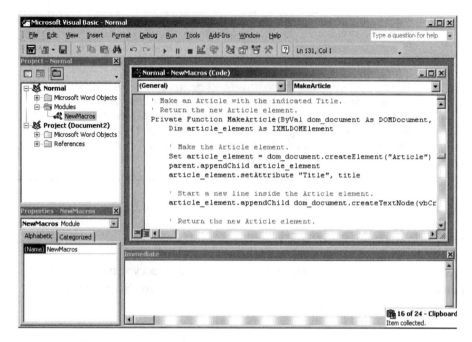

Figure 2-23. The VBA IDE should look familiar to you.

If you're experienced with Visual Basic or VBA, the IDE should look very familiar. You can drag around the different windows (Project, Properties, Immediate,
and so forth) and dock, hide, or display them to suit your personal preferences.
Their basic contents are pretty much the same in any Office application.

You open the IDE the same way in all Office applications, too. Select the
Tools ➤ Macro ➤ Visual Basic Editor command.

Because this book assumes you already know how to program Visual Basic or
VBA, it presumes you know how to use the IDE, so little more is said about it here.
The Project window, however, deserves a little more discussion.

VBA Modules

Visual Basic stores the code in different modules in separate files. For example,
Figure 2-24 shows the Project window for a Visual Basic 6 application. When you
save this project, Visual Basic creates separate files for the frmRegister form, the
PrintingRoutines module, the two classes Customer and Product, and for the project
itself. When you close the project, Visual Basic creates yet another file (with a .vbw
extension) to record the positions of the modules you had open in the IDE.

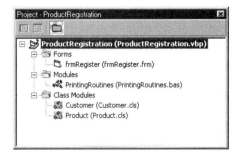

Figure 2-24. Visual Basic 6 stores the code for the different modules in this project in separate files.

Office applications store VBA code inside some other document rather than in separate files. For example, Word keeps code in Word documents and templates. PowerPoint stores code inside PowerPoint presentations. Excel stores code in workbook files. Even if a VBA project contains many code modules, they are all stored in some document.

Figure 2-25 shows the Project window from Word's Visual Basic IDE. At the time, Word had loaded a single document named Invitation.doc. The Invitation project contains a reference to the TemplateProject named GreetingCard because it is based on the GreetingCard.dot template. Word always loads the Normal project shown at the top.

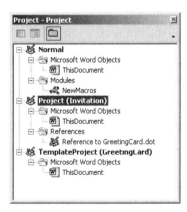

Figure 2-25. This window shows the modules loaded by Word for the document Invitation.doc.

Many of the objects shown in Figure 2-25 can contain code. The ThisDocument module is roughly analogous to a form module in Visual Basic or VBA. It represents a document and provides New, Open, and Close events for the document. For example, if you place the following code in the Normal project's ThisDocument module, Word displays a message whenever you create a new document based on the Normal.dot template.

```
Private Sub Document_New()
    MsgBox "Creating a new document based on Normal.dot."
End Sub
```

If you place a similar event handler in the ThisDocument module in the GreetingCard TemplateProject, Word would display a message whenever you created a new document based on the GreetingCard.dot template.

If you add the same event handler to the Invitation project's ThisDocument module, not much will happen; because that specific file, Invitation.doc, already exists, you cannot create it again. If you place similar code in the project's Document_Open event handler, Word will present a message when you open the file.

The NewMacros module in the Normal project is analogous to a code module (with a .bas extension) in Visual Basic or VBA. You can place macros in this module and call them from other macros, other modules, and even other projects. For instance, suppose the Normal project's NewMacros module contains the SayHello macro shown in the following code.

```
Sub SayHello()
    MsgBox "Hello from NewMacros"
End Sub
```

Then code in the Invitation project's ThisDocument module could call the macro using the following line of code.

```
Application.Run "Normal.NewMacros.SayHello"
```

By default, the SayHello macro is public and is available to code in other modules and other projects. If you want to prevent code in other modules from running the routine, you can declare it with the Private keyword as shown in the following code. Then only other routines in the same module can use the SayHello routine.

```
Private Sub SayHello()
    MsgBox "Hello from NewMacros"
End Sub
```

You can also declare the subroutine with the `Public` keyword if you want to make it absolutely clear that the routine is publicly available.

TIP *It's good programming practice to explicitly declare variables and routines either* `Public` *or* `Private`. *It gives you one less possible source of confusion.*

If you select one of the projects shown in Figure 2-25, you can use the Insert menu to add a `UserForm`, module, or class module to the project. You can then open the new object and add code to it.

Although a project can contain many modules, all code for a project is stored in a single file. Word stores the Normal project's code in the template Normal.dot, it stores the GreetingCard project's code in the GreetingCard.dot, and it saves the code in the Invitation project in the file Invitation.doc.

Excel's Project Window

Excel has no central store for macros that corresponds to Normal.dot. Figure 2-26 shows Excel's Project window while it has two workbooks loaded. Notice that there is no global project corresponding to Normal.dot. Excel stores all macro code in some workbook project.

Figure 2-26. Excel has no project corresponding to Word's Normal.dot.

The Sheet and ThisWorkbook objects shown in Figure 2-26 represent the Excel workbooks and worksheets. Like a form or other object module, they provide event handlers for their objects. For example, if you place the following code in a worksheet's module, Excel beeps every time you give that worksheet the focus.

```
Private Sub Worksheet_Activate()
    Beep
End Sub
```

Similarly, if you place the following code in the SolveQuad.xls project's This-Workbook module, Excel displays a message whenever you open the file Solve-Quad.xls.

```
Private Sub Workbook_Open()
    MsgBox "Welcome!"
End Sub
```

You can add UserForms, modules, and class modules to an Excel project just as you can add them to Word projects using the IDE's Insert menu.

Although a single project can contain many modules, all code in a project is stored in the corresponding workbook file. For example, all modules in the Solve-Quad.xls project are stored together in the file SolveQuad.xls.

PowerPoint's Project Window

Like Excel, PowerPoint has no central storage for code corresponding to Word's Normal.dot. Also like Excel, PowerPoint lets you add UserForms, modules, and class modules to a project. Figure 2-27 shows a PowerPoint project window with the ContainsControls.ppt presentation loaded.

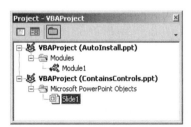

Figure 2-27. PowerPoint projects can contain UserForms, *modules, class modules, and slide modules.*

If a PowerPoint slide contains any controls, it also has a corresponding slide module. This module holds event handlers and other code for the slide. In Figure 2-27, the first slide in the ContainsControls.ppt project contains a control. The corresponding event handler module is Slide1.

Like Excel, PowerPoint stores VBA code in a single file for each project. For example, the presentation file ContainsControls.ppt contains the code for every module in the ContainsControls.ppt project.

Summary

Before you start furiously writing VBA code, make sure you really need to write a macro. One-time tasks and tasks that are easy to do manually are usually not good candidates for encapsulating in a macro. The Office applications are extremely powerful and can do a huge number of things, such as importing and exporting data in a wide variety of formats. Before you start coding, make sure you're not wasting your time duplicating standard Office features.

If you decide you do need to write VBA code, perhaps to perform a complex task or to help someone else do a complicated job, see if you can start with a recorded macro. If you're lucky, you can record much of the code you need so you won't have to write the whole thing from scratch.

Once you've written a macro, you can use the Tools ➤ Macro menu command to manage the macro. You can select it and edit it in the Visual Basic IDE.

Set your Office security to an appropriate level to allow you to run your macros while still protecting yourself from viruses. You may find the high security setting restrictive for your own development use, but it may be appropriate for VBA neophytes and untrained Office users.

The medium security level is usually more appropriate for developers because it lets you enable your macros while disabling those in e-mail messages you receive from disgruntled former coworkers.

Finally, the low security setting is appropriate for computer thrillseekers, those who like experimenting with scrambled hard drives, and those who want an excuse to buy a new computer.

CHAPTER 3

Customizing Office

THERE'S LITTLE POINT in writing or recording a macro if you're never going to use it. One way to invoke a macro is to use the Tools ➤Macro ➤Macros command to open the Macros dialog described in Chapter 2 and shown in Figure 3-1. Select the macro you want to execute and click Run.

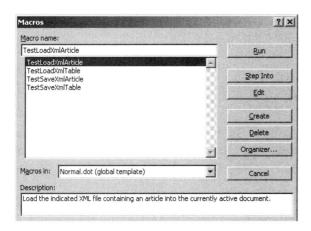

Figure 3-1. You can use Word's Macros dialog to execute macros.

Although this method works, it is somewhat cumbersome. If you have written a lot of macros, finding the right one can be challenging. If you're writing macros for less experienced users to run, forcing them to open this dialog and wander through a list of bewildering choices would be downright cruel.

There are several ways you can make this awkward process easier. First, you can add custom toolbar buttons and menu items that invoke a VBA routine. Instead of opening the Macros dialog and searching for the right routine, a user can simply click the button or invoke the menu item.

You can also tie a macro to a shortcut key. For example, you could make the key sequence Alt-E in Word invoke a VBA subroutine named ShowExpenseForm. This routine would display an expense data form and, after the user clicks OK, it would create a new expense report document using some standardized format that suits your business needs.

This chapter explains how you can use these sorts of customizations to make invoking VBA code easier. It focuses on manually installing customizations. Chapter 4 explains how you can use VBA code to install and remove customizations automatically.

Unfortunately, each Office application handles these tasks in slightly different ways. The basic ideas are the same, but the details are slightly different. Same play, different playbooks.

Customizing Word

Creating custom toolbar buttons and menu items in Word is relatively painless. To start installing a custom toolbar button, menu item, or keyboard shortcut, select Tools ➤ Customize to display the dialog shown in Figure 3-2. The following sections explain how to use this dialog to customize Word.

Figure 3-2. Use Word's Customize dialog to make custom toolbar buttons and menu items.

Keyboard Shortcuts

To bind a macro to a shortcut key, click the Keyboard button shown in Figure 3-2 to display the Customize Keyboard dialog shown in Figure 3-3. Scroll down the left list and select Macros. Then, in the list on the right, select the macro you want to bind.

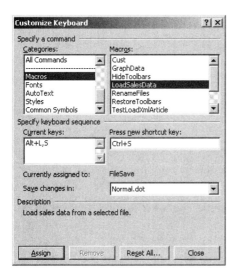

Figure 3-3. The Customize Keyboard dialog lets you bind a macro to a keyboard shortcut.

The "Current keys" list shows shortcut assignments that are already assigned to the macro. In Figure 3-3, Alt-L,S (Alt-L followed by S) is already assigned to the LoadSalesData macro. You can select one of these entries and click Remove to delete that keyboard assignment from the macro.

Click on the "Press new shortcut key" text box and press the key sequence you want to bind to the macro. The "Currently assigned to" label shows what the key sequence currently does, if anything. In Figure 3-3, you can see that Ctrl-S is bound to Word's FileSave method. If you click Assign, Ctrl-S would no longer save the current document; instead it would run the LoadSalesData macro.

 CAUTION *Redefining standard keyboard combinations such as Ctrl-S, or any keyboard combination that users are accustomed to, is risky. The "Currently assigned to" label is a warning that you may be about to confuse users. See the following section for more details.*

Keyboard Confusion

Because Ctrl-S has a standard meaning in most applications (save the current document), changing its definition will almost certainly confuse users. To avoid future headaches, don't reassign a key that already has a standard meaning. Pick a key sequence not already used for something else.

You can also make things less confusing if you use the same key sequences in different Office applications. For example, suppose in Word you make Ctrl-R create a new document based on a performance review template ("R" for Review, get it?). If you make Ctrl-R mean "print a Report" in Excel, users may be confused if they frequently switch between these two applications. It would be better to use similar key sequences for similar purposes.

Unfortunately, the different Office applications provide different capabilities for building keyboard shortcuts. Excel lets you make shortcuts only of the form Ctrl-A and Ctrl-Shift-B. Word allows you to make much more elaborate shortcuts, such as Alt-C, Alt-Ctrl-Shift-D, F5, and Ctrl-E,F (Ctrl-E followed by F). If you want key sequences to match, start with the more restrictive application (Excel in this example) and pick a reasonable sequence there. Then use the same sequence in the more flexible application (Word).

Consider printing out a list of the keyboard shortcuts you have defined and handing them out to your users. Anything you can do to make things less confusing for users now will reduce support calls later.

TIP *In fact, a list of defined key combinations can even help you. If you define more than a couple shortcuts, you'll probably forget some over time.*

Menu Items

To add a custom item to a menu, open the Customize dialog and select Macros in the list on the left as shown in Figure 3-4.

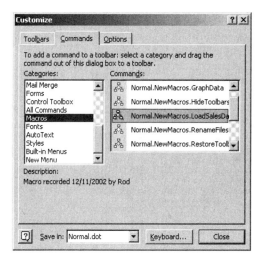

Figure 3-4. To add custom menu items, select the Macros entry in the list on the left.

In the list on the right, find the macro you want to assign. Then click and drag the macro onto Word's top-level menu bar. Hover the mouse over the menu where you want to place the macro and wait until the menu opens. Drag the macro into position in the menu and drop it.

Customizing Menu Items

By default, a new custom menu item shows its completely qualified name. For instance, Figure 3-5 shows a new menu item for the LoadSalesData macro in the NewMacros module contained in the Normal project stored in Normal.dot. You can modify the menu item's appearance to change the text it displays, make it display a button, or change its overall style.

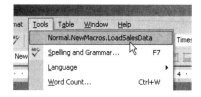

Figure 3-5. Initially, a custom menu item displays a fully qualified path to the macro it executes.

If you closed the Customize dialog shown in Figure 3-4, reopen it using Tools ➤ Customize. Click on the menu that contains the custom menu item to open it. Then right-click on the custom menu item to display the popup menu shown in Figure 3-6. The popup menu holds the commands Reset, Delete, Name, and so forth.

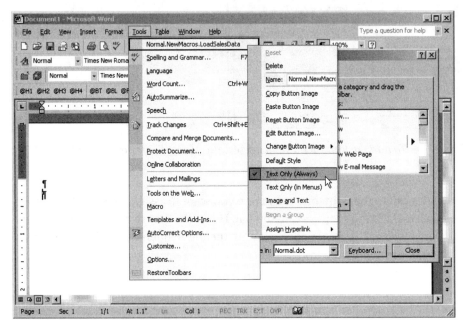

Figure 3-6. Right-click a menu item to customize it.

To change the text displayed in the menu item, click the text box to the right of the Name entry and type the text you want displayed. In this example, you may want to change the entry's name to LoadSalesData or Load Sales Data.

The Copy Button Image, Paste Button Image, and Reset Button Image commands let you borrow images from other menu and toolbar buttons. For example, you can right-click on the File menu's standard Save menu item and select Copy Button Image. If you then right-click on the new LoadSalesData menu item and select Paste Button Image, Word copies the Save button's image onto the new button.

NOTE *Of course the new menu item will display the image only if the item's style (described shortly) is set to display images. Pasting an image onto the item, changing the image with the Change Button Image command, or editing the item's image will automatically switch the item's style from "Text Only (Always)" to "Image and Text." It won't change the style from "Text Only (in Menus)," however. Go figure. If the image doesn't appear, change the style manually.*

The Change Button Image command pops up a menu of several dozen images you can select for the new menu item.

 NOTE *Word includes zillions of other icons, but to get them, you must change the button's image programmatically by using its* FaceId *property. You can also load pictures of your own by setting the button's* Picture *property. Chapter 4 explains how to do this.*

The Edit Button Image command displays the minimalistic button editor shown in Figure 3-7. Click a color to select it, then use the mouse to draw on the large picture. If your first click is on a pixel that already has the color you selected, the mouse erases while you drag it around. If the first click is over any other color, the mouse draws in the color you selected.

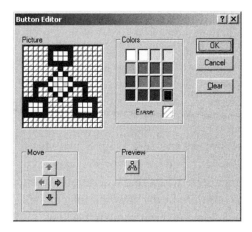

Figure 3-7. Word's spartan button editor lets you modify a button's image.

Unfortunately, the button image editor is very primitive and has no provisions for loading or saving button images to files, selecting areas, copying or pasting, or doing any of the myriad other things you probably expect from a decent graphics editor. Your best bets are to copy and paste an image from another button or use the Change Button Image command to select a standard button image. Then you can modify the image with the editor to get result you want.

NOTE *Again, Chapter 4 explains how you can use code to load a bitmap image from a file into a menu item.*

The Default Style, Text Only (Always), Text Only (in Menus), and Image and Text commands determine how the macro appears in menus and toolbars. The last three options are straightforward, but the first one, Default Style, can be a bit confusing. The Default Style for menus shows the macro's name and button image. In toolbars, the Default Style shows only the image.

In flagrant disregard for the obvious, the Default Style is not the default style when you create a new menu item (or toolbar button). When you first create a menu item or toolbar button, its style is set to Text (Always). This almost makes sense for a menu item (Text (in Menus) would be better) but it seems silly for toolbars. This seems to be fixed in the Office 11 Beta.

You need to right-click and select Default Style to display only the image. Default Style makes more sense when you write code to create menu items and toolbar buttons. In those cases, the code can simply set the new item's style to Default Style to get something reasonable whether the new item is in a menu or toolbar. When the item is in a menu, it displays text and an image. When the item is in a toolbar, it displays only an image.

Toolbar Buttons

Creating toolbar buttons is even easier than creating menu items. Select Tools ➤ Customize to open the Customize dialog shown in Figure 3-4 again. Select Macros from the list on the left and, in the list on the right, find the macro you want to place in the toolbar. Click and drag the macro onto the toolbar where you want it.

Like new menu items, new toolbar buttons initially display their fully qualified names. For example, a button for the LoadSalesData macro stored in the New-Macros module in Normal.dot would display the ungainly title Normal.New-Macros.LoadSalesData. Right-click to modify the text displayed, change the style (toolbar buttons usually have Default Style), edit the button image, and so on exactly as you would for a menu item as described in the previous section.

TIP *You can create your own toolbars and put all your customizations there. You can hide the standard toolbars (use Views ➤ Toolbars and check or uncheck individual toolbar names to show or hide them) and get exactly the tools you use the most. You can easily restore the default toolbars later if you need them.*

Menu Item and Toolbar Button Shortcuts

Once you know how to create custom menu items and toolbar buttons, you can implement a new kind of keyboard shortcut. If a visible item on the active application contains an underlined letter, you can use Alt-<letter> to select that item. For example, in most applications the File menu has F underlined. If you press Alt-F, the menu opens. You can then use Alt-<letter> again to invoke one of the items in the menu. For example, Alt-S saves the current file in Word.

You can use a similar technique to create your own keyboard shortcuts. To create a shortcut for a menu item, place an ampersand (&) before one of the letters in its display text. Word displays that letter underlined without the ampersand, and that letter becomes the item's Alt-<letter> shortcut key.

For instance, suppose you create a new menu named &Macros (Tools ➤ Customize, select New Menu on the left, drag the New Menu item from the right list onto the menu bar). Because the menu's name starts with an ampersand, Word displays its name as Macros.

Now you can add a menu item named &Load Sales Data to the Macros menu. Word would display this item as Load Sales Data. If you hold down the Alt key and press M followed by L, Word opens the Macros menu and then invokes the Load Sales Data item.

Similarly, you can assign an Alt-<letter> shortcut to a toolbar button. Use an ampersand in the button's caption to indicate the letter that should trigger the button. Note that the shortcut will not work unless the button's style is set to display text.

If more than one visible item has the same shortcut key, then pressing Alt-<letter> does not invoke it. Instead, it toggles the focus among the items that share the shortcut. When the one you want is selected, press Enter.

This can make selecting the right item inside a menu tricky, because if you release the Alt key, Word stops looking for accelerators. To select an item in a menu with an ambiguous shortcut key, be sure to hold the Alt key down while you press Enter and any other letters until you have navigated to your final selection.

NOTE *Because all these fingertip gymnastics can be pretty tricky, most users won't bother. Some will use simple key combinations but will just use the mouse if they need to hold down Alt, press the key repeatedly, and hit Enter. You can make things easier by trying hard to ensure that all underlined letters are unique on any given menu.*

Deciding on a shortcut key that is not in use can be tricky because it may depend on the kind of window open at the time. Left to its own devices, Word uses the same menus and toolbars all the time. However, you can hide or show different toolbars and make custom menus, items, toolbars, and buttons. In other Office applications, such as Outlook (which has many different kinds of windows that each has its own menu selections), this can be a big problem.

Creating your own Macros menu and placing all your tools there can make things a little easier. Note that you also can combine all of these techniques. You can make a command available through a menu item, toolbar button, keyboard combination, and Alt-<letter> shortcut. Then users can use the method they find most natural.

Replacing Standard Word Functions

In addition to creating your own custom toolbar buttons and menu items, you can hijack Word's standard functions and replace them with your own VBA subroutines. Overriding standard commands indiscriminately will cause confusion that results in your being paged daily during your vacation. Sometimes, however, it may be worthwhile to add additional functionality to an existing function. For example, you could modify the File ➤ Save command so your code can verify the document's format before saving the user's changes.

Note also that software upgrades may replace any customizations you make with their default actions. Then you would need to reinstall your customizations. If you decide to go ahead anyway, be sure to keep all of the overrides in one place with instructions so you can reapply them later if necessary.

Before you can override Word's standard commands, you must learn what those commands are. One way to do that is to press Ctrl-Alt and the plus sign on the numeric keypad. Find the toolbar button or menu item you want to replace, and click it. That makes Word display the Customize Keyboard dialog shown in Figure 3-8. This figure shows that Word performs the standard New action using the FileNew command.

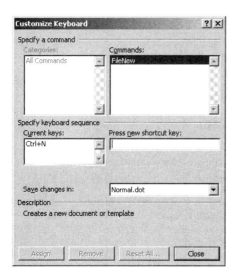

Figure 3-8. Press Ctrl-Alt-Plus and click a menu item or toolbar button to see its definition.

You can also look for standard Word commands by selecting Tools ➤ Customize and clicking the Keyboard button to display the dialog shown in Figure 3-9. Select the category of the command you want on the left. In Figure 3-9, the File category is selected. If you don't know what category you want, select All Commands. After you select a category, scroll through the list on the right to see what commands Word has available.

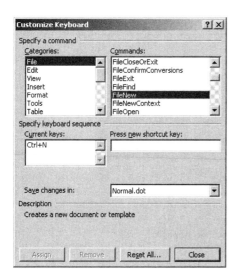

Figure 3-9. Select Tools ➤ Customize and click Keyboard to browse through Word's standard functions.

Once you have found the command you want, you can override it two ways: with a named module or with a named subroutine.

Using Named Modules

The first way you can override Word's standard functions is by creating a standard VBA module named after the command you want to replace. Give this module a subroutine named Main and put the code you want to execute in it.

The following code, placed in a module named `FileOpen`, overrides the File menu's Open command. It prompts the user for a project name, sets the File Open dialog's initial directory appropriately for that project, and then displays the File Open dialog.

 TIP *A more user-friendly application would probably display a list of projects in a combo box on a customized form. Then the user could pick from the list instead of having to type the project name correctly. You could also supply a Cancel button in case the user decides not to open a file after all.*

It may be even better to make this a new menu item or toolbar button and leave Word's standard open command alone.

 FILE *Ch03\BuiltIn.doc*

```
Sub Main()
Dim project_name As String

    ' See which project the user wants to work on.
    project_name = LCase$(InputBox("Project", "Project", ""))

    ' Set an appropriate file open directory.
    If project_name = "amess" Then
        Application.ChangeFileOpenDirectory _
            "C:\Projects\AMess\Current Version\Documents"
```

```
    ElseIf project_name = "foolserrand" Then
        Application.ChangeFileOpenDirectory _
            "C:\Projects\FoolsErrand\Current Version\Documents"
    ElseIf project_name = "ratfink" Then
        Application.ChangeFileOpenDirectory _
            "C:\Projects\Testing"
    Else
        ' Use the current directory.
    End If

    ' Display the file open dialog.
    Application.Dialogs.Item(wdDialogFileOpen).Show
End Sub
```

When you create a new code module, Word initially gives it a catchy name similar to Module1. To rename the module in the IDE, click on it and select View ➤ Properties Window to display the window shown in Figure 3-10. Type the module's new name in the Name property.

Figure 3-10. Select View ➤ Properties Window to rename a module.

As is the case for most operations using Word, you can do the same thing with VBA code.

```
Application.OrganizerRename _
    Source:=ActiveDocument, _
    Name:="Module1", _
    NewName:="FileOpen", _
    Object:=wdOrganizerObjectProjectItems
```

Using Named Subroutines

The second way you can override a standard Word command is to create a VBA subroutine with the same name as the command. You can put the routine in any standard code module.

The following subroutine replaces the `FileSave` command. This code displays a message indicating where you would put validation code if you wanted to check the document's formatting, ensure that necessary data fields were entered, and so forth. It then calls the `ActiveDocument` object's `Save` method to save the document normally.

 FILE *Ch03\BuiltIn.doc*

```
Sub FileSave()
    ' Validate the document's format.
    MsgBox "Validate the document's format here"

    ' Save the document.
    ActiveDocument.Save
End Sub
```

Using New Named Macros

Another way to override a standard Word command is really just a modification on the previous method that uses a named subroutine. This method has two advantages. First, it lets you find and override the standard function in one step. Second, it shows you how the standard Word command works so you can mimic some of its behavior if you like.

Start by selecting Tools ➤ Macro ➤ Macros to open the Macros dialog. In the "Macros in" list, select Word commands. This displays a list of all standard commands available in Word. Scroll through the list and select the command you want to override.

Now, in the "Macros in" list, select the location where you want to save the new macro code. Normally, you would select your current document or Normal.dot if you want to override the command in every Word document.

Finally, click the Create button. Word creates the new macro and gives it the name of the command you want to override. It places the code in the NewMacros module within the project you selected in the "Macros in" list. Word also inserts the code *it* uses to execute the standard command. If you don't change the description entered when you selected the standard command from Word's list, you get the same description, too.

The following code shows an unretouched macro created to replace the File-New command. From this code you can see how to let the user open a new file by using `Dialogs(wdDialogFileNew).Show`.

```
Sub FileNew()
'
' FileNew Macro
' Creates a new document or template
'
    Dialogs(wdDialogFileNew).Show

End Sub
```

Removing Word Customizations

To remove a keyboard shortcut in Word, select Tools ➤ Customize and click the Keyboard button to show the Customize Keyboard dialog in Figure 3-3. Select Macros in the left list and the macro you want to remove in the right list. The "Current keys" list shows the shortcuts you have assigned to this macro. Select the one you want to remove and click the Remove button.

To remove a menu item or toolbar button in Word, select Tools ➤ Customize. Right-click the item you want to remove, and select Delete.

Alternatively, you can drag the item out of its menu or toolbar and drop it somewhere it is not allowed. For example, you can drop it on the Word document, title bar, or the Customize dialog. Figure 3-11 shows the LoadSalesData menu item being dragged over the Customize dialog. The cursor with an arrow, button, and box with an X in it indicates that the item cannot be placed there.

Figure 3-11. To remove a custom toolbar button or menu item, drag it someplace it is not allowed.

Customizing Excel

Customizing Excel is a little different from customizing Word. Although the basic ideas are similar, some details vary. The following sections explain how to make custom keyboard shortcuts, menu items, and toolbar buttons in Excel.

Keyboard Shortcuts

To create a keyboard shortcut in Excel, select Tools ➤ Macro ➤ Macros to display the Macros dialog shown in Figure 3-12.

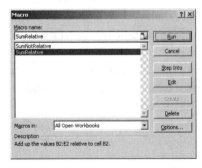

Figure 3-12. Use Excel's Macros dialog to manage macros.

Select the macro you want to assign, then click Options. This displays the dialog shown in Figure 3-13. In the Macro Options dialog, enter the shortcut key you want to associate with the macro. If you enter a capital letter, the dialog automatically adds the word Shift. If you type S, for example, the dialog displays Ctrl+Shift+S.

Figure 3-13. Use the Macro Options dialog to assign a shortcut to an Excel macro.

Excel allows separate macros assignments for upper- and lower-case letters, so you can assign different macros to the shortcuts Ctrl-s and Ctrl-Shift-S.

Menu Items

You create new menu items in Excel much as you do in Word. Select Tools ➤ Customize to display the Customize dialog shown in Figure 3-14. Although this dialog is similar to the one used by Word, there is one big difference. When you select the Macros item in the list on the left, the list on the right does not display a list of available macros. Instead, it displays the two items Custom Menu Item and Custom Button.

Figure 3-14. Excel's Customize dialog is similar to Word's.

To create a menu item, drag the Custom Menu Item object from the list onto the main menu that you want to contain the new item. Hover there until the menu opens. Then drag the new item into position and drop it.

 NOTE *It doesn't matter much whether you use a Custom Menu Item or Custom Button on menus or toolbars; they both do about the same thing. The main difference is their initial appearance. A Custom Menu Item initially displays the name "Custom Menu Item," and the Custom Button initially displays a smiley face button.*

Customizing Menu Items

When you right-click on the new menu item in customize mode, you see the popup menu shown in Figure 3-15.

Figure 3-15. Excel uses this menu to customize menu items and toolbar buttons.

This menu is similar to the one used by Word except for the addition of the Assign Macro command at the bottom. When you select this command, Excel displays the Assign Macro dialog shown in Figure 3-16. Select the macro you want to assign to the menu item and click OK.

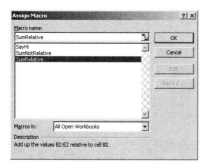

Figure 3-16. Use Excel's Assign Macro command to assign code to a toolbar button.

Toolbar Buttons

To create a new toolbar button in Excel, display the Customize dialog as usual by selecting Tools ➤ Customize. Select Macros in the list on the left. Then click and drag the Custom Button item onto a toolbar and position it where you want it.

Right-click on the new button to change its style, modify the text it displays, copy, paste, and edit its image, and so forth. Use the Assign Macro command to attach the button to a macro.

Removing Excel Customizations

To remove a keyboard shortcut in Excel, open the Macro dialog shown in Figure 3-12 again (Tools ➤ Macro ➤ Macros). Select the macro attached to the shortcut you want to remove and click Options to display the Macro Options dialog shown in Figure 3-13. Select the text in the "Shortcut key" text box and delete it.

You remove a custom menu item or toolbar button the same way you remove these items in Word. Select Tools ➤ Customize. Right-click the item and select Delete to remove it. Alternatively, you can click and drag the item out of its menu or toolbar and drop it somewhere it is not allowed. A cursor with an arrow, button, and box with an X similar to the one shown in Figure 3-11 lets you know where the item cannot be dropped.

Customizing PowerPoint

You make custom menu items and toolbar buttons in PowerPoint in the same way you make them in Word. Use Tools ➤ Customize to open the Customize dialog.

Select Macros on the left and drag the macro you want onto a menu or toolbar. Right-click the newly created item to modify its properties.

Although PowerPoint doesn't have a central location for storing code similar to Word's Normal.dot template, it does let you use code from one presentation while you are designing another. In fact, it will let you use menu items and toolbar buttons that you have attached to any code in any presentation even if you currently have no presentation open.

For example, suppose you have a `MakeJobTable` macro in the presentation Jobs.ppt. You invoke Tools ➤ Customize, select macros on the left, and drag `MakeJobTable` onto a toolbar. Now you close Jobs.ppt so no presentation is loaded. The button you created is still in the toolbar. In fact, if you click the button, it will work despite the fact that the presentation containing the code the button executes isn't loaded. When you click the button, PowerPoint automatically opens Jobs.ppt, digs out the code it needs, and executes it.

The catch is that PowerPoint cannot find the code if you delete or move the file Jobs.ppt. If you delete the file and click the button, PowerPoint displays a message similar to this:

PowerPoint can't run this macro because it can't open C:\OfficeSmackdown\ Src\Ch03\ContainsControls.ppt.

You remove custom menu items and toolbar buttons from PowerPoint just as you do in Word. Open the Customize dialog (Tools ➤ Customize), right-click the item you want to remove, and select Delete. Alternatively, you can drag the item and drop it somewhere is isn't allowed.

Keyboard Shortcuts

Unfortunately, PowerPoint doesn't allow you to create keyboard shortcuts. You can create Alt-<letter> shortcuts by placing an ampersand in the caption displayed by a menu item or toolbar button. For more information, see the section "Menu Item and Toolbar Button Shortcuts" earlier in this chapter.

Customizing Access

Access is not really an end-user tool in the same way Word, Excel, and PowerPoint are. Access is really a programming tool for DBAs (database administrators). It helps you build tables, queries, forms, and reports that you can use to manage the database.

To better understand the difference, think about what the users of these products do. A Word or PowerPoint user composes a more-or-less static document. Once the document is finished, the user can print or display it, but probably won't make changes on a daily basis. An Excel workbook can be somewhat more dynamic, because you may want to make changes to the data over time and let Excel recalculate related values. Often, however, a user creates an Excel workbook to display some data in a report or presentation and it really isn't intended to change daily.

On the other hand, a DBA can use Access on a daily basis to monitor the health of the database and to generate reports that summarize the data. For example, consider a sales database that contains information about customers, orders, inventory, and sales staff. The DBA may run weekly productivity reports to see how much each sales engineer has sold, daily inventory reports to see what supplies are running low, daily order reports to make sure orders are moving through the system, and quarterly sales forecasts to predict future demand. Far from being a static document, the database and its associated forms, reports, and other database tools form a constantly evolving system.

The different focuses of these applications leads to some differences in how you customize them.

Access Macros

Access introduces yet another twist on writing macros and attaching them to menu items and toolbar buttons. To satisfy the more programmatic needs of its users, Access provides more options for writing and executing code. The basic idea is that Access users need powerful programming features but are not necessarily skilled enough to handle the complexities of a programming environment such as VBA by themselves.

To allow users to perform moderately complex tasks, Access includes its own concept of a macro that differs from a simple chunk of VBA code. This is really on the edge of this book's scope because it deals with Access features rather than Office programming. (For comparison, consider instructions for manually indenting paragraphs in Word versus instructions on how to make a VBA program indent the paragraphs.) It's important to understand the difference between the two kinds of macros, however, so this section says a little more about the Access-style macros.

To manage this kind of macro, use Access to select the Macros object category as shown in Figure 3-17. Click the New button at the top to make a new Access-style macro. Select a macro and click Run or double-click the macro to execute it. Select a macro and click Design to open the macro in the Access macro editor.

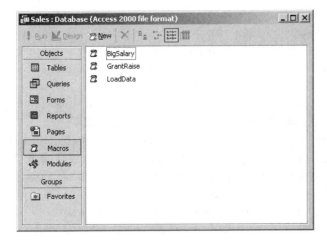

Figure 3-17. Click the Macros object category to manage Access macros.

Figure 3-18 shows the Access macro editor designing a macro named GrantRaise. This kind of macro executes its steps one at a time. In this example, the GrantRaise macro starts by executing the RunCode function. The "Function Name" action argument at the bottom left tells the routine to execute the GiveRaise subroutine. This is a normal VBA subroutine, although RunCode can also execute other Access-style macros.

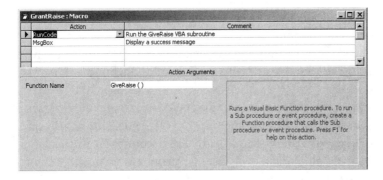

Figure 3-18. The Access macro editor lets you design Access-style macros.

The second statement in the GrantRaise macro is a call to MsgBox. The action arguments, which are hidden because that line isn't selected, tell MsgBox to display the text "Salary increased" with a beep, the information message box icon, and the title "Done."

Access-style macros can be fairly complex, containing branching statements (analogous to If Then statements) and performing complicated tests. Figure 3-19 shows an Access-style macro that validates a ZIP code. If the current record's Country field contains the value USA, and the Zip field has a length other than 5 or 9, the macro displays an error message. The following two lines have an ellipsis (...) in their Condition fields so that they also execute if the previous test succeeds. That means the macro also cancels the current event and stops macro execution.

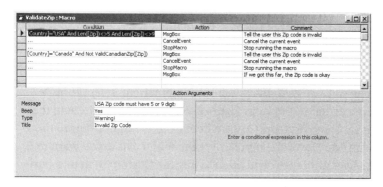

Figure 3-19. This Access-style macro validates ZIP codes.

If the first test fails, the macro continues execution at its fourth line. There it examines the Country field. If the Country is Canada, the test calls the VBA function ValidCanadianZip. That function returns True if the Zip field contains a value of the format A1B 2C3. If this test fails, the macro again displays a message, cancels the current event, and stops running the macro.

The following code shows the ValidCanadianZip function. This code simply uses the VBA Like statement to see if the Zip field contains a string matching the required format. Notice how the Access-style macro's condition code passes the Zip field's value into the function as [Zip].

```
' Return True if the Zip code matches the format A1B 2C3.
Function ValidCanadianZip(Zip As String) As Boolean
    ValidCanadianZip = (Zip Like "[A-Z][0-9][A-Z] [0-9][A-Z][0-9]")
End Function
```

The macro's last line executes if neither of the previous conditions is met. That line simply displays a message saying the ZIP code is valid.

This macro doesn't implement a very robust ZIP code check, but it should give you an idea of how complex some Access macros can be. It also shows how an Access macro can invoke a VBA function (ValidCanadianZip).

Apparently, Microsoft and the Access development team believe that allowing both VBA macros and Access-style macros gives the user extra power and flexibility. In reality, the two styles mostly add to the confusion. Access would be more uniform if it used VBA macros for all of its programming needs. It would be more consistent with the other Office applications and less confusing, at least for Visual Basic and VBA developers.

Menu Items

Now back to customizing Access. To make a custom menu item, select Tools ➤ Customize to display the dialog shown in Figure 3-20. Select the File item in the list on the left. Then click and drag the Custom item from the right list onto the Access top-level menu bar. Hover the mouse over the menu where you want to place the macro and wait until the menu opens. Drag the Custom item into position in the menu and drop it.

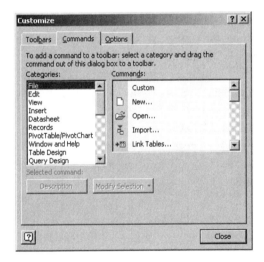

Figure 3-20. Use the Access Customize dialog to make custom toolbar buttons and menu items.

Customizing Menu Items

Initially, the new menu item is labeled Custom and is not attached to any macro. Right-click the item to open the menu shown in Figure 3-21. Change the Name to the text you want the new item to display.

Figure 3-21. Right-click a new menu item to get this customization popup menu.

To attach the item to a macro, right-click the item and select Properties to display the dialog shown in Figure 3-22. In the On Action field, enter the name of the VBA macro you want the new item to execute. Alternatively, you can use the drop-down arrow to select an Access macro for the new item to run.

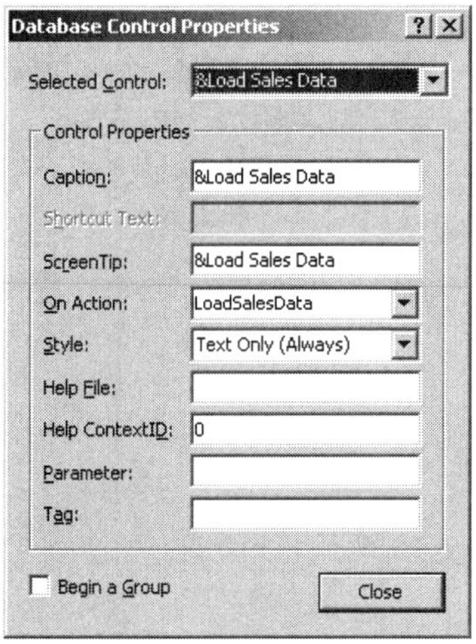

Figure 3-22. The Data Control Properties dialog lets you attach a new menu item to an Access or VBA macro.

The following code shows a simple `LoadSalesData` subroutine that takes no parameters displays a message. You would attach this routine to a menu item as shown in Figure 3-22.

```
Sub LoadSalesData()
    MsgBox "Load sales data here"
End Sub
```

To call a subroutine that needs parameters, open the Database Control Properties dialog and enter the parameter value in the Parameter field as shown in Figure 3-23.

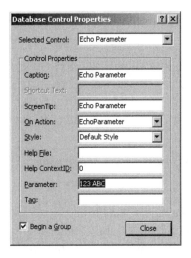

Figure 3-23. Set a subroutine's parameters in the Parameter field.

The subroutine's VBA code should still take no parameters. When it runs, the routine can use `CommandBars.ActionControl` to see what menu item executed it. That object's `Parameter` property gives the parameters you entered in the Data Control Properties dialog. The following code shows a simple subroutine that displays its parameters in a message box.

```
' Echo the button's parameter.
Sub EchoParameter()
    MsgBox CommandBars.ActionControl.Parameter
End Sub
```

Toolbar Buttons

To create a new toolbar button, display the Customize dialog as usual by selecting Tools ➤ Customize. Select File in the list on the left. Then click and drag the Custom item onto a toolbar and position it where you want.

Right-click on the new button to change its style; modify the text it displays; copy, paste, and edit its image; and so forth just as you would with any other Office application.

To bind the button to a macro, right-click on the button and select Properties to open the dialog shown in Figure 3-22. Enter the name of the VBA macro in the On Action box or use the dropdown list to select an Access-style macro for the button to execute.

Keyboard Shortcuts

Just as Access handles menu and toolbar customization differently than the other Office applications do, it also has its own peculiar way for implementing keyboard shortcuts by using an AutoKeys macro group.

To create a macro group, select the Macros objects button as shown in Figure 3-24, then click New. When the new macro form appears, it is initially labeled "Macro1 : Macro."

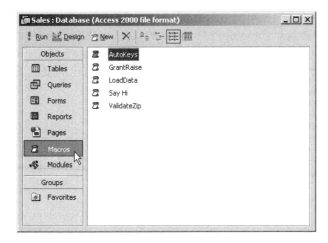

Figure 3-24. Select the Macros object button to manage Access-style macros.

Select View ➤ Macro Names from the main menus to make a Macro Name column appear as shown in Figure 3-25.

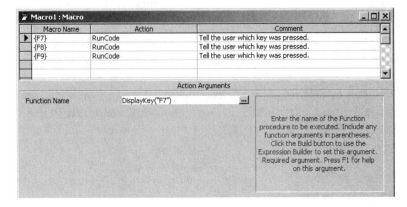

Figure 3-25. View ➤ Macro Names makes the Macro Name column appear.

In the Macro Name column, enter the codes for a key or sequence of keys. You can use four basic kinds of key codes. First, a caret followed by a letter indicates the Control key plus the letter. For example, ^A means Ctrl-A.

Second, the special codes {F1} through {F10} indicate the function keys F1 through F10. Third, the codes {DEL} and {DELETE} mean the Delete key. Finally, the codes {INS} and {INSERT} represent the Insert key.

You can also add ^ to a key code to add the control key to the sequence, or you can add a + to indicate the Shift key. These modifiers allow you to use the same basic key in several different ways. For example, you could have separate actions assigned to Delete, Ctrl-Delete, Shift-Delete, and Ctrl-Shift-Delete. Table 3-1 lists some example key code sequences.

Table 3-1. AutoKeys Key Code Examples

CODE	KEYBOARD COMBINATION
^A	Ctrl-A
{F5}	F5
^{F7}	Ctrl-F7
+{F1}	Shift-F1
^+{F1}	Ctrl-Shift-F1
^+A	Ctrl-Shift-A
^{DEL}	Ctrl-Delete
^+{INSERT}	Ctrl-Shift-Insert

AutoKeys shortcuts have a couple of restrictions. First, you cannot assign keys others than those described here. You cannot assign Alt, Escape, Home, End, and the other keypad keys. You also cannot create multikey combinations the way you can in Word. For example, you cannot assign an action to the sequence Ctrl-X,S.

CAUTION *Note that any AutoKeys assignment you make supercedes any default action the key sequence normally represents. For example, if you assign ^C to some action, you will not be able to use Ctrl-C to copy objects to the clipboard. Similarly, if you assign an action to {DEL}, you will be unable to use the Delete key to delete a selected object or text to the right if the text cursor. (Try it. It's remarkably annoying.) Unfortunately, Access doesn't warn you if you are hiding another key assignment.*

To avoid annoying late-night customer support calls, don't redefine standard keys such as Ctrl-C, Ctrl-X, Ctrl-V, Ctrl-S, Ctrl-O, Ctrl-N, Delete, Insert, and F1. Stick to other function keys such as F9 and shifted key combinations, which are much less common in standard use.

After you enter a key code sequence, enter the action you want the key to perform in the Action column. Enter any parameters necessary for that action in the Action Arguments area. In the example shown in Figure 3-25, the key F7 triggers the RunCode action with the parameter DisplayKey("F7"). That command executes the VBA function named DisplayKey, passing it the string "F7" as a parameter.

All the DisplayKey function does is display a message telling the user which key was pressed (In case the user doesn't know which key he just pressed). The following VBA code shows this function.

```
' Display the parameter string to the user.
Function DisplayKey(txt As String)
    MsgBox txt & " pressed"
End Function
```

You can define other key codes in the Macro form's other rows. The macro group shown in Figure 3-25 defines actions for the F7, F8, and F9 keys.

When you have finished making key assignments, close the Macro form. When Access asks if you want to save the changes, choose Yes. Access then displays an input box asking what you want to name the macro group. Enter AutoKeys and click OK.

TIP *When you close the Macros form and save the changes to the AutoKeys macro, Access will warn you if one of the key codes you entered is invalid.*

As soon as you accept the changes and name the group AutoKeys, the key definitions are ready for use. Press F7, and you should see the message "F7 pressed" (if you have installed the DisplayKey VBA macro).

Removing Access Customizations

Removing customizations from Access is straightforward. Open the customization dialog by using Tools ➤ Customize. Hover the mouse over the menu containing the item until it opens. Then right-click the item and select Delete, or click and drag the item somewhere it is not allowed.

To remove a custom toolbar button, open the customization dialog as before. Then right-click the button and select Delete, or click and drag the button somewhere it is not allowed.

To remove a keyboard shortcut, select the Macros object category. Then select the AutoKeys macro and click the Design button. If you want to change an action's associated keyboard combination, give it a new Macro Name. If you want to delete the action entirely, click the column to the left of the action to select the entire row, then press the Delete key.

Customizing Outlook

Even more than Access, Outlook follows its own path when compared to the other Office applications, and for the same reasons. Like Access, Outlook is a tool for developers so, like Access, Outlook provides a somewhat confusing combination of VBA tools and its own programming tools.

If you think of Outlook as an e-mail application, it may come as a big surprise to you that Outlook is also a developer's tool. Not only does it send and receive e-mail, but it also can manage contact lists, keep track of appointments and other calendar entries, act as a task list, and store miscellaneous notes.

Using Outlook forms, you can design message templates that make the entry of certain kinds of information in a standard format easier. You can use VBScript, another language in the Visual Basic family, to attach code to the forms much as you can add VBA code to VBA forms and Visual Basic code to Visual Basic forms. For example, you can make a standardized requisition form that employees fill out to request supplies.

At the same time, Outlook also allows you to build VBA projects much as you can in other Office applications. With this schizophrenic approach to programming that allows both VBScript and VBA, you might think Outlook would have its own peculiar method for allowing customizations. Fortunately, customization in Outlook works much as it does in Word.

To create a custom menu item, select Tools ➤ Customize to open the Customize dialog. Select Macros on the left and drag the macro you want onto a menu or toolbar. Right-click the newly created item to modify its properties. In particular, the new item initially displays its fully qualified name. For example, an item that invokes the `ListPurchaseRequests` macro in Project1 would display the text Project1.ListPurchaseRequests. You should probably change the item's name to something more appropriate, such as List Purchase Requests.

To create a custom toolbar button, use Tools ➤ Customize to open the Customize dialog again and select Macros. Drag the macro you want onto a toolbar and drop it where you want it. Right-click the new button to modify its appearance. You probably will want to change the button's style to Default Style so it displays a button image rather than a textual description. You may also want to edit the button's image as described earlier in this chapter.

Keyboard Shortcuts

Although Outlook allows you to make custom menu items and toolbar buttons much as Word does, it does not allow you to invent your own keyboard shortcuts. This may be because Outlook provides a huge number of shortcuts. Depending on what kind of window has the focus at the time, Outlook provides approximately 300 different keyboard shortcuts. If you could create your own, you would probably have trouble finding useful combinations that were not already in use somewhere else.

You can still create Alt-<letter> shortcuts by placing an ampersand in the caption displayed by a menu item or toolbar button. For more information, see the section "Menu Item and Toolbar Button Shortcuts" earlier in this chapter.

Removing Outlook Customizations

You remove Outlook customizations much as you remove customizations from Word. Select Tools ➤ Customize to open the customize dialog. Right-click the menu item or toolbar button you want to remove, and select Delete. Alternatively, you can drag the object out of its menu or toolbar and drop it somewhere it is not allowed.

Summary

Although the various Office applications handle customizations differently, they all allow you to create custom toolbar buttons and menu items. These allow you to execute macros much more easily than using Tools ➤ Macro ➤ Macros to open the Macros dialog, selecting the macro you want, and clicking Run.

More importantly, custom toolbar buttons and menu items let relative neophytes use your macros without needing to understand how they work. Many VBA macros are written to make complex tasks easier for less experienced users. It makes little sense to simplify a procedure with a macro and then make invoking the macro difficult. You can install a custom button and let the user invoke the macro with a mouse click.

Of course installing custom toolbar buttons and menu items is itself a relatively complex task that you wouldn't want beginners to tackle on their own. Rather than installing every menu item and toolbar button yourself, you can take the current theme one step further by writing VBA code to automatically install and remove toolbar buttons and menu items. Chapter 4 explains how you can make documents install and remove their own customizations so buttons and menu items are available only when they are most appropriate.

CHAPTER 4

Automatic Customization

USING THE TECHNIQUES described in Chapter 3, you can install buttons and menu items to make using macros easier. That's fine if you're writing macros for your own use, but it can be a real hassle if you're writing tools for someone else.

Suppose you write a routine for use by the two-dozen employees in your finance department. You could write instructions telling the users how to install a button on their toolbars, but you'd probably end up doing it yourself for half of them anyway. You may also waste a lot of time fixing problems that less experienced users caused by accidentally hiding their standard toolbars, deleting the standard buttons they use every day, and turning on the large Office icons.

Installing buttons and menu items also works best with macros that are universally useful. For example, suppose you have a Word macro that inserts the corporate slogan in a specific font. That macro would be useful in many different company documents, so it would be handy to launch with a button.

On the other hand, suppose you write a macro that displays a form in which the user can enter trip expense data. The macro uses the data to create a nicely formatted table and insert it in the current document. This macro is really only useful on trip expense reports. It doesn't make sense on a purchase requisition, meeting summary, or going away party announcement. If you install a button to run this macro in the user's toolbars, the button sits there all the time whether Word is displaying an expense report, requisition form, or lunch menu. You probably don't want the user to click the button while editing a lunch menu.

 TIP *You can make customizations in a template (.dot file), and those customizations show up only in documents attached to the template.*

To make the template, select File ➤ New, select the Template option, and click OK. Make your customizations and save the file in some directory other than the Templates directory (that's for global templates).

To use the template, create a new file or open an existing one. Select Tools ➤ Templates and Add-Ins, click Attach, select the template, and click OK.

The button also takes up some space, which may not be a big deal for one button, but could be annoying if you have a few dozen custom tools loaded. Even when a button is appropriate, the user may have trouble finding it amidst all the clutter. This problem is aggravated by the fact that VBA's button editor is so austere, making it hard to build nice, easily recognizable buttons.

TIP *Sections later in this chapter show how to load a button image from a file. Another interactive trick is to create an image in Microsoft Paint or some other bitmap editor, select the image, and copy it to the clipboard. Then invoke Tools ➤ Customize, right-click the button, and select Paste Button Image.*

You can address these problems a few ways. First, you can make a document install and remove its own customizations when it loads and unloads. This ensures that a document has the buttons it needs available. It reduces the number of buttons you need to keep loaded even though you are not editing a document that can use the button.

A second way you can improve the effectiveness of customizations is to make a macro verify that it is running on the right kind of document before it does anything important. It can see if it is running in an expense report before it trashes your lunch menu.

Finally, you can place buttons and other controls directly inside a document. The document always has the button available even if the user hides every toolbar and fills the menus with hundreds of useless customizations. This also lets you reduce the number of custom buttons on toolbars and menus so the users can find their Tetris button more easily.

These techniques show several approaches to allowing the user to execute VBA code. More importantly, they show techniques for performing actions when the user opens and closes a document. Rather than installing toolbar buttons when the user opens a document, the code could just as easily gather information from the user and search a database to initialize or update the document's text. It could also customize the tools available for different users. Similarly, when the user closes a document, the code could validate information in the document and send updates to databases and other data sources in addition to uninstalling customizations.

In addition to demonstrating these techniques, the examples in this chapter provide a hint of the sorts of VBA programming yet to come. They show how to write and execute VBA code in each major Office application.

Office Application Differences

The following sections explain how you can make different Office applications install and remove custom toolbar buttons and menu items automatically, but that is not always the best solution. All Office applications let you customize their toolbars and menus in more or less the same way, but the details are different in each. They do everything exactly the same way, only differently.

For example, in Word you can add a toolbar button that executes a VBA macro. If the macro is stored globally in Normal.dot, the button is available whenever you open a document that references Normal.dot. On the other hand, if you store the macro in the document's VBA code, the button is available only when that document is loaded. Finally, you can place the code in a customized template so it is available only when that template is attached to the loaded document.

This seems like an ideal situation. If the macro is useful for most documents, place its code in Normal.dot. If it's useful frequently but not universally, put it in a custom template. If you want the macro to apply to only one document, place the code in that document.

If you ever need to modify the code, however, you don't want to have to hunt down every copy of the document and update the code in every one. It would be nice to have the code centralized but still have buttons available only for certain documents.

Excel takes a different approach. When you add a custom toolbar button to Excel, the button is visible whenever Excel runs. Furthermore, the button is tied to a macro in a particular workbook or worksheet, depending on where you place the code. If you load a different workbook and click the button, Excel will try to open the original workbook and execute the macro there.

Access has yet another scheme. If you add a custom button to the Database toolbar, the button is visible no matter what database is loaded. If you click the button while the database containing the button's code is not loaded, Access complains that the macro doesn't exist.

On the other hand, if you give a database a custom toolbar, Access automatically installs and removes the toolbar when you open and close the database. That makes it easy to provide features that apply only to a particular database.

Not particularly consistent.

The following sections explain how to make Office applications install and remove customizations when you open and close documents (or databases or whatever). This approach emphasizes the common features shared by the applications, but it doesn't necessarily guarantee the simplest solution for every application. When you get into this level of customization, you probably will need to experiment a bit with the Office application in question to find the best solution.

This approach does, however, provide you with a good model for performing some action when a document opens and another action when it closes. It also gives you a tour of some of the command bar, menu, and command bar button objects that these applications have in common.

Self-Customizing Documents

You can make customizations automatic by allowing a particular document to install its own buttons and menu items when it opens. When it closes, the document can remove its customizations so they don't clutter up the user's toolbars and menus.

For example, a particular template or document might provide different features for different users. Billing representatives might have access to some features, sales engineers to others, and department managers to more powerful functions.

When the file opens, Word raises the Document_Open event. An event handler can catch this event, check the user's name, and install whatever buttons and menu items are appropriate for that user. Similarly, a Document_Close event handler can remove the buttons and menu items when the user closes the document. A few details must be worked out, but the idea isn't too hard.

Other Office applications use different event handlers when a document is opened or closed. In Excel you can use the Workbook_Open and Workbook_BeforeClose events. In Outlook you can use Application_Startup and Application_Quit. The names are different, but the ideas are similar.

The following sections dealing with Word explain techniques similar to those used to customize the other Office applications, so you should read them even if you aren't planning to use Word in this way.

Word

It's easy to imagine scenarios where a Word document can use specific customization. Any frequently used document that has specific needs can use its own customizations. For example, an employee review template might provide a macro for looking up information about an employee (employee ID, Social Security number, department, phone number, office, and so forth). It makes sense to install this customization only for employee reviews and not for strategic planning documents or garage sale announcements.

The following section explains how a Word document can install customizations when it loads. The subsequent section tells how the document can remove its customizations. You can customize the other Office applications similarly, so you should read these sections even if you aren't particularly interested in Word.

Self-Customizing Word Documents

The natural way to get started with installing buttons using macro code is to record a macro while you install a toolbar button and see how it works. The following code shows a macro recorded while installing a custom toolbar button that invokes the SayHi macro, setting its style to Default Style (display a button only), and using the Change Button Image popup menu item to change its picture to a standard image.

 FILE *Ch04\MakeButton.doc*

```
Sub MakeButton()
'
' MakeButton Macro
' Macro recorded while installing a custom button.
'
    CommandBars("Standard").Controls.Add Type:=msoControlButton, Before:= _
        27
End Sub
```

Unfortunately, this code omits several steps. It shows how to create the button, but the macro doesn't record the steps that set the object's style and change the button's image. It also doesn't give any indication of what macro is assigned to the button. You must learn a bit more about the objects involved in this statement to figure out how to make these modifications. In this case, you can figure out how to customize these objects by using the help files, Visual Basic IDE's IntelliSense feature, and a little trial and error.

A good guess or a little experimentation will tell you that the statement's Before parameter tells where the new button should be created. This code adds the new button before position 27 in the toolbar. This could be a problem if the toolbar doesn't have at least 27 elements. It could also be annoying if the user has a set of custom buttons already in place. Placing the new button in position 27 could split up the user's buttons and make them harder to find.

If you remove the Before parameter from the statement, the new button is placed at the end of the Standard toolbar.

To learn more about the Add statement, set a break point at the beginning of the subroutine in the Visual Basic IDE and press F5 to run the macro. Then type a comma after the statement's last parameter. The IDE's IntelliSense feature will show you a list of parameters the Add method can take as shown in Figure 4-1.

Figure 4-1. IntelliSense tells you what arguments a routine can take.

You can look through the list to figure out what parameters you can use. If you look closely at Figure 4-1, you'll see that the Add method can take the parameters Type, Id, Parameter, Before, and Temporary. With a little experimentation you can probably figure out that these parameters have the meanings shown in Table 4-1.

Table 4-1. CommandBar Controls.Add *Parameters*

PARAMETER	MEANING
Type	The type of control you want to create. This can be one of the constants msoControlButton, msoControlEdit, msoControlDropdown, msoControlComboBox, or msoControlPopup. The following section, "Using Different Control Types," shows how to use each of these control types.
Id	The Id of the standard item you want to install. For example, the Id for the Spelling button is 2 and the Id for the Save button is 3. Omit this argument or set it to 1 to create a new blank item.
Parameter	This parameter is attached to the new item's Parameter property. When the item is invoked, the code can look at this parameter as in the statement MsgBox CommandBars.ActionControl.Parameter.
Before	The control is added before this position in the command bar. If this position doesn't already exist, the code generates the error "Subscript out of range."
Temporary	If you set this to True, the new item is automatically deleted when the Office application closes. If you omit this parameter or set it to False, the item is recreated the next time the Office application starts.

More importantly in this example, the IntelliSense also shows you that the Add method returns a value of type CommandBarControl. To manipulate the newly created item, you should declare a variable with this data type and set it equal to the value returned by the Add method. Because this is an object, you need to use the Set statement.

> **TIP** *As you enter the data type name in the declare statement, IntelliSense will show you possible data types that match what you have typed. You will notice the* CommandBarButton *data type. This is a more specific data type than* CommandBarControl, *and the controls created in these examples are buttons, so that's a better choice.*

Now you can rewrite the Add statement as shown in the following code.

```
' Make a new toolbar button.
Sub MakeButton2()
Dim btn As CommandBarButton

    Set btn = CommandBars("Standard").Controls.Add( _
        Type:=msoControlButton)
End Sub
```

The next step is to figure out how to customize the newly created object btn. Use a With statement to manipulate the btn object. If you type a period inside the With statement, IntelliSense lists the properties and methods provided by the btn object as shown in Figure 4-2. With a little trial and error, you can discover the properties you need to use to customize the button.

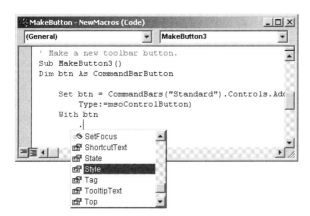

Figure 4-2. IntelliSense lists the properties and methods provided by an object.

The Style property determines whether the button displays an icon, text, or both. When you type .Style =, IntelliSense again comes to the rescue and displays a list of values you can select, as shown in Figure 4-3. This example uses the value msoButtonIcon to indicate an icon only on the toolbar.

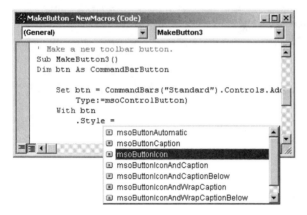

Figure 4-3. When you select a property that takes an enumerated list of values, IntelliSense displays the values.

The btn object's ToolTipText property does exactly what you would imagine: it sets the object's tooltip text. If the user hovers the mouse over the menu item or toolbar button, the tooltip text appears.

The OnAction property gives the name of the macro that runs when object is clicked. The macro can take no parameters, but you can use CommandBars.ActionControl.Parameter to get any data stored in the button's Parameter property.

The Caption property gives the text displayed if the object's style is set to display text. This text also identifies the object in the menu or toolbar that contains it. For example, if you add a button to the Standard toolbar and set its Caption property to People, then your code could later refer to the control as CommandBars("Standard").Controls("People").

One of the more pleasant surprises in the btn object's properties is the Picture property. This is a picture that the control displays if its Style is set to display pictures. Using this property and VBA's LoadPicture method, you can load any picture into a toolbar button or menu item. Although Office provides only a rudimentary button editor, you can create a 16-by-16 pixel button image using any program you like (for example, MS Paint) and then load the picture into the button by using code.

Although the Office button image editor doesn't provide its own means for loading a button image from a file, you can create an image in MS Paint or some other graphics program, select the image, and copy it to the clipboard. Then invoke Tools ➤ Customize, right-click the button, and select Paste Button Image.

TIP *If you are going to install the button on a lot of different users' computers, you may want to store the button image in a directory shared across the network. Then the installation code on each user's computer can load the image from the shared directory.*

The code for creating menu items is very similar. The only real difference between the two kinds of objects is that you may want to set a menu item's Style property to msoButtonCaption so it doesn't display a picture (and, of course, you don't need to load the picture).

The following code shows how a Word program can install a custom toolbar button and menu item when it is opened.

FILE *Ch04\AutoInstall.doc*

```
' Install the Say Hi button and menu item.
Private Sub Document_Open()
Dim btn As CommandBarButton

    ' Create a toolbar button.
    Set btn = CommandBars("Standard").Controls.Add( _
        Type:=msoControlButton)
    With btn
        .Style = msoButtonIcon
        .TooltipText = "Say Hi!"
        .OnAction = "SayHi"
        .DescriptionText = "Execute the SayHi macro"
        .Picture = LoadPicture(ActiveDocument.Path & "\CustomButton.bmp")
        .Caption = "SayHi button"
    End With

    ' Create a Tools menu item.
    Set btn = CommandBars("Tools").Controls.Add( _
        Type:=msoControlButton)
    With btn
        .Style = msoButtonCaption
        .TooltipText = "Say Hi!"
```

```
            .OnAction = "SayHi"
            .DescriptionText = "Execute the SayHi macro"
            .Caption = "SayHi"
        End With
    End Sub
```

Using Different Control Types

The button control type is probably the most commonly used in customizations because it's easy to program, easy to use, and can execute a simple VBA subroutine. The routine can display a `UserForm` if you need to collect extra information from the user.

Sometimes, however, it's more natural to use a combo box, edit box (text box), or popup. The following code shows how to add those controls programmatically to a `CommandBar`.

The `MakeToolbarControls` subroutine begins by deleting the TestControls `CommandBar` if it already exists and creating a new one. Next it creates a button control much as in the previous examples. It sets the button's `FaceId` to 351 to display standard button number 351. It sets the `OnAction` property to "EchoCaption" so the button executes the `EchoCaption` subroutine when it is clicked. It sets the `Caption` property to Button. The button displays only an icon, so the caption is not displayed, but subroutine `EchoCaption` uses it later.

Next the routine creates a combo box (dropdown). It uses the control's `AddItem` method to add items to the list of combo box choices. It sets the control's `OnAction` property to "EchoText" so subroutine `EchoText` executes when the user makes a choice.

`MakeToolbarControls` then creates a popup control, giving it the caption "Suit." It uses the control's `Controls.Add` method to add other controls (in this example, buttons) to the popup.

Finally, `MakeToolbarControls` creates an edit control (text box). It sets the `OnAction` property to "EchoText" to display the text the user enters.

Subroutines `EchoCaption` and `EchoText` are similar. They use the `CommandBars.ActionControl` property to find the control the user is manipulating. They then display the control's `Caption` or `Text` property, respectively.

 FILE   *Ch04\TestControls.doc*

```
' Make some sample CommandBar controls.
Sub MakeToolbarControls()
Dim cbar As CommandBar
Dim cbar_controls As CommandBarControls
Dim new_btn As CommandBarButton
Dim new_cbo As CommandBarComboBox
Dim new_popup As CommandBarPopup
Dim new_edit As CommandBarControl

    ' If the TestControls CommandBar exists, delete it.
    On Error Resume Next
    CommandBars.Item("TestControls").Delete
    On Error GoTo 0

    ' Make the CommandBar.
    Set cbar = CommandBars.Add("TestControls")
    cbar.Visible = True

    ' Make some controls.
    Set cbar_controls = CommandBars.Item("TestControls").Controls

    ' CommandBarButton.
    Set new_btn = cbar_controls.Add(msoControlButton)
    With new_btn
        .FaceId = 351
        .OnAction = "EchoCaption"
        .Caption = "Button"
    End With

    ' CommandBarComboBox.
    Set new_cbo = cbar_controls.Add(msoControlComboBox)
    With new_cbo
        .OnAction = "EchoText"
        .AddItem "Popsicle"
        .AddItem "Ice Cream"
        .AddItem "Cookie"
        .AddItem "Cake"
    End With

    ' CommandBarPopup.
    Set new_popup = cbar_controls.Add(msoControlPopup)
    new_popup.Caption = "Suit"
    With new_popup.Controls.Add(msoControlButton)
```

```
                .FaceId = 481
                .OnAction = "EchoCaption"
                .Caption = "Hearts"
            End With
            With new_popup.Controls.Add(msoControlButton)
                .FaceId = 482
                .OnAction = "EchoCaption"
                .Caption = "Diamonds"
            End With
            With new_popup.Controls.Add(msoControlButton)
                .FaceId = 483
                .OnAction = "EchoCaption"
                .Caption = "Spades"
            End With
            With new_popup.Controls.Add(msoControlButton)
                .FaceId = 484
                .OnAction = "EchoCaption"
                .Caption = "Clubs"
            End With

        ' CommandBarEdit.
        Set new_edit = cbar_controls.Add(msoControlEdit)
        new_edit.OnAction = "EchoText"
    End Sub

' Show the action control's Caption.
Sub EchoCaption()
    MsgBox CommandBars.ActionControl.Caption
End Sub

' Show the action control's Text.
Sub EchoText()
    MsgBox CommandBars.ActionControl.Text
End Sub
```

TIP *The* FaceId *property sets a button's image to a standard button image included with Word. The file Ch04\FaceIds.doc contains the following code that displays 500 buttons with different* FaceId *values. Subroutine* ShowFaceIds *loops through a series of values. For each, it creates a button, sets its* FaceId, *and sets the button's* ToolTipText *property to the* FaceId *so you can get the* FaceId *by hovering over the button.*

Subroutine `ShowFaceIds1_500` calls `ShowFaceIds` to display `FaceIds` between 1 and 500. Change the parameters to view other standard images.

```
' Display FaceIds number min_id through max_id.
Sub ShowFaceIds(ByVal min_id As Long, max_id As Long)
Dim cbar As CommandBar
Dim new_btn As CommandBarButton

    ' If the FaceIds CommandBar exists, delete it.
    On Error Resume Next
    CommandBars.Item("FaceIds").Delete
    On Error GoTo 0

    ' Make the CommandBar.
    Set cbar = CommandBars.Add("FaceIds")

    ' Make some controls.
    For i = min_id To max_id
        With cbar.Controls.Add(msoControlButton)
            .TooltipText = Format$(i)
            .FaceId = i
        End With
    Next i

    ' Display the CommandBar.
    cbar.Visible = True
    cbar.Height = Application.Height * 0.75
End Sub

' Show FaceIds 1 through 500.
Sub ShowFaceIds1_500()
    ShowFaceIds 1, 500
End Sub
```

Removing Word Customizations

Once you've figured out how to install custom toolbar buttons and menu items, it's relatively simple to figure out how to remove them. Begin by recording a macro while you remove a custom button. The following code shows such a macro.

FILE *Ch04\RemoveButton.doc*

```
Sub RemoveButton()
'
' RemoveButton Macro
' Macro recorded while removing a custom button.
'
    CommandBars("Standard").Controls(26).Delete
End Sub
```

Notice that the code finds the button it is removing by its position in the tool-bar, in this case 26. That would be a horrible way to locate the button in code that automatically uninstalls a button. If the user customizes Word, the toolbar may have more or fewer buttons, or this particular button may be in a different position in the toolbar. Blindly removing button number 26 is more likely to be wrong than right.

You can use the button's Caption property as an index to the Controls collection. Changing the index to the button's caption allows the code to remove the button no matter where it appears in the toolbar.

NOTE *More than one button might have the same* Caption. *In that case, the* Controls *collection returns the first control with that caption. Of course, this is one reason it's a bad idea to give two controls the same* Caption.

The following code shows how a Word document can remove the toolbar button and menu item installed by the code in the previous section. This code uses an On Error Resume Next statement to ignore errors if either the button or menu item is missing, which can happen if the user removes the items manually or if you remove one while testing the macro.

TIP *Using* On Error Resume Next *is a rather heavy-handed way to protect your code. By ignoring all errors, you may mask unexpected bugs that you should fix. You may want to use a more detailed error handler that at least records the error so you can decide later if a real problem exists.*

FILE   *Ch04\AutoInstall.doc*

```
' Uninstall the Say Hi button and menu item.
Private Sub Document_Close()
    On Error Resume Next
    CommandBars("Standard").Controls("SayHi button").Delete
    CommandBars("Tools").Controls("SayHi").Delete
End Sub
```

Excel

Word and Excel both allow you to automatically install and uninstall customizations. Although they work similarly, the details are slightly different in a couple of respects.

First, Excel doesn't automatically expose the CommandBars object, so you must refer to the Application object's CommandBars property explicitly, as the following code does.

```
Set btn = Application.CommandBars("Standard").Controls.Add(" _
    Type:=msoControlButton")
```

Second, Excel provides a Workbook_Open event but no Workbook_Close event. You must use the Workbook_BeforeClose event instead.

The following code shows how an Excel workbook can automatically install and uninstall a toolbar button.

TIP *Notice how the* Workbooks_Open *code places the call to* Controls.Add *directly inside the* With *statement so it doesn't need to use a separate variable for the new button. This makes the code a bit more concise and avoids the need for the* btn *variable. If you need to refer to the button later or you find this code more confusing, however, you may want to use a separate variable.*

FILE   *Ch04\AutoInstall.xls*

```
' Install the Say Hi button.
Private Sub Workbook_Open()
    ' Install a button.
    With Application.CommandBars("Standard").Controls.Add( _
        Type:=msoControlButton)
        .Style = msoButtonIcon
        .TooltipText = "Say Hi!"
        .OnAction = "ThisWorkbook.SayHi"
        .DescriptionText = "Execute the SayHi macro"
        .Picture = LoadPicture(ActiveWorkbook.Path & "\CustomButton.bmp")
        .Caption = "SayHi button"
    End With

    ' Install a menu item.
    With Application.CommandBars("Tools").Controls.Add( _
        Type:=msoControlButton)
        .Style = msoButtonCaption
        .TooltipText = "Say Hi!"
        .OnAction = "ThisWorkbook.SayHi"
        .DescriptionText = "Execute the SayHi macro"
        .Caption = "SayHi"
    End With
End Sub

' Uninstall the Say Hi button.
Private Sub Workbook_BeforeClose(Cancel As Boolean)
    On Error Resume Next
    Application.CommandBars("Standard").Controls("SayHi button").Delete
    Application.CommandBars("Tools").Controls("SayHi").Delete
End Sub
```

PowerPoint

A PowerPoint project doesn't have a module representing the presentation itself. That means there is nothing comparable to Word's Document_Open event handler or Excel's Workbook_Open event handler.

Fortunately, the Application object provides a PresentationOpen event. Unfortunately, there is no module corresponding to the Application object, so you cannot use it until you create an instance of the Application object. That means you can catch an event when you open a presentation, but not until you make an

`Application` object. Of course the Application object needs to be declared and instantiated in code somewhere, so you must open a presentation to load code to do all that. This gives you a sort of, "Which came first, the chicken or the egg?" dilemma; you must open a presentation before you can detect the opening of a presentation.

One way around this catch-22 is to create an Add-In.

PowerPoint Add-Ins

A PowerPoint Add-In is nothing more than a normal PowerPoint presentation that has been compiled into an executable form. To make an Add-In, create a fresh presentation. Add whatever code you want in the Add-In to VBA modules.

Two particularly useful routines in an Add-In are `Auto_Open` and `Auto_Close`. If you define those routines in a standard .bas module inside the Add-In template's code, PowerPoint automatically executes them when the Add-In is opened and closed respectively. This happens when the user manually loads and unloads the Add-In, and when PowerPoint starts and stops (assuming the Add-In is loaded).

Typically, you put Add-In startup code in `Auto_Open` and cleanup code in `Auto_Close`.

TIP *Before you compile the Add-In, you might want to digitally sign the code. See the "Digital Signatures" section in Chapter 2 for more information on this.*

When you have finished building your Add-In, select File ➤ Save As. In the "Save as type" combo box, select "PowerPoint Add-In (*.ppa)" and save the file. PowerPoint compiles your code and saves it in an executable Add-In.

If your code doesn't compile correctly, PowerPoint will complain. Try executing your subroutines interactively to verify that they work before you try making the compiled Add-In.

CAUTION *Although you can convert a presentation to an Add-In, you cannot convert an Add-In back to its presentation. After you finish writing the Add-In code, save its presentation somewhere safe. Don't lose it, or you won't be able to make changes to the Add-In later.*

Making Opened and Closed Events

The key feature of PowerPoint Add-Ins that makes them useful here is that an installed Add-In runs before a presentation opens. This means that the Add-In can declare a reference to the `Application` object by using the `WithEvents` keyword and catch its events.

First, create a new presentation. Add a class module and change its name to `OpenWatcher` (click the new module, select View ➤ Properties Window, and change the module's Name property).

Add the following code to the OpenWatcher class module. This code declares a variable named `TheApp` of type `Application`. The `WithEvents` keyword means the module can catch events raised by the `TheApp` object.

Subroutine `TheApp_PresentationOpen` is the event handler for the `TheApp` object's `PresentationOpen` event. This routine receives as a parameter the presentation object `Pres` that is being opened. Subroutine `TheApp_PresentationOpen` uses the new presentation object's `Application.Run` method to execute a macro.

The macro's name is the name of the presentation followed by an exclamation mark and the word "Opened." For example, if you open a presentation named Sales2003.ppt, then the macro's name is Sales2003.ppt!Opened. This name makes the code try to execute the `Opened` macro in the newly opened presentation. If you leave off the name of the presentation, the code could execute an `Opened` macro in some other open presentation.

Note that the code protects itself with an `On Error Resume Next` statement in case the newly opened presentation doesn't contain an `Opened` macro. If the presentation contains an `Opened` macro, it executes. If it doesn't have an `Opened` macro, the Add-In does nothing.

 TIP *Again, consider using a more robust error handler that checks for other possible errors. This version wouldn't know if the* Opened *routine tries to run but has a problem.*

Subroutine `TheApp_PresentationClose` works just as `TheApp_PresentationOpen` does, but it detects when a presentation is closing. This routine invokes the presentation's `Closed` macro.

 TIP *Remove the comment character from the* MsgBox *statement to see when the Add-In catches a* PresentationOpen *event.*

FILE *Ch04\OpenWatcher.ppt*

```
' Declare the variable to catch events.
Public WithEvents TheApp As Application

' A presentation is being opened.
Private Sub TheApp_PresentationOpen(ByVal Pres As Presentation)
'     MsgBox "OpenWatcher: TheApp_PresentationOpen"

    ' Run the presentation's Opened macro.
    On Error Resume Next
    Pres.Application.Run Pres.Name & "!Opened"
End Sub

' A presentation is being closed.
Private Sub TheApp_PresentationClose(ByVal Pres As Presentation)
'     MsgBox "OpenWatcher: TheApp_PresentationClose"

    ' Run the presentation's Closed macro.
    On Error Resume Next
    Pres.Application.Run Pres.Name & "!Closed"
End Sub
```

The OpenWatcher module defines a class that can look for the `Application` object's `PresentationOpen` event, but the Add-In still doesn't have an instance of the class. To create an instance, add a standard BAS module to the Add-In presentation and enter the following code. This code declares a module-level variable named `m_OpenWatcher` of type `OpenWatcher`.

The `Auto_Open` event handler sets this variable to a new `OpenWatcher` object. It then sets the variable's `TheApp` property to a reference to the current application object. Now the `OpenWatcher` object is ready to catch `PresentationOpen` events.

The `Auto_Close` event handler cleans up by setting the `TheApp` reference to `Nothing` and then setting `m_OpenWatcher` to `Nothing`.

TIP *Remove the comment characters from the* `MsgBox` *statements to see when the Add-In is opened and closed.*

FILE *Ch04\OpenWatcher.ppt*

```
Private m_OpenWatcher As OpenWatcher

' The Add-In is opening.
' Set a WithEvents reference to the Application.
Sub Auto_Open()
'     MsgBox "OpenWatcher: Auto_Open"

    Set m_OpenWatcher = New OpenWatcher
    Set m_OpenWatcher.TheApp = Application
End Sub
' The Add-In is closing.
' Clean up.
Sub Auto_Close()
'     MsgBox "OpenWatcher: Auto_Close"

    Set m_OpenWatcher.TheApp = Nothing
    Set m_OpenWatcher = Nothing
End Sub
```

After you have entered all the code, save the presentation as OpenWatcher.ppt. Then use File ➤ Save As to save the file as the PowerPoint Add-In file OpenWatcher.ppa.

Using the Add-In

Before you can use the Add-In, you must install it. In PowerPoint, select Tools ➤ Add-Ins to display the dialog shown in Figure 4-4. Click the Add New button, select the new Add-In, and click OK. Then click Close to close the Add-Ins dialog.

Now you can finally tell when the user opens a particular presentation. Simply give the presentation an Opened macro. When the user opens the presentation, the OpenWatcher Add-In catches the PresentationOpen event and calls the presentation's Opened subroutine.

Give the presentation a Closed macro to take action when the presentation is closed.

The following code shows how a program can install a custom button and menu item when it is opened. The Closed subroutine removes these controls when the presentation closes. The code is very similar to that used by a Word or Excel document.

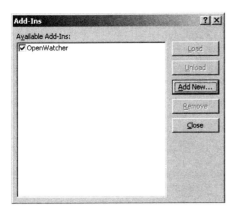

Figure 4-4. This dialog installs PowerPoint Add-Ins.

FILE   *Ch04\AutoInstall.ppt*

```
' This routine is called by the OpenWatcher Add-In.
' Install the Say Hi button and menu item.
Sub Opened()
'     MsgBox "Opened"

    ' Install a button.
    With Application.CommandBars("Standard").Controls.Add( _
      Type:=msoControlButton)
        .Style = msoButtonIcon
        .TooltipText = "Say Hi!"
        .OnAction = "SayHi"
        .DescriptionText = "Execute the SayHi macro"
        .Picture = LoadPicture(ActivePresentation.Path & "\CustomButton.bmp")
        .Caption = "SayHi button"
    End With

    ' Install a menu item.
    With Application.CommandBars("Tools").Controls.Add( _
      Type:=msoControlButton)
        .Style = msoButtonCaption
        .TooltipText = "Say Hi!"
        .OnAction = "SayHi"
        .DescriptionText = "Execute the SayHi macro"
        .Caption = "SayHi"
```

```
        End With
End Sub


' This routine is called by the OpenWatcher Add-In.
' Uninstall the Say Hi button and menu item.
Sub Closed()
'     MsgBox "Closed"

    On Error Resume Next
    Application.CommandBars("Standard").Controls("SayHi button").Delete
    Application.CommandBars("Tools").Controls("SayHi").Delete
End Sub


' Display a message box.
Sub SayHi()
    MsgBox "Hi"
End Sub
```

Access

Philosophically, there is a big difference between Access and the Office applications earlier in this chapter: Word, Excel, and PowerPoint. Typically, people who use these programs are end users. For example, a Word user uses Word to write printed documents.

Access users, on the other hand, come in two distinct classes: end users and database administrators (DBAs). End users generally manage the database by using forms, reports, and other tools that the DBA builds. The DBA builds and maintains the database in addition to creating these end user tools.

Even so, your customization tasks are about the same as they are for Word. You want to add menu items and command bar controls to make the user's lives easier. Although a decent DBA can handle the installation of these tools, there's no reason to make the process harder than necessary.

Custom Toolbars

Philosophical issues about end users and DBAs aside, making custom toolbars for a particular database is practically trivial in Access. Select Tools ➤ Customize to open the Customize dialog, and click the Toolbars tab. Click the New button and enter a name for the new toolbar as shown in Figure 4-5.

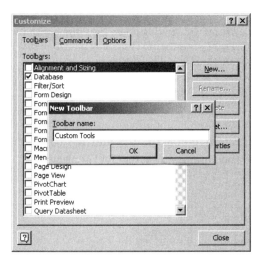

Figure 4-5. The Customize dialog lets you build custom toolbars.

Click OK to make the new toolbar. Initially, the toolbar will be a tiny floating window detached from the other toolbars. Find it and drag it to a position you like. Drag it to the bottom of the other toolbars to attach it to the rest. Next click on the Commands tab and add buttons to the new toolbar manually as described in Chapter 3.

That's all there is to it. This toolbar is associated with the current database. When you open the database, Access displays the toolbar. When you close the database, Access removes the toolbar.

If all you want to do is attach a toolbar to a database, that's the end of the story. To keep this chapter consistent for each of the Office applications, the following sections explain how you can use VBA code to add and remove toolbar buttons and menu items. You can use the same techniques to perform other tasks when Access opens and closes a database.

AutoExec

As Chapter 3 explains, Access has its own type of macro that is not VBA code. An Access-style macro contains a series of statements that Access should execute when it reaches a certain condition. For example, you can build an Access form (which is not the same as a VBA form) and when the form loads, Access can execute an Access-style macro.

If you give a database a special Access-style macro named AutoExec, Access executes that macro when it loads the database. This macro can perform startup tasks such as installing custom menu items and buttons, initializing data structures, checking a file or Web site for updates, and so forth.

NOTE *You can bypass this startup process by holding down the Shift key when you open the database. Start Access and press Ctrl-O to display the Open dialog. Then hold the Shift key while you double-click a database to open it. Access opens the database without executing its AutoExec macro.*

To make an AutoExec macro install custom toolbar buttons and menu items, give it a single RunCode action and specify the parameter Customize() as shown in Figure 4-6.

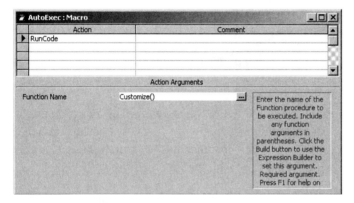

Figure 4-6. This AutoExec macro invokes the Customize *VBA function.*

Next give the database the Customize VBA function shown in the following code. This code adds a new toolbar button and menu item. The controls' OnAction commands make both controls invoke the SayHi macro when the user clicks them.

FILE *Ch04\AutoExec.mdb*

```
' Install the Say Hi button and menu item.
Function Customize()
Dim btn As CommandBarButton

    ' Create a toolbar button.
    Set btn = CommandBars("Database").Controls.Add( _
```

```
            Type:=msoControlButton)
    With btn
        .Style = msoButtonIcon
        .TooltipText = "Say Hi!"
        .OnAction = "SayHi"
        .DescriptionText = "Execute the SayHi macro"
        .Picture = LoadPicture(CurrentProject.Path & "\CustomButton.bmp")
        .Caption = "SayHi button"
    End With

    ' Create a Tools menu item.
    Set btn = CommandBars("Tools").Controls.Add( _
        Type:=msoControlButton)
    With btn
        .Style = msoButtonCaption
        .TooltipText = "Say Hi!"
        .OnAction = "SayHi"
        .DescriptionText = "Execute the SayHi macro"
        .Caption = "SayHi"
    End With
End Function
```

Note that the Access Visual Basic development environment does not auto-matically include a reference to the Office programming objects that you need to execute this code. Without this reference, Visual Basic won't know what a CommandBarButton object is.

To set the reference, open the Visual Basic IDE. Then select Tools ➤ Refer-ences, check the entry named "Microsoft Office 10.0 Object Library," and click OK.

Opened and Closed Events

Using an AutoExec macro to perform database startup actions is reasonable. It's a poor solution for installing custom toolbar buttons and menu items, however, because there's no corresponding "AutoClose" macro for Access to run when it closes a database. That means there's no code for removing the customizations when the database closes.

You could make the customization code for every database remove any cus-tom buttons before installing its own. That would still leave the customizations installed when no database was loaded or when you started a new database. It would also mean adding customization code to every database whether it needed its own buttons or not. Besides, it seems inelegant to make every database contain code to fix problems created by a single other database.

A better solution is to add a hidden form to the Access application. Then you can use that form's Load and Unload events to add and remove customizations.

Start by creating the form. Click the Objects display's Forms category. Next double-click the "Create form in Design view" item (or click the New button and select Design View for them method of creating the new form). This form will be hidden, so you don't need to add any controls to it, and you can shrink it to a reasonably small size if you want.

Right-click on the form and select Properties. In the combo box at the top of the Properties window, select Form. This combo box is only one item tall, so you may need to click on it and then use the arrow keys to find the Form entry.

After you pick the Form entry, select the Event tab and click on the On Load entry. At this point Access displays a dropdown arrow and an ellipsis (...) for that entry as shown in Figure 4-7.

Click the ellipsis to display the Choose Builder dialog shown in Figure 4-8. When you select Code Builder and click OK, Access makes a new code module and attaches it to the form. It builds an empty Form_Load event handler, binds it to the form's On Load event, and opens the code editor so you can edit the event handler. The following code shows the code Access initially creates.

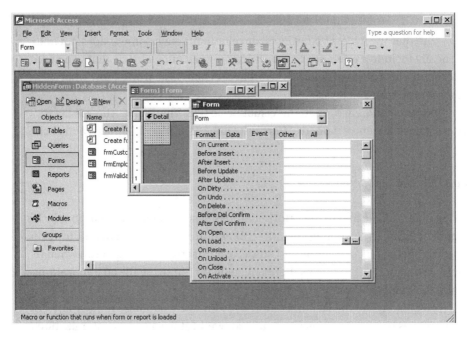

Figure 4-7. When you select the On Load event, Access displays a dropdown arrow and an ellipsis.

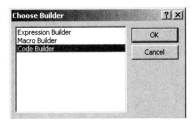

Figure 4-8. Use the Choose Builder dialog to attach VBA code to an event.

```
Option Compare Database

Private Sub Form_Load()

End Sub
```

Add code to the empty event handler so it installs the database's custom toolbar button and menu item.

Repeat these steps to create an Unload event handler. Return to the Properties window, select On Unload, click the ellipsis, select Code Builder, and click OK. Then enter code in the Form_Unload event handler to remove the custom buttons.

The following code shows how these event handlers can add and remove the customizations. Again, this code requires a reference to the Microsoft Office 10.0 Object Library. See the previous section for details.

TIP *Uncomment the* MsgBox *statements to see when the code executes.*

FILE *Ch04\HiddenForm.mdb*

```
Option Compare Database

' Install the Say Hi button and menu item.
Private Sub Form_Load()
Dim btn As CommandBarButton

'    MsgBox "frmHidden.Form_Load"
```

```
' Create a toolbar button.
Set btn = Application.CommandBars("Database").Controls.Add( _
    Type:=msoControlButton)
With btn
    .Style = msoButtonIcon
    .TooltipText = "Say Hi!"
    .OnAction = "SayHi"
    .DescriptionText = "Execute the SayHi macro"
    .Picture = LoadPicture(CurrentProject.Path & "\CustomButton.bmp")
    .Caption = "SayHi button"
End With

' Create a Tools menu item.
Set btn = Application.CommandBars("Tools").Controls.Add( _
    Type:=msoControlButton)
With btn
    .Style = msoButtonCaption
    .TooltipText = "Say Hi!"
    .OnAction = "SayHi"
    .DescriptionText = "Execute the SayHi macro"
    .Caption = "SayHi"
End With
End Sub

' Uninstall the Say Hi button and menu item.
Private Sub Form_Unload(Cancel As Integer)
'    MsgBox "frmHidden.Form_Unload"

    On Error Resume Next
    Application.CommandBars("Database").Controls("SayHi button").Delete
    Application.CommandBars("Tools").Controls("SayHi").Delete
End Sub
```

After you finish entering the code, return to Access and close the new form. When Access asks if you want to save the form's design, click Yes. Then enter a meaningful name for the form, such as frmHidden or frmCustomize.

Next create an Access-style AutoExec macro as described in the previous section. This time give the macro the single command OpenForm. Set the Form Name parameter to the form you just created and set the Window Mode to Hidden as shown in Figure 4-9.

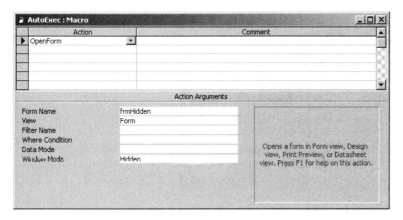

Figure 4-9. This AutoExec macro opens the form frmHidden and hides it.

Now when the database opens, its AutoExec macro opens frmHidden and hides it. When the form opens, its Form_Load event handler executes and installs the custom toolbar button and menu item.

When you are finished working with the database and close it, Access automatically closes the form, and that triggers the form's Form_Unload event handler, which removes the custom button and menu item.

Normally, the form remains hidden while you work with the database. If you manually open the form (select the Forms category and double-click the form), it will appear. If you then close the form, its Form_Unload event handler executes and removes the customizations.

Outlook

Because Outlook has no concept of a document, it makes little sense to talk about automatically adding and removing custom toolbar buttons and menu items in Outlook. Each user can have only one Outlook session, so if you want to use a custom tool, you'll probably want to use it whenever Outlook is running. You can simply place it in a toolbar or menu and leave it at that.

On the other hand, if you work with Outlook long enough, you'll probably find reasons to execute code when Outlook starts and stops, so this section explains how to do that.

From Outlook, select Tools ➤ Macros ➤ Visual Basic Editor. In the Project window, open the Microsoft Outlook Objects item and double-click ThisOutlookSession to open the code window. In the dropdown list on the left, select Application. Then use the dropdown list on the right to select events that the Application object provides, as shown in Figure 4-10.

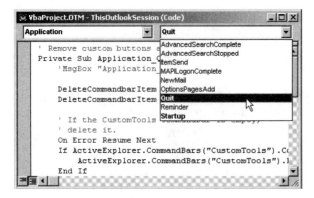

Figure 4-10. Outlook's Application *object provides events dealing with the application itself.*

In particular, Outlook's Application object provides Startup and Quit events. You can use those events to install and remove customizations (or do something more useful). The following code shows how an Outlook session can install a custom toolbar button and menu item when it starts and remove them when it quits.

TIP *Uncomment the* MsgBox *statements to see when the code executes.*

FILE *Ch04\AutoInstallOutlook.cls*

```
' Install the Say Hi button and menu item.
Private Sub Application_Startup()
    'MsgBox ("Application_Startup")

    ' Create the CustomTools CommandBar
    ' and ensure it is visible.
    MakeCommandBarVisible "CustomTools"

    ' Create the toolbar button.
    MakeCommandbarItem "CustomTools", "SayHi button", _
        msoButtonIcon, "SayHi", "Say Hi!", _
        "Execute the SayHi macro", _
        481
```

```
     ' Create a Tools menu item.
    MakeCommandbarItem "Tools", "SayHi", _
        msoButtonCaption, "SayHi", "Say Hi!", _
        "Execute the SayHi macro"
End Sub

' Remove custom buttons and menu items.
Private Sub Application_Quit()
    'MsgBox ("Application_Quit")

    DeleteCommandbarItem "CustomTools", "SayHi button"
    DeleteCommandbarItem "Tools", "SayHi"

    ' If the CustomTools CommandBar is empty,
    ' delete it.
    On Error Resume Next
    If ActiveExplorer.CommandBars("CustomTools").Controls.Count = 0 Then
        ActiveExplorer.CommandBars("CustomTools").Delete
    End If
End Sub
```

Multiple Self-Customizing Documents

The previous method (making a document install its own customizations as it is opened and remove them when it is closed) has trouble if the user opens more than one such document at a time.

For instance, suppose a user opens the file ExpenseReport.doc, which installs some buttons customized for that user. Next the user opens an earlier expense report file Trip091902.doc to copy and paste some data. When the user opens this file, it also installs the user's customizations. Now the user sees two copies of the customizations. If the user opens other documents with the same Document_Open event handler, the menus and command bars will soon be cluttered with duplicate buttons. To see for yourself, make a few copies of Ch04\AutoInstall.doc and open them all at the same time.

It's easy enough to make the Document_Open event handler check whether a button already exists before creating a new one, but that also leads to trouble. If the user opens several documents that use the same button and then closes one of them, the Document_Close event handler deletes the button even though other documents that need it remain open.

One way to solve this problem is to require the event handlers to track the number of open documents that need the button. For instance, the event handlers can store the number of documents that need a button in the button's Tag property. When a document opens, its Document_Open event handler looks for the button. If the button doesn't yet exist, the event handler creates it and sets its Tag property to 1. If the Document_Open event handler finds that the button already exists, it increments the Tag value.

When a document closes, its Document_Close event handler decrements the Tag property. If the result is 0, the event handler removes the button. If you place custom buttons on a special toolbar, the event handler can also check whether the toolbar is empty. If it contains no more buttons, the code can hide or delete the toolbar.

The following code shows revised event handlers for a Word document. The Document_Open event handler calls subroutine MakeCommandBarVisible to ensure that the command bar named CustomTools is visible. It then calls subroutine MakeCommandbarItem twice to add a button to the command bar and a menu item to the Tools menu.

The Document_Close event handler calls subroutine DeleteCommandbarItem to remove the custom command bar button and menu item created by the Document_Open event handler. Then if the CustomTools command bar is empty, the Document_Close event handler deletes it.

 FILE   *Ch04\AutoInstall2.doc*

```
' Install the Say Hi button and menu item.
Private Sub Document_Open()
    ' Create the CustomTools CommandBar
    ' and ensure it is visible.
    MakeCommandBarVisible "CustomTools"

    ' Create the toolbar button.
    MakeCommandbarItem "CustomTools", "SayHi button", _
        msoButtonIcon, "SayHi", "Say Hi!", _
        "Execute the SayHi macro", _
        ActiveDocument.Path & "\CustomButton.bmp"

    ' Create a Tools menu item.
    MakeCommandbarItem "Tools", "SayHi", _
        msoButtonCaption, "SayHi", "Say Hi!", _
        "Execute the SayHi macro"
End Sub
```

```
' Uninstall the Say Hi button and menu item.
Private Sub Document_Close()
    DeleteCommandbarItem "CustomTools", "SayHi button"
    DeleteCommandbarItem "Tools", "SayHi"

    ' If the CustomTools CommandBar is empty,
    ' delete it.
    If Application.CommandBars("CustomTools").Controls.Count = 0 Then
        Application.CommandBars("CustomTools").Delete
    End If
End Sub
```

MakeCommandBarVisible looks for a particular command bar. If the command bar doesn't exist, the routine creates it and sets its Position property to msoBarTop, which indicates that the bar should sit where command bars normally live above any open Word document. Whether it creates a new command bar or finds that one already exists, the subroutine sets the command bar's Visible property to True.

 FILE *Ch04\AutoInstall2.doc*

```
' If the CommandBar doesn't exist, create it.
' Then ensure that the CommandBar is visible.
Sub MakeCommandBarVisible(ByVal commandbar_name As String)
Dim command_bar As CommandBar

    ' See if the CommandBar exists.
    On Error Resume Next
    Set command_bar = Application.CommandBars(commandbar_name)
    If Err.Number <> 0 Then
        ' The CommandBar doesn't exist. Create it.
        Set command_bar = CommandBars.Add(Name:=commandbar_name)
        command_bar.Position = msoBarTop
    End If

    ' Make the CommandBar visible.
    command_bar.Visible = True
End Sub
```

Subroutine `MakeCommandbarItem` looks in a command bar to see if a control with the given name already exists. If `MakeCommandbarItem` finds the control, it increments its `Tag` property value.

If the `MakeCommandbarItem` subroutine doesn't find the control in the command bar, it creates a new button control. Then the routine uses its parameters to set the control's `Style`, `TooltipText`, `OnAction`, `DescriptionText`, and `Caption` properties. If the `picture_file` property is nonblank, the routine sets the button's `Picture` property to the picture in the indicated file. This is useful if the button is in a toolbar, but it may not be necessary if the new button is a menu item. Finally, the code sets the new control's `Tag` property to 1.

TIP *If you want others to use your code to load custom toolbar buttons, store the button pictures in a shared directory so the code can load them.*

FILE *Ch04\AutoInstall2.doc*

```
' Make a toolbar button or menu item.
Sub MakeCommandbarItem(ByVal commandbar_name As String, _
   ByVal item_caption As String, ByVal button_style As MsoButtonStyle, _
   ByVal on_action As String, Optional ByVal tooltip_text As String = "", _
   Optional ByVal description_text As String = "", _
   Optional ByVal picture_file As String = "")
Dim btn As CommandBarButton

    ' See if the button already exists.
    On Error Resume Next
    Set btn = Application.CommandBars(commandbar_name).Controls(item_caption)
    If Err.Number = 0 Then
        ' The button exists. Increment Tag.
        btn.Tag = CInt(btn.Tag) + 1
    Else
        ' The button doesn't exist. Create it.
        With Application.CommandBars(commandbar_name).Controls.Add( _
          Type:=msoControlButton)
            .Style = button_style
            .TooltipText = tooltip_text
            .OnAction = on_action
```

```
            .DescriptionText = description_text
            If Len(picture_file) Then
                .Picture = LoadPicture(picture_file)
            End If
            .Caption = item_caption
            .Tag = "1"
        End With
    End If
End Sub
```

The DeleteCommandbarItem subroutine obtains a reference to the item it should delete and decrements that item's Tag property. If the result is less than or equal to 0, the last document that needs the control is closing, so the subroutine deletes it.

FILE   *Ch04\AutoInstall2.doc*

```
' Delete a toolbar button or menu item.
Sub DeleteCommandbarItem(ByVal commandbar_name As String, _
  ByVal item_caption As String)
Dim btn As CommandBarButton

    ' Get a reference to the button.
    On Error Resume Next
    Set btn = Application.CommandBars(commandbar_name).Controls(item_caption)
    If Err.Number = 0 Then
        ' The button exists.
        ' Decrement its Tag property.
        btn.Tag = CInt(btn.Tag) - 1

        ' See if the count is zero.
        If CInt(btn.Tag) <= 0 Then
          ' No document needs this button.
          ' Delete it.
          Application.CommandBars(commandbar_name).Controls(item_caption).Delete
        End If
    End If
End Sub
```

The final helper subroutine is `DeleteCommandBar`. This routine simply finds the target command bar and calls its `Delete` method.

FILE *Ch04\AutoInstall2.doc*

```
' Delete this CommandBar.
Sub DeleteCommandBar(ByVal commandbar_name As String)
    On Error Resume Next
    Application.CommandBars(commandbar_name).Delete
End Sub
```

You could write similar code that automatically installs and removes toolbar buttons and menu items in Excel. In PowerPoint, you can modify the code described earlier that uses the OpenWatcher Add-In to tell when a presentation is opening or closing. See the files Ch04\AutoInstall2.xls and Ch04\AutoInstall2.ppt for sample code.

In Access, there's less reason to bother with this sort of customization because you can make a custom toolbar in a particular database. The toolbar automatically appears when the database is loaded and disappears when it is closed.

In Outlook, there's pretty much no reason to use this kind of code because you can have only one Outlook session running at a time. If you close the session, you close the entire Outlook application, so it makes little sense to uninstall any customizations.

Disappearing Toolbars

A user can hide or display a toolbar by using the View ➤ Toolbars command. Once users grow comfortable customizing Office applications, it's only a matter of time until someone hides the toolbar that contains your custom buttons. If a toolbar is hidden, your code that adds and removes toolbar commands still works. The user won't see your buttons, however, so you can expect a confused phone call asking why you deleted the tool remotely when the user wasn't looking.

One solution to this problem is to use the `MakeCommandBarVisible` subroutine shown in the previous section. Automatically making the user's toolbars appear and disappear can be annoying, however, and might result is less confused but more irate phone calls. You might be better off just leaving the toolbar visibility alone and letting meddlesome users live with the consequences of their customizations.

You may also want to place your tools on a special toolbar just for that purpose. Name it CustomTools or something else appropriate. Then users can hide or show your tools and the application's standard toolbars separately. If someone calls asking what happened to your tool, you can explain how to unhide the CustomTools toolbar rather than explaining why the user shouldn't hide the Formatting toolbar.

TIP *Another strategy is to remove the novice users' ability to remove the command bar as shown in the following code.*

```
CommandBars("CustomTools").Protection = _

    msoBarNoCustomize Or _

    msoBarNoChangeDock Or _

    msoBarNoChangeVisible Or _

    msoBarNoMove Or _

    msoBarNoResize
```

This strategy is a bit more totalitarian, but it can save a lot of confusion. And when a user knows enough to want to customize the command bars, you can probably remove these restrictions safely.

Verifying Document Type

Even this system isn't completely idiot-proof. Suppose the user opens an expense report document that installs a button, and then opens a shopping list. The button is still visible when the shopping list is the active document even though the shopping list document doesn't use the button. If the user presses the button, the associated macro could become confused at the file's format and crash or, even worse, mess up the shopping list so badly the user cannot figure out how to undo the damage.

Here's one solution for this predicament: Before it executes its code, make the macro attached to the button decide whether the currently active document is the proper type. You might make the macro try to determine this from the document's title, but that will probably work in only very special circumstances. After all, the user can rename a document to just about anything.

One way to mark a document as appropriate for a particular macro is to give it a *custom document property*. In Word, Excel, or PowerPoint, invoke the Tools ➤ Properties command and click the Custom tab to see the dialog shown in Figure 4-11.

Enter the name of the new property in the Name field. Use the Type combo box to set the property's data type to Text, Date, Number, or "Yes or no" (Boolean). Enter or select the value you want to assign to the property and click Add.

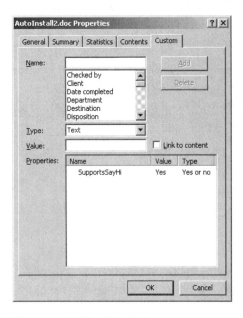

Figure 4-11. Use this dialog to create a custom property for a Word or Excel document.

The Properties list in Figure 4-11 shows this document has a custom property named SupportsSayHi. This property has type "Yes or no" (Boolean) and value Yes. The intent is to indicate that a SayHi macro will work for this document. More generally, any macro can check the active document to see if it has a specific custom property indicating that the macro should work properly.

The following code shows how the SayHi macro verifies that the active document has a custom SupportsSayHi property set to True before it displays a message box. The routine uses an On Error Resume Next statement to protect itself in case the document doesn't have a value for the property. It then looks for the property in the active document's CustomDocumentProperties collection. If an error occurs, the code sets the variable supports_say_hi to False. Next, if supports_say_hi is True, the macro displays a message box.

```
Sub SayHi()
Dim supports_say_hi As Variant

    ' Verify that the document has a SupportsSayHi setting of True.
    On Error Resume Next
    supports_say_hi = ActiveDocument.CustomDocumentProperties("SupportsSayHi")
    If Err.Number <> 0 Then supports_say_hi = False
    If supports_say_hi Then MsgBox "Hi"
End Sub
```

In Word, you can make a template that defines the property. Any documents the user creates based on the template inherit the property.

In Access and PowerPoint, you can create a template, give it the property, and post the template document for users to copy. When users copy the document and save it with a new name, the custom property goes along for the ride. The macro can check the property on the copy of the document and verify that it should run properly.

In addition to retrieving a custom property's value, you can create, modify, and delete custom properties with VBA code. The following code shows a few additional subroutines that you can use to manipulate custom properties for a Word document more easily. The routines in the code do the following:

- Subroutine CustomPropertyCreate creates a property with a given data type and assigns it a value.

- Function CustomPropertyValue uses an On Error Resume Next statement to protect itself in case the document doesn't have a value for the property. It then looks for the property in the active document's CustomDocumentProperties collection. If an error occurs, the document doesn't have the property defined, so the function returns a default value.

- Subroutine CustomPropertySet changes a property's value. Note that this routine cannot change the property's data type. For example, if you initially create the property as a "Yes or no" (Boolean) type, you can use CustomPropertySet to assign the property the value False, but you cannot use this routine to change the value to "Hello."

- Subroutine CustomPropertyDelete deletes a custom property. If you want to change a property's data type, use CustomPropertyDelete to delete it, then use CustomPropertyCreate to create it again with the new data type.

FILE *Ch04\CustomProperty.doc*

```
' Create a custom property and set its value.
Sub CustomPropertyCreate(ByVal property_name As String, _
  ByVal property_type As MsoDocProperties, ByVal property_value As Variant)
    ActiveDocument.CustomDocumentProperties.Add _
        Name:=property_name, _
        LinkToContent:=False, _
        Type:=property_type, _
        Value:=property_value
End Sub

' Return a custom property's value.
Function CustomPropertyValue(ByVal property_name As String, _
  Optional ByVal default As Variant = Empty) As Variant
    On Error Resume Next
    CustomPropertyValue = ActiveDocument.CustomDocumentProperties(property_name)
    If Err.Number <> 0 Then CustomPropertyValue = default
End Function

' Change a custom property's value.
' Note that this cannot change the data type.
Sub CustomPropertySet(ByVal property_name As String, _
  ByVal property_value As Variant)
    ActiveDocument.CustomDocumentProperties(property_name).Value = _
        property_value
End Sub

' Delete a custom property.
Sub CustomPropertyDelete(ByVal property_name As String)
    On Error Resume Next
    ActiveDocument.CustomDocumentProperties(property_name).Delete
End Sub
```

The following code shows how a macro can use these helper routines to verify that the document has a SupportsSayHi property value of True before presenting its message box.

FILE   *Ch04\CustomProperty.doc*

```
Sub SayHi()
    ' Verify that the document has a SupportsSayHi setting of True.
    If CustomPropertyValue("SupportsSayHi", False) Then MsgBox "Hi"
End Sub
```

The code for manipulating custom properties in Excel and PowerPoint is basically the same, so it is not shown here. The only difference is that the Excel code uses the `ActiveWorkbook` object to refer to the currently open document instead of the `ActiveDocument` object used by Word. Similarly, the PowerPoint code uses the `ActivePresentation` object instead of the `ActiveDocument` object.

To see examples for Excel and PowerPoint, look at the files Ch04\CustomProperty.xls and Ch04\CustomProperty.ppt.

Documents Containing Controls

For some documents, command bar buttons and menu items are inconvenient. Too many command bar buttons clutter the user's desktop. If you have a lot of tools, the menu item or button the user wants might be hidden in the confusion.

Keeping track of whether a tool applies to a particular document is also relatively complicated. You must prevent the tool from acting on an inappropriate document (such as adding an expense table to an annual performance review), and you must keep track of whether the tool should be displayed.

Even with all the tricks presented so far in this chapter, toolbar buttons and menu items are often visible even if they don't apply to a particular type of document. Before it does any damage, the VBA code can verify that it is operating on a document with a custom property, but the user can still click the button while viewing the wrong kind of document.

Another way to give the user easy access to a VBA routine is to place a control directly in the document. For example, Figure 4-12 shows a small Word document that contains a command button. If the user clicks the button, VBA code executes and displays a message box.

FILE   *Ch04\ContainsControls.doc*

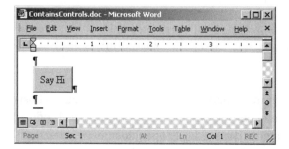

Figure 4-12. You can embed command buttons directly inside a Word document.

This method is handy because the button is integrated into a particular document. That means you know the button is appropriate for the document and that it is always available when that document has the focus.

TIP *In Word, you can also place a button on a template. Any document based on the template gets the button, too.*

For example, suppose you create an expense report template with a button that presents an expense entry form. A user creates a new document based on the template and saves it. The user then opens a memo document and makes another document based on the expense report template. The two expense report documents have their own buttons. When one of them has the focus, its button is available. When the memo document has the focus, the buttons are hidden so they cannot cause trouble.

Word

To add a button to Word, select the View ➤ Toolbars ➤ Control Toolbox menu item. This displays the Control toolbox shown in Figure 4-13. If you wish, you can drag this toolbox into the toolbar area and dock it so it becomes another toolbar.

Figure 4-13. Word's Control toolbox lets you add controls to a document.

The icon in the upper-left corner of the toolbox is the Design Mode tool. Clicking this icon turns design mode on and off. When you are in design mode, you can click on command buttons and other controls without invoking their functions. That lets you easily move them, resize them, and modify their properties without executing the underlying VBA code.

When you turn design mode on, Word displays the small toolbox shown in Figure 4-14. You can hide the Control toolbox and still use the icon on this toolbox to close design mode.

Figure 4-14. This toolbox lets you exit design mode.

After you display the Control toolbox, click on one of its control tools to add an instance of that control to the Word document. Word automatically enters design mode when you create a new control.

Initially, the control is placed at the current cursor position (wherever you were typing last), has a default size determined by Word, is selected, and displays drag handles on its corners and sides as shown in Figure 4-15. Use the drag handles to resize the control.

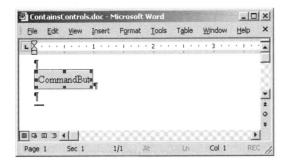

Figure 4-15. A new command button in design mode displays drag handles.

While Word is in design mode, the other two icons at the top of the Control toolbox are enabled. The one under the design mode icon that looks like a little magnifying glass over a document is the View Code tool. If you select a control and click this button, Word opens the Visual Basic editor and displays the code for the control you selected. While in design mode, you can also double-click a control to jump to its associated code. Figure 4-16 shows the code assigned to the button shown in Figure 4-12.

Figure 4-16. The Say Hi button executes this code when you click it, not in design time.

The final icon at the top of the Control toolbox is the Properties tool. If you select a control and click this tool, Word displays the properties dialog shown in Figure 4-17. You can also display the Properties dialog by right-clicking on the control in design mode and selecting the Properties command. Use this dialog to change the control's name, caption, font, color, and other properties.

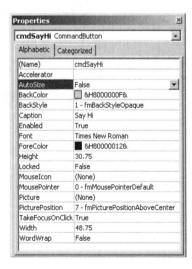

Figure 4-17. The Properties dialog lets you modify a control's appearance.

When you have finished editing a control's properties, click the Design Mode tool either in the Control toolbox or in the Exit Design Mode toolbox (see Figures 4-13 and 4-14) to end design mode. Word automatically closes the Properties dialog if it is open.

Now that you have exited design mode, you can click on the command button to execute its associated code.

Excel

You create command buttons and other controls for Excel in more or less the same way you do in Word, with the usual few obligatory differences. As in Word, you display the Control Toolbox with the View ➤ Toolbars ➤ Control Toolbox menu item.

To create a new control, select the appropriate tool from the Control Toolbox. Rather than immediately creating the control, however, Excel changes the mouse pointer into a crosshair. Click and drag on the Excel document to define the control's new position. When you release the mouse, Excel creates and selects the control, and enters design mode. The new control displays round grab handles as shown in Figure 4-18. Click and drag the handles to resize the control. Click and drag the control itself to move it.

 FILE *Ch04\ContainsControls.xls*

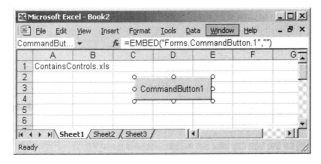

Figure 4-18. Excel displays controls in design mode with round grab handles.

Sometimes you may want to create several controls one after another. For example, you may want to make a series of text boxes or check boxes. Instead of clicking the text box tool and then clicking and dragging to make each control individually, you can save a little time by double-clicking the text box tool. When you click and drag on the document, Excel creates a new control as before.

This time, however, Excel does not automatically select the new control. Instead it keeps the text box tool selected so you can click and drag to create another control. You can continue clicking and dragging to create as many text boxes as you like. When finished, click the text box tool one more time to deselect it.

You can use one other trick for quickly making new controls. Instead of clicking and dragging to position the new control, press the Ctrl key and click on the document. Excel immediately creates a new control with a default size of its choosing at the position you clicked.

If you combine these two tricks, double-clicking a control tool and Ctrl-clicking to make controls, you can plaster a workbook with controls in no time. With a little practice, you can Ctrl-click with machine-gun rapidity to build a worksheet tiled with an artistic but useless display of text boxes. For added thrills, try clicking and dragging while pressing the Ctrl key, the Shift key, or both at the same time.

After you create a series of controls, you need a way to format them quickly. One way is to Shift-click on each to select them all at once. Click the Properties tool and use the Properties dialog to modify all of the controls at once. For example, you can change the controls' height, width, caption or text, and so forth. Some properties, however, you will need to set one at a time, different labels need different captions, text boxes need different meaningful names, and so forth. At least you may be able to set a few values all at once by selecting them all.

You can assign VBA code to a control the same way you do in Word. In design mode, select the control and click the View Code tool or double-click the control to open the Visual Basic IDE. Add the code you want to execute, and the control is ready to go.

PowerPoint

You add controls to a PowerPoint presentation much as you add them to an Excel workbook. Use View ➤ Toolbars ➤ Control Toolbox to display the Control toolbox shown in Figure 4-19. Note that this toolbox doesn't include a Design Mode tool. A PowerPoint presentation is always in design mode until you run it as a presentation so you don't need a tool to switch modes. For example, while you are designing a presentation, you can click a control to select it. Then you can drag it to a new position or use its drag handles to change its size. If you click the button while running the presentation, PowerPoint executes the button's associated code.

FILE *Ch04\ContainsControls.ppt*

Figure 4-19. PowerPoint's control toolbox contains no Design Mode tool.

You create and work with controls in PowerPoint much as you do in Excel. Select a control tool and click and drag to create a new control. Double-click a tool to keep the tool selected while you make several controls one after another. Ctrl-click to create a control with a default size at the mouse's position.

Select the control and click the View Code tool or double-click the control to open the Visual Basic IDE and assign code to the control.

Access

Once again Access's focus on DBAs makes it take a different approach than other Office applications do. An Access database doesn't really correspond to a single document like those used by Word, Excel, and PowerPoint, so it doesn't make sense to think about placing a control on a database.

However, Access provides its own flavor of form object. Usually, you use Access forms to enter, view, modify, or otherwise manipulate data, but you can just as easily use a form to provide a convenient toolbox for your VBA macros.

Select the Forms category and double-click the "Create form in Design view" entry to make a new form. Select View ➤ Toolbox to display the control toolbox shown in Figure 4-20. Click on a tool to select it. Then click and drag to position the new control on the form.

 FILE *Ch04\ContainsControls.mdb*

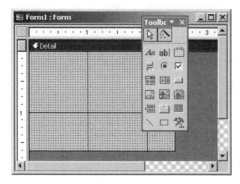

Figure 4-20. The Access control toolbox contains a Control Wizards tool.

If the Control Wizards tool (in the upper middle in Figure 4-20) is selected, Access creates the control and may launch a Wizard that it thinks is appropriate for the kind of control you created. Figure 4-21 shows the Command Button Wizard. At this first stage, you can select a category and action for the new control. Remember that Access typically uses forms to view and manipulate data, so typical button actions deal with record navigation and modification. To make a button execute a VBA macro, select the Miscellaneous category and the Run Macro action.

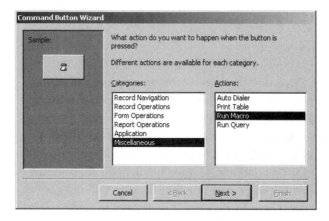

Figure 4-21. The Command Button Wizard helps you initialize a new button control.

When you click Next, the Command Button Wizard displays the dialog shown in Figure 4-22, which lists the Access-style macros available in the database. Select one and click Next.

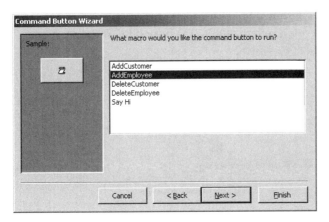

Figure 4-22. The Command Button Wizard lets you select the new button's Access-style macro to execute.

The Command Button Wizard then displays the dialog shown in Figure 4-23. If you want the button to display text, select the Text option and enter the words you want displayed. If you want the button to display an image, select the Picture option. Then you can select the MS Access Macro picture as shown in Figure 4-23, or you can select the Run Macro picture (which looks almost like the MS Access Macro picture followed by a red exclamation mark). If you check the Show All Pictures box, the list shows a couple hundred standard pictures you can assign to the button. You can also click the Browse button to select your own picture from a file.

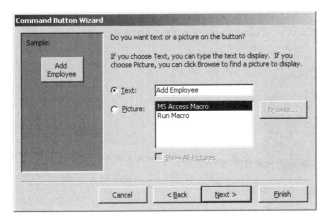

Figure 4-23. Use this dialog to determine the new button's appearance.

Click Next to see the dialog shown in Figure 4-24. Enter a descriptive name for the new button. You can use this name to refer to the button in VBA code. When you finish entering the name, click Finish.

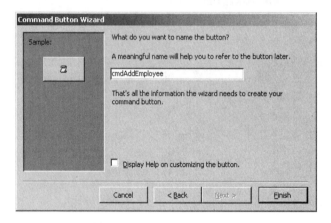

Figure 4-24. Enter a descriptive name for the new button.

Normally, Access adds all sorts of database-related bells and whistles to its forms. Because this form is intended as a macro button toolbox, you can remove these extra features.

Close the control toolbox and double-click the form to open its Properties window shown in Figure 4-25. In the combo box at the top, select Form. Then set these form properties: Scroll Bars = Neither, Record Selectors = No, and Navigation Buttons = No. You can set other properties, such as Auto Center, Border Style, Control Box, and Min Max Buttons, if doing so suits your purpose.

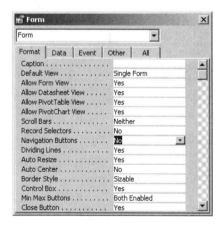

Figure 4-25. Use the form's Properties window to remove the form's database-related features.

When you have finished designing the form, close it. When Access asks if you want to save the changes, say Yes and tell Access what to name the form. To run the form, select the Forms category and double-click it. Figure 4-26 shows the result.

FILE   *Ch04\ContainsControls.mdb*

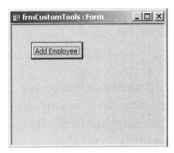

Figure 4-26. The frmCustomTools form holds buttons that execute handy macros.

Outlook

Like Access, Outlook has no single object that corresponds to a document in Word, a workbook in Excel, or a presentation in PowerPoint. You can have only one Outlook session running at a time, and when you close it, you close the entire Outlook application. Because of this, it doesn't make a lot of sense to try to tie customizations to a particular Outlook session. Just create toolbar buttons and menu items to execute your custom tools and leave it at that.

On the other hand, Outlook does include a whole bunch of different kinds of objects, such as mail items, folders, contacts, notes, and so forth. It makes sense to build customized forms to help input and format some kinds of these items, and it might make some sense to add buttons and other controls to make using these objects easier.

Unfortunately, Outlook, like Access, has its own set of tools for building different kinds of forms. Also like Access, Outlook uses its own style of code behind the scenes. Whereas Access uses Access-style macros, Outlook uses Visual Basic Scripting Edition (VBScript).

The controls on Outlook forms are not tied nicely to VBA code. Instead, these controls generally perform Outlook-specific actions, such as filling in a return address, closing the form, or opening a new custom-built Outlook form. A few of these objects, such as a command button, can execute more general events, but they are tied to VBScript code rather than VBA code.

VBScript

VBScript gives you access to the same Outlook-defined objects that you would use in VBA code, such as `Application`, `CommandBars`, `Recipient`, `Selection`, and so forth. The Script Editor is much more limited than the Visual Basic IDE, however.

VBScript is also more limited than VBA. A few of the more obvious differences include:

- All variables have the `Variant` data type. It is illegal to declare a variable with any other data type. In fact, it is illegal to explicitly declare a variable to be a `Variant`. You must simply use `Dim X` and leave off the type.

- The code editor does not have IntelliSense.

- The code editor does not know which objects are available on the form or what their events are. For example, you cannot use dropdown lists to help make an event handler for a command button. You must type in all of the event handler's code correctly with no formatting help.

- The Object Browser is much weaker than the one in the Visual Basic IDE, although it's certainly better than nothing.

- The Object Browser doesn't list objects such as `CommandBarButton`, so it won't help with you its properties, methods, and events.

The support provided by the Visual Basic IDE is so much better than that provided by the VBScript code editor that it's usually easiest to write and test a subroutine in VBA first. When the routine is working properly, you can copy and paste it into the VBScript code editor. Then you can comment out the variable type declarations, which are not allowed in VBScript. For example, the VBA declaration `Dim i As Integer` becomes `Dim i ' As Integer` in VBScript.

A trick that can make working with these events even easier is to make a VBScript subroutine invoke a VBA macro. One relatively simple way to do that is to install a toolbar button that executes the VBA macro. Then the VBScript code can find the button in Outlook's command bars and call its Execute method. The following code shows how the Click event handler for the cmdRunSayHi button on an Outlook message form can invoke the macro tied to the "SayHi button" control in the CustomTools command bar.

```
Sub cmdRunSayHi_Click()
    Application.ActiveExplorer.CommandBars("CustomTools"). _
        Controls("SayHi button").Execute
End Sub
```

Using code similar to this, you can work exclusively in VBA and leave VBScript more or less alone.

Whither Contained Controls?

So where does this leave Outlook and contained controls? The short answer is: Don't bother. Build your tools in VBA and provide access to them through custom toolbar buttons and menu items.

If you want to provide controls to help perform specific tasks, such as filling in fields for a new requisition request e-mail, use Outlook's forms and controls tied to VBScript. This topic is outside this chapter's scope and mostly out of this book's scope. For more information on building forms, see a book on Outlook programming, such as *Microsoft Outlook Version 2002 Step by Step*.

When to Use Embedded Controls

Embedded controls are convenient and easy to use—at least they are in Word, Excel, and PowerPoint, and you don't really need them much in Access and Outlook. Embedded controls attach macros to specific documents, so they are most useful when the code applies only to a particular type of document. If a macro is useful on a wide variety of documents, you'll probably be better off running it with a normal toolbar button or menu item.

Embedded controls are also most useful when the document is small or when you place the control so the user can find it easily. If you place a button in the middle of a 150-page Word document, the user will have trouble finding it. If you put the button at the top of the document, the user can always find it easily, although it means moving to the top of the file and possibly losing the user's place.

Note that clicking on an embedded control moves focus to that control, so the code should not try to manipulate the document's current selection. For example, suppose you have a Word macro that applies a specific format to the selected text. If you click a button to run the code, the selection moves to the button. When the code runs, only the button is selected so the text you had selected is not formatted.

Toolbar buttons and menu items, on the other hand, do not change a document's current selection. If you attach the same code to a toolbar button and click it, your selected text remains selected while the code executes so that the code can manipulate that text.

In some cases, you can use the fact that clicking a button selects it to your advantage. For example, you can place a button at the top of a Word document and mark the document read-only. A user opens the document and saves it with a new name. Then the user clicks the button and VBA code does something appropriate to initialize the document. For instance, it might prompt the user for an employee name, look up the employee in a database, and copy employee information into the document. When it is finished initializing the document, the code can then delete the button that invoked it. Because clicking the button selects it, the code knows that the button is currently selected (unless the code changes the selection), so it's easy to delete. The following code shows how a Word document can provide this kind of initialization.

FILE   *Ch04\InitializeButton.doc*

```
' Initialize the document.
Private Sub cmdStartDocument_Click()
    MsgBox "Do something to initialize the document here."

    ' Delete the selection (which is the button).
    Selection.Delete
End Sub
```

NOTE *You can also run initialization code in a* Document_New *event handler in the ThisDocument module in either the Normal.dot template or a template you create.*

Summary

Chapter 3 explains how to manually install custom toolbar buttons and menu items that execute VBA code. This chapter explains how to make the Office applications automatically install and remove their own customizations. You can use these techniques to ensure that a document provides only the tools it needs. You can also make different tools available to users who have different jobs and skill levels.

More generally, the examples contained in this chapter show how to make the Office applications perform tasks automatically. They show where you would place code to initialize or update a document when it opens, and to validate a document's contents when it closes. After you study the chapters later in this book so you understand each application's object model in greater detail, you'll be able to use these techniques to write more powerful and flexible Office applications.

CHAPTER 5

Office Programming
the Easy Way: OLE

OBJECT LINKING AND EMBEDDING (OLE—usually pronounced olé, just as you'd shout at a bullfight) is pretty much what its name says: It's a method for linking objects and embedding one object in another. Unfortunately, knowing what the words mean individually doesn't really give you a sense of what they mean together. To really understand the power of OLE, you must dig into it a bit and study a few examples.

In a sense, OLE is just a feature provided by the Office applications that lets them interact with each other. (Actually, many other applications support OLE, and your programs can use OLE to interact with them, too.) As a feature of the Office applications, it's reasonable to ask if OLE should even be covered in an Office programming book. After all, this book doesn't explain how to format paragraphs in Word or change the master slide layout for PowerPoint (well, not much anyway). So why is this feature so important to Office programmers?

OLE is described in this chapter for one main reason: It does something that many VBA programmers do using VBA code. OLE is usually faster, more effective, and more flexible than the VBA code you would write yourself. It lets you skip the possibly lengthy debugging process and avoid excessive maintenance costs later.

For example, suppose you are writing a production report in Word and you want to include a table of figures drawn from an Excel workbook. You could approach this problem several ways. If you're going to do this only once, you could export the Excel data and import it into Word. Alternatively, you could copy the data in Excel and paste it into Word.

If you foresee a need to do this more than once (perhaps every three months for quarterly reports), you might write VBA code to automate the process. The code could run in Word, open the Excel workbook, find the data, create a new Word table, and fill the table with numbers. This wouldn't be too difficult and is actually an interesting exercise. However, this solution requires you to debug the code and maintain it over time.

On the other hand, with just a few clicks of the mouse you can use OLE to drop the Excel data directly into the Word document. Problem solved. You don't have to spend a lot of time figuring out how to open Excel, find the data, create a new Word table, and copy the data into it. These are all things worth knowing, but in this case OLE lets you display the data with minimal work.

This chapter explains how to use OLE to integrate Office applications with each other and with your Visual Basic programs. OLE certainly won't solve all your problems. It won't even do everything you might want to do when it comes to displaying data from one application in another. If you want to reformat the data as you display it, you may need to roll up your sleeves and write some VBA code. However, if you want to use one Office application to display data in another, OLE can save you a huge amount of effort.

What Is OLE?

The Microsoft Office applications support OLE. That means you can place an instance of one Office application inside another. Big deal. Word and Excel are quite complicated enough without glomming them together. So why should you bother? Even the previous example of copying data from an Excel workbook into a Word table isn't very hard to handle with copy and paste.

To see how OLE can help, consider a more complicated example. Suppose you want to make a report using Word and you want to include a graph of some sales figures. There are many ways you could handle this problem. For instance, you could whip up a nice three-dimensional graph in Excel with a fancy legend and pretty colors. Then you could take a screen capture of the result, massage it with an image-editing tool, and paste the result it into the Word document.

This would let you use the best features of both applications. You could use Word's document layout features to produce brilliantly formatted text that wraps nicely around the graph's image. You could also use Word's index and table of contents features. At the same time, you could use all of Excel's powerful graphing features to produce line graphs, scatter diagrams, pie charts, surface diagrams—just about anything you need in a graph.

Unfortunately, this method requires a lot of manual intervention. Suppose you present your report to your boss and he says, "That's wonderful! But the graph would look better in red." Now you need to modify the Excel workbook (which you hope you saved), take a new screen capture, reedit it with an image-editing tool, and replace the old image with the new. Then your boss will say, "Oh yeah. Include the East Coast sales, too," and you get to start all over.

A better solution is to use OLE to place an instance of Excel directly inside the Word document. You can link this instance to the Excel workbook containing the graph you want to display. Then if you need to make changes, all you must do is update the Excel workbook, and the Word document immediately displays the new graph. Making modifications is so easy that you may even be able to tell your boss to make them himself (although you may have to make him think it's his idea).

Figure 5-1 shows an Excel graph linked inside a Word document. This is not just a simple picture. It's a living, breathing link to an Excel document. If you double-click the graph, Excel opens and lets you modify the graph and its data. If you make changes, save them, and close Excel, the picture in the Word document immediately shows the new results.

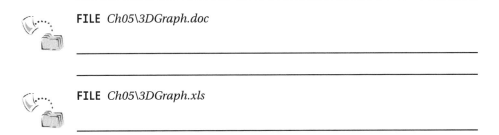

FILE *Ch05\3DGraph.doc*

FILE *Ch05\3DGraph.xls*

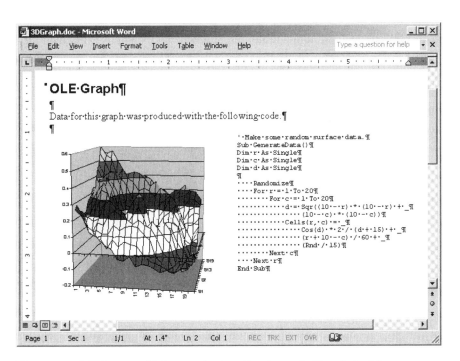

Figure 5-1. OLE lets you link or embed an Excel graph directly inside a Word document.

The name "Object Linking and Embedding" mentions two related but different techniques: object linking and object embedding. The following section explains the difference between the two and describes when you might want to use one or the other.

The rest of this chapter explains how to use OLE with the Microsoft Office applications and Visual Basic. Once you understand how you can use OLE to make Office applications work together, you'll find ways to use OLE to avoid writing rather complicated VBA applications. You could probably write code to copy and paste the image of an Excel chart into a Word document, but it would be a lot of work. Using OLE, you can do this faster, more effectively, and with less work. Best of all, you won't need to debug your code and maintain it over time.

Linking Versus Embedding

When you create an OLE object inside an application, you can either link to an external document or embed a document inside the current application. If you link to an external document, the application shows any changes you make to that document. If you embed a document inside the application, a copy of the embedded document is stored inside the main application's document. Any changes you make to the original external document or to the embedded copy are independent of each other.

Consider again the example of a sales report written in Word that includes an Excel graph showing sales data. If you want the report to continually reflect the most recent data stored in the Excel workbook, you can *link* to the workbook. When you enter new data in Excel, the Word report updates automatically.

 NOTE *Interestingly, if you rename the linked file, Word can use the link to update the link itself. Word will still be able to find the linked file with its new name. But if you delete the linked file, Word will not be able to find it. If you try to update a link to a missing file, Word will display an error message and keep whatever data it currently has.*

On the other hand, suppose you want the report to contain a snapshot of the data as it currently appears. For instance, you might want to freeze the report to show the state of the data at the end of the third quarter. In that case, you can embed the Excel workbook in the Word document. This makes Word save a copy of the data inside the report document so later changes to the external Excel workbook do not appear in the report.

 CAUTION *The difference between linking and embedding is particularly important if you send the main document to other users. If the subordinate document is embedded in the main document, the recipients can see the embedded document. However, if the subordinate document is linked, the recipients may not be able to access the link. Unless the link refers to a network share or the recipients have the exact same subordinate document on their local computers, the link won't work.*

OLE provides additional features for determining exactly when a linked object is updated. For example, you can mark a link so it is only updated manually. The container application stores a copy of the linked data and doesn't update it until you explicitly tell it. In this example, you might link the Excel graph to your Word report and let the link to update itself automatically. At the end of the quarter, you could make a copy of the report, open it, and set the link to manual update so it will not update itself again. That gives you a snapshot of the data for the end of the quarter while allowing the original report to keep tracking any new data.

You can also *lock* a link so it cannot be updated later. That makes it less likely that someone will accidentally update the link manually. If you really need to, you can unlock the link and update the data, but requiring the extra unlocking step helps prevent accidents.

If you are certain you will never want to modify the data in the report again, you can even break the link. That makes Word replace the linked object with a picture of the object. After this, you cannot update the graph. This provides the greatest assurance that the report data will not be modified later.

Converting the linked data into an image is also useful if you want to send the report to a recipient using a computer without Excel. If you just sent someone the Word report, the OLE link would be unable to find the Excel workbook it needs to display the graph. If you copy the original Word report and convert the OLE link to a picture, you can send the report to recipients without worrying whether Excel is present.

There is also a resource tradeoff between linked and embedded documents. Because an embedded document is a new copy of the document, it takes up additional space. If the documents are small, this may be no big deal. If the embedded document is large, it's an issue worth considering.

Which kind of linking you should use depends on your specific needs. By providing enough flexibility to update an object automatically, manually, or not at all, OLE can handle most scenarios.

OLE in Word, Excel, and PowerPoint

The way you add an OLE object to Word, Excel, PowerPoint, Access, or Outlook is basically the same. A few of the details about how the host application holds the OLE object differ slightly. For instance, if you embed text from a Word document inside an Excel workbook, Excel lets you easily rotate the text so it sits at an angle. If you embed Word text in a PowerPoint presentation, PowerPoint doesn't provide the same features for rotating the text. The way you create OLE objects and invoke their native host applications (Word in this example) is the same, however, so the rest of this section assumes you are inserting an object in Word. The others are very similar.

To create a linked or embedded object in Word, invoke the Insert ➤ Object menu item. Word displays the dialog shown in Figure 5-2. Select the object you want to create and click OK. The following sections describe in detail some of the available options.

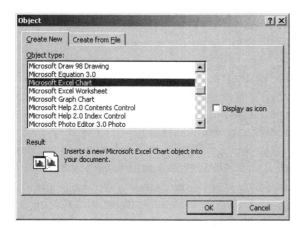

Figure 5-2. Use this dialog to insert an embedded or linked object in Word.

Display Icons

If you check the "Display as icon" box, Word displays the object as an icon in the Word document. If you double-click on the icon, Word invokes the linked object's host application so you can view and edit the object.

For example, suppose you embed an Excel worksheet in a Word document and display it as an icon. When you double-click the icon, Excel opens in its own window and shows you the embedded worksheet. You can then edit the data and save the results. When you close Excel, Word stores the modified data in the Word document and still displays the icon.

If you leave the "Display as icon" box unchecked, Word displays the object directly in the document. If the object is an Excel worksheet, you will see an array of rows and columns containing data much as a Word table does.

Displaying an icon instead of the object itself is faster because Word doesn't need to interact with Excel to generate an image of the data. In some cases it is less convenient, however, because the user cannot see the data integrated into Word.

To change the way Word displays the object, right-click on the object and select the "Object" command's Convert item. The exact menu items you see depend on the type of object. For an Excel chart object, select Chart Object ➤ Convert. For an Excel worksheet object, select Worksheet Object ➤ Convert. In the Convert dialog, check or uncheck the "Display as icon" box and click OK.

NOTE *Before you can find the Convert menu item, you must be sure the object is not open for editing. If you can interact with the object as if it were open in its native application (for example, Excel), click somewhere else in Word to deactivate the object. Then try right-clicking it again.*

Embedded Objects

To make an embedded object, click the Create New tab and select the type of object you want to create from the list. Figure 5-3 shows a Microsoft Excel Chart object selected.

Figure 5-3 shows a newly created embedded Excel chart. When you first create it, the chart is open for editing in Excel. Initially, the chart contains default data added so you can see something more than a blank chart.

FILE *Ch05\Embedded.doc*

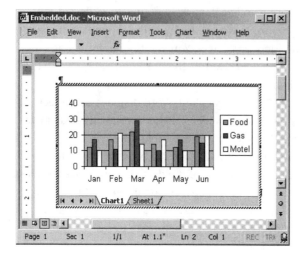

Figure 5-3. A new embedded Excel chart is initially open for editing with Excel.

Notice that the Excel workbook includes a chart sheet and a worksheet. The worksheet contains the data displayed by the chart. Click on the Sheet1 tab at the bottom of the object to switch to the worksheet and modify the data. Figure 5-4 shows the worksheet data open for editing.

FILE *Ch05\Embedded.doc*

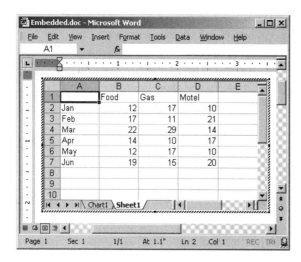

Figure 5-4. Click the Sheet1 tab to edit the chart's data.

When you click outside the object, Excel closes and the object is no longer editable. Double-click the object to reopen it in Excel and edit the data again.

The Word document shows the last sheet you viewed with Excel. If you were viewing Chart1 when you close Excel, Word displays the chart. If you last viewed Sheet1, Word displays the worksheet.

When the embedded document is open, you have access to all of the tools provided by the object's provider application. For Excel objects, you have access to the Excel menu bars and popup menus. For example, in Figure 5-3 notice that Word displays a Chart menu in its menu bar, and that in Figure 5-4 it displays a Data menu. You can use those menus to modify the embedded Excel data.

You can also right-click on the chart to see the standard Excel chart popup menu items Format Chart Area, Chart Type, Chart Options, 3-D View, and so forth.

When you click outside the object, its provider application closes and the object becomes just another graphic in Word. You can use the Word menus to modify the object. If you right-click on the object, the popup menu offers standard Word commands, such as Copy, Cut, Paste, and Borders and Shading.

The Chart Object popup menu item offers three commands: Edit, Open, and Convert. The Edit command opens the object for editing with Excel within the Word window. The Open command opens the object in a new Excel window. You may be more comfortable editing the object in Excel rather than Word. Excel provides more space to work than a Word document, which must handle margins, text, and other items on the same page.

The third command, Convert, lets you convert the object from a chart to a worksheet or vice versa. It also lets you determine whether the object should be displayed as an icon as described in the previous section.

Linked Objects

To make a linked object in Word, invoke the Insert ➤ Object menu item and click the "Create from file" tab as shown in Figure 5-5. Enter the name of the document you want to link or click Browse and find it. Check the "Link to file" box (and the "Display as icon" box if you like) and click OK.

 CAUTION *It's very easy to forget to check the "Link to file" box. After you create a new linked object, right-click on it and make sure the popup menu contains the Update Link command. If this command is missing, you forgot to check the box. (Of course, if you forgot to check the box, chances are good you'll forget to right-click the object to verify that it is linked properly, too.)*

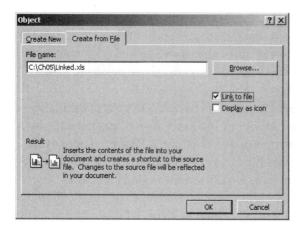

Figure 5-5. Select the "Create from file" tab to make a linked object.

 NOTE *If you leave the "Link to file" box unchecked, Word copies the contents of the document you selected into the document as an embedded object. The only difference between this and the embedded documents described in the previous section is that this time the object starts with a copy of an existing document. The preceding section explained how to make a new embedded object from scratch.*

To outward appearances, a linked object looks exactly the same as an embedded object. The difference is in what you can do with the object. If you right-click on the object, Word provides a couple new commands not offered for embedded objects. Figure 5-6 shows the popup menu Word provides for a linked PowerPoint presentation.

FILE *Ch05\Linked.doc*

FILE *Ch05\OLE.ppt*

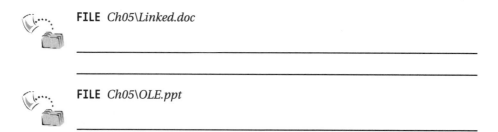

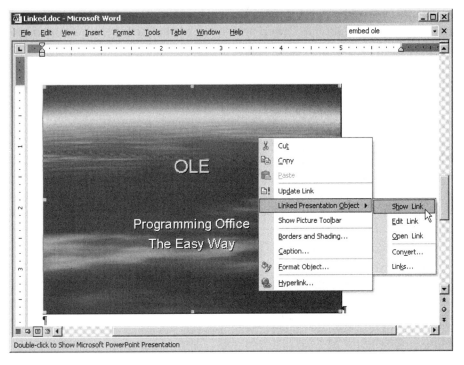

Figure 5-6. Word offers a few new commands for linked objects that are unavailable for embedded objects.

The Update Link command updates the data displayed by the object in Word. If the object is set up to automatically update its data (it is by default), you shouldn't need to do this. When you modify the linked document in its native application (PowerPoint in this example), Word automatically updates the data.

 TIP *To update all the linked objects in the document at once, press Ctrl-A to select the entire document. Right-click anywhere and select Update Link.*

The Linked Presentation Object ➤ Show Link command runs the linked Power-Point presentation. You use the normal PowerPoint popup menu to navigate through the presentation, or click the mouse to move from slide to slide. When the presentation ends, Word reappears. The Show Link command is available to PowerPoint because it makes sense for a PowerPoint presentation. Because you don't "execute" an Excel worksheet, the command is not available for linked Excel objects.

The Linked Presentation Object menu's Edit Link and Open Link commands both open the presentation in PowerPoint so you can edit it. When you close the presentation, Word reappears.

The Linked Presentation Object ➤ Convert command lets you convert between different object types and determine whether the object is displayed as an icon. See the "Display Icons" section earlier in this chapter for more information.

Managing Object Links

The Linked Presentation Object ➤ Links command shown in Figure 5-6 opens the dialog shown in Figure 5-7. You can also open this dialog by using the Edit ➤ Links menu command.

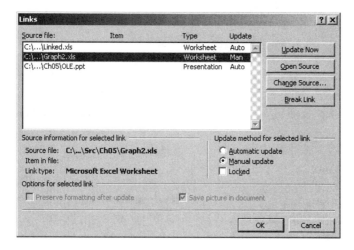

Figure 5-7. Use this dialog to manage linked objects.

Select one or more links from the list, then click the Update Now button to make the links reload from their linked documents.

TIP *Use Shift-click to select a group of sequential links. Use Ctrl-click to select a set of nonsequential links.*

Click the Open Source button to open a single link in the provider application. This button is available only when a single link is selected.

Click Change Source to replace the selected links with links to new documents. This is more or less equivalent to deleting the linked objects from Word and then creating new ones in the same positions. You can even change the type of the source document. For example, you could change a link's source from an Excel worksheet to a PowerPoint slide.

Click Break Link to break the selected links and convert their objects into text or pictures. After doing this, you cannot update the objects or edit their data by using their native applications. About all you can do is edit the results by using Word's text or picture editing tools.

Select the "Automatic update" button to make the selected links update automatically whenever their source documents change.

Select "Manual update" to prevent the links from updating automatically. To manually update a link, right-click a linked object in the Word document and select Update Link. Alternatively, you can open this dialog, select the links, and click Update Now.

If you check the Locked box, the selected links will not automatically update, and both the Update Link popup command and the Update Now button are disabled. You cannot update these links until you use this dialog again to uncheck the Locked box. This doesn't stop you from updating the link if you really need to, but it makes it harder to do so accidentally if you want the data to remain unchanged.

Copying and Pasting Excel Data

An additional method for creating linked and embedded objects uses copy and paste. Start Excel and open the Excel workbook you want to use in the Word document. Select the data you want to insert and use Edit ➤ Copy or Ctrl-C to copy it to the clipboard. Next open the Word document that you want to display the data and select Edit ➤ Paste Special. After you select options telling Word how to create the OLE object and close the dialog, Word creates the appropriate kind of object.

For example, suppose the file Sales.xls contains sales data for 12 months across 4 regions. You might open this workbook in Excel, use the mouse to select just the first two regions, and then press Ctrl-C to copy this data.

 NOTE *Because you aren't pasting the entire workbook into Word, you can save the Word document some space. If you need only a little data from the workbook, paste only that.*

Next open the Word document that should hold this data and move the cursor where you want the worksheet. When you invoke the Edit ➤ Paste Special command, Word displays the dialog shown in Figure 5-8.

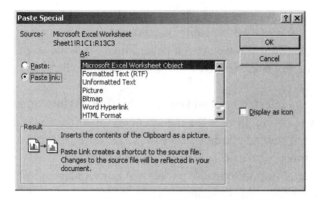

Figure 5-8. The Paste Special dialog lets you create a linked or embedded object.

If you look closely at the top of this figure, you'll see that the Source object is Microsoft Excel Worksheet, Sheet1!R1C1:R13C3. This means the selection includes the region defined by cells R1C1 (A1) through R13C3 (C13) in Sheet1 of an Excel document.

Pick the format you wish the data to have in Word. Select Microsoft Excel Worksheet Object if you want the data to stay in its original Excel format. Select the "Paste" option to create an embedded object. Select the "Paste link" option to create a linked object.

Check the "Display as icon" box if you wish and click OK to create the new object. The result is the same as if you had created the OLE object using any of the methods described earlier in this chapter. The one big difference is that the previous methods didn't allow you to restrict the data selected.

Copying and Pasting PowerPoint Slides

Just as you can copy and paste Excel ranges into Word, you can do the same with one or more PowerPoint slides. To copy a single slide, open a presentation in PowerPoint, select the slide you want, and press Ctrl-C. Then switch to Word, position the cursor where you want the slide, and select Edit ➤ Paste Special. In the Paste Special dialog, select the Paste option to create an embedded object or select "Paste link" to create a linked object. Check the "Display as icon" box if you want, then click OK.

Because it doesn't make a lot of sense to step through a single slide (not a very interesting presentation), Word assumes you just want to display the slide inside the document. If you double-click on the object, it opens in PowerPoint so you can edit it.

To link to more than one slide, select the slides in PowerPoint's Slide view. Click, Shift-click, or Ctrl-click to select the slides you want. Then press Ctrl-C to copy them to the clipboard. Open Word and select Edit ➤ Paste Special. Now when the Paste Special dialog opens, the "Paste link" option is disabled. You can paste the group of slides only as an embedded object, not as a linked object. Check the "Display as icon" box if you like, then click OK.

Because this object contains more than one slide, it makes sense to display them as a presentation. In Word, if you double-click the object or right-click it and select Presentation Object ➤ Show, PowerPoint displays the slides as a presentation. If you right-click and select Presentation Object ➤ Edit, a copy of PowerPoint opens inside the Word document to let you edit the slides. If you right-click and select Presentation Object ➤ Open, PowerPoint opens in its own window to let you edit the slides. Remember that these slides are an embedded copy, so any changes you make are not reflected in the original PowerPoint presentation.

Object Sizes

Sometimes, an OLE object has a size or shape that doesn't match what you want in Word. For example, Figure 5-9 shows an Excel chart embedded in a Word document. As you can see from the box and grab handles, the chart object contains a large amount of space on either side of the actual graph.

 FILE *Ch05\Graph3.doc*

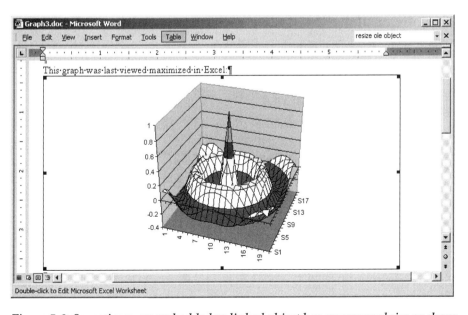

Figure 5-9. Sometimes, an embedded or linked object has an unusual size or shape.

In this situation, you probably would like to remove that empty space. Then you could make the picture bigger and it would still fit on the page. Or you could allow text to wrap around the area that actually contains the picture.

If you click and drag the grab handles shown in Figure 5-9, Word will happily resize the object. Unfortunately, the empty space is inside the object, so that is resized, too. If you make the picture thinner without changing its height, the result is a squeezed graph still surrounded by empty space.

Because the empty space is inside the object, you need to use the object's native application to remove it. In this case, you would right-click the object and select Worksheet object ➤ Open. In Excel, you would resize the chart sheet so it didn't contain all that white space. In this particular example, the sheet was maximized in Excel when it was embedded in the document, so it kept its maximized shape in Word. To fix it, you would open the worksheet, click the Restore button so it is no longer maximized, and resize it so the chart fills it nicely. When you close Excel, the object in Word looks much better, as shown in Figure 5-10.

FILE *Ch05\Graph3.doc*

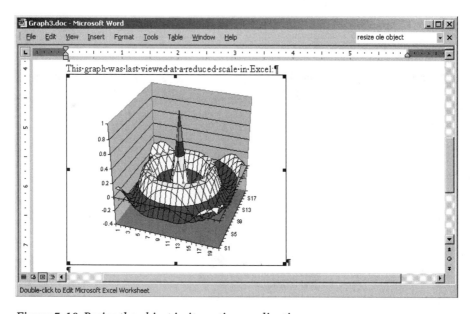

Figure 5-10. Resize the object in its native application.

When you create an OLE object, the object retains whatever size and layout it had when you last viewed it in its native application.

OLE in Access

As usual, Access takes a different approach than Word, Excel, and PowerPoint do. You can place an OLE object inside an Access form or report much as you can add one to these other applications. However, Access also allows another type of OLE use. It lets you use OLE DB (Object Linking and Embedding Database) to connect to data sources. Different OLE DB providers allow programs to connect to different data sources.

The Office XP setup installs the Microsoft Jet 4.0 OLE DB Provider and the OLE DB Provider for SQL Server automatically. You can also install other OLE DB providers for data sources such as ODBC (Open Database Connectivity) and Oracle.

To see a list of the OLE DB providers installed on your computer, display a Data Link Properties dialog and click the Provider tab. One way to display this dialog is to create a Data Access Page (select the Pages object and click "Create data access page in Design View"). Open the page in design view, right-click it, and select Page Properties. On the Data tab, select the ConnectionString property and click the ellipsis to the right. This displays the Data Link Properties dialog shown in Figure 5-11.

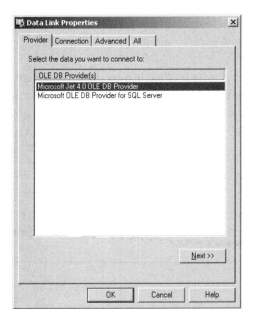

Figure 5-11. The Data Link Properties dialog's Provider tab shows the OLE DB providers installed on the computer.

If you search the Access help files for OLE, you'll learn a lot about OLE DB but very little about other uses of OLE. Fortunately, you use OLE in other ways much as you do in Word, Excel, or PowerPoint. Open a form or report. Select Insert ➤ Object and create the OLE object as before.

You can also select data in another application and copy it to the clipboard. Then in an Access form or report, you can select Edit ➤ Paste Special to create an OLE object that links or embeds the data you copied.

If the OLE object is linked rather than embedded, the form or report shows the most current view of the object each time you display it. For example, you could make a corporate sales report display an Excel chart showing your company's stock price over the last few months in its header. Each time you ran the report, it would display the latest data in the linked Excel chart.

OLE in Outlook

Like Access, Outlook has its own peculiar view of the world, and this view affects the way Outlook handles OLE. Outlook focuses on items that include notes, calendar entries, and e-mail messages. These items tend to be relatively self-contained. For example, when you send an e-mail message, you usually expect the recipient to be able to read it without logging on to a network and downloading other files. To keep a message self-contained, you would usually include as an attachment any file you refer to.

If you really want to, however, you can include an OLE link to an object inside an e-mail message. If you use Word as your Outlook e-mail editor, you can insert an OLE object if you are using HTML or Rich Text Format. If you do not use Word as your e-mail editor, you can insert an OLE object into the message only if you are using Rich Text Format.

 TIP *To make Rich Text your default message format, close any open messages and select Tools ➤ Options. Go to the Mail Format tab and in the "Compose in this message format" dropdown select Rich Text.*

To start a new message in Rich Text Format, select Actions ➤ New Mail Message Using ➤ Rich Text. Then, to create an OLE object, click on the message body and select Insert ➤ Object.

At this point, you're back to the normal OLE object creation dialog used by the other Office applications. Create a new object embedded in the e-mail message or open an existing file. Click the Link button if you want the OLE object to link to the file rather than embedding a copy.

 NOTE *If you send a message linked to a file and you want the recipients to be able to edit the file, it must be stored in a directory where the recipients have permission to edit the file.*

Similarly, you can add OLE objects to calendar entries, journal items, and tasks. Open the item and select Insert ➤ Object or Edit ➤ Paste Special. Then create the new object as described earlier in this chapter.

Programming OLE Objects

Practically anything you can do interactively with Office XP you can also do programmatically, so it should come as little surprise that you can use VBA code to create and manipulate OLE objects. You won't need to do this often, because usually you can use the Office XP applications' menus and dialogs to do everything you need to do with OLE objects interactively. However, VBA is all about handling those other occasions when it makes more sense to do something programmatically.

For example, consider again the example of writing a report in Word that includes an Excel chart showing sales data. Suppose the data is saved in an Access database and you don't really need or want an Excel workbook to display the data. You could make an Excel workbook anyway, copy the data into it, build the chart, and use OLE to display the results.

Alternatively, you could write a VBA subroutine that opens the Access database, opens Excel as an automation server, and uses the server object to build an Excel workbook displaying the data. Then it could create an OLE object that embeds the workbook in the report's Word document. Finally, the routine could delete the Excel workbook, leaving only the chart embedded in the report's Word document.

The following sections describe some of the objects you can use to create and manipulate OLE objects with VBA code. As usual, each Office application puts its own particular spin on OLE objects, so these sections explain how to use OLE objects in each Office application. The basic plan is similar, however, so you may want to read the following section, "Word," to get an idea of how this works no matter which application you will be using.

A Word of Warning

Before you read about how the different Office XP applications let you manipulate OLE objects in code, you should be aware of some misleading similarities among the applications. The Office XP applications have many objects with identical names and similar purposes. Unfortunately, the objects are not necessarily identical.

For example, Word and Excel both have Shape objects that describe "shapes." Word and Excel handle shapes very differently, however, so it should come as no surprise that these objects are different.

More troublesome examples include objects that represent virtually identical OLE concepts. For instance, both Word and Excel have a LinkFormat object that describes an OLE object's link parameters. Although these classes have the same name and purpose, they have different properties and methods.

For example, Word's version provides SourceName and SourcePath properties that describe the OLE object's source document, and a BreakLink method that converts an OLE object to a snapshot of its last appearance. Excel's version of the LinkFormat object doesn't provide any of these.

Worse still, both the Word and Excel versions of the LinkFormat object provide a Locked property, but they have different meanings. In Word's version, when Locked is True, the user cannot manually or automatically update the OLE object without first setting Locked to False. In Excel, if Locked is True, the user cannot update an OLE object when the worksheet that contains it is protected.

All these objects with similar names and purposes can be very confusing. It can also be confusing for a VBA program. Suppose you write some Excel code that manipulates an embedded Word document. To make things easier, you use the Tools ➤ References command to include a reference to the Microsoft Word 10.0 Object Library. That library defines Word's version of the LinkFormat object. Excel also defines its own version of LinkFormat, so which version does the following code mean?

```
Dim lf As LinkFormat
```

Because this code is running in Excel, the Excel object library has a higher priority than the Word library, so this variable is an Excel-style LinkFormat object. To prevent confusion, however, you may want to explicitly define the library for ambiguous variables as shown in the following code.

```
Dim lf1 As Excel.LinkFormat
Dim lf2 As Word.LinkFormat
```

NOTE *To change the priority of referenced libraries, select Tools ➤ References. Click on a library and use the up and down priority arrows to move the library up and down in the priority list. Note that Excel will not let you move any additional libraries above the VBA and Excel libraries.*

Excel increases the potential for confusion by removing library specifications from type names. For example, if you try to set these two variables equal to each other, VBA raises a "Type mismatch" error. If you use the TypeName statement to check a LinkFormat variable's type, VBA returns the string "LinkFormat" without telling you which library it is using.

Suppose you assign an Excel-style LinkFormat variable to an object, and you assign a Word-style LinkFormat variable to a Word object. Now you try to assign one variable to the other's value. Because their LinkFormat types come from different libraries, the code raises a "Type mismatch" error. If you use TypeName to display their data types, however, you'll see that both are of type LinkFormat. Figuring out how two objects with the same data type can cause a type mismatch can be downright maddening.

You can do two things to prevent unnecessary confusion. First, be aware that the different Office applications use classes with similar purposes and names but with different implementations. Second, when working with more than one Office application in the same program, qualify variable declarations so it is obvious which library you are using. You can also include a hint in variables names. For example, you might name a Word LinkFormat variable wlf_sales and an Excel LinkFormat variable elf_forecasts. (The second variable will also give you plenty of chances for Santa Clause jokes during code reviews.)

Programming OLE Objects in Word

Word stores OLE objects as shapes and inline shapes. The following sections describe the Shape and InlineShape objects, and several other object types you can use to understand and manipulate OLE objects.

Creating OLE Objects

You can create an OLE object in Word as either a Shape or InlineShape. Both represent a nontext area drawn on a Word document. A Shape has an anchor point that determines the paragraph near which it is located. You can position the Shape anywhere on the page that contains the anchor.

In contrast, an InlineShape object is located at a specific place within the text of a Word document. You cannot move the InlineShape relative to that position.

If necessary, you can convert an OLE object from an InlineShape to a Shape or vice versa. Select the object and invoke the Format ➤ Object command. On the Layout tab shown in Figure 5-12, select the "In line with text" wrapping style to make the object an InlineShape. Select one of the other wrapping styles to make the object a Shape.

Figure 5-12. Select the "In line with text" wrapping style to use an InlineShape *object.*

Both the Shapes and InlineShapes collections provide an AddOLEObject method that you can use to create a new OLE object. The two methods take slightly different parameters because you can position a Shape object anywhere on the page, whereas an InlineShape's position is determined by its location in the Word document.

The following code shows the syntax for creating an InlineShape object. The AddOLEObject method returns a reference to the new object.

```
InlineShapes.AddOLEObject(ClassType, FileName, LinkToFile, DisplayAsIcon, _
    IconFileName, IconIndex IconLabel, Range)
```

Table 5-1 describes these parameters, all of which are optional.

Table 5-1. `InlineShapes.AddOLEObject` *Parameters*

PARAMETER	PURPOSE
ClassType	The name of the class of object you are creating. For example, Excel.Sheet.8 or PowerPoint.Slide.8. Omit the version number to get the most current version available on the computer. For instance, Excel.Chart or Word.Document.
DisplayAsIcon	True to display the object as an icon.
FileName	The file name from which the object should be created.
IconFileName	The name of the file containing the icon to display.
IconIndex	The index of the icon in the icon file.
IconLabel	The label that should be displayed below the icon.
LinkToFile	True for a linked object, False for an embedded object.
Range	The range where the new InlineShape should be created.

The following code shows how VBA code can make a new OLE object linking to an Excel workbook. The Range parameter uses the ActiveDocument.Range method to create a new Range object. That method's parameter, ActiveDocument.Range.End - 1, sets the new Range's start position to the second-to-last position in the document. This makes the new InlineShape object replace the final character in the file, which is a paragraph mark. Word then automatically adds a new paragraph mark at the end.

 FILE *Ch05\MakeOle.doc*

```
' Create an OLE object linked to an Excel chart.
Private Sub cmdLinkChart_Click()
    ActiveDocument.InlineShapes.AddOLEObject _
        ClassType:="Excel.Sheet.8", _
        FileName:=txtChartFile.Text, _
        LinkToFile:=True, _
        DisplayAsIcon:=False, _
        Range:=ActiveDocument.Range(ActiveDocument.Range.End - 1)
End Sub
```

The `AddOLEObject` method provided by the Shapes collection offers a few new parameters for positioning the new `Shape` object. The following code shows the syntax for the `Shapes` collection's `AddOLEObject` method. This method returns a reference to the new object.

```
Shapes.AddOLEObject(ClassType, FileName, LinkToFile, DisplayAsIcon, _
    IconFileName, IconIndex, IconLabel, Left, Top, Width, Height, Anchor)
```

The first seven parameters are the same as those used by the `InlineShapes` collection's `AddOLEObject` method. The `Left`, `Top`, `Width`, and `Height` parameters specify the new object's position and size in points.

 TIP *An inch equals 72 points. The* `Application` *object provides several functions, such as* `InchesToPoints` *and* `PointsToPixels`, *to convert between different units. These functions are described further in Chapter 7.*

The `Anchor` parameter specifies a `Range` object. The new `Shape` object's anchor is bound to the first paragraph in this range.

When you create an OLE object interactively, Word makes an `InlineShape` object rather than a `Shape` object. Word also associates each OLE object in an `InlineShape` with a `Field` object. You can find this object in the document's `Fields` collection.

Word does not associate a `Field` object with an OLE object stored as a `Shape` object. If you use VBA code to make an OLE object in the `Shapes` collection, or if you use the Format ➤ Object command to convert an `InlineShape` into a `Shape`, there is no corresponding `Field` object. Word also does not make a `Field` object for embedded objects.

You can use a Word document's `Fields`, `Shapes`, and `InlineShapes` collections to refer to OLE objects. The `Field`, `Shape`, and `InlineShape` objects in these collections let you learn about and manipulate the OLE objects. The following sections explain only the most useful properties and methods provided by these objects. For complete descriptions of these objects, see the online help or go to Microsoft's Web page for Word's Document object at `http://msdn.microsoft.com/library/en-us/vbawd10/html/woobjDocument.asp` and look at its `Fields`, `Shapes`, and `InlineShapes` properties.

Shape *Objects*

The Shape object provides general information about an OLE object stored in the Shapes collection. Table 5-2 describes the most useful properties provided by a Shape object that represents an OLE object. Table 5-3 lists the Shape object's most useful methods.

Table 5-2. Useful Shape *Object Properties*

PROPERTY	PURPOSE
Anchor	The Range object that determines the Shape's anchoring location. The object is anchored to the first paragraph in the range.
Height, Left, Width, Top	These properties determine the shape's size and position on the page in points.
LinkFormat	A LinkFormat object representing the link parameters. Because this object represents link parameters, it only applies to linked objects, not embedded objects. This object is described further in a later section.
LockAnchor	If this is True, the anchor doesn't move if you drag the shape.
Name	The name of the object. Initially this is something relatively useless such as "Object 5" but you can change it to something meaningful such as "Sales Figures." After that, you can use the Name as an index into the Shapes collection as in the statement ActiveDocument.Shapes("Sales Figures").Activate.
OLEFormat	An OLEFormat object that provides additional information about the OLE object (other than linking information). This object is described further in a later section.
Type	The type of the Shape object. This value has data type MsoShapeType. For an OLE object, this should be either msoLinkedOLEObject or msoEmbeddedOLEObject.
Visible	This property indicates whether the object should be visible.

Table 5-3. Useful Shape *Object Methods*

METHOD	PURPOSE
Activate	Uses the OLE object's native application to edit the object in a separate window
Delete	Removes the object from the Word document
Duplicate	Makes a duplicate of the object

CAUTION *Note that the* Duplicate *method copies the object's* Name *property as well as its other information. If you duplicate a* Shape *object named "Sales Figures," then the* Shapes *collection will contain two objects named "Sales Figures." To avoid confusion, you should probably keep a reference to the newly created object and change its name as shown in the following code:*

```
Dim new_shape As Shape

    Set new_shape = ActiveDocument.Shapes("Sales Figures").Duplicate
    new_shape.Name = "New Sales Figures"
```

InlineShape *Objects*

The InlineShape object provides properties and methods similar to those of the Shape object. See the previous section for information on most of these. This section describes only the differences between Shape and InlineShape objects used to hold OLE objects.

Because an InlineShape object is positioned within the stream of the document's text, it has no properties for changing size and position, or for manipulating an anchor. Instead it has a Range property that indicates the object's position in the document.

The InlineShape object has a Field property that gives a reference to the Field object associated with the OLE object. This object is described in a later section.

Unlike the Shape object, the InlineShape object has no Name property, so you must find objects in the InlineShapes collection by index.

The InlineShape object also has no Duplicate method. You can make a copy of an InlineObject by using its Field object's Copy method and then pasting the results into the document. For example, the following code copies the fifth InlineShape object to the end of the document.

```
ActiveDocument.InlineShapes(5).Field.Copy
ActiveDocument.Range(ActiveDocument.Range.End - 1).Paste
```

The final interesting difference between Shape and InlineShape objects is that the Type property has data type WdInlineShapeType instead of MsoShapeType. For an OLE object, this should be either wdInlineShapeLinkedOLEObject or wdInlineShapeEmbeddedOLEObject.

LinkFormat *Objects*

As its name implies, a LinkFormat object provides information about how an OLE object is linked. Because this object describes a link, it isn't needed for embedded objects. The LinkFormat property for a Shape or InlineShape object representing an embedded OLE object is Nothing.

Tables 5-4 and 5-5 list the most interesting properties and methods provided by the LinkFormat object.

Table 5-4. Useful LinkFormat *Object Properties*

PROPERTY	PURPOSE
AutoUpdate	True if the OLE object should automatically update when its source is modified
Locked	True if the OLE object is locked against automatic or manual updating
SourceFullName	The full path and file name of the object's source file
SourceName	The file name of the object's source file without the path
SourcePath	The path of the object's source file without the file name
Type	The type of the link (for an OLE object, this should bewbLinkTypeOLE)

Table 5-5. Useful LinkFormat *Object Methods*

METHOD	PURPOSE
BreakLink	Breaks the link between the object and its document (this converts the OLE object into a picture of its last appearance)
Update	Makes Word update the OLE object

OLEFormat *Objects*

The OLEFormat object represents an OLE object's non-linking characteristics. Table 5-6 describes the OLEFormat object's more useful properties.

Table 5-6. Useful OLEFormat *Object Properties*

PROPERTY	PURPOSE
ClassType	The name of the object's class. For example, Excel.Sheet.8, Excel.Chart.8, Word.Document.8, PowerPoint.Slide.8, or PowerPoint.Show.8 (the "8" means version 8).
DisplayAsIcon	True to display the object as an icon.
IconIndex	The index of the icon in the icon file.
IconLabel	The label that should be displayed below the icon.
IconName	The name of the file containing the icon to display.
IconPath	The path to the icon file, not including the file's name.
Label	A string identifying the part of the source document used by the OLE object. For instance, if you copy cells A1 through E3 from the first worksheet in an Excel workbook and use Edit ➤ Paste Special to create a linked OLE object, the Label property for the new OLEFormat object would be Sheet1!R1C1:R3C5.
Object	The object representing the OLE object's top-level interface. This will be something like an Excel Workbook, Word Document, or PowerPoint Presentation. Use that object's Application property to get a reference to the source application object.

To see how the four icon properties work, suppose you create a new embedded Excel chart displayed as an icon, and you don't change the default values. The new OLEFormat object will have IconIndex = 3, IconLabel = Microsoft Excel Chart, and IconName = xlicons.exe. The IconPath depends on your system, but is probably similar to the following value.

```
C:\WINNT\Installer\{90280409-6000-11D3-8CFE-0050048383C9}
```

Table 5-7 describes the OLEFormat object's most useful methods.

Table 5-7. Useful `OLEFormat` *Object Methods*

METHOD	PURPOSE
Activate	Activates the OLE object. The object must be activated before you can use its `Object` property.
ConvertTo	Converts the object to a new class. This method takes the parameters `ClassType`, `DisplayAsIcon`, `IconFileName`, `IconIndex`, and `IconLabel`. The `DisplayAsIcon` and icon properties work as usual. The `ClassType` property indicates the class to which the object should be converted. For example, the following code converts a Word.Document class object into the Word.Picture class. `ActiveDocument.InlineShapes(5).OLEFormat.ConvertTo "Word.Picture"` To see a list of possible conversions, right-click the object and select Object ➤ Convert. To see the corresponding class name, make an `InlineShape` with that class and then look at the `ClassType` property as shown in the following code. `MsgBox ActiveDocument.InlineShapes(5).OLEFormat.ClassType`
DoVerb	Asks the OLE object to perform one of several actions. The single `VerbIndex` parameter tells the object which action to perform. Table 5-8 lists `VerbIndex` values.
Edit	Opens the OLE object for editing in the application that created it. For example, if you use Word to create an embedded Excel worksheet, this method opens the object inside Word. If you use Excel to create a work sheet in a separate file and then use Word to link to it, this method opens the worksheet in a separate Excel window.
Open	Opens the OLE object in its native application. For example, if you use Word to create an embedded Excel worksheet, this method opens the object in a separate Excel window. In contrast, the `Edit` method would open the worksheet inside Word because Word created it.

Note that the `Object` property is usable only if the object has been activated and it is embedded rather than linked.

The `OLEFormat` object's `DoVerb` method takes a single parameter, `VerbIndex`, that tells the object what to do. This parameter can be any constant of the type `WdOLEVerb` listed in Table 5-8. If the OLE object doesn't support a particular verb, VBA code that invokes it will raise an error.

Table 5-8. VerbIndex *Values*

VALUE	PURPOSE
wdOLEVerbDiscardUndoState	Makes the object discard any undo information it is holding.
wdOLEVerbHide	Activates the object but hides its user interface elements (menus, toolbars, and so forth) from view.
wdOLEVerbInPlaceActivate	Activates the object but doesn't display any user interface elements.
wdOLEVerbOpen	Opens the object for editing in a separate window much as the Open method described in Table 5-7 does.
wdOLEVerbPrimary	Does the same thing the object does if you double-click it.
wdOLEVerbShow	Opens the OLE object for editing in the application that created it much as the Edit method described in Table 5-7 does.
wdOLEVerbUIActivate	Activates the object and displays its user interface elements (menus and toolbars).

CAUTION *If the object will be opened within Word, you should select it first. If you do not, focus moves away from the object after it opens, so the object immediately closes again.*

```
ActiveDocument.InlineShapes(1).Select
ActiveDocument.InlineShapes(1).OLEFormat.Edit
```

If the object opens in a separate window, it is unaffected by the focus in Word, so you don't need to worry about selecting it.

TIP *Type* "Word.WdOLEVerb." *to make IntelliSense list the available* VerbIndex *values.*

If you want to do something programmatically to the object, but you don't want to open it for interactive editing, use wdOLEVerbHide to activate the object. To manipulate the object with VBA code, you must access the OLEFormat.Object property, but that property is not available unless you activate the object.

The following VBA code uses wdOLEVerbHide to increment the value in the first cell in an embedded Excel worksheet without opening the worksheet for interactive editing.

```
Dim wb As Workbook
Dim ws As Worksheet

    ' Activate the object while hiding its user interface elements.
    ActiveDocument.InlineShapes(1).OLEFormat.DoVerb _
        Word.WdOLEVerb.wdOLEVerbHide

    ' Get the Workbook.
    Set wb = ActiveDocument.InlineShapes(i).OLEFormat.Object

    ' Get the Worksheet.
    Set ws = wb.Sheets(1)

    ' Increment the cell's value.
    ws.Cells(1, 1) = ws.Cells(1, 1) + 1
```

Field *Objects*

The InlineShape object's Field property returns a Field object that provides several interesting values. Table 5-9 describes the object's most interesting properties.

Table 5-9. Useful Field *Object Properties*

PROPERTY	PURPOSE
Code	A Range object that contains the field's code. A typical field code for a linked OLE object might look like this: LINK Excel.Sheet.8 "C:\\OfficeSmackdown\\Src\\Ch05\\3DGraph.xls" "" \a \f 0 \p
InlineShape	The InlineShape object representing this OLE object. Use this object to invoke properties and methods not provided by the Field object.
LinkFormat	A LinkFormat object representing the link parameters. Because this object represents link parameters, it only applies to linked objects, not embedded objects. This object is described further in an earlier section.
Locked	This is True if the object is locked to prevent automatic updating.
OLEFormat	An OLEFormat object that provides additional information about the OLE object, other than linking information. This object is described further in the previous section.
ShowCodes	This is True if this object should display its field codes instead of the OLE object itself.

The Field object also provides some useful methods. Table 5-10 lists the most useful.

Table 5-10. Useful Field *Object Methods*

METHOD	PURPOSE
Copy	Copies the field to the clipboard.
Cut	Copies the field to the clipboard and removes it from the document.
Delete	Deletes the field. This has the same effect as invoking the InlineShape object's Delete method.
DoClick	Clicks the field. The precise effect depends on the object. This selects a linked object but opens an embedded object.
Select	Selects the object much as invoking the InlineShape object's Select method does.
Unlink	Breaks the link and coverts the object into a textual or picture representation. After doing this, you cannot edit the object using its native application.

The following example code demonstrates the Field object's Copy method. The subroutine copies the field information for the object stored in InlineShapes(4) to the clipboard. It then creates a Range object at the end of the document and pastes the field into that range. If InlineShapes(4) is an embedded Excel worksheet, this makes a copy of the worksheet.

NOTE *Note that the newly pasted copy has its own embedded data, so a change to either one of these embedded worksheets does not affect the other.*

FILE *UseOle.doc*

```
' Copy the object in InlineShapes(4).
Sub CopyWorksheet()
Dim rng As Range

    ' Copy the worksheet's field info.
    ActiveDocument.InlineShapes(4).Field.Copy

    ' Make a range at the end of the document.
    Set rng = ActiveDocument.Content
    rng.Collapse Direction:=wdCollapseEnd

    ' Paste the copied worksheet field.
    rng.Paste
End Sub
```

Examples

The following code shows how VBA code in a Word document can create an embedded Excel worksheet from scratch. The subroutine uses the InlineShapes object's AddOLEObject method to create a new OLE object. The ClassType parameter indicates that this should be an Excel worksheet, and the Range parameter puts the object at the end of the Word document. The call to AddOLEObject does not include a file name, so this is an embedded object.

The subroutine uses a With statement to work with the new worksheet object. The new object's OLEFormat.Object property represents the workbook containing the new worksheet. The subroutine saves a reference to the workbook and uses its Sheets collection to get a reference to the new worksheet. It uses this object to place a value in the new worksheet's upper-left cell.

Finally, the routine activates the OLE object so the user can enter other values in the worksheet.

FILE *Ch05\UseOle.doc*

```
' Make an embedded worksheet.
Private Sub cmdEmbeddedWorksheet_Click()
Dim excel_workbook As Excel.Workbook
Dim excel_worksheet As Excel.Worksheet

    ' Make the new Excel worksheet at the end.
    With ActiveDocument.InlineShapes.AddOLEObject( _
        ClassType:="Excel.Sheet", _
        Range:=ActiveDocument.Range(ActiveDocument.Range.End - 1))

        ' Activate the object without opening
        ' it for interactive editing.
        .OLEFormat.DoVerb Word.WdOLEVerb.wdOLEVerbHide

        ' Get the workbook.
        Set excel_workbook = .OLEFormat.Object

        ' Get the worksheet.
        Set excel_worksheet = excel_workbook.Sheets.Item(1)
```

```
        ' Set the first cell's value.
        excel_worksheet.Cells(1, 1) = 1

        ' Activate the worksheet so the user
        ' can enter values.
        .Activate
    End With
End Sub
```

The following code creates an OLE object linking to a PowerPoint slide. It uses the InlineShapes object's AddOLEObject method to create a new OLE object. The ClassType parameter indicates that this is a PowerPoint presentation (show). The FileName parameter gives the name of the PowerPoint file that the OLE object should load. If you omit the ClassType parameter, VBA uses the file to decide that you want to link to a PowerPoint presentation.

The LinkToFile parameter is True, indicating that this OLE object should be linked rather than embedded. The Range parameter puts the object at the end of the Word document.

 FILE *Ch05\UseOle.doc*

```
' Make a linked PowerPoint slide.
Private Sub cmdLinkedPresentation_Click()
    ' Make the new Excel worksheet at the end.
    ActiveDocument.InlineShapes.AddOLEObject _
        ClassType:="PowerPoint.Show", _
        FileName:=ActiveDocument.Path & "\OLESource.ppt", _
        LinkToFile:=True, _
        Range:=ActiveDocument.Range(ActiveDocument.Range.End - 1)
End Sub
```

The following code increments the value in the first cell in an embedded Excel worksheet. First it loops through the active document's InlineShapes collection until it finds one with a field code that includes the text EMBED Excel.Sheet. It invokes that InlineShape object's DoVerb method with the wdOLEVerbHide parameter to activate the object without opening it for interactive editing. It uses the object's OLEFormat.Object method to get a reference to the object's workbook and uses the workbook's Sheets collection to get a reference to the worksheet. It then uses the worksheet's Cells collection to increment the value in the first cell.

FILE *Ch05\UseOle.doc*

```
' Increment the first cell in the embedded worksheet.
Private Sub cmdIncrementCell_Click()
Dim i As Integer
Dim excel_workbook As Excel.Workbook
Dim excel_worksheet As Excel.Worksheet

    For i = 1 To ActiveDocument.InlineShapes.Count
        ' See if this is an embedded Excel.Sheet.
        With ActiveDocument.InlineShapes(i)
            If InStr(.Field.Code, "EMBED Excel.Sheet") > 0 Then
                ' This is the one.
                ' Activate the object without opening
                ' it for interactive editing.
                .OLEFormat.DoVerb Word.WdOLEVerb.wdOLEVerbHide

                ' Get the workbook.
                Set excel_workbook = .OLEFormat.Object

                ' Get the worksheet.
                Set excel_worksheet = excel_workbook.Sheets.Item(1)

                ' Increment the first cell's value.
                excel_worksheet.Cells(1, 1) = excel_worksheet.Cells(1, 1) + 1
            End If
        End With
    Next i
End Sub
```

Programming OLE Objects in Excel

Word stores an OLE object as a free-floating shape or as an inline shape located within the flow of the text. Excel doesn't have the same concept of "flow of text," so an Excel worksheet stores all of its OLE objects in a Shapes collection. For convenience, a Worksheet object also provides an OLEObjects collection that contains references to the worksheet's OLE objects.

The following section explains how your VBA code can create OLE objects in Excel. The sections after that describe the objects you can use to manipulate OLE objects in Excel.

Creating OLE Objects

Just as a Word document's Shapes collection provides an AddOLEObject method for creating new OLE objects, so too does an Excel worksheet's Shapes collection. The following code shows the syntax for the Shapes collection's AddOLEObject method. This method returns a reference to the new object.

```
Shapes.AddOLEObject(ClassType, FileName, LinkToFile, DisplayAsIcon, _
    IconFileName, IconIndex, IconLabel, Left, Top, Width, Height)
```

This is the same syntax used by the AddOLEObject method provided by Word's Shapes collection, except it doesn't include Word's final Range parameter. Excel doesn't have a concept of paragraphs, so it doesn't make sense to anchor the Shape to a paragraph represented by a Range. The other parameters have the same meanings they do for Word and you can read about them earlier in this chapter. They are described in detail in Table 5-1.

The following code shows how an Excel macro can create an embedded Word document. The subroutine first obtains a reference to the active worksheet. It uses the worksheet's Shapes.AddOLEObject method to create a new embedded Word document.

Next the routine gets a reference to the newly created object stored at the last position in the OLEObjects collection. Alternatively, the code could have used the OLEFormat.Object property of the last item in the Shapes collection.

The code finishes by setting the object's Name property. You can later use this name to find the object in the Shapes or OLEObjects collection.

 FILE *Ch05\MakeOle.xls*

```
' Create an embedded Word document.
Sub EmbedWordDocument()
Dim ws As Worksheet
Dim ole_obj As OLEObject

    ' Create the new OLE object.
    Set ws = Application.ActiveSheet
```

```
    ws.Shapes.AddOLEObject _
        ClassType:="Word.Document", _
        Link:=False

    ' Set the new object's name.
    Set ole_obj = ws.OLEObjects(ws.OLEObjects.Count)
'    Set ole_obj = ws.Shapes(ws.Shapes.Count).OLEFormat.Object
    ole_obj.Name = "Word Document"
End Sub
```

The following version of this code uses a slightly different approach. When it uses the AddOLEObject method to make the new embedded Word document, it saves a reference to the newly created Shape object. It uses the object's OLEFormat.Object property to get a reference to the new OLE object. The code then sets that object's position and Name property.

 FILE *Ch05\MakeOle.xls*

```
' Create an embedded Word document.
Sub EmbedWordDocument2()
Dim ws As Worksheet
Dim ole_obj As OLEObject
Dim new_shape As Excel.Shape

    ' Create the new OLE object.
    Set ws = Application.ActiveSheet
    Set new_shape = ws.Shapes.AddOLEObject( _
        ClassType:="Word.Document", _
        Link:=False, _
        Left:=20, Top:=20, Height:=100, Width:=100)

    ' Set the new object's name.
    Set ole_obj = new_shape.OLEFormat.Object
    With ole_obj
        .Top = 50
        .Left = 50
        .Width = 50
        .Height = 50
        .Name = "New Word Document"
    End With
End Sub
```

The following sections describe some of the classes you can use to manipulate OLE objects in Excel.

Shape *Objects*

The Shape object provides general information about an OLE object stored in the Shapes collection. Table 5-11 describes the most useful properties provided by a Shape object representing an OLE object. Table 5-12 lists the Shape object's most useful methods.

NOTE *The* Shape *object contains many other properties that do not relate to OLE objects. For many of those properties, accessing the property for an OLE object causes an error. For example, the* Diagram *property only applies to shapes that are* Diagram *objects. If your code tries to access an OLE object's* Diagram *property, Excel raises the runtime error 1004, "This member can only be accessed for a Diagram object."*

Table 5-11. Useful Shape *Object Properties*

PROPERTY	PURPOSE
AutoShapeType	Returns the Shape's autoshape type. For OLE objects, this is msoShapeMixed.
BottomRightCell	Returns the lowermost, rightmost cell that is at least partly covered by the Shape.
ControlFormat	Returns an object that describes the control's properties. This is a catch-all object intended to describe objects such as scrolled lists rather than OLE objects. The two most useful ControlFormat properties for OLE objects are ControlFormat.Enabled (True if the control is enabled) and ControlFormat.PrintObject (True if the object will be printed when the document is printed).
Height	The OLE object's height in points.
Left	The OLE object's left edge position in points.
LinkFormat	A LinkFormat object representing the link parameters. Because this object represents link parameters, it only applies to linked objects, not embedded objects. This object is described further in a later section.

(continued)

Table 5-11. Useful Shape *Object Properties (continued)*

PROPERTY	PURPOSE
Locked	If True, the user cannot update the OLE object while the worksheet is locked. Use Tools ➤ Protection ➤ Protect Sheet to protect a worksheet. Use Tools ➤ Protection ➤ Unprotect Sheet to unprotect a worksheet. Note that VBA code cannot change an OLE object's Locked property while its worksheet is protected. You can also use the Worksheet object's Protect and Unprotect methods to protect and unprotect it.
Name	A unique identifier for the OLE object. You can use this name to quickly locate objects in a worksheet's Shapes or OLEObjects collections, as in: Sheets(1).OLEObjects("SalesFigures").Update. Note that two objects cannot have the same name. Note also that this is the OLE object's name, not the Shape's name. That means it has the same value as the corresponding OLEObject's Name property. The OLEObject class is described in the next section.
OLEFormat	An OLEFormat object that provides additional information about the OLE object (other than linking information). This object is described further in a later section.
Placement	Indicates the way in which the object is attached to the cells beneath it. This can be xlFreeFloating (does not move or resize with the cells beneath), xlMove (moves with the cells beneath), or xlMoveAndSize (moves and resizes with the cells beneath). For example, if you use Insert ➤ Rows to insert a row above an OLE object with Placement = xlMove, the object moves down a row.
Rotation	The angle at which the object is rotated. You may not be able to rotate some OLE objects.
Top	The OLE object's top position in points.
TopLeftCell	Returns the uppermost, leftmost cell that is at least partly covered by the Shape.
Type	The type of Shape object. For an OLE object, this should be msoEmbeddedOLEObject or msoLinkedOLEObject.
Visible	Indicates whether the object should be visible. This can take the values msoTrue, msoCTrue, msoFalse, or msoTriStateToggle (toggles between msoTrue and msoFalse).
Width	The OLE object's width in points (remember that 1 inch equals 72 points).

CAUTION *When you first create an OLE object, Excel gives it a default name, such as Object 1, Object 2, and so forth. Excel may not let you give an object a default name that has been used even if you have changed that object's name. For example, suppose you create an OLE object linked to a Word document, Excel gives it the name Object 27, and you change the object's name to Sales Figures. If you create another OLE object, you may not be able to change that object's name to Object 27 even though that name is not currently in use. You can avoid this unpleasantness by not naming your objects Object <number>. That's not a very meaningful name anyway.*

Table 5-12 describes the Shape object's most useful methods.

Table 5-12. Useful Shape *Object Methods*

METHOD	PURPOSE
Copy	Copies the OLE object to the clipboard.
CopyPicture	Copies a picture of the OLE object to the clipboard. This method takes optional parameters Appearance (which can be xlPrinter or xlScreen) and Format (which can be xlBitmap or xlPicture).
Cut	Copies the OLE object to the clipboard and removes it from the worksheet.
Delete	Deletes the OLE object from the worksheet.
Duplicate	Creates a duplicate of the object, positioning it on top of the original object. This method returns a reference to the new Shape.
IncrementLeft	Moves the left edge of a Shape the specified number of points to the right.
IncrementTop	Moves the top edge of a Shape the specified number of points down.
Select	Selects the Shape.

OLEObject *Objects*

An Excel Worksheet object has an OLEObjects collection containing references that represent each OLE object on the worksheet. Tables 5-13 and 5-14 describe the OLEObject's most useful properties and methods.

Table 5-13. Useful OLEObject *Properties*

PROPERTY	PURPOSE
AutoLoad	True if the OLE object is loaded when the Excel document is opened. This property applies only to linked objects, not embedded. If AutoLoad is False, Excel asks if it should update a workbook's links when you open it. If you know the data has not changed, you can save some time by clicking the Don't Update button.

(continued)

Table 5-13. Useful OLEObject *Properties (continued)*

PROPERTY	PURPOSE
AutoUpdate	True if the OLE object should update whenever the source document changes. This property applies only to linked objects, not embedded.
BottomRightCell	Returns the lowermost, rightmost cell that is at least partly covered by the OLE object.
Enabled	If this is False, the OLE object does not automatically update when the linked document changes.
Height	The OLE object's height in points.
Index	The OLE object's position in the OLEObjects collection.
Left	The OLE object's left edge position in points.
Locked	If True, the user cannot update the OLE object while the worksheet is locked. Use Tools ➤ Protection ➤ Protect Sheet to protect a work sheet. Use Tools ➤ Protection ➤ Unprotect Sheet to unprotect a worksheet. Note that VBA code cannot change an OLE object's Locked property while its worksheet is protected. You can also use the Work sheet object's Protect and Unprotect methods to protect and unprotect it.
Name	A unique identifier for the OLE object. You can use this name to quickly locate objects in a worksheet's Shapes or OLEObjects collections as in: Sheets(1).OLEObjects("SalesFigures").Update. Note that two objects cannot have the same name. Note also that this is the OLE object's name, not the OLEObject's name. That means it has the same value as the corresponding Shape's Name property (see the previous section).
Object	The object representing the OLE object's top-level interface. This will be something like an Excel Workbook, Word Document, or PowerPoint Presentation. Use that object's Application property to get a reference to the source application object.
OLEType	Returns either xlOLELink or xlOLEEmbed.
Placement	Indicates the way in which the object is attached to the cells beneath it. This can be xlFreeFloating (does not move or resize with the cells beneath), xlMove (moves with the cells beneath), or xlMoveAndSize (moves and resizes with the cells beneath). For example, if you use Insert ➤ Rows to insert a row above an OLE object with Placement = xlMove, the object moves down a row.
PrintObject	True if the object will be printed when the document is printed.
SourceName	The source document for a linked OLE object. For example: Word.Document.8|C:\OfficeSmackdown\Src\Ch05\OLESource.doc!'
Top	The OLE object's top position in points.
TopLeftCell	Returns the uppermost, leftmost cell that is at least partly covered by the Shape.
Visible	Indicates whether the object should be visible. This can take the values msoTrue, msoCTrue, msoFalse, or msoTriStateToggle (toggles between msoTrue and msoFalse).
Width	The OLE object's width in points.

Table 5-14. Useful `OLEObject` *Methods*

METHOD	PURPOSE
Activate	Activates the object and opens it for editing the application that created it. For example, if you use Insert ➤ Object to create an embedded Word document, Excel created the object, so this method opens it for editing within Excel. If you link to an external Word document created in Word, this method opens it in a new Word window.
Copy	Copies the OLE object to the clipboard.
CopyPicture	Copies a picture of the OLE object to the clipboard. This method takes optional parameters `Appearance` (which can be `xlPrinter` or `xlScreen`) and `Format` (which can be `xlBitmap` or `xlPicture`).
Cut	Copies the OLE object to the clipboard and removes it from the worksheet.
Delete	Deletes the OLE object from the worksheet.
Duplicate	Creates a duplicate of the object, positioning it on top of the original object. This method returns a reference to the new `Shape`.
Select	Selects the `Shape`.
Update	Updates the OLE object. For example, if `AutoUpdate` is False, use this method to update the object's contents.
Verb	Sends a verb to the OLE object's server application. The verbs you can use depend on the server application, but they usually include `xlOpen` (which opens the document in the application that created it) and `xlPrimary` (which opens the document using its native application in a separate window).

LinkFormat *Objects*

Like Word's `LinkFormat` objects, Excel's version provides information about how an OLE object is linked. Because this object describes a link, it isn't needed for embedded objects. Unlike the case with Word, however, the `LinkFormat` property for a `Shape` representing an embedded OLE object is not `Nothing`. Instead, some of the object's properties and methods don't make sense. For example, executing the `Update` method of a `LinkFormat` object representing an embedded object raises an error.

Excel's `LinkFormat` object has two important properties: `AutoUpdate` and `Locked`. These are the same as those provided by the `OLEObject` described in the previous section.

The `LinkFormat` object also provides an `Update` method that makes a linked OLE object refresh its data from its data source.

OLEFormat *Objects*

The OLEFormat object represents an OLE object's nonlinking characteristics. Its most useful property is Object. This property returns a reference to the OLEObject representing the OLE object. See the "OLEObject Objects" section earlier in this chapter for information on the OLEObject class.

The OLEFormat object also provides two methods, Activate and Verb, that work much as the corresponding OLEObject methods do.

Examples

The following code shows how VBA code in an Excel workbook can create an embedded PowerPoint slide from scratch. The subroutine uses the Shapes collection's AddOLEObject method to create a new OLE object. It saves the returned Shape object and sets its Name property to PowerPoint Slide.

 FILE *Ch05\MakeOle.xls*

```
' Create an embedded PowerPoint slide.
Sub EmbedPowerPointSlide()
Dim ws As Worksheet
Dim new_shape As Shape

    ' Create the new OLE object.
    Set ws = Application.ActiveSheet
    Set new_shape = ws.Shapes.AddOLEObject( _
        ClassType:="PowerPoint.Slide", _
        Link:=False)

    ' Set the new object's name.
    new_shape.Name = "PowerPoint Slide"
End Sub
```

The following code places text on the new PowerPoint slide. It finds the OLEObject corresponding to the slide in the OLEObjects collection. It uses the OLEObject's Object property to get a reference to the slide.

Next the routine locates the shape named Rectangle 2 in the slide's Shapes collection. Rectangle 2 is the default name for a new slide's title area. The shape's TextFrame property is an object that represents the shape's text, including its alignment and anchoring information.

The TextFrame object's TextRange property is another object representing the contents of the text. This object also represents the text's font and provides methods for manipulating the text by line, sentence, and paragraph. Finally, the TextRange object's Text property contains the text itself. The program sets this property so the slide's title displays the text "PowerPoint."

The code then locates the shape named Rectangle 3, the default name for the new slide's content area. The routine chases down the same sequence of properties, TextFrame.TextRange.Text, to set this shape's text to "This is an embedded PowerPoint slide."

 FILE *Ch05\MakeOle.xls*

```
' Place text on a PowerPoint slide.
Sub WritePowerPointSlide()
Dim ws As Worksheet
Dim ole_obj As OLEObject
Dim ppt_slide As PowerPoint.Slide

    ' Get the OLE object.
    Set ws = Application.ActiveSheet
    Set ole_obj = ws.OLEObjects("PowerPoint Slide")

    ' Get the PowerPoint slide and application.
    ole_obj.Verb xlVerbPrimary
    Set ppt_slide = ole_obj.Object

    ppt_slide.Shapes("Rectangle 2").TextFrame.TextRange.Text = _
        "PowerPoint"
    ppt_slide.Shapes("Rectangle 3").TextFrame.TextRange.Text = _
        "This is an embedded PowerPoint slide."
End Sub
```

The following code displays information for the OLE objects on a worksheet. It saves a reference to the first worksheet and then activates worksheet 2. It clears the worksheet and writes column headers in cells A1 through Q1.

The routine then loops through the first worksheet's OLEObjects collection. For each object, the code displays various properties. Note that a few properties depend on whether the object is linked or embedded. For example, the AutoUpdate and SourceName properties exist only if the object is linked. If the code tried to access those properties for an embedded object, it would raise error 1004, "Application-defined or object-defined error" (not terribly informative, I know).

 FILE *Ch05\MakeOle.xls*

```
' List information about OLE objects.
Sub DescribeOLEObjects()
Dim ws As Worksheet
Dim obj As OLEObject
Dim next_row As Integer
Dim c As Integer

    ' Save a reference to Sheet 1.
    Set ws = Sheets(1)

    ' Show results in Sheet2.
    Worksheets("Sheet2").Activate

    ' Clear everything and write column headers.
    Cells.Clear
    Range("A1:Q1") = Array( _
        "Name", "OLEType", "AutoLoad", "AutoUpdate", _
        "Enabled", "Locked", "Visible", "PrintObject", _
        "Placement", "Left", "Top", "Width", "Height", _
        "TopLeftCell", "BottomRightCell", "Application", _
        "SourceName")
    Range("A1:Q1").Font.Bold = True

    ' Loop through the OLE objects.
    On Error Resume Next
    next_row = 2
    For Each obj In ws.OLEObjects
        ' Display properties that apply to both
```

```
            ' linked and embedded objects.
            Cells(next_row, 1) = obj.Name
            Cells(next_row, 3) = obj.AutoLoad
            Cells(next_row, 5) = obj.Enabled
            Cells(next_row, 6) = obj.Locked
            Cells(next_row, 7) = obj.Visible
            Cells(next_row, 8) = obj.PrintObject
            Select Case obj.Placement
                Case xlFreeFloating
                    Cells(next_row, 9) = "xlFreeFloating"
                Case xlMove
                    Cells(next_row, 9) = "xlMove"
                Case xlMoveAndSize
                    Cells(next_row, 9) = "xlMoveAndSize"
            End Select
            Cells(next_row, 10) = obj.Left
            Cells(next_row, 11) = obj.Top
            Cells(next_row, 12) = obj.Width
            Cells(next_row, 13) = obj.Height
            Cells(next_row, 14) = "(" & _
                obj.TopLeftCell.Row & ", " & _
                obj.TopLeftCell.Column & ")"
            Cells(next_row, 15) = "(" & _
                obj.BottomRightCell.Row & ", " & _
                obj.BottomRightCell.Column & ")"
            Cells(next_row, 16) = obj.Object.Application.Name

            ' See if the object is linked.
            If obj.OLEType = xlOLELink Then
                Cells(next_row, 2) = "xlOLELink"
                Cells(next_row, 4) = obj.AutoUpdate
                Cells(next_row, 17) = obj.SourceName
            Else
                Cells(next_row, 2) = "xlOLEEmbed"
            End If

            ' Move to the next row.
            next_row = next_row + 1
        Next obj

        ' Autofit.
        Columns("A:Q").Select
        Selection.Columns.AutoFit
        Range("A" & next_row).Select
    End Sub
```

Programming OLE Objects in PowerPoint

Like Excel, PowerPoint stores OLE objects in shapes. A Slide object's Shapes collection provides an AddOLEObject method that creates new OLE objects.

The following sections describe the Shape class and other classes you can use to manipulate OLE objects in PowerPoint.

Shape *Objects*

As is the case in Excel, PowerPoint's Shape object provides general information about an OLE object stored in the Shapes collection. Table 5-15 describes the most useful properties provided by a Shape object representing an OLE object. Table 5-16 lists the Shape object's most useful methods.

Table 5-15. Useful Shape *Object Properties*

PROPERTY	PURPOSE

AnimationSettings	An AnimationSettings object that describe the OLE object's animation settings. For example, the following code applies an animation to the Shape named "Embedded Word Document" on the slide named "Embedded Word Slide."
	
	`ActivePresentation.Slides("Embedded Word Slide"). _`
	    `Shapes("Embedded Word`
	`Document").AnimationSettings.EntryEffect = _`
	       `ppEffectBlindsVertical`

AutoShapeType	Returns the Shape's autoshape type. For OLE objects, this is msoShapeMixed.
Height	The OLE object's height in points (remember, one inch equals 72 points).
Left	The OLE object's left edge position in points.
LinkFormat	A LinkFormat object representing the link parameters. Because this object represents link parameters, it only applies to linked objects, not embedded objects. This object is described further in a later section.
Name	A unique identifier for the OLE object. You can use this name to quickly locate objects in a slide's Shapes collection. Note that two objects in the same Shapes collection cannot have the same name, although objects in the Shapes collections of different Slide objects *can* have the same name.
OLEFormat	An OLEFormat object that provides additional information about the OLE object (other than linking information). This object is described further in a later section.

(continued)

Table 5-15. Useful Shape *Object Properties (continued)*

PROPERTY	PURPOSE
Parent	Returns a reference to the Slide containing the OLE object.

Shadow	A ShadowFormat object that describes the object's display shadow. For example, the following code gives the OLE object a shadow in the color scheme's shadow color, offset 5 points to the right and 3 points down.
	
	`With ActivePresentation.Slides("Embedded Word Slide"). _`
	`        Shapes("Embedded Word Document").Shadow`
	`    .ForeColor.SchemeColor = ppShadow`
	`    .OffsetX = 5`
	`    .OffsetY = 3`
	`End With`

Tags	A dictionary containing values you can store and retrieve for later use. This is similar to a collection and provides an Add method that lets you add a name and value pair of strings. Unlike normal collections, however, you must later refer to values by name not index. Also unlike regular collections, if you add a value with the same name as a previous value, the new value replaces the old with no error.
Top	The OLE object's top position in points.
Type	The type of Shape object. For an OLE object, this should be msoEmbeddedOLEObject or msoLinkedOLEObject.
Visible	Indicates whether the object should be visible. This can take the values msoTrue, msoCTrue, msoFalse, or msoTriStateToggle (toggles between msoTrue and msoFalse). Note that if you set this value to msoFalse, the OLE object is invisible during presentation design time as well as when you run the presentation. You will need to make the object visible again before you can work with it at design time.
Width	The OLE object's width in points.

When you first create an OLE object, PowerPoint gives it a default name such as Object 1, Object 2, and so forth. Right after you create the object, you may want to give it a more meaningful name.

Table 5-16 describes the Shape object's most useful methods.

Table 5-16. Useful Shape *Object Methods*

METHOD	PURPOSE
Copy	Copies the OLE object to the clipboard.
Cut	Copies the OLE object to the clipboard and removes it from the worksheet.
Delete	Deletes the OLE object from the worksheet.
Duplicate	Creates a duplicate of the object, positioning it slightly offset from the original object. This method returns a reference to a ShapeRange object containing the new Shape object.
IncrementLeft	Moves the left edge of a Shape the specified number of points to the right.
IncrementTop	Moves the top edge of a Shape the specified number of points down.
Select	Selects the Shape.

Although your code cannot give a Shape the same name as another Shape on the same slide, the Duplicate method can. When you use a Shape object's Duplicate method, the new object has the same Name property as the original. To avoid confusion, you should rename the duplicate right away.

The same thing happens if you copy and paste a Shape object either interactively or with VBA code. For example, the following code copies the Shape object named "Linked Word Document" from the slide "Linked Word Slide" and pastes it onto the same slide. It uses the returned ShapeRange object to get a reference to the new Shape and renames it. Unlike the Duplicate method, Copy and Paste places the new object directly on top of the original, so this code also moves the new object down slightly.

 FILE *Ch05\MakeOLE.ppt*

```
Sub CopyShape()
Dim sr As ShapeRange
Dim new_shape As Shape

    ActivePresentation.Slides("Linked Word Slide").Shapes("Linked Word
Document").Copy
    Set sr = ActivePresentation.Slides("Linked Word Slide").Shapes.Paste
    Set new_shape = sr(1)
    new_shape.Name = "Copy of " & new_shape.Name
    new_shape.IncrementTop 20
    new_shape.Delete
End Sub
```

LinkFormat *Objects*

Like Word's and Excel's LinkFormat objects, PowerPoint's version provides information about how an OLE object is linked. Because this object describes a link, it isn't needed for embedded objects.

PowerPoint's LinkFormat object has two important properties: AutoUpdate and SourceFullName. AutoUpdate is True if the OLE object should automatically update when its source is modified. SourceFullName returns the complete path and file name of the document linked by the OLE object.

The LinkFormat object also provides an Update method that makes a linked OLE object refresh its data from its data source.

OLEFormat *Objects*

The OLEFormat object represents an OLE object's nonlinking characteristics. Its most useful properties are described in Table 5-17.

Table 5-17. Useful OLEFormat *Object Properties*

PROPERTY	PURPOSE
FollowColors	Determines the extent to which the object follows the presentation's color scheme. This value can be ppFollowColorsNone (ignore the color scheme), ppFollowColorsMixed, ppFollowColorsScheme (follow the color scheme), or ppFollowColorsTextAndBackground (the text and background follow the color scheme). Note that this property applies only to embedded objects, and the actual effect depends on the application you are embedding.
Object	The object representing the OLE object's top-level interface. This will be something like an Excel Workbook, Word Document, or Power Point Presentation. Use that object's Application property to get a reference to the source application object.
ObjectVerbs	A collection listing the verbs understood by the source application. For example, the ObjectVerbs collection for a linked Word document contains the strings Edit and Open.

The OLEFormat object provides two methods: Activate and DoVerb. As its name implies, the Activate method activates the object.

The DoVerb method makes the object perform an action defined by its native application. This method's parameter is the index of the verb in the ObjectVerbs collection. For example, the following code finds a linked object's Open action and invokes it.

FILE *Ch05\MakeOLE.ppt*

```
' Find and execute an object's Open verb.
Sub OpenObject()
Dim target_slide As Slide
Dim i As Integer

    ' Select the slide in Normal view.
    Set target_slide = ActivePresentation.Slides("Linked Word Slide")
    With Application.ActiveWindow
        .ViewType = ppViewNormal
        .View.GotoSlide target_slide.SlideIndex
    End With

    ' Find and execute the Open verb.
    With ActivePresentation.Slides("Linked Word Slide"). _
            Shapes("Linked Word Document").OLEFormat
        For i = 1 To .ObjectVerbs.Count
            ' See if this is Open.
            If .ObjectVerbs(i) = "Open" Then
                .DoVerb i
                Exit For
            End If
        Next i
    End With
End Sub
```

Examples

The following code adds a new embedded Word document to a PowerPoint presentation. It begins by adding a new slide to the presentation and changing the new slide's name to Embedded Word Slide. It calculates the new OLE object's size and position so it will be 80 percent of the slide's width and height, and centered on the slide.

Next the code makes a new OLE object by using the AddOLEObject method provided by the new slide's Shapes collection. Parameters give the object's size and position, and indicate that the new object should be an embedded Word document. After creating the object, the code gives it a meaningful name.

The code switches PowerPoint to Normal view and moves to the new slide. Some operations, including activating the new OLE object, work only if PowerPoint is displaying the object's slide.

The code uses the OLEFormat object's Object property to get a reference to the embedded Word document. It uses that object's Application property to get a reference to the Word application server. The code uses these objects to initialize the embedded document.

The routine uses the Word application object to enter text in the document. It then uses the document object to give the first paragraph the style Heading 1, and the second and third paragraphs the style Heading 2. It also sets the paragraphs' font sizes to match those of the PowerPoint presentation's title and body styles. The code explicitly sets the paragraphs' colors, although with a little more work you could set them based on the presentation's colors instead.

 FILE *Ch05\MakeOLE.ppt*

```
' Create a new embedded Word document.
Sub EmbedWordDocument()
Dim new_slide As Slide
Dim new_shape As Shape
Dim X As Single
Dim Y As Single
Dim wid As Single
Dim hgt As Single
Dim word_doc As Word.Document
Dim word_app As Word.Application

    ' Make a new slide.
    With Application.ActivePresentation.Slides
        Set new_slide = .Add(.Count + 1, ppLayoutBlank)
        new_slide.Name = "Embedded Word Slide"
    End With

    ' Add a Word document to the slide.
    X = ActivePresentation.SlideMaster.Width * 0.1
    Y = ActivePresentation.SlideMaster.Height * 0.1
    wid = ActivePresentation.SlideMaster.Width * 0.8
    hgt = ActivePresentation.SlideMaster.Height * 0.8
```

```
    Set new_shape = new_slide.Shapes.AddOLEObject( _
        ClassName:="Word.Document", _
        Link:=msoFalse, _
        Left:=X, Top:=Y, Width:=wid, Height:=hgt)
    new_shape.Name = "Embedded Word Document"

    ' Display the new slide in a normal view.
    With Application.ActiveWindow
        .ViewType = ppViewNormal
        .View.GotoSlide Application.ActivePresentation.Slides.Count
    End With
    new_shape.OLEFormat.Activate

    ' Get the Word document and application.
    Set word_doc = new_shape.OLEFormat.Object
    Set word_app = word_doc.Application

    ' Create some text.
    With word_app
        .Selection.WholeStory
        .Selection.TypeText Text:="Word"
        .Selection.TypeParagraph
        .Selection.TypeParagraph
        .Selection.TypeText Text:="This is an embedded Word document."
    End With
    With word_doc
        With .Paragraphs(1).Range
            .Style = word_doc.Styles("Heading 1")
            .Font.Size = _
                ActivePresentation.SlideMaster. _
                TextStyles(ppTitleStyle).Levels(1). _
                Font.Size
            .Font.Color = wdColorSkyBlue
        End With
        With .Range(.Paragraphs(2).Range.Start, .Paragraphs(3).Range.End)
            .Style = word_doc.Styles("Heading 2")
            .Font.Size = _
                ActivePresentation.SlideMaster. _
                TextStyles(ppBodyStyle).Levels(1). _
                Font.Size
            .Font.Color = wdColorWhite
        End With
    End With
End Sub
```

The following code adds a new linked Word document to a PowerPoint presentation. Like the previous code, this routine creates a new slide. It then uses the AddOLEObject method to create a new OLE object linked to a Word document. It centers the object, switches PowerPoint to Normal view, and moves to the new slide.

 FILE *Ch05\MakeOLE.ppt*

```
' Create a new linked Word document.
Sub LinkWordDocument()
Dim new_slide As Slide
Dim new_shape As Shape

    ' Make a new slide.
    With Application.ActivePresentation.Slides
        Set new_slide = .Add(.Count + 1, ppLayoutBlank)
        new_slide.Name = "Linked Word Slide"
    End With

    ' Add a Word document to the slide.
    Set new_shape = new_slide.Shapes.AddOLEObject( _
        FileName:="C:\OfficeSmackdown\Src\Ch05\OLESource.doc", _
        Link:=msoTrue)
    new_shape.Name = "Linked Word Document"

    ' Center the shape.
    With new_shape
        .Left = (ActivePresentation.SlideMaster.Width - .Width) / 2
        .Top = (ActivePresentation.SlideMaster.Height - .Height) / 2
    End With

    ' Display the new slide in a normal view.
    With Application.ActiveWindow
        .ViewType = ppViewNormal
        .View.GotoSlide Application.ActivePresentation.Slides.Count
    End With
End Sub
```

Programming OLE Objects in Access

As is the case with so many other topics, the programming-oriented approach used by Access makes it look at OLE objects differently than Word, Excel, and PowerPoint do. Access doesn't really intend you to build and manipulate OLE objects at run time. You are supposed to build them interactively at design time and then *use* them at run time, either interactively or through VBA code.

This division between design-time creation and run-time use carries into the tools Access gives you for manipulating OLE objects. At design time, you can use VBA code to build a new OLE object, but you cannot initialize it. At run time, you can use VBA to initialize an OLE object that already exists, but you cannot create a new one.

The following section explains how to create ObjectFrame objects at design time. The section after that describes the most useful properties and methods provided by the ObjectFrame object. The next section provides several examples that manipulate ObjectFrames.

Creating and manipulating OLE objects in this way can be somewhat confusing. It is often simpler to create the object manually at design time by using Insert ➤ Object. Use the Properties window to give the object a meaningful name. Then you can manipulate the object at run time by using VBA code. For example, you can change the Excel worksheet or chart displayed by the object relatively easily. Using this technique, you don't need to worry about creating the object with code at design time. Unless you are building tools for other database form designers, you probably won't need to create a huge number of these objects at design time anyway, so making them interactively shouldn't be a major burden.

Creating ObjectFrame Objects

Access stores OLE objects by using the ObjectFrame class. It keeps a form's Object-Frame objects in the form's Controls collection. For example, the following code finds the form named frmEmployees and looks in its Controls collection for the ObjectFrame control named olePicture. It sets that control's Enabled property to False.

```
Application.Forms("frmEmployees").Controls("olePicture").Enabled = False
```

You can create an ObjectFrame control interactively by using the Insert ➤ Object menu, much as you can make OLE controls in other Office applications. When you have a form open for design, you can also use the control toolbox to place an ObjectFrame or BoundObjectFrame on the form.

Also when you have a form open for design, you can create a new `ObjectFrame` control by using the `Application` object's `CreateControl` method. The `CreateControl` method has the following syntax.

```
CreateControl(form_name, control_type, [section], [parent], [column_name], _
    [left], [top], [width], [height])
```

Table 5-18 describes the `CreateControl` method's parameters.

Table 5-18. `CreateControl` *Method Parameters*

PARAMETER	PURPOSE
column_name	The name of the field to which the control should be bound. For an unbound `ObjectFrame`, set this parameter to an empty string ("") or omit it.
control_type	The type of control. For an `ObjectFrame`, this should be `acObjectFrame`. You can also use the value `acBoundObjectFrame` to make a bound object frame that you can bind to OLE fields inside the database.
form_name	The name of a form open in design mode.
left, top, width, height	The position and size of the control in twips (1 inch equals 1,440 twips).
parent	The name of the parent control. To place the control directly on the form, set this to an empty string ("") or omit it.
section	The section on the form that should contain the new control. This should be one of the following values: `acDetail`, `acHeader`, `acFooter`, `acPageHeader`, `acPageFooter`.

The `CreateControl` method returns a reference to the newly created control. You can use that reference to set the new control's properties. In particular, you may want to give the control a more meaningful name than the default name of OLEUnbound1, OLEUnbound2, and so forth.

The following code adds an `ObjectFrame` control to the form named frmMakeOle. It then sets the control's name to ofEmbeddedWorksheet.

FILE *Ch05\MakeOLE.xls*

```
Sub MakeObjectFrame()
Dim object_frame As ObjectFrame

    Set object_frame = CreateControl("frmMakeOle", acObjectFrame)
    object_frame.Name = "ofEmbeddedWorksheet"
End Sub
```

The following version is slightly more concise. It calls the CreateControl method and sets the Name property of the returned object.

```
Sub MakeObjectFrame()
    CreateControl("frmMakeOle", acObjectFrame).Name = "ofEmbeddedWorksheet"
End Sub
```

 TIP *This version is more concise, but you may find that it is harder to read. If you find this kind of code confusing, use the previous version.*

ObjectFrame *Objects*

Having created a new ObjectFrame control, you can use its properties and methods to manipulate it. Some of these work only at run time. See the online help to determine which work when.

Table 5-19 describes the ObjectFrame properties most useful for working with OLE objects.

Table 5-19. Useful ObjectFrame *Properties*

PROPERTY	PURPOSE
Action	This is one of the ObjectFrame's most important properties. When you set its value, the control performs some action. Table 5-20 describes the values this property can take.
AutoActivate	Indicates how the control is activated. If this value is acOLEActivateManual, the object can only be activated by VBA code setting its Action property to acOLEActivate (calling this AutoActivate value "acOLEActivateCode" might have been better, because acOLEActivateManual implies that the user can activate the control manually when actually the opposite is true). The value acActivateGetFocus means the control activates whenever it receives the focus. The value acActivateDoubleClick means the control activates when the user double-clicks it or presses Ctrl-Enter when the control has focus.

(continued)

Table 5-19. Useful ObjectFrame *Properties (continued)*

PROPERTY	PURPOSE
Class	Sets the class name for an embedded OLE object. Examples include Word.Document, Excel.Sheet, and PowerPoint.Slide.
ControlType	For OLE objects, this is acObjectFrame or acBoundObjectFrame.
DisplayType	Determines whether the form displays the OLE object's data or an icon. Allowed values are acOLEDisplayContent and acOLEDisplayIcon.
DisplayWhen	Determines when the control is displayed. Set this value to 0 (always), 1 (print only), or 2 (screen only). Note that some other operations may not be allowed when the control has a particular DisplayWhen value. For example, if DisplayWhen is 1 (print only), the control is effectively hidden when running onscreen. In that case, you cannot set the Action property to acOLECreateLink.
Enabled	When the control is disabled, your code cannot set the Action property to certain values, such as acOLECreateLink. At run time, the user cannot open a control if Enabled is False.
Height	The control's height in twips (remember that 1 inch equals 1,440 twips).
Left	The coordinate of the control's left edge in twips.
Locked	Determines whether you can edit the control at run time. The default value is False for unbound object frames.
Name	The name of the object. Initially, this is something relatively useless, such as "OLEUnbound23," but you can change it to something meaningful, such as "Sales Figures." After that, you can use the Name as an index into the form's Controls collection as in this statement: Application.Forms("frmEmployees").Controls("Sales Figures").Locked = True.
Object	A reference to the OLE object. For example, if the ObjectFrame contains an embedded Excel workbook, then the Object property returns a reference to an Excel.Workbook object.
ObjectVerbs	A zero-based collection of the verbs understood by the OLE object.
ObjectVerbsCount	The number of verbs in the ObjectVerbs collection.
OLEClass	Contains a description of the OLE object's type. This is related but not identical to the Class property. For example, if you link the control to an Excel worksheet, Class might be Excel.Sheet.8 while OLEClass is Microsoft Excel 2000.
OLEType	Indicates the type of OLE object loaded into the control. This will be acOLELinked, acOLEEmbedded, or acOLENone. When you create the control, use the OLETypeAllowed property to specify the kinds of OLE objects the control can contain.
OLETypeAllowed	Determines the type of objects the control can contain. This should be acOLELinked, acOLEEmbedded, or acOLEEither. Set this property before you use the Action property to create the object.

(continued)

Table 5-19. Useful ObjectFrame *Properties (continued)*

PROPERTY	PURPOSE
SizeMode	Determines how the OLE object fits into the control. This property can have the values acOLESizeClip (clips off parts that don't fit), acOLESizeStretch (stretches the object to fill the control, possibly distorting the object), or acOLESizeZoom (scales the object to fit without distorting it).
SourceDoc	Use this property to specify which source document the Action property should link or embed.
SourceItem	Use this property to specify the data inside the source document that should be linked or embedded. For example, to link to an Excel workbook's sheet 2, cells A1 through E8, set SourceItem to Sheet2!R1C1:R8C5. To link to the bookmark Greeting in a Word document, set SourceItem to Greeting. To link to a specific slide in a PowerPoint presentation, set SourceItem to the slide's SlideID.
SourceObject	A string giving the full path and file name of the linked OLE object.
Top	The coordinate of the control's top edge in twips.
UpdateOptions	Specifies when the linked OLE object is updated. This value can be acOLEUpdateAutomatic (updates whenever the source document is changed) or acOLEUpdateManual (updates only when you set the Action property to acOLEUpdate, or the user selects Edit ➤ OLE/DDE Links, selects the link, and clicks the Update button).
Verb	Set this value to tell the control what to do when activated. Set this property to the index of the verb you want to use in the ObjectVerbs collection. For example, setting Verb = 1 makes the object execute ObjectVerb number 1 when it is activated. Table 5-21 describes additional values you can assign to this property.
Visible	Indicates whether the control is visible on the form. You cannot set the Action property while Visible is False.
Width	The control's width in twips.

Table 5-20 lists values you can assign to an ObjectFrame's Action property. Most values are not allowed when the control's Enabled property is False, its Locked property is True, or its Visible property is False. The exceptions are acOLECopy and acOLEActivate (which are always allowed), and acOLEClose and acOLEFetchVerbs (which are allowed when Enabled is True even if Locked is also True or Visible is False).

Table 5-20. ObjectFrame Action *Property Values*

VALUE	PURPOSE
acOLEActivate	Activates the control. Before using this Action, you must set the control's Verb property to tell it what to do when it activates.
acOLEClose	Closes the connection between an embedded OLE object and its native application.
acOLECopy	Copies the object to the clipboard.
acOLECreateEmbed	Creates an embedded OLE object in the ObjectFrame. Before using this Action, you should set the OLETypeAllowed property to acOLEEmbedded or acOLEEither, and set the Class property to the type of OLE object you want to create (for example, Word.Document). You can set the SourceDoc property if you want the object to copy its data from an external document.
acOLECreateLink	Creates a linked OLE object in the ObjectFrame. Before using this Action, you should set the OLETypeAllowed and SourceDoc properties. You can also set the SourceItem property if you want to specify only part of the source document. For example, if you are linking to an Excel worksheet, the value R1C1:R5C10 specifies the cells A1 through J5.
acOLEDelete	Deletes the OLE object and frees its resources.
acOLEFetchVerbs	Builds the control's list of allowed verbs. See the ObjectVerbs and ObjectVerbsCount properties.
acOLEInsertObjDlg	Displays the Insert Object dialog and lets the user select the control's object linked or embedded OLE object. Use the OLETypeAllowed property to specify the type of object the user is allowed to create.
acOLEPaste	Pastes data from the clipboard to the control. For example, suppose you select a range of cells from an Excel worksheet and copy it to the clipboard. Using this Action would paste the data into the control.
acOLEPasteSpecialDlg	Displays the Paste Special dialog and lets the user determine how the data is pasted into the control. For example, if you copy a range of Excel cells to the clipboard, this dialog lets the user decide whether to paste the data as an Excel worksheet, picture, bitmap, or text. Use the OLETypeAllowed property to specify the type of object the user is allowed to create (linked, embedded, or either).

You can set an `ObjectFrame`'s `Verb` property to the index in the `ObjectVerbs` collection of the command you want the object to execute when it is activated. For example, if you want the object to perform verb number 2 in this collection, set `Verb` to 2.

Note that `ObjectVerbs` is a zero-based collection, so the first verb has index 0. This first verb is the object's default action, and it is probably duplicated in the remaining verbs, usually in the second verb (depending on the application).

For example, the form frmListVerbs in database MakeOLE.mdb uses the following code to list the verbs supported by a linked Excel worksheet object and display them in a list. When you run this form, it should display the verbs &Edit, &Edit, and &Open. The first entry is the default action for this object. Setting the `ObjectFrame`'s `Verb` property to 2 would make it perform its Open action when it was activated.

 FILE *Ch05\MakeOLE.mdb*

```
' Build the list of verbs.
Private Sub ListVerbs()
Dim i As Integer

    ' Empty the list.
    Do While lstVerbs.ListCount > 0
        lstVerbs.RemoveItem 0
    Loop

    ' Do no more if no object is loaded.
    If ofWorksheet.OLEType = acOLENone Then Exit Sub

    ' Update the ObjectFrame's verbs.
    ofWorksheet.Enabled = True
    ofWorksheet.Locked = False
    ofWorksheet.Action = acOLEFetchVerbs

    ' Display the ObjectFrame's verbs.
    For i = 0 To ofWorksheet.ObjectVerbsCount - 1
        lstVerbs.AddItem ofWorksheet.ObjectVerbs(i)
    Next i
End Sub
```

In addition to indexes in the ObjectVerbs collection, you can set the Verb property to one of the constants listed in Table 5-21.

Table 5-21. Special ObjectFrame Verb Property Values

VALUE	PURPOSE
acOLEVerbOpen	Opens the object for editing in its native application in a separate window.
acOLEVerbPrimary	Invokes the object's default action. This constant has value 0, so it is the same as using the first verb in the ObjectVerbs collection.
acOLEVerbShow	Opens the object for editing in the application that created it. If the object is linked, this opens it in its native application in a separate window. If the object is embedded and was created by Access, it opens in-place inside the Access form.

ObjectFrame *Examples*

The following sections describe some simple examples that manipulate Object-Frames and the OLE objects they contain. Remember that you can create these objects only at design time and populate them only at run time.

Creating an ObjectFrame

The following code adds a new ObjectFrame to a form. It then sets the object's name and position.

If you create an ObjectFrame using code, you will almost certainly need to refer to it again later if for no other reason than to put a linked or embedded document in it. You might be able to dig through the form's Controls collection and use the controls' properties, such as OLEType, to find the ObjectFrame you created, but you can make this a lot easier by naming the object right after you create it. Remember that the name must be unique among the controls on this form.

FILE *Ch05\MakeOLE.xls*

```
' Open frmMakeOle for design and then execute
' this routine to make a new ObjectFrame control.
Sub MakeAndPositionObjectFrame()
    With CreateControl("frmMakeOle", acObjectFrame)
        .Name = "ofPositionedObjectFrame"
        .Left = 1440 / 4     ' 1/4 inch.
        .Top = 1440 / 4      ' 1/4 inch.
        .Width = 1440 * 3    ' 3 inches.
        .Height = 1440 * 2   ' 2 inches.
    End With
End Sub
```

This code uses a With statement to operate on the newly created ObjectFrame without needing to declare a separate variable for it. This is concise, but it limits the amount of IntelliSense help the Visual Basic IDE can provide. The IDE knows that the CreateControl method returns a control, but it doesn't know which kind of control. If you type a period inside the With block, IntelliSense lists the properties and methods of a generic Control object, not those of an ObjectFrame.

NOTE *The Office 11 Beta's IntelliSense seems to be a lot better at knowing what's going on in cases such as this.*

The following version of this routine saves a reference to the new control in a variable of type ObjectFrame and uses that variable in the With statement. The Visual Basic IDE knows the variable is an ObjectFrame, so it can provide more complete IntelliSense. If you type a period inside the With block, you'll see a list of the ObjectFrame's properties and methods, not just those for a generic Control. The end result of the code is the same, but this version makes programming easier.

FILE *Ch05\MakeOLE.xls*

```
' Open frmMakeOle for design and then execute
' this routine to make a new ObjectFrame control.
Sub MakeAndPositionObjectFrame2()
Dim object_frame As ObjectFrame

    Set object_frame = CreateControl("frmMakeOle", acObjectFrame)
    With object_frame
        .Name = "ofPositionedObjectFrame"
        .Left = 1440 / 4     ' 1/4 inch.
        .Top = 1440 / 4      ' 1/4 inch.
        .Width = 1440 * 3    ' 3 inches.
        .Height = 1440 * 2   ' 2 inches.
    End With
End Sub
```

Embedding an Object Interactively

You can create an ObjectFrame at design time. Then at run time, you can execute code to manipulate the ObjectFrame control, possibly linking or embedding an OLE object. You can execute the code interactively through the Visual Basic IDE or using a customized menu item or toolbar button.

The following code embeds an Excel worksheet in a running form. The code finds the form named frmMakeOle and uses its Controls collection to find the ObjectFrame named ofEmbeddedWorksheet. It then sets the control's properties to create an embedded worksheet.

Note that the code clears the control's SourceDoc and SourceItem properties. If the object previously contained some other OLE object and had these properties set, the control would use the data source document as a template for the embedded object instead of creating a fresh Excel worksheet. It would even override the Class property if necessary. For example, if the SourceDoc property indicated a Word document, the control would make an embedded Word document even though the Class property says Excel.Sheet.

FILE *Ch05\MakeOLE.xls*

```
Sub EmbedWorksheetInForm()
    With Application.Forms("frmMakeOle").Controls("ofEmbeddedWorksheet")
        .Enabled = True
        .Locked = False
        .OLETypeAllowed = acOLEEmbedded
        .SourceDoc = ""
        .SourceItem = ""
        .Class = "Excel.Sheet"
        .Action = acOLECreateEmbed
    End With
End Sub
```

Embedding an Object at Form Load

You can use the Visual Basic IDE, a menu item, or a toolbar button to execute the code shown in the previous section and embed a worksheet in an ObjectFrame. Alternatively, you can attach the code to one of the form's events.

For example, the following code in the frmMakeOle form executes when the form loads. The Form_Load event handler calls subroutine EmbedWorksheet. That routine enables and unlocks the ofEmbeddedWorksheet control, sets its OLETypeAllowed property to indicate the object will be an embedded OLE object, and sets its Class property to indicate an Excel worksheet. Then it sets the object's Action property to acOLECreateEmbed. That makes the object initialize itself as an embedded Excel worksheet.

With this code, all you need to do is open the form, and the form automatically makes the embedded worksheet.

FILE *Ch05\MakeOLE.xls*

```
Private Sub Form_Load()
    EmbedWorksheet
End Sub

' Embed an Excel worksheet.
Private Sub EmbedWorksheet()
    With ofEmbeddedWorksheet
        .Enabled = True
        .Locked = False
        .OLETypeAllowed = acOLEEmbedded
        .Class = "Excel.Sheet"
        .Action = acOLECreateEmbed
    End With
End Sub
```

Filling an Embedded Object

An embedded worksheet isn't tremendously useful if it just sits there empty. The following code embeds a worksheet just as the previous version does. Then it uses the ObjectFrame's Object property to get a reference to the embedded Excel Workbook object. It finds the Excel Worksheet object displayed by the control and gives it some data. A real application would probably display data more interesting than just the worksheet's cell names.

FILE *Ch05\MakeOLE.xls*

```
Private Sub Form_Load()
    FillEmbeddedWorksheet
End Sub

' Embed an Excel worksheet and fill it
' with data.
```

```
Private Sub FillEmbeddedWorksheet()
Dim excel_book As Excel.Workbook
Dim excel_sheet As Excel.Worksheet
Dim r As Integer
Dim c As Integer

    With ofEmbeddedWorksheet
        .Enabled = True
        .Locked = False
        .OLETypeAllowed = acOLEEmbedded
        .Class = "Excel.Sheet"
        .Action = acOLECreateEmbed

        ' Save a reference to the Excel
        ' workbook object.
        Set excel_book = .Object
    End With

    ' Put some data in the workbook.
    Set excel_sheet = excel_book.Sheets(1)
    For r = 1 To 10
        For c = 1 To 4
            excel_sheet.Cells(r, c) = "(" & _
                r & ", " & c & ")"
        Next c
    Next r
End Sub
```

Linking an Object at Form Load

Embedding a new Excel worksheet when a form opens is a bit unusual because it starts empty every time the form loads. You could add code to save and restore values when the form loads and unloads, but in that case you may as well use a linked Excel worksheet and let it save and restore the data for you.

The following code shows how a form might link to an Excel chart when it opens. This code sets the OLETypeAllowed property to allow linked objects, sets the SourceDoc property to give the path and file name of the Excel document that it should link, and sets the Action property to acOLECreateLink to make the link.

FILE *Ch05\MakeOLE.xls*

```vba
Private Sub Form_Load()
    LinkWorksheet
End Sub

' Link an Excel worksheet.
Private Sub LinkWorksheet()
    With ofEmbeddedWorksheet
        .Enabled = True
        .Locked = False
        .OLETypeAllowed = acOLELinked
        .SourceDoc = "C:\OfficeSmackdown\Src\Ch05\Linked.xls"
        .Action = acOLECreateLink
    End With
End Sub
```

By linking an OLE object when a form loads, you can display the most current version of a document on the form. For example, you might use this technique to display summary sales data from an Excel chart at the top of a form that manages sales data. If the file containing the Excel chart changes daily (for example, 022104.xls for February 21, 2004) then your code could determine the current day's file and link to it when the form loads.

Displaying Record-Related Data

It is sometimes more useful to display data that depends on the record currently displayed by the form. For example, you might build an Employee table that includes a PictureFile field. This field could hold the name of a file containing a picture of the corresponding employee. When the form moves to display a new record, VBA code can link an OLE object to that employee's picture file.

The following code shows how the frmOleSources form displays Excel data selected by the user. When the user moves to a new record in the OleSources table, the Form_Current event handler runs. The code finds the form's ObjectFrame control named ofExcelData. It updates the control's SourceDoc property to indicate the file name stored in the table's SourceFile field. It sets the control's OLETypeAllowed property to allow only linked documents and uses the control's Action method to link to the file.

FILE *Ch05\MakeOLE.xls*

```
' Display the currently selected Excel data.
Private Sub Form_Current()
    With ofExcelData
        .Enabled = True
        .Locked = False
        .SourceDoc = Me!SourceFile
        .OLETypeAllowed = acOLELinked
        .Action = acOLECreateLink
    End With
End Sub
```

Linking a PowerPoint Slide

Sometimes you don't want to link to an entire document. You can use the SourceItem property to tell the ObjectFrame which part of the source document you want. The following code shows how a program can link to a specific PowerPoint slide.

The code finds the control and sets its properties to create the link much as previous examples have done. It sets the SourceDoc property to the name of the PowerPoint file and sets the SourceItem property to the SlideID of the slide it wants to link.

FILE *Ch05\MakeOLE.xls*

```
Sub LinkPowerPointSlide()
    With Application.Forms("frmMakeOle").Controls("ofEmbeddedWorksheet")
        .Enabled = True
        .Locked = False
        .OLETypeAllowed = acOLELinked
        .Class = "PowerPoint.Slide"
        .SourceDoc = "C:/OfficeSmackdown/Src/Ch05/OLESource.ppt"
        .SourceItem = "257"
        .Action = acOLECreateLink
    End With
End Sub
```

PowerPoint automatically assigns a unique SlideID whenever you create a new slide. This value remains unchanged if you move the slides around so you can use it to identify the slide even if the presentation has been rearranged.

Unfortunately, there's no easy way to find out a slide's ID value. One method is to use VBA code in PowerPoint. For example, if you enter the following code in Visual Basic's Immediate window and press Return, the IDE displays the SlideID property of the second slide in the active presentation.

```
?ActivePresentation.Slides(2).SlideID
```

Linking a Word Bookmark

Just as you can link to a specific PowerPoint slide, you can link an ObjectFrame to a bookmark defined in a Word document. Set the SourceDoc property to the document's name and set SourceItem to the name of the bookmark. The following code links an ObjectFrame to the bookmark named Greeting in the file HasBookmark.doc.

FILE *Ch05\MakeOLE.xls*

```
Sub LinkWordBookmark()
    With Application.Forms("frmMakeOle").Controls("ofEmbeddedWorksheet")
        .Enabled = True
        .Locked = False
        .OLETypeAllowed = acOLELinked
        .Class = "Word.Document"
        .SourceDoc = "C:/OfficeSmackdown/Src/Ch05/HasBookmark.doc"
        .SourceItem = "Greeting"
        .Action = acOLECreateLink
    End With
End Sub
```

To create a bookmark in Word, select the text you want the bookmark to contain. Then use the Insert ➤ Bookmark menu item to open the Bookmark dialog shown in Figure 5-13. Enter the new bookmark's name and click Add.

Figure 5-13. Use the Bookmark dialog to insert and manage bookmarks in Word.

Linking an Excel Range

To link to a range of cells in an Excel worksheet, set SourceItem to the name of the worksheet or chart you want to use, followed by the cell range in RC notation. For example, the following code sets SourceItem to Sheet2!R1C1:R3C5. This selects cells A1 through E3 from worksheet Sheet2.

FILE *Ch05\MakeOLE.xls*

```
Sub LinkExcelRange()
    With Application.Forms("frmMakeOle").Controls("ofEmbeddedWorksheet")
        .Enabled = True
        .Locked = False
        .OLETypeAllowed = acOLELinked
        .Class = "Excel.Sheet"
        .SourceDoc = "C:/OfficeSmackdown/Src/Ch05/3Sheets.xls"
        .SourceItem = "Sheet2!R1C1:R3C5"
        .Action = acOLECreateLink
    End With
End Sub
```

Programming OLE Objects in Outlook

Like Access, Outlook adds it own unique perspective to OLE. Although you can use OLE objects in an Outlook item (mail message, contact item, journal entry, or whatever), Outlook doesn't provide great support for managing those objects programmatically. However, it does provide some useful alternatives in the form of attachments. It lets you attach a link to a file, an embedded copy of a file, or an embedded copy of another Outlook item. This gives you functionality similar to that provided by OLE.

The following section explains how to create and use OLE objects interactively in Outlook. The section after that describes the Attachment class that you can use to manage attachments. Subsequent sections explain how you can use Outlook file attachments to perform some of the tasks you might otherwise handle with OLE.

Using OLE Objects

It is simple to add an OLE object interactively to an Outlook item. Open the item for editing, place the cursor in the item's body area where you want to add the OLE object, and use the Insert ➤ Object menu command to display the dialog shown in Figure 5-14.

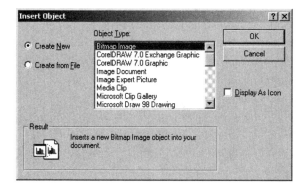

Figure 5-14. Use this dialog to insert an OLE object in an Outlook item.

To create an embedded OLE object from scratch, select the type of object from the list. Check the Display As Icon box if you want to display the object as an icon rather than display its current contents. Click OK when finished.

To make a linked OLE object, click the Create From File option button to see the dialog shown in Figure 5-15. Enter the file's path and name or click Browse to find the file. Check the Link button to make a linked object. Leave this box unchecked to make an embedded object. It's easy to forget to check the Link button, so take an extra second to think about it before you click OK. Check the Display As Icon box if you want to show the OLE object as an icon. Click OK when finished with your selections.

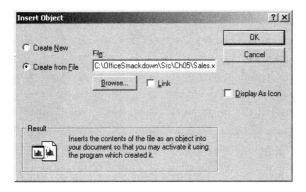

Figure 5-15. Use this dialog to select an existing file for linking or embedding.

You can also add an OLE object by selecting the object in another application such as Word or Excel and copying it to the clipboard. Then position the cursor in the Outlook item's body and select Edit ➤ Paste Special.

When you add an OLE object to an item, Outlook makes the object an attachment. Your VBA code can find the object in the item's Attachments collection. For example, the following code looks in the Drafts folder for a mail message with subject Progress Report. It examines the item's attachments and deletes those that are OLE objects.

FILE *Ch05\OlCh05.bas*

```
' Delete all OLE attachments from this item.
Sub DeleteOleAttachments()
Dim ns As NameSpace
Dim draft_folder As MAPIFolder
Dim mail_item As MailItem
Dim i As Integer
Dim att As Attachment
```

```
' Find the "Progress Report" mail item.
Set ns = GetNamespace("MAPI")
Set draft_folder = ns.GetDefaultFolder(olFolderDrafts)
Set mail_item = draft_folder.Items("Progress Report")

' Examine the attachments.
For i = mail_item.Attachments.Count To 1 Step -1
    Set att = mail_item.Attachments(i)
    If att.Type = olOLE Then att.Delete
Next i

' Save the changes.
mail_item.Save
End Sub
```

Using Attachment *Objects*

An item's Attachments collection contains Attachment objects describing its attachments (pretty obvious, huh?). This includes OLE attachments and the Outlook file attachments described in the following sections. Table 5-22 describes the Attachment object's most useful properties.

Table 5-22. Useful Attachment *Object Properties*

PROPERTY	PURPOSE
DisplayName	Indicates the text Outlook should display under the attachment's icon when it is displayed as an icon. This may or may not be the same as the attachment's file name.
FileName	The attached file's name without the directory path. This applies only to the Outlook file attachments described in the following section. If you try to access this property for an OLE attachment, Outlook raises an error.
Index	The index of the attachment in the Attachments collection.
Parent	A reference to the object containing the attachment. For example, if the attachment belongs to a mail item, this is a MailItem object.
PathName	The attached file's complete directory path including the file name. This applies only to the Outlook file attachments described in the following section. If you try to access this property for an OLE attachment, Outlook raises an error. If the attachment is a linked Outlook file attachment (shortcut), this property returns the linked file's path. If the attachment is an embedded Outlook file attachment, this property returns an empty string.

(continued)

Table 5-22. Useful Attachment *Object Properties (continued)*

PROPERTY	PURPOSE
Position	The character position where the attachment should be located in the mail message. This is really just advice to the mail display application. For example, the mail application may display all attachments at the end of the message. For that reason, it may be best to ignore this property.
Session	Returns a reference to the NameSpace object for the Outlook session. Currently, Outlook only supports one name space called MAPI (Mail Application Programming Interface). The NameSpace object provides properties and methods for managing the MAPI session: logging in and out, accessing folders, identifying the current user, dialing a contact's phone number, and so forth.
Type	A constant that identifies the kind of attachment. This can be olByReference (Outlook linked file attachment or shortcut), olByValue (Outlook embedded file attachment), olEmbeddedItem (an embedded Outlook item such as another mail message, contact entry, or task), or olOLE (an OLE object).

The Attachment object provides only two methods. The Delete method removes the attachment from the item to which it is attached. If the attachment is an embedded OLE object or an embedded Outlook file attachment, the object is permanently removed. If the object is a linked OLE object or a linked Outlook file attachment, the link is removed, but the file remains.

 NOTE *Changes to an item are not saved until you call the item's* Save *method. For example, your code can delete all of an item's attachments. If it exits without calling the item's* Save *method, the item is unchanged and keeps its attachments.*

The Attachment object's second method is SaveAsFile. This method saves the attachment in a file.

Outlook Attachments

In addition to OLE objects, Outlook has its own method for attaching files and other objects to an item. Outlook supports four kinds of attached object: OLE, by value, by reference, and embedded item. The previous sections discussed OLE objects in Outlook. The following sections describe the other three kinds of attachment.

"By Value" Attachments

An object attached by value is copied into the item much as an OLE embedded document is. The mail message shown in Figure 5-16 contains an attachment by value to the file Colors.doc.

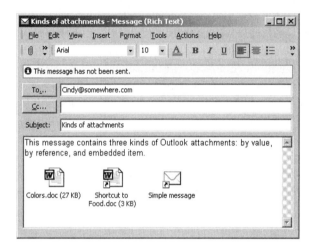

Figure 5-16. This message contains three attachments of different types.

If you double-click the attachment, Outlook displays the warning shown in Figure 5-17. If you select the "Open it" option and click OK, Outlook opens the attachment by using its default application. Normally, it would open the file Colors.doc using Word.

Figure 5-17. If you double-click a "by value" or "by reference" attachment, Outlook displays this warning.

TIP *If you are uncertain whether a Word document is safe, save it instead of opening it right away. Then open the file in WordPad. WordPad cannot execute macros, so it can safely read the file even if it contains a VBA virus.*

When you edit the attachment, you can make changes and save those changes into the attachment. If you open it again later, the changes will be there. Because the file is attached by value, however, the changes do not affect the original file on which the attachment was based.

"By Reference" Attachments

An object attached by reference (an Outlook shortcut) is represented as a shortcut in the Outlook item. In Figure 5-16, the second attachment is a shortcut to the file Food.doc.

If you double-click the attachment, Outlook again displays the warning shown in Figure 5-17. Because the attachment is just a shortcut to the actual file on disk, any changes you make to it are saved in the file. If you later open the attachment, you will see the changes. If you open the original file, you will also see the changes. In fact, anyone else who opens the file will see the changes. This can be useful if you need several people to examine and modify the same file.

 NOTE *If you plan to send a file as a "by reference" attachment to people, you should be sure they that can read the file. Place it in a publicly shared folder or network share. If people must edit the file, be sure the file gives them edit permission.*

 CAUTION *An evildoer could change the file even after you have looked at it the first time. For instance, long after the file was created, someone could open it and insert a virus even if you have previously examined the file and decided it was safe. To be prudent, you probably shouldn't place a "by reference" attachment on a system where people you don't trust can modify it.*

Embedded Item Attachments

In the third kind of attachment, you embed one Outlook item (mail message, contact entry, task, or whatever) in another. In Figure 5-16, the third attachment is an embedded item attachment to a mail item with subject "Simple message."

If you double-click this attachment, Outlook displays the warning shown in Figure 5-18. If you click Yes, Outlook opens the embedded item.

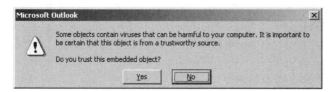

Figure 5-18. If you double-click an "embedded item" attachment, Outlook displays this warning.

CAUTION *Don't open embedded items unless you are sure they are safe! Outlook displays this warning message for a reason.*

Making Attachments

The following code shows how to make a simple Outlook item containing only text. The code calls the Application object's CreateItem method, passing it the parameter olMailItem to create a new mail item. It sets the message's To, Subject, and Body fields. It then calls the item's Save method. This is very important; if the code doesn't call the Save method, the new item is discarded.

The new mail item is saved in the appropriate default folder for its type of item. For example, Outlook saves new mail message items in the Drafts folder.

FILE *Ch05\OlCh05.bas*

```
' Make a simple text-only mail item.
Sub MakeSimpleMailItem()
Dim new_item As MailItem
```

```
    ' Create a new mail item.
    Set new_item = Application.CreateItem(olMailItem)
    new_item.To = "Bob@somewhere.com"
    new_item.Subject = "Simple message"
    new_item.Body = _
        "This is a simple mail message containing only text." & _
        vbCrLf & vbCrLf & _
        "Another example attaches this message as an embedded item."
    new_item.Save
End Sub
```

The following code shows how to make a new item with three kinds of attachments. It begins much as the previous example does, creating a new mail message item and filling in its To, Subject, and Body fields.

Next the routine creates a new attachment by using the Add method provided by the new mail item's Attachments collection. It passes the Add method a file name and the parameter olByValue to indicate that the file should be attached by value. The code repeats this step, passing Add the parameter olByReference to create a second attachment by reference.

The code then makes an embedded item attachment. To do that, it must first find the item it wants to embed. The code begins by using the Application object's GetNamespace method to retrieve a reference to the MAPI name space. This NameSpace object provides a starting point your code can use to examine all of the data contained in Outlook.

Next the routine uses the NameSpace object's GetDefaultFolder method to get a reference to the Drafts folder's MAPIFolder object. It uses that object's Items collection to find an item with subject "Simple message."

Now that the code has a reference to the object it wants to link, it calls the Attachments collection's Add method to attach the item to the new mail item, using the olEmbeddeditem parameter to indicate that this attachment should be an embedded Outlook item.

Finally, the code calls the new mail item's Save method.

FILE *Ch05\OlCh05.bas*

```
' Make a mail item with three different kinds
' of attachments.
Sub MakeMailWithAttachments()
```

```
Dim new_item As MailItem
Dim ns As NameSpace
Dim draft_folder As MAPIFolder
Dim attachment_item As MailItem

    ' Create a new mail item.
    Set new_item = Application.CreateItem(olMailItem)
    new_item.To = "Cindy@somewhere.com"
    new_item.Subject = "Kinds of attachments"
    new_item.Body = _
        "This message contains three kinds of Outlook attachments: " & _
        "by value, by reference, and embedded item." & vbCrLf & vbCrLf
    new_item.Attachments.Add _
        "C:\OfficeSmackdown\Src\Ch05\Colors.doc", _
        olByValue
    new_item.Attachments.Add _
        "C:\OfficeSmackdown\Src\Ch05\Food.doc", _
        olByReference

    ' Find the "Simple message" mail item.
    Set ns = GetNamespace("MAPI")
    Set draft_folder = ns.GetDefaultFolder(olFolderDrafts)
    Set attachment_item = draft_folder.Items("Simple message")

    ' Attach this item as an embedded item.
    new_item.Attachments.Add _
        attachment_item, _
        olEmbeddeditem
    new_item.Save
End Sub
```

The following code shows how to position an attachment inside a new mail message. The routine makes the new mail item as usual. After it creates the message body, it calls the new mail item's Save method.

Then it calls the Attachments object's Add method, passing it the character number where it wants the attachment positioned as an argument. Note that the message body contains an X at that position. The display program (Outlook in this case) replaces the character at that position with the attachment.

After creating the attachment, the code again calls the new item's Save method to save the attachment.

Note that the code calls the Save method twice: once after it creates the message body and once after it creates the attachment. If you don't call Save after creating the message body, the attachment is not positioned correctly. Possibly, the new item needs to save the body first so it knows where to position the attachment. The online help states, "To ensure consistent results, always save an item before adding or removing objects in the Attachments collection of the item."

```
' Make a mail item with a "by reference"
' attachment in a specific position.
Sub MakePositionedAttachment()
Dim new_item As MailItem
Dim txt1 As String
Dim txt2 As String

    ' Create a new mail item.
    Set new_item = Application.CreateItem(olMailItem)
    new_item.To = "Alice@somewhere.com"
    new_item.Subject = "1Q Sales Figures"
    txt1 = _
        "Alice," & vbCr & vbCr & _
        "Here are the final sales figures for the first quarter." & _
        vbCr & "X"
    txt2 = _
        vbCrLf & _
        "I hope you find them useful." & vbCr & vbCr & _
        "Rod"
    new_item.Body = txt1 & txt2
    new_item.Save

    ' Add an attachment.
    new_item.Attachments.Add _
        "C:\OfficeSmackdown\Src\Ch05\Sales.xls", _
        olByReference, Len(txt1)
    new_item.Save
End Sub
```

NOTE *If you step through this code in the Visual Basic development environment, you may notice something peculiar. If you examine the new item's* Body *property after the code assigns it, you'll discover that the object has converted the* vbCr *characters in the string into* vbCrLf *character combinations. That's a little strange, but what's really weird is that the attachment is positioned correctly based on the length of the first string, which includes only the* vbCr *characters. The three additional line feeds should make the attachment appear in the wrong place, but they don't!*

What seems to be happening is this: If you place a carriage return in the item's Body *property and don't follow it with a line feed, the object adds a line feed. It probably does that for the convenience of the text boxes that will later display the body. However, the position of an attachment doesn't seem to count the line feed characters. Using the length of the first string without line feeds puts the attachment in the right spot.*

If you use vbCrLf *in the body instead of* vbCr, *the object doesn't add the three line feeds because they are unnecessary. The attachment's position becomes messed up, and the attachment appears three places later than it should.*

Summary

Although OLE isn't exclusively an Office tool, it is still particularly useful in Office programming. It lets you link or embed information from one Office application in another without a whole bunch of conversion or import routines. OLE objects let you give users access to data in its original format. Using linked objects, you can let the user edit the data and save it into its original file where other users and possibly other documents using OLE can share it.

OLE may not solve all of your needs when it comes to displaying data from one application in another, but it can save you a huge amount of time under some circumstances. Whenever you need to display data from one application in another, consider OLE before you dive in and start churning out unnecessary code.

CHAPTER 6

Introduction to Office XP Object Models

IN A NUTSHELL, an object model describes the features that an application makes available to a developer. It tells what objects and methods a developer must use to make the application do whatever it needs to do.

Learning the specific features provided by an Office application's object model is a big part of learning how to program that application. For example, you cannot reasonably manipulate the text in a Word document until you understand the Word application's Range object and its properties and methods. The chapters later in this book describe specific details of the different Office applications' object models.

This chapter describes object models in general. It explains why object models typically include only objects and classes, and shows how you can expose object models in Visual Basic applications. Finally, it talks about some of the object model features shared by all of the Microsoft Office applications. This information provides the background you need to study the applications' specific object models described later in this book.

If you are familiar with object models, you may want to skim this chapter and move on. Even if you know basically what an object model is, however, it may be worth your time to at least scan this chapter. It tells where you can get additional information about an object model, how to implement your own object models and make them available for scripting, and how to bind objects defined in the Office applications' object models.

Object Model Basics

In the last few years, the term *object model* has been stretched a bit thin through overuse. For a term so heavily used, finding a concrete, generic definition is surprisingly hard. One fairly general definition says that an object model consists of the class definitions and specific objects that make up an application, and the relationships among them. For the purposes of this book, an Office application's object model describes the classes and objects available to the VBA developer.

The Application Class

All Office applications define an Application class that sits at the top of the object hierarchy. When you start one of the applications, it creates an instance of its Application class named Application.

 NOTE *Yes, creating an object of type* Application *named "Application" can be a little confusing at first. You almost never need to think about the class, however. Your code will almost always deal with the object named "Application," so you can usually ignore the class.*

Your VBA code can use that object to manipulate the application itself. The Application object's properties also contain references to other objects in use by the application. Many of those objects, in turn, contain references to objects that provide references to still other objects. Starting at the Application object and digging deeply enough through the object hierarchy, you can get into every niche and crevice provided by the application.

For example, Word's Application class has an ActiveDocument property. When a document is loaded, ActiveDocument returns a reference to an object of the Document class representing the document that's currently displayed. The Document object contains references to other objects, such as Paragraphs, Sentences, and Shapes collections, that you can use to manipulate the document. The Paragraphs property is a collection of Paragraph objects. Those provide a Range property that returns an object representing the contents of a paragraph. Like the Document object, the Range object has a Sentences collection representing the sentences in the text it represents. The following code digs down to this level to make the second paragraph in the fourth sentence in the active document bold. You can continue digging into the object hierarchy just about as far as you'd like.

```
Application.ActiveDocument.Paragraphs(4).Range.Sentences(2).Bold = True
```

NOTE *Microsoft's documentation and online help is inconsistent in classifying class members. At different times they call these items properties, methods, or objects. For example, in many places the online help describes the* Document *object's* Range *member as an object. Usually, however, you use that member as a function to return a* Range *object representing part of the document. Microsoft doesn't help matters by reusing names like this (a method named* Range *returns an object of class* Range*). Most of the time you'll do just fine if you ignore whether the documentation claims an item is an object, property, or method and just think about what it does. If it looks, acts, and feels like a property, think of it as a property. If it feels like a method, think of it as a method.*

Same Play, Different Playbook

All Office applications provide an Application object for you to use in manipulating the application and burrowing through the object hierarchy. It's important to note, however, that the different applications have different Application classes. The applications have many similar classes with similar names, and they perform roughly the same functions, but their details may be very different. It's as if they are using the same play but taken from different playbooks.

For instance, Excel doesn't work with text documents, so it doesn't have a Document class. Instead it has a Workbook class to represent an Excel workbook. The ActiveWorkbook object provides a reference to the currently active workbook, just as Word's ActiveDocument object gives a reference to the currently active document. Instead of breaking a document into paragraphs as Word does, Excel breaks a workbook into worksheets. Instead of a Paragraph class, Excel uses a Worksheet class. Just as Word's Document class contains a Paragraphs collection, Excel's Workbook class contains an analogous Worksheets collection.

The Office applications' object models have many similarities. All have Application objects. All have some sort of object to represent whatever kind of document-like thing the application manipulates (Word has Document, Excel has Workbook, PowerPoint has Presentation, Access has Database, and Outlook has several item classes including MailItem and ContactItem). All except Access have a Selection class that represents a group of objects the user has selected. All except Outlook and Access have a Range class that represents some sort of group of objects.

Although the parallels between the Office applications' object models are strong, it is important not to confuse them. In particular, be careful to use the right kind of object when you manipulate a particular application. For example, suppose you are writing a Word macro that opens an Excel workbook and interacts with it using a Range object. Your code must use Excel's Range class when it is working with Excel and Word's version when it is working with Word. The section "Cross-Application Development" later in this chapter has more to say about declaring and using objects defined by the different Office applications.

Object Models Resources

The Microsoft Office applications have truly enormous object models, exposing literally thousands of classes, properties, methods, enumerations (predefined constants), collections, and events for use by VBA programs. Later chapters describe some of the most useful pieces of the applications' object models, but it would be impractical (not to mention a waste of time) to describe every last inconsequential detail.

If you need to use some obscure part of an application's object model, you'll need to dig out the information on your own. Office comes with two tools to help: the online help and the Object Browser.

Online Help

The first place to look is the online help. Use the Tools ➤ Macro ➤ Visual Basic Editor command to open the Visual Basic development environment. Then select Help ➤ Microsoft Visual Basic Help.

Some developers prefer to work the other way around. You can open the Object Browser, find a likely looking method, property, enumeration, or whatever, highlight it and press F1 to display the corresponding help.

NOTE *The online help is different depending on whether you access it from the Visual Basic development environment or the application itself. The application's help is intended for end-users who want to know how to format a paragraph or make a chart. The Visual Basic development environment's help is aimed at developers who need to know what parameters the* Document *object's* Close *method takes.*

Using the online help, you can search for specific classes, properties, and methods. If you search for "application object," the help will give you information about the Application class. You can sift through the object's properties and methods to find the other classes at the next level of the object hierarchy.

TIP *You can also use the MSDN library at* http://msdn.microsoft.com/library, *which gives you complete help without requiring you to open the IDE for each application individually. This can be particularly handy when working with more than one Office application at once.*

Each help file also contains a graphical object model diagram for its application. To find it, search for "Microsoft Xxx Objects" where *Xxx* is the name of the application. For example, if you search for "Microsoft Excel Objects" in Excel and then click on the topic with that name (not the one named "Microsoft Excel Objects (Worksheet)"), you'll see the diagram shown in Figure 6-1. You can see by the vertical scrollbar on the right that less than half of the object model is visible in this picture.

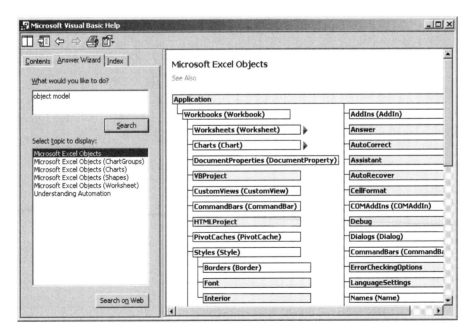

Figure 6-1. Help for Excel provides nice, graphical, and clickable object model diagrams.

Online, you can find the objects models at the following URLs.

Word—http://msdn.microsoft.com/library/en-us/vbawd10/html/
wotocObjectModelApplication.asp

Excel—http://msdn.microsoft.com/library/en-us/vbaxl10/html/
xltocObjectModelApplication.asp

PowerPoint—http://msdn.microsoft.com/library/en-us/vbapp10/html/
pptocObjectModelApplication.asp

Access—http://msdn.microsoft.com/library/en-us/vbaac10/html/
acsumAccessObjHierarchy.asp

Outlook—http://msdn.microsoft.com/library/en-us/vbaol10/html/
oltocObjectModelApplication.asp

Office (general)—http://msdn.microsoft.com/library/en-us/vbaof10/html/
oftocObjectModelApplication.asp

You can click on any object in this diagram to jump to that object's help entry. Objects with an arrow on the right, such as the Application.Workbooks.Worksheets and Application.Workbooks.Charts objects in Figure 6-1, have their own object model diagrams. If you click on the arrow, the help jumps to the expanded object model.

Office comes with some other help files that you may find useful. They describe VBA for a particular Office application and are stored in the directory C:\Program Files\Microsoft Office\Office10\1033 or somewhere similar on your system. Table 6-1 lists the help files and the applications they describe. The file VBAOF10.CHM describes Office components, such as menu items, toolbars, and the Office Assistant, shared among all the applications. All of these help files initially display their object model diagrams when you open them.

Table 6-1. Useful Office Application-Specific VBA Help Files

HELP FILE	APPLICATION
VBAAC10.CHM	Access
VBAOF10.CHM	Office
VBAOL10.CHM	Outlook
VBAPP10.CHM	PowerPoint
VBAWD10.CHM	Word
VBAXL10.CHM	Excel

The Object Browser

In addition to the online help, another tool you can use to learn about object models is the Object Browser. If you open the Visual Basic development environment and select View ➤ Object Browser or press F2, the Object Browser shown in Figure 6-2 appears.

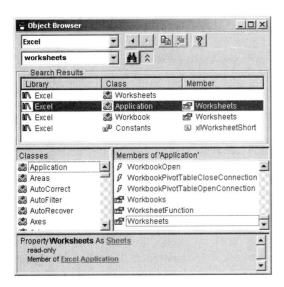

Figure 6-2. You can use the Object Browser to learn about the object hierarchy.

Initially, the library dropdown at the top selects all libraries. You can select a specific library, such as the Excel library chosen in Figure 6-2, to narrow the number of choices displayed. Enter text in the second dropdown and press Enter or click the binoculars button to search for the text. Figure 6-2 shows the results of searching for the text "worksheets."

Click on a returned entry to learn more about the entry. In Figure 6-2, the Application class's Worksheets member is selected. The lists below the search results area let you browse through the application's classes and a class's methods. The area at the very bottom gives additional information about the item selected. In Figure 6-2, this area says that the Application object's Worksheets member is a read-only property that returns an object of type Sheets. If you click the link to Sheets, the Object Browser displays information about the Sheets class.

The Object Browser doesn't provide as much information as the online help, but it is sometimes faster to use if you know more or less what you want to do. You can also highlight an item and press F1 to see its help.

TIP *Highlight an item and press Ctrl-C (or right-click and select Copy) to copy the item to the clipboard. Then you can paste it into your code quickly and without typing errors.*

The Global Object

Earlier, this chapter defined an object model as describing the classes and objects available to the developer. That definition works pretty well in a strictly object-oriented environment, but what if the program also uses variables and subroutines not contained in any class? For example, a Visual Basic code module (.bas file) can hold private and global variables and routines that are available to code throughout the project.

There are many occasions for which it may be reasonable for an Office application to create a global property or function. For example, suppose you have several forms that all need to verify that a particular text value has a valid phone number format. If you place the code in a particular form, it is hard for the other forms to share the code. If you place the IsValidPhoneNumber function in a code module, all the forms can share it.

Some things, such as a Document object, are clearly objects, but where do things like the Answer Wizard fit in? Auto Corrections and other options? What about menus, toolbars, custom dictionaries, and the recent file list? All of these things have an existence independent of any particular document, so it doesn't make sense to put them in the Document class.

The only reasonable choices are to make them public variables and routines, or to put them in a catchall class. Word puts these kinds of items in the Application class. When it starts, Word creates an instance of this class named Application. Your VBA code can use the Application object to access these global features. For example, the following VBA code changes the directory where Word looks when you want to open a new file. This method isn't a feature of a particular document, so it's dumped in the Application object.

```
Application.ChangeFileOpenDirectory "C:\Proposals"
```

To provide the best features of global routines and a catchall object (while making things a bit more confusing in the process), Word also provides a Global "object" that allows you to access many of the Application object's properties and methods without typing Application. For example, the following two VBA statements do the same thing.

```
MsgBox Application.RecentFiles(1).Name     ' Using the Application object.
MsgBox RecentFiles(1).Name                 ' Using the Global "object."
```

Although Global is referred to as an object in Word's online help, there seems to be no way to directly use it as an object. Its main purpose is to give you access to these features without typing an object name such as Application in front.

NOTE *Actually, it may very well be the other way around. It's likely that these features were implemented globally in Word, and then they were added to the* Application *object so they would have a home in the object model.*

The Global object also provides a handy categorization that you can use with the Object Browser. Open the browser and select the <globals> entry in the Classes list on the left as shown in Figure 6-3. The list on the right shows the objects, routines, and variables available without using Application or any other object.

NOTE *Word's help refers to the* Global *object, but the other Office applications' help files do not. Their Object Browsers do have a <globals> entry, however.*

Figure 6-3. Select the Object Browser's <globals> item to view globally available items.

These globally available items are also sometimes called convenience, short-cut, or shorthand items. They can sometimes shorten your code, but they can also cause some confusion if you are working with more than one Office application at a time. For example, suppose you write a Word VBA program that manipulates an Excel workbook and you copy and paste some Excel code into your new program. Now suppose the Excel code invokes Excel's global Selection object. When it runs in your Word macro, the code invokes Word's version of the object instead. That's likely to cause problems as your code tries to invoke Excel methods on the Word object. Usually, this sort of thing will cause a problem quickly, and you won't have too much trouble figuring out what's going wrong. Nevertheless, it's an issue you should keep in mind as you write code that will be shared among different Office applications.

One particularly useful global object is the Application object. Because it's global, you can refer to the Application object without prefixing it with the Application object. Yes, that sounds weird, but the Application object actually does contain a reference to itself, so the code Application.Application makes sense.

 NOTE *Of course this wouldn't work if the first instance weren't available globally. Then you would have a recursive "Which came first, the chicken or the egg?" type of problem.*

Many other objects in the Office applications' object models also contain a reference to the Application object. In Word, for example, the Document, Dictionary, Paragraph, Selection, and a couple hundred other classes include references to the Application object. If you are working with a reference far down the object hierarchy, these references let you get quickly back to the Application object if you need it.

Do-It-Yourself Object Models

There are several reasons why Microsoft may have decided to put the global objects and methods in the object model instead of just leaving them globally available. Perhaps it was to make it easier to figure out which version your code means when it refers to an object. For example, if word_app is a Word Application object, then you can use word_app.Selection to unambiguously refer to Word's Selection object whether the code runs in Word, Excel, or some other Office application.

Microsoft may have had some mysterious architectural reason for putting the global items in the object model. They may even have done this out of a sense of object-oriented aesthetics.

Whatever Microsoft's reasons, you have good reason to follow their example if you are a Visual Basic programmer and you want to allow other programs to control yours in a similar manner. In Visual Basic 6, you can build an ActiveX DLL that exposes classes for other programs to use. A client program creates a new instance of your class and can then use its properties and methods.

CAUTION *These sections are intended for Visual Basic 6 developers, not VBA developers.*

NOTE *Instead of an ActiveX DLL, you can also create an ActiveX EXE. This is a library of classes much as an ActiveX DLL. While an ActiveX DLL runs in the client program's address space (an* in-process server*), an ActiveX EXE runs in its own address space (an* out-of-process server*). That makes it a little slower, because calls to the library's routines and methods must cross address space boundaries in a process called* marshalling. *However, marshalling can work across computer boundaries, so a program on one computer can call routines in an ActiveX EXE running on a different computer. This may be useful for some applications. Out-of-process servers also cannot crash the main program as easily as in-process servers.*

This is very similar to the way the Microsoft Office applications let you create application servers and use their methods. For example, a PowerPoint application can create an instance of a Word server and use it to open and manipulate a Word document.

Unlike the Office applications, however, an ActiveX DLL cannot expose purely global variables, routines, and object instances. For example, your DLL cannot have a global object corresponding to Word's RecentFiles collection. You would need to make the collection a property of some object that the client application can create.

A good way to build this kind of ActiveX DLL is through the three steps described in the following sections. These and the following sections explain how you can expose object models for your Visual Basic applications.

A Separate Server Class

First, build a test program that includes the DLL's code in a separate class. The main program creates an instance of the class and uses its properties and methods to test the DLL code.

For example, suppose you have a MortgageSolver class that provides a public ShowVersion subroutine. The program could use the following code to execute that routine.

FILE *Ch06\FinancialFunctions 1\Form1.frm*

```
Private Sub cmdShowVersion_Click()
Dim mortgage_solver As MortgageSolver

    Set mortgage_solver = New MortgageSolver
    mortgage_solver.ShowVersion
End Sub
```

Debugging becomes harder as you move to the following steps, so you'll save time if you test and debug the DLL's code thoroughly before you move to the next step.

Separate Projects

Next, move the class into a new project. From Visual Basic's File menu, select Add Project and select the ActiveX DLL choice. Delete the MortgageSolver class from the main program. Select the new project and delete the default class named Class1. Then press Ctrl-D to add the MortgageSolver class to this project. Change its Instancing property to MultiUse. See the online help for more information on the Instancing property.

To make the server project easier to use, select the Project menu's Properties command. In the Project Name box, enter a name for the server project. Other applications that use the server will need to select this name from a list of references, so name it something meaningful and reasonably concise. For example, if you are building a library of financial functions, you might call the server FinancialFunctions.

Now select the main test program again. From the Project menu select References. Check the box next to the server project in the list as shown in Figure 6-4 and click OK.

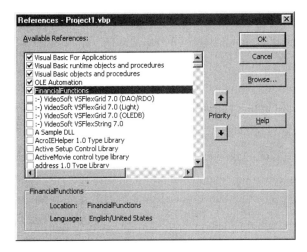

Figure 6-4. Select the test server project in the References list.

The main test program can create instances of the server library's public classes and use their methods exactly as before. You can also include the library's name in the class declarations if you like. For example, if the program uses more than one library that defines public classes with the same names, you can use the library names to let Visual Basic know which version you mean. This is similar to the way you might declare a variable of type Word.Application or Excel.Application to tell the program whether to use Word's or Excel's version of the Application class.

The following code shows how the program could declare and use a MortgageSolver object defined by the FinancialFunctions library.

FILE *Ch06\FinancialFunctions 2\Form1.frm*

```
Private Sub cmdShowVersion_Click()
Dim mortgage_solver As FinancialFunctions.MortgageSolver

    Set mortgage_solver = New FinancialFunctions.MortgageSolver
    mortgage_solver.ShowVersion
End Sub
```

Once again, debugging becomes harder when you move to the next phase, so test and debug the server as much as possible now.

A Separate Server DLL

The third step in building the server is to separate the test project and server project and debug them separately. Close the project group you have created and open the server's .vbp project file. That opens the server project without the main test project. In the File menu, select Make FinancialFunctions.dll to build the ActiveX DLL.

Now open the test program's .vbp project file. Visual Basic will complain that it cannot create a reference to the server's project file. It's really saying that the test server is not part of the same project group, so it cannot make a reference to it automatically. You must make the reference.

To make the reference, select the Project menu's References command and select the DLL as shown in Figure 6-5. Notice that the References dialog displays the DLL's location. This should match the location where you built the DLL.

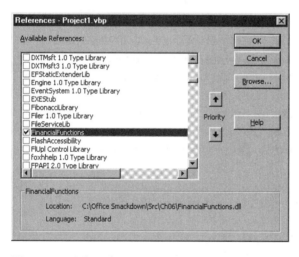

Figure 6-5. Select the test server project in the References list.

Contrast this with Figure 6-4, which shows a reference to a server project contained inside the same program group as the test program. Figure 6-4 doesn't show the server DLL's location because you hadn't built the DLL yet.

The main test program can create and use the server DLL's classes exactly as the previous version did. You shouldn't need to make any changes to the main program at this point.

A More Realistic Example

The FinancialFunctions example is similar in essence to the Microsoft Office applications, but it's much simpler. It's intended to provide a few straightforward subroutines and functions while the Office applications manipulate complicated documents. The LittleDraw example program is a bit more realistic.

The LittleDraw server project provides one public class named `ld_Picture`. This class represents a LittleDraw drawing. The server also provides several classes with `Instancing` property set to PublicNotCreatable. Because they are marked PublicNotCreatable, the program cannot create instances of the classes by using the `New` keyword. Instead it must use the methods provided by the `ld_Picture` class to make them. Once it has created an object using those methods, the program can manipulate them normally.

For example, the following code shows how a program can make a new `ld_Picture` object and use its `NewCircle` method to make a new `ld_Circle` object. Once it has created the object, the program uses its `FillStyle` and `FillColor` properties to make the circle red.

```
Dim new_circle As LittleDrawServer.ld_Circle

Set new_circle = ld_picture.NewCircle(1440, 1440, 1440)
new_circle.FillStyle = vbFSSolid
new_circle.FillColor = vbRed
```

The LittleDraw server DLL provides methods for creating a picture object, adding and manipulating objects (circles, ellipses, rectangles, and lines), and for saving and loading picture files.

Program LittleDrawUI provides a test user interface for the LittleDraw server. Its menus let the user create a new picture, add objects to it, save the results, and reload a saved picture file. This is analogous to the way the Office applications provide user interfaces to their underlying servers. For example, Word provides a user interface that lets you manipulate the Word application server.

Although the LittleDraw server provides only methods for manipulating a picture, the Office application servers provide a selection of tools for working with the associated user interface. For example, they allow you to manipulate the application's menus, command bars, and the currently selected text. They even provide access to the application's dialogs. For instance, a VBA program can make a Word server display a dialog asking the user what OLE object it should load. The Office applications are similar to LittleDraw, just a lot more powerful and complex.

Server Benefits

The most obvious benefit to building your own server is that it lets developers invoke your server from other programs. If the server is useful under a wide variety of circumstances, it can be used in many applications.

Even if the server has relatively limited usefulness, it can be handy to allow other programs to control it. Then if you think of a complex operation that the original program cannot handle, you may be able to write a helper program to get the job done.

For example, the LittleDrawTest program uses the following code to generate 561 line segments and save the results into a file. Generating those segments by hand using the original LittleDrawUI program would be next to impossible.

 FILE *Ch06\LittleDraw Cycloid\LittleDrawTest.frm*

```
Private Sub cmdGenerate_Click()
Const PI = 3.14159265
Const DT = PI / 40

Dim ld_picture As LittleDrawServer.ld_picture
Dim t As Double
Dim X1 As Single
Dim Y1 As Single
Dim X2 As Single
Dim Y2 As Single
Dim file_name As String
Dim file_title As String
Dim pos As Long

    ' Make a new LittleDraw picture.
    Set ld_picture = New LittleDrawServer.ld_picture
```

```
        ' Generate line segments for the picture.
        t = 0
        X2 = X(t)
        Y2 = Y(t)
        Do While t < 14 * PI
            t = t + DT
            X1 = X2
            Y1 = Y2
            X2 = X(t)
            Y2 = Y(t)
            ld_picture.NewLine X1, Y1, X2, Y2
        Loop

        ' Generate the final segment.
        X1 = X2
        Y1 = Y2
        t = 14 * PI
        X2 = X(t)
        Y2 = Y(t)
        ld_picture.NewLine X1, Y1, X2, Y2

        ' Save the picture.
        file_name = txtFileName.Text
        pos = InStrRev(file_name, "\")
        file_title = Mid$(file_name, pos + 1)
        ld_picture.DataSave file_name, file_title
        MsgBox "Ok"
End Sub

Private Function X(ByVal t As Double) As Double
    X = 2000 + 2000 * (27 * Cos(t) + 15 * Cos(t * 20 / 7)) / 42
End Function

Private Function Y(ByVal t As Double) As Double
    Y = 2000 + 2000 * (27 * Sin(t) + 15 * Sin(t * 20 / 7)) / 42
End Function
```

Figure 6-6 shows the resulting file displayed in the LittleDrawUI program.

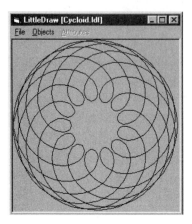

Figure 6-6. Program LittleDrawTest uses the LittleDraw server to generate this cycloid.

A less obvious benefit to publishing a server is that it lets users help test your code. At this point, thousands and perhaps millions of VBA programmers have extensively exercised the functions provided by the Microsoft Office application server classes. If those classes contain bugs, they have almost certainly been found. Whether all of those bugs have been reported and acted upon is another issue.

If you provide a server to an active group of developers, they will surely give it a good workout. If you provide a good forum for discussion and an easy way for developers to report bugs, they can help you improve your product, at least in subsequent releases.

Do-It-Yourself Scripting

The previous sections explain how you can expose an object model to developers through a public class in an ActiveX DLL or EXE. You can go one step further and give users the ability to execute a script inside your application just as the Microsoft Office applications do. The Microsoft Windows Script Control allows a program to execute script code relatively painlessly.

If you have Microsoft Windows 2000 or a later version of Windows, this control should already be installed. If you are running Windows 98, Windows ME, or Windows NT 4.0, you'll need to install it yourself.

NOTE *Microsoft has dropped support for these operating systems, so the scripting control may not work exactly as it would in the most recent operating systems.*

To install the control, go to Microsoft's scripting Web page at `http://msdn.microsoft.com/scripting`. In the Related Links section on the right side of the page, click the Windows Script Control link. Download the control and install it on your system.

 NOTE *Currently, you can find the Microsoft Windows Script Control at* `http://www.microsoft.com/downloads/details.aspx?FamilyId=D7E31492-2595-49E6-8C02-1426FEC693AC&displaylang=en` *(enter this whole mess all on one line in your browser's Address bar). Microsoft occasionally rearranges its links, however, so this download may have moved by the time you read this.*

To use the control, open your Visual Basic project. Select the Project menu's Components command or press Ctrl-T to open the Components dialog. Check the box next to the script control as shown in Figure 6-7 and click OK.

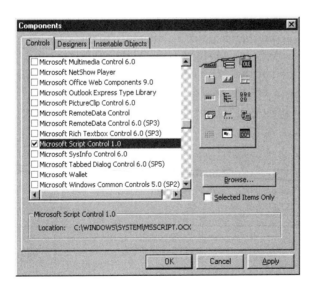

Figure 6-7. Add the Microsoft Windows Script Control to Visual Basic's control toolbox.

Next use the control toolbox to add an instance of the control to your Visual Basic application. Now the program's code can use the control's properties and methods to execute VBScript code.

Three of the control's most useful methods are AddCode, AddObject, and Run. The AddCode method adds a text string to the control's library of VBScript code. Note that you don't need to add all the code at once. For example, your program might call AddCode once, passing it a string containing a subroutine's definition. Later it could call AddCode again, passing it the definition of another subroutine. The control would add the new routine to its library of routines, and later it could use them all.

The control's AddObject method defines an object that the control can use when executing script code. This method takes as parameters the name the control should use for the object and a reference to the object itself. For example, a program could pass the routine the name LittleDrawPicture and a reference to an ld_Picture object. When the control saw a reference to an object named Little-DrawPicture in its script code, it would replace it with the object.

The control's Run method takes as a parameter the name of a subroutine. The method simply executes that routine.

Example program LittleDrawScript uses a Microsoft Windows Script Control to let the user execute script code that manipulates the program's ld_Picture object. The program executes the following code when the user selects the Script menu's Execute command. The code displays the form frmScript. This form isn't very interesting; it just lets the user enter the script text.

If the user presses OK, the program calls the AddCode method to tell the control about the user's script code. It uses the AddObject method to tell the control to replace the name LittleDrawPicture in the script with a reference to the m_LittleDrawPicture object. The code then calls the Run method, telling it to run the DrawBowditch subroutine defined by the script code. The program then calls the control's Reset method to clear the code and object references so they can be replaced the next time the user runs a script. The routine finishes by redrawing its picture to display the results.

 FILE *Ch06\LittleDraw Script\LittleDrawScript.frm*

```
Private Sub mnuScriptExecute_Click()
Dim script_text As String

    ' Let the user enter the script.
```

```
    If frmScript.ShowDialog(script_text) = vbOK Then
        ' Execute the script.
        ScriptControl1.AddCode script_text
        ScriptControl1.AddObject _
            "LittleDrawPicture", m_LittleDrawPicture
        ScriptControl1.Run "DrawBowditch"
        ScriptControl1.Reset
        m_LittleDrawPicture.Redraw
    End If
    Unload frmScript
End Sub
```

The sample program starts with the following sample code already filled in, so you can just click OK if you like. Subroutine DrawBowditch calls functions X and Y to get coordinates along a Bowditch curve as variable t moves from 0 to 2π.

Notice how the script calls the LittleDrawPicture object's NewLine to create new ld_Line objects. It then sets those objects' ForeColor and DrawWidth properties to make thick red lines.

Notice also that none of the variable or function declarations include a data type. This code is VBScript, not Visual Basic or VBA, so all variables are Variants. If you declare a variable with a specific data type, the script control raises an error when it executes the script.

```
Sub DrawBowditch()
Const PI = 3.14159265

Dim t
Dim dt
Dim X1
Dim Y1
Dim X2
Dim Y2
Dim new_line

    t = 0
    dt = PI / 100
    X2 = X(t)
    Y2 = Y(t)
    Do While t < 2 * PI
        t = t + dt
        X1 = X2
        Y1 = Y2
        X2 = X(t)
```

```
            Y2 = Y(t)
            Set new_line = LittleDrawPicture.NewLine(X1, Y1, X2, Y2)
            new_line.ForeColor = vbRed
            new_line.DrawWidth = 3
        Loop

        ' Generate the final segment.
        X1 = X2
        Y1 = Y2
        t = 2 * PI
        X2 = X(t)
        Y2 = Y(t)
        Set new_line = LittleDrawPicture.NewLine(X1, Y1, X2, Y2)
        new_line.ForeColor = vbRed
        new_line.DrawWidth = 3
End Sub

Function X(t)
    X = 2200 + 2000 * Sin(4 * t)
End Function

Function Y(t)
    Y = 2200 + 2000 * Sin(5 * t)
End Function
```

Figure 6-8 shows the LittleDrawScript program after it has executed this script.

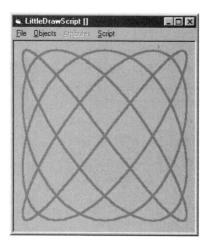

Figure 6-8. Program LittleDrawScript executes a script to draw a Bowditch curve.

Cross-Application Development

The early sections in this chapter focus on using object models to understand how to program an application. For example, you can use Word's object model to figure out how to write a Word VBA program to manipulate a document.

The previous section showed how the LittleDrawScript program uses the object model provided by the LittleDrawServer library to display and manipulate pictures. Using one application's object model from another like this is called *cross-application development*.

Just as you can write a Visual Basic program to use the LittleDrawServer routines, you can write a VBA program that manipulates the objects provided by an Office application. For example, you can write a Word VBA program that opens an Excel server and uses its properties and methods to manipulate Excel workbooks.

To invoke an Office server, a program must declare a reference to the server's top-level Application object and then instantiate the object. After that, the program can use the server object's properties and methods almost exactly as if the program were running inside the corresponding Office application. For instance, a Word VBA program that creates an Excel server can use the server to do just about anything Excel can do.

There are two ways you can declare and initialize a reference to one of these server objects: early binding and late binding. The following sections describe these two methods and give some examples.

Early Binding

In early binding, the program declares the reference to a server giving an explicit data type. For example, the following code shows how a Word program would declare an Excel Application object. This code declares an object of type Application defined in the library named Excel.

```
Dim excel_app As Excel.Application
```

If you simply type this line into the code editor, VBA will flag the line as an error because it doesn't know what the Excel.Application type is. To make it understand, you must add a reference to the Excel object model. To add the reference, select the Tools ➤ References command, check the box next to the Excel 10.0 Object Library reference as shown in Figure 6-9, and click OK.

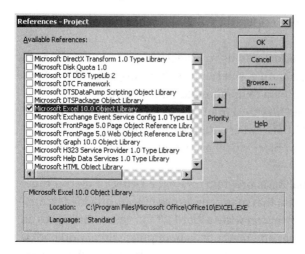

Figure 6-9. To use Excel data types, set a reference to the Excel object library.

To initialize the variable, the code can use the New keyword just as it would to initialize any other object. For example, the following code creates a new Excel server.

```
Set excel_app = New Excel.Application
```

The following code shows how a Word VBA program can manipulate an Excel workbook by using early binding. It declares variables to represent the Excel Application object and a Workbook object. It creates the Application instance and uses its Workbooks collection's Open method to open the workbook file, saving a reference to the returned Workbook object. It writes text into the workbook's first worksheet, closes the workbook, and makes the server quit.

 CAUTION *If you do not use the* Quit *method to close the server, it remains running and takes up resources on your computer. Even worse, it may cause side effects, such as keeping a file locked so you cannot edit it and save your changes. To stop rogue servers, use the Task Manager to list the processes running on your system. Look for processes named WINWORD.EXE, EXCEL.EXE, POWERPNT.EXE, MSACCESS.EXE, and OUTLOOK.EXE.*

 FILE *Ch06\UseExcel.doc*

```
' Write to an Excel workbook using early binding.
Private Sub cmdEarlyBinding_Click()
Dim excel_app As Excel.Application
Dim excel_workbook As Excel.Workbook
Dim file_name As String

    ' Open the Excel server.
    Set excel_app = New Excel.Application

    ' Open the workbook.
    file_name = Application.ActiveDocument.Path
    If Right$(file_name, 1) <> "\" Then file_name = file_name & "\"
    file_name = file_name & "UseWord.xls"
    Set excel_workbook = _
        excel_app.Workbooks.Open(file_name)

    ' Write data into cell A4.
    excel_workbook.Sheets(1).Cells(4, 1) = _
        "This text was written by Word using early binding"

    ' Save and close.
    excel_workbook.Close True
    excel_app.Quit
End Sub
```

TIP *When done with an object variable, you can set it equal to* Nothing. *That allows VBA to free any resources associated with the object. In this code, the* excel_app *and* excel_workbook *objects go out of scope when the subroutine ends, so they are automatically freed. Many programmers always explicitly set objects to* Nothing, *however, to make it obvious that the objects are freed. This also frees the objects' resources sooner if it will be a while before the objects go out of scope.*

CAUTION *Only one instance of a PowerPoint server can run on a computer at one time. If you quit a PowerPoint server after you are done with it, any PowerPoint session you may have running will also disappear.*

The following code shows how an Excel VBA program manipulates a Word document using early binding. It declares variables to represent the Word Application object, a Document object, and a Range object.

Next the code creates the Application instance and uses its Documents collection's Open method to open the Word document, saving a reference to the returned Document object.

The program uses the Document object's Range method to create a reference to a Range object representing the bookmark named EarlyBinding. It places text in that Range, saves the closes the document, and quits the Word application server.

FILE *Ch06\UseWord.xls*

```vba
' Write to a Word document using early binding.
Private Sub cmdEarlyBinding_Click()
Dim word_app As Word.Application
Dim word_document As Word.Document
Dim bookmark_range As Word.Range
Dim file_name As String

    ' Open the Word server.
    Set word_app = New Word.Application

    ' Open the document.
    file_name = Application.ActiveWorkbook.Path
    If Right$(file_name, 1) <> "\" Then file_name = file_name & "\"
    file_name = file_name & "UseExcel.doc"
    Set word_document = _
        word_app.Documents.Open(file_name)

    ' Select the EarlyBinding bookmark.
    Set bookmark_range = word_document.GoTo( _
        What:=wdGoToBookmark, _
        Name:="EarlyBinding")

    ' Write text.
    bookmark_range.Text = _
        "This text was written by Excel using early binding"

    ' Save and close.
    word_document.Close True
    word_app.Quit
End Sub
```

Take a few moments to compare these two programs. Both declare Application objects for the Office application they will be using. Both declare a document-like object (Workbook for Excel, Document for Word) and use an Application collection's Open method to open the object. They manipulate the document object quite differently because Word and Excel perform very different tasks. When they are finished, both programs call their documents' Close methods to save their results and close the document, and both call the Application object's Quit method.

The similarities between these programs highlight the places where the Office applications have similar features. They both have an Application class at the tops of their object models. Both have collections that hold the document-like objects that the program manipulates. Those collections provide methods for opening documents, and the documents have methods for saving any changes.

Late Binding

In late binding, the program declares references to server objects by using the generic type Object. It then uses the CreateObject function to create an instance of the server object. The following code shows how a Word VBA program might declare and initialize an Excel Application object.

```
Dim excel_app As Object

Set excel_app = CreateObject("Excel.Application")
```

When a program uses late binding, it does not need to have a reference to the server application's object model. In this case, VBA doesn't need to know what the Excel.Application type is because no variable is declared using that type.

The following code shows how a Word VBA program can manipulate an Excel workbook. This code is similar to the previous Word example, but it uses late binding instead of early binding.

The code declares variables to represent Excel application and workbook objects, but it declares them by using the generic Object data type. It creates the application instance by using CreateObject. It uses that object's Workbooks collection's Open method to open the workbook file as before, saving a reference to the returned Workbook object. It writes text into the workbook's first worksheet, closes the workbook, and makes the server quit.

FILE *Ch06\UseExcel.doc*

```
' Write to an Excel workbook using late binding.
Private Sub cmdLateBinding_Click()
Dim excel_app As Object
Dim excel_workbook As Object
Dim file_name As String

    ' Open the Excel server.
    Set excel_app = CreateObject("Excel.Application")

    ' Open the workbook.
    file_name = Application.ActiveDocument.Path
    If Right$(file_name, 1) <> "\" Then file_name = file_name & "\"
    file_name = file_name & "UseWord.xls"
    Set excel_workbook = _
        excel_app.Workbooks.Open(file_name)

    ' Write data into cell A5.
    excel_workbook.Sheets(1).Cells(5, 1) = _
        "This text was written by Word using late binding"

    ' Save and close.
    excel_workbook.Close True
    excel_app.Quit
End Sub
```

The following code shows the late binding version of the previous Excel example. It declares variables to represent Word application, document, and range objects, declaring them with the generic Object data type. It uses CreateObject to initialize the application object. It uses the Documents collection's Open method to open the Word document, saving a reference to the returned Document object.

The program then uses the document's Range method to create a reference to a Range object representing the bookmark named EarlyBinding. It places text in the Range, saves and closes the document, and quits the Word application server.

FILE *Ch06\UseWord.xls*

```
' Write to a Word document using late binding.
Private Sub cmdLateBinding_Click()
Dim word_app As Object
Dim word_document As Object
Dim bookmark_range As Object
Dim file_name As String

    ' Open the Word server.
    Set word_app = CreateObject("Word.Application")

    ' Open the document.
    file_name = Application.ActiveWorkbook.Path
    If Right$(file_name, 1) <> "\" Then file_name = file_name & "\"
    file_name = file_name & "UseExcel.doc"
    Set word_document = _
        word_app.Documents.Open(file_name)

    ' Select the LateBinding bookmark.
    Set bookmark_range = word_document.GoTo( _
        What:=wdGoToBookmark, _
        Name:="LateBinding")

    ' Write text.
    bookmark_range.Text = _
        "This text was written by Excel using late binding"

    ' Save and close.
    word_document.Close True
    word_app.Quit
End Sub
```

If you compare these programs to their early binding versions, you'll find that
the only difference is in how the variables are declared and how the application
objects are created. The early and late binding versions both use exactly the same
object methods to do their work.

Picking Early or Late Binding

Objects created using early binding work a bit faster than those created with late binding, because VBA can more quickly figure out which methods an object supports and it can execute them faster. For example, consider the following statement.

```
bookmark_range.Text = "This text was written by Excel using late binding"
```

If the variable bookmark_range is declared to be of type Word.Range, then VBA knows that the object supports a Text property, and it knows how to access that property.

On the other hand, if the object is declared using the generic Object data type, VBA must query the object at run time and ask it if it supports a Text property. This takes considerably longer.

TIP *This is true when working with other kinds of objects as well. More specific data types such as* TextBox *give better performance than more generic ones such as* Control *or* Object.

For the speed difference alone, many programmers prefer early binding to late binding. However, the Office application servers are quite large and take a considerable amount of time to load. If the program performs only a few operations using the server objects, adding a few milliseconds to the time needed to invoke the objects' properties and methods won't make a huge difference to the overall time. If the program makes many calls to those methods, the difference may be noticeable.

An even better reason to prefer early binding is that it allows VBA to provide IntelliSense. If you declare a variable using the Object data type, VBA has no idea what properties and methods the object supports until run time.

On the other hand, if you declare it using an explicit data type such as Word.Document (after including a reference to the Word object library), the development environment knows which properties and methods the object supports. If you type the variable's name followed by a period, IntelliSense pops up and shows you a list of the possibilities.

After you select a method, IntelliSense shows the list of parameters the method takes. This can be particularly useful for Office applications, because many of the Office methods take a large number of parameters and it can be hard to remember all of their names. For example, in Word the Documents collection's

Open method takes 15 parameters. IntelliSense lists those parameters and tells you that the method returns an object of type Document.

Although early binding has a lot of advantages, there are a few smaller reasons to pick late binding. First, the CreateObject function allows you to create a server object on a remote computer. It's hard to imagine a good reason for running an Office application on someone else's computer, but it's conceivable.

Using late binding, you might be able to write some general-purpose routines that work with more than one Office application. For instance, you could write a subroutine that takes a generic object as a parameter and then performs different actions depending on the type of object it receives. Again, it's hard to imagine doing this very often, but it is possible.

A better reason to use late binding is that it doesn't require a reference to a specific object library. Suppose you write a VBA program using a reference to the Word 10.0 Object Library. You then copy the code onto a different computer that has a different version of Word installed. The code will not be able to find the library on that computer, so it won't run. If you use generic objects and initialize them using CreateObject, the code may still run. Naturally, it will fail if the code tries to invoke a feature that is not provided by the other computer's version of Word. Many of Word's most useful functions remain relatively stable across releases, however, so there is at least some chance that the program will still work.

If you do decide to use late binding, initially you may want to develop using early binding to take advantage of VBA's IntelliSense support. When you have debugged the code, you can remove the reference to the object library, replace specific variables declarations with generic ones, and initialize the application server objects by using CreateObject.

Remote Macros

Sometimes, a cross-application macro is useful only for a particular combination of Office applications. For example, you might write a PowerPoint macro that opens an Excel workbook and uses its data to build a PowerPoint slide. It would make little sense to use that code in Word because Word doesn't include slides. It also wouldn't make sense for PowerPoint to try to use the code to pull data from Access, because data stored in Access has a different format than data stored in Excel.

Sometimes, however, a macro may make sense for more than one combination of Office applications. For example, you might like to create a certain type of chart in Excel whether you are running code in Excel, Word, PowerPoint, or some other application. In that case, you could write separate VBA subroutines to generate the chart from each of those applications. That would give you several different but almost identical routines stored in different places. If you needed to change the code, you would have to make the same changes in each of the places it was stored.

A better solution is to place the code in the application that is common to each of these scenarios: Excel. Then you can use VBA code in each of the other applications to invoke the Excel macro that creates the chart. Later, if you need to change the chart's appearance, you need to change only the Excel macro; the code in the other applications remains unchanged.

The Application provided by each of the Office applications has a Run method that executes a macro by name. This macro can be a built-in routine, such as FileOpen in Word, or it can be a macro of your own. The following sections show examples of one Office application calling macros written in another.

Excel Calling Word

The following code shows how an Excel VBA program can invoke a Word macro. It begins by creating a Word Application object and opening a document. It then calls the Application object's Run method, passing it the name of the WriteSomething macro with the string parameter "Excel." After the macro executes, the code saves the document's changes, closes it, and quits the Word server.

NOTE *Word's version of the* Run *method can take up to 30 parameters that it passes to the macro it is running.*

FILE *Ch06\CallMacros.xls*

```
' Call the WriteSomething macro in a Word document.
Private Sub cmdCallWordMacro_Click()
Dim word_app As Word.Application
Dim word_document As Word.Document
Dim file_name As String

    ' Open the Word server.
    Set word_app = New Word.Application

    ' Open the document.
    file_name = Application.ActiveWorkbook.Path
```

```
        If Right$(file_name, 1) <> "\" Then file_name = file_name & "\"
        file_name = file_name & "CallMacros.doc"
        Set word_document = _
            word_app.Documents.Open(file_name)

        ' Invoke the Word document's WriteSomething macro.
        word_app.Run "WriteSomething", "Excel"

        ' Save and close.
        word_document.Close True
        word_app.Quit
        MsgBox "Okay"
End Sub
```

The following code shows the Word document's WriteSomething macro. This subroutine finds the WriteSomethingHere bookmark and adds the text it receives as a parameter.

FILE *Ch06\CallMacros.doc*

```
' Write a text string.
Public Sub WriteSomething(ByVal txt As String)
Dim write_here As Range

    ' Get the bookmark.
    Set write_here = ActiveDocument.GoTo( _
        What:=wdGoToBookmark, _
        Name:="WriteSomethingHere")

    ' Write the text.
    write_here.Text = _
        "Called from: " & txt & vbCrLf
End Sub
```

If the macro were a function that returned a value, the application's Run method would return the macro's result. For example, the following code shows how a Word program might display the result returned by an Excel VBA function named CalculateInterest.

```
MsgBox word_app.Run("CalculateInterest", "Excel")
```

Word Calling PowerPoint

The following code shows how a Word VBA program can invoke a PowerPoint macro. It begins by creating a PowerPoint `Application` object and opening a presentation.

It then calls the `Application` object's `Run` method, passing it the name of the `WriteSomething` macro and the string parameter "Word." Notice how the program specifies the macro's name as the complete PowerPoint file name, an exclamation point, the code module containing the macro, a dot, and finally the macro's name. This tells PowerPoint exactly where the macro is.

After the macro executes, the code saves the document's changes and closes it. Notice that this code doesn't quit the PowerPoint server. Only one instance of the PowerPoint server can run on a computer at one time. When you create a server instance in code, the result is a reference to the existing server if one is already running. Making that instance quit would also close the existing server. This code leaves the server running so it won't close an existing instance.

NOTE *PowerPoint's version of the* Run *method can take any number of parameters that it passes to the macro it is running.*

FILE *Ch06\CallMacros.doc*

```
' Call a PowerPoint macro.
Private Sub cmdCallPowerPointMacro_Click()
Dim ppt_app As PowerPoint.Application
Dim ppt_presentation As PowerPoint.Presentation
Dim file_name As String

    ' Open the PowerPoint server.
    Set ppt_app = New PowerPoint.Application

    ' Open the presentation.
    file_name = Application.ActiveDocument.Path
    If Right$(file_name, 1) <> "\" Then file_name = file_name & "\"
    file_name = file_name & "CallMacros.ppt"
    Set ppt_presentation = _
        ppt_app.Presentations.Open(file_name)
```

```
' Call the WriteSomething macro.
ppt_app.Run _
    file_name & "!GlobalRoutines.WriteSomething", _
    "Word"

' Save and close.
ppt_presentation.Save
ppt_presentation.Close

' Because there can only be one PowerPoint
' server running at a time, closing this
' server closes all open PowerPoint sessions.
'    ppt_app.Quit
    MsgBox "Okay"
End Sub
```

The following code shows the PowerPoint WriteSomething macro. The code adds a new slide to the end of the active presentation. It moves to the new slide and selects the shape named Rectangle 2, which holds the new slide's title by default. The macro then sets the shape's text to the value it received as a parameter.

 FILE *Ch06\CallMacros.ppt*

```
' Add a new slide with the given text.
Public Sub WriteSomething(ByVal txt As String)
Dim new_slide As Slide

    Set new_slide = _
        ActivePresentation.Slides.Add( _
            Index:=ActivePresentation.Slides.Count + 1, _
            Layout:=ppLayoutText)
    ActiveWindow.View.GotoSlide new_slide.SlideIndex
    ActiveWindow.Selection.SlideRange.Shapes("Rectangle 2").Select
    ActiveWindow.Selection.TextRange.Text = txt
End Sub
```

PowerPoint Calling Excel

The following code shows how a PowerPoint VBA program can invoke an Excel macro. It begins by creating an Excel `Application` object and opening a workbook.

It then calls the `Application` object's `Run` method, passing it the name of the `WriteSomething` macro and the string parameter "PowerPoint." Notice how the program specifies the macro's name as the code module containing the macro (ThisWorkbook), a dot, and the macro's name. This tells Excel exactly where the macro is.

After the macro executes, the code saves the workbook's changes, closes it, and quits the Excel server.

 NOTE *Excel's version of the* Run *method can take up to 30 parameters to pass to the macro it is executing.*

 FILE *Ch06\CallMacros.ppt*

```vba
' Execute an Excel macro.
Private Sub cmdCallExcelMacro_Click()
Dim excel_app As Excel.Application
Dim excel_workbook As Excel.Workbook
Dim file_name As String

    ' Open the Excel server.
    Set excel_app = New Excel.Application

    ' Open the workbook.
    file_name = Application.ActivePresentation.Path
    If Right$(file_name, 1) <> "\" Then file_name = file_name & "\"
    file_name = file_name & "CallMacros.xls"
    Set excel_workbook = _
        excel_app.Workbooks.Open(file_name)

    ' Call the WriteSomething macro.
    excel_app.Run _
        "ThisWorkbook.WriteSomething", _
        "PowerPoint"
```

```
    ' Save and close.
    excel_workbook.Close True
    excel_app.Quit
    MsgBox "Okay"
End Sub
```

The following code shows the Excel WriteSomething macro. The code finds the last row currently in use by the active workbook's first worksheet and adds one. If the result is less than 4, the program makes it 4 so the text doesn't appear beneath the Excel worksheet's command buttons. The code then uses the worksheet's Cells method to display some text.

FILE *Ch06\CallMacros.xls*

```
' Write a text string.
Public Sub WriteSomething(ByVal txt As String)
Dim r As Long

    r = Sheets(1).UsedRange.Rows.Count + 1
    If r < 4 Then r = 4
    Sheets(1).Cells(r, 1) = "Called from: " & txt
End Sub
```

Summary

An object model defines the class definitions and specific objects that you can use to manipulate an application. The Office applications have many objects in common. All have an Application object at the top of the object model. All provide some sort of document-like object, most have a Selection object, and several have a Range class. These objects serve similar purposes, but they may differ greatly in detail.

Just as the Office applications expose their object models for use in your programs, you can expose object models for your own Visual Basic libraries. You can allow other programs to manipulate your server objects. Using the Microsoft Windows Script Control, those programs can even allow the user to execute scripts that manipulate your library.

Once you understand an Office application's object model, you can manipulate that application from another Office application. For example, you can write a Word VBA program that opens Excel, PowerPoint, any of the other Office applications, or even libraries of your own. Using the `Application` object's `Run` method, you can even invoke macros you have written in one of the other applications.

The final piece to the puzzle is to understand the Office applications' object models. The chapters that follow discuss the most useful objects exposed for your use by the Office applications. Using those objects, you can take advantage of the applications' most important features. By combining the applications, you can build even more powerful solutions that merge each application's strengths.

CHAPTER 7

Word

THE OFFICE XP WORD object model contains thousands of objects, properties, methods, and predefined values. Fortunately, you only need to understand a handful of key objects to handle most chores. Many of the other items are esoteric trappings that you will rarely need. Others will be easy to figure out if and when you need them. For example, you don't need to memorize the 50 or so predefined WdTextureIndex enumerated values. You can look up the value you need when you want to specify a texture index.

This chapter describes some of the most useful items provided by the Word object model. The following section gives an overview of some of those objects; it will help you figure out what objects you must use to perform various tasks. Subsequent sections describe key pieces of the Word object model in greater detail.

This chapter doesn't explain every detail of these objects; its aim is to provide you with enough detail so you can easily figure out what objects you need to accomplish most common tasks. You can discover others when you need them by looking at the online help and by examining recorded macros.

Overview

The Application object sits at the top of the Word object hierarchy. It provides properties and collections that let you find the application's other objects. It also includes methods for working with the Word application rather than with a specific document. For example, it includes properties and methods that search for files, bind keys to macros, manipulate the recent file list, and manage styles.

The Global "object" provides a collection of globally available properties and methods that you can use without referring to the Application object. For example, the global ActiveDocument property returns the same reference that the Application.ActiveDocument property does.

A Document object represents a specific Word file. If you need to modify a file, you will probably need to use a Document object. This object provides methods for modifying the file's text and styles, saving changes to the file, managing the file's headers and footers, and accessing the file's contents by paragraph, word, or letter.

As you can probably guess, the Template object represents a template. Usually, a VBA project works with a document rather than its template because there's more stuff in a document to manipulate. As a VBA *programmer*, however, you may find templates very useful because you can place important code in them. For example, you can make a purchase order template that contains code that is useful for the purchase order documents based on it.

The Selection object represents the currently selected text in a document. In one common scenario, the user selects some text and then invokes a macro that acts upon the selected text in some way.

If a macro needs to make extensive changes to the document, particularly parts of the document that the user has not selected, the Selection object is rather cumbersome. One natural approach many beginners take is to move the Selection to contain the required text and then operate on it. Unfortunately, that makes the changes visible to the user as the code makes them. When the code moves the Selection, Word jumps to show the newly selected text. If the code moves the Selection around several times, Word will visibly jump back and forth through the file.

Instead of using the Selection object in this case, the program can use Range objects. A Range object represents a piece of the document and provides roughly the same features as the Selection object without forcing the user interface to jump all over the place.

The Selection object's Find property returns a Find object that your code can use to control search and replace operations. Using a Find object, your code can search a document for specific text, styles, or formatting and optionally change its text, style, or formatting.

A Bookmark object represents a named location in the text. A program can use a Bookmark to quickly locate an important part of a document. For example, it could jump to the body portion of a report and enter text there.

The following sections describe these objects in more detail.

Global Objects

The Global "object" contains properties and methods that don't have to be preceded by an Application object. For example, the following two lines of code both display the number of documents currently loaded by Word. The first line explicitly references the Application object's Documents collection. The second line uses the global reference to the Documents collection.

```
Debug.Print Application.Documents.Count
Debug.Print Documents.Count
```

These properties and methods are the same as those provided by the Application object, so they are not described here. The following section describes the most useful Application object properties and methods, and indicates which are available globally.

Note that the Global "object" isn't really an object. You cannot refer to it explicitly in code and you cannot create an instance of the Global class. The concept of a Global object is simply a device for categorizing these globally available properties and methods. For more information on this "object," see the section "The Global Object" in Chapter 6.

Note also that the result returned by some global objects depends on the context. For example, the ActiveWindow object returns a reference to the window with current input focus. If VBA code is running in Normal.dot or some other template, this is the window containing the active document, much as you would expect. However, if the code is contained in a document's code modules, ActiveWindow returns a reference to that document's window.

For example, suppose you have two documents, Top.doc and Bottom.doc, open in Word, and that Top.doc has the focus. Now suppose the following code is contained in Bottom.doc's code module. The first Print statement displays "Bottom.doc" because it refers explicitly to ThisDocument, the document containing the code. The second Print statement also displays "Bottom.doc" because it implicitly uses the ThisDocument object. The third Print statement uses the Application object's ActiveWindow property, which refers to the active document's window, so it displays "Top.doc." The final Print statement explicitly refers to the ActiveDocument object, so it displays the caption on the active document's window: "Top.doc."

 FILE *Ch07\Bottom.doc*

```
' The following displays "Bottom.doc."
Debug.Print ThisDocument.ActiveWindow.Caption

' The following displays "Bottom.doc."
Debug.Print ActiveWindow.Caption

' The following displays "Top.doc."
Debug.Print Application.ActiveWindow.Caption

' The following displays "Top.doc."
Debug.Print ActiveDocument.ActiveWindow.Caption
```

To avoid confusion, you can explicitly specify an object to give the statement a clear context. For example, use ThisDocument if you want to work with the document that contains the code no matter which document has the input focus. Use ActiveDocument to refer to the active document no matter which file contains the code.

Application

The Application object serves two purposes. First, it provides access to features that don't apply to a particular Word document. For example, its RecentFiles collection allows your code to manipulate the recent file list shown in Word's File menu. The recent file list exists whether or not a particular document is loaded, so the Application object provides it. Code in any Word document can read the list and see what file names it contains.

 TIP *A different application can load a Word server and use its* RecentFiles *collection to see what file names it contains.*

The Application object's second purpose is to provide access to the objects representing documents. It does this mainly with its ActiveDocument property and its Documents collection. ActiveDocument gives your code a reference to the document with current input focus. The Documents collection provides methods for opening and closing documents. It also lets your code retrieve references to Document objects representing all of the loaded documents.

If you are working with Word from another application, such as Excel or PowerPoint, you will probably begin with the Word Application object and then use its properties and methods to load and manipulate documents. If you are working within Word, you may sometimes want to use the globally available objects described briefly in the previous section.

The following sections describe the Application object's most useful properties and methods. Those marked with a G are available globally. Those marked with a C are collections.

Application *Object Properties and Methods*

The following sections describe some of the Application object's most useful properties and methods. They are grouped together here because many of the properties behave like methods, and many of the methods behave like properties. For example, the FindKey property returns an object representing a particular key combination. It may be implemented as a property internally within Word, but to the programmer it looks more like a function. On the other hand, DefaultWebOptions, which Word's online help classifies as a method, simply returns a reference to an object, so it looks like more like a property to a VBA programmer.

Many of these properties return collections of objects. Usually, a collection's name is the plural of the name of the type of objects it contains. For example, the Documents collection contains objects of type Document.

Be aware that Application is the name of an object class as well as a specific predefined object. You can create a new instance of the Application class to create a new Word server. You would use the Application object already running to use the server in which the code is running.

In the following code, the first Set statement makes the variable app point to the predefined Application object representing the Word server running the code. The second Set statement creates a new server.

```
Dim app As Application

    ' This line makes app refer to the server running this code.
    Set app = Application

    ' This line makes app refer to a new server.
    Set app = New Application
```

If the code creates a new server, you may want it to call that server's Quit method when the code is finished with it. If the code uses the predefined Application object, it should probably not call the Quit method, because that would close the server running the code. For example, imagine pressing a button to run a macro that formats the text you have selected. After the macro is done, your Word session disappears. Not a very friendly macro!

General Macro Execution

Several properties and methods are important for macro execution in general, and it's vital that you understand these items whenever you write and execute macros. Some of these issues deal with macro security, and understanding how they work can save you from a potentially devastating virus.

CustomizationContext (G) is the template or document where changes to menu bars, command bars, and key bindings are saved. If you write code that customizes Word or examines customizations, you need to set CustomizationContext to the appropriate object before you start. For example, if you want to display a particular command bar in one document, you need to set `CustomizationContext` to that document before you start. Otherwise, the change may be saved in Normal.dot, and the customization will apply to all documents.

The `DisplayAlerts` property determines how a macro responds if a dialog is displayed. If this is `wdAlertsAll`, all message boxes and alerts are displayed to the user. If this is `wdAlertsMessageBox`, Word displays only messages and not alerts. If this is `wdAlertsNone`, Word displays no alerts or message boxes. If a message box should appear, Word automatically selects the default choice.

TIP *Try to write macros that do not make Word display dialogs on its own. If you succeed, you won't need to worry about this property. For example, if your code blithely closes a document, Word may want to ask the user whether it should save any pending changes. Do you want your macro interrupted by a dialog? Do you want to accept the default behavior? Do you even know offhand what the default behavior is? A better solution is to have the macro tell Word whether it should save the changes so it doesn't need to ask the user. Of course this doesn't mean you cannot display your own forms, message boxes, and other dialogs to get input from the user or to tell the user what your code is doing.*

The `EnableCancelKey` property determines whether Word allows the user to interrupt a macro by pressing Ctrl-Break. Set this to `wdCancelEnabled` (macros cannot be interrupted) or `wdCancelInterrupt` (the user can interrupt a macro). For examples, see subroutines `Interruptable` and `NonInterruptable` in file Ch07\Word.doc.

TIP *Generally, you will not want less experienced users to be able to interrupt your macros, because that might leave things in a half-baked state. However, you will want to be able to use Ctrl-Break while programming so you can break out of infinite loops and such.*

The `MacroContainer` (G) property returns a `Template` or `Document` object representing the object containing the executing macro. This can be useful, for example, if the code needs to know whether a default `Document` object is present (if the code is running in a document module, it is) or whether it should use `ActiveDocument` (probably correct if the code is in a template).

The Run method executes a VBA macro by name, passing up to 30 parameters to the macro. For example, the following code executes the UpdateSales function, passing it the current date and saving the returned value in the variable result.

```
result = Application.Run("UpdateSales", Date)
```

The ListCommands method creates a new document containing a table listing all Word commands, their shortcut keys, and the menus in which they appear. If the method's ListAllCommands parameter is False, the command lists only commands with customized assignments. You can print the file to get a handy reference list.

Conversion Functions (G)

Word performs almost all of its measurements in printer's points, where a point is defined as 1/72 of an inch. To make working with points easier, the Application object provides several functions, listed in Table 7-1, that convert distances between points and other units of measurement.

Table 7-1. Application *Object Conversion Functions*

FUNCTION	FROM	TO	NOTES
CentimetersToPoints	Centimeters	Points	--
InchesToPoints	Inches	Points	--
LinesToPoints	Lines	Points	1 line = 12 points
MillimetersToPoints	Millimeters	Points	--
PicasToPoints	Picas	Points	1 pica = 12 points
PixelsToPoints	Pixels	Points	--
PointsToCentimeters	Points	Centimeters	--
PointsToInches	Points	Inches	--
PointsToLines	Points	Lines	1 line = 12 points
PointsToMillimeters	Points	Millimeters	--
PointsToPicas	Points	Picas	1 pica = 12 points
PointsToPixels	Points	Pixels	--

Depending on your system, the number of pixels per inch may be different vertically and horizontally. In that case, the PixelsToPoints and PointsToPixels functions need to return different values depending on whether you are measuring vertically or horizontally. Both of those functions take a second parameter that you should set to True if you want vertical measurements.

Visual Basic often measures in twips, where a twip is defined as 1/1,440 of an inch. The Application object doesn't provide functions for using twips, but you can easily plug in the following formulas.

```
twips = points * 20
points = twips / 20
```

All of these conversion functions are available globally.

ActiveDocument *(G)*

This property returns a Document object representing the Word document that has the input focus. In a very common scenario, a macro uses ActiveDocument to perform some task for the document the user is currently editing. For example, the following code deletes all of the current document's shapes and inline shapes.

 FILE *Ch07\Word.doc*

```
' Remove all Shape and InlineShape objects.
Sub DeleteShapes()
    Do While ActiveDocument.Shapes.Count > 0
        ActiveDocument.Shapes(1).Delete
    Loop

    Do While ActiveDocument.InlineShapes.Count > 0
        ActiveDocument.InlineShapes(1).Delete
    Loop
End Sub
```

When you write VBA code that deals with a document, you must be aware of which document you want to manipulate and which document contains the code. Usually, it makes the most sense for code to work with the currently active document, particularly if the code is contained in Normal.dot or some other template. In that case, you can use the ActiveDocument object to be certain you are working with the correct object. If you sometimes need to use the code for a document that is not active, you may want to have the subroutine take the document it should manipulate as a parameter.

ActiveDocument is a read-only property, so you cannot use it to change which document has the input focus. To give a particular document the focus, find the document in the Documents collection by using either its index or name, and call its Activate method. For example, the following code makes the file named Resume.doc the active document.

```
Application.Documents("Resume.doc").Activate
```

AutoCaptions *(G, C)*

The AutoCaptions property is a collection of AutoCaption objects representing captions created automatically when you add certain items to a document. For example, you can make Word automatically provide a caption of the form "Table 1" when you create a new table.

The AutoCaption object's most useful properties are Name, AutoInsert, and CaptionLabel. The Name property gives the name of the type of object the AutoCaption represents. For instance, the name "Microsoft Word Table" means the AutoCaption represents new Word tables.

The AutoInsert property is a Boolean value that determines whether Word uses the AutoCaption object's information. If AutoInsert is True, Word inserts captions for the object automatically.

The CaptionLabel property is a CaptionLabel object that determines how Word creates captions. The CaptionLabel object has several useful properties of its own. The Name property identifies the CaptionLabel in the CaptionLabels collection. It also determines the text displayed in the caption. The Position property determines whether the caption is added above (wdCaptionPositionAbove) or below (wdCaptionPositionBelow) the new object. The NumberStyle property determines whether the table number is shown in Arabic (1, 2, 3), Roman (I, II, III), lowercase letter (a, b, c), or one of about 30 other formats.

If certain paragraphs in the document have headings numbered with a chapter numbering style, you can use the CaptionLabel object's IncludeChapterNumber, ChapterStyleLevel, and Separator properties to add chapter numbers to the captions. If IncludeChapterNumber is True, then the caption includes the chapter number. The Separator property determines the character that appears between the chapter title and the table number. The ChapterStyleLevel property gives the heading level of the chapter numbers. For example, if the chapter titles have style Heading 2, then this value should be 2.

The following code demonstrates the AutoCaption and CaptionLabel objects. It starts by creating a new document. It then makes a new CaptionLabel object named My Table. This identifies the object in the CaptionLabels collection and indicates that a new table's caption should say My Table. The code sets this object's properties to include the chapter number, take the chapter number from text with style Heading 1, display table numbers in Arabic numerals (1, 2, 3), position captions below their tables, and use a colon between the chapter number and the table number.

Next the code finds the AutoCaption named "Microsoft Word Table." It sets that object's AutoInsert property to True to activate it, and makes its CaptionLabel property refer to the CaptionLabel object it just created.

Now the code creates some chapters containing tables. Subroutine MakeChapter adds a new chapter to the end of the document. It creates a Range object that contains the entire document and then collapses it so it is positioned at the end of the document.

MakeChapter adds the title text and a paragraph mark to the Range and sets its style to Heading 1. It then applies a list template to the title. This particular template makes the title a numbered field using Roman numerals (I, II, III). MakeChapter finishes by adding a blank line to the end of the document.

Subroutine MakeTableByRows takes as a parameter an array of arrays. It loops through the arrays, building a string that separates the values in a row with tabs, and separates the rows with paragraph marks. It makes a Range at the end of the document and adds the text. Then it calls the Range's ConvertToTable method to convert the text to a table. At this point, Word automatically adds a caption to the table. MakeTableByRows finishes by adding two blank lines after the table.

After it finishes making chapters and tables, the main MakeAutoCaptionTables subroutine sets the table AutoCaption object's AutoInsert property to False so Word does not automatically add captions to tables in the future. It then deletes the CaptionLabel entry.

 FILE *Ch07\Word.doc*

```
' Make some tables with AutoCaptions.
Sub MakeAutoCaptionTables()
Dim caption_label As CaptionLabel
Dim pos As Long
Dim new_range As Range
Dim txt As String
Dim i As Long

    ' Make a new document.
    Documents.Add
```

```
    ' Make the CaptionLabel entry.
    On Error Resume Next
    Set caption_label = CaptionLabels("My Table")
    On Error GoTo 0
    If caption_label Is Nothing _
        Then Set caption_label = CaptionLabels.Add("My Table")
    With caption_label
        .IncludeChapterNumber = True
        .ChapterStyleLevel = 1
        .NumberStyle = wdCaptionNumberStyleArabic
        .Position = wdCaptionPositionBelow
        .Separator = wdSeparatorColon
    End With

    ' Activate the table AutoCaption.
    With AutoCaptions("Microsoft Word Table")
        .AutoInsert = True
        .CaptionLabel = caption_label
    End With

    ' Make some chapters.
    MakeChapter "Fruit"
    MakeTableByRows Array( _
        Array("Citrus", "Other, Tree", "Bush/Vine"), _
        Array("Orange", "Apple", "Grape"), _
        Array("Lemon", "Banana", "Strawberry"), _
        Array("Grapefruit", "Date", "Blackberry"))

    MakeChapter "Dessert"
    MakeTableByRows Array( _
        Array("Icecream", "Cake", "Cookie", "Mint"))
    MakeTableByRows Array( _
        Array("Pecan Sandy", "Chocolate Chip", "Oatmeal"), _
        Array("Peanut Butter", "Snickerdoodle", "Anzac Crisp"))

    ' Remove the AutoCaption information.
    AutoCaptions("Microsoft Word Table").AutoInsert = False
    CaptionLabels("My Table").Delete
End Sub

' Make a chapter.
Sub MakeChapter(ByVal title_text As String)
Dim new_range As Range
```

```
        ' Make a Range at the end of the document.
        Set new_range = ActiveDocument.Range
        new_range.Collapse wdCollapseEnd

        ' Type the title.
        new_range.InsertAfter title_text & vbCrLf

        ' Give the title Heading 1 style.
        new_range.Style = wdStyleHeading1

        ' Apply the Heading 1 style.
        new_range.ListFormat.ApplyListTemplate _
            ListGalleries(wdOutlineNumberGallery).ListTemplates(6)

        new_range.Collapse wdCollapseEnd
        new_range.InsertParagraph
End Sub

' Make a table at the end of the file.
Sub MakeTableByRows(data As Variant)
Dim r As Long
Dim c As Long
Dim txt As String
Dim new_range As Range

        ' Compose the table's text.
        For r = LBound(data, 1) To UBound(data, 1)
            For c = LBound(data(r), 1) To UBound(data(r), 1)
                txt = txt & data(r)(c) & vbTab
            Next c
            txt = Left$(txt, Len(txt) - 1) & vbCrLf
        Next r

        ' Make a Range at the end of the document.
        Set new_range = ActiveDocument.Range
        new_range.Collapse wdCollapseEnd

        ' Insert the text and convert it to a table.
        new_range.InsertAfter txt
        new_range.ConvertToTable vbTab

        ' Add a blank line.
        Set new_range = ActiveDocument.Range
```

```
    new_range.Collapse wdCollapseEnd
    new_range.InsertParagraph
    new_range.Collapse wdCollapseEnd
    new_range.InsertParagraph
End Sub
```

The file Ch07\AutoCaptionResults.doc, shown in Figure 7-1, contains this code's output.

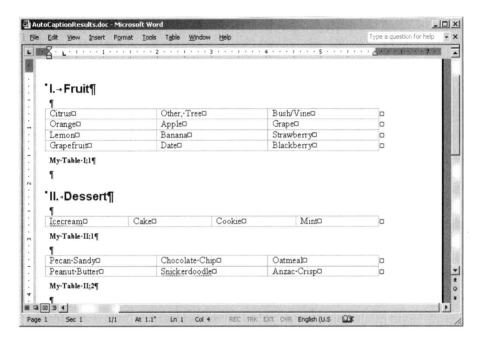

Figure 7-1. These table captions were automatically generated by Word.

See also the CaptionLabels property, which contains a collection of CaptionLabel objects that determine how captions are formatted.

AutoCorrect *(G)*

The AutoCorrect object determines how Word automatically corrects text as the user types. You can use this object's methods to determine whether Word corrects initial capitalization errors, whether it automatically capitalizes the first letter in weekday names, and what substitutions it makes automatically as you type. For example, the following code makes Word replace "tot he" (one of my favorite typos) with "to the" whenever you type it.

```
AutoCorrect.Entries.Add "tot he", "to the"
```

Browser

This property is completely unrelated to Web browsers, the objects you probably think about when someone says "browser" these days. Instead a Browser object lets the program jump to the next or previous object of a certain type: footnote, page, table, heading, or whatever. For example, the following code moves the insertion position to the next text with a heading style.

```
Application.Browser.Target = wdBrowserHeading
Application.Browser.Next
```

The code can call Application.Browser.Next repeatedly to move through the document. Similarly, the Browser's Previous method moves to the previous instance of the target type.

When the Browser reaches the last target in the document, calling Next does nothing. Unfortunately, the Next method doesn't return a value, so it won't tell you when it reaches the last target instance. However, you can use the Selection object's Start property to tell where the selection position is within the file. When the Browser's Next method does nothing, Selection.Start will not change.

The following code uses the Browser object to jump through the active document's text with a heading style. The code prints each heading's text indented to show its heading level.

 FILE *Ch07\Word.doc*

```
Sub ListHeadings()
Dim last_position As Long
Dim heading_style As String

    ' Start at the beginning.
    Selection.SetRange 0, 0
```

```
' Look for headings.
Application.Browser.Target = wdBrowseHeading

' Loop through them.
last_position = -1
Do
    ' Find the next heading.
    Application.Browser.Next

    ' See if we moved.
    If last_position = Selection.Start Then Exit Do
    last_position = Selection.Start

    ' Display the heading.
    Selection.Expand wdParagraph
    Debug.Print _
        Space$(4 * (CInt(Right$(Selection.Style, 1)) - 1)) & _
        Selection.Text;
Loop
End Sub
```

See also the Document object's GoTo method, which is described in the online help and briefly mentioned in the "Bookmarks" section later in this chapter.

Dialogs *(G, C)*

This collection represents all of Word's built-in dialogs. The Dialog object's Display method shows the dialog and returns one of the following values to indicate whether the user clicked Close, OK, Cancel, or some other button.

VALUE	MEANING
-2	Close
-1	OK
0	Cancel
> 0	A command button numbered 1, 2, 3, and so forth

The program can then decide what action to take. For example, if the user clicks OK on a file selection dialog, the program can open the file. Unfortunately, it's not always easy to figure out what properties you need to use to get the dialog's results. The following code displays an Open File dialog. If the user clicks OK, the dialog automatically sets the Application.Options.DefaultFilePath(wdCurrentFolderPath) property to the path the user selected. The dialog's Name property gives the file's name.

FILE *Ch07\Word.doc*

```
' Let the user select a file and display the
' file's path and name.
Sub PickFile()
Const OK_PRESSED = -1
Dim dlg As Dialog

    Set dlg = Application.Dialogs(wdDialogFileOpen)
    If dlg.Display = OK_PRESSED Then
        MsgBox "Selected file " & _
            Application.Options.DefaultFilePath(wdCurrentFolderPath) & _
            "\" & dlg.Name
    End If
End Sub
```

NOTE *The dialog's* Name *and other properties specific to a particular dialog are not documented in the online help for the* Dialog *object.*

Notice how this code saves a reference to the dialog it uses and then works with the reference. The statement Application.Dialogs(wdDialogFileOpen) returns a new instance of the dialog. If the code used that statement to display the dialog and then a similar statement to check the dialog's Name property, it would be working with two different Dialog objects, and the second object's Name property would be blank.

You can use the Show method to display the dialog and have Word automatically process the result. For example, the following code displays the File Open dialog and automatically opens the file the user selects.

```
Application.Dialogs(wdDialogFileOpen).Show
```

A Dialog object's Execute method makes the dialog apply its present values to the current selection. For example, the following code indents the paragraph that contains the insertion point by half an inch.

```
With Dialogs(wdDialogFormatParagraph)
    .LeftIndent = 0.5
    .Execute
End With
```

Using the Execute method like this is quite cumbersome, however. The properties that a particular dialog supports (LeftIndent in this example) don't seem to be documented. The property's units also do not necessary match those of similar properties supported by other objects. For example, the Paragraph object's LeftIndent property measures in points, but this dialog measures LeftIndent in inches.

NOTE *This makes some sense, because the Format Paragraph dialog measures the indentation in inches. It's inconsistent from a programming point of view, however.*

The real purpose of the Execute method is let the program modify or examine the dialog's selections before applying its results. For example, the following code displays the Format Paragraph dialog. If the user presses the OK button, it sets the dialog's LeftIndent and RightIndent properties to 1 inch and calls the Execute method to apply the dialog's settings. That lets the user format the paragraph but not change its indentation.

FILE *Ch07\Word.doc*

```
' Format the selected paragraph but set
' left and right indentation to 1 inch.
Sub FormatParagraphWithoutIndent()
Const OK_PRESSED = -1

    With Dialogs(wdDialogFormatParagraph)
        If .Display() = OK_PRESSED Then
            .LeftIndent = 1
            .RightIndent = 1
            .Execute
        End If
    End With
End Sub
```

If you simply want to take some action, for example opening a specific file or setting a piece of code's indentation level, it is almost always simpler and faster to perform the action directly without using a dialog.

The dialog type constants are named `wdDialog` followed by a menu name and the dialog name. For example, `wdDialogFileOpen` is the File menu's Open dialog. To see a list of the 200+ values available, search the online help for `Dialog Object`, select the Properties dropdown's Type entry, open the entry for the `Dialog` object, and click the link to the `WdWordDialog` constant.

Documents *(G, C)*

This collection contains `Document` objects representing each of the loaded Word documents. If you need to manipulate a document other than the active one, you will probably need to work with this collection.

The `Documents` collection also provides a few methods for working with documents in general rather than with a particular document. The `Add` method creates a new `Document` object and adds it to the collection. The `Open` method opens a document, adds it to the collection, and returns a reference to the new `Document` object.

The following code checks the `Documents` collection to see if a particular file is already open. If it is not, the subroutine uses the `Open` method to open the file. If the file is already open, the code calls its `Document` object's `Activate` method to make it the active document.

FILE *Ch07\Word.doc*

```
' If the document is not yet open, open it.
' Then activate the document.
Sub ActivateDocument(ByVal file_name As String)
Dim doc As Document

    ' See if the document is already loaded.
    On Error Resume Next
    Set doc = Documents(file_name)
    On Error GoTo 0
    If doc Is Nothing Then
        ' Open the document.
        Set doc = Documents.Open(file_name)
    Else
        ' Make this the active document.
```

```
        doc.Activate
    End If
End Sub
```

 TIP *Notice how this code disables error handling with* On Error Resume Next *and then reenables it with* On Error GoTo 0. *It disables error handling before looking for the document in the* Documents *collection so the program doesn't crash if the document isn't already open. It reenables error handling so it won't silently ignore unexpected errors later (for example, if the file isn't open and doesn't exist).*

The Documents collection's Save method saves every open document. If you set the method's NoPrompt parameter to True, the Save method saves each file without prompting the user. If you set NoPrompt to False or omit it, the Save method asks the user whether it should save each file. (This seems a little silly because if you are calling the Save method, you probably want to save the files, but you might sometimes want to give the user the choice.)

The Documents collection's Close method closes every open document. The first parameter, SaveChanges, indicates whether you want to save any changes to the files. If you omit this parameter or set it to wdPromptToSaveChanges, the Save method prompts the user for any document that has unsaved changes. If you set SaveChanges to wdDoNotSaveChanges, any changes are discarded. If you set SaveChanges to wdSaveChanges, Close automatically saves all modified files.

To save or close a specific document, find its Document object in the Documents collection and use its Save or Close method. Like the Close method described in the previous paragraph, the Document object's version takes a SaveChanges parameter that tells Word whether to save changes, discard changes, or prompt the user.

FileDialog *(C)*

FileDialog is a collection of dialog objects similar to the Dialogs collection. The key into this collection should be one of the following constants.

VALUE	DIALOG PURPOSE
msoFileDialogFilePicker	Lets the user select a file
msoFileDialogFolderPicker	Lets the user select a folder
msoFileDialogOpen	Displays the File Open dialog
msoFileDialogSaveAs	Displays the File Save As dialog

The items in the FileDialog collection are FileDialog objects rather than the more generic Dialog objects returned by the Dialogs collection. That allows IntelliSense to provide better support for the dialogs' properties and methods. Table 7-2 lists the FileDialog object's most useful properties.

Table 7-2. Useful FileDialog *Properties*

PROPERTY	PURPOSE
AllowMultiSelect	Determines whether the user can select multiple files.
ButtonName	The text displayed on the default button (normally OK).
FilterIndex	Gets or sets the index of the filter initially selected when the dialog displays.
Filters	A collection of FileDialogFilter objects representing the dialog's file filters.
InitialFileName	Gets or sets the path and/or file name initially displayed. The file name can include the * and ? wildcards.
InitialView	The initial file view displayed by the dialog. This can be msoFile DialogViewDetails, msoFileDialogViewLargeIcons, msoFileDialogViewList, msoFileDialogViewPreview, msoFileDialogViewProperties, msoFileDialogViewSmallIcons, or msoFileDialogViewThumbnail (Windows 2000, ME, or later).
SelectedItems	A collection of the selected file names.
Title	The text displayed in the dialog's title bar.

The FileDialog object provides only two methods: Show and Execute. Show displays the dialog and returns –1 if the user clicked the OK button or 0 if the user clicked Cancel. The Execute method makes the dialog perform its associated action. The following code shows how a program might let the user open several files at once.

 FILE *Ch07\Word.doc*

```
' Let the user open files.
Sub OpenMultipleFiles()
Dim dlg As FileDialog

    Set dlg = Application.FileDialog(msoFileDialogOpen)
    dlg.AllowMultiSelect = True
    If dlg.Show() Then dlg.Execute
End Sub
```

The following code shows a more elaborate example. It creates a File Picker dialog, allows multiselect, and changes the default button's text to List. Then it clears the filter list and adds filters for Image Files and All Files. It sets FilterIndex to 1 to select the first filter.

The code then displays the dialog. If the user clicks the List button, the code loops through the selected files and prints them in the Debug window.

 FILE *Ch07\Word.doc*

```
' Let the user select multiple files.
Sub SelectMultipleFiles()
Const OK_PRESSED = -1
Dim i As Integer

    ' Create and use the dialog.
    With Application.FileDialog(msoFileDialogFilePicker)
        .AllowMultiSelect = True
        .ButtonName = "List"
        .Filters.Clear
        .Filters.Add "Image Files", "*.bmp;*.gif;*.jpg"
        .Filters.Add "All Files", "*.*"
        .FilterIndex = 1
        .Title = "Select File"

        ' Show the dialog.
        If .Show() = OK_PRESSED Then
            ' The user pressed OK.
            ' Display the selected items.
            For i = 1 To .SelectedItems.Count
                Debug.Print .SelectedItems(i)
            Next i
        End If
    End With
End Sub
```

Key Bindings

Word lets you bind certain key combinations to actions. For example, you might make Ctrl-Alt-F10 execute a macro you have written.

Word represents key combinations with numeric key codes. The BuildKeyCode (G) function returns a key code for a combination. For instance, the following statement returns the key code for the sequence Shift-F10.

```
key_code = BuildKeyCode(wdKeyF10, wdKeyShift))
```

The KeyBindings (G, C) collection contains KeyBinding objects that represent custom key bindings. The following code lists any custom key bindings.

 FILE *Ch07\Word.doc*

```
' List custom key bindings.
Sub ListKeyBindings()
Dim key_binding As KeyBinding

    For Each key_binding In Application.KeyBindings
        Debug.Print key_binding.KeyString & ": " & key_binding.Command
    Next key_binding
End Sub
```

You can use the KeyBindings collection's Add method to create a new key binding as shown in the following code. This code sets the CustomizationContext to save the key binding in the template Normal.dot. It then creates the new key binding.

 FILE *Ch07\Word.doc*

```
' Make Control-Shift-C execute the ConvertToCode macro.
Sub InstallConvertToCode()
    CustomizationContext = NormalTemplate
    Application.KeyBindings.Add _
        wdKeyCategoryMacro, _
        "Normal.NewMacros.ConvertToCode", _
        BuildKeyCode(wdKeyControl, wdKeyShift, wdKeyC)
End Sub
```

NOTE *If the key binding already exists, the* KeyBindings *collection silently over-writes the old entry. You can use the* KeysBoundTo *and* FindKey *functions described shortly to see if a particular key binding is already defined.*

To remove an entry from the KeyBindings collection, find the item and invoke its Clear method. The UninstallConvertToCode subroutine in the following code calls subroutine RemoveKeyBinding, passing it the ConvertToCode macro's name. RemoveKeyBinding searches the KeyBindings collection and calls the Clear method of any bindings it finds that match that command.

FILE *Ch07\Word.doc*

```
' Remove any key bindings that execute the
' ConvertToCode macro.
Sub UninstallConvertToCode()
    RemoveKeyBinding "Normal.NewMacros.ConvertToCode"
End Sub

' Remove key bindings with the indicated command.
Sub RemoveKeyBinding(ByVal command_text As String)
Dim key_binding As KeyBinding

    For Each key_binding In Application.KeyBindings
        If key_binding.Command = command_text Then
            key_binding.Clear
        End If
    Next key_binding
End Sub
```

TIP *When you need to delete more than one item from a collection, search the collection by using a* For Each *loop rather than iterating over the items' indexes. When you delete an item, the indexes of the remaining items change, so using indexes to iterate over the collection can be confusing and error prone.*

The KeysBoundTo (G, C) method returns a collection of KeyBinding objects representing keys bound to a particular command. The following code uses the KeysBoundTo property to list the keys bound to a particular command.

FILE *Ch07\Word.doc*

```
' List keys bound to the command.
Sub ListKeysBoundTo(ByVal command_text As String)
Dim key_binding As KeyBinding

    For Each key_binding In Application.KeysBoundTo( _
        wdKeyCategoryMacro, command_text)
          Debug.Print key_binding.KeyString
    Next key_binding
End Sub
```

The following code shows another way to remove key bindings that execute a particular command. It iterates through the collection returned by KeysBoundTo and clears each key binding.

```
' Remove key bindings with the indicated command.
Sub ClearKeyBinding(ByVal command_text As String)
Dim key_binding As KeyBinding

    For Each key_binding In Application.KeysBoundTo( _
        wdKeyCategoryMacro, command_text)
          key_binding.Clear
    Next key_binding
End Sub
```

The FindKey (G) property returns a KeyBinding object representing a particular key combination. Its two parameters give the key codes you want to examine. You can use the BuildKeyCode method to calculate the key codes you need.

For example, the following code uses BuildKeyCode to build a key code for the Shift-F10 key combination. It passes that value to FindKey to get the KeyBinding object for this key. If that object's Command property is nonblank, the key has already been assigned. In that case, the code displays a message giving the key combination and its command. For example, the message might read:

```
Shift+F10 is already bound to command 'Normal.NewMacros.SayHi'
```

If the `KeyBinding` object's `Command` is blank, the code uses the `KeyBinding` object's `Rebind` method to assign the key to the `SayHi` macro in the `NewMacros` module contained in Normal.dot. After running this code, if you are using Word and press Shift-F10, the `SayHi` macro executes and displays a message box.

 FILE *Ch07\Word.doc*

```
' Make Shift-F10 execute the SayHi macro.
Sub BindShiftF10()
Dim key_binding As KeyBinding

    ' Make sure Shift-F10 isn't already bound.
    Set key_binding = FindKey(BuildKeyCode(wdKeyF10, wdKeyShift))
    If Len(key_binding.Command) > 0 Then
        MsgBox key_binding.KeyString & _
            " is already bound to the command '" & _
            key_binding.Command & "'"
    Else
        key_binding.Rebind _
            wdKeyCategoryMacro, _
            "Normal.NewMacros.SayHi"
    End If
End Sub
```

Finally, the `KeyString` (G) method takes as a parameter a key code and returns a textual representation of the code, such as ALT+F10.

GoBack, GoForward

These methods move the insertion point backward and forward through the last three places where the active document was edited. Those places are saved with the file, so the code can use `GoBack` and `GoFoward` even if the file has not been edited since it was opened.

The following code shows one particularly handy use for `GoBack`. This routine has the same name as the standard `FileOpen` method, so Word runs it when the user selects File ➤ Open. The routine displays the standard file open dialog. If the user selects a file, the dialog automatically opens it, and its `Show` method returns

True. Then the code executes the GoBack method to move to the place where the file was last edited. This lets you open the file and resume editing where you left off.

 FILE *Ch07\Word.doc*

```
' Open a file and go back to the last place it was edited.
Sub FileOpen()
    ' Display the file open dialog.
    If Application.Dialogs.Item(wdDialogFileOpen).Show() Then
        ' The user selected a file.
        Application.GoBack
    End If
End Sub
```

Note that this routine executes only if it is active. For example, if it is in a specific document's code, it runs only if that document is active when you open a file. Usually, you would save this code in a module inside Normal.dot.

Quit

This method makes Word exit. The method takes three optional parameters: SaveChanges, Format, and Route.

The SaveChanges parameter can be wdDoNotSaveChanges (discard changes to all open documents), wdPromptToSaveChanges (prompt the user for any documents with unsaved changes), or wdSaveChanges (save all modified documents).

The Format parameter tells Quit what format to use when saving a document that was not originally a Word document. It can have the values wdOriginalDocumentFormat, wdPromptUser, or wdWordDocument.

If the Route parameter is True and the document has a routing slip attached, Word sends the document to the next recipient.

To save changes to specific documents, use the Document object's Save method. To close specific documents without saving changes, use the Document object's Close method.

ScreenUpdating

The ScreenUpdating property enables or disables most of Word's screen updates. Sometimes you can make a routine run significantly faster by disabling updates before it starts and enabling them after it finishes.

This technique also hides changes from the user as they are applied to the document. If the program jumps back and forth all over the document, the user may become confused (or even dizzy). Use ScreenUpdating to hide the changes until they are all complete.

TIP *If you have a very long update, the user may find it disconcerting if the screen doesn't update once in a while. This is largely a matter of preference, but you may want to leave screen updating on for very long operations. You can also set* Application.StatusBar *to a message telling the user what is going on periodically. This message is small, however, so you will need to tell users where to look for it.*

Note that you can often avoid jumping back and forth through the file by using the correct object. For example, the following code uses the Find object provided by the Selection object to add the word *Section* to the beginning of each level 1 heading. Because it uses the Selection object, Word moves the document to show the new selection as it does its work. In the end, it displays the end of the document.

Repositioning the document like this can be very annoying to the user. If the code needs to make several passes through the document while making different substitutions and complex calculations, the user might see the document strobe back and forth in a headache-inducing way.

FILE *Ch07\SelectionVsContent.doc*

```
' Add the word "Section" to each level 1 head
' using the Selection object.
Private Sub cmdSelection_Click()
    ActiveDocument.Content.Select
    With Selection.Find
        .ClearFormatting
```

```
            .Style = wdStyleHeading1
            Do While .Execute(FindText:="", _
               Forward:=True, Format:=True)
                With .Parent
                    .StartOf Unit:=wdParagraph, Extend:=wdMove
                    .InsertAfter "Section "
                    .Move Unit:=wdParagraph, Count:=1
                End With
            Loop
        End With
End Sub
```

The following code makes the same substitution by using the Find object provided by the ActiveDocument.Content object. Because this object is not tied to the current selection, Word does not need to reposition the document to show a new selection as it works. When it finishes, the document shows the same position it had when the code started. The user sees only the changes visible from that position.

 FILE *Ch07\SelectionVsContent.doc*

```
' Add the word "Section" to each level 1 head
' using the Document.Content object.
Private Sub cmdContent_Click()
    With ActiveDocument.Content.Find
        .ClearFormatting
        .Style = wdStyleHeading1
        Do While .Execute(FindText:="", _
           Forward:=True, Format:=True)
            With .Parent
                .StartOf Unit:=wdParagraph, Extend:=wdMove
                .InsertAfter "Section "
                .Move Unit:=wdParagraph, Count:=1
            End With
        Loop
    End With
End Sub
```

When you record a macro, the automatically generated code often uses the Selection object because that makes the most sense interactively. The user selects some text and performs some action on the selection. If you want code to perform the same action, however, you often don't want to change the user's selection.

Even if you do want to operate on the selected text, you may not want to modify the selection. In that case, you can make a Range object that contains the same region as the Selection and then work with the Range. The following code adds the word Hello after the selected text and leaves the selection unchanged.

```
Dim new_range As Range

    Set new_range = Selection.Range
    new_range.Collapse wdCollapseEnd
    new_range.InsertAfter "Hello"
```

In contrast, the following code adds the word Hello to the end of the selection and automatically expands the selection to include the new text.

```
Selection.InsertAfter "Hello"
```

Whenever you write code that uses the Selection object, you should spend a little time deciding whether you could accomplish the same task by using a different object. Remember to give the user feedback, however. If the screen is too quiet for too long, the user may pull up the task manager and kill Word before your macro is finished.

Selection *(G)*

The Selection object represents the user's currently selected text. Many Word macros use this object to perform some action on text the user has selected. In a very common scenario, the user selects some text and clicks a button to run a macro that formats the text in a special way. For example, the following macro formats the selected text as Visual Basic source code for an Apress book.

If the selection contains a single paragraph, the code sets its style to Code Single. That style defines the basic code font and adds a little blank vertical space above and below the single line of code.

If the selected text includes more than one sentence, the macro sets the entire selection's style to Code to define the basic code font. It then switches the first and last paragraphs to style Code First and Code Last. These styles add a little extra vertical space before the first paragraph and after the last paragraph.

Having set the text's style, the macro saves the current value of the AutoFor-matAsYouTypeReplaceQuotes option. It then sets this option's value to False so Word will not automatically replace apostrophes and single quotes (' ' and "") with "smart" (curly) quotes (' ' and " "). Next the code replaces apostrophes with new apostrophes and double quotes with new double quotes. That makes Word replace any existing apostrophes and quotes with straight ones, the desired format for Visual Basic code.

The code finishes by restoring the original value of the AutoFormatAsYouTypeReplaceQuotes option.

FILE *Ch07\Word.doc*

```
' Convert the selected text to code style.
Sub ConvertToCode()
Dim para As Range
Dim replace_quotes As Boolean

    If Selection.Paragraphs.Count = 1 Then
        ' A single paragraph. Use "Code Single" style.
        Selection.Style = ActiveDocument.Styles("Code Single")
    Else
        ' Multiple lines. Set all lines to "Code" style.
        Selection.Style = ActiveDocument.Styles("Code")

        ' Set the first paragraph to "Code First" style.
        Set para = Selection.Paragraphs(1).Range
        ExcludeTrailingParagraphs para
        para.Style = ActiveDocument.Styles("Code First")

        ' Set the last line to "Code Last" style.
        Set para = Selection.Paragraphs(Selection.Paragraphs.Count).Range
        ExcludeTrailingParagraphs para
        para.Style = ActiveDocument.Styles("Code Last")
    End If

    ' Straighten quotes.
    replace_quotes = Options.AutoFormatAsYouTypeReplaceQuotes
    Options.AutoFormatAsYouTypeReplaceQuotes = False
    With Selection.Find
```

```
        .ClearFormatting
        .Replacement.ClearFormatting
        .Forward = True
        .Wrap = wdFindStop
        .Format = True
        .MatchCase = False
        .MatchWholeWord = False
        .MatchWildcards = False
        .MatchSoundsLike = False
        .MatchAllWordForms = False
        .Text = "'"
        .Replacement.Text = "'"
        .Execute Replace:=wdReplaceAll

        .ClearFormatting
        .Replacement.ClearFormatting
        .Forward = True
        .Wrap = wdFindStop
        .Format = True
        .MatchCase = False
        .MatchWholeWord = False
        .MatchWildcards = False
        .MatchSoundsLike = False
        .MatchAllWordForms = False
        .Text = """"
        .Replacement.Text = """"
        .Execute Replace:=wdReplaceAll
    End With
    Options.AutoFormatAsYouTypeReplaceQuotes = replace_quotes
End Sub

' Exclude any trailing empty paragraphs from the range.
Private Function ExcludeTrailingParagraphs(ByVal rng As Range)
    Do While rng.Characters(rng.Characters.Count) = vbCr
        rng.SetRange rng.Start, rng.End - 1
    Loop
End Function
```

This code demonstrates a couple of important techniques. First, it saves the value of the AutoFormatAsYouTypeReplaceQuotes option so it can restore the value when it is finished.

The code also does not change the Selection object's location. The user selects some text and runs the macro. When the code finishes, the text selected by the user is still selected. Both of these leave things as much as possible as they were before the user ran the macro.

The Selection object is so important that it has its own section describing its most important properties and methods later in this chapter.

System (G)

The System object represents various accessible system parameters. For example, its properties include OperatingSystem, Version, ProcessorType, ComputerType, FreeDiskSpace, HorizontalResolution, VerticalResolution, and MathCoprocessorInstalled. Some of these properties may not be available on all systems.

The System.PrivateProfileString method gets or sets a value saved in a settings file or in the system Registry much as Visual Basic's SaveSetting and GetSetting methods get and set values in the Registry. The syntax is:

```
System.PrivateProfileString(file_name, section, key)
```

Here the parameters have the following meanings:

- **file_name**—The name of the settings file in which the value should be stored or retrieved. To save or restore a value in the Registry, this parameter must be blank.

- **section**—The section within the settings file. To save or restore a value in the Registry, this must include the complete Registry path to the value.

- **key**—The name of the setting to set or get. To save or restore a value in the Registry, this should be the name of the Registry subkey.

For example, the following code saves the Telephone value in the Settings section of the file Customers.dat. Because the file name does not include a path, the file is created in the Windows directory by default.

```
System.PrivateProfileString("Customers.dat", "Settings", "Telephone") = _
    "123-456-7890"
```

After executing this code, the file contains the following text.

```
[Settings]
Telephone=123-456-7890
```

The following code displays the value stored in a Registry key. Note that PrivateProfileString returns an empty string if the required value is not found in the Registry or the setting file. The code checks for missing values and supplies appropriate defaults if necessary.

FILE *Ch07\Word.doc*

```
' Display the registered Windows NT
' user and organization.
Sub DisplayRegistration()
Dim user_name As String
Dim organization As String

    organization = System.PrivateProfileString("", _
        "HKEY_LOCAL_MACHINE\SOFTWARE\Microsoft\Windows NT\CurrentVersion\", _
        "RegisteredOrganization")
    If Len(organization) = 0 Then organization = "<organization>"

    user_name = System.PrivateProfileString("", _
        "HKEY_LOCAL_MACHINE\SOFTWARE\Microsoft\Windows NT\CurrentVersion\", _
        "RegisteredOwner")
    If Len(user_name) = 0 Then user_name = "<user>"

    MsgBox "User: " & user_name & vbCrLf & _
        "Organization: " & organization
End Sub
```

For a couple years now, Microsoft has discouraged the use of settings files (although it still uses a few of its own in some applications) and has recommended that programmers store values in the Registry. In Visual Basic, this is somewhat easier using the GetSetting and SaveSetting methods, so you should probably use them rather than System.PrivateProfileString when possible. However, System.PrivateProfileString does provide access to existing setting files and Registry values that are not accessible by using GetSetting and SaveSetting.

> **NOTE** *Lately, Microsoft has even moved beyond the Registry and is making noises about storing data in XML files and Active Directory. Who knows what the fad will be tomorrow?*

The Document object's Variables collection provides an alternative to these methods. Using this collection, VBA code can save and restore values inside a document. For more information, see the "Variables" section later in this chapter. There are two main drawbacks to document variables. First, they are tied to the document, not to the user. If another user logs on or you copy the document to another computer, it keeps the same values. On the other hand, the Registry is user-specific, so different users can have different values. Whether you want one common value or different values for each user depends on your application.

A second disadvantage to document variables is that they are not very secure. Anyone who can read the document can read them, too. You have more control over access to the Registry on a particular computer.

Application *Object Events*

The Application object supports several events that you can use to tell what's going on in the Word application. You can capture these events by creating a variable that refers to the Application object by using the WithEvents keyword.

To catch all of the most useful events, it would make sense to initialize this variable in the Normal.dot template's AutoExec module so the variable would be assigned as soon as Word starts. Unfortunately, VBA lets you use the WithEvents keyword only in class modules, not in code modules such as AutoExec.

To get around this problem, you can create an ApplicationEventWatcher class that contains the WithEvents variable. Then the AutoExec module can create an instance of the ApplicationEventWatcher class.

In the following code, the AutoExec module's Main subroutine instantiates an ApplicationEventWatcher object.

FILE *Ch07\AutoExec.bas*

```
' An instance of this object to watch events.
Public g_ApplicationEventWatcher As ApplicationEventWatcher
```

```
' Create the ApplicationEventWatcher instance.
Sub Main()
    Set g_ApplicationEventWatcher = New ApplicationEventWatcher
End Sub
```

The ApplicationEventWatcher class defines its own variable TheApplication of type Application by using the WithEvents keyword. When an instance of this class is created, the Class_Initialize event handler executes. That routine makes TheApplication refer to the Application object.

When you declare a variable by using WithEvents, the development environment adds the variable to the code window's left dropdown list. When you select the variable from that list, the right dropdown list shows events supported by the object. Select one to open the corresponding event handler code. The following code defines event handlers that display messages when the Application object receives a DocumentBeforeClose, DocumentBeforeSave, DocumentChange, DocumentOpen, or NewDocument event.

```
' A variable to catch Application events.
Public WithEvents TheApplication As Application

' Set a reference to the Application object.
Private Sub Class_Initialize()
    Set TheApplication = Application
End Sub

Private Sub TheApplication_DocumentBeforeClose(ByVal Doc As Document, _
  Cancel As Boolean)
    Debug.Print "DocumentBeforeClose"
End Sub
Private Sub TheApplication_DocumentBeforeSave(ByVal Doc As Document, _
  SaveAsUI As Boolean, Cancel As Boolean)
    Debug.Print "DocumentBeforeSave"
End Sub
Private Sub TheApplication_DocumentChange()
    Debug.Print "DocumentChange"
End Sub
Private Sub TheApplication_DocumentOpen(ByVal Doc As Document)
    Debug.Print "DocumentOpen"
End Sub
Private Sub TheApplication_NewDocument(ByVal Doc As Document)
    Debug.Print "NewDocument"
End Sub
```

You could also use an `Application` variable declared `WithEvents` to hold a new instance of the `Application` class. For example, the following line of code saves a reference to a new `Application` object in the `app` variable.

```
Set app = New Application
```

A new instance of the `Application` class such as this one makes a new Word server. If the app variable is declared `WithEvents`, this code could catch the new server's events.

One more oddity bears mention here. When your code initializes the `With-Events` variable, VBA seems to create the object as its code exists at that moment. If you later modify the event handler code, the new code is not installed until a new instance of the object is created. You will probably need to close Word (not just the document) to get it to load the new code.

Table 7-3 describes some of the most useful `Application` object events.

Table 7-3 Useful Application *Object Events*

EVENT	DESCRIPTION
DocumentBeforeClose	Occurs before a document closes. Set the Cancel parameter to True to cancel the document's closing.
DocumentBeforePrint	Occurs before a document prints. Set the Cancel parameter to True to cancel the document's printing.
DocumentBeforeSave	Occurs before a document closes. Set the SaveAsUI parameter to True to make Word display the Save As dialog. Set the Cancel parameter to True to cancel the document's saving.
DocumentChange	Occurs when Word switches the active document. This happens when a document is created or opened, or when a new document is activated.
DocumentOpen	Occurs when Word opens a new document.
NewDocument	Occurs after Word creates a new document. See also DocumentOpen.
Quit	Occurs when Word quits. The DocumentBeforeClose event occurs for any open documents before this event fires. If any document does not close, either because the DocumentBeforeClose event sets its Cancel parameter to True or because the user clicks Cancel when prompted to save changes, the quit is canceled.
WindowActivate	Occurs when a document window activates.
WindowDeactivate	Occurs when a document's window deactivates.
WindowSelectionChange	Occurs when the selection in the active window changes.

Because there really isn't a Global object that you can reference, it doesn't make sense to think of these events as having a global scope. You need to make a reference to an Application object to catch them.

Document

A Document object represents a specific Word file. If you need to modify a file, you will probably need to use a Document object. This object provides methods for modifying the file's text and styles, saving changes to the file, managing the file's headers and footers, and accessing the file's contents by paragraph, word, or letter.

The following sections describe some of the most important of the Document object's properties and methods.

Document *Object Properties and Methods*

Like the Application object, the Document object has several properties that return collections. Most have names that reflect the objects they contain. For example, the Fields collection contains Field objects that describe fields in the document. The following sections are marked (C) to indicate properties that return collections.

Unlike the Application object, Document object properties make sense only in the context of a particular document, so they cannot have global scope.

The Documents collection described earlier in this chapter and a Document object are very closely related. A Document object applies to a particular Word document, but the Documents collection provides properties and methods that deal with all open documents. For example, the Documents.Add method creates a new Document object and adds it to the Documents collection.

If you need to work with a particular document, you need to use a Document object. If you want to work with the open documents (add new ones, open a document, and so forth), you need to use the Documents collection. See the "Documents" section earlier in this chapter for more on the Documents collection.

Bookmarks *(C)*

The Bookmarks collection contains objects representing bookmarks in the document. You can use bookmarks to indicate special places within the document. For example, you could use a bookmark to indicate where the monthly cafeteria menu begins.

Later, a user can quickly navigate to a bookmark by selecting Insert ➤ Bookmark, selecting the desired bookmark, and clicking Go To as shown in Figure 7-2.

Figure 7-2. Bookmarks let you quickly navigate through a document.

Often it is simpler for a user to find a position in the document by searching
for a piece of text. In this example, the user might search for the section name
Cafeteria Menu.

Bookmarks are very useful in code, however. They let the code locate a spot in
the document unambiguously. For instance, you could define a newsletter template with bookmarks indicating locations for the cafeteria menu, conference
schedules, birthday announcements, and so forth. VBA code could then easily
jump to the bookmarks and insert the appropriate text.

The following code shows how a program might replace the Menu bookmark
with a table.

FILE *Ch07\Word.doc*

```
' Insert a menu at the Menu bookmark.
Sub InsertMenu()
Dim menu_range As Range

    ' Get the Range representing the bookmarked text.
    Set menu_range = ActiveDocument.Bookmarks("Menu").Range
```

```
    ' Remove the existing text.
    menu_range.Delete

    ' Add the menu text.
    menu_range.InsertAfter vbTab & "Monday" & vbTab & _
        "Tuesday" & vbTab & "Wednesday" & vbTab & _
        "Thursday" & vbTab & "Friday" & vbCrLf
    menu_range.InsertAfter "Breakfast" & vbTab & "Eggs" & vbTab & _
        "Pancakes" & vbTab & "Donuts" & vbTab & _
        "French Toast" & vbTab & "Bagels" & vbCrLf
    menu_range.InsertAfter "Lunch" & vbTab & "Club Sand" & vbTab & _
        "Tacos" & vbTab & "Pizza" & vbTab & _
        "Soup" & vbTab & "Fish" & vbCrLf
    menu_range.InsertAfter "Dinner" & vbTab & "Lasagna" & vbTab & _
        "Mac/Cheese" & vbTab & "Quiche" & vbTab & _
        "Stew" & vbTab & "Salad" & vbCrLf

    ' Convert the text to a table.
    menu_range.ConvertToTable vbTab

    ' Add a blank line.
    menu_range.Collapse wdCollapseEnd
    menu_range.InsertParagraphAfter
End Sub
```

You can also use the GoTo method to retrieve a Range representing a bookmark. For example, the following two statements both display the text contained in the Menu bookmark.

```
Debug.Print ActiveDocument.Bookmarks("Menu").Range.Text
Debug.Print ActiveDocument.GoTo(What:=wdGoToBookmark, Name:="Menu").Text
```

The GoTo method also allows you to navigate to other objects in the document such as comments, pages, sections, and tables. See the online help for a more complete description.

Document Properties

A document property in this context is some value defined for the document, such as the author's name, not a Document object property. Word defines two kinds of document properties: built-in properties and custom properties. Built-in properties include predefined values, such as the document's title, subject, and author name. You can access these properties interactively by using the File ➤ Properties command.

The Document object's BuiltInDocumentProperties (C) collection lets you get and set built-in property values in VBA code. The following code displays the value of the Author property.

```
MsgBox ActiveDocument.BuiltInDocumentProperties("Author")
```

The following code lists a document's built-in properties.

FILE *Ch07\Word.doc*

```
' List all the built in properties.
Sub ListBuiltInDocumentProperties()
Dim new_range As Range
Dim prop As DocumentProperty
Dim prop_value As Variant

    ' Make a Range at the end of the document.
    Set new_range = ActiveDocument.Range
    new_range.Collapse wdCollapseEnd

    ' Insert the text.
    For Each prop In ActiveDocument.BuiltInDocumentProperties
        ' Get the property value. This is protected by
        ' On Error because it can cause an automation error.
        On Error Resume Next
        prop_value = prop.Value
        If Err.Number <> 0 Then prop_value = "<unknown>"
        On Error GoTo 0

        ' Display the property information.
        new_range.InsertAfter prop.Name & vbTab & prop_value & vbCrLf
    Next prop

    ' Convert the text to a table.
    new_range.ConvertToTable vbTab
```

```
    ' Add a blank line.
    Set new_range = ActiveDocument.Range
    new_range.Collapse wdCollapseEnd
    new_range.InsertParagraph
    new_range.Collapse wdCollapseEnd
    new_range.InsertParagraph
End Sub
```

Custom properties can be just about anything you want. They are simply pairs of names and values. For example, you could define a new Priority property and set its value to High, Medium, or Low. You can access these properties interactively by invoking the File ➤ Properties command and clicking on the Custom tab.

The CustomDocumentProperties (C) collection contains objects representing the document's custom properties. The collection's Add method lets you add a new custom property to the document.

After you add a custom property, you can use its name as an index into the CustomDocumentProperties collection. Use the returned CustomDocumentProperty object's Delete method to remove that property.

The following code shows how to add, access, and delete a custom property. Subroutine AddCustomProperty creates a property named Usefulness of type string and having value High. Subroutine ShowCustomProperty prints the property's value in the debug window. Subroutine DeleteCustomProperty deletes the Usefulness property.

FILE *Ch07\Word.doc*

```
' Add a new custom property to the document.
Sub AddCustomProperty()
Dim custom_properties As DocumentProperties

    Set custom_properties = CustomDocumentProperties
    custom_properties.Add _
        Name:="Usefulness", _
        LinkToContent:=False, _
        Type:=msoPropertyTypeString, _
        Value:="High"
End Sub
```

```
' Show a custom property's value.
Sub ShowCustomProperty()
    Debug.Print CustomDocumentProperties("Usefulness").Value
End Sub


' Delete a custom property.
Sub DeleteCustomProperty()
    CustomDocumentProperties("Usefulness").Delete
End Sub
```

If your code tries to access a property that doesn't exist, VBA raises an error. Use an `On Error` statement to catch the error and take appropriate action as shown in the following code.

```
' Show a custom property's value.
Sub ShowCustomProperty()
    On Error Resume Next
    Debug.Print CustomDocumentProperties("Usefulness").Value
    If Err.Number <> 0 Then Debug.Print "Unknown property"
End Sub
```

CommandBars *(C)*

The `CommandBars` collection represents the command bars associated with the document. You can use this collection to customize the document's tools. Use the `Application.CustomizationContext` property to set the document or template before accessing `CommandBars`. See Chapter 3 and Chapter 4 for more information on using `CommandBars` interactively and with VBA code.

Passwords

The `HasPassword` property returns True if the document has a password.

A VBA program can use the `Password` property to set the document's password. Setting `Password` to an empty string removes the password. Changing the password in this way does not give the user a chance to confirm the password, however, so it's a fairly unusual operation. If the code changes it to something the user cannot remember, there may be no way to open the document later. Also note that an attacker who can get hold of the code that sets the password can simply read the password out of the code.

The following code shows some simple uses of the HasPassword and Password properties.

FILE *Ch07\Password.doc*

```
' Tell if the document has a password.
Sub ShowHasPassword()
    If HasPassword Then
        MsgBox "Has a password"
    Else
        MsgBox "No password"
    End If
End Sub

' Set the document's password.
Sub SetPassword()
    Password = "password"
End Sub

' Clear the document's password.
Sub RemovePassword()
    Password = ""
End Sub
```

A more interesting use of the password property would be to let the user enter a password and then check the password before it is added to the document. The following code verifies that the user's password contains between 6 and 15 characters and that it contains at least one letter and one nonletter. A more elaborate routine might check that the password isn't a name, date, single word, and so forth.

FILE *Ch07\Password.doc*

```
' Let the user pick a new password.
Sub SetNewPassword()
Dim pwd As String
Dim has_letter As Boolean
Dim has_non_letter As Boolean
Dim i As Integer

    ' Get the password.
    pwd = InputBox("Password", "Password", "")
    If Len(pwd) = 0 Then Exit Sub

    ' See if the password has at least 6 characters.
    If (Len(pwd) < 6) Or (Len(pwd) > 15) Then
        MsgBox "The password must have between 6 and 15 characters"
        Exit Sub
    End If

    ' See if the password has at least 1 letter
    ' and 1 non-letter.
    For i = 1 To Len(pwd)
        Select Case Mid$(pwd, i, 1)
            Case "A" To "Z", "a" To "z"
                has_letter = True
            Case Else
                has_non_letter = True
        End Select
    Next i
    If (Not has_letter) Or (Not has_non_letter) Then
        MsgBox "The password must contain at least one letter and one non-letter"
        Exit Sub
    End If

    ' Set the new password.
    Password = pwd
End Sub
```

The Document object's WritePassword property sets a password that the user must enter to save changes to the document. The Boolean WriteReserved property returns True if the document is protected with a write password. The following code sets a document's write password.

FILE *Ch07\WritePassword.doc*

```
' Set the document's write password.
Sub SetWritePassword()
    Me.WritePassword = "write"
End Sub
```

When a user tries to open a file that has a write password, the dialog shown in Figure 7-3 appears. The user must either enter the write password or click the Read Only button to open the file as a read-only document.

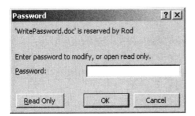

Figure 7-3. When you open a file with a write password, Word displays this dialog.

After you open the file, you can use VBA code to change the write password. Set WritePassword to an empty string to remove the password. Of course if you clicked the Read Only button in the dialog, you won't be able to save the document with its new write password.

To set a document's open and write passwords interactively, select Tools ➤ Options, click the Security tab, and enter the new values in the "Password to open" and "Password to modify" text boxes.

A Word document also provides another kind of document security. The Protect method allows you to restrict the kinds of modifications a user can make to the document. The method's Type parameter indicates the type of access you want to allow a user to have. This parameter can take the values wdAllowOnlyComments, wdAllowOnlyFormFields, wdAllowOnlyRevisions, and wdNoProtection. The Password parameter sets the password you must later use to unprotect the document by using the Unprotect method. The following code shows routine statements that protect and unprotect a document.

FILE *Ch07\Protected.doc*

```
' Protect the document to allow only comments.
Sub SetProtection()
    Me.Protect Type:=wdAllowOnlyComments, Password:="protected"
End Sub

' Remove the protection.
Sub RemoveProtection()
    Me.Unprotect "protected"
End Sub
```

TIP *You can omit the* Password *parameter from the* Protect *method if you want to protect the document from accidental changes, but you want to allow the user to remove the protection (by omitting the* Password *parameter from the* Unprotect *method) if necessary. This can help prevent simple accidents.*

The Document object's read-only ProtectionType property tells what kind of protection the document has.

Directory and File Properties

The Path property gives the document's directory path. Name gives the name of the file. The FullName property gives the document's directory path and file name together.

The PathSeparator property returns the character used to separate the document's directory path and file name. That means the following two statements are roughly equivalent.

```
MsgBox ActiveDocument.Path & ActiveDocument.PathSeparator & ActiveDocument.Name
MsgBox ActiveDocument.FullName
```

If the document is new and has not yet been saved, its Path property returns a blank string. In that case, the document's Name property returns the default name Word originally assigned to it, such as Document 3, and the FullName property returns the same value as the Name property.

Word also lets you use a field containing the file's name. For example, you could add the file name field to the document's page headers so the file name appears at the top of every page. To do that interactively, invoke the View ➤ Header and Footer command. Then invoke Insert ➤ Field and select the FileName entry as shown in Figure 7-4. Select a field formatting option, check the "Add path to file-name" option if you like, and click OK.

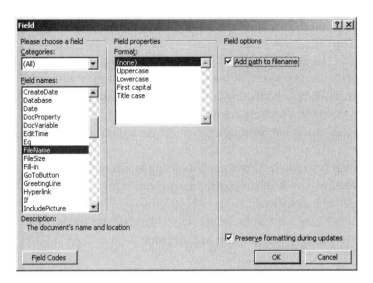

Figure 7-4. Use Insert ➤ Field to insert a FileName field.

The following code inserts this field automatically.

FILE *Ch07\Word.doc*

```
' Display a FILENAME field in the document's header.
Sub MakeHeader()
Dim header_range As Range

    ' Get the primary header range.
    Set header_range =
ActiveDocument.Sections(1).Headers(wdHeaderFooterPrimary).Range
```

```
    ' Add a FILENAME field to the range.
    Selection.Fields.Add _
        Range:=header_range, _
        Type:=wdFieldEmpty, _
        Text:="FILENAME  \p ", _
        PreserveFormatting:=True
End Sub
```

Grammar and Spelling

The Document object's CheckGrammar function returns True if its string argument has no grammatical errors. You probably shouldn't rely on this for anything terribly important because grammar checkers are notoriously easy to fool. Note that CheckGrammar is not globally available, although the closely related CheckSpelling method is.

The CheckSpelling (G) function returns True if its string argument has no spelling errors. This function can be useful, particularly if you want to spell individual words, but beware of homonyms.

For example, both CheckGrammar and CheckSpelling return True for the following text, indicating that it has no grammar or spelling errors:

Mare he hat a lid tell lamb. It fleas was wide as know.

The GetSpellingSuggestions (G, C) method returns a collection of spelling suggestions for a word. The following function returns a string containing spelling suggestions separated by carriage returns.

 FILE *Ch07\Word.doc*

```
' Return a list of spelling suggestions for a word.
Function GetSpellingSuggestions(ByVal the_word As String) As String
Dim spelling_suggestions As SpellingSuggestions
Dim i As Long
Dim results As String
```

```
    Set spelling_suggestions = _
        Application.GetSpellingSuggestions( _
            Word:=the_word, _
            SuggestionMode:=wdSpellword)
    For i = 1 To spelling_suggestions.count
        results = results & _
            spelling_suggestions(i).Name & vbCrLf
    Next i

    GetSpellingSuggestions = results
End Function
```

The Document object's GrammarChecked and SpellingChecked properties return True if the document has been checked for grammar or spelling, respectively.

You can set a Document object's ShowGrammaticalErrors property to True to make the document display grammatical errors with a wavy green underline. This property works only if you have also set the Options object's CheckGrammarAsYouType property to True.

Similarly, the Document object's ShowSpellingErrors property determines whether the document underlines spelling errors with a wavy red line. This property works only if you also set the Options object's CheckSpellingAsYouType property to True.

These properties are related to the Options object's CheckGrammarWithSpelling property. As its name implies, this property indicates whether a spelling check should also automatically perform a grammar check.

The Options object's SuggestSpellingCorrections property determines whether Word displays spelling suggestions when it checks spelling. To see the difference, set this property to True, highlight some misspelled text in Word, and select Tools ➤ Spelling and Grammar. The resulting dialog lists spelling suggestions. Now set SuggestSpellingCorrections to False and spell check the text again. This time the dialog doesn't display spelling suggestions.

TIP *Right-click on text that has a red or green wavy underline to make Word display grammar or spelling suggestions.*

The GrammaticalErrors (C) and SpellingErrors (C) properties contain Range objects representing grammatical and spelling errors in the document. The following code shows how you might list the errors in a document.

 FILE *Ch07\Word.doc*

```
' List the document's spelling errors.
Sub ListSpellingErrors()
Dim i As Long

    For i = 1 To ActiveDocument.SpellingErrors.Count
        Debug.Print i & ": " & ActiveDocument.SpellingErrors(i).Text
    Next i
End Sub

' List the document's grammar errors.
Sub ListGrammaticalErrors()
Dim i As Long

    For i = 1 To ActiveDocument.GrammaticalErrors.Count
        Debug.Print i & ": " & ActiveDocument.GrammaticalErrors(i).Text
    Next i
End Sub
```

PageSetup

The PageSetup object gives VBA code access to the properties you manipulate interactively using the File ➤ Page Setup command. This object lets you define the page size, orientation, margins, gutters, and other page layout properties. See the online help for a complete list of this object's properties.

Printing

The Document object's `PrintOut` method prints the document. Parameters let you define the part of the document printed, the number of copies, whether copies should be collated, and other print characteristics.

The `Range` parameter can be one of the constants `wdPrintAllDocument`, `wdPrintSelection`, `wdPrintCurrentPage`, `wdPrintFromTo`, or `wdPrintRangeOfPages`. If the value is `wdPrintCurrentPage`, the document prints the page containing the start of the current selection. If Range is `wdPrintFromTo`, the `From` and `To` parameters tell `PrintOut` which pages to print. If Range is `wdPrintRangeOfPages`, then the `Pages` parameter should contain a list of page ranges to print, separated by commas. For example, the value "1-5,6,8-10" makes the document print pages 1 through 5, 6, and 8 through 10.

In addition to printing areas in the document, you can also print types of information in the document. You can set the `Item` parameter to `wdPrintAutoTextEntries`, `wdPrintComments`, `wdPrintDocumentContent`, `wdPrintKeyAssignments`, `wdPrintProperties`, or `wdPrintStyles` to make the document print different kinds of information.

Using the `PageType` parameter, you can restrict the pages printed. You can set `PageType` to `wdPrintAllPages`, `wdPrintEvenPagesOnly`, or `wdPrintOddPagesOnly`.

See the online help for more information on the `PrintOut` parameters.

The `Document` object's `PrintRevisions` property determines whether tracked revisions are printed as if they have been accepted or whether the document prints with revision marks.

The `Document` object's `PrintPreview` property is only somewhat related to printing. It returns True if the document is currently being viewed in print preview mode. You cannot set the value of this property, but you can use the document's `PrintPreview` method to enter print preview mode. You can also set the `Application` object's `PrintPreview` property to True to display the currently active document in print preview mode.

Yes, it's confusing. To summarize, `Application.PrintPreview` is a read/write property, `Document.PrintPreview` is a read-only property, and `Document.PrintPreview()` is a method that makes the document enter print preview mode.

The `ClosePrintPreview` method returns the document to the view it had before entering print preview mode. The following code shows how a program might display the active document in print preview mode, let the user look at it, and the return to the previous mode.

FILE *Ch07\Word.doc*

```
' Display the active document in print preview mode,
' let the user look at it, and then return to the
' previous display mode.
Sub ShowPrintPreview()
    ' Use either of the following two statements
    ' to display the print preview.
'    Application.PrintPreview = True
    ActiveDocument.PrintPreview

    MsgBox "Click when ready"

    ActiveDocument.ClosePrintPreview
End Sub
```

The following, more interesting example generates a series of invoice documents and prints them. The code is rather long, and some pieces are similar to others, so some code has been omitted. Download PrintInvoices.doc to take a look at the complete code.

The cmdPrintInvoices_Click event handler starts by calling subroutine GenerateInvoiceData. This routine generates some bogus test data and leaves it in the array m_InvoiceData, which contains items of the type InvoiceData. A real application would gather this data from some sort of time-tracking data stored in Access. (Chapter 11 explains how a VBA program can fetch data from such a database.) After loading the data, the event handler calls subroutine PrintCustomerInvoice for each customer.

Subroutine PrintCustomerInvoice creates a new document based on the template Invoice.dot. In this example, the template is stored in the same directory as the file PrintInvoices.doc, but you might prefer to save it as a global template.

Next the routine uses the customer data values to drop information into the document at positions marked by bookmarks. It creates a string representing some table data and places it in a Range defined by a bookmark. It calls the Range's ConvertToTable method to make a table and uses the resulting Table's AutoFormat method to make the table look nice.

After it finishes filling in the document's data, the code uses the Document object's SaveAs, PrintOut, and Close methods to save, print, and close the document.

FILE *Ch07\PrintInvoices.doc*

```
' Generate invoices for customers.
Private Sub cmdPrintInvoices_Click()
Dim cust_number As Integer

    ' Generate some data. (Normally you would pull
    ' this data from some sort of timecard database.
    ' See the later chapters on Access and ADO
    ' for information on fetching data.)
    GenerateInvoiceData

    ' Create invoices for each customer.
    For cust_number = LBound(m_InvoiceData) To UBound(m_InvoiceData)
        ' Print this customer's invoice.
        PrintCustomerInvoice cust_number
    Next cust_number
End Sub

' Print this customer's invoice.
Sub PrintCustomerInvoice(ByVal cust_num As Integer)
Dim new_doc As Document
Dim start_date As Date
Dim end_date As Date
Dim total_due As String
Dim txt As String
Dim new_table As Table

    ' Create a new invoice document based on the
    ' Invoice.dot template.
    Set new_doc = Documents.Add( _
        Template:=ActiveDocument.Path & "\Invoice.dot", _
        Visible:=False)

    ' Add the invoice data.
    With m_InvoiceData(cust_num)
        ' Code omitted ...
        ' Fill in header information.
        new_doc.Bookmarks("ContractNumber").Range.Text = .ContractNumber
        new_doc.Bookmarks("InvoiceDate").Range.Text = _
```

```
              Format$(Date, "short date")
        ' Code omitted...

        ' Build text describing the item table.
        ' Headers.
        txt = "Date" & vbTab & "Item" & vbTab & "Hours" & vbTab & _
            "Rate" & vbTab & "Total" & vbCrLf

        ' The real information.
        txt = txt & Format$(start_date, "short date") & "-" & _
                Format$(end_date, "short date") & vbTab
        txt = txt & .Description & vbTab
        txt = txt & .TotalHours & vbTab
        ' Code omitted...

        ' Build the item table.
        With new_doc.Bookmarks("ItemTable").Range
            .Text = txt
            Set new_table = .ConvertToTable()
            new_table.AutoFormat Format:=wdTableFormatGrid1, _
                ApplyBorders:=True, ApplyShading:=True, ApplyFont:=True, _
                ApplyColor:=True, ApplyHeadingRows:=True, _
                ApplyLastRow:=False, ApplyFirstColumn:=True, _
                ApplyLastColumn:=False, AutoFit:=True
            new_table.Rows(1).Range.Bold = True
            new_table.Rows(3).Range.Font.Size = 3
        End With

        new_doc.Bookmarks("TotalDue").Range.Text = total_due

        ' Save the document.
        new_doc.SaveAs FileName:=.ContractNumber & "-" & _
            Format$(.InvoiceDate, "yymm") & ".doc"

        ' Print it.
        new_doc.PrintOut

        ' Close it.
        new_doc.Close
    End With
End Sub
```

Revision Properties and Methods

The Document object provides several properties and methods for tracking and displaying revisions. The TrackRevisions property determines whether the document keeps a record of changes made to the document. ShowRevisions determines whether the document displays the revisions onscreen. PrintRevisions (see the previous section "Printing") determines whether the document shows revisions when printing.

The Protect method allows you to restrict the kinds of modifications a user can make to the document. If you pass this method the parameter wdAllowOnlyRevisions, the document automatically tracks revisions and disables the Tools ➤ Track Changes command so the user cannot turn change tracking off. See the "Passwords" section earlier in this chapter for more information on the Protect method.

As their names imply, the AcceptAllRevisions and RejectAllRevisions methods accept and reject all pending revisions respectively. Similarly, the DeleteAllComments method removes all comments from the document.

The Compare method creates a new copy of the document with revision marks showing where the document differs from another document. This can be useful for determining what has changed in different versions of a document. For instance, legal and real estate firms must know exactly what changes are made between versions of a contract. They could use this method to see exactly what has changed.

The Compare method is not particularly useful with completely unrelated documents because it basically flags everything as different.

Routing Properties

The Document object has a couple of properties and methods related to routing documents to several users either simultaneously or consecutively. The RoutingSlip property returns an object that represents the document's routing information. You can use that object to do such things as add recipients to the routing list, specify how the recipients can modify the document (if at all), and indicate whether the recipients should all receive the document at the same time or one after another.

The HasRoutingSlip property returns True if the document has an associated routing slip. VBA code can set this property to True to create a routing slip or set it to False to delete an existing routing slip.

The Route method sends the document off to the recipients. The Routed property indicates whether the document has been routed. The RoutingSlip object's Status property provides more information, returning the values wdNotYetRouted, wdRouteInProgress, and wdRouteComplete.

Saving and Closing

The Document object's Save method saves any changes to the document. If the file is new and has never been saved, the Save method prompts the user for a file name.

The SaveAs method allows the code to save the file with a new file name. This method's most important parameter is the file's name. Other useful parameters include an optional password and the file's format (text, Word document, RTF, HTML, and so forth).

NOTE *Word 2003 will also allow you to save the document as WordML (an XML-like Word format) or as XML.*

The Document object's Close method closes the document. Its SaveChanges parameter can be wdSaveChanges, wdPromptToSaveChanges, or wdDoNotSaveChanges.

The Saved property tells whether the document has been modified since it was last saved or opened. You can set this property to True to make the document think it has been saved. If you then close the document, any changes will be lost because Word thinks they have already been saved. This is a pretty strange thing to do, however, because it gives the document an incorrect view of its modification status. If you just want to close the document without saving changes, it would be less confusing to call the Close method, passing it the parameter wdDoNotSaveChanges.

Shapes *(C) and* InlineShapes *(C)*

These collections represent the document's shapes (which sit in boxes around which the text can flow) and inline shapes (which appear in the flow of text).

One use for these collections is to remove all of the shapes and inline shapes. Many professional publishing packages handle pictures differently than Word does, so one step in producing a book may be to remove any pictures in the document. The following code removes all of the shapes from these collections.

FILE *Ch07\Word.doc*

```
' Remove all Shape and InlineShape objects.
Sub DeleteShapes()
    Do While ActiveDocument.Shapes.Count > 0
        ActiveDocument.Shapes(1).Delete
    Loop

    Do While ActiveDocument.InlineShapes.Count > 0
        ActiveDocument.InlineShapes(1).Delete
    Loop
End Sub
```

Groups of Text

The Document object provides several properties for manipulating groups of text. The Paragraphs (C), Sentences (C), Words (C), and Characters (C) collections return objects that let you access the text by progressively smaller units. For example, the following code changes the 12th word in the document to Dog.

```
ActiveDocument.Words(12) = "Dog"
```

 NOTE *This doesn't mean Word stores the document internally in any of these forms. It is unlikely that Word actually ever builds a collection containing one item for every character in the document. It simply provides an object that lets you access the characters as if they were contained in a collection. How Word actually does this behind the scenes is irrelevant.*

Manipulating the smaller units of text is generally slower than working with larger units. Examining the document one character at a time and converting each letter into uppercase would be quite slow. It would be much more efficient to work with the text as a whole. For example, the following code converts the first sentence to uppercase. Performing this conversion one character at a time would be more time consuming.

```
ActiveDocument.Sentences(1).Text = UCase$(ActiveDocument.Sentences(1).Text)
```

Also note that the Range object provides its own Paragraphs, Sentences, Words, and Characters properties. That means, for example, that your code can easily work with the third word in the fourth sentence in the ninth paragraph, as in this code.

```
ActiveDocument.Paragraphs(9).Range.Sentences(4).Words(3).Font.Bold = True
```

Story Properties

A *story* is an area in the document representing a particular type of document content. These areas include the main text, footnotes, endnotes, even and odd page headers, and so forth.

The Document object provides several methods for working with the document's stories. The Comments (C), Endnotes (C), and Footnotes (C) collections provide access to the items in their respective stories. These items do not provide direct access to the text they contain, however. Instead they contain Range objects representing the text. For example, the following code displays the contents of the first footnote.

```
MsgBox ActiveDocument.Footnotes(1).Range.Text
```

The StoryRanges (C) collection gives information about each of the document's stories. This collection contains room for entries representing each of the possible story types. You can use a story type constant as an index into StoryRanges to get a range representing that story. The following list shows the allowed story type constants.

- wdCommentsStory

- wdEndnotesStory

- wdEvenPagesFooterStory

- wdEvenPagesHeaderStory

- wdFirstPageFooterStory

- wdFirstPageHeaderStory

- wdFootnotesStory

- wdMainTextStory

- wdPrimaryFooterStory

- wdPrimaryHeaderStory

- wdTextFrameStory

Unfortunately, if you try to access a story not present in the document, VBA raises an error. You need to catch the error to see if the story is present. The following code shows how a program might access the footnotes story and display all of its text if it is present.

 FILE *Ch07\Stories.doc*

```
' Show the text in the footnotes story.
Sub ShowFootnotesStory()
Dim story_range As Range

    ' See if this story exists.
    On Error GoTo NoFootnotes
    Set story_range = StoryRanges(wdFootnotesStory)
    On Error GoTo 0

    MsgBox story_range.Text
    Exit Sub

NoFootnotes:
    MsgBox "This document has no footnotes"
    Exit Sub
End Sub
```

The following code lists all of the stories that are present in a document and shows their start and end positions.

FILE *Ch07\Stories.doc*

```vba
' Describe the document's stories.
Sub ListStories()
Dim i As Long
Dim story_range As Range

    For i = 1 To StoryRanges.Count
        ' See if this story exists.
        On Error Resume Next
        Set story_range = Nothing
        Set story_range = StoryRanges(i)
        On Error GoTo 0

        If Not (story_range Is Nothing) Then
            Debug.Print i & ": ";
            Select Case story_range.StoryType
                Case wdCommentsStory
                    Debug.Print "wdCommentsStory";
                Case wdEndnotesStory
                    Debug.Print "wdEndnotesStory";
                Case wdEvenPagesFooterStory
                    Debug.Print "wdEvenPagesFooterStory";
                Case wdEvenPagesHeaderStory
                    Debug.Print "wdEvenPagesHeaderStory";
                Case wdFirstPageFooterStory
                    Debug.Print "wdFirstPageFooterStory";
                Case wdFirstPageHeaderStory
                    Debug.Print "wdFirstPageHeaderStory";
                Case wdFootnotesStory
                    Debug.Print "wdFootnotesStory";
                Case wdMainTextStory
                    Debug.Print "wdMainTextStory";
                Case wdPrimaryFooterStory
                    Debug.Print "wdPrimaryFooterStory";
                Case wdPrimaryHeaderStory
                    Debug.Print "wdPrimaryHeaderStory";
                Case wdTextFrameStory
                    Debug.Print "wdTextFrameStory";
```

```
            Case Else
                Debug.Print "<unknown story>";
        End Select
        Debug.Print " (" & _
            story_range.Start & "-" & _
            story_range.End & ")"
    End If
  Next i
End Sub
```

Although not exactly a story property, the ListParagraphs (C) collection is closely related. It contains Paragraph objects representing the paragraphs with bulleted or numbered list styles.

Sections *(C)*

The Sections collection contains a series of objects representing the document's sections. You can interactively create a section by selecting Insert ➤ Break, selecting the type of section break you want to add (shown in Figure 7-5), and clicking OK.

Figure 7-5. Use the Break dialog to insert a section break.

TIP *Ctrl-Enter also creates a page break.*

VBA code can use the Sections collection's Add method to create a new section. The Section objects contained in the collection have their own Headers and Footers collections that you can use to manipulate a section's headers and footers.

The Section object also provides a Range property that you can use to modify the section's text.

Style Properties

One of the most important tasks of a word process is formatting text. Using various menus, you can interactively make text **bold**, <u>underlined</u>, *italicized*, and so forth. Word also allows you to format paragraphs so they are aligned on the left, right, or center; so they do not break across pages; and so on.

Often, your code should use a Range object to format a piece of text. For example, a Range object's Font property lets you set the text's font size, whether it is a subscript, and its color. See the "Range" section later in this chapter for more information on the Range object.

To make more complex formatting easier, Word also lets you define *styles* that define a combination of formatting elements. For example, a chapter title style might indicate text that is larger than usual, bold, left aligned, followed by a little extra vertical space, and automatically followed by the Body Text style.

The Document object's Styles (C) property returns a collection of objects that define the styles available for use by the document. The following code lists the styles in the active document.

FILE *Ch07\Word.doc*

```
' List the document's styles.
Sub ListStyles()
Dim i As Long

    For i = 1 To ActiveDocument.Styles.Count
        Debug.Print i & " (" & _
            ActiveDocument.Styles(i).NameLocal & ") " & _
            ActiveDocument.Styles(i).Description
    Next i
End Sub
```

The Style objects in this collection have a lot of properties that you can use to examine and modify the styles. For example, the Font property determines the style's font-related formatting. See the online help for a list of the Style object's properties.

To assign a style to a piece of text, VBA code can build a Range object representing the text and then set its Style property to an appropriate value. You can set the Style property to the name of a style such as "Normal," "Heading 1," or "Footer."

Alternatively, you can set it to a Style object selected from the Styles collection. For example, the following two statements give the same result.

```
Selection.Range.Style = "Heading 2"
Selection.Range.Style = ActiveDocument.Styles("Heading 2")
```

You can also set Style to one of about a hundred numeric constants predefined by Word. Unfortunately, the allowed style constants are not listed in the online help. To see a list of the style constants, open the Visual Basic development environment, select View ➤ Object Browser, enter the value WdBuiltinStyle in the search box, and click the search button (which looks like a pair of binoculars). Some of the more useful style constants include wdStyleNormal, wdStyleBodyText, and wdStyleHeading1.

TIP *You can find many of these styles listed at*
http://msdn.microsoft.com/library/en-us/off2000/html/woprostyle.asp.

Use the Styles collection's Add method to create a new Style object. The following code creates a new style named Skinny Caps that increases the text's font sizes, squeezes it horizontally, and makes it use small caps (lowercase letters appear as smaller capital letters).

FILE *Ch07\Word.doc*

```
' Create a new style.
Sub CreateStyle()
Dim new_style As Style

    ' Remove the style if it already exists.
    On Error Resume Next
    ActiveDocument.Styles("Skinny Caps").Delete
    On Error GoTo 0
```

```
' Create the style.
Set new_style = ActiveDocument.Styles.Add("Tiny Caps")
new_style.BaseStyle = wdStyleNormal
With new_style.Font
    .Grow            ' Larger font size.
    .Grow            ' Larger font size.
    .Scaling = 75    ' Half normal width.
    .Bold = True
    .Name = "Times New Roman"
    .SmallCaps = True
    .Color = wdColorRed
End With
End Sub
```

Table Properties

The Document object's Tables (C) property contains objects representing the document's tables. These Table objects provide properties and methods for modifying the table's appearance (table style, auto fit, and so on), and for accessing the data inside the table.

The following code uses a Range object's ConvertToTable method to turn the selected text into a table. It uses the resulting Table object's Style property to make the table use the Table List 4 style. It makes the font in the first row bigger and bold, and finally makes the table size itself to fit its contents.

 FILE *Ch07\Word.doc*

```
' Make the selected text into a table.
Sub MakeTable()
    With Selection.Range.ConvertToTable(vbTab)
        ' Use the Table List 4 style.
        .Style = "Table List 4"

        ' Set the first row's style.
        With .Rows(1).Range.Font
            .Grow            ' Bigger.
            .Bold = True     ' Bold.
        End With
        .AutoFitBehavior (wdAutoFitContent)
    End With
End Sub
```

Variables *(C)*

The Document object's Variables (C) collection allows VBA code to save and restore values inside the document. Use the collection's Add method to add a value to the document.

NOTE *The "System" section earlier in this chapter discusses the pros and cons of storing values inside the document with document properties versus storing values in the system Registry. The same issues apply here too.*

Use the value's name as a key to locate its entry in the collection. Then use the entry's Value property to get the item's value, or use its Delete method to remove it from the collection.

The following code shows one way to create, examine, and delete variables.

FILE *Ch07\Word.doc*

```
' Save some variables in the document.
Sub SaveVariables()
    ActiveDocument.Variables.Add "Cookie", "Chocolate Chip"
    ActiveDocument.Variables.Add "Dessert", "Ice Cream"
    ActiveDocument.Variables.Add "Food", "Pizza"
End Sub

' List variables defined in the document.
Sub ListVariables()
Dim i As Long

    For i = 1 To ActiveDocument.Variables.Count
        Debug.Print i & ": " & ActiveDocument.Variables(i).Name & " = " & _
            ActiveDocument.Variables(i).Value
    Next i
End Sub
```

```
' Delete some variables from the document.
Sub DeleteVariables()
    ActiveDocument.Variables("Cookie").Delete
    ActiveDocument.Variables("Dessert").Delete
    ActiveDocument.Variables("Food").Delete
End Sub
```

Document *Object Events*

The Document object provides three events: New, Open, and Close. To create an event handler for one of these, open a ThisDocument object in the Visual Basic development environment. Select the Document entry in the left combo box. Then, in the right combo box, select the type of event you want to catch.

For example, in Figure 7-6 the Normal project's ThisDocument object is open for editing. The Document object is selected in the left combo box and New is selected in the right.

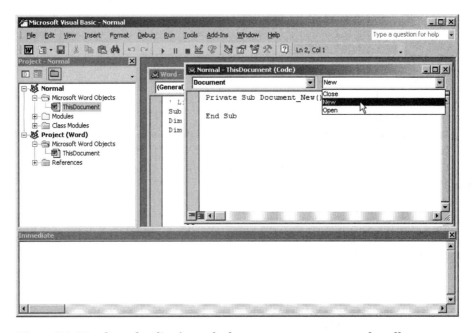

Figure 7-6. Use the code editor's combo boxes to create new event handlers.

If you make a New, Open or Close event handler in a template, the event handler fires whenever any document is created, opened, or closed while the template is loaded. For example, you could place these event handlers in Normal.dot.

If you place an Open or Close event handler in a document's ThisDocument module, the events fire when you open or close that document.

The New event handler works a little differently. Normally, if a document contains a New event handler, the document already exists, so you probably don't need to create it, and therefore the New event handler never fires. There is one case, however, in which a document's New event handler comes into play. If you select File ➤ New, Word presents a New Document pane. In the "New from existing document" section, you can select "Choose document" and pick the file that contains the New event handler. In that case, you are creating a new document based on a file that includes the event handler, so the event handler fires.

Selection **and** Range

The Selection and Range classes represent parts of a document. Because these objects are so similar, they are described together in the following sections. The biggest difference between the two is that the Selection object represents the unique piece of the active document currently selected by the user, whereas a Range object can represent any chunk of document independent of what the user is doing.

Object Selection

Word's object model is filled with objects that provide a Select method that selects the object. The Bookmark, Cell, Document, Field, Range, Table, and even the Selection objects provide a Select method. For example, the following code selects the active document's first table.

```
ActiveDocument.Tables(1).Select
```

After you select an object, you can use the Selection object to work with it. You can also extend the selection to include more than one object. Methods for extending the selection are described shortly in the section "Movement and Extension."

Many of Word's objects also provide methods that return Range objects. Document, Bookmark, Table, Selection, Footnote, Paragraph, Cell, and many other objects have Range properties that return a Range representing all or some of the corresponding object. For example, the following code makes a Range object represent the active document's first table and then makes the text in the range italic.

```
Set table_range = ActiveDocument.Tables(1).Range
table_range.Italic = True
```

The following code makes a Range refer to all of a document before the user's selection. It then makes the text in the Range bold.

```
Set front_range = Selection.Document.Range(0, Selection.Start - 1)
front_range.Bold = True
```

 TIP *The* Range *object doesn't have its own* Range *method, but you can make one* Range *refer to the same chunk of text as another by using the* SetRange *method, as in* range2.SetRange range1.Start, range1.End.

Properties

Many of the Selection and Range properties let you work directly with objects in the selection. For example, Selection.Tables(1) returns a Table object representing the first table that is at least partially contained in the selection.

The Selection and Range objects have many properties that correspond to properties provided by the Document, Table, and other objects representing part of a document. They contain properties representing bookmarks, fields, headers and footers, comments, footnotes, and text.

Many of these properties apply only if the selection contains items of the appropriate type. For example, the Selection.Tables property is empty if the selection doesn't contain part of any table.

Unfortunately, some properties don't even *exist* under certain circumstances depending on the kind of object. For instance, the Selection.Cells collection contains objects representing cells inside tables within the selection. This property exists only if the selection begins with part of a table. In that case, the Cells collection only includes cells in that first table and not cells in any other table that may occur later in the selection.

For example, suppose the selection starts in the middle of a table containing colors, continues past the end of the table to include some text, and then includes another table containing car models. The Cells collection contains references to only the cells in the first table containing colors that are also within the selection.

If the selection doesn't begin with part of a table, then the Cells property is not merely an empty collection; it doesn't even exist. If your code tries to access the property, VBA raises a run time error. The following code shows one way to watch for this error.

FILE *Ch07\Word.doc*

```
' List the contents of cells in the Selection.Cells property.
Sub ListSelectionCells()
Dim num_cells As Long
Dim c As Cell

    ' See if the Cells collection exists.
    On Error Resume Next
    num_cells = Selection.Cells.Count
    If Err.Number = 0 Then
        For Each c In Selection.Cells
            Debug.Print c.Range.Text
        Next c
    End If
End Sub
```

Most of the Selection and Range objects' properties are straightforward once you understand these sorts of issues. Spend some time browsing through the online help to get a feel for the kinds of properties and methods available.

One set of methods unique to the Selection and Range classes are those that deal with changing the pieces of the document represented by these classes. The following section describes the most important of these.

Formatting Properties

The Selection and Range objects provide several properties for formatting the regions they represent. The Bold, Case, Italic, and Underline properties let you format text quickly and easily. The Font property returns a Font object you can use to perform more extensive font formatting, such as changing the font name, color, strikethrough, embossing or engraving, scaling, and spacing.

TIP *In VBA macros, the* Font *object's* Grow *and* Shrink *methods are particularly handy. Those methods enlarge or reduce the font to the next standard size. You can use them to make text that is an appropriate amount larger or smaller than the surrounding text.*

For even fancier formatting, use the Selection or Range object's properties to obtain another object representing the items you want to format. For example, the following statement centers the second paragraph in the current selection.

```
Selection.Paragraphs(2).Alignment = wdAlignParagraphCenter
```

Many collections in the Word object model have their own methods that apply some function to all items in the collection. For example, the following code uses the Paragraphs collection to center all of the currently selected paragraphs.

```
Selection.Paragraphs.Alignment = wdAlignParagraphCenter
```

The Selection and Range objects have a Shading property that determines how the region should be shaded. This property is a Shading object with its own properties that define the effect. The following code sets the shading's background pattern colors to yellow and a slightly darker yellow, and its texture to cross (vertical and horizontal lines). It then slightly enlarges the selection's font and makes it bold.

```
' Shade the selection.
Sub ShadeSelection()
    With Selection.Shading
        .BackgroundPatternColor = RGB(255, 255, 0) ' Yellow.
        .ForegroundPatternColor = RGB(224, 224, 0) ' Slightly darker yellow.
        .Texture = wdTextureCross
    End With
    With Selection.Font
        .Grow
        .Bold = True
    End With
End Sub
```

Movement and Extension

The Selection and Range classes provide several methods for changing the selected parts of the document. Some are described in the following sections. Before you can use these methods, however, you must create the object in the first place.

The Selection object is created for you, but your code must create any Range objects it wants to use. Unfortunately, the Range class is "not creatable," so you cannot create an instance of the Range object by using the New keyword. Instead you must use some other object's property or method that returns a Range object. For example, you can use a Document object's Range method.

The Document object's Range method takes as parameters the start and end positions the new Range object should have. If the document contains only text, these positions are character positions. If the document contains pictures, fields, or other nontext objects, the positions are not as easy to calculate. To avoid problems in these situations, it's more common to set the start and end positions by using the location of some other object.

For example, the following code makes a Range object include all the text between the end of the bookmark Name and the beginning of the bookmark Address. It then uses the Range object's Delete method to remove that text.

```
' Delete the text between the Name and Address bookmarks.
Sub DeleteBetweenBookmarks()
Dim between_range As Range

    ' Make the Range include the desired area of the document.
    Set between_range = Me.Range( _
        Bookmarks("Name").Range.End, _
        Bookmarks("Address").Range.Start)

    ' Delete the text.
    between_range.Delete
End Sub
```

After you have created a new Range object, you can use its methods to change the part of the document it represents. The SetRange method sets the object's start and end positions much as the Document object's Range method does. If the code has somehow created the between_range object, the following code makes it represent the text between the Name and Address bookmarks.

```
between_range.SetRange _
    Bookmarks("Name").Range.End, _
    Bookmarks("Address").Range.Start
```

You can also set a Range object's Start and End positions explicitly, as in this code.

```
between_range.Start = Bookmarks("Name").Range.End
between_range.End = Bookmarks("Address").Range.Start
```

Although a Selection or Range object's start and end positions are useful, it is probably more common to "grow" them by using their Expand, Extend, and other growth methods described in the following sections.

Collapse

The Collapse method shrinks the Selection or Range to either its beginning or its end depending on whether the method's parameter is wdCollapseStart or wdCollapseEnd. Note that this does not affect the text in the document. It simply changes the location of the Selection or Range.

Expand *and* Extend

The Expand method grows a Selection or Range to include a unit of text. This method takes as a parameter the unit by which the object should be expanded. The unit can be one of the constants wdCharacter, wdWord, wdSentence, wdParagraph, wdSection, wdStory, wdCell, wdColumn, wdRow, or wdTable. For the Selection object, the unit can also be wdLine.

For example, suppose a Range object has Start and End properties positioning it in the middle of a sentence. Then the statement the_range.Expand wdSentence enlarges the Range to include the entire sentence from beginning to end. The statement the_range.Expand wdParagraph then enlarges the Range to include its entire paragraph.

If you call Expand when the object spans parts of more than one unit, all of the units are selected. For instance, if the Selection includes the second half of one sentence and the first half of the next, then calling Selection.Expand wdSentence makes the selection grow to include all of both sentences.

Calling Expand with a unit smaller than the one already selected by the Select or Range does nothing. For example, Selection.Expand wdSentence makes the selection grow to include any partly included sentences. Calling Selection.Expand wdSentence again does nothing.

The Extend method works much as the Expand method does, except it doesn't apply to the Range object, and it grows the Selection by the next larger unit each time you call it. The first call turns on the Selection's ExpandMode. The second extends to the word level. Subsequent calls enlarge the Selection to the sentence, paragraph, and finally the entire document.

```
' Expand the Selection by a word, sentence, paragraph,
' and finally to include the whole document.
Sub ExpandSelection()
    ' Start with just a location.
    Selection.Collapse
'    Selection.ExtendMode = True
    Selection.Extend     ' Turn it ExpandMode onSelection.
    Selection.Extend     ' Word
```

```
    Selection.Extend      ' Sentence
    Selection.Extend      ' Paragraph
    Selection.Extend      ' Whole document
End Sub
```

The Extend method can also take a character as a parameter. In that case, it grows the selection until it reaches the specified character. For example, the statement Selection.Extend "-" grows the selection until it includes the next "-" character.

Movement Methods

The Selection and Range objects provide many methods for moving through the document. The Next and Previous methods return a Range object representing the next or previous item of a particular type. For example, the following statement makes the variable next_paragraph represent the paragraph following the current selection.

```
Set next_paragraph = Selection.Next(wdParagraph)
```

 TIP *To select the following paragraph, use the returned object's* Select *method, as in* Selection.Next(wdParagraph).Select.

The GoTo, GoToNext, and GoToPrevious methods return ranges representing objects inside the document. For example, the following code set a Range to the bookmark named Address and makes its text italic.

```
Set addr_range = ActiveDocument.Range
Set addr_range = addr_range.GoTo(What:=wdGoToBookmark, Name:="Address")
addr_range.Italic = True
```

When you use the Selection object's GoTo method, the selection moves to the indicated item. For instance, the following code makes the Address bookmark bold and, as a side effect, selects it.

```
Set addr_range = Selection.GoTo(What:=wdGoToBookmark, Name:="Address")
addr_range.Italic = True
```

The StartOf and EndOf methods move or extend the start or end of a Selection or Range to the next unit. For example, the following code extends the selection to include the beginning and end of the current paragraph.

```
Selection.StartOf wdParagraph, wdExtend
Selection.EndOf wdParagraph, wdExtend
```

The Move method collapses the Selection or Range and moves it to the next or previous unit (word, sentence, paragraph, and so on). The following code moves the selection forward one sentence and then moves it back three words. The move back from the beginning of the second paragraph to the end of the first counts as moving a word, so the result of these two lines is to position the Selection at the beginning of the second-to-last word in the currently selected sentence.

```
Selection.Move wdSentence, 1
Selection.Move wdWord, -3
```

The MoveEnd method moves the end of the Selection or Range a certain number of units. The following code extends the Range to the end of the next sentence.

```
name_range.MoveEnd wdSentence, 1
```

Similarly, the MoveStart method moves the start of the Selection or Range. The following code makes a Range representing the current selection, collapses it, uses MoveStart and MoveEnd to make it include the sentence in which it lies, and then italicizes the sentence.

```
' Italicize the sentence containing the selection.
Sub ItalicizeSentence()
Dim r As Range

    Set r = Selection.Range
    r.Collapse
    r.MoveEnd wdSentence, 1
    r.MoveStart wdSentence, -1
    r.Italic = True
End Sub
```

The MoveEndUntil and MoveStartUntil methods move the Selection's or Range's end or start until they encounter one of a set of characters. The following code enlarges the selection until the next character is an uppercase or lowercase vowel.

Note that the vowel is not included in the selection. If you want to include it, use the MoveEnd method to move the selection's end position one character.

```
Selection.MoveEndUntil "aeiouAEIOU"
```

Conversely, the MoveEndWhile and MoveEndUntil methods move the Selection's or Range's end or start as long as the next character is in the specified set. The following code enlarges the selection until the next character is *not* a vowel. Again, the next nonvowel is not included in the selection.

```
Selection.MoveEndWhile "aeiouAEIOU"
```

The MoveUntil and MoveWhile methods move the entire Selection or Range rather than just its start and end positions. The following code moves the insertion point until the next character is a vowel.

```
Selection.MoveUntil "aeiouAEIOU"
```

The Selection object has a few additional movement methods not supported by Range objects. The MoveDown and MoveUp methods move the selection a certain number of lines, paragraphs, windows, or screens up or down. The optional Extend parameter lets you decide whether the Selection should be extended to the new location instead of being moved.

Similarly, the MoveLeft and MoveRight methods move the Selection object a certain number of cells, characters, words, or sentences left or right.

Finally, the Selection object provides several methods for extending the selection until text properties change. The SelectCurrentAlignment method extends the selection until the following paragraph has a different alignment. The SelectCurrentColor, SelectCurrentFont, SelectCurrentIndent, SelectCurrentSpacing, and SelectCurrentTabs methods extend the selection until they find a change in the corresponding text properties.

Text Addition Methods

The Selection and Range objects provide several methods for adding text. The InsertBefore and InsertAfter methods add text at the beginning or end of the region, respectively. Both methods expand the region to include the new text.

The following code uses the Selection object's InsertAfter method to create a series of paragraphs containing values separated by tabs. It then uses the Selection object's ConvertToTable method to convert the new text into a table.

```
' Use InsertAfter to add text to the Selection.
' Then convert it into a table.
Sub MakeTable()
    ' Add the rows of text with cells separated by tabs.
    Selection.InsertAfter "Color" & vbTab & "Example" & vbCrLf
    Selection.InsertAfter "Yellow" & vbTab & "Banana" & vbCrLf
    Selection.InsertAfter "Red" & vbTab & "Apple" & vbCrLf
    Selection.InsertAfter "Orange" & vbTab & "Orange" & vbCrLf
    Selection.InsertAfter "Blue" & vbTab & "Grape" & vbCrLf

    ' Convert to a table.
    Selection.ConvertToTable
End Sub
```

Notice how this code uses the VBA constant vbTab to add tabs between the items that will fill the table. Notice also how it uses the constant vbCrLf to add a carriage return/linefeed pair to the end of each paragraph. The InsertParagraphBefore and InsertParagraphAfter methods also add paragraph marks before or after the Selection or Range so the following two statements are equivalent to the first InsertAfter statement in the previous code.

```
Selection.InsertAfter "Color" & vbTab & "Example"
Selection.InsertParagraphAfter
```

Table 7-4 lists several methods that the Selection and Range objects provide for inserting special items into the document. Some of these methods replace the Selection's or Range's current contents with the new item. If you don't want to replace the contents, use the Collapse method to move the Selection or Range to its start or end before calling these methods. See the online help for more details.

Table 7-4. Special Item Insertion Methods

METHOD	PURPOSE
InsertBreak	Replaces the region with a page break, section break, line break, or some other kind of break
InsertCaption	Adds an equation, table, or figure caption above or below the region
InsertDateTime	Replaces the region with the current date and time in a specified format
InsertFile	Replaces the region with a file
InsertParagraph	Replaces the region with a paragraph mark
InsertSymbol	Replaces the region with a symbol from a font

The Selection object also provides InsertCells, InsertColumns, InsertColumnsRight, InsertFormula, InsertRows, InsertRowsAbove, and InsertRowsBelow methods.

The Selection object's TypeBackspace, TypeParagraph, and TypeText methods provide more ways to add text to the document. These routines replace the current selection if it is not empty, or add new text if the selection is empty. Normally, Word works this same way when you type interactively. For example, if you select some text and press Backspace, Word deletes the text. If you don't select text and you press Backspace, Word deletes whatever comes before the insertion position.

TypeText works this way if the Options.ReplaceSelection property is True. If this property is False, TypeText inserts the new text in front of the current selection.

Find

The last major class described here is Find. Both the Range and Selection classes have a Find property that returns a reference to a Find object. This object represents a find or replace operation similar to those you can perform interactively using the Find and Replace dialog. Using a Find object, your code can search all or part of a document for specific text, styles, or formatting. You can also use this object to change text, style, or formatting.

The Find object is rather complicated and has many properties that affect its behavior in ways that aren't obvious. The rest of this section describes some of the object's more important properties and methods. Usually, the easiest way to perform a search or replace in VBA code, however, is to record a macro performing the same search interactively and modify the code if necessary.

The Find object has lots of properties that specify the type of text it should locate and ways in which it should modify the things it finds. The ClearFormatting method resets all of these properties. Before starting a new search, your code should call ClearFormatting and then explicitly set any properties it needs to use.

Forgetting to clear formatting can make the code fail to work properly even though it looks correct. Sometimes you can stare at the code for quite a while without realizing that a property set previously is causing the problem. For instance, a simple find operation may fail because the code didn't clear the Find object's MatchCase property.

After setting the appropriate formatting parameters, the code calls the Find object's Execute method to perform the find or replace. The following code shows one way to replace all occurrences of the letter "a" in the document with a dash.

FILE *Ch07\Find.doc*

```
' Replace all lowercase a's with -'s.
Sub GlobalReplace()
    ' Work with the entire document's range.
    With Me.Range.Find
        .Text = "a"
        .MatchCase = True
        .Replacement.Text = "-"
        .Execute Replace:=wdReplaceAll
    End With
End Sub
```

The Execute method takes 15 parameters, many of which override the object's
formatting properties. For example, the MatchCase parameter overrides the value in
the Find object's MatchCase property. The method's FindText and ReplaceText
parameters indicate the text the method should find and replace. Using those
properties, code can perform simple replacements without setting any of the Find
object's properties. The following code makes the same replacement as the previous version by using only the Execute method.

FILE *Ch07\Find.doc*

```
' Replace all lowercase a's with -'s.
Sub GlobalReplace2()
    ' Work with the entire document's range.
    With Me.Range.Find
        .Execute FindText:="a", _
            MatchCase:=True, _
            ReplaceWith:="-", _
            Replace:=wdReplaceAll
    End With
End Sub
```

If the Find object is a member of a Range object, the Execute method searches the Range's text.

If the Find object is a member of the Selection object, the Execute method searches the current selection. If the selection is empty, Execute searches the entire document. If the operation finds text without replacing it or if it makes one replacement, the selection is updated to hold the text that was found or replaced. If the operation cannot find any occurrences of the search string or if it makes more than one replacement, it leaves the selection unchanged.

During a repeated search, the Execute method moves the Selection or Range to the next occurrence of the target text. It also returns True if it successfully finds or replaces some text. This can be useful if you want to use VBA code to provide further processing for the pieces of text that match some criterion.

TIP *The* Find *object's* Found *property is also set to True if* Execute *finds or replaces some text.*

For example, the following code uses a Find object to display all of the sentences in a document that contain the word *find*. The code calls the Execute method repeatedly as long as it finds a new piece of text matching the target string *find*. Each time Execute returns True, the code makes a new Range that contains the found text. It expands the Range to include the sentence holding the text. If this sentence is different from the previously examined sentence, the program prints it.

FILE *Ch07\Search.doc*

```
' Find sentences that contain the word Find.
Sub FindFind()
Dim search_range As Range
Dim hit_range As Range
Dim last_start As Long
Dim i As Long

    ' Make sure we use the first hit.
    last_start = -1
```

```
            ' Search the entire document.
        Set search_range = Me.Range
        With search_range.Find
            Do While .Execute(FindText:="Find")
                ' Make hit_range include the found text.
                Set hit_range = Me.Range(search_range.Start, search_range.End)

                ' Expand hit_range to include the whole sentence.
                hit_range.Expand wdSentence

                ' See if this is the same as the last one.
                If last_start <> hit_range.Start Then
                    ' This is a new sentence.
                    last_start = hit_range.Start

                    ' Remove trailing CRs.
                    Do While hit_range.Characters(hit_range.Characters.Count) = vbCr
                        hit_range.End = hit_range.End - 1
                    Loop

                    ' Display it.
                    i = i + 1
                    Debug.Print i & ". " & hit_range.Text
                End If
            Loop
        End With
    End Sub
```

As is mentioned earlier, the Find object is quite complex. Use the macro recorder and the online help to learn about other details.

Summary

The Word object model is far too large for this chapter to cover every object, property, method, event, and constant in detail. Doing so would be a waste of time, because you will probably never need many of these items anyway. On the other hand, you can't do much if you don't know what objects are in the Word object model.

To help you understand what is possible and what basic approaches you can take, this chapter describes many of the most important and useful objects provided by Word. You might also want to spend an hour or two browsing through the online help. Start by searching for "Microsoft Word Objects" to get a feel for the other objects not mentioned in this chapter. After you have an idea of the kinds of objects available to your code, you can pick up extra details as you need them from the online help.

CHAPTER 8

Excel

THE EXCEL OBJECT MODEL contains thousands of objects, properties, methods, and predefined enumerated values. Even mentioning them all here would be a huge waste of space, because you will probably never need them all, and you probably know better than to squander your time reading about all the inconsequential constants that you'll never need anyway.

This chapter describes some of the most useful items provided by the Excel object model. The following section gives an overview of the most important objects to help you determine which objects are necessary to perform various tasks. The subsequent sections describe different objects and pieces of the Excel object model in greater detail.

This chapter is not intended to explain every detail of these objects. It merely provides enough detail for you to figure out which objects you need to accomplish most common tasks. For more details, consult the online help. You may want to start with the entry for "Microsoft Excel Objects," which shows a diagram of the Excel object model.

Overview

Like other Office applications, Excel begins its object model with the Application object. This object provides properties and collections that let you find the application's other objects. It also includes methods for working with the Excel application itself rather than with a specific workbook or worksheet. For example, it includes properties and methods that search for files, generate speech, manipulate the recent file list, and evaluate numeric expressions.

The Workbook object represents an Excel workbook file containing one or more worksheets. The Workbook's methods allow you to find and manipulate the worksheets. It also provides a natural place to store code that deals with more than one worksheet.

A Worksheet object represents a worksheet in a workbook. This object's properties and methods let you manipulate the contents of the worksheet's cells. Collections allow you to manipulate objects such as charts, query tables, and shapes on the worksheet.

The Worksheet object's Range property returns a Range object that represents a rectangular block of cells on the worksheet. As in other Office applications, your code can use Range objects to easily manipulate groups of data in the application.

The following sections describe some general concepts important in Excel programming, such as where Excel workbooks store code and how to refer to cells and ranges of cells. The sections after those describe the most generally useful Excel objects in greater detail.

Code Storage

Excel stores VBA code in just one place: inside an Excel workbook file. It has no central location similar to Normal.dot and other template files used by Word.

 TIP *However, you can create your own central repository. Place code that you plan to use in more than one project in a central workbook. Then you can refer to its VBA routines when working in other workbooks. You can also save code modules into .bas files that you can load into other projects later.*

When you create a workbook, it initially has modules named Sheet1, Sheet2, Sheet3, and ThisWorkbook. If you place code in one of the three worksheet modules, objects default to worksheet scope.

For instance, both the Application and Worksheet objects have a Names collection. The following statement displays the number of items in the Names collection.

```
MsgBox Names.Count
```

If this code is in ThisWorkbook, it displays the number of items in the Application.Names collection. If this code is in one of the worksheet code modules, it displays the number of items in the corresponding Worksheet object's Names collection.

In addition to these default modules, you can add code modules, UserForms, and class modules to an Excel project. Objects in those modules default to the Application object's scope, much as objects in ThisWorkbook do.

Cell Addresses

You frequently must refer to a cell or group of cells when working with Excel. You refer to cells to format them, change their values, delete them, and use them in aggregate functions, such as AVERAGE, SUM, and MAX.

There are a couple ways you can specify a cell or range depending on what you want to do and when. The most common method is the "A1" notation. You usually use this notation when you refer to a cell inside another cell's formula. You also use A1 notation most of the time you need to refer to cells in VBA code.

In some code, you can use cell indexing instead of A1 notation. A Worksheet object's Cells collection takes as parameters the indexes of the row and column you want to use. This can be handy if you want to use a For loop to examine a series of rows or columns.

Occasionally, you can also use "R1C1" notation. Whether you should use A1 or R1C1 notation is mostly a matter of preference. R1C1 may be a little more intuitive if you're used to thinking in terms of array indexes, although A1 is probably more common among nonprogrammer end-users.

The following sections describe these kinds of notations and show how to convert among them.

A1 Notation

In A1 notation, you specify a cell by giving its column letter (A, B, C) and its row number (1, 2, 3). So, cell A1 is the cell in the upper-left corner, in the first column (A) and the first row (1). The following statement makes the text in the third cell in the first column blue.

```
Range("A3").Font.Color = vbBlue
```

You specify a rectangular region by giving the positions of the cells in two opposite corners of the region, separated by a colon. For example, the following three statements all make the eight cells in the first two rows of the first four columns use a bold font. These statements are equivalent; they simply specify different corners for the region.

```
Range("A1:D2").Font.Bold = True
Range("A2:D1").Font.Bold = True
Range("D2:A1").Font.Bold = True
```

If you specify two column values without row values, Excel uses the entire columns between the values you specify. For example, the following code gives columns B, C, and D a red background.

```
Range("B:D").Interior.Color = vbRed
```

Similarly, if you specify only row values, Excel uses the whole rows. The following code deletes row 2.

```
Range("2:2").Delete
```

Mixing and matching these formats causes a syntax error. For example, the cell ranges A1:B, A:2, and A don't make sense.

You can specify a union of rectangular regions by separating them with commas. The following statement erases the contents of cells A1:B2 and C3:D4.

```
Range("A1:B2,C3:D4").Clear
```

Use a space to indicate the intersection of two regions. The following statement makes text bold in the area that is in both of the regions A1:C3 and C2:F5. That area includes the cells C2 and C3. Figure 8-1 shows this intersection graphically.

```
Range("A1:C3 C2:E5").Font.Bold = True
```

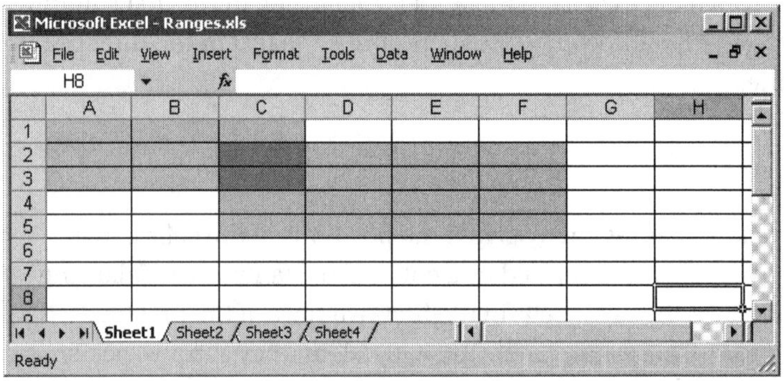

Figure 8-1. A space in A1 notation indicates the intersection of two regions.

You can mix and match the row, column, cell, and rectangular formats in the same region specification as long as all are individually formatted properly. The following code uses commas to form the union of four areas to make the text blue in column E, row 5, the region G7:I9, and the single cell J10.

```
Range("E:E,5:5,G7:I9,J10").Font.Color = vbBlue
```

Index Numbers

Sometimes in VBA code you can refer to a cell by using row and column indexes. The Worksheet object's Cells property takes a cell's row and column numbers as indexes. For example, the following statement sets the text in cell A3 to Hello.

```
Worksheets(1).Cells(3, 1) = "Hello"
```

 CAUTION *Note that the order of the cell's coordinates in A1 notation is the reverse of the order when you use row and column indexes. In A1 notation, the column letter comes first and the row number comes second. With index numbers, the row index comes first and the column index comes second. For instance, A3 corresponds to* Cells(3, 1). *Mixing up the row and column is a fairly common mistake.*

Sometimes, using indexes is more convenient than A1 notation. This is particularly true if you want some code to loop over a sequence of cells. You can use For loop variables as indexes into the Cells property. For example, the following code loops through a series of cells and makes any with values greater than 1.0 red.

```
For r = 1 To 5
    For c = 1 To 10
        If Cells(r, c) > 1.0 Then Cells(r, c).Font.Color = vbRed
    Next c
Next r
```

R1C1 Notation

R1C1 is a notation similar to using indexes. You can use it instead of A1 notation when entering formulas interactively. The format is the letter R, followed by the row number, followed by C, followed by the column number. For example, R3C2 refers to the cell in row 3, column 2. That's the cell B3 in A1 notation.

 CAUTION *Like row and column indexes, the R1C1 notation places the row number first and the column number second. This is the reverse of A1 notation, so the two orders are easily confused.*

If you prefer R1C1 notation to A1 notation, you can make Excel use it when you enter values interactively. Select Tools ➤ Options, click on the General tab, and check the box labeled "R1C1 reference style." That lets you enter formulas into cells by using R1C1 notation. It also makes Excel display R1C1 notation in the formula bar when you click on a cell that contains a reference.

Referencing Other Worksheets and Workbooks

Referencing cells in another worksheet is fairly simple. Just add the name of the worksheet followed by an exclamation point in front of the region specification. For instance, the following statement makes the first column in the worksheet named Employee bold.

```
Range("Employees!B:B").Font.Bold = True
```

NOTE *A Range cannot span worksheets, so you cannot do something like* Range("Employees!B:B,Managers!A:A").Font.Bold = True.

In some cases, you can also refer to another workbook. For example, the following formula entered in a worksheet cell calculates the average of the values in cells E1 through E10 on the Bonuses worksheet in the workbook named Salaries.

```
=AVERAGE([Salaries.xls]Bonuses!A1:A10)
```

NOTE *After you enter this formula, Excel expands the other workbook's path and adds quotes, so the formula looks like this if you click on the cell later:* =AVERAGE('C:\Wherever\[Salaries.xls]Bonuses'!A1:A10)

Using Absolute and Relative References

Excel supports two kinds of cell references: absolute and relative. If you're an experienced Excel user, you already know what these mean and how to use them interactively. If you don't know what absolute and relative references are, see the Excel user help.

Once you understand what absolute and relative references are, you can learn how to specify them in your VBA code by using index numbers and A1 and R1C1 notation.

Index numbers are always absolute. If you want to work with relative values when using index numbers, you must calculate them yourself. However, you can use a Range object's Offset property to make working with another Range relative to the first Range easier. The Offset property takes as parameters the row and column offsets you want to use. For example, the following statement makes the background behind the cell below the active cell yellow.

```
ActiveCell.Offset(1, 0).Interior.Color = vbYellow
```

In A1 notation, a letter followed by a number is relative. For example, suppose cell C5 contains the formula =C4. This refers to the cell one row above cell C5. Because this is a relative reference, if you copy and paste it to cell D5, that cell will contain the formula =D4.

Adding a $ symbol before the column letter or row number makes that part of the reference absolute. For example, suppose cell C10 contains the formula =$C$5. Both the C and the 5 are absolute, so if you copy this cell to any other cell, the new cell will contain the same value =$C$5.

On the other hand, suppose cell C10 contains the formula =C$5. Here the column C is relative but the row number is absolute. If you copy this cell to cell D7, the relative column and absolute row give the new cell the value =D$5.

In R1C1 notation, you surround relative row and column numbers with square brackets, and the value [0] is omitted. For example, the formula =R[-1]C represents a relative reference to the cell one row above (here an implied [0] is omitted from the column). The formula =R[3]C5 refers to the cell three rows below the one containing the formula and in column 5.

Named Ranges

Another powerful way to manipulate groups of cells is with *named ranges*. As you can probably guess, a named range is a group of cells that you can refer to with a name. For example, you might gather cells A1:O1 into a range named Headers. Then your code could manipulate those cells as a unit. For example, the following code changes the background color in the Headers range to green.

```
Range("Headers").Interior.Color = vbGreen
```

To create a named range interactively, click and drag to select the cells. Then click on the Name Box on the left of the Formula Bar and enter the name you want to give to the cells. Later, you can use the dropdown arrow next to the Name Box to select a named range quickly.

To make a named range programmatically, create a Range object. Next add an entry to the Names collection, specifying the name you want to give the Range.

The following code creates a Range object representing row 12. It uses the Names collection's Add method to create a new entry named Row12 that refers to the new Range object. The code sets the variable row_12 to Nothing to destroy it. Finally, the routine uses the name Row12 as a parameter to the Range method and uses the returned named range to make the text in row 12 bold.

 FILE *Ch08\CellNames.xls*

```
' Make a named range.
Sub MakeNamedRange()
Dim row_12 As Range

    ' Make the range.
    Set row_12 = Range("12:12")

    ' Add it to the Names collection.
    Application.Names.Add Name:="Row12", RefersTo:=row_12
    Set row_12 = Nothing

    ' Use the named range to make the row bold.
    Range("Row12").Font.Bold = True
End Sub
```

Code can use a range's name as a parameter to the Range method, as shown in this code. It can also find the named range in the Names collection. The following code lists the names in the Names collection, and their values in A1 and R1C1 notation.

 FILE *Ch08\CellNames.xls*

```
' List all named ranges.
Sub ListNamedRanges()
Dim i As Long

    For i = 1 To Application.Names.Count
        With Application.Names(i)
            Debug.Print i & ": " & _
                .Name & _
                " (" & .RefersTo & _
                " or " & .RefersToR1C1 & ")"
        End With
    Next i
End Sub
```

 CAUTION *The* Application, Workbook, *and* Worksheet *objects all have* Names *collections. Code that simply uses* Name *without a prefix can be very confusing. Depending on where the code runs, you may end up storing named ranges in the* Application's Names *collection and trying to locate them in a* Worksheet's *collection.*

The following shows this routine's results with two named ranges defined.

```
1: Header (=Sheet1!$1:$1 or =Sheet1!R1)
2: Row12 (=Sheet1!$12:$12 or =Sheet1!R12)
```

The Name objects contained in the Names collection also have a RefersToRange property that returns a Range representing the named object. Note, however, that the Names collection may contain formulas and other items that are not Ranges. If you try to access the RefersToRange property for an object that isn't a Range, VBA raises an error. Use an On Error statement to protect your code.

Application

The Application object provides access to features that do not relate directly to a specific worksheet inside the workbook. For example, it provides properties and methods for generating speech, manipulating the recent file list, and evaluating numeric expressions.

The `Application` object also provides properties and methods for accessing the other objects in the Excel object model. For instance, its `Workbooks` collection contains `Workbook` objects representing each of the workbook files currently loaded into Excel. The `ActiveWorkbook` property returns a reference to the currently active `Workbook`.

The following sections describe the most useful `Application` object properties, methods, and events.

Properties

Here we describe some of the `Application` object's most useful properties. Those that are collections are followed with a (C).

In many cases, these properties behave as much like methods as they do properties. For example, the documentation lists `Range` as a property, but it takes a wide variety of parameters and returns an object that represents what may be quite a complicated set of worksheet cells. So, it may seem more natural to think of `Range` as a function rather than a property.

Active Object Properties

The `Application` object provides several properties that identify currently active objects. For example, the `ActiveWorkbook`, `ActiveSheet`, and `ActiveCell` properties return references to the currently active workbook, worksheet, and cell respectively. VBA code often needs to use these objects to interact with the cells the user has selected.

The `Application` object's `Selection` property returns an object representing the user's current selection. For example, if the user clicks and drags to select a region of cells, this is a `Range` object. If the user clicks a chart, this object is a `ChartArea`.

Workbooks *(C)*

The `Workbooks` collection contains `Workbook` objects representing open Excel files. You can use a file's name or position in the `Workbooks` collection as an index. For example, if the file Income.xls is the first workbook in the collection, then the following two statements are equivalent.

```
MsgBox Workbooks(1).Name
MsgBox Workbooks("Income.xls").Name
```

Use the Workbooks collection's Add method to create a new workbook. The following code creates a new workbook, initializes it with some data, and saves it in the file Test Scores.xls in the same directory as the file containing this code.

NOTE *Because Excel code must reside in some workbook file, you know a file must be loaded when this code executes. That means the* ThisWorkbook *object must exist, so it's safe to use in the* SaveAs *statement.*

FILE *Ch08\CellNames.xls*

```
' Make a new workbook.
Sub MakeNewWorkbook()
Dim work_book As Workbook
Dim work_sheet As Worksheet
Dim i As Long

    ' Make the workbook.
    Set work_book = Workbooks.Add()

    ' Create some column headers.
    Set work_sheet = work_book.Sheets(1)
    work_sheet.Name = "Test Scores"
    work_sheet.Cells(1, 1) = "Last Name"
    work_sheet.Cells(1, 2) = "First Name"
    For i = 1 To 10
        work_sheet.Cells(1, i + 2) = i
    Next i

    work_sheet.Range("A1:B1").ColumnWidth = 20
    work_sheet.Range("C1:L1").ColumnWidth = 5

    work_book.SaveAs ThisWorkbook.Path & "\Test Scores.xls"
End Sub
```

Sheets *(C)*, Charts *(C)*, *and* Worksheets *(C)*

The Sheets collection holds objects representing each of the sheets in the active workbook. The collection contains Worksheet objects to represent worksheets and Chart objects to represent chart sheets.

The Worksheets collection contains only the Sheets collection's Worksheet objects. Similarly, the Charts collection contains only the Sheets collection's Chart objects. If you want to work with only worksheets or charts, you can use these collections instead of the Sheets collection.

If your code needs to work with a particular worksheet or chart, it can use these collections to get a reference to the appropriate object. The following statements show how VBA code might locate worksheets or charts by name or index.

```
Set name_sheet = Sheets("Names")
Set first_sheet = Worksheets(1)
Set salary_chart = Charts("Salaries")
```

Range

The Range property returns a Range object representing some or all of the active worksheet. This property takes two parameters that ordinarily identify cells defining the Range's corners. For example, the following code selects cells A1:D5.

```
Application.Range("A1", "D5").Select
```

If you omit the second parameter, the returned Range includes only the first cell. The following statement selects only cell J4.

```
Application.Range("J4").Select
```

Either of the parameters can also define a region by using A1 notation. The returned Range includes the smallest rectangular region that contains both of the areas defined by the parameters. For example, the following statement selects the cells in the rectangular region surrounding the ranges B2:D4 and D3:G6.

```
Application.Range("B2:D4", "D3:G6").Select
```

Figure 8-2 shows this situation graphically. The range B2:D4 is the shaded rectangle on the upper left. The range D3:G6 is the shaded rectangle on the lower right. The intersection of the ranges is shaded darker. The large speckled rectangle containing both ranges is the area selected by the previous code.

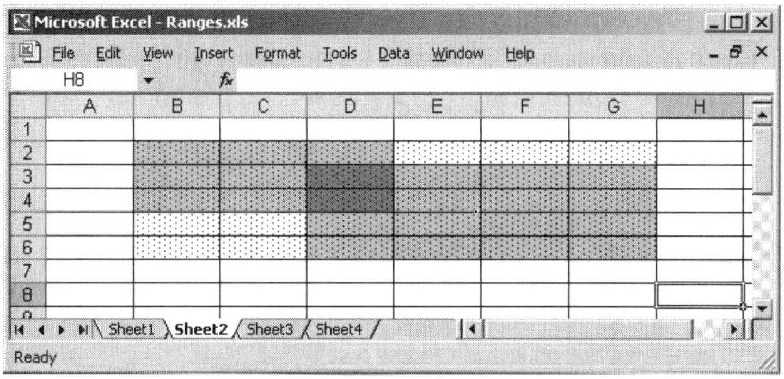
Microsoft Excel - Ranges.xls
File Edit View Insert Format Tools Data Window Help
H8
A B C D E F G H
1 2 3 4 5 6 7 8
Sheet1 Sheet2 Sheet3 Sheet4
Ready

Figure 8-2. The `Range` *property returns the smallest rectangular region containing the ranges defined by its two parameters.*

The two parameters can also be `Range` objects rather than A1 notations representing ranges. The following code selects the same cells as the previous code, but this time by using `Range` objects.

```
Dim r1 As Range
Dim r2 As Range

    Set r1 = Range("B2:D4")
    Set r2 = Range("D3:G6")
    Application.Range(r1, r2).Select
```

NOTE *Usually, you would not create* Range *objects just to use them to create a new* Range *as in this example. If you're not going to use them for something, there's little point in creating extra objects that consume resources, clutter your code, and possibly cause extra confusion. You would probably use* Range *objects only if you had already created them for some other purpose.*

Finally, you can use A1 notation that specifies more than one region for the property's first parameter. In this case, the resulting region is the union of the regions specified in the parameter, not the rectangular region containing them all. The following code selects the cells in the ranges C2:D6 and B3:G4.

```
Application.Range("C2:D6,B3:G4").Select
```

Figure 8-3 shows this situation graphically. The code selects all of the shaded cells in Figure 8-2. Note that cells such as B2 and E2 are not contained in this Range. Also note that you must omit the Range property's second parameter if the first parameter selects multiple regions like this.

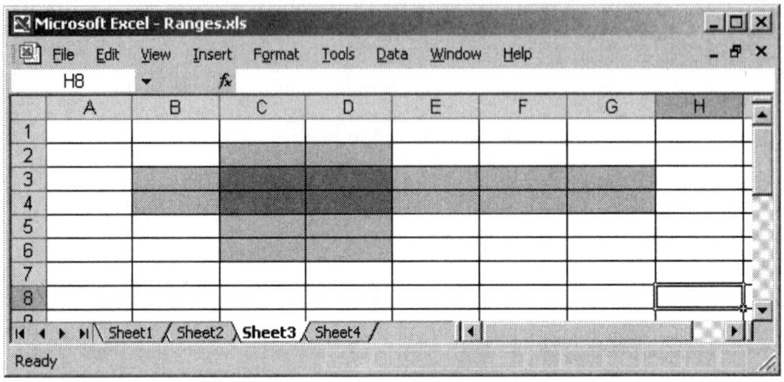

Figure 8-3. If the Range property's first parameter specifies multiple regions, the result is the union of the regions.

CommandBars *(C)*

The CommandBars collection represents the command bars displayed by Excel. You can use this collection to customize Excel's tools. For instance, the following code adds a new button to the Standard CommandBar that executes the SayHi macro in the ThisWorkbook module when pressed.

```
' Make a command bar button.
Sub MakeToolbarItem()
    With Application.CommandBars("Standard").Controls.Add( _
      Type:=msoControlButton)
        .Style = msoButtonIcon
        .TooltipText = "Say Hi!"
        .OnAction = "ThisWorkbook.SayHi"
        .DescriptionText = "Execute the SayHi macro"
        .Picture = LoadPicture(ActiveWorkbook.Path & "\CustomButton.bmp")
        .Caption = "SayHi button"
    End With
End Sub
```

The Workbook object also has a CommandBars property, but it's not very useful when programming Excel itself. If a workbook is embedded in another application, its CommandBars property describes the Excel tools available within that application. This property is Nothing when your code accesses it from within Excel.

Columns, Rows, *and* Cells

The Columns and Rows properties are multiple-area Range objects. They are Ranges containing unions of other Ranges.

The Columns property contains a series of Range objects representing the worksheet's columns. For example, the following code sets the variable col3 to a Range representing the worksheet's third column.

```
Dim col3 As Range

    Set col3 = Application.Columns(3)
```

Similarly, the Rows property contains a series of Range objects representing the worksheet's rows.

These properties represent *all* of the worksheet's rows and columns, not just those in use. That means Application.Columns.Count = 256 and Application.Rows.Count = 65,536 because Excel could define 256 columns and 65,536 rows.

The Cells property is a Range object representing all of the worksheet's cells. Those are the same 256 * 65,536 = 16,777,216 possible cells represented by the Rows and Columns properties, not the cells actually used. The Cells property is a convenient way to manipulate a worksheet's contents programmatically.

Accessing any of these properties causes an error unless the currently selected object is a worksheet. For example, if the user clicks and drags to select one or more cells, the properties exist. If the user clicks on a chart, the properties raise errors if you try to use them. The following code shows one way your code can tell if the active sheet is a worksheet or chart.

```
If TypeOf Application.ActiveSheet Is Worksheet Then
    ' Do stuff for a Worksheet...
Else ' It's a Chart.
    ' Do stuff for a Chart...
End If
```

The Worksheet object has its own versions of the Columns, Rows, and Cells properties. They have the same general meanings as the corresponding Application object properties. One big difference is that these properties are always defined for a worksheet even if the user selects a chart or some other nonworksheet object.

The Worksheet also has a UsedRange property that returns a Range representing only the cells actually used. See the "UsedRange" section later in this chapter for more information.

Dialogs *(C)*

The Dialogs collection contains Dialog objects representing all of Excel's built-in dialogs. You can use a dialog's Show methods to display it. The dialogs generally return True if the user pressed OK, and False if the user pressed Cancel.

Excel defines several hundred numeric constants you can use as indexes into the Dialogs collection. Many of the dialogs take optional parameters that indicate initial values they should display. For example, the following code displays the Format Cells Font dialog with the font initially set to Times New Roman. If the user clicks OK, the code displays a message box.

```
If Application.Dialogs(xlDialogActiveCellFont).Show("Times New Roman") Then
    MsgBox "Font changed"
End If
```

Search the online help for "Built-In Dialog Box Argument List" for a list of defined dialog boxes and the parameters they take. For dialog box information on the Web, see http://msdn.microsoft.com/library/en-us/off2000/html/xlmscDialogArgLists.asp.

FileDialog *(C)*

FileDialog is a collection of objects representing standard open and save file dialogs. The index into this collection should be one of the following values.

VALUE	DIALOG PURPOSE
msoFileDialogFilePicker	Lets the user select a file
msoFileDialogFolderPicker	Lets the user select a folder
msoFileDialogOpen	Displays the File Open dialog
msoFileDialogSaveAs	Displays the File Save As dialog

The items in the `FileDialog` collection are `FileDialog` objects rather than the more generic `Dialog` objects returned by the `Dialogs` collection. The more specific type lets IntelliSense provide better support for the dialogs' properties and methods. Table 8-1 lists the `FileDialog` object's most useful properties.

Table 8-1. Useful `FileDialog` *Properties*

PROPERTY	PURPOSE
AllowMultiSelect	Determines whether the user can select multiple files.
ButtonName	The text displayed on the default button (normally OK).
FilterIndex	Gets or sets the index of the filter initially selected when the dialog displays.
Filters	A collection of objects representing the dialog's file filters.
InitialFileName	Gets or sets the path and/or file name initially displayed. The file name can include the * and ? wildcards.
InitialView	The initial file view displayed by the dialog. This can be msoFileDialogViewDetails, msoFileDialogViewLargeIcons, msoFileDialogViewList, msoFileDialogViewPreview, msoFileDialogViewProperties, msoFileDialogViewSmallIcons, or msoFileDialogViewThumbnail (Windows 2000, ME, or later).
SelectedItems	A collection of the selected file names.
Title	The text displayed in the dialog's title bar.

The `FileDialog` object provides only two methods: `Show` and `Execute`. `Show` displays the dialog and returns True if the user clicked the OK button, or False if the user clicked Cancel. The `Execute` method makes the dialog perform its associated action.

The `Filters` collection contains objects representing the filters the user can select to pick different kinds of files. The following code lists the filters available by default to the open file dialog.

 FILE *Ch08\CellNames.xls*

```
' List the filters available for the File Open dialog.
Sub ListOpenFilters()
Dim i As Long

    With Application.FileDialog(msoFileDialogOpen)
        For i = 1 To .Filters.Count
```

```
            Debug.Print .Filters(i).Description & _
                " (" & .Filters(i).Extensions & ")"
        Next i
    End With
End Sub
```

Your code can use the Filters collection to modify the filters available to the user. When it does this, the dialog's filters remain modified until Excel needs to recreate that particular dialog. This occurs when your code accesses a different dialog and then accesses the dialog you modified again.

The following code sets the open file dialog's AllowMultiSelect property to True so the user can select more than one file. It sets the InitialFileName property to the active workbook's path so the dialog begins in that workbook's directory.

Next the code removes all of the dialog's predefined filters and adds two of its own. It then prints the number of filters (currently two).

The code selects the first filter and displays the dialog. If the user clicks OK, the code lists the files selected.

To reset the filter list, the program then accesses the Save As dialog. It finishes by printing the number of filters available to the open file dialog.

 FILE *Ch08\CellNames.xls*

```
' Select a file using *.xls and *.* filters only.
Sub SelectFile()
Dim i As Long

    With Application.FileDialog(msoFileDialogOpen)
        .AllowMultiSelect = True
        .InitialFileName = ActiveWorkbook.Path
        .Filters.Clear
        .Filters.Add "All Files", "*.*"
        .Filters.Add "Worksheets", "*.xls"
        Debug.Print .Filters.Count & " filters"

        ' Select the first filter (All Files).
        .FilterIndex = 1
```

```
        ' Display the dialog and see if the user clicks OK.
        If .Show Then
            ' Display the selected files.
            For i = 1 To .SelectedItems.Count
                Debug.Print .SelectedItems(i)
            Next i
        End If
    End With

    ' Access another dialog to reset the filters.
    i = Application.FileDialog(msoFileDialogSaveAs).Filters.Count

    ' Display the number of file open filters now.
    Debug.Print Application.FileDialog(msoFileDialogOpen).Filters.Count & _
        " filters"
End Sub
```

For some more information on finding and opening files, see the section "FindFile, GetOpenFilename, and GetSaveAsFilename" later in this chapter.

Names *(C)*

The Names collection contains Name objects representing named items in the active workbook. These include the named ranges described in the section "Named Ranges" earlier in this chapter as well as named areas and formulas.

 CAUTION *The* Workbook *object's* Names *collection represents named objects in the workbook, including any names defined for worksheets. A* Worksheet *object's* Names *collection represents named objects in that worksheet only. Be sure you are using the right collection when you create or access named objects.*

ReferenceStyle

This property determines whether Excel displays formulas in R1C1 notation (ReferenceStyle = xlR1C1) or A1 notation (ReferenceStyle = xlA1). It affects only Excel's interactive display format, not how objects such as Range process cell specifications. The Range property takes as parameters locations specified in A1 notation whether ReferenceStyle is xlR1C1 or xlA1.

ScreenUpdating

ScreenUpdating determines whether Excel displays changes to the screen. If a routine makes many changes to the screen, you can often improve performance by setting ScreenUpdating to False when the routine starts, then setting it back to True when the routine ends.

TIP *If the update will take a while, hiding all the screen updates may confuse the user. Users may think Excel is stuck and use the Task Manager to kill the application. If you know the update will take a while, you may want to keep the updates visible or display some sort of progress indicator so users know something is happening.*

The following code changes the font of every cell in the active worksheet's used range. It does this twice, once with ScreenUpdating set to True and again with ScreenUpdating set to False. When ScreenUpdating is True, Excel refreshes the display each time a cell's font changes. When ScreenUpdating is False, Excel doesn't show any changes until every cell has been updated.

FILE *Ch08\CellNames.xls*

```
' See how much difference ScreenUpdating can make.
Sub TestScreenUpdating()
Dim i As Long
Dim start_time As Double
Dim stop_time As Double
Dim times(1 To 2) As Double
Dim cell As Range

    For i = 1 To 2
        ' Set ScreenUpdating for this run.
        If i = 1 Then
            Application.ScreenUpdating = True
        Else
            Application.ScreenUpdating = False
        End If
        DoEvents
```

```
        ' Time the operation.
        start_time = Timer
        For Each cell In ActiveSheet.UsedRange
            If cell.Font.Name = "Times New Roman" Then
                cell.Font.Name = "Arial"
            Else
                cell.Font.Name = "Times New Roman"
            End If
        Next cell
        stop_time = Timer
        times(i) = stop_time - start_time
    Next i
    Application.ScreenUpdating = True

    ' Display the results.
    MsgBox _
        "ScreenUpdating True:  " & _
        Format$(times(1), "0.00") & " seconds" & vbCrLf & _
        "ScreenUpdating False: " & _
        Format$(times(2), "0.00") & " seconds"
End Sub
```

In one test, this routine took approximately 0.57 seconds to modify each cell with ScreenUpdating set to True. It took only 0.08 seconds with ScreenUpdating set to False. In many cases, including this example, both versions are probably fast enough for most uses. Before you worry about ScreenUpdating, just try running the program to see if it is already fast enough.

See the "StatusBar" section later in this chapter for one way to keep the user informed while a long process is running.

Selection

The Selection property returns an object representing whatever the user has currently selected. If the user has selected one or more cells, this object is a Range, but it is important to realize that the Selection can be other types of objects if other things are selected. For example, if the user clicks on different parts of a chart, the Selection object might return a Series, Gridlines, Legend, ChartArea, or PlotArea object.

Your code can use the TypeOf operator to verify that the Selection property contains a certain kind of object before trying to manipulate it. For example, the following code ensures that the Selection contains a Range object before it gets to work.

```
If TypeOf Selection Is Range Then
    ' Do something with the Range...
Else
    MsgBox "No Range selected"
End If
```

You can also use the TypeName statement to see what kind of object is selected, as the following code does.

FILE *Ch08\CellNames.xls*

```
' Display the selected object's type in the status bar.
Sub SayType()
    Application.StatusBar = TypeName(Selection)
End Sub
```

Speech

The Speech property returns a Speech object that you can use to make Excel talk (if the speech features have been installed). This object's SpeakCellOnEnter property determines whether Excel reads a cell's value after you enter it. The object's Speak method makes Excel say something, such as in the following statement.

```
Application.Speech.Speak "Enter number of employees"
```

NOTE *Speech can be annoying in a typical cube-farm environment where nearby coworkers will overhear it. Speech can be useful, however, if you need to implement accessibility features or if you are working on a kiosk system or other system with limited input and output capabilities. In particular, speech and audio input may become more useful in the future as handheld and phone-based applications become more common.*

StatusBar

The StatusBar property gets or sets the value displayed in Excel's status bar. You can use this area to keep the user posted while you perform long calculations. This is particularly useful if you disable screen updating by setting ScreenUpdating to False. See the "ScreenUpdating" section earlier in this chapter for more on this property.

When Excel controls the status bar (it's not displaying something set by your code), the StatusBar property returns False. To return control of the status bar to Excel, set StatusBar to False.

The following code shows how a program might display messages to let the user know what the code is doing. When finished, the code returns control of the status bar to Excel.

```
Application.StatusBar = "Loading data..."
...

Application.StatusBar = "Searching for customers..."
...

Application.StatusBar = "Searching for delinquent customers..."
...

Application.StatusBar = "Disconnecting delinquent customers..."
...

' Return control of the StatusBar to Excel.
Application.StatusBar = False
```

ThisCell *and* ThisWorkbook

The ThisCell property returns a Range object representing the cell in which a function is executing. For example, suppose a workbook contains a code module that holds the following function.

 FILE *Ch08\CellNames.xls*

```
' Return the address of the cell calling this function.
Function CellAddress() As String
    CellAddress = Application.ThisCell.Address
End Function
```

Now suppose you enter the formula =CellAddress() in cell B25. To evaluate the cell's value, Excel calls the CellAddress function. That function uses the ThisCell property to get a Range representing the cell being evaluated, B25. CellAddress returns the cell's address, which in this case is $B$25, and Excel places that value in the cell.

For a more interesting scenario, select cell B25 containing the formula, press Ctrl-C to copy it, select a range of cells, and press Ctrl-V to paste. As Excel pastes the formula into each cell, it evaluates the CellAddress function and displays the correct cell address.

A more realistic example might use the cells' positions to determine how they should be formatted or how their values should be calculated.

The ThisWorkbook property returns a Workbook object representing the workbook in which the current code is executing.

WorksheetFunction

The WorksheetFunction object is a container for all the Excel workbook functions your code can invoke. For instance, the following statement calculates the standard deviation of the values in the Range B12:B21.

```
Debug.Print WorksheetFunction.StDev(Range("B12:B21"))
```

The WorksheetFunction object provides almost 200 functions that handle everything from calculating inverse hyperbolic tangents, to finding standard deviations in a population, to deciding whether a value is odd or even. For a list of functions available to a VBA program, search the online help for "List of Worksheet Functions Available to Visual Basic" or go to http://msdn.microsoft.com/library/en-us/off2000/html/xlmscListOfWorksheetFunctions.asp.

Methods

The following sections describe some of the Application object's most useful methods.

Calculate, CalculateFull, *and* CalculateFullRebuild

The Calculate method makes Excel recalculate all open workbooks. Usually, this isn't necessary because Excel automatically recalculates cells when you change those they depend upon.

One case where the Calculate method can be useful is if you change the definition of a VBA function used to calculate cell values. For example, suppose you write a VBA function named CalcBonus, and some cells use a formula such as =CalcBonus(50000). If you change the code used by CalcBonus, you can call the Calculate method to make Excel recalculate all cell values.

Another case where this might be useful is if you write a VBA function that uses data that may be changing. For example, a function might read values from a database that tracks stock prices. You could periodically call Calculate to refresh the function's values.

 TIP *The* Worksheet *and* Range *objects also provide a* Calculate *method that you can use to recalculate a more restricted group of cells. If you know that only one cell's value may have changed, it's silly to recalculate every cell in every workbook.*

When you call the Calculate method, Excel recalculates only the cells it thinks may need to be recalculated. The CalculateFull method forces it to recalculate everything.

The CalculateFullRebuild method forces Excel to recalculate everything and rebuild dependencies (the relations among cells).

Unit Conversion Functions

Excel measures distances in points. To make working with points easier, the Application object provides CentimetersToPoints and InchesToPoints functions for converting values into points.

The Application object provides no other unit conversion functions, but several others are easy to derive. The following formulas show how to convert from points into inches or centimeters.

```
inches = points / Application.InchesToPoints
centimeters = points / Application.CentimetersToPoints
```

It's also easy to convert between points and twips or picas.

```
twips = points * 20
points = twips / 20
picas = points / 12
points = picas * 12
```

ConvertFormula

The ConvertFormula function converts the cell references in a formula between A1 notation and R1C1 notation, or between relative and absolute addresses. This method takes five parameters that give the formula, the formula's current notation style (xlA1 or xlR1C1), the desired new style (xlA1 or xlR1C1), the desired addressing style (xlAbsolute, xlAbsRowRelCol, xlRelRowAbsCol, or xlRelative), and a Range object representing the cell to which addresses should be relative.

The following output from the Debug window shows some example statements and their results. The following statement converts the A1-style absolute reference $A$1:$C$3 into the R1C1-style absolute reference R1C1:R3C3.

```
?Application.ConvertFormula("=MyFunction($A$1:$C$3)", xlA1, xlR1C1)
=MyFunction(R1C1:R3C3)
```

The following statement converts the relative reference D1 into R1C1-style notation. The reference is relative to the cell C3. The cell D1 is two rows up and one column right from cell C3 so the result is a relative shift of two rows and one column.

```
?Application.ConvertFormula("=MyFunction(D1)", xlA1, xlRC1, _
    xlRelative, Range("C3"))
=MyFunction(R[-2]C[1])
```

The following code takes the relative address R[1]C[1], converts it relative to the cell C3, and gives the result one row down and one column right of cell C3, which is R4C4.

```
?Application.ConvertFormula("=MyFunction(R[1]C[1])", xlR1C1, xlR1C1, _
    xlAbsolute, Range("C3"))
=MyFunction(R4C4)
```

Evaluate

The Evaluate function evaluates a formula and returns the result. For example, the following statement displays the sine of Pi / 5.

```
MsgBox Evaluate("Sin(Pi()/5)")
```

Evaluate can calculate expressions that involve cell and range references in A1 notation. The following statement displays the sum of the values in cells A12 through A21.

```
MsgBox Evaluate("Sum(A12:A21)")
```

The Evaluate function can also decipher the names of certain Excel objects. In the following code, the Evaluate function returns a Range object representing the cells in the intersection of ranges A4:H6 and A1:C10,F1:G10. The code then sets the interior color of the resulting Range object to yellow.

```
Evaluate("A4:H6 (A1:C10,F1:G10)").Interior.Color = vbyellow
```

FindFile, GetOpenFilename, *and* GetSaveAsFilename

The FindFile method displays a File Open dialog with filters appropriate for Excel. If the user selects a file, the method opens the file and returns True. If the user cancels, the method returns False.

The following example lets the user search for a workbook. If the user selects one and clicks OK, the code adds a new worksheet to the current workbook and copies the newly opened workbook's first worksheet into it. It then closes the newly opened workbook.

 FILE *Ch08\CopyWorksheet.xls*

```
' Copy a workbook's first worksheet.
Private Sub cmdCopyFirstWorksheet_Click()
Dim dest_ws As Worksheet
Dim source_ws As Worksheet
```

```
    If Application.FindFile() Then
        ' Make a new worksheet.
        Set dest_ws = ThisWorkbook.Worksheets.Add(, _
            ThisWorkbook.Worksheets(ThisWorkbook.Worksheets.Count))

        ' Get the first worksheet in the newly loaded workbook.
        Set source_ws = ActiveWorkbook.Sheets(1)

        ' Copy the worksheet.
        source_ws.UsedRange.Copy dest_ws.Range("A1")

        ' Close the newly opened worksheet.
        ActiveWorkbook.Close
    End If
End Sub
```

The GetOpenFilename method displays a File Open dialog. If the user selects a file, the method returns the selected file's name.

If the method's MultiSelect parameter is True, the user can select more than one file. In that case, the method returns an array of variants containing the names of the files selected. In either case, the method returns False if the user cancels. GetOpenFilename does not automatically open any files the user selects. Your code can take whatever action is appropriate with the files.

> **NOTE** *If* MultiSelect *is True,* GetOpenFilename *returns an array of values even if the user selects only one file.*

The following code lets the user select one or more files and then displays the files selected, if any. A real application would do something more involved than simply listing the files. For example, it could open the files and search for particular values, copy data into or out of the workbooks, change the workbooks' formatting, and so forth.

FILE *Ch08\CopyWorksheet.xls*

```
' Let the user select one or more files.
Private Sub cmdSelectFiles_Click()
Dim result As Variant
Dim txt As String
Dim i As Integer

    ' Let the user select files.
    result = Application.GetOpenFilename(MultiSelect:=True)

    ' See what kind of result this is.
    If VarType(result) = vbBoolean Then
        ' The user canceled.
        MsgBox "Canceled"
    Else
        ' The user selected one or more files.
        ' This is an array of variants.
        txt = "Selected:" & vbCrLf
        For i = LBound(result) To UBound(result)
            txt = txt & "    " & result(i) & vbCrLf
        Next i
        MsgBox txt
    End Select
End Sub
```

The GetSaveAsFilename method displays a Save As dialog. Like the GetOpenFilename method, this routine returns a file name if the user selects a file and it returns False if the user cancels. GetSaveAsFilename does not automatically do anything with the file the user selects. Your code must do the work. For instance, the code might save the current workbook with a new file name, save a copy of the workbook with that name, or automatically generate a new workbook and save it with that file name.

See also the sections "Dialogs" and "FileDialog" earlier in this chapter for information on some related dialog objects.

Goto

The Goto method makes Excel select a Range. If the Range's worksheet is not the currently active one, Excel activates it. If the Range is not initially visible on the worksheet, Excel scrolls so it is visible.

If the Goto method's optional second parameter, Scroll, is True, then Excel scrolls so the Range is visible in the upper-left visible cell. For complex Ranges, this may produce slightly unexpected results. For example, the following two statements both go to the range consisting of the two cells W45 and Z40. While executing the first statement, Excel scroll so cell W45 is in the upper-left corner of the screen. While executing the second statement, Excel scroll so cell Z40 is in the upper-left corner of the screen. In both cases, the entire region is probably not visible (unless you have a huge screen and tiny font) because one cell is cut off either on the top or on the left.

```
Application.Goto Worksheets("Names").Range("W45,Z40"), True
Application.Goto Worksheets("Names").Range("Z40,W45"), True
```

TIP *Usually, people expect to see the upper-left corner of the range and don't mind as much if cells on the lower-right are cut off. Whether that's true for you depends on the application and why you want to scroll to the data.*

If you set the Scroll parameter to False in these statements, one of the cells is still cut off, this time on the right or bottom. If you want both cells to be visible, you can find the smallest row and column used by the Range, use Goto with Scroll parameter True to position the cell using that row and column in the upper-left corner of the screen, and then use the original Range's Select method to select the Range.

```
Application.GoTo Worksheets("Names").Range("W40"), True
Range("W45,Z40").Select
```

InputBox

Like VBA's InputBox function, this method displays a dialog where the user can input a value. This method takes an additional Type parameter at the end, however, that lets you specify the type of data that the user should enter. Figure 8-4 shows a dialog that requires a number as input. Because the value entered is not a number, when the user clicked OK, the dialog automatically displayed an error message.

CAUTION *Because VBA has its own* InputBox *function, you must be sure to specify the* Application *namespace to get this version.*

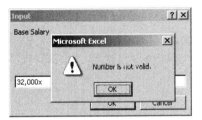

Figure 8-4. The Application.InputBox *method can require the user to enter data in a particular format.*

Table 8-2 lists the values the Type parameter can take.

Table 8-2. Application.InputBox Type *Parameter Values*

VALUE	INPUT TYPE
0	Formula
1	Number
2	String
4	Boolean
8	Range specification
16	An error value
64	Array of values

A Boolean value can be True, False, 0 (False), or any other numeric value (True).

When you set Type to 8 (to require a Range specification), InputBox returns a Range object. You can use a Set statement to save the result in a Range variable as shown in the following code.

```
Set selected_range = Application.InputBox("Range", Type:=8)
```

If you assign the result of a Range selection to a string, Excel copies the contents of the Range into the string. This works only if the Range contains a single cell, however. If the user enters a multiple-cell Range, its text value is not easily defined, so Excel raises an error. To avoid this problem, you should save the returned value in a Range variable and then examine the result to see whether it contains a single cell.

You can combine Type values to allow more than one kind of input. For example, the following statement allows the user to enter a number or Boolean value.

```
Dim v As Variant
v = Application.InputBox("Number or Boolean", Type:=1 + 4)
```

There seem to be some exceptions, however. For instance, if you set Type equal to 1 + 8 to allow numbers or Range specifications, the dialog allows only numbers. You also cannot allow a formula plus any other type (how would Excel know if you added 0 for a formula to any other value?).

If you want to restrict the user's input slightly, InputBox can be handy. If you have complicated data checking needs, however, you will probably be better off building your own dialog by using a UserForm. On a UserForm, you can also let the user enter several related values all at once (and you can make the form look consistent with the rest of your application, providing nice colors, a logo, and so forth).

Intersect *and* Union

The Intersect function returns a Range object representing the intersection of two or more Range objects. For example, the following code creates two L-shaped Ranges as shown in Figure 8-5. The intersection contains the two isolated cells C5 and F2 shown in the figure.

 FILE *Ch08\CellNames.xls*

```
' Select the intersection of two ranges.
Sub SelectIntersection()
Dim r1 As Range
Dim r2 As Range
Dim r3 As Range

    ' Make the first range yellow.
    Set r1 = Range("C2:C6,C2:G2")
    r1.Interior.Color = vbYellow

    ' Make the second range red.
    Set r2 = Range("B5:F5,F1:F5")
    r2.Interior.Color = vbRed
```

```
' Make the intersection orange.
Set r3 = Application.Intersect(r1, r2)
r3.Interior.Color = RGB(255, 128, 0)
End Sub
```

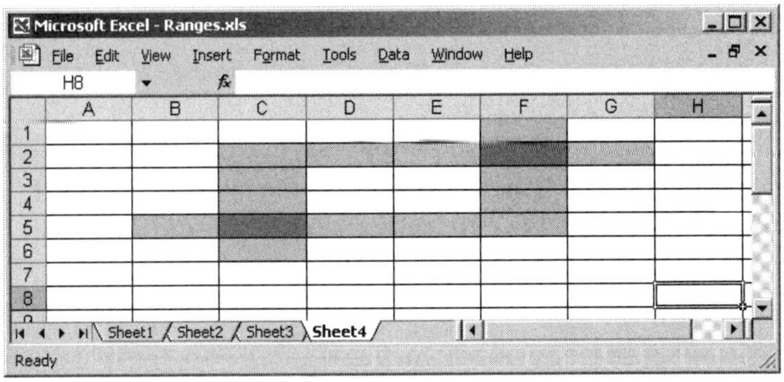

Figure 8-5. The intersection of two Range *objects need not be contiguous.*

If the Intersect function's Range parameters do not intersect, the function returns Nothing.

The Union function returns a Range object representing the union of two or more Range objects. For example, the following code creates the same two L-shaped Ranges shown in Figure 8-5 and then selects their union. The union contains all of the cells shaded in the figure.

FILE *Ch08\CellNames.xls*

```
' Select the union of two ranges.
Sub SelectUnion()
Dim r1 As Range
Dim r2 As Range

    ' Make the ranges.
    Set r1 = Range("C2:C6,C2:G2")
    Set r2 = Range("B5:F5,F1:F5")
```

```
    ' Select the union.
    Application.Union(r1, r2).Select
End Sub
```

OnKey

The OnKey method installs a keyboard shortcut. When the user presses a certain key combination, Excel runs the associated macro.

The InstallF8 subroutine shown in the following code makes Excel run subroutine ThisWorkbook.F8Pressed when the user presses the F8 key. Subroutine UninstallF8 omits the OnKey's method's macro name parameter, restoring F8 to its default use.

FILE *Ch08\CellNames.xls*

```
' Run subroutine F8Pressed when the user presses F8.
Sub InstallF8()
    Application.OnKey "{F8}", "ThisWorkbook.F8Pressed"
End Sub

' Just say that F8 was pressed.
Sub F8Pressed()
    MsgBox "F8 pressed"
End Sub

' Uninstall subroutine F8Pressed.
Sub UninstallF8()
    Application.OnKey "{F8}"
End Sub
```

TIP *To override a key sequence and make it do nothing, set the macro name parameter to a blank string.*

See the online help for OnKey or go to http://msdn.microsoft.com/library/en-us/vbaxl10/html/xlmthOnKey.asp to learn about allowed key sequence formats.

OnTime

The OnTime method schedules Excel to execute a macro at a later time. The method's first two parameters indicate the time at which the macro should execute and the macro's name.

The optional third parameter gives the latest time at which the macro will run. If Excel is busy performing a long calculation when the macro should run, the macro needs to wait until Excel is finished. If the time indicated by this third parameter has passed before Excel has a chance to run the macro, the event is skipped.

The optional Boolean fourth parameter, Schedule, tells Excel whether you are trying to schedule an event or cancel one. To cancel an event, set the time and macro name to the same values you used to schedule the event, and set Schedule to False. If the time and macro name don't match the values you used originally, VBA raises an error.

The following code schedules three events for 5, 10, and 15 seconds in the future. It then cancels the event in 10 seconds. When the events fire, the DisplayTime subroutine prints the current time in the Debug window.

 FILE *Ch08\CellNames.xls*

```
' Display the time in 5 and 15 seconds.
Sub ScheduleTimes()
Dim t1 As Date
Dim t2 As Date
Dim t3 As Date

    ' Caculate Now plus 5, 10, and 15 seconds.
    t1 = Now + TimeValue("00:00:05")
    t2 = t1 + TimeValue("00:00:05")
    t3 = t2 + TimeValue("00:00:05")

    ' Set up to run DisplayTime in 5, 10, and 15 seconds.
    Application.OnTime t1, "DisplayTime"
    Application.OnTime t2, "DisplayTime"
    Application.OnTime t3, "DisplayTime"

    ' Unschedule DisplayTime in 10 seconds.
    Application.OnTime t2, "DisplayTime", Schedule:=False
```

```
    ' Display the time now.
    Debug.Print Now & " (start)"
End Sub

' Display the current time.
Sub DisplayTime()
    Debug.Print Now
End Sub
```

Quit

This method makes Excel exit. If any open workbooks have unsaved changes, Excel asks the user whether it should save changes to the files.

To save the changes automatically before quitting, execute each open Workbook's Save method. To silently discard the changes in a Workbook, set its Saved property to True. That essentially "fools" Excel into thinking the Workbook has been saved.

To silently discard changes to all open Workbooks, you can set Application.DisplayAlerts to False.

TIP *In general, silently discarding changes is a bad idea. Your users won't thank you if you throw away an afternoon's work without asking them. One case in which you may want to discard changes is if the user is working on a training workbook, so you know you don't want to save the changes.*

CAUTION *When* Application.DisplayAlerts *is False, Excel doesn't display any prompts; it simply selects each dialog's default action instead. Using this method to discard changes relies on the fact that the default action when closing a workbook is to not save changes. That's not at all obvious because, if you interactively close a workbook that has changes, pressing Enter on the Save Changes dialog does the opposite and saves the changes. Won't you feel silly if Microsoft changes the default behavior in some later release? They've done similar things before! Setting each* Workbook's Saved *property to True is less ambiguous.*

You can also call a Workbook's Close method by passing it False as its SaveChanges parameter. Overall, this is a much less confusing strategy that doesn't rely on tricks or default behavior.

Run

The Run method executes a macro by name. In addition to the name of the macro, Run can take up to 30 parameters, which it passes to the macro. Run returns whatever value the macro returns.

Normally, VBA code can simply call a macro itself. One advantage of using Run rather than directly invoking a macro is that the name of the macro can be stored in a string. Then you can pass the macro's name to a different routine that can execute it without needing to know exactly what macro it is.

Volatile

The Volatile method takes a Boolean parameter indicating whether the function containing it should be marked volatile. When any cell's value on a worksheet changes, all cells that refer to volatile functions are recalculated.

For example, suppose you write a VBA function named CombinedResults that examines some of the cells on the worksheet and returns a result based on their values. Suppose also that cell A1 contains the formula =CombinedResults(). If the user changes the value of one of the cells that this function examines, Excel does not automatically update cell A1 because it doesn't know that the change affects the value returned by CombinedResults.

If you add the statement Application.Volatile to the beginning of function CombinedResults, then Excel automatically recalculates cell A1 whenever any other cell's value changes.

To mark a function as nonvolatile, remove the Application.Volatile statement or pass it the parameter False. The next time Excel executes the function, it will mark it as nonvolatile.

Events

The Application object provides four groups of events. First, it has its own NewWorkbook event that fires when the user creates a new workbook.

Second, the Application object has several events that deal with worksheets. Events such as SheetActivate (fires when a sheet activates), SheetBeforeDoubleClick (fires after the user double-clicks the sheet but before any other processing of the double-click), and SheetDeactivate (fires when the sheet deactivates) are fairly self-explanatory. Some particularly useful events are SheetCalculate (fires when the sheet performs any calculation), SheetChange (fires when a cell changes), and SheetSelectionChange (fires when the sheet's selection changes).

The third group of events includes the window events WindowActivate, WindowDeactivate, and WindowResize.

The last group of events deals with workbooks: WorkbookOpen, WorkbookActivate, WorkbookNewSheet, WorkbookBeforeSave, and WorkbookBeforeClose. These events are generally similar to the group dealing with worksheets.

See the online help for details about these events. On the Web, go to http:// msdn.microsoft.com/library/en-us/vbax110/html/xlevtWorkbookBeforeClose.asp to learn about WorkbookBeforeClose. Use the navigation panel on the left to look up other events.

Unfortunately, Excel doesn't create an Application object module, so there is no predefined place where you can catch these events. To use these events, you must declare a variable by using the WithEvents keyword and assign it to the Application object. You cannot use the WithEvents keyword in a normal code module, however. You can declare a variable WithEvents only in an object module.

An Excel workbook's VBA project typically contains a ThisWorkbook module representing the workbook as a whole, and possibly many sheet and chart modules representing the items contained in the workbook. Each module represents an object, so it can contain the WithEvents keyword.

To catch Application events, declare a variable by using the WithEvents keyword in one of those modules. The ThisWorkbook module is often the best place for this kind of code because it doesn't deal directly with a specific worksheet. Now you can select the variable in the code editor's left combo box and select the event you want to catch in the right combo box.

You must initialize the variable somewhere by setting it equal to the Application object. You can do that in a subroutine. If you want to catch these events any time the workbook is open, you can do it in the workbook's Workbook_Open event handler.

The following code declares the m_App variable using the WithEvents keyword. The CatchApplicationEvents subroutine initializes this variable. Event handlers catch the SheetCalculate, SheetChange, and SheetSelectionChange events. Subroutine StopCatchingApplicationEvents sets the variable to Nothing so the program no longer catches Application events.

 FILE *Ch08\CellNames.xls*

```
' Catch Application events.
Dim WithEvents m_App As Application

' Set m_App so we can catch Application events.
Sub CatchApplicationEvents()
    Set m_App = Application
End Sub

' Stop catching Application events.
Sub StopCatchingApplicationEvents()
    Set m_App = Nothing
End Sub

Private Sub m_App_SheetCalculate(ByVal Sh As Object)
    Debug.Print "SheetCalculate"
End Sub

Private Sub m_App_SheetChange(ByVal Sh As Object, ByVal Target As Range)
    Debug.Print "SheetChange"
End Sub

Private Sub m_App_SheetSelectionChange(ByVal Sh As Object, -
  ByVal Target As Range)
    Debug.Print "SheetSelectionChange"
End Sub
```

NOTE *When you are working with these events interactively using the VBA debugger, setting the* WithEvents *variable to* Nothing *can be tricky sometimes. Executing the code in the* Debug *window doesn't always work. Instead, set and clear this variable by using subroutines so they execute in the same program context. Note also that changes to subroutines may clear the variables. If you suddenly stop receiving* Application *events, set the variable to the* Application *object again.*

Workbook

The Workbook object represents an Excel workbook file containing one or more worksheets and chart sheets. The Workbook's methods allow you to find and manipulate the sheets it contains. It also provides a natural place to store code that is not specific to a particular sheet.

Properties

The following sections describe the Workbook object's most useful properties. Those that return collections are marked with a (C).

Active Object Properties

The Workbook object's ActiveSheet and ActiveChart properties return the currently active worksheet or chart sheet. These two properties are mutually exclusive, so if one returns a value, the other returns Nothing. For instance, if the Workbook is currently displaying a worksheet, then no chart sheet is active, so ActiveChart is Nothing.

Note that a workbook defines an active sheet even if the workbook itself is not active. Also note that a workbook must always contain at least one visible sheet, so either ActiveSheet or ActiveChart should not be Nothing.

Sheets *(C),* Worksheets *(C), and* Charts *(C)*

The Sheets collection contains Worksheet and Chart objects representing the worksheets and charts in the workbook. You can use an object's position or name as an index into this collection. For instance, the following code activates the object named Employees. Note that this code will work whether Employees is a worksheet or a chart.

```
Sheets("Employees").Activate
```

The Worksheets and Charts collections contain the objects representing the workbook's worksheets and charts. No objects are in both of these collections, and collectively, these two collections contain all the objects in the Sheets collection.

As with the Sheets collection, you can use an object's position or name as an index into these collections. Note, however, that an object's position is not necessarily the same in this collection and the other collections. For example, suppose the workbook's first object is a worksheet and its second is a chart sheet. Then the chart sheet is at Sheets(2) and Charts(1).

BuiltinDocumentProperties *(C) and* CustomDocumentProperties *(C)*

The BuiltinDocumentProperties collection contains DocumentProperty objects that define predefined workbook properties. Those objects contain Name, Type, and Value properties that define the items' values.

The ListBuiltInDocumentProperties subroutine shown in the following code lists a workbook's built-in properties. It activates the BuiltInProperties worksheet, creating it if necessary, and then calls subroutine ListProperties to display the properties.

Subroutine ListProperties fills in some column headers and then loops through the property collection, listing each property's name, type, and value.

 FILE *Ch08\CellNames.xls*

```
' Display the built-in document properties.
Sub ListBuiltInDocumentProperties()
    ' If there isn't a BuiltInProperties sheet, make one.
    On Error Resume Next
    Worksheets("BuiltInProperties").Activate
    If Err.Number <> 0 Then
        Worksheets.Add After:=Worksheets(Worksheets.Count)
        ActiveSheet.Name = "BuiltInProperties"
    Else
        ActiveSheet.Clear
    End If
    On Error GoTo 0

    ' List the properties.
    ListProperties BuiltinDocumentProperties
End Sub

' Display the built-in document properties.
Sub ListProperties(ByVal properties As DocumentProperties)
Dim i As Long
```

```
' Write the column headings.
Cells(1, 1) = "Name"
Cells(1, 2) = "Type"
Cells(1, 3) = "Value"
Range("A1:C1").Font.Bold = True

' Display the properties.
For i = 1 To properties.Count
    With properties(i)
        Cells(i + 1, 1) = .Name
        Select Case .Type
            Case msoPropertyTypeBoolean
                Cells(i + 1, 2) = "Boolean"
            Case msoPropertyTypeDate
                Cells(i + 1, 2) = "Date"
            Case msoPropertyTypeFloat
                Cells(i + 1, 2) = "Float"
            Case msoPropertyTypeNumber
                Cells(i + 1, 2) = "Number"
            Case msoPropertyTypeString
                Cells(i + 1, 2) = "String"
        End Select

        On Error Resume Next
        Cells(i + 1, 3) = .Value
        On Error GoTo 0
    End With
Next i

Range("A:C").Columns.AutoFit
End Sub
```

The CustomDocumentProperties collection is similar to BuiltinDocumentProperties except that you can add and remove items from it. The following code removes any existing custom properties and then creates some new ones.

 FILE *Ch08\CellNames.xls*

```
' Add a couple custom document properties.
Sub AddCustomProperties()
Dim prop As DocumentProperties

    ' Delete all current properties.
    Do While CustomDocumentProperties.Count > 0
        CustomDocumentProperties(1).Delete
    Loop

    ' Add some new properties.
    CustomDocumentProperties.Add "A string", False, _
        msoPropertyTypeString, "http://www.vb-helper.com/office.htm"
    CustomDocumentProperties.Add "A number", False, _
        msoPropertyTypeNumber, 20
    CustomDocumentProperties.Add "A float", False, _
        msoPropertyTypeFloat, 1.23
    CustomDocumentProperties.Add "A Boolean", False, _
        msoPropertyTypeBoolean, False
    CustomDocumentProperties.Add "A date", False, _
        msoPropertyTypeDate, #1/30/1983#
End Sub
```

Subroutine ListCustomDocumentProperties in Ch08\CellNames.xls lists custom document properties much as subroutine ListBuiltInDocumentProperties lists built-in properties. See the code for details.

Note that these properties are attached to the workbook, so they are appropriate when you want to save values that should travel with the workbook data. For example, you might use them to store information about the data loaded, such as the last date it was updated from the Internet.

These properties are not particularly appropriate for values that depend on the user accessing the workbook. For example, if you build a user-based system of tools to help different users perform different jobs, you won't want the user's configuration to be part of the workbook. Instead it would be better to store the configuration information in the system Registry by using VBA's SaveSetting and GetSetting methods. Then different users would have their own configurations.

DisplayDrawingObjects

This property determines whether the workbook displays drawing objects (DisplayDrawingObjects = xlDisplayShapes), displays drawing objects as placeholders (DisplayDrawingObjects = xlPlaceholders), or hides drawing objects (`DisplayDrawingObjects = xlHide`). Depending on what the user is doing, you may want to hide drawing objects or show them as placeholders to reduce clutter or to remove information that certain types of users may not understand.

Name, Path, *and* FullName

The `Name` property gives the workbook's file name. `Path` returns the file's path. `FullName` returns the complete file name including path.

HasPassword, Password, *and* WritePassword

The `HasPassword` property returns True if the workbook is password-protected. VBA code can use the `Password` property to set the file's password. Excel assumes that if the file is open, you have entered the password, so the code you execute should have permission to change the password. To remove password protection, set the `Password` property to an empty string.

NOTE *Code can read the* Password *property, but it always returns the string* ******** *whether a password exists or not, so this isn't terribly useful. It's important, however, that the property does not return the password so your archenemy in the accounting department can't read it, but Microsoft could have just made this property write-only.*

The `WritePassword` property works much as the `Password` property does. Set its value to place a write password on the workbook and prevent users from modifying the file without the password. Set `WritePassword` to an empty string to remove the write password.

NOTE *To set a password or write password interactively, select File ➤ Save As, click the dialog's Tools menu, and select General Options. Setting these properties in code lets you easily protect or unprotect the workbook without saving the file with a new name using Save As.*

Routing Properties

The Workbook object has a few properties and methods that let you route a workbook to several users either at the same time or consecutively. This can be handy if you want several people to review or add data to a workbook.

The RoutingSlip property returns an object that represents the document's routing information. You can use that object to do such things as add recipients to the routing list, specify a message to travel with the workbook, and indicate whether the recipients should all receive the document simultaneously or consecutively.

The HasRoutingSlip property returns True if the document has an associated routing slip. VBA code can set this property to True to create a routing slip or set it to False to delete an existing routing slip.

The Route method sends the document off to the recipients. The Routed property indicates whether the document has been routed. The RoutingSlip object's Status property provides more information, returning the values wdNotYetRouted, wdRouteInProgress, and wdRouteComplete.

Names *(C)*

The Names collection contains Name objects representing the workbook's named objects. These include the named ranges described in the section "Named Ranges" earlier in this chapter and named areas and formulas. See that section for more information and examples.

ReadOnly

This property returns True if the workbook was opened read-only. In multiple-user environments, it's relatively common for a user to open a file read-only because someone else already has it open. Note that VBA code can change whether the file is open for writing with the ChangeFileAccess method described later in this chapter.

Saved

Normally, this property returns True if no changes have been made to the workbook since the last time it was saved. However, VBA code can set this property to True to mark the document as saved without actually saving it. This fools Excel into thinking the document has no unsaved changes when actually it might. You can use this trick to close a workbook while preventing Excel from asking the user whether it should save changes.

CAUTION *This is a somewhat dangerous trick, so use it with caution. If you aren't careful, the user whose changes you throw away may come after you looking for trouble (or at least a good explanation).*

Styles (C)

The Styles collection contains objects representing defined formatting styles. You can use this collection and its contents to add, modify, and delete styles.

Methods

The following sections describe some of the Workbook object's most useful methods.

Activate

This method activates the workbook, making it appear on top of other open workbooks.

Note that many of the Application object's properties and methods refer to the active workbook or its active worksheet. For example, the Range and Cells methods return objects in the active worksheet. You can refer to these objects on a worksheet that is not active, but the notation is often simpler if you activate the workbook first.

For example, the following code shows three ways to place values in a sequence of cells. The first method activates the target worksheet and then uses the Application object's Cells collection to set the values. The second method refers directly to the target worksheet's cells without activating the worksheet. The third method also refers directly to the target cells, but it uses a With statement. Although all three methods do the same thing, the first is the most concise, and the final version is a bit simpler than the second.

```
' Active the worksheet first.
Workbooks(1).Sheets(1).Activate
Cells(1, 1) = "First Name"
Cells(1, 2) = "Last Name"
Cells(1, 3) = "Address"
...
' Without activating the worksheet.
```

```
Workbooks(1).Sheets(1).Cells(1, 1) = "First Name"
Workbooks(1).Sheets(1).Cells(1, 2) = "Last Name"
Workbooks(1).Sheets(1).Cells(1, 3) = "Address"
...
' Without activating the worksheet.
With Workbooks(1).Sheets(1)
    .Cells(1, 1) = "First Name"
    .Cells(1, 2) = "Last Name"
    .Cells(1, 3) = "Address"
End With
...
```

ChangeFileAccess

This method can change a file's access method between read-only and read-write. The first parameter specifies the new access mode and should be xlReadWrite or xlReadOnly.

The second parameter specifies the file's write password and is required if the workbook has a write password and the code is changing the access mode to xlReadWrite.

NOTE *When you change the access mode to* xlReadWrite, *Excel reloads the file in case someone else modified it while you had it opened read-only. Reloading the file also lets Excel confirm that there is no sharing violation.*

Close

The Close method closes the workbook. The first parameter, SaveChanges, can be True or False to indicate whether Excel should save any changes. If you omit this parameter, Excel asks the user if it should save changes.

The method's second parameter gives a new file name in which to save the file. (This probably should have been a job left to the SaveAs method.)

If the final parameter RouteWorkbook is True or False, it tells Excel whether it should send the workbook to the next recipient listed in its routing slip. If you omit this parameter and the workbook has a routing slip, Excel asks the user if it should route the workbook.

NewWindow

This method creates a new window for the workbook. Using multiple windows, you can view different parts of the same workbook at the same time.

Printing Methods

The `PrintPreview` method displays a picture of how the workbook would appear printed. The `PrintOut` method prints some or all of the workbook. Parameters let you specify the printer, pages to print, number of copies, and other options. See the online help or go to `http://msdn.microsoft.com/library/en-us/vbaxl10/html/xlmthPrintOut.asp` for details.

Protect *and* Unprotect

The `Protect` method protects the workbook's structure or windows from modification. `Protect` takes three parameters. The first is the protection password. The second is a Boolean value that determines whether Excel protects the workbook's structure (whether the user can rearrange the sheets). The third parameter is a Boolean value that determines whether Excel protects the workbook's windows (whether the user can resize windows).

 TIP *Once you have nicely arranged the workbook, you can protect its structure and windows without using a password. This prevents you from making accidental changes, and you can easily unprotect the workbook if you need to make changes.*

The `Unprotect` method removes the workbook's protection. If you protected the workbook with a password, you must pass the password to the `Unprotect` method.

Route

The `Route` method routes the workbook according to its routing slip. See the section "Routing Properties" earlier in this chapter for more information on routing.

Save, SaveAs, *and* SaveCopyAs

These methods save the workbook in various ways. The Save method simply saves the workbook with its current name. If the workbook is new and has not yet been saved, Excel saves it in the current directory. For example, suppose you create a new workbook and Excel assigns it the initial name Book7. If you execute the workbook's Save method, Excel saves it in the current directory as Book7.xls.

The SaveAs method allows you to specify several options, including the file's name, format (such as Excel, CSV, text, XML spreadsheet, or one of about three dozen other formats), password, write password, and so forth.

The SaveCopyAs method saves a copy of the workbook but leaves the open copy unchanged. Any changes you later make to the open workbook apply to the original file, not the copy.

Contrast this with SaveAs, which saves the workbook under a new name and updates the open workbook's name. Any changes you later make to the open workbook apply to the new file and not to the original.

TIP *You could use* SaveAsCopy *to make a series of checkpoint versions of the file while working on it.*

UpdateFromFile

If you open a workbook read-only, another user could modify the original document while you are looking at the file. The UpdateFromFile method makes Excel see if the workbook has been modified in this way and, if it has, reload the workbook.

Events

The Workbook object provides two main groups of events. First, it has events that relate to the workbook itself. These are more or less self-explanatory and include Activate (fires when the workbook activates), BeforeClose (fires before the workbook closes), BeforePrint (fires before the workbook prints), BeforeSave (fires before the workbook saves), Deactivate (fires when the workbook deactivates), NewSheet (fires when the workbook adds a new sheet), and Open (fires when the workbook opens).

The second group of events includes those related to the workbook's worksheets. These events include SheetActivate (fires when a new sheet activates), SheetBeforeDoubleClick (fires when the user double-clicks a sheet before other double-click processing takes place), SheetBeforeRightClick (fires when the user right-clicks a sheet before other right-click processing takes place), SheetCalculate (fires when a sheet calculates), SheetChange (fires when a sheet's data is modified), SheetDeactivate (fires when a sheet deactivates), and SheetSelectionChange (fires when the user changes a sheet's selection).

Excel doesn't provide an Application object module, but it does provide a ThisWorkbook module that lets you easily catch Workbook events. Open that module in the code editor and select Workbook from the left dropdown. Then select an event name in the right dropdown and enter the code you want to execute. The rest is automatic. You do not need to create a variable using the WithEvents keyword to respond to Workbook events.

Worksheet

A Worksheet object represents a worksheet in a workbook. This object's properties and methods let you manipulate the contents of the worksheet's cells. Collections allow you to manipulate objects on the worksheet such as charts, query tables, and shapes.

If you need to change something on a worksheet, you almost certainly need to use a Worksheet object either directly or indirectly. Excel provides many convenience functions that work with the active worksheet. For example, the Application object's Range, Cells, ActiveCell, Rows, Columns, and Selection properties all return objects that represent parts of the active worksheet. The ActiveSheet property returns a reference to the active Worksheet object itself.

All of these objects have global scope, so you can refer to them without using a prefix. For instance, the following code uses the Application object's Range property to select the active worksheet's third row.

```
Range("3:3").Select
```

Several other objects provide their own versions of these properties and methods, however. For example, the Worksheet object provides its own Range and Cells properties. To avoid confusion, you might want to always use explicit prefixes so it's obvious which object is providing a property. Then if you have code in a workbook's Sheet1 module, you won't need to wonder whether a Range statement refers to the active worksheet, Sheet1, or something else. (In case you're wondering, it refers to Sheet1.)

Worksheet Properties

The following sections describe some of the most useful properties provided by the Worksheet object. The sections after those describe the Worksheet object's most useful methods and events.

Cells *(C)*

The Cells property lets code address cells by row and column number rather than by using A1 or R1C1 notation. This can be particularly helpful when you want to loop over a group of cells. For example, the following code fills the first eight columns of the first ten rows with random values between 1 and 100.

```
For r = 1 To 10
    For c = 1 To 8
        Cells(r, c) = Int(100 * Rnd) + 1
    Next c
Next r
```

Columns *(C) and* Rows *(C)*

The Columns and Rows properties return Range objects representing the worksheet's columns or rows, respectively. Each column or row is itself represented by a Range object. For example, Rows(1) is a Range object representing the active worksheet's first row.

Note that these collections represent all of the columns and rows that *might* exist in the worksheet, not those actually in use. The value Columns.Count is always 256 and Rows.Count is always 65,536 no matter how many cells are actually used. You can use these Ranges to manipulate columns and rows that you know exist, but you should not loop through the entire worksheet this way (it would take a while). Instead use the UsedRange property described shortly.

CustomProperties *(C)*

This collection contains CustomProperty objects representing values you have assigned for the worksheet. You can use this property to save and restore values that should be associated with the worksheet. For example, you could store values in a worksheet that relate to the worksheet's data, such as the time when you last updated values from the Internet or the last modification date of a file from which you loaded data.

To associate properties with the workbook as a whole, see the Workbook properties BuiltinDocumentProperties and CustomDocumentProperties described earlier in this chapter. Also see that section for a discussion of when it makes sense to store values in the workbook rather than in an external location such as the system Registry.

Index

The Index property gives the Worksheet's index in its Workbook object's Sheets collection. This is not necessarily the Worksheet's index in the Workbook's WorkSheets collection. For instance, suppose the workbook contains a worksheet, a chart sheet, and another worksheet. Then the second Worksheet object's Index property is 3. It is third in the Sheets collection but second in the Worksheets collection.

To avoid confusion with worksheet indexing, particularly if users can add, remove, and rearrange worksheets, locate worksheets by using their names instead of their indexes. For example, the following code clears the worksheet named People no matter where it appears in the Sheets collection.

```
Worksheets("People").UsedRange.Clear
```

Name

This is simply the name of the worksheet. Your code can get and set this property. It can also use a worksheet's Name to get a reference to the corresponding Worksheet object in the Worksheets or Sheets collection.

Names (C)

This collection holds named objects defined for the Worksheet. Note that the Workbook's Names collection includes any name defined within a Worksheet's Names collection. See also the section "Names (C)" describing the Workbook object's Names collection earlier in this chapter.

Range

This property returns a Range object representing some or all of the worksheet's cells. See the "Range" section earlier in this chapter for a description of the Application object's Range property.

Shapes *(C)*

This collection contains Shape objects representing the worksheet's drawing objects, including AutoShapes, OLE objects, and pictures. Many applications don't need to work with shapes. Still others can get by with Excel's standard diagrams that display organizational charts, cyclic processes, Venn diagrams, and so forth.

Once in a while, however, it's useful to build a drawing programmatically. For example, you could write code that uses lines to connect worksheet cells to show various relationships. Subroutine ConnectCells, shown in the following code, creates a new Shape object that draws a line between the centers of two cells. It takes as parameters an optional dash style and color to give the line. Subroutine TestConnectCells shows how to use this routine.

 FILE *Ch08\CellNames.xls*

```
' Draw a line between two cells.
Sub ConnectCells(ByVal cell1 As Range, ByVal cell2 As Range, _
  Optional ByVal dash_style As MsoLineDashStyle = msoLineSolid, _
  Optional ByVal fore_color As OLE_COLOR = &H808080)
Dim new_line As Shape
Dim x1 As Single

    Set new_line = Worksheets(1).Shapes.AddLine( _
        cell1.Left + cell1.Width / 2, _
        cell1.Top + cell1.Height / 2, _
        cell2.Left + cell2.Width / 2, _
        cell2.Top + cell2.Height / 2)
    new_line.Line.DashStyle = dash_style
    new_line.Line.ForeColor.RGB = fore_color
End Sub

' Draw a red dashed line from A1 to E10.
Sub TestConnectCells()
    ConnectCells Range("A1"), Range("E10"), msoLineDash, vbRed
End Sub
```

For more elaborate drawings, you can use an AutoShape. The following code shows how a program could draw a cycloid on a worksheet. The code is defined by the functions Xt and Yt, which give coordinates of points on the cycloid for different values of the parametric variable T.

The code starts by finding the first point on the cycloid. It calls the `Shapes.BuildFreeform` method to make a `FreeformBuilder` object for the new shape. Then while the value T loops from 0 to 14 *π, the code calculates the next point on the cycloid and uses the `FreeformBuilder's` `AddNodes` methods to add the point to the shape.

After it has added all of the cycloid's points, the code calls the `FreeformBuilder's` `ConvertToShape` method. The code sets the resulting `Shape` object's `Fill.Visible` property to False so the shape isn't filled. It then selects the `Shape` so you can immediately work with it.

FILE *Ch08\CellNames.xls*

```
' Draw a cycloid.
Sub DrawCycloid()
Const PI = 3.14159265
Dim X As Single
Dim Y As Single
Dim T As Single
Dim dT As Single

    ' Find the first point.
    T = 0
    dT = PI / 20
    X = Xt(T)
    Y = Yt(T)

    ' Create the FreeformBuilder object.
    With ActiveSheet.Shapes.BuildFreeform(msoEditingAuto, X, Y)
        ' Add the rest of the points.
        T = T + dT
        Do While T < 14 * PI
            X = Xt(T)
            Y = Yt(T)
            .AddNodes msoSegmentCurve, msoEditingAuto, X, Y
            T = T + dT
        Loop
```

```
        ' Add the last point.
        X = Xt(T)
        Y = Yt(T)
        .AddNodes msoSegmentCurve, msoEditingAuto, X, Y

        ' Convert the FreeformBuilder into a Shape.
        With .ConvertToShape
            .Fill.Visible = msoFalse
            .Select
        End With
    End With
End Sub


Function Xt(ByVal T As Single) As Single
    Xt = 150 * (27 * Cos(T) + 15 * Cos(T * 20 / 7)) / 42 + 180
End Function


Function Yt(ByVal T As Single) As Single
    Yt = 150 * (27 * Sin(T) + 15 * Sin(T * 20 / 7)) / 42 + 180
End Function
```

Figure 8-6 shows the results of this code.

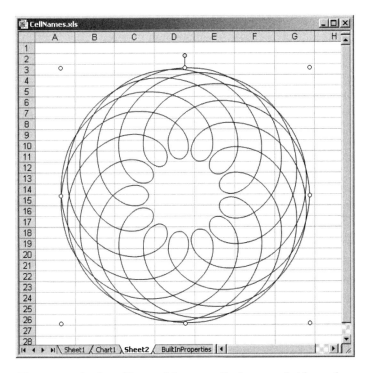

Figure 8-6. An AutoShape object can display a cycloid or other complex figure.

TIP *You must know the right formulas if you want to draw a cycloid, but you can figure out what objects and properties are necessary for building one by recording a macro while you draw and then examining its code.*

The FreeformBuilder, Shape, and other drawing objects are fairly complicated in their own rights. See the online help or go to http://msdn.microsoft.com/library/ en-us/vbaxl10/html/xlobjFreeformBuilder.asp and http://msdn.microsoft.com/ library/en-us/vbaxl10/html/xlobjShape.asp for information about their properties and methods.

UsedRange

UsedRange is one of the Worksheet object's most useful properties. It simply returns a Range object consisting of the smallest rectangular area that includes all of the worksheet's used cells. If the worksheet has no used cells, UsedRange returns the single cell A1.

NOTE *Inserted objects such as charts, drawing objects, and OLE objects don't count as part of the* UsedRange.

CAUTION *Some programmers who don't know about* UsedRange *loop through cells looking for used and empty entries to figure out what the used range is. Others loop through the* Rows *and* Columns *collections, unnecessarily examining millions of empty cells and wondering why their code takes so long. Of course, now you know about* UsedRange, *so you won't have these problems.*

Note that the UsedRange returns a rectangular region, not just the cells actually in use. For example, if the worksheet has values only in cells C3 and E5, UsedRange contains all of the cells in the rectangular region C3:E5, not just the two cells. If you want to operate only on the used cells, you must check each cell to see if it is empty. The following code examines all of the cells in the UsedRange and displays the values of those that are not empty.

FILE *Ch08\CellNames.xls*

```
' List only the worksheet's used cells.
Sub ListUsedCells()
Dim cell As Range

    For Each cell In ActiveSheet.UsedRange
        If Not IsEmpty(cell.Value) Then
            Debug.Print cell.Address & ": " & cell.Value
        End If
    Next cell
End Sub
```

Visible

This property determines whether the worksheet is visible. You can use a hidden worksheet as a scratch pad for intermediate calculations. You can also use different worksheets to provide different views of the same data, hiding those you don't want to display.

Worksheet Methods

The following sections describe the Worksheet object's most interesting methods. See the online help for a complete list of methods and additional details.

Activate *and* Select

The Activate method makes the Worksheet the currently active Worksheet. Many of the Application object's properties and methods, such as Range, Cells, Rows, and Columns, apply to the active Worksheet.

The Select method also activates the Worksheet, although most developers use the Activate method.

Calculate

The `Calculate` method makes Excel recalculate the Worksheet. Usually, this isn't necessary, because Excel automatically recalculates cells when you change those they depend upon. For examples where calling this method is useful, see the section "`Calculate`, `CalculateFull`, and `CalculateFullRebuild`" earlier in this chapter.

Evaluate

The `Evaluate` function evaluates a formula or object name and returns the result. For more information and examples, see the "`Evaluate`" section covering the `Application` object's `Evaluate` method earlier in this chapter.

Copy, Delete, *and* Move

The `Copy` method makes a copy of the `Worksheet`. This method takes two optional parameters, `Before` and `After`, that you can use to position the new worksheet. For example, the following code makes a copy of the active worksheet and places it after the existing worksheets and chart sheets.

```
ActiveSheet.Copy After:=Sheets(Sheets.Count)
```

If you omit both the `Before` and `After` parameters, Excel places the copy of the worksheet in a new workbook.

The `Delete` method deletes the `Worksheet` from the `Workbook`. Before it does so, however, it displays a message telling the user that the `Worksheet` will be permanently deleted and asking the user to confirm the deletion. To prevent that message from appearing, set the `Application` object's `DisplayAlerts` property to False, as shown in the following code.

```
Application.DisplayAlerts = False
Sheets(Sheets.Count).Delete
Application.DisplayAlerts = True
```

The `Move` method moves the `Worksheet` to a new position in the `Workbook`. `Before` and `After` parameters let you specify the `Worksheet`'s new position. The first statement in the following code moves the active `Worksheet` to the end of the `Workbook`. The second statement moves it to the beginning.

```
ActiveSheet.Move After:=Sheets(Sheets.Count)
ActiveSheet.Move Before:=Sheets(1)
```

PrintPreview *and* PrintOut

The PrintPreview method displays a picture of how the workbook would appear printed. The PrintOut method prints the worksheet. Parameters let you specify the printer, pages to print, number of copies, and other options. See the online help or go to http://msdn.microsoft.com/library/en-us/vbaxl10/html/xlmthPrintPreview.asp and http://msdn.microsoft.com/library/en-us/vbaxl10/html/xlmthPrintOut.asp for details.

Worksheet Events

The Worksheet object provides only a handful of events, all of which are fairly self-explanatory. Briefly, the most useful are Activate (fires when the Worksheet activates), BeforeDoubleClick (fires when the user double-clicks the Worksheet), BeforeRightClick (fires when the user right-clicks the Worksheet), Calculate (fires when the Worksheet calculates), Change (fires when a Worksheet cell changes), Deactivate (fires when the Worksheet deactivates), and SelectionChange (fires when the user changes the Worksheet's selection).

Like the Workbook object, Excel creates a module for each Worksheet object. Initially, this module has the same name as the Worksheet. For example, suppose you create a new worksheet, and Excel names it Sheet4. Excel also creates a module named Sheet4.

If you open a Worksheet's module in the code editor, you can add event handlers to it. In the left combo box, select Worksheet. Then in the right combo box, select the event you want to catch. The code editor creates en empty event handler where you can place your code.

Range

Whenever you work with one or more cell values, you use a Range object. Practically every property or method that returns an object related to one or more cells returns a Range object. For information on creating Range objects using the Application object's Range property, see the "Range" section earlier in this chapter.

A Range can represent a cell, rectangular group of cells, or a collection of other Range objects. Because a Range can hold many different items, the online help refers to Range as a collection. To find more information on the Range object, search the online help for "Range Collection" or go to http://msdn.microsoft.com/library/en-us/vbaxl10/html/xlobjRange.asp.

The following sections describe some of the most useful Range properties and methods. The Range object supports no events.

Many of these properties apply only to a Range's first area. For instance, the address A1,D4 specifies two areas, each consisting of a single cell. Some properties, such as Columns, apply only to the first area. That means Range("A1,D4").Columns.Count returns 1 rather than 2 as you might expect. If you need to work with a Range that might contain more than one area, loop through the Areas collection described later.

Activate, Select, *and* Show

The Range object's Show method makes Excel scroll until the first cell in the Range is visible. Excel scrolls the worksheet to place the cell in the center of the window unless the cell occupies an early row (Z2) or column (A50) in which case placing it in the center of the screen would be impossible. If the Range is large or has multiple pieces spaced far apart, they may not all be visible after scrolling. Using Show does not change the worksheet's current selection.

The Select method selects the cells in the Range, scrolling to make the cells visible if necessary. After the Range is selected, the user can easily manipulate it interactively. VBA code can interact with the selected cells through the Selection object.

The online help says the Activate method selects a Range containing a single cell and tells you to use Select to select a Range containing more than one cell. In practice, Activate seems to be a bit more complicated. In at least some cases, if the current selection contains part of the Range you want to activate, the Activate method does nothing. For example, in the following code the first two statements both select their indicated Ranges as expected. For some reason, the third statement fails.

```
Range("Z20,Z30").Activate    ' Works.
Range("Y20,Z20").Activate    ' Works.
Range("Z20,Z30").Activate    ' Doesn't work.
```

To avoid confusing behavior, use the Select method instead of Activate.

Address

The Address property returns a string giving a Range's A1 or R1C1 specification. Parameters let you specify whether the row or column should be relative or fixed, and whether the address should use A1 or R1C1 notation. The following Debug window output shows a simple example. The code creates a Range including cells

Z20 through Z30. It then invokes that Range's Address method, indicating that the column should be relative and the result should use the R1C1 notation.

```
?Range("Z20:Z30").Address(ColumnAbsolute:=False, ReferenceStyle:=xlR1C1)
R20C[25]:R30C[25]
```

Areas *(C)*

The Areas collection contains Range objects representing the rectangular areas in the Range. These may not match the Range objects you used to compose the larger Range. For instance, the expression Range("C1:D10 A4:G5") specifies the intersection of the Ranges C1:D10 and A4:G5. That intersection is the Range C4:D5, which is neither of the Ranges used in the original statement.

The Areas collection also seems to produce incorrect results in some cases. The first two lines in the following output show that the Areas property for the Range defined by the previous example contains four Ranges. However, the next lines show that the first Range contains the entire area of intersection. If the code attempts to access the other three entries that the Areas collection thinks it contains, Excel raises an error. Use an On Error statement to protect your code against nonexistent areas.

```
?Range("C1:D10 A4:G5").Areas(1).Count
 4
?Range("C1:D10 A4:G5").Areas(2).Address
$C$4:$D$5
```

Formatting Properties and Methods

The Range object provides several properties and methods for formatting the cells it contains. Some of the more straightforward include Font, Style, NumberFormat, and Orientation.

The AutoFit method makes the Range adjust its row or column sizes to fit the values it contains. One quirk of this method is that the Range must contain only rows or only columns. You can use the Range's Rows and Columns properties to get new Ranges containing only rows or columns. The following code makes the current selection adjust its rows and columns to fit.

```
Selection.Rows.AutoFit     ' Fit row heights.
Selection.Columns.AutoFit  ' Fit column widths.
```

As you can probably guess from their names, the RowHeight and ColumnWidth properties let you adjust the Range's row heights and column widths explicitly. These properties make the sizes of all rows or columns in the Range the same. For example, the statement Selection.RowHeight = 10 makes all rows in the current selection have the same height. In contrast, the AutoFit method gives each row a size that fits its own contents.

The Interior property returns an object representing the Range's background area. It's the property you must use if you want to give the Range a colored background.

The Borders collection lets you specify border colors and styles for the Range. This collection's entries specify border styles for different borders. For example, the following code adds a red double line to the top of the selected cells.

```
With Selection.Borders(xlEdgeTop)
    .LineStyle = xlDouble
    .Color = vbRed
End With
```

Rather than defining borders one at a time for the top, bottom, and sides of a Range, you can use the BorderAround method to define them all at once. This method lets you specify the borders' line style, weight, and color. The following code makes a blue double border around cells B28 and C29.

 FILE *Ch08\CellNames.xls*

```
' Make a border around some cells.
Sub MakeBorders()
    Range("B28,C29").BorderAround LineStyle:=xlDouble, Color:=vbBlue
End Sub
```

To remove borders, loop through the items in the Borders collection and set each border's LineStyle to xlNone. The following code removes the border created by the previous code.

FILE *Ch08\CellNames.xls*

```
' Remove the borders.
Sub RemoveBorders()
Dim b As Border

    For Each b In Range("B28,C29").Borders
        b.LineStyle = xlNone
    Next b
End Sub
```

Item, Cells, Range, *and* Count

These properties provide different ways to access a Range's cells. The Item property provides access to the cells in the Range. You can provide either an item number or row and column offsets as parameters. If you provide an item number and the Range represents a rectangular area such as C2:E3, then Item returns the Range's cells as if they were reordered in a one-dimensional array. For the area C2:E3, the cells would be returned in the order C2, D2, E2, C3, D3, E3.

NOTE *You can use* Item *to refer to cells outside the* Range*. For the area C2:E3,* Item(7) *returns the cell C4. The* Item *property just extends the area as if it had more rows. This is a rather obscure trick, however, and it's possible that Microsoft could change this extended behavior of the* Item *property in some future release, so you should probably not do this.*

CAUTION *You can also use negative parameters to the* Item *method to access cells before the* Range*. These locations are harder to understand, however. For the area C2:E3, the value* Item(0) *returns cell B2, which is outside the* Range*. If you need to access cells relative to the beginning of the* Range *like this, use the row and column parameters described further on. This is another obscure trick that Microsoft could change in a later release, so you're better off leaving this alone.*

If the Range is not a simple rectangular area—for example Range("A1,C3,E5"), which selects three disconnected cells—the Item method gets somewhat confused and returns cells on the Range's first row. In the case of Range("A1,C3,E5"), Item returns the cells A1, A2, A3, and so forth.

If you provide the Item property with row and column offsets, the property acts as a two-dimensional array with position (1, 1) at the Range's starting cell. For example, Range("C3:H5").Item(1, 1) returns the cell C3. The statement Range("C3:H5").Item(2, 4) returns the cell one row down from C3 and three columns to the right, giving cell F4.

 TIP *You can pass negative row and column parameters to* Item *to find other cells outside the* Range. *For example,* Range("C3:H5").Item(0, –2) *returns cell A2. This isn't completely obvious, but it's a lot easier to understand than the fact that* Range("C3:H5").Item(–1) *returns cell A3.*

The Cells property returns a Range object that contains the cells in the Range. Because the Range object's default property is Item, you can follow Cells with row and column indexes to get a cell relative to the Range's starting cell. That makes the following three statements equivalent.

```
name_range.Item(4, 5).Select
name_range.Cells(4, 5).Select
name_range(4, 5).Select
```

Like the Cells property, the Range property returns a new Range object positioned relative to the current Range. The Range property, however, can return a Range object containing more than one cell. It also specifies the relative position of the new Range by using A1 notation instead of the more natural R1C1 notation.

For example, the following statement begins with the four cells C3:D4. It then selects the cells in B2:C3 relative to the Range. The value B2 adds one row and one column to the cell C3, giving cell D4. The value C4 adds three rows and two columns to the cell C3, giving cell E6. The result is the Range D4:E6.

```
Range("C3:D4").Range("B2:C4").Select
```

The Count property returns the number of cells in the Range. This includes only the cells actually part of the Range and not those that lie within the Range's rectangular bounds. For example, Range("A1,B2,C3").Count returns three because this Range contains only the three cells A1, B2, and C3.

Note that the `Item` and `Cells` properties will let you access cells such as A2 and B1, which lie within the `Range`'s bounds but are not part of the `Range`. This means you cannot use a `For` loop running from 1 to the `Range.Count` value to examine only the `Range`'s values. Instead you should use a `For Each` loop similar to the following.

FILE *Ch08\CellNames.xls*

```
' List the cells in a non-rectangular Range.
Sub ListRangeCells()
Dim rng As Range
Dim cell As Range

    Set rng = Range("A1,B2,C3")
    For Each cell In rng
        Debug.Print cell.Address
    Next cell
End Sub
```

Row and Column Properties

The `Range` object provides several properties for working with the rows and columns that contain it. The `EntireRow` and `EntireColumn` properties return `Ranges` that contain other `Ranges` representing the rows and columns containing the original `Range`, respectively. For example, the following statement works with a `Range` containing two `Ranges` representing columns B and E.

```
Range("B3,E1:E4").EntireColumn.Select
```

The `Range` object's `Rows` and `Columns` properties also return `Ranges` representing the original `Range`'s rows and columns. However, these `Ranges` represent the original `Range`'s cells more closely. For instance, the first statement in the following code makes every cell in columns B and C use a bold font. The second statement affects only the cells that are part of the `Range`.

```
Range("B2:C3").EntireColumns.Font.Bold = True
Range("B2:C3").Columns.Font.Bold = True
```

Both sets of properties define rows and columns, however, so you can use the AutoFit method with their resulting Ranges. Even then, the difference between the two sets of routines is significant. The first statement in the following code makes columns B and C resize to fit their contents. The second statement does almost the same thing, except it only considers the cells within the Range. If cell B5 (outside the Range) is wider than cells B2 and B3 (inside the Range), then it won't fit when the column resizes.

```
Range("B2:C3").EntireColumns.AutoFit
Range("B2:C3").Columns.AutoFit
```

Compared to these properties, the Row and Column properties are straightforward. They simply return the number of the first row and column in the Range's first area. For example, Range("D5:B3").Column returns 2 (B is the worksheet's second column).

Value Properties

The Value property sets or returns the value for the cells in a Range. You can set Value to a constant, such as 3.14159265, or to a formula, such as =SUM(A1:A10). When you read the Value property, it returns a cell's current evaluated result. For example, if you set a cell's Value to the formula =SUM(A1:A10), the Value property returns whatever the sum adds up to.

If the Range includes more than one cell, then the Value property returns a two-dimensional array of values. The following code shows how you can display the returned values.

 FILE *Ch08\CellNames.xls*

```
' List the values in a Range.
Sub ShowValues()
Dim v As Variant
Dim i As Long
Dim j As Long
```

```
    v = Range("B25:C26").Value
    For i = LBound(v, 1) To UBound(v, 1)
        For j = LBound(v, 2) To UBound(v, 2)
            Debug.Print v(i, j) & vbTab;
        Next j
        Debug.Print
    Next i
End Sub
```

The Formula property returns or sets the formula for a Range's cells. The Value property returns the formula's currently calculated result, and the Formula property returns the underlying formula.

The FormulaR1C1 property sets or returns the formula for a Range's cells in R1C1 notation.

If you use relative addressing with the Formula or FormulaR1C1 property, each cell is adjusted accordingly.

The HasFormula property returns True if all of the cells in a Range contain formulas, False if none of the cells contain formulas, or Null if some but not all of the cells contain formulas.

Clearing Methods

The Clear method clears the values and formatting from a Range. ClearContents removes the Range's values but not its formatting.

The Delete method removes the Range's cells. Its optional Shift parameter can be either xlShiftToLeft or xlShiftUp, which tell Excel whether to shift other cells left or up to fill the hole. If you omit the parameter, Excel decides based on the shape of the Range. For basically vertical Ranges such as B3:B9, Excel shifts cells left to fill in the hole. For mostly horizontal Ranges such as C5:E7, Excel shifts cells up to fill in the hole. If the Range is square, Excel shifts cells up. For strangely shaped disconnected regions, explicitly specify the direction you want cells moved.

 NOTE *The* Delete *method doesn't remove entire rows or columns, it just removes the cells in the* Range. *For example, if the* Range *includes C2:C3, then Excel moves all the cells to the right of those two cells left one position to fill in the missing positions. Cells on other rows are not moved.*

Fill Methods

The `FillDown`, `FillRight`, `FillLeft`, and `FillUp` methods fill a `Range` based on values already in it. For example, `Range("A1:G1").FillRight` fills in cells B1 through G1 based on the value currently in A1. If cell A1 contains the formula =SUM(A2:A11), then cell B1 receives the formula =SUM(B2:B11) and so forth.

Printing Methods

The `PrintPreview` method displays a picture of how the workbook would appear printed. The `PrintOut` method prints some or all of the workbook. Parameters let you specify the printer, pages to print, number of copies, and other options. See the online help or go to `http://msdn.microsoft.com/library/en-us/vbaxl10/html/xlmthPrintOut.asp` for details.

Sort

The `Sort` method makes Excel sort the data in a `Range`. Parameters tell it such things as which items to use as sorting keys, whether to sort ascending or descending, whether to perform a case-sensitive sort, and whether the `Range` contains a header row that should not be sorted with the rest of the data.

Summary

As you can see, the Excel object model is quite complicated. This chapter doesn't list every nook and cranny of the object model, but it does explain some of the objects that are most useful when writing Excel programs.

You may also want to spend some time exploring the online help. Search the online help for Microsoft Excel Objects to find a good starting place, or on the Web go to `http://msdn.microsoft.com/library/en-us/vbaxl10/html/xltocObjectModelApplication.asp`. The help for the basic object model provides links to the objects described here and others that may come in handy under different circumstances.

The objects described in this chapter should get you started when you need to perform a specific task. The online help and a few recorded macros can help fill any missing details.

CHAPTER 9

PowerPoint

ALTHOUGH POWERPOINT'S OBJECT MODEL is a bit smaller than Word's and Excel's, it's still a pretty hefty application. Fortunately, as is the case with the other Office applications, you don't really need to know every niggling detail of the object model. Instead, you can focus on understanding the objects that you need to perform most common PowerPoint programming tasks, such as creating slides, adding text, building tables, and working with animation settings. You can dig any remaining details out of the online help as necessary.

Microsoft Word groups a document's contents into text-like entities: sections, paragraphs, sentences, words, and so forth. Excel deals primarily with computations and values in a grid, so it provides tools for calculating values and formatting the results.

It helps to think of PowerPoint as basically a drawing program. Its purpose is to display simple graphics and pictures in a slide show. It just so happens that many of the graphics include text. Viewed in that light, it almost makes sense to set a slide's title using the following code. This statement begins with the second slide in the active presentation. It finds the Shape object named Rectangle 2 and sets its TextFrame property's TextRange value.

```
ActivePresentation.Slides(2).Shapes("Rectangle 2").TextFrame.TextRange = _
    "New Title"
```

If you think in terms of paragraphs and sentences, you will find PowerPoint's object model frustrating. Instead, think in terms of Shapes containing TextFrames that have TextRange properties.

The following section gives a brief overview of the PowerPoint object model. You can find more information on the PowerPoint object model by searching the online help for "Microsoft PowerPoint Objects" or by going to http://msdn.microsoft.com/library/en-us/vbapp10/html/pptocObjectModelApplication.asp.

The rest of the chapter explains some of the most important objects in greater detail.

Overview

Like the other Office applications, PowerPoint begins its object model with the `Application` object. This object contains properties and methods that let you access other PowerPoint objects representing presentations, slides, and so forth. It also includes methods for managing the PowerPoint application itself rather than a specific presentation or slide. For example, it includes properties for selecting printers, customizing command bars, selecting and searching for files, and creating new presentations. It also supports several events that your VBA code can catch.

The `Presentation` object represents a PowerPoint presentation. It provides tools for managing the presentation as a whole. For example, it includes properties for handling the presentation's color scheme, master slides, file location, and password protection.

The `Slide` object represents a slide in a presentation. This object includes properties and methods for managing the slide's appearance, contents, and position in the presentation.

The `Shape` object represents some sort of shape, such as a freeform drawing, picture, or text. Its properties allow you to specify the `Shape`'s appearance and contents. The related `ShapeRange` class lets you gather `Shapes` and manipulate them as a group. `ShapeRange` also provides methods for aligning and distributing `Shapes`.

The following section talks about where PowerPoint stores VBA code and how you can catch events. The rest of this chapter describes some of the most useful PowerPoint objects in greater detail.

Code Storage

Like Excel, PowerPoint stores VBA code inside a specific document. It has no central location similar to Normal.dot and other template files used by Word. One way you can provide shared VBA code is to make a PowerPoint Add-In. Chapter 4 tells how to build Add-Ins.

When you create a new PowerPoint presentation, it initially contains no code modules. You can add your own by using the Visual Basic IDE's Insert menu. For example, Insert ➤ Module adds a new code module to the project.

Although you can create your own modules, PowerPoint doesn't automatically associate any object modules with presentations or the slides contained by a presentation. That means you cannot easily catch events for those objects. The fact that the `Slide` and `Presentation` objects provide no events explains part of the reason for this problem.

The Application object does provide some support for events, however. It includes events generated by many of the objects in the PowerPoint object model, including events that arise at the presentation and slide level.

Like Excel, however, PowerPoint doesn't create an instance of the Application object for you, so catching its events is not trivial. If you want to catch the Application object's events, you must create a variable of type Application declared using the WithEvents keyword. VBA only allows the WithEvents keyword in an object module, so you need some kind of object to contain the variable.

One way to declare this variable is to use the Insert ► Class command to create a new class module. Give the module a variable declaration similar to the following.

```
Public WithEvents App As Application
```

Now you can select the App variable from the module's left dropdown. Then select the event you want to catch from the right dropdown and enter the code you want to execute when the event occurs. The following code shows event handlers triggered when PowerPoint moves to the next slide in a presentation and when it finishes a presentation.

 FILE *Ch09\Samples.ppt*

```
' The Application object whose events we will catch.
Public WithEvents App As Application

' Beep when we move to the next slide.
Private Sub App_SlideShowNextSlide(ByVal Wn As SlideShowWindow)
    Beep
End Sub

' The slide show is finished. Say "Ta da!"
Private Sub App_SlideShowEnd(ByVal Pres As Presentation)
    MsgBox "Ta da!"
End Sub
```

This code defines event handlers for the `Application` object stored in the variable `App`, but you still need to instantiate the class and make `App` refer to the main `Application` object. You can do that using code similar to the following. You should place this code in a normal code module and execute it before you want to catch the events.

 FILE *Ch09\Samples.ppt*

```
' The object that watches for Application events.
Private m_ApplicationWatcher As ApplicationWatcher

' Prepare an ApplicationWatcher object to catch Application events.
Sub LoadApplicationWatcher()
    Set m_ApplicationWatcher = New ApplicationWatcher
    Set m_ApplicationWatcher.App = Application
End Sub
```

If you execute this code and then run a presentation, PowerPoint beeps before it displays each slide. It displays the "Ta da!" message box after you view the last slide and close the presentation.

Unfortunately, this method requires you to manually execute code that initializes the `ApplicationWatcher`. One way to make the process more automatic is to create an Add-In. Chapter 4 explains how to build a PowerPoint Add-In that automatically initializes a variable declared using the `WithEvents` keyword when PowerPoint starts.

Application

The top-level object in the PowerPoint hierarchy is the `Application` object. This object provides access to features that do not relate directly to a specific presentation or slide inside a PowerPoint document. For example, it includes properties for selecting printers, customizing command bars, and creating new presentations.

The `Application` object also provides properties and methods for accessing the other objects in the PowerPoint object model. For instance, its `Presentations` collection contains `Presentation` objects representing each of the presentation files currently loaded into PowerPoint. The `ActivePresentation` property returns a reference to the currently active `Presentation`.

The following sections describe the most useful `Application` object properties, methods, and events.

Properties

The following sections describe some of the `Application` object's most useful properties. Those that are collections are followed with a (C).

Active Object Properties

The `ActivePresentation`, `ActivePrinter`, and `ActiveWindow` properties tell you which objects are currently active. When you write a tool to help interactively build a PowerPoint presentation, your code will probably use the `ActivePresentation` property to work with the presentation the user is currently editing.

CommandBars (C)

The `CommandBars` collection represents the command bars displayed by PowerPoint. You can use this collection to customize PowerPoint's tools. Often you can make customizations manually, but automatic customization can be helpful for giving different users different tools or for performing complex customizations quickly (for example, if you need to install the same customizations for several users).

The following code adds a new button to the Standard `CommandBar` that executes the `MakeNewSlide` macro when pressed. `MakeNewSlide` adds a new slide to the `ActivePresentation`'s `Slides` collection, selects it, and sets the text in its title and bulleted list.

 FILE *Ch09\Samples.ppt*

```
' Make a new CommandBar button.
Sub MakeButton()
Dim new_button As CommandBarButton
Dim file_name As String

    ' Create the button.
```

```
    Set new_button = Application.CommandBars("Standard").Controls.Add( _
        Type:=msoControlButton)

    ' Give it a picture.
    file_name = ActivePresentation.Path & "\NewSlideButton.bmp"
    new_button.Picture = LoadPicture(file_name)
    new_button.OnAction = "MakeNewSlide"
End Sub


' Add a new slide.
Sub MakeNewSlide()
    With ActivePresentation.Slides.Add( _
            ActivePresentation.Slides.Count + 1, ppLayoutText)
        .Select
        .Shapes("Rectangle 2").TextFrame.TextRange.Text = "This is the Title"
        .Shapes("Rectangle 3").TextFrame.TextRange.Text = _
            "Bullet Point 1" & vbCrLf & _
            "Bullet Point 2" & vbCrLf & _
            "Bullet Point 3"
    End With
End Sub
```

DisplayAlerts

The DisplayAlerts property determines whether code that encounters a dialog displays it or silently accepts the dialog's default. This property is described here mostly to contrast it with similar properties provided by Excel.

If an Excel macro tries to close a document that has unsaved changes, the program normally displays a dialog asking the user to decide whether to save the changes, discard the changes, or cancel the document closure. One trick for closing a document without saving the changes in Excel is to set DisplayAlerts to False. Then, when the code closes the document, Excel silently takes the default action of not saving the changes (an odd default).

 TIP *It's better to use an Excel document's Close method, explicitly telling it to discard the changes.*

This trick isn't necessary with PowerPoint. If a PowerPoint macro calls a `Presentation` object's `Close` method, it closes immediately without saving any changes. The code must explicitly call the `Presentation` object's `Save` or `SaveAs` method first to save the changes.

CAUTION *This could cause a nasty bug if you are expecting behavior similar to Excel's. If your code simply closes* Presentation *objects, expecting PowerPoint to protect against lost changes, your users may come after you with pitchforks.*

FileDialog *(C)*

`FileDialog` is a collection of objects representing standard file open and save dialogs. The index into this collection should be one of the values `msoFileDialogFilePicker`, `msoFileDialogFolderPicker`, `msoFileDialogOpen`, or `msoFileDialogSaveAs`.

The `FileDialog` object provides only two methods: `Show` and `Execute`. `Show` displays the dialog and returns True if the user clicked the OK button or False if the user clicked Cancel. The `Execute` method makes the dialog perform its associated action. For example, it makes an open dialog open the selected file.

The `Filters` collection contains objects representing filters the user can select to pick different kinds of files. The following code lists the filters available by default to the open file dialog.

FILE *Ch09\Samples.ppt*

```
' List the filters available for the File Open dialog.
Sub ListOpenFilters()
Dim i As Long

    With Application.FileDialog(msoFileDialogOpen)
        For i = 1 To .Filters.Count
            Debug.Print .Filters(i).Description & " (" & _
                .Filters(i).Extensions & ")"
        Next i
    End With
End Sub
```

The following text shows the output on one computer. Note that the All Out-
lines entry is broken across two lines.

```
All Files (*.*)
All PowerPoint Presentations (*.ppt;*.pps;*.pot;*.htm;*.html;*.mht;*.mhtml)
Presentations and Shows (*.ppt;*.pps)
Web Pages and Web Archives (*.htm, *.html, *.mht, *.mhtml)
Design Templates (*.pot)
Harvard Graphics 3.0 Shows (*.sh3)
Harvard Graphics 3.0 Charts (*.ch3)
Freelance Windows 1.0-2.1 (*.pre)
All Outlines
(*.txt;*.rtf;*.doc;*.xls;*.xlw;*.wps;*.wpd;*.wk1;*.wk3;*.wk4;*.mcw;*.wpt)
PowerPoint Add-Ins (*.ppa)
```

The following code provides a more interesting example. It loads an open file
dialog, removes its existing filters, and adds filters to select .ppt files or all files. It
displays the dialog and, if the user clicks OK, prints the names of the selected files.

The code then selects another `FileDialog` entry to reset the filters for the file
open dialog. It finishes by displaying the current number of filters for a file open
dialog.

FILE *Ch09\Samples.ppt*

```
' Select a file using *.ppt and *.* filters only.
Sub SelectFile()
Dim i As Long

    With Application.FileDialog(msoFileDialogOpen)
        .AllowMultiSelect = True
        .InitialFileName = ActivePresentation.Path
        .Filters.Clear
        .Filters.Add "All Files", "*.*"
        .Filters.Add "Presentations", "*.ppt"
        Debug.Print .Filters.Count & " filters"

        ' Select the first filter (All Files).
        .FilterIndex = 1
```

```
        ' Display the dialog and see if the user clicks OK.
        If .Show Then
            ' Display the selected files.
            For i = 1 To .SelectedItems.Count
                Debug.Print .SelectedItems(i)
            Next i
        End If
    End With

    ' Access another dialog to reset the filters.
    i = Application.FileDialog(msoFileDialogSaveAs).Filters.Count

    ' Display the number of file open filters now.
    Debug.Print Application.FileDialog(msoFileDialogOpen).Filters.Count & _
        " filters"
End Sub
```

The `FileDialog` property is very similar to the version provided by Excel. The difference is that the Excel version provides Excel-related filters whereas the PowerPoint version provides PowerPoint-related filters. For more information, see the "FileDialog" section in the Chapter 8. You can also check PowerPoint's online help or go to http://msdn.microsoft.com/library/en-us/vbaof10/html/zofobjFileDialog.asp.

Presentations *(C)*

The `Presentations` collection contains `Presentation` objects representing each of the currently open PowerPoint presentations. This collection's `Add` method lets you programmatically create a new presentation. For example, the following code creates a new presentation, saves it in the file NewPresentation.ppt, and closes it.

FILE *Ch09\Samples.ppt*

```
' Make a new presentation.
Sub MakePresentation()
Dim new_presentation As Presentation

    ' Make the new presentation telling Add to not
    ' display the presentation in a visible window.
    Set new_presentation = Presentations.Add(msoTrue)
```

```
    ' Add a slide.
    With ActivePresentation.Slides.Add(1, ppLayoutText)
        .Select
        .Shapes("Rectangle 2").TextFrame.TextRange.Text = "This is the Title"
        .Shapes("Rectangle 3").TextFrame.TextRange.Text = _
            "Bullet Point 1" & vbCrLf & "Bullet Point 2" & _
            vbCrLf & "Bullet Point 3"
    End With

    ' Save the new presentation.
    new_presentation.SaveAs "NewPresentation.ppt"
    new_presentation.Close
End Sub
```

NOTE *When you first create it, a new presentation contains no slides. Use the* Presentation *object's* Slides.Add *method to give it slides as shown in this example.*

Methods

The Application object's two most useful methods are Run and Quit.

Run executes a macro by name. The method's first parameter is the macro's name. The method can take any number of following parameters to pass to the macro. Run returns whatever value the macro returns.

The DemonstrateRun subroutine shown in the following code calls the Run method passing it the macro name MakeNewListSlide. It passes the word Color and some color names as parameters for the macro.

The MakeNewListSlide macro makes a new slide and uses its first parameter as the new slide's title. It concatenates its remaining parameters, separating them with carriage returns, and sets the new slide's list text to the result.

FILE *Ch09\Samples.ppt*

```
' Demonstrate the Application.Run method.
Sub DemonstrateRun()
    Application.Run "MakeNewListSlide", "Colors", "Red", "Green", "Blue", _
        "Yellow", "Orange", "Purple"
End Sub


' Add a new list slide.
Sub MakeNewListSlide(ParamArray parameters() As Variant)
Dim i As Long
Dim txt As String

    With ActivePresentation.Slides.Add( _
            ActivePresentation.Slides.Count + 1, ppLayoutText)
        .Select
        ' Use the first parameter as the title.
        .Shapes("Rectangle 2").TextFrame.TextRange.Text = parameters(0)

        ' Combine the other parameters into a string.
        For i = 1 To UBound(parameters)
            txt = txt & vbCrLf & parameters(i)
        Next i
        If Len(txt) > 0 Then txt = Mid$(txt, Len(vbCrLf) + 1)

        ' Set the list.
        .Shapes("Rectangle 3").TextFrame.TextRange.Text = txt
    End With
End Sub
```

The Application object's Quit method immediately closes PowerPoint. Any unsaved changes to open files are discarded. If you want to save the changes, use the Presentation object's Save or SaveAs methods before you call Quit.

Events

The Application object provides the only really useful events supported by the PowerPoint object model. Most of these events are self-explanatory. The most useful are described in Table 9-1.

Table 9-1. Application *Object Events*

EVENT	WHEN IT FIRES
ColorSchemeChanged	The presentation's color scheme changes.
NewPresentation	The PowerPoint user creates a new presentation.
PresentationBeforeSave	A presentation is about to be saved.
PresentationClose	A presentation closes.
PresentationNewSlide	A presentation adds a new slide.
PresentationOpen	PowerPoint opens a presentation.
PresentationPrint	PowerPoint is printing.
PresentationSave	PowerPoint saves a presentation.
SlideSelectionChanged	The slide selection changes.
SlideShowBegin	A presentation starts.
SlideShowEnd	A presentation ends.
SlideShowNextSlide	A presentation displays its next slide.

See the online help for more information on particular events.

NOTE *Remember that PowerPoint doesn't automatically create an object module that you can use to catch these events. You must declare your own variable of type* Application *by using the* WithEvents *keyword and initialize it. For more information on this, see the section "Code Storage" earlier in this chapter.*

Presentation

The Presentation object represents a PowerPoint presentation. It provides tools for managing a presentation as a whole, as opposed to working with the slides within the presentation.

The following sections describe the most useful of the Presentation object's properties and methods. This object provides no events. The Application object described earlier in this chapter provides events you can use instead.

Properties

The following sections describe the Presentation object's most useful properties. See the online help for other properties.

BuiltinDocumentProperties *(C) and* CustomDocumentProperties *(C)*

The BuiltinDocumentProperties collection contains DocumentProperty objects that define built-in workbook properties. Those objects have Name, Type, and Value properties that define the items.

The ListBuiltInDocumentProperties subroutine shown in the following code calls subroutine ListProperties, passing it the BuiltInDocumentProperties collection. That routine loops through the collection printing each property's name, data type, and value.

 FILE *Ch09\Samples.ppt*

```
' Display the built-in document properties.
Sub ListBuiltInDocumentProperties()
    ' List the properties.
    ListProperties ActivePresentation.BuiltInDocumentProperties
End Sub

' Display the document properties.
Function ListProperties(ByVal properties As DocumentProperties) As String
Dim i As Long
Dim col_wid As Long

    ' Get the first column's width.
    For i = 1 To properties.Count
        If col_wid < Len(properties(i).Name) Then
            col_wid = Len(properties(i).Name)
        End If
    Next i

    ' Add some padding.
    col_wid = col_wid + 3

    ' Display the properties.
    For i = 1 To properties.Count
        With properties(i)
            Debug.Print Format$(.Name, "!" & String(col_wid, "@"));
            Select Case .Type
                Case msoPropertyTypeBoolean
```

```
                    Debug.Print "Boolean    ";
                Case msoPropertyTypeDate
                    Debug.Print "Date       ";
                Case msoPropertyTypeFloat
                    Debug.Print "Float      ";
                Case msoPropertyTypeNumber
                    Debug.Print "Number     ";
                Case msoPropertyTypeString
                    Debug.Print "String     ";
            End Select

            On Error Resume Next
            Debug.Print Format$(.Value);
            On Error GoTo 0
            Debug.Print
        End With
    Next i
End Function
```

The CustomDocumentProperties collection is similar to BuiltinDocumentProperties except that you can add and remove items from it. The following code removes any existing custom properties and then creates some new ones.

The CustomDocumentProperties's Add method (which is the collection's most interesting feature) takes parameters giving the value's name, a flag telling whether the property should be linked to data, the value type (msoPropertyTypeBoolean, msoPropertyTypeDate, msoPropertyTypeFloat, msoPropertyTypeNumber, or msoPropertyTypeString), the value itself, and a link data source (if the earlier parameter indicates that the value should be linked).

NOTE *Both the* BuiltinDocumentProperties *and* CustomDocumentProperties *collections have type* DocumentProperties. *To learn more about their properties and methods, search the online help for "DocumentProperties Collection Object."*

FILE *Ch09\Samples.ppt*

```
' Add a couple custom document properties.
Sub AddCustomProperties()
    With ActivePresentation
        ' Delete all current properties.
        Do While .CustomDocumentProperties.Count > 0
            .CustomDocumentProperties(1).Delete
        Loop

        ' Add some new properties.
        .CustomDocumentProperties.Add "A string", False, _
            msoPropertyTypeString, "http://www.vb-helper.com/office.htm"
        .CustomDocumentProperties.Add "A number", False, _
            msoPropertyTypeNumber, 20
        .CustomDocumentProperties.Add "A float", False, _
            msoPropertyTypeFloat, 1.23
        .CustomDocumentProperties.Add "A Boolean", False, _
            msoPropertyTypeBoolean, False
        .CustomDocumentProperties.Add "A date", False, _
            msoPropertyTypeDate, #1/30/1983#
    End With
End Sub
```

Subroutine `ListCustomDocumentProperties` in Ch09\Samples.ppt lists custom document properties much as subroutine `ListBuiltInDocumentProperties` does. See the code for details.

Fonts *(C)*

The `Fonts` collection lists the fonts currently used by the presentation. You cannot add or remove items from this collection. This collection updates itself as you change the fonts in the presentation. For instance, if you create some text using a new font, the `Fonts` collection updates to include the new font.

While you cannot add or remove fonts using the `Fonts` collection, this property provides a `Replace` method that you can use to replace one font with another. For instance, if you decide to change all instances of the Arial font to Comic Sans MS, you can use the `Replace` method to make the change in one step as shown in the following code.

```
ActivePresentation.Fonts.Replace "Arial", "Comic Sans MS"
```

You can also change the font for a specific piece of text as shown in the following rather sprawling statement.

```
ActivePresentation.Slides(1).Shapes(2).TextFrame.TextRange.Font.Name = "Arial"
```

Master Properties

PowerPoint lets you define standard presentation features by using *masters*. These are similar to templates that apply to different pieces of the presentation. Different masters define the appearance of slides, handouts, notes, and titles.

For example, the slide master defines the general appearance of slides. The slide master can define the slides' background (color, shading, fill style, and so forth), color scheme, logos or drawings, and text styles.

 NOTE *Masters are not quite the same as the templates used by Word. A Word template can define a document's initial text, VBA code, events, command bar buttons, and other functional items. A PowerPoint master defines the appearance of part of the presentation.*

The Presentation object's SlideMaster, HandoutMaster, NotesMaster, and TitleMaster properties return masters that determine the appearance of the slides, handouts, notes, and slides that use the title layout.

Changes to a master immediately affect all of the items that refer to that master. For instance, if you change the background shading on the slide master, all of the slides use the same shading.

You can find a particular slide's master by using the Slide object's Master property. For example, the following code changes the background on the master associated with the active presentation's second slide to a gradient. If this slide is a title slide, its master is the title master, so any other title slides would immediately change to display the gradient. If the slide is not a title slide, its master is the slide master, so all other nontitle slides would switch to display the gradient.

```
ActivePresentation.Slides(2).Master.Background.Fill.PresetGradient _
    Style:=msoGradientHorizontal, _
    Variant:=1, _
    PresetGradientType:=msoGradientDaybreak
```

The following code sets the background for the same slide. This version first sets the slide's `FollowMasterBackground` property to `msoFalse` so that changing its master doesn't affect the other slides.

FILE *Ch09\Samples.ppt*

```
' Give a single slide a gradient background.
Sub SingleSlideMasterGradient()
    ActivePresentation.Slides(2).FollowMasterBackground = msoFalse
    ActivePresentation.Slides(2).Background.Fill.PresetGradient _
        Style:=msoGradientHorizontal, _
        Variant:=1, _
        PresetGradientType:=msoGradientDaybreak
End Sub
```

Your code can also use a `SlideRange` object to modify several slides' masters at once. The following code changes the background style of the active presentation's slides number 2 and 4.

FILE *Ch09\Samples.ppt*

```
' Give a SlideRange a gradient background.
Sub SlideRangeMasterGradient()
    With ActivePresentation.Slides.Range(Array(2, 4))
        .FollowMasterBackground = msoFalse
        .Background.Fill.OneColorGradient _
            Style:=msoGradientVertical, _
            Variant:=1, _
            Degree:=1
        .Background.Fill.BackColor.RGB = RGB(0, 128, 255)
        .Background.Fill.ForeColor.RGB = RGB(255, 128, 0)
    End With
End Sub
```

The title master applies to slides that have a title layout. The `Presentation` object's `HasTitleMaster` property returns True if the presentation has a title master. The `AddTitleMaster` method creates a new title master.

 CAUTION *If the presentation already has a title master, trying to create a new one raises an error. Trying to access the title master when the presentation does not have one also causes an error. Use the* HasTitleMaster *property to see if the title master exists before you do anything with it.*

The following code creates a new title master and gives it a gradient background. The background affects title slides but not other slides.

 FILE *Ch09\Samples.ppt*

```
' Give the title master a gradient background.
Sub TitleMasterGradient()
    If Not ActivePresentation.HasTitleMaster Then
        ActivePresentation.AddTitleMaster
    End If

    ActivePresentation.TitleMaster.Background.Fill.PresetGradient _
        Style:=msoGradientHorizontal, _
        Variant:=1, _
        PresetGradientType:=msoGradientDaybreak
End Sub
```

The following code deletes the presentation's title master. After this code runs, all title slides revert to the settings defined by the slide master.

```
If ActivePresentation.HasTitleMaster Then
    ActivePresentation.TitleMaster.Delete
End If
```

Name, Path, *and* FullName

The Name property gives the presentation's file name. Path returns the file's path. FullName returns the complete file name including the path.

Password *and* WritePassword

The Password property sets the presentation's password. PowerPoint assumes that if the file is open, the code you execute should have permission to change the password. Set the Password property to an empty string to remove password protection.

NOTE *Code can read the Password property, but it always returns the string ******** whether there is a password or not, so this isn't terribly useful. It probably would have made more sense if Microsoft had made this a write-only property.*

The WritePassword property works much as the Password property does. Set its value to place a write password on the presentation and prevent users from modifying the file without the password. Set WritePassword to an empty string to remove the write password.

NOTE *Unfortunately, the* Application.Presentations.Open *method doesn't take a password as a parameter, so your code cannot open a password-protected file without the user's help. When your code tries to open a protected file, Power-Point prompts the user for the password.*

Saved

The Saved property indicates whether the Presentation has been saved since its last modification.

When VBA code calls a Presentation object's Close method, PowerPoint closes the presentation without saving any changes and without warning the user. On the other hand, if the user closes a presentation that has unsaved changes, Power-Point warns the user and asks if it should save the modifications. Your VBA code can set the Presentation object's Saved property to true to "trick" PowerPoint into thinking the presentation has no unsaved changes. Then if the user closes the presentation, PowerPoint discards any changes without warning.

This trick could make PowerPoint discard changes the user has made, thus really annoying the user. You may be able to find a valid use for this technique, but you had better ensure that the users' changes are safe if you don't want a small-scale riot on your hands.

SlideShowSettings

This property returns an object of type SlideShowSettings that contains an assort-ment of properties and methods for controlling the presentation's slide show. Table 9-2 describes some of the most useful of these properties. You can set these properties to control how the slide show runs.

Table 9-2. Useful SlideShowSettings *Properties*

PROPERTY	PURPOSE
AdvanceMode	Indicates how the presentation should move from one slide to the next. This property can take the values ppSlideShowManualAdvance (you must manually move from slide to slide), ppSlideShowUseSlideTimings (the presentation automatically moves from slide to slide using previously recorded slide timings), or ppSlideShowReherseNewTimings. (I haven't figured out what ppSlideShowReherseNewTimings does, if anything. E-mail me if you know.)
EndingSlide	Determines the index of the last slide to run.
LoopUntilStopped	Determines whether the slide show continues looping until the user presses Escape. For example, you can set AdvanceMode to ppSlideShowUseSlideTimings and LoopUntilStopped to msoTrue to make the presentation run in a loop noninteractively.
StartingSlide	Determines the index of the first slide to run.
RangeType	Indicates the set of slides to display. This property can take the values ppShowAll (display all slides), ppShowNamedSlideShow (display a particular slide), or ppShowSlideRange (display a Range of slides).

NOTE *If your code programmatically sets* SlideShowSettings *properties, the values are saved with the presentation and are used later even if you run the presentation interactively. For example, if you set* RangeType = ppShowSlideRange, StartingSlide = 2, *and* EndingSlide = 3, *then when you later run the presentation interactively, you will only see slides 2 and 3. (Of course, if you close the presentation you must save changes to save these values.)*

The SlideShowSettings object's only method, Run, displays the slide show. The following example sets the slide show transition for slides 2, 3, and 4 so they automatically advance after two seconds. It then uses SlideShowSettings properties to prepare for a continuous loop of those slides and runs the presentation.

FILE *Ch09\Samples.ppt*

```
' Display slides 2-4 in a loop until the user presses Escape.
Sub ShowSlides2to4()
    ' Make all slides advance after 2 seconds.
    With ActivePresentation.Slides.Range(Array(2, 3, 4)).SlideShowTransition
        .AdvanceOnTime = msoTrue
        .AdvanceTime = 2
    End With

    ' Display the presentation.
    With ActivePresentation.SlideShowSettings
        ' Show slides 2-4 in a loop.
        .RangeType = ppShowSlideRange
        .StartingSlide = 2
        .EndingSlide = 4
        .LoopUntilStopped = msoTrue

        ' Start the presentation.
        .Run().Activate
    End With
End Sub
```

The Run method launches the presentation asynchronously and immediately returns control to the VBA code. The VBA code that starts the presentation cannot take further action after the presentation finishes because Run doesn't wait until the presentation is over. That means a single VBA routine cannot change a presentation's properties, run, and then reset the properties. If you need to reset properties or take other action after the presentation finishes, use the Application object's SlideShowEnd event.

The RunPresentationLoop subroutine, shown in the following code and contained in a normal code module, creates a new ApplicationWatcher object (described shortly). It sets that object's App property to refer to the current Application object so the ApplicationWatcher can receive application events.

The routine saves the presentation's AdvanceMode and LoopUntilStopped properties. It then loops through the presentation's slides, saving their timing information and setting each to advance automatically after one second.

Finally, the routine uses the SlideShowSettings object to display the presentation in a loop until stopped. The Run method returns immediately and the code ends, but the presentation keeps running.

FILE *Ch09\Loop.ppt*

```
' The object that watches for Application events.
Private m_ApplicationWatcher As ApplicationWatcher


' Prepare an ApplicationWatcher object to catch
' Application events. Save the presentation's
' settings.
Sub RunPresentationLoop()
Dim the_slide As Slide

    ' Prepare the ApplicationWatcher object.
    Set m_ApplicationWatcher = New ApplicationWatcher
    Set m_ApplicationWatcher.App = Application

    ' Save AdvanceMode and LoopUntilStopped.
    m_ApplicationWatcher.OldAdvanceMode = _
        ActivePresentation.SlideShowSettings.AdvanceMode
    m_ApplicationWatcher.OldLoopUntilStopped = _
        ActivePresentation.SlideShowSettings.LoopUntilStopped
```

```
    ' Save the slide timings and set them to 1 second.
    Set m_ApplicationWatcher.OldAdvanceOnTime = New Collection
    Set m_ApplicationWatcher.OldAdvanceTime = New Collection
    For Each the_slide In ActivePresentation.Slides
        m_ApplicationWatcher.OldAdvanceOnTime.Add _
            the_slide.SlideShowTransition.AdvanceOnTime
        m_ApplicationWatcher.OldAdvanceTime.Add _
            the_slide.SlideShowTransition.AdvanceTime
        the_slide.SlideShowTransition.AdvanceOnTime = msoCTrue
        the_slide.SlideShowTransition.AdvanceTime = 1
    Next the_slide

    ' Display the presentation in an
    ' automatically advancing loop.
    ActivePresentation.SlideShowSettings.AdvanceMode = _
        ppSlideShowUseSlideTimings
    ActivePresentation.SlideShowSettings.LoopUntilStopped = True
    ActivePresentation.SlideShowSettings.Run().Activate
End Sub
```

The ApplicationWatcher class, shown in the following code, catches the presentation's SlideShowEnd event. It restores the application and slide properties saved by subroutine RunPresentationLoop. The routine finishes by setting the ApplicationWatcher object's App variable to Nothing so the object no longer receives application events.

 FILE *Ch09\Loop.ppt*

```
' The Application object whose events we will catch.
Public WithEvents App As Application

Public OldAdvanceMode As PpAdvanceMode
Public OldLoopUntilStopped As Boolean
Public OldAdvanceOnTime As Collection
Public OldAdvanceTime As Collection

' Restore saved slide show settings.
Private Sub App_SlideShowEnd(ByVal Pres As Presentation)
Dim i As Integer
```

```
          Debug.Print "Restoring saved values"

          ' Restore AdvanceMode and LoopUntilStopped.
          ActivePresentation.SlideShowSettings.AdvanceMode = OldAdvanceMode
          ActivePresentation.SlideShowSettings.LoopUntilStopped = OldLoopUntilStopped

          ' Restore the slide timings.
          For i = 1 To ActivePresentation.Slides.Count
              ActivePresentation.Slides(i).SlideShowTransition.AdvanceOnTime = _
                  OldAdvanceOnTime(i)
              ActivePresentation.Slides(i).SlideShowTransition.AdvanceTime = _
                  OldAdvanceTime(i)
          Next i
          Set OldAdvanceOnTime = Nothing
          Set OldAdvanceTime = Nothing

          ' Don't catch events any more.
          Set App = Nothing
      End Sub
```

Slides *(C)*

The Slides collection provides access to the slides in the presentation. A slide's position in the collection is the same as its position in the presentation. In other words, Slides(3) is the third slide you would see while running the presentation.

This collection provides several methods for finding and creating slides. The Add method makes a new slide. The InsertFromFile method copies slides from an existing PowerPoint presentation into the current one. The Paste method copies the slides in the clipboard into the presentation. All three of these methods take parameters that indicate the position where the new slides should be created.

 TIP *One way to place slides in clipboard is to use a* SlideRange *object's* Copy *or* Cut *method. You can also interactively select one or more slides in the Slide Sorter, Outline, or Slides views and press Ctrl-C.*

The Slides collection's Range method returns a SlideRange object representing a subset of the presentation's slides. If you use Range without any parameters, the SlideRange represents all the slides in the collection. This method can also take as a parameter either the index of a single slide or an array of slide indexes. For instance, the following code makes a SlideRange object representing slides 3, 5, 7, and 9. It then calls the SlideRange's Delete method to remove the slides from the presentation.

```
ActivePresentation.Slides.Range(Array(3, 5, 7, 9)).Delete
```

The Slides collection's last interesting method is FindSlideByID. When you create a new slide, PowerPoint assigns it a unique slide ID. Unlike a slide's position in the Slides collection, this ID never changes, even if you move the slide to a different part of the presentation.

Unfortunately, slide IDs are not particularly meaningful values and you have no control over their assignment. About all they are good for is returning to a previously visited slide. For example, when a program creates a new slide, it can save the slide's ID in a variable. Later it can use that value to quickly relocate the slide.

You could also create a slide ID database. Then you could look up the slide using its title, name, or some piece of data stored in the database. You could then use the saved ID to quickly find the slide again.

Usually, it's easier to loop through the Slides collection searching for the slide you want. If you need to work with a slide often, you can also set its Name property and use that value as an index into the Slides collection as in ActivePresentation.Slides("Overview").Delete. See the section "SlideID, SlideIndex, SlideNumber, and Name" later in this chapter for more information on slide names.

Methods

The following sections describe some of the Presentation object's more useful methods. Note that this object provides no events.

AddTitleMaster

This method adds a title master to the presentation. Any slide that uses a title style follows the format of this master if it exists. Note that trying to access the title master if it doesn't exist raises an error, as does trying to add a title master when one already exists. For more information on masters, see the section "Master Properties" earlier in this chapter.

Close

The Close method immediately closes the presentation without saving any recent changes. If you want to save changes, you must call the Presentation object's Save or SaveAs method before you call Close.

Merge

The Merge method merges another presentation into the one currently open. The following code provides an example that merges file A.ppt into the active presentation.

 FILE *Ch09\Merge.ppt*

```
' Merges the presentation with A.ppt.
Sub MergePresentation()
    ActivePresentation.Merge "A.ppt"
End Sub
```

PowerPoint places a marker at the beginning of the presentation to represent the new slides. Click the marker and select one or more slides to add them to the presentation. Figure 9-1 shows the marker as a little document with a pencil above it. The marker is just to the left of the four-item popup menu.

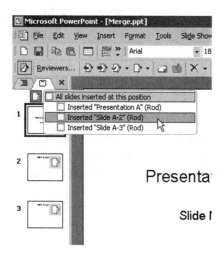

Figure 9-1. Use the marker's popup menu to insert some or all of the merged presentation's slides.

Even after you save the presentation, the markers represent any merged slides. You can click on the markers to show or hide specific slides. Right-click on a marker and select Delete Marker to remove it permanently.

PrintOut

The `PrintOut` method lets you print some or all of the presentation's slides. The `Presentation` object's `PrintOptions` property sets such options as how many slides should go on a page, whether PowerPoint should print hidden slides, and whether it should draw a frame around the slides.

Save, SaveAs, *and* SaveCopyAs

The `Save` method saves the presentation in its original file.

The `SaveAs` method saves the presentation in a new file. It also lets you specify the file format. For example, if you select the GIF file format, `SaveAs` creates a new directory with the name you specify and places one GIF image file for each slide in the new directory.

When you create a new presentation, PowerPoint initially assigns it a catchy name such as Presentation4. If you call the `Save` method for this new file, Power-Point saves the file as Presentation4.ppt in the current directory. Use the `SaveAs` method to give the new file a more meaningful name.

The `SaveCopyAs` method saves the presentation in a new file but keeps it open with its original name. For example, suppose you are working on the file Budget.ppt. Every so often you could call `SaveCopyAs` to save a new version of the presentation in the files Budget001.ppt, Budget002.ppt, Budget003.ppt, and so forth. Better still, your code could put the current date and time in the file names. When you were finished, you could use the `Save` method to save the presentation in its original file Budget.ppt. You would end up with a series of versions of the file saved as you worked.

Slide **and** SlideRange **(C)**

The `Slide` object represents a slide in a presentation. This object includes proper-ties and methods for managing the slide's appearance, contents, and position in the presentation.

The `SlideRange` collection represents a notes page or a group of slides. The `SlideRange` object provides many of the same properties and methods that the `Slide` object provides. You can use these properties to modify all of the slides in the `SlideRange` at once rather than modifying the slides separately.

The most common way to make a SlideRange is to use the Slides collection's Range method. If you use this method with no parameters, it returns a SlideRange representing all of the slides. If you pass Range the name or index of a slide in the Slides collection, the resulting SlideRange represents the single slide. Finally, you can pass Range an array of indexes and slide names to make a SlideRange representing a group of slides.

For example, the following code makes a SlideRange containing slide 3 and the slide named Authors. It then calls the SlideRange's Delete method to delete the slides.

```
Dim target_range As SlideRange

Set target_range = ActivePresentation.Slides.Range(Array(3, "Authors"))
target_range.Delete
```

NOTE *When you create a slide, PowerPoint initially gives it a name like Slide7. You can programmatically set a* Slide *object's* Name *property; for example,* ActivePresentation.Slides(7).Name = "Authors".

The following sections describe some of the Slide object's most useful properties and methods. The SlideRange provides many of the same features, where they make sense. For instance, all slides must have unique names so the SlideRange object's Name property only works if the SlideRange represents a single slide.

Properties

The following sections describe the Slide object's most useful properties. Those that are collections are followed by (C). See the online help to learn which also apply to the SlideRange object.

Background *and* FollowMasterBackground

Use this property to specify the slide's background appearance. Note that the slide displays the appearance of its corresponding master unless you set its FollowMasterBackground property to msoFalse. For example, the following code gives slide 6 its own background.

```
ActivePresentation.Slides(6).FollowMasterBackground = msoFalse
ActivePresentation.Slides(6).Background.Fill.PresetGradient _
    Style:=msoGradientDiagonalDown, _
    Variant:=1, _
    PresetGradientType:=msoGradientCalmWater
```

The following code makes slide 6 once again follow the style specified by its master.

```
ActivePresentation.Slides(6).FollowMasterBackground = msoTrue
```

NOTE *The slide's master is either the slide master or, if this is a title slide and the title master exists, the title master.*

ColorScheme

This property returns a `ColorScheme` object representing the slide's colors in RGB (red, green, and blue) numeric values. The `ColorScheme` object's `Colors` property is a collection of eight `RGBColor` objects that represent the colors used by the slide. The `RGBColor` object's most useful property is `RGB`, which gets or sets the color's numeric value. For example, the following code sets the title color of the active presentation's seventh slide to a dark red.

```
ActivePresentation.Slides(7).ColorScheme(ppTitle).RGB = RGB(192, 0, 0)
```

The index into the `ColorScheme` collection can take the predefined values `ppTitle` (title color), `ppShadow` (color for object shadows), `ppBackground` (the slide background color), `ppForeground` (nontitle text and other foreground objects such as lines), `ppFill` (color for filled objects such as AutoShapes), `ppAccent1` ("accent" color), `ppAccent2` (hyperlink color), and `ppAccent3` (color for hyperlinks that have been followed). These colors are also used by default to fill in chart regions.

The following code sets the colors for a slide's color scheme. Download the ColorScheme.ppt presentation and look at the slide to see the results.

FILE *Ch09\ColorScheme.ppt*

```
' Set the ColorSamples slide's color scheme colors.
Sub SetColorScheme()
    With ActivePresentation.Slides("ColorSamples")
        With .ColorScheme
            .Colors(ppTitle) = vbRed
            .Colors(ppForeground) = vbBlue
            .Colors(ppBackground) = RGB(192, 192, 192)
            .Colors(ppFill) = vbYellow
            .Colors(ppShadow) = vbWhite

            .Colors(ppAccent1) = RGB(0, 128, 255)    ' Accent.
            .Colors(ppAccent2) = RGB(255, 128, 0)    ' Hyperlink.
            .Colors(ppAccent3) = RGB(255, 128, 128) ' Followed hyperlink.
        End With

        ' Make the title's shadow visible.
        With .Shapes("Title").Shadow
            .Visible = True
            .OffsetX = 3
            .OffsetY = 3
        End With
    End With
End Sub
```

DisplayMasterShapes

This property determines whether the slide displays any shapes that are on its master. For example, you can place rectangles, ovals, and other shapes on the slide master to create a generally pleasant (or unpleasant) appearance. By default, slides will display those shapes. You can set DisplayMasterShapes to False on certain slides to make them omit the shapes so they are less cluttered or easier to understand.

Layout

The Layout property determines the slide's general layout. Changing the layout of an existing slide will not remove objects that it already contains, although it may move them around and change their appearance.

For instance, a slide with Layout set to ppLayoutText normally displays a centered title at the top and a bulleted list of items beneath, as shown in Figure 9-2.

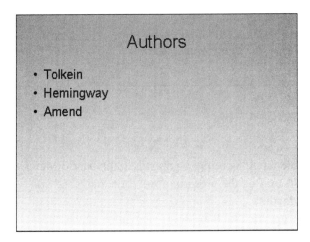

Figure 9-2. When Layout = ppLayoutText, *the slide displays a centered title and bulleted list.*

If you change Layout to ppLayoutTitle, PowerPoint applies the title master format, which can rearrange things significantly, as shown in Figure 9-3.

Figure 9-3. When Layout = ppLayoutTitle *style, the slide uses the title master.*

The Layout property can take one of more than two-dozen values. To see a list of the allowed values, see the online help for the Layout property or got to http://msdn.microsoft.com/library/en-us/vbapp10/html/ppproLayout.asp. Open the Slide and SlideRange topic and click the PpSlideLayout link.

TIP *You should manually review any slide whose layout you change to make sure it looks OK. For instance, the change may make text wrap at awkward places.*

Master

This property returns a `Master` object representing the master that currently determines the slide's appearance. This may be the presentation's slide master or title master, depending on the slide's layout.

The `Master` object provides properties such as `Background`, `ColorScheme`, `Shapes`, and `TextStyles` to determine the appearance of the slides it controls.

SlideID, SlideIndex, SlideNumber, *and* Name

When you create a new slide, PowerPoint assigns it a numeric `SlideID`. This ID doesn't change even if you reorder the slides, so you can use it to permanently identify a particular slide. Unfortunately, PowerPoint doesn't assign meaningful values, and you cannot change them. There's little reason for you to remember that the Productivity slide was assigned ID 9. If you build a similar presentation later, PowerPoint may assign the same slide a different number, so your code can't rely on a particular ID number in different presentations.

 TIP *You could build a database listing the IDs assigned for one or more presentations.*

The `SlideIndex` property returns a slide's position in the `Slides` collection. This value changes when you reorder the slides, so it's not a great way to identify a particular slide.

`SlideNumber` is the number displayed in the slide's lower-right corner if slide numbers are displayed. The `Presentation` object's `PageSetup.FirstSlideNumber` property determines the number displayed for the first slide. For instance, the following code sets the presentation's first slide number to 100. It then displays the first slide's `SlideIndex` and `SlideNumber` properties. In this example, `SlideIndex` is 1 and `SlideNumber` is 100.

```
ActivePresentation.PageSetup.FirstSlideNumber = 100
Debug.Print ActivePresentation.Slides(1).SlideIndex      ' 1
Debug.Print ActivePresentation.Slides(1).SlideNumber     ' 100
```

As you can surely guess, the Name property gives the slide's name. Like the SlideID property, Name doesn't change if you rearrange the slides. If you assign a slide a meaningful name, this property is much more meaningful than a number arbitrarily assigned by PowerPoint.

The following code creates a new slide and sets its name. Later, the code finds the slide and changes its title.

```
' Add a new Productivity slide.
With ActivePresentation.Slides.Add( _
        ActivePresentation.Slides.Count + 1, ppLayoutText)
    .Name = "Productivity"
    ' Set the title, text, etc.
    ...
End With

' Change the title.
ActivePresentation.Slides("Productivity"). _
    Shapes("Rectangle 2").TextFrame.TextRange.Text = "Employee Productivity"
```

TIP *Right after you create a new slide, assign it a unique, meaningful name so you can find it easily later.*

NotesPage

This property returns a SlideRange object representing the slide's notes page. Use its properties and methods to add or modify the slide's notes. For instance, the following code adds a note to slide 8.

FILE *Ch09\Samples.ppt*

```
' Add some notes to slide 8.
Sub MakeNotes()
    With ActivePresentation.Slides(8).NotesPage
        .Shapes("Rectangle 3").TextFrame.TextRange.Text = _
            "These are some authors." & vbCrLf
    End With
End Sub
```

Shapes *(C)*

The Shapes collection holds references to the slide's objects. These shapes can include rectangles containing text, stars, action buttons, arcs, balloons, arrows, and a whole host of other items.

The Shapes collection provides special methods to make creating different kinds of objects easier. For example, it has AddCurve, AddLabel, AddLine, AddPicture, AddPolyline, AddShape, and AddTitle methods.

Some of these methods have restrictions. For instance, the AddTitle method only restores a title that you previously removed. If you call AddTitle on a slide that already contains a title or that cannot contain a title (for example, on a slide with blank nontitle layout), PowerPoint raises an error.

The following code uses the Shapes collection in a couple ways. First, it creates a new slide of type text. Next, it finds the new slide's shapes named Rectangle 2 and Rectangle 3, and changes their names to the more meaningful values Title and ListItems, respectively. The program sets values for those shapes, does some formatting of the ListItems object's fonts, and then calls subroutine DrawCycloid.

DrawCycloid generates a series of line segments that define a cycloid and uses the Shapes collection's AddLine method to draw them on the slide. Don't worry too much about the mathematics behind subroutine DrawCycloid. The important point is to notice how the routine creates lines on the slide. The result is shown in Figure 9-4 on page 447.

 FILE *Ch09\Samples.ppt*

```
' Add a new slide.
Sub MakeCycloidSlide()
Dim new_slide As Slide
```

```
        Set new_slide = ActivePresentation.Slides.Add( _
            ActivePresentation.Slides.Count + 1, ppLayoutText)
        With new_slide
            ' Give the title and list shapes more
            ' meaningful names.
            .Shapes("Rectangle 2").Name = "Title"
            .Shapes("Rectangle 3").Name = "ListItems"

            ' Set the title and list text.
            .Shapes("Title").TextFrame.TextRange.Text = "Cycloid"
            .Shapes("ListItems").TextFrame.TextRange.Text = _
                "Defined by the equations:" & vbCrLf & _
                vbCrLf & _
                "    Xt = 150 * (27 * Cos(t) + 15 * Cos(t * 20 / 7)) / 42 + 400" & _
                vbCrLf & _
                "    Yt = 150 * (27 * Sin(t) + 15 * Sin(t * 20 / 7)) / 42 + 300" & _
                vbCrLf & vbCrLf & _
                "where 0 <= t <= 14 * Pi"
            With .Shapes("ListItems").TextFrame.TextRange
                .Paragraphs.Font.Size = 16
                .Paragraphs.ParagraphFormat.Bullet.Visible = msoFalse
                .Paragraphs(1).Font.Size = 20
                .Paragraphs(.Paragraphs.Count).Font.Size = 20
            End With

            ' Add a cycloid.
            DrawCycloid new_slide
        End With
End Sub

' Draw a cycloid.
Sub DrawCycloid(ByVal new_slide As Slide)
Const PI = 3.14159265
Dim X1 As Single
Dim Y1 As Single
Dim X2 As Single
Dim Y2 As Single
Dim t As Single
Dim dT As Single

    ' Find the first point.
    t = 0
    dT = PI / 30
```

```
        next_pt = 1
    X2 = Xt(t)
    Y2 = Yt(t)

    ' Add the rest of the points.
    t = t + dT
    Do While t < 14 * PI
        next_pt = next_pt + 1
        X1 = X2
        Y1 = Y2
        X2 = Xt(t)
        Y2 = Yt(t)
        new_slide.Shapes.AddLine X1, Y1, X2, Y2

        t = t + dT
    Loop

    ' Add the last point.
    t = 0
    X1 = X2
    Y1 = Y2
    X2 = Xt(t)
    Y2 = Yt(t)
    new_slide.Shapes.AddLine X1, Y1, X2, Y2
End Sub

Function Xt(ByVal t As Single) As Single
    Xt = 150 * (27 * Cos(t) + 15 * Cos(t * 20 / 7)) / 42 + 530
End Function

Function Yt(ByVal t As Single) As Single
    Yt = 150 * (27 * Sin(t) + 15 * Sin(t * 20 / 7)) / 42 + 350
End Function
```

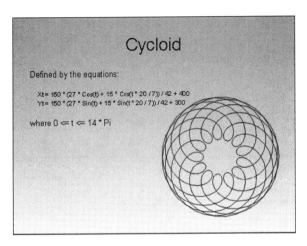

Figure 9-4. The Shapes *collection's AddLine method can draw complex shapes such as cycloids.*

Methods

The following sections describe the Slide object's most useful methods.

Copy, Cut, Delete, *and* Duplicate

The Copy, Cut, and Delete methods work as you would expect. Copy places a copy of the slide on the clipboard. Cut places a copy on the clipboard and removes the slide from the presentation. Delete simply removes the slide from the presentation.

> **NOTE** Cut *and* Delete *remove slides from the presentation, so the remaining slides are renumbered. Their* SlideID *values don't change, but their* SlideIndex *and* SlideNumber *properties may.*

The Duplicate method makes a new copy of the slide and places it after the slide being duplicated. It returns a SlideRange object representing the new slide so you can work with it immediately. (Hint: give it a meaningful name!)

You can then use the MoveTo method to move the new slide to some other location. For example, the following code makes a copy of the slide named Section2 and moves it to the end of the presentation.

FILE *Ch09\Samples.ppt*

```
' Make a copy of the Section2 slide and move it to the end.
Sub DuplicateSectionSlide()
Dim new_slide As SlideRange

    Set new_slide = ActivePresentation.Slides("Section2").Duplicate
    new_slide.Name = "Section3"
    new_slide.MoveTo ActivePresentation.Slides.Count

    ' Modify the slide...
    ' ...
End Sub
```

Export

This method lets you save a file in a different format. For example, you could save a slide in EMF, GIF, or JPEG format. Use the File ➤ Save As command and click the "Save as type" combo box to get an idea of what export formats are supported.

The following code saves the active presentation's first slide in the file Start Slide.gif. The final parameters give the dimension of the saved picture in pixels.

FILE *Ch09\Samples.ppt*

```
' Export slide 1 as a GIF.
Sub ExportSlide1()
    ActivePresentation.Slides(1).Export _
        "Start Slide.gif", ".gif", 400, 300
End Sub
```

If you call this method for a `SlideRange` containing more than one slide, PowerPoint saves only the first slide. You can use the `Presentation` object's `SaveAs` method to quickly export more than one slide. For example, the following code makes a `SlideRange` holding the slides it wants to export. It calls that object's `Copy` method to copy the slides onto the clipboard.

Next, it creates a temporary `Presentation` object without giving it a window. It pastes the copied slides into the presentation and calls `SaveAs` to save the result in a series of GIF files within the directory named Slides 1 to 3. It finishes by deleting the temporary presentation.

 FILE *Ch09\Samples.ppt*

```
' "Export" slides 1 through 3 as GIFs in the
' directory "Slides 1 to 3".
Sub ExportSlides1to3()
    ' Copy slides 1 through 3 to the clipboard.
    ActivePresentation.Slides.Range(Array(1, 2, 3)).Copy

    ' Make a temporary presentation.
    With Application.Presentations.Add(WithWindow:=msoFalse)
        ' Paste slides 1 through 3 into it.
        .Slides.Paste

        ' Save the temporary presentation as type GIF.
        .SaveAs "Slides 1 to 3", ppSaveAsGIF

        ' Delete the temporary presentation.
        .Close
    End With
End Sub
```

 CAUTION *In this code, the new presentation doesn't have the same master settings as the original, so the slides don't look exactly the same when you use* SaveAs *versus* Export. *If you want them to look exactly the same, you must copy the master values over to the new presentation. It may be easier just to use* Export *to save each slide individually.*

MoveTo

This method moves the slide to a new position in the presentation. Its parameter gives the new index that the slide should have. The slide is first removed, then the remaining slides are moved to close the gap. Next, the slide is inserted in its new position, pushing back the slides after it to make room if necessary.

Select

This method selects the slide. If the presentation is in Normal or Slide Sorter view (View ➤ Normal or View ➤ Slide Sorter), this displays the slide.

Shape **and** ShapeRange **(C)**

The Shape object represents an object in a Slide's drawing layer. That includes AutoShapes, freeform shapes, OLE objects, and pictures.

The ShapeRange collection represents a group of Shapes much as a SlideRange represents a group of Slides. The ShapeRange provides properties and methods for modifying the Shapes it contains. It also provides methods for aligning and distributing its Shapes.

Properties

The following section describes use properties provided by the Shape and ShapeRange objects. Those that are collections are followed by (C).

Just as most Slide properties and methods also apply to SlideRanges, most of the Shape properties and methods apply to ShapeRanges, where they make sense. For instance, the Name property only works for a ShapeRange that contains exactly one Shape, because it wouldn't make sense to get or set the name for more than one Shape at a time.

ActionSettings *(C)*

This collection holds two ActionSetting objects that determine the actions the object takes when the mouse interacts with it during a presentation. Use the predefined indexes ppMouseClick and ppMouseOver to identify the ActionSetting object you want.

For example, the following statement sets a Shape's mouse click action to ppActionEndShow so it ends the presentation if the user clicks it.

```
the_shape.ActionSettings(ppMouseClick).Action = ppActionEndShow
```

The following more complex example creates a new slide and adds a rectangular Shape to it. It sets the Shape's actions so that it runs the SayTada macro when clicked and plays a chime sound effect when the mouse moves over it.

NOTE *The* Shapes.AddShape *method takes parameters that give the new shape's type (rectangle in this example), left coordinate, top coordinate, width, and height. It returns a* Shape *object.*

FILE *Ch09\Samples.ppt*

```
' Make a slide with a shape that has actions.
Sub MakeActionSlide()
Dim new_shape As Shape

    ' Make the slide.
    With ActivePresentation.Slides.Add( _
            ActivePresentation.Slides.Count + 1, ppLayoutText)
        .Select
        .Name = "ActionSlide"
        .Shapes("Rectangle 2").TextFrame.TextRange.Text = "Action!"
        .Shapes("Rectangle 3").Delete

        ' Make the shape, centered.
        Set new_shape = .Shapes.AddShape( _
            msoShapeRectangle, _
            (ActivePresentation.PageSetup.SlideWidth - 300) / 2, _
            (ActivePresentation.PageSetup.SlideHeight - 200) / 2, _
            300, 200)
        new_shape.ActionSettings(ppMouseClick).Action = ppActionRunMacro
        new_shape.ActionSettings(ppMouseClick).Run = "SayTada"
        new_shape.ActionSettings(ppMouseOver).SoundEffect.Name = _
            "chime"
```

```
        End With
End Sub


' Display a message box.
Sub SayTada()
    MsgBox "Tada!"
End Sub
```

See the online help or go to `http://msdn.microsoft.com/library/en-us/` `vbapp10/html/ppobjActionSetting.asp` for more information on `ActionSetting` objects.

AnimationSettings

This property returns an object of type `AnimationSettings` that determines how the `Shape` is animated. For example, you could make a shape glide smoothly onto the slide from the left. (For an example, see the "List" section in the code described shortly.)

Table 9-3 describes some of the `AnimationSettings` object's more useful properties.

Table 9-3. Useful `AnimationSettings` *Properties*

PROPERTY	MEANING
AdvanceMode	Determines whether the animation happens when the user clicks the slide or after a specified amount of time.
AdvanceTime	The time to wait before running the animation.
AfterEffect	Determines what the Shape does after the animation has finished. For example, it might dim or hide.
Animate	Must be msoTrue for animation to occur.
AnimationOrder	The order in which the Shape is animated on the slide if the slide contains more than one animated shape.
DimColor	The color the Shape should become when it dims because of AfterEffect.
EntryEffect	Determines how the Shape appears on the slide. Examples include ppEffectAppear (it just pops up), ppEffectCrawlFromRight, ppEffectDissolve, and ppEffectFlyFromLeft.
SoundEffect	The sound to play while the animation occurs.

The following example demonstrates several animation techniques. The code creates a new slide and sets its title so that after half a second, it animates using a dissolve effect and playing the standard "chime" sound. The text starts bright blue and dims to a darker blue when the animation finishes.

Next, the code adds three items to the slide's list area. It makes the text fly in from the right while playing the "whoosh" sound. This text also dims when its animation finishes. PowerPoint is smart enough to figure out that this text is in a list, so it automatically animates the lines in the list one at a time.

The program then creates a 16-point star shape with a light blue background and a thick border. The star's animation makes it simply appear while playing the "laser" sound.

 FILE *Ch09\Samples.ppt*

```
' Make a slide with animation settings.
Sub MakeAnimatedSlide()
Dim new_shape As Shape

    ' Remove the slide if it exists.
    On Error Resume Next
    ActivePresentation.Slides("AnimatedSlide").Delete
    On Error GoTo 0

    ' Make the slide.
    With ActivePresentation.Slides.Add( _
            ActivePresentation.Slides.Count + 1, ppLayoutText)
        .Select
        .Name = "AnimatedSlide"

        ' Title.
        With .Shapes("Rectangle 2")
            .TextFrame.TextRange.Text = "Animated Slide"
            .TextFrame.TextRange.Font.Color.RGB = RGB(0, 0, 255)
            With .AnimationSettings
                .Animate = msoTrue
                .AdvanceMode = ppAdvanceOnTime
                .AdvanceTime = 0.5
                .TextLevelEffect = ppAnimateByFirstLevel
                .EntryEffect = ppEffectDissolve
                .AfterEffect = ppAfterEffectDim
                .DimColor.RGB = RGB(0, 0, 128)
                .AnimationOrder = 1
                .SoundEffect.Name = "chime"
```

```
                End With
            End With

            ' List.
            With .Shapes("Rectangle 3")
                .TextFrame.TextRange = "Animal" & vbCrLf _
                    & "Mineral" & vbCrLf & "Vegetable"
                .TextFrame.TextRange.Font.Color.RGB = RGB(255, 0, 0)
                With .AnimationSettings
                    .Animate = msoTrue
                    .AdvanceMode = ppAdvanceOnTime
                    .AdvanceTime = 0.5
                    .TextLevelEffect = ppAnimateByFirstLevel
                    .EntryEffect = ppEffectFlyFromRight
                    .AfterEffect = ppAfterEffectDim
                    .DimColor.RGB = RGB(128, 0, 0)
                    .AnimationOrder = 2
                    .SoundEffect.Name = "whoosh"
                End With
            End With

            ' Make an animated star.
            With .Shapes.AddShape( _
                    msoShape16pointStar, _
                    (ActivePresentation.PageSetup.SlideWidth - 300) / 2, _
                    ActivePresentation.PageSetup.SlideHeight - 300, _
                    300, 200)
                .Fill.BackColor.RGB = RGB(0, 128, 255)
                .Line.Weight = 10
                With .AnimationSettings
                    .Animate = msoTrue
                    .AdvanceMode = ppAdvanceOnTime
                    .AdvanceTime = 0.5
                    .EntryEffect = ppEffectAppear
                    .AnimationOrder = 3
                    .SoundEffect.Name = "laser"
                End With
            End With
        End With
    End Sub
```

AutoShapeType

This property determines the kind of figure an AutoShape object displays. Power-Point defines more than 100 AutoShape types, a few of which are shown in Figure 9-5.

Figure 9-5. PowerPoint defines more than 100 AutoShape *types.*

The following code generated the slide shown in Figure 9-5.

  FILE *Ch09\Samples.ppt*

```
' Make a slide demonstrating some AutoShapes.
Sub MakeAutoShapes()
Dim shape_types As New Collection
Dim R As Long
Dim C As Long
Dim col_wid As Single
Dim row_hgt As Single

    shape_types.Add msoShapeFlowchartOr
    shape_types.Add msoShapeIsoscelesTriangle
    shape_types.Add msoShapeLeftRightArrow
    shape_types.Add msoShapeLightningBolt
    shape_types.Add msoShapeMoon
```

```
        shape_types.Add msoShapePentagon
        shape_types.Add msoShapePlaque
        shape_types.Add msoShapeQuadArrow
        shape_types.Add msoShape8pointStar
        shape_types.Add msoShapeWave
        shape_types.Add msoShapeBalloon
        shape_types.Add msoShapeSmileyFace
        shape_types.Add msoShapeUTurnArrow
        shape_types.Add msoShapeCube
        shape_types.Add msoShapeCircularArrow
        shape_types.Add msoShapeDonut

        ' Remove the slide if it exists.
        On Error Resume Next
        ActivePresentation.Slides("AutoShapes").Delete
        On Error GoTo 0

        ' Make the slide.
        With ActivePresentation.Slides.Add( _
                ActivePresentation.Slides.Count + 1, ppLayoutBlank)
            .Select
            .Name = "AutoShapes"

            col_wid = ActivePresentation.PageSetup.SlideWidth \ 4
            row_hgt = ActivePresentation.PageSetup.SlideHeight \ 4
            For R = 0 To 3
                For C = 0 To 3
                    .Shapes.AddShape _
                        shape_types(R * 4 + C + 1), _
                        C * col_wid, R * row_hgt, col_wid, row_hgt
                Next C
            Next R
        End With
End Sub
```

To see the complete list of AutoShape types, search the online help for
"AutoShapeType Property" or go to http://msdn.microsoft.com/library/en-us/
vbapp10/html/ppproAutoShapeType.asp and click the MsoAutoShapeType link.

BlackWhiteMode

This property determines how the Shape should appear when viewed in black-and-white mode, as on a printer. Table 9-4 describes the allowed values.

Table 9-4. BlackWhiteMode *Values*

VALUE	MEANING
msoBlackWhiteAutomatic	PowerPoint decides how to draw the shape.
msoBlackWhiteBlack	PowerPoint draws the shape as black.
msoBlackWhiteBlackTextAndLine	PowerPoint draws the shape's text and lines. Results may vary and may look like msoBlackWhiteGrayScale.
msoBlackWhiteDontShow	PowerPoint doesn't draw the shape.
msoBlackWhiteGrayOutline	PowerPoint draws the shape as a gray outline.
msoBlackWhiteGrayScale	PowerPoint draws the shape using a grayscale. This generally gives the best noncolor results if your printer can handle it.
msoBlackWhiteHighContrast	PowerPoint draws the shape's lines.
msoBlackWhiteInverseGrayScale	PowerPoint draws the shape using an inverted grayscale so dark areas appear light and vice versa.
msoBlackWhiteLightGrayScale	PowerPoint draws the shape using a lighter grayscale. The shapes may look washed out.
msoBlackWhiteWhite	PowerPoint draws the shape in white.

Fill *and* Line

The Fill property returns a FillFormat object that determines how the object is filled. Using this object's properties and methods, you can define the Shape's fill color, background pattern, color gradient, and other background properties.

The FillFormat object provides several methods for defining fill types. These include OneColorGradient, Patterned, PresetGradient, PresetTextured, Solid, TwoColorGradient, UserPicture, and UserTexture.

For example, the following code fragment creates a new slide and adds a rectangle. It then sets the new Shape's foreground and background colors, and calls its TwoColorGradient method. It passes this method the parameter msoGradientHorizontal, so the result is a horizontal color gradient shaded smoothly from red at the top (the foreground color) to blue at the bottom (the background color).

```
With ActivePresentation.Slides.Add( _
        ActivePresentation.Slides.Count + 1, ppLayoutBlank)
    .Name = "FilledShapes"
    With .Shapes.AddShape(msoShapeRectangle, GAP, GAP, wid, hgt).Fill
```

```
        .ForeColor.RGB = vbRed
        .BackColor.RGB = vbBlue
        .TwoColorGradient msoGradientHorizontal, 1
    End With
End With
```

The other `FillFormat` methods are similar. See the online help for details.

The `Line` property returns a `LineFormat` object that determines how the `Shape` should draw lines. This object's properties let you specify line characteristics including color, thickness, dash style (solid, dashed, dotted, dash-dotted, and so forth), pattern, and arrowheads at both ends.

The following example creates a new slide and adds a rectangle to it. The code then formats the rectangle's border blue, dashed, and extra thick.

```
With ActivePresentation.Slides.Add( _
        ActivePresentation.Slides.Count + 1, ppLayoutBlank)

    ' Make the shape, centered.
    With .Shapes.AddShape( _
            msoShapeRectangle, _
            (ActivePresentation.PageSetup.SlideWidth - 300) / 2, _
            (ActivePresentation.PageSetup.SlideHeight - 200) / 2, _
            300, 200).Line
        ' Set line properties.
        .ForeColor.RGB = vbBlue
        .DashStyle = msoLineDash
        .Weight = 5
    End With
End With
```

GroupItems *(C)*

This property returns a `GroupShapes` collection containing individual `Shapes` in a group. For example, you might draw a series of lines to represent some business process. You can group the lines to make working with them easier.

A `ShapeRange` object's `Group` method joins its `Shapes` into a group represented by a single `Shape` object in the slide's `Shapes` collection. You can use the `Shape`'s `GroupItems` property to work with the `Shapes` contained inside the group without ungrouping them.

HasDiagram, HasDiagramNode, HasTable, *and* HasTextFrame

These properties indicate whether the Shape contains a diagram, diagram node, table, or text frame, respectively. You can use them to determine which of these items is available before you work with them. For example, you can verify that a Shape has a TextFrame before you try to set its TextFrame.TextRange.Text property.

left, Top, Width, *and* Height

These properties specify in points the Shape's size and position.

NOTE *One point is defined as 1/72nd of an inch.*

Id *and* Name

When you create a new Shape, PowerPoint assigns it an Id and Name. The Id identifies the Shape, but it is not a particularly meaningful number.

The Name property is slightly more descriptive. Initially, PowerPoint assigns a name, such as Rectangle 1, Oval 3, or AutoShape 2. These names are unique on a particular slide, although different slides could have Shapes that share the same name.

TIP *Even these names tell only what the shape is, not what it means. If you will need to refer to a* Shape *later, set its* Name *property to something more descriptive right after you create it.*

LockAspectRatio

This property determines whether the Shape preserves its aspect ratio (ratio of height to width) when the user resizes it. Normally, a user can click and drag a shape's corner drag handle to change its height and width at the same time. If LockAspectRatio is msoTrue, then dragging the corner drag handle changes the shape's size while preserving the aspect ratio.

> **NOTE** *The user can still drag the side grab handles to change the shape's width or height without modifying the other dimension, thus changing the aspect ratio.*

Programmatically, if your VBA code changes a Shape's width or height while LockAspectRatio is msoTrue, PowerPoint automatically changes the other dimension to keep the same aspect ratio.

For example, the following code sets LockAspectRatio to msoTrue for the second Shape on slide 15. It then doubles the Shape's Width. PowerPoint automatically doubles the Shape's height to preserve the aspect ratio.

```
ActivePresentation.Slides(15).Shapes(2).LockAspectRatio=msoTrue
ActivePresentation.Slides(15).Shapes(2).Width = _
    2 * ActivePresentation.Slides(15).Shapes(2).Width
```

Table

This property returns a Table object for a Shape that contains a table. This object's properties and methods let you work with the table's rows, columns, and cells.

The following code makes a new slide and uses its AddTable method to add a table Shape to it. It uses the new Shape's Table property to get a reference to the Table object. It then uses that object's Cell method to place text in the table.

FILE *Ch09\Samples.ppt*

```
' Make a slide containing a table.
Sub MakeTableSlide()
Const NUM_ROWS = 8
Const NUM_COLS = 4
Dim new_slide As Slide
Dim new_shape As Shape
Dim new_table As Table
Dim R As Long
Dim C As Long
```

```
    ' Make a new slide.
    Set new_slide = ActivePresentation.Slides.Add( _
        ActivePresentation.Slides.Count + 1, ppLayoutTitleOnly)
    new_slide.Shapes("Rectangle 2").TextFrame.TextRange.Text = "New Table Slide"

    ' Add a table.
    Set new_shape = new_slide.Shapes.AddTable(NUM_ROWS, NUM_COLS)
    Set new_table = new_shape.Table

    ' Fill in some table values.
    For R = 1 To NUM_ROWS
        For C = 1 To NUM_COLS
            new_table.Cell(R, C).Shape.TextFrame.TextRange.Text = _
                "(" & R & ", " & C & ")"
        Next C
    Next R
End Sub
```

TextFrame

This property returns a TextFrame object that represents the Shape's text and positioning. The following example creates a new slide and adds three rectangles. It uses the Shapes' TextFrame properties to position text in different parts of the rectangles.

```
' Make a slide showing text justification.
Sub JustifyText()
    ' Remove the slide if it exists.
    On Error Resume Next
    ActivePresentation.Slides("Justify").Delete
    On Error GoTo 0

    ' Make the new slide.
    With ActivePresentation.Slides.Add( _
      ActivePresentation.Slides.Count + 1, ppLayoutBlank)
        .Name = "Justify"

        With .Shapes.AddShape(msoShapeRectangle, 260, 50, 200, 100)
            .TextFrame.TextRange.Text = "Top Left"
            .TextFrame.TextRange.ParagraphFormat.Alignment = ppAlignLeft
            .TextFrame.VerticalAnchor = msoAnchorTop
        End With
```

```
        With .Shapes.AddShape(msoShapeRectangle, 50, 50, 200, 100)
            .TextFrame.TextRange.Text = "Centered"
        End With
        With .Shapes.AddShape(msoShapeRectangle, 470, 50, 200, 100)
            .TextFrame.TextRange.Text = "Bottom Right"
            .TextFrame.TextRange.ParagraphFormat.Alignment = ppAlignRight
            .TextFrame.VerticalAnchor = msoAnchorBottom
        End With
    End With
End Sub
```

One of the most important properties of the TextFrame object is TextRange. The TextRange object has its own properties and methods for manipulating the text contained in the Shape. The most important of those is the Text property, which sets the Shape's text. The following statement shows the complete path you must follow through the objects to set the text in the first slide's first object.

```
ActivePresentation.Slides(1).Shapes(1).TextFrame.TextRange.Text = "Hello"
```

Type

This read-only property returns the type of the Shape. Values include msoAutoShape, msoGroup, msoTable, and msoTextBox. You set the Shape's type when you create it using a method similar to Shapes.AddShape or Shapes.AddTable.

Methods

The following sections describe some of the most useful methods provided by the Shape and ShapeRange objects.

PickUp *and* Apply

The PickUp method copies the Shape's formatting. Apply applies the copied formatting to a Shape. The following code shows how you might copy the formatting from Shape(1) to Shape(2) on the active presentation's first slide.

```
With ActivePresentation.Slides(1)
    .Shapes(1).PickUp
    .Shapes(2).Apply
End With
```

Copy, Cut, Delete, *and* Duplicate

The Copy and Cut methods perform their usual functions—copying or cutting the Shape to the clipboard. Use the Shapes.Paste method to paste the copy onto another slide. For instance, the following code copies the third Shape from slide 11 onto slide 15.

```
ActivePresentation.Slides(11).Shapes(3).Copy
ActivePresentation.Slides(15).Shapes.Paste
```

Delete removes the Shape from its slide.

Duplicate makes a copy of the Shape on the same slide. The new Shape is offset slightly so it doesn't sit exactly on top of the original Shape.

Align, Distribute, Group, *and* Ungroup

The ShapeRange object provides these methods for arranging Shapes on a slide.

The Align method lines up Shapes along their edges or centers. Align takes two parameters. The first tells which part of the objects to align and can take the values msoAlignBottoms, msoAlignCenters (horizontally), msoAlignLefts, msoAlignMiddles (vertically), msoAlignRights, and msoAlignTops.

The second parameter indicates whether the Shapes should be aligned to the slide's edge or center. For example, if this parameter is msoTrue and the first parameter is msoAlignLefts, the Shapes are aligned so their left edges lie along the slide's left edge. If this parameter is msoFalse and the first parameter is msoAlignLefts, the Shapes are aligned so their left edges lie along the leftmost of the Shapes' left edges.

The first statement in the following code aligns all the Shapes on slide 16 so they line up with the left edge of the leftmost Shape. The second statement aligns the Shapes on slide 17 so they all have top edges along the top of the slide.

```
ActivePresentation.Slides(16).Shapes.Range().Align msoAlignLefts, msoFalse
ActivePresentation.Slides(17).Shapes.Range().Align msoAlignTops, msoTrue
```

The Distribute method spaces the Shapes evenly. This method's parameters indicate whether the Shapes should be spaced vertically (msoDistributeVertically) or horizontally (msoDistributeHorizontally), and whether they should be spaced across the whole slide (msoTrue) or only the area they currently occupy (msoFalse). The following statement distributes the Shapes on slide 18 horizontally across the slide.

```
ActivePresentation.Slides(18).Shapes.Range().Distribute _
    msoDistributeHorizontally, msoTrue
```

NOTE Distribute *leaves a margin around the edge of the slide, but* Align *does not.* Align *will move* Shapes *right to the slide's edge.*

The Group method groups the Shapes in the ShapeRange and converts them into a single Shape object. Ungroup breaks up any Shapes that represent groups and replaces them with their individual members.

Selection

The Selection object often plays a key role in Office programming. The user selects something and clicks a button. A macro executes and performs some action on the selection. In Word or Excel, the Selection represents text or worksheet cells in a fairly simple and uniform way, so this isn't too complicated. PowerPoint's Selection object is slightly different, however.

The location of the Selection object is different from its location in other Office applications. In Word and Excel, Selection is a property of the Application object. In PowerPoint, the Selection object is a property of a DocumentWindow, an object that represents an open window in PowerPoint.

Normally, it's the selection in the active window that you want to manipulate. You can use the ActiveWindow object to get a reference to that window. For example, the following statement displays the currently selected text (if text is selected).

```
MsgBox ActiveWindow.Selection.TextRange.Text
```

PowerPoint's Selection object is complicated by the fact that it might contain several different types of objects that depend on two variables: what the user has selected and the current PowerPoint view. Depending on the circumstances, the Selection object can represent a shape containing text, multiple shapes with or without text, or slides. These items are represented by the Selection object's TextRange, ShapeRange, and SlideRange properties.

For example, when PowerPoint is in Normal view (View ➤ Normal), you can select a Shape object containing text on the current slide. In that case, the Selection.TextRange.Text property gets or sets the text inside the selected Shape. If you click and drag on part of the text so only some of the text is selected, then Selection.TextRange.Text applies only to the selected text.

If you select more than one Shape, the TextRange property is invalid. You would need to loop through the Selection object's ShapeRange collection to work with the selected Shapes individually.

If you select one or more slides from the slide list, the Selection object's SlideRange property contains Slide objects representing the selected slides. To work with the selected slides, you must loop through this collection.

Other views let you work with the selection in different ways. For example, in Notes view (View ➤ Notes Page) you can click the slide at the top to select it into the Selection object's SlideRange property. If you select some or all of the slide's note text, the Selection object's TextRange property works.

It's probably not worth the effort of working through all of the combinations of what objects might be selected in what view. Instead, you can check the Selection object's Type property to see what is selected. This property can have the values ppSelectionNone, ppSelectionShapes, ppSelectionSlides, and ppSelectionText. Once you know what the Selection contains, you can use its ShapeRange, SlideRange, or TextRange properties to access the selected items.

 NOTE *The* Type *property tells you the most specific type of object selected, but other objects may also be represented by the* Selection *object's properties. For example, if you select a single* Shape *containing some text,* Type *is* ppSelectionText, *and you can manipulate the text using the* TextRange *property. However, the* Shape *containing the text is also stored in the* ShapeRange *collection, and the slide containing the shape is stored in the* SlideRange *collection.*

In some cases, your code should simply exit or display an error message if the wrong types of objects are selected. For example, the following code first checks that the active window's selection contains Shapes. If the selection doesn't contain Shapes, the code displays an error message and exits.

If the selection does contain Shapes, the code iterates through them to find the largest and smallest Y coordinate midpoints. It then sets the Shapes' colors so they change smoothly from green at the top to blue at the bottom. The result is striking for a set of shapes such as those making up the cycloid shown earlier in Figure 9-4.

```
' Color the selected shapes in shades of red.
Sub ShadeSelectedShapes()
Dim clr As Single
Dim dclr As Single
Dim i As Integer
Dim Y As Single
Dim ymin As Single
Dim ymax As Single
```

```
With ActiveWindow.Selection
    ' Make sure Shapes are selected.
    If .Type <> ppSelectionShapes Then
        MsgBox "You must select shapes."
        Exit Sub
    End If

    ' Find bounds on the shapes' Y midpoints.
    With .ShapeRange(1)
        Y = .Top + .Height / 2
        ymin = Y
        ymax = Y
    End With
    For i = 2 To .ShapeRange.Count
        With .ShapeRange(i)
            Y = .Top + .Height / 2
            If ymin > Y Then ymin = Y
            If ymax < Y Then ymax = Y
        End With
    Next i

    ' Shade the shapes.
    If ymax = ymin Then
        dclr = 0
    Else
        dclr = 255 / (ymax - ymin)
    End If
    For i = 1 To .ShapeRange.Count
        With .ShapeRange(i)
            ' Set the shape's color.
            clr = (.Top + .Height / 2 - ymin) * dclr
            .Line.ForeColor.RGB = RGB(0, 255 - clr, clr)
        End With
    Next i

    .Unselect
End With
End Sub
```

Summary

Although not as complex as the Word and Excel object models, PowerPoint's object model holds plenty of complexity. The `Application`, `Presentation`, `Slide`, and `Shape` objects give you access to the basic structure of a presentation.

There are a few key differences between the way PowerPoint's object model works and the general approach taken by Word and Excel. Word and Excel use the single `Range` object to represent groups of text or cells. PowerPoint uses `TextRange`, `ShapeRange`, and `SlideRange` objects to represent different types of selections. This may seem awkward if you think of PowerPoint as basically displaying text. It makes more sense if you think of PowerPoint as mainly a drawing program that sometimes happens to draw shapes that contain text.

A second difference between PowerPoint and Word and Excel is their implementation of the `Selection` object. Just as Word and Excel use a single `Range` object to represent text or cells, they use a relatively simple `Selection` object to represent the user's current selection. Because PowerPoint deals explicitly with the differences between text, shapes, and slides, its `Selection` object also deals explicitly with the differences.

If you don't keep these differences in mind, what you know about Word and Excel programming may make working with PowerPoint more confusing than necessary. If you allow for these differences, you should have little trouble working with PowerPoint. The objects described in this chapter will get you started. Use the online help and recorded macros to help fill in any details when you approach a specific problem.

CHAPTER 10

Access

ACCESS AND OUTLOOK are a bit different from the other Office applications. Word, Excel, and PowerPoint are primarily end-user applications. You use them to generate some kind of document (text file, workbook, or slide presentation), and that's that. You can write VBA macros to automate things for yourself or for other users (that's what this book is all about, after all), but you are not really intended to write a complete application by using Word, Excel, or PowerPoint. For example, you could build UserForms that let a user fill in expense report data in PowerPoint and then automatically print them. That would certainly work, but it's not really the main purpose of PowerPoint. Its main purpose is to create presentations.

On the other hand, a database is much more complicated than a simple document. A moderately complex database may contain several dozen or even hundreds of tables with intricate validation schemes and linked in complex relationships spanning multiple fields. Many databases also allow multiple users to access data simultaneously, an operation that is rarely necessary for text documents, workbooks, or slide shows. Because databases can be so complex, Access includes powerful tools to help the DBA design, build, and manage databases.

At the same time, Access provides simple tools that let end-users perform day-to-day data entry. Its built-in development environment lets the DBA define customized forms and reports that make these tasks easier.

You can also use VBA UserForms to build yet another kind of data entry form. As if this schizophrenic focus weren't bad enough, there's yet another way to use Access. After you build an Access database, code running in another application can use a database engine to manipulate the database without using Access itself. For example, you might build a customer database using Access. Then a program written in C++, Visual Basic, VBA, or some other language can open the database and add, update, and delete records without using Access. This technique is generally more common than using Access itself from another application.

Over the years, Microsoft has published several tools for accessing and manipulating data, including DAO (Data Access Objects), RDO (Remote Data Objects), OLE DB (Object Linking and Embedding Database), ADO (ActiveX Data Objects), and ADO.NET (the .NET version of ADO). It has also provided controls that a Visual Basic or other program can use to make connecting to databases easier.

Currently, ADO is one of the more popular methods for accessing databases. It is powerful and relatively simple. It's also fairly recent, so Microsoft gives it more support than some of the older technologies, although ADO.NET will undoubtedly push it out in time.

Lest you think you can settle on ADO and ignore all other database access methods, however, you should be at least somewhat aware of DAO, because it provides features for creating and modifying databases that are not provided by ADO. The ADO-related tool ADOX (Microsoft ActiveX Data Objects Extensions for Data Definition Language and Security) provides these features, but to use ADOX you must learn the ADOX object model (as if you didn't have enough to learn already). DAO also provides better performance than ADO under some circumstances by using Microsoft's Jet database engine, which is used by Access databases.

The Access object model includes several DAO-related objects. For example, the `Application.CurrentDb` property returns a DAO `Database` object that you can use to manipulate the database by using DAO. Meanwhile, `Application.CurrentProject.Connection` returns an ADO Connection object that you can use to manipulate the database by using ADO. Whether you decide to use ADO or DAO, you should be aware that Access has many objects to support both.

To recap, there are several main kinds of Access programming. First, you can use Access's tools to build forms that allow users to perform day-to-day data entry tasks, but this functionality is really about Access as a product rather than a subject for VBA programming (it's analogous to using Word to build a document). Because this isn't really VBA programming, it's not covered in detail in this book.

A second form of Access programming uses VBA to automate tasks within Access. For example, you can write code that loads a Word document and uses its contents to build a new Access table. To perform this sort of task, your VBA code must work with the Access object model. This chapter covers programming of this kind.

Third, you can build `UserForms` to allow the user to interact with your VBA code. This is really an issue of placing a front end on your VBA code, so it's not explicitly covered here.

Finally, you can use database access technologies such as ADO and DAO to manipulate an Access database from another program, such as one you've written in Visual Basic, C++, or some other language. It can also be a VBA program running within Word, Excel, or another Office application, or VBScript running on an ASP Web page. These applications use the database access tool's object model rather than the Access object model.

In a way, this last type of Access programming is more important than working within Access itself, because it applies to programs written in a wide variety of languages and running other applications. It's very common to build a database using Access, SQL Server, Oracle, or some other database product, and then build the main application using Visual Basic, C++, or another programming language. The next chapter provides an introduction to this type of programming by using ADO to work with data in an Access database.

The following section briefly describes the key classes in the Access VBA object model. The rest of the chapter describes these objects in greater detail.

Overview

Access may be different from Word, Excel, and PowerPoint in many respects, but it too starts its object model with the `Application` object. This object provides properties and methods for working with Access as a whole rather than with a particular database. For example, the `Application` object lets you customize the Access command bars, open a database, create a new database, or search for files.

The `Application` object also provides properties that provide entry to the rest of the Access object model. For instance, its `Forms` and `Modules` collections let you manipulate the forms and code modules stored in an Access project.

Many of the `Application` object's properties and methods deal with the current database. For example, the `CodeProject` property returns an object representing the currently loaded Access project and lets you examine such things as the reports and forms defined in the project.

Several objects, such as `CodeProject`, include collections holding other objects by category. For instance, the `CodeProject` object has collections representing forms, reports, macros, modules, and data access pages. The objects in these collections are of type `AccessObject`. The `AccessObject` has informational properties that tell you the item's name, creation and modification date, type, and whether the item is currently loaded.

Other `Application` object properties contain collections of loaded objects. For instance, the `Forms`, `Reports`, and `Modules` collections contain objects representing any open forms, reports, and modules. These objects are more specific than the generic `AccessObject`. For example, the `CodeProject.AllForms` collection holds `AccessObjects` that tell you the names of all the project's forms. The `Application.Forms` collection contains `Form` objects representing only the currently open forms. These `Form` objects let you work directly with the open forms.

The following sections describe the most useful Access objects in more detail. They cover only the more important objects, properties, and methods. For information on other types of objects, search the online help for Microsoft Access Objects or go to `http://msdn.microsoft.com/library/en-us/vbaac10/html/ acsumAccessObjHierarchy.asp`. For further information on a particular object's properties and methods, search the help for that object.

Application

The `Application` object is the gateway to the Access object model. Its properties and methods lead to other objects in the object model.

The following sections describe the most useful `Application` object properties and methods.

Properties

The following sections describe some of the Application object's most useful properties. Those that are collections are followed with a (C).

CodeContextObject

This property returns an object that defines the instance of the code currently executing. For instance, if the VBA code is running in a button's event handler, this object will be the form that contains the button.

The following code is in the Click event handler for a button on the form frmGetCodeContextObject. It calls subroutine ShowCodeContextObject contained in the module Samples.

FILE *Ch10\Customers.mdb*

```
' Display the CodeContextObject's name
' and class name.
Private Sub cmdGetCodeContextObject_Click()
    ShowCodeContextObject
End Sub
```

The following code shows the ShowCodeContextObject subroutine. When the click event handler calls this subroutine, the code displays the name and class name of the object that contains the click event handler.

FILE *Ch10\Customers.mdb*

```
' Display the CodeContextObject's name
' and class name.
Public Sub ShowCodeContextObject()
    MsgBox "Name: " & CodeContextObject.Name & vbCrLf & _
        "Type: " & TypeName(CodeContextObject)
End Sub
```

The following text shows the results. Note that this object represents the form containing the click event handler, not the module containing the ShowCodeContextObject subroutine.

```
Name: frmGetCodeContextObject
Type: Form_frmGetCodeContextObject
```

The CodeContextObject property has the generic Object type, so it can return different kinds of objects, depending on what object contains the executing code. For example, suppose you have defined a report named CustomerAddresses and a form named Customers. VBA code running in those objects would have CodeContextObject objects of type Report_CustomerAddresses and Form_Customers, respectively. Use the CodeContextObject object's Name property or VBA's TypeOf or TypeName statement to figure out what kind of object you have.

Because CodeContextObject is a generic Object, IntelliSense isn't very helpful. VBA doesn't know ahead of time what type of object it will be, so it cannot provide much information about the object's properties and methods. You can make IntelliSense work by creating an object of an appropriate type and setting it equal to the CodeContextObject object. For example, the following code checks whether the CodeContextObject object is of type Form_frmGetCodeContextObject. If it is, the code saves a reference to the object in the variable frm declared with the appropriate type. Later, the code can use IntelliSense to work with the variable frm. For example, IntelliSense shows that frm has the WindowWidth and WindowHeight properties.

 FILE *Ch10\Customers.mdb*

```
' If the CodeContextObject is a Form_frmGetCodeContextObject,
' display the form's window size.
Public Sub CodeContextObjectIntellisense()
Dim frm As Form_frmGetCodeContextObject

    If TypeOf CodeContextObject Is Form_frmGetCodeContextObject Then
        Set frm = CodeContextObject
        MsgBox "Size: " & _
            Format$(frm.WindowWidth / 1440, "0.00") & "x" & _
            Format$(frm.WindowHeight / 1440, "0.00") & " inches"
    End If
End Sub
```

CodeData, CurrentData, CodeProject, *and* CurrentProject

The CodeData and CurrentData properties return objects holding five collections representing parts of the database design. These collections are AllDatabaseDiagrams, AllTables, AllQueries, AllStoredProcedures, and AllViews. The CodeData object represents the database in which the code is stored. The CurrentData object represents the current database.

Suppose you open the CustomerData database and add a reference to the CustomerTools database project, which contains handy VBA macros. Now suppose you run one of those macros, and its code refers to CodeData and CurrentData. The CodeData object refers to the database containing the executing code (CustomerTools) while CurrentData refers to the current database in which the code is executing via a reference (CustomerData).

The following code lists all of the tables in the current database and tells you which are loaded.

 FILE *Ch10\Customers.mdb*

```
' List all tables.
Sub ListAllTables()
Dim table_object As AccessObject

    ' List the tables.
    For Each table_object In Application.CurrentData.AllTables
        ' Print the table's name and tell
        ' if it is loaded.
        If table_object.IsLoaded Then
            Debug.Print table_object.Name & " (Loaded)"
        Else
            Debug.Print table_object.Name
        End If
    Next table_object
End Sub
```

If you run this code on a new database, you may be surprised to find that the database already contains tables. The following output shows the tables created by Access XP.

```
MSysAccessObjects
MSysAccessXML
MSysACEs
MSysObjects
MSysQueries
MSysRelationships
```

Note that if the database doesn't contain a particular type of item, the corresponding collection may not exist. For instance, if the database doesn't contain any stored procedures, the AllStoredProcedures collection may not exist. If you try to use it in any way, including testing to see if it's Nothing, VBA raises an error. Use an On Error GoTo statement, as shown in the following example, to protect your code from this error.

 FILE *Ch10\Customers.mdb*

```
' List the database's store procedures.
Sub ListAllStoredProcedures()
Dim sp_object As AccessObject

    ' Display the names of the stored procedures.
    On Error GoTo ListStoredProceduresError
    For Each sp_object In Application.CurrentData.AllStoredProcedures
        Debug.Print sp_object.Name
    Next sp_object
    Exit Sub

ListStoredProceduresError:
    Debug.Print Err.Description
    Exit Sub
End Sub
```

The CodeProject object contains a similar set of collections representing objects in the Access project. These collections are AllDataAccessPages, AllForms, AllReports, AllMacros, and AllModules. The following code lists the project's forms and tells which are currently loaded.

FILE *Ch10\Customers.mdb*

```
' List all forms.
Sub ListAllForms()
Dim form_object As AccessObject

    ' List forms.
    For Each form_object In Application.CodeProject.AllForms
        ' Print the form's name and tell
        ' if it is loaded.
        If form_object.IsLoaded Then
            Debug.Print form_object.Name & " (Loaded)"
        Else
            Debug.Print form_object.Name
        End If
    Next form_object
End Sub
```

NOTE *Unlike the* CodeData *and* CurrentData *objects, the* CodeProject *object contains valid collections even if the database contains no relevant items. For example, if the database contains no macros, then* CodeProject.AllMacros *exists and* CodeProject.AllMacros.Count *is zero.*

A few paragraphs back in this section, I explained that the CodeData object represents the database containing the executing code, while the CurrentData object represents the database that is actually loaded. Similarly, the CodeProject object represents Access objects in the project that contains the executing code, and the CurrentProject object represents objects in the project that is actually loaded.

The differences between CodeData and CurrentData and between CodeProject and CurrentProject are subtle but usually don't make any difference. If you have a single database that contains its own VBA code, you don't need to worry about the differences.

DataAccessPages *(C)*, Forms *(C)*, Reports *(C)*, *and* Modules *(C)*

Like the `AllDataAccessPages`, `AllForms`, `AllReports`, and `AllModules` collections, these properties give you access to the project's data access pages, forms, reports, and modules. These collections only contain references to open objects, however.

The following code lists the open standard and class modules.

 FILE *Ch10\Customers.mdb*

```
' List the modules that are open.
Sub ListOpenModules()
Dim i As Long

    For i = 0 To Application.Modules.Count - 1
        Debug.Print Application.Modules(i)
    Next i
End Sub
```

The following example opens the Samples code module. Then it uses that module's `InsertText` method to add a subroutine at the end.

 FILE *Ch10\Customers.mdb*

```
' Add a subroutine to the end of the Samples module.
Sub AddSayHiSub()
    ' Open the module if it's not already open.
    DoCmd.OpenModule "Samples"

    ' Work Get a reference to the Module object.
    With Modules("Samples")
        ' Insert the subroutine.
        .InsertText _
            "' Say Hi." & vbCrLf & _
            "Sub SayHi()" & vbCrLf & _
```

```
              "    MsgBox ""Hi""" & vbCrLf & _
            "End Sub"
    End With
End Sub
```

CommandBars *(C)*

The CommandBars collection represents the command bars displayed by Access. You can use this collection to customize Access's tools. For instance, the following code adds a new button to the Database CommandBar that executes the MakeRandomCustomers macro when pressed.

 FILE *Ch10\Customers.mdb*

```
' Add a button for the MakeRandomCustomers VBA routine.
Sub CustomizeMakeRandomCustomers()
Dim new_button As CommandBarButton
Dim file_name As String

    ' Create the button.
    Set new_button = Application.CommandBars( _
        "Database").Controls.Add( _
            Type:=msocontrolbutton)

    ' Give it a picture.
    file_name = CurrentDb.Name
    file_name = Left$(file_name, InStrRev(file_name, "\"))
    file_name = file_name & "RandomCustomers.bmp"
    new_button.Picture = LoadPicture(file_name)
    new_button.OnAction = "MakeRandomCustomers"
End Sub
```

Chapter 4 says more about using VBA code to customize CommandBars.

CurrentObjectName, *and* CurrentObjectType

These properties give information on the database object from which the code is running. For example, the form frmGetCodeContextObject in the Ch10\ Customers.mdb database has a button named cmdCurrentObject. When you run the form and click this button, the following code displays the current object's name (frmGetCodeContextObject) and type (Form).

NOTE CurrentObjectType *returns an enumerated value unless the object is* Nothing *or ambiguous (for example, if a dialog has the input focus), in which case it returns True. Yes, that's just as silly as it sounds. Why the Access design team didn't simply define another constant* acUnknown *is a mystery.*

FILE *Ch10\Customers.mdb*

```
' Display current object information.
Private Sub cmdCurrentObject_Click()
Dim type_name As String

    Select Case Application.CurrentObjectType
        Case acDataAccessPage
            type_name = "Data Access Page"
        Case acDiagram
            type_name = "Diagram"
        Case acForm
            type_name = "Form"
        Case acMacro
            type_name = "Macro"
        Case acModule
            type_name = "Module"
        Case acQuery
            type_name = "Query"
        Case acReport
            type_name = "Report"
        Case acServerView
            type_name = "Server View"
        Case acStoredProcedure
```

```
            type_name = "Stored Procedure"
        Case acTable
            type_name = "Table"
        Case True
            type_name = "(nothing)"
        Case Else
            type_name = "Unknown current object " & _
                Application.CurrentObjectType
    End Select

    MsgBox _
        "Name: " & Application.CurrentObjectName & vbCrLf & _
        "Type: " & type_name
End Sub
```

You can use these properties to identify the object and then take appropriate action. For example, the following code decides whether the object is the frmGetCodeContextObject form and, if it is, closes it.

```
If Application.CurrentObjectName = "frmGetCodeContextObject" Then _
    Form_frmGetCodeContextObject.Visible = False
```

DBEngine

The DBEngine object sits at the top of the DAO object model. Generally, you should use the newer ADO (or possibly even ADO.NET) to work with the database, but the DBEngine object can make some operations a little easier. For instance, the following code uses the DBEngine object to create a test database.

 FILE *Ch10\Customers.mdb*

```
' Create a test database using DAO. Note that to define the
' constant dbLangGeneral you need to set a reference to the
' Microsoft DAO 3.51 Object Library (or whatever
' version you have on your system).
Sub DAOCreateTestDatabase()
Dim db_name As String
```

```
    ' Get the path from the current database's full name.
    db_name = CurrentDb.Name
    db_name = Left$(db_name, InStrRev(db_name, "\"))

    ' Add the name Test1.mdb.
    db_name = db_name & "Test1.mdb"

    ' Create the database.
    DBEngine.CreateDatabase db_name, dbLangGeneral
End Sub
```

DBEngine also provides a convenient CompactDatabase method. CompactDatabase copies and compacts a closed database to reclaim unused space in the tables. Parameters let you specify the database's current name, name of the new compacted copy, locale (which determines the database's collating order), options (for encryption and Jet database version), and password (if the database is password protected).

DoCmd

This property returns a reference to the DoCmd object. You can use this object's methods to perform Access actions from within VBA code. For example, the following code opens the Customers form. It then moves to the first record that contains the value 25. In this database, that's the record with CustomerNumber = 25.

FILE *Ch10\Customers.mdb*

```
' Display the Customers form and go to the first
' record containing 25.
Sub ShowCustomer()
    Application.DoCmd.OpenForm _
        FormName:="Customers"
    Application.DoCmd.FindRecord "25", _
        OnlyCurrentField:=acAll, _
        FindFirst:=True
End Sub
```

FileDialog

FileDialog is a collection of objects representing standard open and save file dialogs. The index into this collection should be one of the values msoFileDialog-FilePicker, msoFileDialogFolderPicker, msoFileDialogOpen, or msoFileDialogSaveAs.

The FileDialog objects contained in this collection provide only two methods: Show and Execute. Show displays the dialog and returns True if the user clicked the OK button or False if the user clicked Cancel. The Execute method makes the dialog perform its associated action. For example, it makes an open dialog open the selected file.

The following example uses the file picker dialog to let the user select one or more files by using the *.mdb and *.* filters. It displays the user's selections in the Debug window.

 FILE *Ch10\Customers.mdb*

```
' Select a file using *.mdb and *.* filters only.
Sub SelectFile()
    With Application.FileDialog(msoFileDialogFilePicker)
        .AllowMultiSelect = True
        .InitialFileName = CurrentDBPath()
        .Filters.Clear
        .Filters.Add "All Files", "*.*"
        .Filters.Add "Access Databases", "*.mdb"

        ' Select the first filter (Access Databases).
        .FilterIndex = 2

        ' Display the dialog and see if the user clicks OK.
        If .Show Then
            ' Display the selected files.
            For i = 1 To .SelectedItems.Count
                Debug.Print .SelectedItems(i)
            Next i
        End If
    End With
End Sub
```

The `FileDialog` property is very similar to the versions provided by Word and Excel. For more information, see the "FileDialog" sections in the Chapters 7 and 8, the online help, or the Web page `http://msdn.microsoft.com/library/en-us/vbaof10/html/ofobjFileDialog.asp`.

References *(C)*

This collection gives information about the project's references set by the Tools ➤ References command. The following code lists the names, major and minor versions, and complete paths for the loaded references.

FILE *Ch10\Customers.mdb*

```
' List the project's references.
Sub ListReferences()
Dim ref As Reference

    For Each ref In Application.References
        Debug.Print _
            ref.Name & " " & ref.Major & "." & ref.Minor & _
            " (" & ref.FullPath & ")"
    Next ref
End Sub
```

The following output shows this code's results in one test. Your results will vary depending on Office's installation directory, version, and features installed. They will also vary depending on the references you have added to the VBA project and their order.

```
VBA 4.0 (C:\Program Files\Common Files\Microsoft Shared\VBA\VBA6\VBE6.DLL)
Access 9.0 (C:\Program Files\Microsoft Office\Office10\MSACC.OLB)
stdole 2.0 (C:\WINNT\System32\stdole2.tlb)
Office 2.2 (C:\Program Files\Common Files\Microsoft Shared\Office10\MSO.DLL)
DAO 4.0 (C:\Program Files\Common Files\Microsoft Shared\DAO\DAO350.DLL)
VBIDE 5.3 (C:\Program Files\Common Files\Microsoft Shared\VBA\VBA6\VBE6EXT.OLB)
ADODB 2.7 (C:\Program Files\Common Files\System\ADO\msado15.dll)
```

Normally, you use the Tools ➤ References command to manage references, but the References collection also provides methods for adding and removing references. For example, suppose you write some VBA code that uses features of ADODB 2.7 and then you distribute it on a bunch of different computers. The following code fragment shows how your routine could verify that the IDE has a reference to ADODB 2.7.

```
Dim ref As Reference

    On Error Resume Next
    Set ref = Application.References("ADODB")
    If Err.Number = 0 Then
        ' There's some reference to ADODB.
        ' See if it's the right one.
        If ref.Major = 7 And ref.Minor = 2 Then
            ' Do stuff that requires ADODB 2.7.
            ...
        End If
End If
```

More elaborate code could check for an older version of ADODB, remove it, and create a new reference to the version 2.7 DLL. That might mess up other code, however, so it may be better to just warn the user and stop.

Methods

The following sections describe some of the Application object's most useful methods.

CloseCurrentDatabase, OpenCurrentDatabase, *and* NewCurrentDatabase

As you can probably guess, CloseCurrentDatabase closes the current database. This statement is not as useful as you may think in Access VBA code, because the closing database takes its code modules with it, so the code immediately stops executing. That means, for example, that you cannot write a subroutine that closes one database and opens another. When the first database closes, the code stops working.

CloseCurrentDatabase is more useful when you are not trying to use VBA code to work with its own Access application. For instance, a Word macro could create an Access Application object and open another database. Later, it would use CloseCurrentDatabase to close that database and then use OpenCurrentDatabase to open a different one.

TIP *It's usually simpler to use ADO to work with databases than it is to open an Access* Application. *An Access application server would be more appropriate if you wanted to modify the Access objects (reports, forms, and so forth), but ADO is easier and uses fewer resources if you want to manipulate the data itself. See Chapter 11 for more information on ADO.*

The NewCurrentDatabase method creates a new Access database and loads it into Access. Unfortunately, Access will not let you open a database while another is open (an Access session can have only one database session open at a time), so you face a conundrum similar that with the CloseCurrentDatabase method. Before you can create and load a new database, you must close the current one. When you close the current one, however, the code stops working.

As with CloseCurrentDatabase, you can use the NewCurrentDatabase method in VBA code that doesn't try to use its own Access application. For example, the following code creates another Access Application object. It calls that object's NewCurrentDatabase method to make a new database and then quits that application.

FILE *Ch10\Customers.mdb*

```
' Create a test database using NewCurrentDatabase.
Sub CreateTestDatabase()
Dim app As Access.Application
Dim db_name As String

    ' Get the database name.
    db_name = CurrentDBPath() & "Test2.mdb"

    ' Create a new Access Application object.
    Set app = New Access.Application
    app.NewCurrentDatabase db_name
    app.Quit acQuitSaveNone
End Sub
```

TIP *You could use ADOX or DAO to create a new database instead of using* `NewCurrentDatabase`.

The `OpenCurrentDatabase` method will not let you open a database while one is already open. As before, closing the current database makes any VBA code stop running, so you cannot close one database and open another using code inside the first database.

CompactRepair

This method compacts and repairs a database and saves the result in a new database. The database cannot be open during this operation because Access needs to open it for exclusive use. In particular, code cannot repair and compact the database that is executing the code.

The following example uses this method to compact the database Sales.mdb into the new database new_Sales.mdb.

FILE *Ch10\Customers.mdb*

```
' Compact and repair the database.
Sub CompactDb()
Dim old_db_name As String
Dim new_db_name As String

    old_db_name = CurrentDBPath() & "Sales.mdb"
    new_db_name = CurrentDBPath() & "new_Sales.mdb"
    On Error GoTo CompactError
    If Application.CompactRepair( _
        old_db_name, new_db_name) _
    Then
        MsgBox "Success"
    Else
        MsgBox "Error compacting database " & old_db_name
    End If
    Exit Sub
```

```
CompactError:
    MsgBox "Error compacting database " & old_db_name & vbCrLf & _
        Err.Description
    Exit Sub
End Sub
```

TIP *There are many ways this method can fail. For instance, the database may be open or might not exist, or the output database name may be invalid. Use an error handler to catch these errors.*

CreateForm, CreateControl, *and* DeleteControl

CreateForm and CreateControl create forms and controls on forms. You can use these methods to build wizard applications that automatically build forms.

For example, the following code makes a new form, saves its default name (which is something like Form3), and attaches it to the CustomerAddresses table. Next the code initializes an array listing the fields in the CustomerAddresses table that should go on the form, then it loops through the array. For each field name, the code uses the CreateControl method to create a new TextBox. It sets the new control's name to "txt" followed by the field name, as in txtStreet. The control then creates a label control as a child of the TextBox.

To finish the new form, the code uses the DoCmd object to close the form, saving changes. It then uses DoCmd to rename the form to something more meaningful than Form3.

NOTE *The form's* Name *property is available only while the form is open. The* DoCmd.Rename *command cannot rename an open form, so the form must be closed, but* DoCmd.Rename *needs to know the form's current name. That's why the code saves the name in a variable before closing the form.*

FILE *Ch10\Customers.mdb*

```
' Make a new CustomerAddresses form.
Sub MakeNewCustomerAddressesForm()
Dim frm As Form
Dim form_name As String
Dim control_names As Variant
Dim txt_control As TextBox
Dim Y As Single
Dim i As Long

    ' Create a new form.
    Set frm = CreateForm()
    form_name = frm.Name

    ' Set the form's RecordSource property to
    ' the CustomerAddresses table.
    frm.RecordSource = "CustomerAddresses"

    ' Initialize the list of fields we will create.
    control_names = Array( _
        "CustomerNumber", _
        "ContactName", _
        "Street", _
        "City", _
        "State", _
        "Zip", _
        "Phone")

    ' Create the fields.
    Y = 120
    For i = LBound(control_names) To UBound(control_names)
        ' Make the TextBox.
        Set txt_control = CreateControl( _
            form_name, acTextBox, , _
            "", control_names(i), 1600, Y)
        txt_control.Name = "txt" & control_names(i)

        ' Add a child label to the TextBox.
        CreateControl _
            form_name, acLabel, , _
            txt_control.Name, control_names(i), _
            120, Y
        Y = Y + 360
    Next i
```

```
    ' Close the form, saving changes.
    ' (Rename only works on closed objects.)
    DoCmd.Close acForm, form_name, acSaveYes

    ' Rename the object.
    ' Note that the form's name is not available
    ' when the form is closed so the code saves
    ' it earlier.
    DoCmd.Rename "NewCustomerAddresses", acForm, form_name
End Sub
```

The DeleteControl method removes a control from a form. This method is straightforward, aside from the fact that the form must be open in design mode for the method to work. To remove a control at run time, you can disable it and set its Visible property to False.

CreateReport, CreateReportControl, *and* DeleteReportControl

These methods are analogous to the CreateForm, CreateControl, and DeleteControl methods described in the previous section. The following code uses these methods to build a report. It uses CreateReport to make the new report. It saves the report's initial name (something like Report6) and sets its RecordSource property to the Customers table.

Next the code uses CreateReportControl to place a TextBox in the report's detail section and a Label in the page header section. It makes the Label bold and calls its SizeToFit method to make it big enough to hold the bold text.

The subroutine sizes the detail section to fit the TextBox. It then uses DoCmd to close the report (saving changes) and to rename the report.

 FILE *Ch10\Customers.mdb*

```
' Make a new Customers report.
Sub MakeNewCustomersReport()
Dim rpt As Report
Dim report_name As String
Dim txt_control As TextBox
Dim lbl_control As Label
```

```
    ' Create a new report.
    Set rpt = CreateReport()
    report_name = rpt.Name

    ' Set the report's RecordSource property to
    ' the Customers table.
    rpt.RecordSource = "Customers"

    ' Make the TextBox.
    Set txt_control = CreateReportControl( _
        report_name, acTextBox, acDetail, _
        "", "CompanyName", 120)
    txt_control.Name = "txtCustomerName"

    ' Add a label for this column.
    Set lbl_control = CreateReportControl( _
        report_name, acLabel, acPageHeader, _
        "", "Company Name", 120)
    lbl_control.FontBold = True
    lbl_control.SizcToFit

    rpt.Section(acDetail).Height = _
        txt_control.Top + txt_control.Height + 120

    ' Close the report, saving changes.
    ' (Rename only works on closed objects.)
    DoCmd.Close acReport, report_name, acSaveYes

    ' Rename the object.
    ' Note that the report's name is not available
    ' when the report is closed so the code saves
    ' it earlier.
    DoCmd.Rename "CustomerNames", acReport, report_name
End Sub
```

The DeleteReportControl method removes a control from a report. This method is straightforward aside from the fact that the report must be open in design mode for the method to work.

At run time, you can use event handlers to set a control's Visible property to False. For instance, the following code runs when the report formats its page header. If the current user's name is Bob, the code hides the Phone TextBox and its corresponding Label.

FILE *Ch10\Customers.mdb*

```
' Hide the phone number field from user Bob.
Private Sub PageHeaderSection_Format(Cancel As Integer, FormatCount As Integer)
    If Application.CurrentUser = "Bob" Then
        Me.Phone_Label.Visible = False
        Me.Phone.Visible = False
    End If
End Sub
```

A more elaborate application might look up user records in the database itself to determine whether the current user had permission to view specific fields.

CurrentDb *and* CodeDb

The CurrentDb method returns a DAO Database object representing the currently loaded database. The CodeDb method returns a DAO Database object representing the database that is running the current code.

For instance, suppose you open the CustomerData database and add a reference to the CustomerTools project, which contains some useful VBA macros. Now suppose you run one of those macros. While that code is running, CodeDb refers to CustomerTools (which contains the running code) and CurrentDb refers to CustomerData (the currently loaded database).

NOTE *This is similar to the way the* CodeData, CurrentData, CodeProject, *and* CurrentProject *properties refer to objects describing the current and code databases. See the section "CodeData, CurrentData, CodeProject, and CurrentProject" earlier in this chapter for more information.*

You can use these Database objects to manipulate the database with DAO. For example, the DAOListTables subroutine, shown in the following code, loops through the current database's TableDefs collection to display the names of the database's tables. The subroutine DAOMakeTable shows how to use the Database object's methods to create a new table.

FILE *Ch10\Customers.mdb*

```vb
' Use DAO to list the database's tables.
Sub DAOListTables()
Dim i As Integer

    For i = 0 To CurrentDb.TableDefs.Count - 1
        Debug.Print CurrentDb.TableDefs(i).Name
    Next i
End Sub

' Make a table using DAO.
Sub DAOMakeTable()
Dim table_def As TableDef
Dim new_field As DAO.Field
Dim new_index As Index

    ' Define the table.
    Set table_def = CurrentDb.CreateTableDef("InventoryItems")

    ' Define the ItemNumber field.
    Set new_field = table_def.CreateField("ItemNumber", adInteger)
    table_def.Fields.Append new_field

    ' Define the ItemName field.
    Set new_field = table_def.CreateField("ItemName", dbText, 40)
    table_def.Fields.Append new_field

    ' Define the ItemDescription field.
    Set new_field = table_def.CreateField("ItemDescription", dbText, 80)
    table_def.Fields.Append new_field

    ' Define the primary key index.
    Set new_index = table_def.CreateIndex("idxItemNumber")
    new_index.Primary = True
    new_index.Fields.Append table_def.CreateField("ItemNumber", adInteger)
    table_def.Indexes.Append new_index

    ' Create the table.
    CurrentDb.TableDefs.Append table_def
End Sub
```

TIP *Because ADO is the newer technology, you may want to avoid using these DAO methods and use the ADO equivalents instead. ADO's methods for manipulating data tend to be somewhat easier and have better support from Microsoft. On the other hand, ADO doesn't provide methods for manipulating the database structure, so you would need to use ADOX (yet another thing to learn) or execute SQL statements to create a new table. In cases such as this, developers often make the final decision to use ADO or DAO based on personal preference or previous experience.*

CurrentUser

This property returns the name of the user connected to the database. If you are not using workgroups, this property returns the name of the default account (usually Admin).

 NOTE *Early beta versions indicate that this behavior may change in Office 2003.*

If you are using workgroups, this method can be useful in applications that track user activities. For example, a VBA program that adds data to the database can also add the user's name so you can later tell who entered the data. A program can also use this method to determine what customizations and tools it should provide for particular users.

Calculation Functions

These functions perform various calculations on database values. For example, the DAvg function calculates an average. Its three parameters give an expression naming the fields to average, a domain identifying the records to search, and an optional search criterion to restrict the records found.

For instance, the following VBA code displays the average of the Salary field in the Employees table for records where the JobLevel is 8.

```
MsgBox DAvg("Salary", "Employees", "JobLevel = 8")
```

The DAvg, DCount, DMax, DMin, DStDev, DStDevP, DSum, DVar, and DVarP functions are relatively straightforward. Respectively, they return the average, count, maximum value, minimum value, standard deviation, standard deviation for a population, sum, variance, and variance for a population. (The last several are statistical functions. If you don't know what they are, you probably don't need them. If you're curious, you can find some mathematical definitions at http://mathworld.wolfram.com/StandardDeviation.html or more intuitive information at http://www.animatedsoftware.com/statglos/sgstdev.htm.)

The DFirst and DLast functions return the first and last values selected. Those are not necessarily the largest and smallest values. They are just the first and last values in the order in which the values are selected. Use DMin and DMax to get the largest and smallest values.

TIP DMin *and* DMax *work on textual fields, too. They return the alphabetically first and last values according to the database's collating order.*

The DLookup function returns a single value. If the domain and criterion select more than one value, DLookup returns the first value it encounters. Normally, this function is used to return a single value from a particular table, often selected by the table's primary key. For instance, a report based on one table could make a calculated field that uses DLookup to get a value from some other table. It may be more efficient (and would certainly be less confusing) to join the other table into the query that generates the report.

Echo

This method tells Access whether to update the screen. It takes two parameters: a Boolean indicating whether the screen should be updated, and text to display in the Access status bar. If your VBA code makes a lot of visible changes, it may be faster to turn screen updating off before starting, then turn it back on when the changes are finished.

ExportXML

This method exports a piece of the database as XML data, optionally with an XSD schema (XML Schema Definition). (If you're unfamiliar with XML and XSD, see a book on XML.) The following code saves the Customers table's data and schema.

FILE *Ch10\Customers.mdb*

```
' Export the Customers table as XML and its XSD schema.
Sub ExportCustomers()
    Application.ExportXML _
        acExportTable, _
        "Customers", _
        CurrentDBPath() & "Customers.xml", _
        CurrentDBPath() & "CustomersSchema.xsd"
End Sub

' Return the database's path.
Function CurrentDBPath() As String
Dim db_name As String

    db_name = CurrentDb.Name
    CurrentDBPath = Left$(db_name, InStrRev(db_name, "\"))
End Function
```

The following text shows part of the resulting XML file. This table has only two fields: CompanyName and CustomerNumber. Here the CustomerName values are filled with random strings of characters. CustomerNumber is an AutoNumber field.

The records in the table are represented in the XML file with tags named after the table: Customers. The tags representing field values are named after the database fields: CompanyName and CustomerNumber. The whole thing is contained in a <dataroot> tag.

```
<?xml version="1.0" encoding="UTF-8"?>
<dataroot xmlns:od="urn:schemas-microsoft-com:officedata"
xmlns:xsi="http://www.w3.org/2000/10/XMLSchema-instance"
xsi:noNamespaceSchemaLocation="CustomersSchema.xsd">
<Customers>
<CompanyName>PZVUYFPPUK</CompanyName>
<CustomerNumber>21</CustomerNumber>
</Customers>
<Customers>
<CompanyName>GBDRCLMHPZ</CompanyName>
<CustomerNumber>22</CustomerNumber>
</Customers>
```

```
<Customers>
<CompanyName>EYHDXCVNFF</CompanyName>
<CustomerNumber>23</CustomerNumber>
</Customers>
<Customers>
<CompanyName>MKUNDKFDVA</CompanyName>
<CustomerNumber>24</CustomerNumber>
</Customers>
</dataroot>
```

The following output shows the schema created for this table. If you are unfamiliar with XML and schemas, it may not make complete sense, but you can probably still pick out key elements. For instance, the main element named dataroot is a complex type containing any number (maxOccurs="unbounded") of Customers objects. The Customers element contains some information describing the table's fields and index. Customers is a complex type containing a sequence of elements including CompanyName and CustomerNumber.

CompanyName has the Jet database engine type of text and SQL type of varchar. It is based on the XSD string type and is restricted to a maximum of 50 characters.

CustomerNumber has Jet type autonumber and SQL type int. It is an Auto-Number field (od:autoUnique="yes") and must not be empty (od:nonNullable="yes"). It is based on the XSD integer type.

 NOTE *The schema also says CompanyName is optional (*minOcccurs="0"*), but that's not true in the original database table. Schemas can be extremely complicated, and it's likely that it will be a while before this method is perfected.*

```
<?xml version="1.0" encoding="UTF-8"?>
<xsd:schema xmlns:xsd="http://www.w3.org/2000/10/XMLSchema" xmlns:od="urn:schemas-
microsoft-com:officedata">
<xsd:element name="dataroot">
<xsd:complexType>
<xsd:choice maxOccurs="unbounded">
<xsd:element ref="Customers"/>
</xsd:choice>
</xsd:complexType>
</xsd:element>
<xsd:element name="Customers">
<xsd:annotation>
```

```
<xsd:appinfo>
<od:index index-name="CustomerNumber" index-key="CustomerNumber " primary="no"
unique="yes" clustered="no"/>
<od:index index-name="PrimaryKey" index-key="CustomerNumber " primary="yes"
unique="yes" clustered="no"/>
<od:index index-name="CompanyName" index-key="CompanyName " primary="no"
unique="no" clustered="no"/>
</xsd:appinfo>
</xsd:annotation>
<xsd:complexType>
<xsd:sequence>
<xsd:element name="CompanyName" minOccurs="0" od:jetType="text"
od:sqlSType="nvarchar">
<xsd:simpleType>
<xsd:restriction base="xsd:string">
<xsd:maxLength value="50"/>
</xsd:restriction>
</xsd:simpleType>
</xsd:element>
<xsd:element name="CustomerNumber" od:jetType="autonumber" od:sqlSType="int"
od:autoUnique="yes" od:nonNullable="yes">
<xsd:simpleType>
<xsd:restriction base="xsd:integer"/>
</xsd:simpleType>
</xsd:element>
</xsd:sequence>
</xsd:complexType>
</xsd:element>
</xsd:schema>
```

For more information on XML and schemas, see a book on XML.

InsertText

The InsertText method appends text to a VBA module. Note that the module must be open for editing when you call this method.

The following routine adds a SayHi subroutine to the end of the Samples module.

```
' Add a subroutine to the end of the Samples module
' using the Application object.
Sub ApplicationAddSayHiSub()
    Application.InsertText _
```

```
            "' Say Hi." & vbCrLf & _
            "Sub SayHi()" & vbCrLf & _
            "    MsgBox ""Hi""" & vbCrLf & _
            "End Sub", _
            "Samples"
    End Sub
```

The following code shows the result.

```
' Say Hi.
Sub SayHi()
    MsgBox "Hi"
End Sub
```

Quit

The Quit method closes the Access application. This method can take a parameter telling Access whether to save changes to the database. This parameter can take the values acQuitPrompt (ask the user whether to save changes), acQuitSaveAll (save all changes), or acQuitSaveNone (discard all changes). The default is acQuit-SaveAll.

Run *and* RunCommand

The Run method executes an Access method or a routine defined by your VBA code. This method can take up to 30 parameters that it passes to the routine it calls. It returns whatever value the function it calls returns.

Normally, your code can simply call a subroutine directly, so it doesn't need Run. This method is convenient if you want to compose the name of the routine in a string or if you want to call a routine from another application. For example, a Word macro might open Access and use the Run method to execute a subroutine defined in the database project.

The RunCommand method executes an Access menu or toolbar command. For instance, the following code minimizes the Access application.

```
Application.RunCommand acCmdAppMinimize
```

Form

A Form object represents an open Access form. Note that these objects only exist in the Forms collection when a form is open.

Note also that any changes your VBA code makes while a form is in run mode are reset when the user closes and reopens the form. For example, your code might set a Form object's Filter property to select particular records. When the user closes and reopens the form, the Filter property will not have the value your code gave it.

If you want to change a form's properties permanently, use Access to open the form in design mode, right-click the form, and select Properties.

Note also that VBA can modify some Form properties only in particular views. For example, the ControlBox property determines whether the close button (the little X in the upper-right corner) is enabled. VBA code can only set that property when the form is open in design view. Search the online help for a property to see in which views you can change it.

Properties

The following sections describe some of the Form object's most useful properties.

Event Properties

The Form object provides a host of properties that define events for the form. These properties are strings that give the name of an Access or VBA macro that should be executed when the event occurs.

For example, the database Customers.mdb contains an Access macro (not a VBA macro) named SayClosed that presents a message box that says "Closed." The following code makes the Customers form call that macro when its OnClosed event fires.

 FILE *Ch10\Customers.mdb*

```
' Define an OnClose event for the Customers form.
Sub SetFormEvent()
    Forms("Customers").OnClose = "SayClosed"
End Sub
```

For a list of the Form object's event properties, search the online help for "Form Object." For more information on event properties, search the online help for "Event Properties" or go to http://msdn.microsoft.com/library/en-us/vbaac10/html/acproeventproperties.asp. For a list of event properties for various objects, search the help for "Event Properties and Objects They Apply To" or go to http://msdn.microsoft.com/library/en-us/vbaac10/html/acproevents.asp.

Permission Properties

The Form object has several properties that determine what the user can do with the form. These are reasonably self-explanatory, and include AllowAdditions, AllowDatasheetView, AllowDeletions, AllowEdits, AllowFilters, AllowFormView, AllowPivotChartView, and AllowPivotTableView. For example, the following code in a form's Load event handler ensures that only the user named Supervisor can edit records on the form.

```
Private Sub Form_Load()
    If Application.CurrentUser <> "Supervisor" Then Me.AllowEdits = False
End Sub
```

User Interface Properties

The Form object provides a reasonable number of properties for modifying the form's appearance. VBA code can change most of these properties only when the form is open in design view. When the form is open in run mode, these properties are read-only.

Some of the more useful properties are described here.

AutoCenter is a Boolean that determines whether the form is automatically centered when it is opened.

AutoResize determines whether the form is automatically resized to fit a complete record.

BorderStyle determines the form's border type. This property can have the values 0 (none), 1 (thin, nonresizable), 2 (sizable, the default), or 3 (dialog, nonresizable).

CloseButton determines whether the close button (the little X on the right end of the title bar) is enabled. When CloseButton is False, the button is still visible, but it's grayed out and the user cannot click it. The Close command in the control menu (at the left end of the title bar) is also disabled. If you disable this button, you should probably provide some other method for the user to close the form, such as a command button. The user can also close the form by pressing Ctrl-F4.

Disabling the Close button encourages the user to close the form normally by clicking the Close button or whatever other control you place on the form for that purpose. For example, you don't want the user to close a login form without giving your program a chance to validate the user name and password. Because the user can still press Ctrl-F4, however, your code should be prepared if the user doesn't click the button.

For example, the following code shows how the Login form protects itself. If the user clicks the OK button, the code validates the user name and password. If the values match, the code sets the variable m_OkClicked to flag the form as ready to unload and uses the DoCmd object to unload the form. (A real application would perform more useful checks, such as looking up the password in a database. It would also do something about the password, such as setting a global variable indicating that the user had supervisor permissions.)

If the user name and password fail validation, the OK button's event handler displays a message and leaves the form running.

The Close button's event handler sets m_OkClicked to True and uses the DoCmd object to close the form.

When the form is ready to close (either because the user clicked OK or Cancel, or because the user pressed Ctrl-F4), the Form_Unload event handler checks the m_OkClicked variable. If m_OkClicked is True, it is safe to close the form so the event handler sets Cancel to False. If m_OkClicked is False, the form is trying to close because the user pressed Ctrl-F4. In that case, the code sets Cancel to True so the form stays loaded and displays a message.

FILE *Ch10\Customers.mdb*

```
Private m_OkClicked As Boolean

' The user clicked OK.
' Validate the username and password.
Private Sub cmdOk_Click()
    ' Validate the username and password.
    If Len(txtUserName) > 0 And txtUserName = txtPassword Then
        ' The username and password are okay. Close the form.
        m_OkClicked = True
        Application.DoCmd.Close acForm, "Login"
        MsgBox "Password accepted.", vbExclamation, "Password Okay"
    Else
```

```
        ' The username and password are bad. Say so.
        MsgBox "Invalid user name/password.", vbExclamation, "Invalid Password"
        txtUserName = ""
        txtPassword = ""
        txtUserName.SetFocus
    End If
End Sub


' The user clicked Cancel.
' Close the form.
Private Sub cmdCancel_Click()
    m_OkClicked = True
    Application.DoCmd.Close acForm, "Login"
End Sub


' The form is unloading. Make sure the user clicked
' a button rather than pressing Ctrl-F4.
Private Sub Form_Unload(Cancel As Integer)
    Cancel = Not m_OkClicked
    If Cancel Then MsgBox "Please click OK or Cancel"
End Sub
```

ControlBox determines whether the control menu (on the left side of the title bar) is visible. If ControlBox is False, the menu is hidden. Because the menu includes commands to minimize, maximize, and close the form, those buttons are also removed from the right end of the title bar. If you hide the control box and the close button, you should probably provide some other way for the user to close the form such as a command button.

Hiding the control box can be particularly useful for login forms and other fixed-sized dialogs where minimizing or maximizing the form would make the form more confusing. In these cases, you might also want to set the form's border style to 3 (dialog, nonresizable).

CurrentView is a read-only property that returns a value indicating the form's current view. It can take the values 0 (design view), 1 (form view), or 2 (datasheet view).

Cycle determines the action the form takes when the user tabs off the current record's last field. This property can take the values 0 (move to the first field in the next record), 1 (move to the first field in the same record), or 2 (move to the first field in the same page).

MinMaxButtons determines whether the form's minimize and maximize buttons are present. This property can take the values 0 (none), 1 (minimize is visible), 2 (maximize is visible), or 3 (both buttons are visible). If the minimize or maximize button is removed, the corresponding Minimize or Maximize command in the control menu is disabled.

Modal determines whether the form is modal. If it is, the user must close it before interacting with any other form in the application.

Moveable determines whether the user can move the form. The Move command in the form's control menu remains enabled but doesn't do anything. The following code makes the Customers form auto-center and auto-sized, nonmovable, and nonresizable.

FILE *Ch10\Customers.mdb*

```
' Make the Customer form centered, auto-resized, and immovable.
Sub FixSize()
    ' Make sure the Customer form is open in design view.
    On Error GoTo FixSizeError
    With Forms("Customers")
        .Moveable = False    ' Not movable.
        .MinMaxButtons = 0    ' No min or max buttons.
        .AutoCenter = True    ' Auto-center.
        .AutoResize = True    ' Auto-size.
        .BorderStyle = 3    ' Dialog border (no resizing).
    End With
    Exit Sub

FixSizeError:
    MsgBox "Error fixing the form's size." & _
        vbCrLf & vbCrLf & Err.Description & _
        vbCrLf & vbCrLf & _
        "Make sure the Customers form is open in Design view", _
        vbExclamation, "Error"
    Exit Sub
End Sub
```

NavigationButtons is a Boolean that determines whether the form supplies record navigation buttons. If you set NavigationButtons to False, the user can still navigate between records by using Tab and Shift-Tab to move off the record's last and first fields, respectively (see the Cycle property described a few paragraphs earlier). This is somewhat awkward, so you may want to provide some other navigation method.

Picture sets the file name for the form's background picture. If your code sets this property while the form is in design view, the picture is permanently attached to the form. If it sets this property in run mode, the picture goes away when the user closes and reopens the form. Set the Picture property to an empty string "" to remove the current picture.

PictureAlignment determines how the picture is aligned on the form. This property can take the values 0 (top left), 1 (top right), 2 (center), 3 (bottom left), 4 (bottom right), or 5 (form center).

PictureData is an image of the form's picture. You can set this property to the PictureData property of another form or object that has a PictureData property.

PictureSizeMode determines how the picture is resized if it doesn't exactly fit the form. It can take the values 0 (display the picture at its true size), 1 (stretch the picture to fill the form, possibly stretching the picture out of shape), or 3 (enlarge the picture as much as possible while maintaining aspect ratio).

PictureTiling is a Boolean that determines whether the picture is tiled to fill the form.

PictureType can be 0 to embed the picture in the form's definition or 1 to save only the picture's file name in the form. Setting this property to 1 can save a little space in the application if the picture file will always be available when you run the form.

Data Properties

The Form object provides several properties for determining how it handles data. Some of the most useful are described here.

BatchUpdates is a Boolean that determines whether the form performs batch updates.

Bookmark is a string value your code can use to return later to a specific record. For example, the following code shows the event handlers for two buttons. When the user clicks the Save Bookmark button, the cmdSaveBookmark_Click event handler saves the form's current Bookmark value in a string and makes the Return To Bookmark button visible. When the user clicks the Return To Bookmark button, the cmdReturnToBookmark_Click event handler restores the saved Bookmark value. The form immediately moves to display the corresponding record.

FILE *Ch10\Customers.mdb*

```
Private m_Bookmark As String

' Save the current bookmark.
Private Sub cmdSaveBookmark_Click()
    m_Bookmark = Me.Bookmark

    ' Enable the Return To Bookmark button.
    cmdReturnToBookmark.Visible = True
End Sub

' Return to the saved bookmark.
Private Sub cmdReturnToBookmark_Click()
    Me.Bookmark = m_Bookmark
End Sub
```

The CommitOnNavigation and CommitOnClose properties determine whether the form saves changes to the current record when the user moves to a different record or closes the form, respectively.

CurrentRecord returns the index of the current record in the current Recordset. This property is read-only in the form and datasheet views, so it's not really intended to let you navigate through the records. You should use the Bookmark property to move to specific records. CurrentRecord is more often used to display the record number to the user.

Dirty returns True if the current record has been modified since it was loaded or last saved.

NewRecord returns True if the current record is a new record that the user is still creating. When the record is saved, it is no longer a new record.

Recordset returns the ADO Recordset object the form uses to manipulate its selected records. Your VBA code can use this object to affect the records, too. For instance, the following code lets the cmdFirst, cmdPrevious, cmdNext, and cmdLast command buttons perform basic navigation functions.

FILE *Ch10\Customers.mdb*

```
Private Sub cmdFirst_Click()
    Me.Recordset.MoveFirst
End Sub

Private Sub cmdLast_Click()
    Me.Recordset.MoveLast
End Sub

Private Sub cmdNext_Click()
    Me.Recordset.MoveNext
End Sub

Private Sub cmdPrevious_Click()
    Me.Recordset.MovePrevious
End Sub
```

The Filter property specifies a WHERE clause that the form should use to filter the records it displays. The FilterOn property is a Boolean value that determines whether the form should actually use the filter. For example, the following code makes the Customers form display only records where the CompanyName field contains the letter P.

FILE *Ch10\Customers.mdb*

```
' Set a filter for the Customers form that
' selects records where CompanyName contains P.
Sub SetFilter()
    Forms("Customers").Filter = "Customers.CompanyName Like '*P*'"
    Forms("Customers").FilterOn = True
End Sub
```

Similarly, the OrderBy property specifies an ORDER BY clause the form should use to order its data. The OrderByOn property determines whether the form uses the OrderBy clause. By default, OrderByOn is False.

The NewCustomerAddresses form contains option buttons for each of its records' fields. The following code shows how those buttons' event handlers make the form order its data by each of those fields.

The ClearOptions subroutine clears all of the option buttons except one and sets focus to a particular control. The option buttons' event handlers use this routine to clear all other option buttons and set the focus to the appropriate field. For instance, the optOrderByCity_Click event handler clears the other option buttons and sets focus to the City field. It then sets the form's OrderBy property to "City" and sets OrderByOn to True. This makes the form order its data by using the City field.

FILE *Ch10\Customers.mdb*

```
' Select none of the option buttons.
Private Sub Form_Load()
    ClearOptions optOrderByStreet, txtStreet
End Sub

' Clear all option buttons.
Sub ClearOptions(ByVal except As Control, ByVal focus_control As Control)
Dim ctl As Control

    For Each ctl In Controls
        If TypeName(ctl) = "OptionButton" Then
            ctl.Value = False
        End If
    Next ctl
    except.Value = True

    focus_control.SetFocus
End Sub

Private Sub optOrderByCity_Click()
    ClearOptions optOrderByCity, txtCity
    OrderBy = "City"
```

```
        OrderByOn = True
    End Sub

    Private Sub optOrderByNone_Click()
        ClearOptions optOrderByNone, txtStreet
        OrderByOn = False
    End Sub

    Private Sub optOrderByState_Click()
        ClearOptions optOrderByState, txtState
        OrderBy = "State"
        OrderByOn = True
    End Sub

    Private Sub optOrderByStreet_Click()
        ClearOptions optOrderByStreet, txtStreet
        OrderBy = "Street"
        OrderByOn = True
    End Sub

    Private Sub optOrderByZip_Click()
        ClearOptions optOrderByZip, txtZip
        OrderBy = "Zip"
        OrderByOn = True
    End Sub
```

HasModule *and* Module

The HasModule property determines whether the form has an associated code module. If the form doesn't need any code, setting this to False removes any previously
created code module. That saves some space in the database and can improve
performance, particularly if you open the database across a network connection.
For example, suppose you add an event handler to the form and then decide to
remove it. The form's module remains even though it doesn't contain any code.
You can open the form in design view and set its HasModule property to False to
remove the module.

   If the form has a code module, the Module property returns a reference to a
Module object representing the form's code.

Properties *(C)*

The Properties property is a collection giving the names and values for all of the form's properties. The following code shows how you can use this collection to list every property for the NewCustomerAddresses form.

 FILE *Ch10\Customers.mdb*

```
' List the NewCustomerAddresses form's properties.
Sub ListNewCustomerAddressesProperties()
Dim i As Long

    With Forms("NewCustomerAddresses")
        For i = 0 To .Properties.Count - 1
            Debug.Print i & ". " & .Properties(i).Name & _
                " = " & .Properties(i).Value
        Next i
    End With
End Sub
```

You can also set values using this collection. For example, the following code makes the NewCustomerAddresses form immovable.

```
Forms("NewCustomerAddresses").Properties("Moveable").Value = False
```

Usually, it's easier to set the form's properties directly as in the following code.

```
Forms("NewCustomerAddresses").Moveable = False
```

You can use this technique to set values for properties whose names are stored in strings. For example, based on the user's name, you could create two collections giving property names and values that are appropriate for that user. Later, when the user opened a particular form, you could loop through those collections to set the property values that are appropriate for the user.

Methods

The Form object provides only a few methods. Move lets you move or resize the form. Recalc makes the form update any calculated fields. Refresh updates the records selected by the form.

Repaint finishes any pending calculations and finishes drawing the form. It does not requery the database; that's what the Requery method does.

The Undo method cancels any changes to the current record. You can use this method to give the user a Cancel button.

 NOTE *If the user navigates to another record (and* CommitOnNavigation *is True), the changes are saved and cannot later be undone.*

Report

The Report object is similar to the Form object in many ways. Both appear in Windows forms, so they share all the properties that deal with window appearance. These include the AutoCenter, AutoResize, BorderStyle, CloseButton, ControlBox, MinMaxButtons, Modal, Moveable, Picture, PictureAlignment, PictureData, PictureSizeMode, PictureTiling, and PictureType properties. See the earlier sections on the Form object for information about these properties.

Like the Form object, the Report object provides an assortment of event properties such as OnActivate, OnError, and OnClose. These properties are strings that tell which Access or VBA macro to execute when an event occurs. For a list of the Report object's event properties, search the online help for "Report Object." For more information on event properties, search the online help for "Event Properties" or go to http://msdn.microsoft.com/library/en-us/vbaac10/html/acproeventproperties.asp. For a list of event properties for various objects, search the help for "Event Properties and Objects They Apply To" or go to http://msdn.microsoft.com/library/en-us/vbaac10/html/acproevents.asp.

The Report object also shares many of the Form's data-related properties. For example, it provides CurrentRecord, Dirty, Filter, FilterOn, HasData, OrderBy, OrderByOn, RecordSource, and Recordset properties. See the earlier sections discussing the Form object and the online help for more information about these.

Finally, a Report can be associated with a code module much as a Form can, so it has similar HasModule and Module properties.

The Report object does have several properties and methods not supported by the Form object. The following sections describe the most useful Report properties. The sections after that describe its most valuable methods.

Properties

Although the Form object doesn't provide methods for drawing directly on the form's surface, the Report object does. Many of the Report object's unique properties and methods deal with drawing and writing on the report surface.

A Report is also naturally broken into sections and pages. Whereas a form typically displays one record at a time, a report may display data from hundreds of records and it may require many pages.

The following sections describe these properties that deal with drawing, writing, and pages, in addition to a few other interesting properties.

Page and Section Properties

The Page property returns the page number currently being printed. Pages returns the total number of pages in the report. Typically, you would use these properties to display the number of the page currently being printed.

The PageHeader and PageFooter properties determine how page headers and footers are printed with the report header and footer. These properties can take the values 0 (print the page header/footer on all pages, the default), 1 (don't print on the page containing the report header), 2 (don't print on the page containing the report footer), or 3 (don't print on the page containing the report header or footer). If these properties are set to 2 or 3, Access prints the report footer on a new page at the end.

The PicturePages property determines where the report's picture is displayed. This property can take the values 0 (on all pages, the default), 1 (on the first page only), or 2 (on no pages).

The Section property is a collection that returns Section objects representing the different areas on the report. The index into the Section collection can be acDetail, acHeader, acFooter, acPageHeader, acPageFooter, acGroupLevel1Header, acGroupLevel1Footer, acGroupLevel2Header, or acGroupLevel2Footer.

TIP *The Form object has a similar* Section *property, although it doesn't support the group level sections.*

For example, the following code draws circles on the CustomerAddresses report's header and then sets background colors for the report's header and page footer sections.

 FILE *Ch10\Customers.mdb*

```
' Draw on the report header and set colors for
' the header and page footer sections.
Private Sub ReportHeader_Print(Cancel As Integer, PrintCount As Integer)
Dim i As Single

    For i = 1 To 20
        Me.Circle (i * 120, i * 120), i * 120 - 20
    Next i

    With Reports("CustomerAddresses")
        .Section(acHeader).BackColor = vbRed
        .Section(acPageFooter).BackColor = vbBlue
        .Section(acDetail).BackColor = vbWhite
    End With
End Sub
```

The PrintSection property determines whether the current section is displayed. For instance, the following code runs when the CustomerAddresses report generates its report header. It sets the PrintSection property to False so the report header is not shown.

```
Private Sub ReportHeader_Print(Cancel As Integer, PrintCount As Integer)
    Reports("CustomerAddresses").PrintSection = False
End Sub
```

Text and Drawing Properties

When Access formats part of a report, it raises an appropriate event. For example, when it generates a report's header section, it raises a ReportHeader_Print event.

You can catch these events and draw directly on the appropriate part of the report. For example, in the ReportHeader_Print event handler, you can draw on the report's header area. You cannot draw on other parts of the report at that time. If you try to draw outside the header area, Access clips off your drawing.

NOTE *In the names of these event handlers, the word "Print" refers to printing to the screen and to a printer, so the event handlers fire whether you are printing the report or viewing it on the screen.*

While the event handler is executing, the report's ScaleLeft, ScaleTop, ScaleWidth, and ScaleHeight properties give you the dimensions of the appropriate area. To continue the same example, while the ReportHeader_Print event handler is executing, these properties give the dimensions of the report's header area.

The Report object has several properties for positioning and drawing text. CurrentX and CurrentY get or set the position inside the current area (header or whatever) for text output using the Print method. The FontBold, FontItalic, FontName, FontSize, and FontUnderline properties determine the font's characteristics. ForeColor determines the text's color.

The following code, when called from a report's Detail_Print event handler, draws the first letter of the ContactName field using a customized font. The code begins by setting the font's size, color, bold, italic, and name properties. It gets the letter it will print and sets CurrentX and CurrentY to position the text. Then it calls the Print method to draw the text. The TextWidth and Print methods are described shortly in the Report object's "Methods" section.

FILE *Ch10\Customers.mdb*

```
' Draw the ContactName's first letter in a large,
' red, bold, italicised Comic Sans MS font.
Private Sub DetailPrintInitial()
Dim ch As String

    ' Set the font characteristics.
    Me.FontSize = 16
    Me.ForeColor = vbRed
```

```
        Me.FontBold = True
        Me.FontItalic = True
        Me.FontName = "Comic Sans MS"

        ' Place the initial just left of the StreetName.
        ch = Left$(Me.ContactName, 1)
        CurrentX = Me.Controls("Street").Left - Me.TextWidth(ch) * 1.5
        CurrentY = 0

        ' Draw the initial.
        Me.Print ch
    End Sub
```

Figure 10-1 shows the results at a zoom factor of 200 percent.

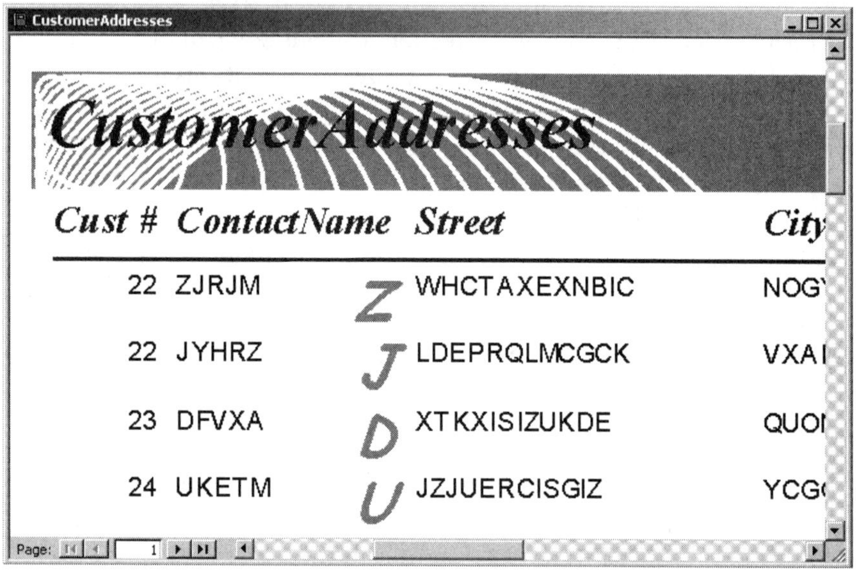

Figure 10-1. The Report *object lets you draw text where and how you want it.*

The Report object provides several properties that control the appearance of drawings. The ForeColor property, which you've already seen in the previous code, determines the color of any text or other graphics drawn.

DrawMode determines how the ForeColor is used to produce the output color. The different values this property can take are somewhat confusing. For example, the value 1 means Access should draw in black no matter what value ForeColor has and no matter what color is already on the report. The value 13 is the default and tells Access to draw using the ForeColor value. The value 6 inverts whatever color is on the report. For example, if you draw a line across a white area, the result is the bitwise inverse of white (that is, black). This setting is useful for ensuring that a line drawn across a very complicated area is visible no matter what colors it crosses. Other values for DrawMode are even more confusing. See the online help for more details.

NOTE *Actually, using* DrawMode *6 is a little more confusing. If you invert a color such as RGB(128, 128, 128) you get RGB(127, 127, 127) which is pretty much the same. If your system uses 8-bit color or some lower color model, the bitwise inversion applies to the color palette. If you know nothing about the colors on the report, however,* DrawMode *6 gives you a decent chance of making a line visible.*

DrawStyle determines the dash style of lines and circles. This property can take the values 0 (solid), 1 (dashed), 2 (dotted), 3 (dash-dotted), 4 (dash-dot-dotted), 5 (invisible lines with transparent interior), and 6 (invisible lines with solid interior). (The last two values are rather strange and less common than the others. Their exact behavior depends on whether you are drawing a line, rectangle, or circle. If you need them, a little experimentation should give you the result you need.)

DrawWidth determines how thick, in pixels, lines are drawn. The special value 0 means draw a line one pixel wide. If DrawWidth is greater than 0, the report ignores DrawStyle and draws a solid line.

FillColor and FillStyle determine how the report fills closed areas such as circles. FillColor applies only to the interior of the object, and ForeColor determines the color of the object's border. FillStyle can take the values 0 (opaque), 1 (transparent), 2 (horizontal line), 3 (vertical line), 4 (upper-left to lower-right diagonal), 5 (lower-left to upper-right diagonal), 6 (cross), and 7 (diagonal cross).

NOTE *Some combinations of* DrawStyle *and* FillStyle *may be contradictory. For example, if* DrawStyle *is 6 (transparent with solid interior) and* FillStyle *is 5 (lower-left to upper-right diagonal),* FillStyle *wins. So, a rectangle, for example, is filled with diagonal lines. You can use a little experimentation to get the results you want.*

For instance, when a report's `Detail_Print` event handler calls the following code, it sets `DrawStyle` to 5 and draws a box using the `Line` statement (described shortly). The result is shown in Figure 10-2 at a 200 percent zoom.

 FILE *Ch10\Customers.mdb*

```
' Draw a filled box.
Sub DetailPrintBox()
Dim wid As Single

    wid = Me.Controls("CustomerNumber").Left + _
        Me.Controls("CustomerNumber").Width * 0.6
    Me.FillStyle = 5
    Line (0, 0)-Step(wid, ScaleHeight - 30), , B
End Sub
```

Figure 10-2. `FillStyle` *5 fills areas with slanted lines going from lower-left to upper-right.*

Methods

Most of the Report object's methods are drawing routines. The Circle method draws a circle, an ellipse, or an arc of an ellipse depending on its parameters. Its flexibility makes it a bit confusing. The basic syntax is:

```
Circle (X, Y), Radius, Color, StartAngle, EndAngle, AspectRatio
```

Here X and Y give the coordinates of the circle's center. Radius gives the circle's radius. The StartAngle and EndAngle parameters tell where an arc should begin and end. If you omit these parameters, the method draws a whole circle. If one of these values is negative, the Circle method draws a line from the center of the circle to the corresponding point on the circle.

AspectRatio is the ellipse's ratio of height to width. If this value is 1.0, the ellipse is a circle. When this value is not 1.0, the Radius parameter really gives the ellipse's horizontal radius. The vertical radius is the AspectRatio times the Radius value. For example, the following code draws an ellipse centered at (400, 200) with width 800 (2 * 400) and height 200 (2 * 400 * 0.25).

```
Circle (400, 200), 400, , , , 0.25
```

The Report object's Line method draws a line. Its syntax is:

```
Line [Step](X1, Y1)-[Step](X2, Y2), Color, [B][F]
```

Here Step, B, and F are literal values that you may optionally add to the statement. Step means the following coordinates are relative to the previous coordinates. The first Step option makes the first point relative to the position (CurrentX, CurrentY). The second Step option means the second point is relative to the first. For example, the following two statements are equivalent.

```
Line (100, 100)-Step(200, 300)
Line (100, 100)-(300, 400)
```

The X1, Y1, X2, and Y2 parameters give the coordinates of the points to join with the line. These values may be absolute or relative, depending on whether you include the Step keywords.

Color specifies the line's color. If you specify Color, it overrides the Report object's ForeColor property.

The B option means the Line method should draw a box rather than a line. The following statement draws a box with opposite corners at (100, 100) and (300, 500).

```
Line (100, 100)-(300, 500), , B
```

The F option makes the box filled. You cannot specify F unless you also specify B.

The following more interesting example draws a face next to each record in the CustomerAddresses report. Depending on the first letter in the ContactName field, the code draws a yellow smiley face, a green neutral face, or a blue frowning face.

TIP *A more appropriate criterion for deciding on the type of face might be the customer's account balance, account status, shipping status, and so forth.*

FILE *Ch10\Customers.mdb*

```
' Draw a face next to the customer detail line
' depending on the first letter of their names
'
' A-I   Happy
' J-R   Neutral
' S-Z   Sad
Private Sub DetailPrintFaces()
Const PI = 3.14159265

Dim Cx As Single
Dim Cy As Single
Dim R As Single

    ' Center the face near the left side
    ' of this record's detail area.
    Cy = ScaleHeight / 2
    R = Cy * 0.8
    Cx = ScaleLeft + 1.2 * R

    ' Draw the face.
    Me.DrawWidth = 0
    Me.FillStyle = 0            ' Opaque.
    Select Case Left$(Me.ContactName, 1)
        Case "A" To "I"     ' Happy
            Me.FillColor = vbYellow         ' Yellow.
            Me.Circle (Cx, Cy), R
```

```
            Me.Circle (Cx, Cy), R * 0.7, vbBlack, PI, 2 * PI
        Case "J" To "R"      ' Neutral
            Me.FillColor = RGB(0, 192, 0)    ' Green.
            Me.Circle (Cx, Cy), R
            Me.Line (Cx - R * 0.4, Cy + R * 0.4)-Step(R * 0.8, 0)
        Case "S" To "Z"      ' Sad
            Me.FillColor = RGB(0, 128, 255) ' Blue.
            Me.Circle (Cx, Cy), R
            Me.Circle (Cx, Cy + R), R * 0.7, vbBlack, PI * 0.25, PI * 0.75
    End Select

    Me.FillColor = vbBlack
    Me.Circle (Cx, Cy), R * 0.2
    Me.Circle (Cx - R * 0.4, Cy - R * 0.3), R * 0.2
    Me.Circle (Cx + R * 0.4, Cy - R * 0.3), R * 0.2
End Sub
```

Figure 10-3 shows the results at 200 percent zoom.

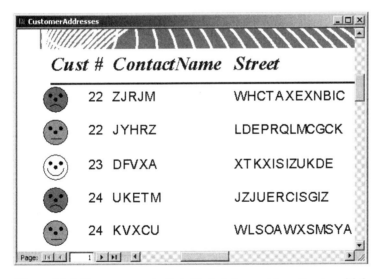

Figure 10-3. You can use the Detail_Print *event handler to add drawings to the lines on a report.*

The Report object's PSet method sets the color of a single pixel. The syntax is:

```
PSet (X, Y), Color
```

In practice, setting individual pixels in a report sometimes leads to unexpected results. You may be better off using the Line statement with the BF options to make a small filled box.

Two final Report methods are useful for formatting text. The TextWidth and TextHeight methods return the width and height of a string, respectively.

CAUTION *Be sure to set the report's font properties before you use* TextWidth *and* TextHeight. *Otherwise, these methods will return the size of the text in the previously selected font, not the font you are going to use.*

Module

The Module object represents a standard code module or a class module. The Modules collection contains a Module object for each module that is open in the VBA development environment.

A Form or Report object's Module property returns a Module object representing its code. This Module is available when the form or report is open and is not necessarily also contained in the Modules collection, depending on whether the module is also open in the IDE.

The Module object's Type property returns either acClassModule or acStandardModule to indicate the module's type.

Other properties give you access to parts of the module. For instance, the following code displays all lines in the Samples module. The Lines property takes as parameters a starting line number and the number of lines to return. The CountOfLines property returns the total number of lines in the module.

FILE *Ch10\Customers.mdb*

```
' Display this module's code.
Sub ShowModuleLines()
    With Modules("Samples")
        Debug.Print .Lines(1, .CountOfLines)
    End With
End Sub
```

The following example displays the lines in the ListAllTables subroutine. The ProcStartLine and ProcCountLines properties give the start line and number of lines in the indicated routine, respectively.

FILE *Ch10\Customers.mdb*

```
' Display the code for the ListAllTables routine.
Sub ShowListAllTables()
    With Modules("Samples")
        Debug.Print .Lines( _
            .ProcStartLine("ListAllTables", vbext_pk_Proc), _
            .ProcCountLines("ListAllTables", vbext_pk_Proc))
    End With
End Sub
```

The Module object also provides a few methods for manipulating the code. The AddFromFile and AddFromString methods insert code into the module from a file or a string passed as a parameter. InsertLines adds text at a specific position. Insert-Text adds text at the end of the module.

NOTE *Yes, it's a bit silly to have all these different methods that do more or less the same thing. It probably would have been fine to have one or two methods with a few extra parameters to indicate where the new text belonged.*

The Module object also provides DeleteLines, ReplaceLine, and Find methods.

See the online help for a complete list of the Module's properties and methods, and for more detailed descriptions.

Summary

Seen from a developer's point of view, Access appears somewhat schizophrenic. It includes its own system of forms, reports, and Access-style macros that you can use to build a complete user interface using only Access tools. At the same time, Access supports UserForms and VBA macros. It also has an Application object that lets you program Access from within VBA, from another Office application, or from some other program written in another language, such as Visual Basic or C++.

As if that weren't bad enough, you can also take several different approaches to using an Access database after you create it. For example, you can use the Application object to manipulate Access objects. You can also use DAO, RDO, ADO, or some other database access technology to manipulate the data.

Describing all of these methods in detail is outside the scope of this book and wouldn't do you much good anyway. Few developers need to use all of these techniques.

This chapter describes many of the objects you can use to manipulate Access itself at design time or while running Access forms and reports. It doesn't explain every detail of the Access object model, but it should be enough to get you started. Use the online help to fill in any details you might need to solve specific problems.

The following chapter provides an introduction to using ADO to manipulate a database after you create it with Access. ADO is probably the most common method for handling Access data, at least for now.

NOTE *Microsoft's favorite database access method shifts periodically. Currently, they seem to be moving toward ADO.NET. In practice, your development environment will probably determine the method you use. If you use VB 6 or an earlier version, you should use ADO. If you're using VB .NET, you should use ADO.NET.*

Unfortunately, despite the similarity of name, ADO.NET is very different from ADO. At least they both use an object model to allow access to the data. If you are unfamiliar with using object models in this way, working with ADO will be reasonably good practice.

CHAPTER 11

Access and ADO

OVER THE PAST FEW YEARS, Microsoft has gone through a series of tools for letting a program access a database. These have included DAO, RDO, OLE DB, ADO, and ADO.NET. Each had its moment in the sun before being superceded by a newer technology.

One of the more recent and most effective of these technologies is ADO. ADO provides objects you can use to open a database and then read, update, delete, and otherwise manipulate the database.

NOTE *ADO.NET is Microsoft's latest and greatest database access technique designed for manipulating databases in its Visual Studio .NET languages, such as Visual Basic .NET. Despite the similar name, ADO.NET is very different from ADO. Both use objects to manipulate the database, but the objects they provide are quite different.*

ADO and ADO.NET also use fundamentally different approaches to retrieving and storing data. ADO.NET assumes a much more disconnected approach through which the program fetches data into local data structures, works with it for a while, and then moves any changes back into the database. This type of access is particularly appropriate for Web-based client/server applications. ADO allows this type of access, but it also lets you maintain a cursor on the database so changes are more immediate.

If you want to use databases from Office 2000 or from Visual Basic 6 (or earlier versions), you can use ADO. If you want to use databases from Visual Basic .NET, you should probably skip this chapter and learn ADO.NET instead. For an overview of ADO.NET, see the Microsoft articles "ADO.NET for the ADO Programmer" (http://msdn.microsoft.com/library/en-us/ dndotnet/html/adonetprogmsdn.asp), *"Using ADO.NET"* (http:// msdn.microsoft.com/library/en-us/Dndotnet/html/Usingadonet.asp), *and "Accessing Data with ADO.NET"* (http://msdn.microsoft.com/library/ en-us/cpguide/html/cpconaccessingdatawithadonet.asp?frame=true). *For more in-depth information, see a book that covers ADO.NET in more detail, such as* Visual Basic .NET Database Programming *by Rod Stephens (Que, 2002).*

This chapter explains the basics of ADO: how to open, manipulate, and close a database using ADO. This should be sufficient for most common Office 2000 applications. If you need to work with ADO at a much greater level of detail, you should read a book specifically about ADO programming.

CAUTION *As is mentioned several times in this book, ADO is very different from ADO.NET. If you want to learn about ADO, don't get a book about ADO.NET! And vice versa.*

TIP *Microsoft's ADO reference is located at* http://msdn.microsoft.com/ library/en-us/ado270/htm/adostartpage1.asp. *Use the navigation frame on the left to search for ADO-related topics, including the ADO Programmer's Guide and ADO Programmer's Reference.*

Late and Early Binding

There are two general approaches to using ADO in Visual Basic or VBA code: late binding and early binding.

To use late binding, you declare the various ADO objects you will use with the generic type Object. Then you use the CreateObject function to instantiate the objects. For example, the following code creates a Connection object.

```
Dim conn As Object
Set conn = CreateObject("ADODB.Connection")
```

A big disadvantage to this method is that the VBA development environment doesn't know in advance what types of objects these variables represent. It can't tell from the declaration that conn is an ADODB.Connection object, so it can't tell what properties and methods that object might provide. It doesn't learn these things until run time, when you actually initialize the variable and try to use its properties and methods. This means that it cannot provide IntelliSense support as you write the code. It also gives the program slightly worse performance at run time.

To use early binding, you must give your application a reference to the ADO library so the VBA development environment understands the objects' types. This lets it know in advance what properties and methods the objects provide, and that gives generally better performance. Perhaps even more importantly to a developer, it also allows the development environment to provide IntelliSense.

To add a reference to the ADO library, select Tools ➤ References, check the box next to Microsoft ActiveX Data Objects 2.8 Library (or whatever version you have installed), and click OK.

TIP *If you don't have ADO installed on your computer, you can download it from Microsoft's Web site. It is included in MDAC (Microsoft Data Access Components). Currently, you can download MDAC at* www.microsoft.com/ data/download.htm.

Many of the objects defined by ADO have names similar to those provided by DAO. If you use both in the same application, you can avoid confusion by explicitly listing the library that defines the class you are using in object declarations.

TIP *It's not a bad idea to explicitly give the library even if you only use one of ADO and DAO. Then, if you (or someone else) later add the other database access method to the project, your code won't break.*

For instance, both ADO and DAO have a Recordset class. If you declare the variable rs to be of type Recordset, it's not immediately obvious which version you'll get. You may be able to figure it out, but you run the risk of mixing ADO objects with DAO objects and becoming very confused. For example, suppose you call an ADO function that returns an ADO Recordset. If you try to assign the result to a DAO Recordset variable, VBA will complain that the variable has the wrong data type. You can plainly see that variable is of type Recordset and that the function returns a Recordset, so what's the problem? It's a bad way to spend an afternoon.

To avoid this kind of trouble, explicitly declare libraries for all ADO and DAO variables. For instance, the following code declares both ADO and DAO Recordset objects.

```
Dim ado_rs As ADODB.Recordset    ' An ADO Recordset.
Dim dao_rs As DAO.Recordset      ' A DAO Recordset.
```

TIP *To further reduce confusion if you use both ADO and DAO, consider including the strings "ado" and "dao" in variable names, as shown in this example.*

Connection

A Connection object represents a conduit to a database. You can obtain a connection several ways. For example, in Access VBA, the Application.CurrentProject.Connection object is a reference to the connection to the current database.

You can also build and open a Connection yourself. The Connection object provides several ways to do this. The basic idea is to set the Connection object's ConnectionString property to define the connection. Then you call the object's Open method. You can set the ConnectionString and call Open as separate steps, or you can pass the ConnectionString value as a parameter to the Open method.

The ConnectionString *Property*

The ConnectionString contains a series of name and value pairs separated with semicolons. For example, the following value specifies a connection to the database file C:\Foods.mdb using the Microsoft Jet database engine.

```
Provider=Microsoft.Jet.OLEDB.4.0;Data Source=C:\Foods.mdb
```

ConnectionString can hold a variety of other parameters that define security settings, user ID, and database password. It may also contain other parameters that depend on the database provider.

The ConnectionString format can be quite confusing. Fortunately, you can use several techniques to automatically generate a ConnectionString. These are particularly useful when you must use a data provider that you haven't used before. After you've built one ConnectionString, you can usually copy and paste it with appropriate changes to use in other programs.

The following sections explain two of the simpler of these methods for building ConnectionStrings.

Using the ADO Data Control

If you are programming in Visual Basic, you can make an ADO Data Control build a ConnectionString.

Start a Visual Basic project, select Project➤Components, check the box next to the Microsoft ADO Data Control 6.0 (OLEDB) (or whatever version is installed on your system), and click OK. Add a new ADO Data Control to your form, click on the control's ConnectionString property in the Properties window, and click the ellipsis to the right to display the dialog shown in Figure 11-1.

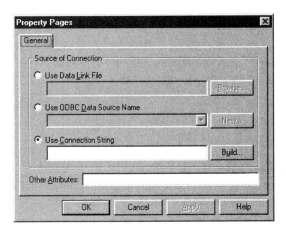

Figure 11-1. You can use Visual Basic's ADO Data Control to compose a ConnectionString.

Select the Use Connection String option (if it isn't already selected) and click Build to display the Data Link Properties dialog shown in Figure 11-2.

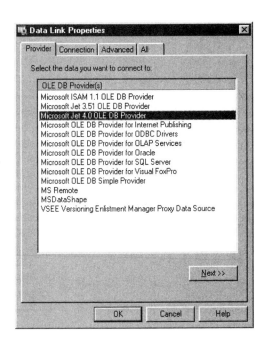

Figure 11-2. The Data Link Properties dialog defines a database connection.

Select the data provider you want to use (you can use Jet for Access databases) and click Next to see the Connection tab shown in Figure 11-3.

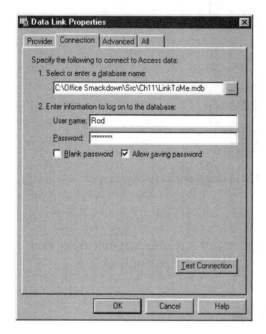

Figure 11-3. Specify the database name, user, and password information on this tab.

Enter the database name or click the button with the ellipsis to select the database file. Enter the user name you want to use when connecting to the database. If you want to specify a password, uncheck the "Blank password" box and enter the password (the password box is disabled if the "Blank password" box is checked).

TIP *If you uncheck the "Allow saving password" property, the dialog sets the* ConnectionString's *Persist Security Info property to False and doesn't include the user name or password in the string. If you want to see how the password is included in the string, check this box.*

TIP *If you leave the user name with its default value Admin, the dialog omits the user name parameter from the string. To see how this parameter is included, change the user name to something else.*

If you click the Test Connection button, the system tries to connect to the database using the parameters you entered. This verifies that the database exists, that the data provider can understand it, and that the user name and password you entered work. If you can test the database in this way, it's a good idea.

NOTE *Sometimes you may want to fill in the database, user name, or password at run time. In that case, you may not be able to test the connection now.*

Click on the Advanced tab, shown in Figure 11-4, to specify database access and sharing parameters.

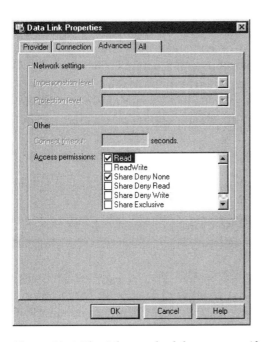

Figure 11-4. The Advanced tab lets you specify data access parameters.

When you click OK, the Property Pages dialog shown in Figure 11-5 contains the completed ConnectionString (highlighted in the figure). You can copy and paste this string, or you can click OK and then copy the value from the control's ConnectionString property in the Properties window.

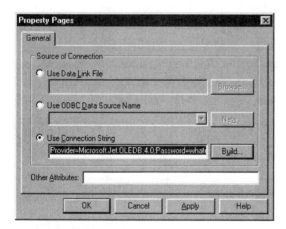

Figure 11-5. The Property Pages dialog shows the ConnectionString *you built.*

The following text shows typical results. The different parameter statements are shown on separate lines to make them easier to read, but you should put them all in one long string without carriage returns in your program's code.

Note that each parameter clause is separated from the next by a semicolon. The last parameter is not followed by a semicolon because nothing follows it. The Mode parameter contains a series of data access and sharing values separated by vertical bars (|).

```
Provider=Microsoft.Jet.OLEDB.4.0;
Password=whatever;
User ID=Rod;
Data Source=C:\Office Smackdown\Src\Ch11\LinkToMe.mdb;
Mode=Read|Share Deny None;
Persist Security Info=True
```

You can use this string as a template for your Visual Basic code. For instance, the following code composes a ConnectionString with user name and password values entered by the user.

Notice how the code uses line breaks to make the string more readable. Also notice that the code has changed the Persist Security Info parameter to False. This tells the data provider not to save the password and other sensitive information.

```
connect_string = _
    "Provider=Microsoft.Jet.OLEDB.4.0;" & _
    "Password=" & txtPassword.Text & ";" & _
    "User ID=" & txtUserName.Text & ";" & _
    "Mode=Read|Share Deny None;" & _
    "Data Source=C:\Office Smackdown\Src\Ch11\LinkToMe.mdb;" & _
    "Persist Security Info=False"
```

Using Data Link Files

Another way to build a ConnectionString uses a data link file. This is a file that defines a database connection, basically by holding a ConnectionString.

To build a data link file, right-click on your Windows desktop and select New➤Microsoft Data Link.

If your system's shortcut menu doesn't have a New➤Microsoft Data Link option, select New➤TXT File (or New➤Text Document or whatever it's called on your system). Right-click the new file, select Rename, and change the file's extension to .udl.

Having created a data link file, double-click it to open a dialog similar to the one shown in Figure 11-3. Click the Provider tab to select a provider as shown in Figure 11-2. Click Next to return to the Connection tab and enter the database name, user name, and password. Test the connection if you want, then click OK.

Now open the data link file using your favorite text editor. Figure 11-6 shows the file open in WordPad. The lines below the comment "; Everything after this line is an OLE DB initstring" gives the ConnectionString that you can copy and paste into your code. The string is wrapped in WordPad because it is so long (they always are for all but the simplest connection strings), but it will appear on one line when you paste it.

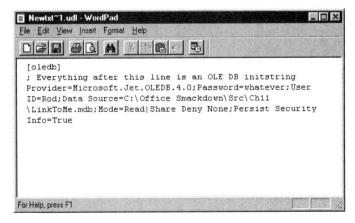

Figure 11-6. WordPad can show you the contents of the data link file.

An Example

Once you have built a ConnectionString, you can use it to connect to a database. The following code shows how to make a Word table from data in an Access database. It starts by declaring some variables including ADO Connection, Recordset, and Field objects. It composes the database file's name. Then it creates the Connection object, sets its Mode property to allow read-only access, and defines the object's ConnectionString. This string says that the Connection should use the Microsoft Jet database engine and tells where the database is. The code then calls the Connection object's Open method.

Next the code calls the object's Execute method. It passes the method a SQL statement telling it to select data from the database's CustomerAddresses table. When you pass the Execute method a SQL SELECT statement such as this one, Execute returns a Recordset object representing the selected rows of data. Each row of data contains fields that hold the data values.

The program iterates through the Recordset's Fields collection and adds the names of the selected fields to a string, separating them with tabs. Then it calls the Recordset's GetString method to shovel all of the Recordset's data into a string all at once. Parameters tell GetString to separate fields with tabs and records with the string vbCrLf, and to represent NULL database values with the string "<null>".

At this point, the program has all the data it needs, so it closes the Recordset and Connection objects. Closing these objects when you don't need them frees system and database resources. Freeing those resources makes it more likely that the database will be able to satisfy other users' requests for data. Closing objects you no longer need is also good programming practice. If an object isn't connected to the database, your code cannot accidentally mess up the data.

Now that the program has its data, it turns to Word VBA code. It makes a Range object pointing to the end of the document, adds the text containing the data, and converts the Range into a table. The carriage returns in the data string make Word place different database records in different table rows. The tabs characters make Word place data fields in different table cells. The code makes the table size itself to fit the data and adds a blank line at the end of the document.

FILE *Ch11\UseAdo.doc*

```
Sub ListCustomers()
Dim db_name As String
Dim conn As ADODB.Connection
Dim rs As ADODB.Recordset
Dim new_field As ADODB.Field
Dim txt As String
Dim new_range As Range

    ' Compose the database name.
    db_name = Me.Path & "\Customers.mdb"

    ' Connect to the database.
    Set conn = New ADODB.Connection
    conn.Mode = adModeRead
    conn.ConnectionString = _
        "Provider=Microsoft.Jet.OLEDB.4.0;" & _
        "Data Source=" & db_name
    conn.Open

    ' Select all of the records in the Customers table.
    Set rs = conn.Execute( _
        "SELECT DISTINCT ContactName, Street, City, State, Zip, Phone " & _
        "FROM CustomerAddresses ORDER BY ContactName")

    ' Add a row containing the field names.
    For Each new_field In rs.Fields
        txt = txt & vbTab & new_field.Name
    Next new_field
    txt = Mid$(txt, 2) & vbCrLf      ' Remove leading tab.

    ' Get the Recordset's data as a single string
    ' with vbTab between fields and vbCrLf between rows.
    txt = txt & rs.GetString( _
        ColumnDelimeter:=vbTab, _
        RowDelimeter:=vbCrLf, _
        NullExpr:="<null>")
```

```
    ' Close the Recordset and Connection.
    rs.Close
    conn.Close

    ' Make a Range at the end of the Word document.
    Set new_range = ActiveDocument.Range
    new_range.Collapse wdCollapseEnd

    ' Insert the text and convert it to a table.
    new_range.InsertAfter txt
    new_range.ConvertToTable vbTab

    ' Autofit to the contents.
    new_range.Tables(1).AutoFitBehavior wdAutoFitContent

    ' Add a blank line.
    Set new_range = ActiveDocument.Range
    new_range.Collapse wdCollapseEnd
    new_range.InsertParagraph
    new_range.Collapse wdCollapseEnd
    new_range.InsertParagraph
End Sub
```

The `Connection` object's `ConnectionString` property and its `Open` and `Execute` methods are its most useful features and are enough for many applications. With some more advanced work, you can make this object connect to a database asynchronously, execute an SQL statement asynchronously, manage transactions, or get schema information describing the database's structure.

 NOTE *A transaction is a series of database commands that should be executed as a unit. Your code starts a transaction and executes a series of database commands. Later, it can accept the transaction, making the changes permanent, or it can rollback the transaction, canceling all of its actions.*

See the online help at http://msdn.microsoft.com/library/en-us/ado270/htm/ mdaobj01_7.asp for more information about the `Connection` object.

Recordset

A Recordset object represents a set of data returned by a database query. You can think of the Recordset as representing a particular record in the returned data. Its Fields collection gives you access to the fields within the record. Each Field object has Name, Value, and other properties that let you know the field's type of data and its value.

Many applications step through the Recordset's records one at a time, using the MoveNext method to go to the next record. The EOF (End Of File) function returns True when the Recordset is at the end of its data. The following code fragment shows a typical loop through a Recordset's data.

```
' Connect to the database and build the Recordset rs.
...
' Loop through the data.
Do While Not rs.EOF
    ' Do something with this record.
    ...
    ' Get the next record.
    rs.MoveNext
Loop
```

CAUTION *Forgetting to call* MoveNext *is a common mistake. The result is an infinite loop processing the first record over and over again.*

The Recordset also has MovePrevious, MoveFirst, and MoveLast methods for navigating through the data. The BOF (Beginning Of File) method returns True if the Recordset is at the first record and you use MovePrevious to try to move before the first record. If you use MovePrevious to loop backward through a Recordset, you can use BOF to see when you have visited all of the records.

TIP *Both* EOF *and* BOF *are True if the* Recordset *is empty.*

NOTE *Not all* Recordsets *support all navigation methods. The* adOpenForwardOnly CursorType *described shortly prevents you from moving backward through the* Recordset.

The Move method can move a specific number of records or jump to a particular bookmarked location. The Recordset's Bookmark property returns a Variant you can use to record the Recordset's position. For example, the following code fragment records a bookmark and later returns to it.

```
' Create the Recordset rs and move through the records for a while.
...
' Save the bookmark.
Dim saved_bookmark As Variant
saved_bookmark = rs.Bookmark

' Move through the records some more.
...
' Return to the bookmark.
rs.Bookmark = saved_bookmark
```

Although the Recordset's various movement methods let you cruise through the data, often they are not the most efficient way to process the Recordset, depending on what you need to do with the data. The GetRows method grabs all of the Recordset's data at once and stuffs it into a two-dimensional variant array. If you aren't selecting too many records (so the memory usage doesn't swamp your computer) and you need to process most of the records, the GetRows method can be faster than stepping through the records one at a time (particularly if you are fetching the data across a network). See the online help for a discussion of parameters that tell GetRows which rows and which columns to return.

Similarly, the GetString method may be faster if you need to build a string containing the Recordset's data anyway. For instance, the code example in the previous section uses GetString to copy a Recordset's data into a string with fields separated by tabs and records separated by vbCrLf. This is exactly the format the code needs to create a table in Word.

In addition to creating a Recordset using the Connection object's Execute method, you can define a Recordset object and then call its Open method. For example, the following code opens a Recordset using its Open method.

```
' Open the Connection conn.
...
' Define and open the Recordset.
Dim rs As ADODB.Recordset
Set rs = New ADODB.Recordset
' Open the Recordset.
rs.Open "SELECT * FROM Employees", conn, , , adCmdText
```

There seems to be no big performance difference between these two methods for opening a Recordset, but the second method lets you set the Recordset's properties before calling Open, and this gives you some extra control. For example, it lets you specify the Recordset's cursor type, cursor location, and lock type.

A *cursor* controls Recordset navigation, whether you can update the data, and whether you can see changes made by other users. The Recordset object provides a couple properties that affect the cursor.

The CursorLocation property determines whether the cursor is located on the client computer (where your application is running) or on the database server (where the database lives). This property can take the values adUseClient and adUseServer.

Briefly, when you use a client-side cursor, the database passes all of the data back to your program, and the cursor running on your computer manages it. This can be fast and may provide easy navigation if the total amount of data isn't too big, but it can swamp your computer if you fetch too much data at once.

A server-side cursor manages the selected data on the database's end. It returns data to your computer only when you actually need it. This will require more trips to the database if you step through many records, but it doesn't require your computer to hold all the data at once. Server-side cursors also support dynamic and keyset cursors (described shortly). For a more detailed comparison, see the Microsoft article "Client-Side Cursors Versus Server-Side Cursors" at http://msdn.microsoft.com/library/en-us/vsentpro/html/veconclientsidecursorsversusserversidecursors.asp.

The CursorType property determines the types of actions the Recordset can take. This property can take the following values.

CURSORTYPE	MEANING
adOpenStatic	Takes a snapshot of the data so any changes made by other users are not shown in the Recordset.
adOpenForwardOnly	Similar to adOpenStatic, except you can only move forward through the data. This gives better performance and is the default.
adOpenDynamic	If other users modify the data, the Recordset shows the changes. This CursorType also allows you to use all of the Recordset's movement methods.
adOpenKeyset	Similar to adOpenDynamic, except you cannot see records that other users add (but you can see changes or deletions).

TIP *If using a static cursor, you can use the* Recordset*'s* Requery *method to refresh the data and show any changes that have been made in the database.*

Set the CursorType property before you open the Recordset or pass the CursorType as the third parameter to the Open method.

 NOTE *Client-side cursors don't support dynamic or keyset cursor types. This makes sense if you think about it. If all the data is copied to the client at once, the* Recordset *cannot know if the data has changed on the server.*

The LockType property determines the kinds of locks placed on a record when you edit it. This property can take the following values.

LOCKTYPE	MEANING
adLockOptimistic	The idea here is that another user probably won't try to access a record while you are modifying it. The data provider only briefly locks the record when you call Update.
adLockPessimistic	The idea here is that another user may try to access a record while you are modifying it. The data provider locks the record as soon as you modify any of its values. It unlocks the record only when you call Update.
adLockBatchOptimistic	Optimistic locking in batches. All changes are saved to the database when you call the Recordset's BatchUpdate method. (Imagine a client-side cursor that downloads all the data to your computer. You make a bunch of changes and then upload the results in a big batch.)
adLockReadOnly	You cannot modify the Recordset's data.

The Recordset object provides methods for adding, updating, and deleting records (assuming the Recordset type allows those operations). AddNew creates a new blank record. Set the new record's field values, then call the Update method to save the new record or the CancelUpdate method to cancel it.

The following code shows how to add a record using a Recordset. The frmNewCustomer UserForm executes this code when the user clicks the OK button. The code opens a Connection to a database. It then defines a Recordset attached to the Customers table. It calls the Recordset's AddNew method and fills in the user-entered CustomerName value. It leaves the auto-number field CustomerNumber alone. Next the code calls the Recordset's Update method to save the new record. At that point, the database fills in the CustomerNumber value and makes the new record the Recordset's current record. The code reads the auto-generated CustomerNumber value and displays it to the user. Finally, the code closes the Recordset, Connection, and UserForm.

FILE *Ch11\UseAdo.doc*

```vb
' Create the new record.
Private Sub cmdOk_Click()
Dim db_name As String
Dim conn As ADODB.Connection
Dim rs As ADODB.Recordset

    ' Compose the database name.
    db_name = ActiveDocument.Path & "\Customers.mdb"

    ' Connect to the database.
    Set conn = New ADODB.Connection
    conn.Mode = adModeReadWrite
    conn.ConnectionString = _
        "Provider=Microsoft.Jet.OLEDB.4.0;" & _
        "Data Source=" & db_name
    conn.Open

    ' Open a Recordset connected
    ' to the CustomerAddresses table.
    Set rs = New ADODB.Recordset
    Set rs.ActiveConnection = conn
    rs.CursorType = adOpenDynamic
    rs.Source = "Customers"
    rs.LockType = adLockOptimistic
    rs.Open

    ' Add the new record.
    rs.AddNew
    rs.Fields("CompanyName") = Me.txtCompanyName
    ' Leave the auto-number CustomerNumber field blank.
    rs.Update

    ' Display the new record's CustomerNumber.
    MsgBox "New CustomerNumber: " & rs.Fields("CustomerNumber").Value

    rs.Close
    conn.Close

    Unload Me
End Sub
```

To change a record, simply set a `Recordset` field to the new value. The following statement changes the rs `Recordset`'s LastName value to Stephens.

```
rs.Fields("LastName").Value = "Stephens"
```

Call the `Recordset`'s `Delete` method to remove its current record from the database.

 TIP *You can also add, update, and delete records without a* `Recordset` *by executing an appropriate SQL statement using the* `Connection` *object. For example, the following code adds a new record with CompanyName RMCC. It doesn't specify a value for the auto-number field CompanyNumber, so the database can fill it in.*

```
conn.Execute "INSERT INTO Customers (CompanyName) VALUES ('RMCC')"
```

The `Recordset` object provides many other methods that let you find particular records, requery the database, limit the number of records fetched, sort the records using different fields, and so forth. See the online help at `http://msdn.microsoft.com/library/en-us/ado270/htm/mdaobj01_19.asp` for additional details.

Field

The `Recordset` object's `Fields` collection contains `Field` objects representing the values in the selected records. You can use this collection to access specific fields by name or by position in the record. You can also use an exclamation mark followed by a field's name as shorthand for the field's value. The following three statements are equivalent (assuming the LastName field is number 2 in the Fields collection).

```
rs.Fields("LastName") = "Stephens"
rs.Fields(2) = "Stephens"
rs!LastName = "Stephens"
```

You can also loop through the `Fields` collection by using a `For Each` loop or an index loop as shown in the following code.

```
' List the field names.
For i = 0 To rs.Fields.Count - 1
    Debug.Print rs.Fields(i).Name
Next i
```

The `Field` object's most important properties are `Name` and `Value`. As you can probably guess, `Name` gives the database field's name, and value gives its value for the `Recordset`'s current record.

NOTE *The* `Name` *and* `Value` *properties may not correspond to an actual database field. If the query defining the* `Recordset` *contains a calculated value or a field with an alias,* `Name` *and* `Value` *give the calculated name and value. For example, the following SQL statement selects the concatenated FirstName and LastName fields, returning the result in a "field" named CombinedName.*

```
SELECT FirstName + ' ' + LastName AS CombinedName
```

The `Field` object provides several other properties that are sometimes useful to programs. The `Type` property returns a value indicating the field's data type. Typical values include `adDouble`, `adInteger`, and `adVarChar` (variable-length string).

The `DefinedSize` property indicates the field's size in bytes. For fixed-size fields such as integers, this value is constant. For variable-size fields such as variable-length strings, this property gives the maximum allowed length in the field. The `ActualSize` property gives the actual length of the field's current value.

Other properties and methods give the field's original value if it has been changed, tell you a numeric field's precision, and let you read and write BLOBs (binary large objects).

Command

The `Command` object represents some sort of database command such as a SQL SELECT, INSERT, or UPDATE statement.

The general idea is that you create a `Command` object and connect it to a `Connection`. You set the object's `CommandText` property to a SQL statement and then use the `Execute` method to execute the command. The `Execute` method returns a `Recordset` object if the command selects records.

You can execute the same SQL statements by using the `Connection` object's Execute method, but there are several reasons why you may prefer to use a `Command` object instead. First, you can create several `Command` objects that perform different tasks and keep them ready for use. Later, you can call their Execute methods without any other preparation.

You can also set a `Command` object's `Prepared` property to True to tell the database that it should compile the `Command`. The database compiles the `Command` the first time you use it. After that, the command executes more quickly.

Compiled `Commands` would be only marginally useful if you couldn't modify their command text. How many times do you need to execute the exact same INSERT statement? Probably just once. However, the `Command` object has a `Parameters` collection that you can use to insert parameters into the command text.

The following example uses a compiled `Command` object to insert three records in the Customers table. It opens a `Connection` as usual, creates a `Command` object, and attaches it to the `Connection`. The code then sets the `Command` object's `CommandText` property to the SQL statement it should execute. It replaces the values it will pass to the `Command` as parameters with @ characters. Next the code sets the `Command`'s `Prepared` property to True.

Now the code creates a new `Parameter` object and appends it to the `Command`'s `Parameters` collection. In this example, the parameter has type `adVarChar` (variable-length string) used as an input to the SQL statement and having maximum length 50.

At this point, the `Command` is ready and the code is finally set to use it. The program simply sets the value of the `Command` object's parameter and calls its Execute method. In this example, compiling the `Command` doesn't make a big difference. If you needed to create thousands of records, it could save a lot of time.

FILE *Ch11\UseAdo.doc*

```
' Insert three records in the Customers table.
Sub AddThreeCustomers()
Dim db_name As String
Dim conn As ADODB.Connection
Dim cmd As ADODB.Command
```

```
' Compose the database name.
db_name = Me.Path & "\Customers.mdb"

' Connect to the database.
Set conn = New ADODB.Connection
conn.Mode = adModeReadWrite
conn.ConnectionString = _
    "Provider=Microsoft.Jet.OLEDB.4.0;" & _
    "Data Source=" & db_name
conn.Open

' Create the Command object.
Set cmd = New ADODB.Command
Set cmd.ActiveConnection = conn
cmd.CommandText = "INSERT INTO Customers (CompanyName) VALUES (@)"

' Compile the Command.
cmd.Prepared = True

' Create the CompanyName parameter (type VarChar,
' as input to the INSERT statement, maximum length 50).
cmd.Parameters.Append _
    cmd.CreateParameter("CompanyName", adVarChar, adParamInput, 50)

' Create some records.
cmd.Parameters(0).Value = "Bob's House O' Software"
cmd.Execute

cmd.Parameters(0).Value = "Penny's Quality Code"
cmd.Execute

cmd.Parameters(0).Value = "Bugzapper Software"
cmd.Execute

conn.Close
End Sub
```

TIP *Your code can also index a parameter by its name, as in*
`cmd.Parameters("CompanyName").Value = "Bugzapper Software"`.
*Alternatively, you could create the parameter as a separate object and set
its value directly as in the following code. Then you don't need to look the
parameter up in the* `Parameters` *collection every time you change its value.*

```
Dim param As ADODB.Parameter

Set param = cmd.CreateParameter("CompanyName", adVarChar, adParamInput, 50)
cmd.Parameters.Append param

param.Value = "Bob's House O' Software"
cmd.Execute
```

Parameterized commands are also useful for executing stored procedures
(code stored within the database itself).

SQL

SQL (Structured Query Language, usually pronounced "sequel") is an industry
standard database manipulation language. You can use it to define statements that
add, update, selected, and delete records. You can also use SQL statements to modify the database by creating and deleting tables and indexes.

SQL is too complicated to cover in any great detail here. For a more complete
discussion, see a book on database programming or go to Microsoft's online help
pages.

TIP *The page* `http://msdn.microsoft.com/library/en-us/tsqlref/`
`ts_tsqlcon_6lyk.asp` *describes the Microsoft Transact SQL language supported by Microsoft's SQL Server database product. Some of these commands
may not work with Access and other databases, but most of the standard commands, such as SELECT, INSERT, UPDATE, and DELETE, should work with
just about any database.*

Even the most commonly used few commands can be quite complicated. For
example, the SELECT statement can select columns from multiple tables satisfy-
ing certain data conditions, grouped by certain fields, and sorted by other fields in

ascending or descending order. It can join more than one SELECT result into a combined group of records, include calculated values (SUM, AVG, MAX, and so forth), and save the results in a new temporary table.

The following sections briefly describe the most common forms of the four SQL statements SELECT, INSERT, UPDATE, and DELETE. For information on more complex SQL statements, consult a book or the online help.

Note that many clauses in SQL statements are optional. For example, if you omit the WHERE clause in a SELECT statement, the database returns every relevant record without checking that it satisfies any condition.

SELECT

The SELECT statement fetches records from the database. The basic syntax is:

```
SELECT select_list FROM table_list WHERE where_clause ORDER BY order_by_clause
```

The `select_list` parameter is a list of fields you want to select. If the `table_list` includes more than one table, the `select_list` must specify the table for any ambiguous fields.

For example, suppose `table_list` includes the tables Customers and CustomerOrders, and that both tables have a CustomerId field. Then if you want to include CustomerId in the `field_list`, you must specify the value from one of the tables as in Customers.CustomerId or CustomerOrders.CustomerId.

TIP *Often, a field like this, which is contained in multiple tables, is used to join the tables together. For example, it could select all Customers and CustomerOrders records where the CustomerId fields match.*

The `field_list` can include calculated fields such as SUM(Salary), where Salary is a table field. It can also use an AS clause to change the result field's name. For example, the following `field_list` concatenates the FirstName and LastName fields into one result field named CombinedName.

```
SELECT FirstName + ' ' LastName AS CombinedName ...
```

The special value * means to take every field from a table. For example, `Customers.*` means to take all of the fields in the Customers table.

The `table_list` parameter lists the tables that contain the fields you want to select. Usually, if the `table_list` contains more than one table, you'll want to use a WHERE clause to join the tables together.

The `where_clause` lists conditions that the fields you select must satisfy to be selected. You can separate different conditions with the AND and OR keywords.

 TIP *SQL is not case-sensitive, so SELECT, select, and Select all mean the same thing. A very useful convention is to set SQL keywords such as SELECT, INSERT, and OR in ALL CAPS, and to set table, field, and other database objects in MixedCase (sometimes called CamelCase because it has humps in the middle).*

The `order_by_clause` lists the fields that should be used to order the results. You can add the keyword ASC or DESC after a field to indicate that the field should be used ascending or descending respectively (the default is ascending).

A textual description of the SELECT statement may be slightly confusing, but a few examples will usually clarify things nicely. SQL isn't all that difficult once you get used to it.

The following example selects all fields in the Customers table and orders them by using the AccountBalance field with the largest values first.

```
SELECT * FROM Customers ORDER BY AccountBalance DESC
```

The following statement selects all fields from the Customers and CustomerAddresses tables where Customers.CustomerNumber equals CustomerAddresses.CustomerNumber.

```
SELECT * FROM Customers, CustomerAddresses
WHERE Customers.CustomerNumber = CustomerAddresses.CustomerNumber
```

The following statement selects Customers and CustomerAddresses records where the CompanyName begins with G or M.

```
SELECT * FROM Customers, CustomerAddresses
WHERE Customers.CustomerNumber = CustomerAddresses.CustomerNumber
AND (CompanyName LIKE 'G%' OR
    CompanyName LIKE 'M%')
```

Joins

A *join* is when you select records from more than one related table. For example, the following statement selects records from the Customers and CustomerAddresses tables where the records have the same CustomerNumber values.

```
SELECT * FROM Customers, CustomerAddresses
WHERE Customers.CustomerNumber = CustomerAddresses.CustomerNumber
```

Unfortunately, this basic form of join doesn't completely specify what the database should do under all circumstances. Suppose a record in one of these tables has a CustomerNumber value that doesn't appear in the other table. What should the database do? Should it return the record with no values for the other table's data? Or should it skip the record? SQL includes a special join syntax that lets you specify exactly what you want done.

By default, the database ignores any records in either table that do not have a corresponding record in the other table. This is called an *inner join.*

A *left outer join* selects all records in the table on the left side of the JOIN keyword plus any matching records in the table on the right. If a record in the left table has no matching records in the other table, the query returns the left record with null data values for the corresponding right table values. The following query is similar to the previous one, except it selects all records from the Customers table even if there is no corresponding record in the CustomerAddresses table. Notice that the WHERE clause has been converted into an ON clause within the table list.

```
SELECT *
FROM Customers LEFT JOIN CustomerAddresses
  ON Customers.CustomerNumber = CustomerAddresses.CustomerNumber
```

A *right outer join* does the opposite of a left outer join: it selects all of the records in the table on the right even if there are no corresponding records in the table on the left.

A *full outer join* selects all records from both tables even if some don't have corresponding records in the other table.

 NOTE *If you like, you can explicitly specify an inner join as in the following SELECT statement.*

```
SELECT *
FROM Customers INNER JOIN CustomerAddresses
  ON Customers.CustomerNumber = CustomerAddresses.CustomerNumber
```

INSERT

The basic syntax for the INSERT statement is:

```
INSERT INTO table (field_list) VALUES (value_list)
```

The `table` parameter gives the name of the database table into which you are inserting a record.

The `field_list` parameter, which is optional, lists the fields for which you are supplying values. The `value_list` gives the values for the `field_list`. The order of the values must match the order of the fields listed. The order need not match the fields' order in the table definition, however.

If you omit `field_list`, you must provide a value for every field in the table in the order they are listed in the table's definition. If you provide a `field_list` that omits some of the table's fields, the database inserts NULL values for those fields.

NOTE *Actually, this depends on how the table is defined. If a field is defined not to allow null values, the database raises an error. If the field defines a default value, the database inserts that value.*

The following example adds a record to the Employees table. This example assumes the table has three fields: LastName, FirstName, and SocialSecurityNumber. If the table doesn't have exactly three fields that can hold the values passed in the INSERT statement in this order, the database raises an error.

```
INSERT INTO Employees VALUES ('Stephens', 'Rod', '123-45-6789')
```

The following statement creates a new Employees record, assigning values to just the LastName and FirstName fields. The database gives the SocialSecurityNumber field a null value.

```
INSERT INTO Employees (LastName, FirstName)
VALUES ('Stephens', 'Rod')
```

If the table contains an auto-number field, you must not assign a value to it either explicitly or implicitly. That means you must use a `field_list` and omit the auto-number field from the list. For example, suppose the Customers table contains two fields: CustomerName and CustomerNumber, which is an auto-number field. The following statement creates a new record for the Coders R Us company.

```
INSERT INTO Customers (CustomerName) VALUES ('Coders R Us')
```

UPDATE

The UPDATE statement changes the values in one or more fields in one or more records. The basic syntax is:

```
UPDATE table SET values_list WHERE where_clause
```

The `table` parameter tells which table you want to update.

The `values_list` parameter is a list of field names and values that you want to assign. It can include constant values such as `LastName = 'Stephens'`. It can also include references to other fields in the selected record. For example, the statement `Bonus = Salary * 0.1` sets a record's Bonus field to 0.1 times its Salary field's value.

The `where_clause` parameter specifies conditions much as a WHERE clause does in a SELECT statement.

The following example sets the LastName value to Stephens for every record in the Employees table where LastName is currently Stevens.

```
UPDATE Employees SET LastName = 'Stephens' WHERE LastName = 'Stevens'
```

The following statement sets the Office and Extension fields for Tiffany Wolfe to explicit values.

```
UPDATE Employees SET Office = 'B-212', Extension = '1234'
WHERE LastName = 'Wolfe' AND FirstName = 'Tiffany'
```

In one common scenario, an application sets some or all of a record's fields and uses a unique key to identify the record. For example, employee ID, Social Security number, and product serial number make good unique identifiers because you know two records must have different values. The following statement updates the values for employee number 61426.

```
UPDATE Employees SET
  LastName = 'Shunk',
  FirstName = 'Marvin',
  Office = 'B-212',
  Extension = '1234',
  ... <other fields> ...
WHERE EmployeeId = 61426
```

DELETE

The DELETE statement removes one or more records from a table. The basic syntax is:

```
DELETE FROM table WHERE where_clause
```

The `table` parameter gives the table from which you want to remove records. The `where_clause` gives conditions that define the records that should be removed.

The following statement removes all Employees records with LastName field Katz.

```
DELETE FROM Employees WHERE LastName = 'Katz'
```

 TIP *This statement could remove many records if several have the same LastName value Katz. In many cases, a program wants to remove exactly one record. In that case, it should use a unique field (such as employee ID) or a unique combination of fields (such as LastName plus FirstName) to ensure that it deletes only the target record.*

The following statement has no WHERE clause, so it removes every record from the Inventory table.

```
DELETE FROM Inventory
```

The DELETE statement is instant and unforgiving. If you accidentally delete a record, you cannot get it back later.

 CAUTION *A particularly devastating bug is to use code that accidentally creates an empty WHERE clause or forgets to add the WHERE clause to the statement. Then every record in the table is deleted!*

 TIP *To prevent disastrous deletions with a missing WHERE clause, some programs precede a DELETE statement with a SELECT statement using the same WHERE clause to see how many records would be deleted. It can then ask the user if that makes sense. A user who wants to delete one or two records should be suspicious if the program asks if it should delete 2,615 records.*

Read-Only Databases

This is a small matter, but it's a common enough and tricky enough situation to deserve its own section. When you open an Access database using ADO, the Jet database engine normally creates an .ldb file in the database's directory. It uses this file to keep track of locks that allow multiple users to access the database without interfering with each other.

This is fine as long as your program has permission to write into the database's directory. If it doesn't have permission, however, ADO fails to open the database because it cannot create this lock file. A particularly annoying case occurs when the database is on a read-only CD-ROM. Because you cannot write on the CD-ROM, ADO certainly cannot create the lock file.

To avoid this problem, your program can open the database for exclusive read-only access. If you open the database in this way, the database engine knows it doesn't have to worry about anyone else using the database and that you won't modify the data. In that case, it doesn't need to worry about locks, so it doesn't need to create the lock file.

The following code opens a database connection exclusively with read-only access. It then selects records from a database on a CD-ROM and displays the results.

FILE *Ch11\UseAdo.doc*

```
' Execute a query on the CD-ROM database D:\Customers.mdb.
Sub ExecuteReadOnlyQuery()
Dim conn As ADODB.Connection
Dim rs As ADODB.Recordset
Dim i As Integer

    ' Connect to the database.
    Set conn = New ADODB.Connection
    conn.Mode = adModeRead Or adModeShareExclusive
    conn.ConnectionString = _
        "Provider=Microsoft.Jet.OLEDB.4.0;" & _
        "Data Source=D:\Customers.mdb"
    conn.Open
```

```
' Select all of the records in the Customers table.
Set rs = conn.Execute( _
    "SELECT * FROM Customers ORDER BY CompanyName")

' Display the field names.
For i = 0 To rs.Fields.Count - 1
    Debug.Print rs.Fields(i).Name & vbTab;
Next i
Debug.Print

' Display the results.
Debug.Print rs.GetString(ColumnDelimeter:=vbTab, _
    RowDelimeter:=vbCrLf, NullExpr:="<null>")

    rs.Close
    conn.Close
End Sub
```

Database Construction

If you're reading this book, chances are good that you'll use Access to create a database and build its tables, indexes, and other database trappings.

If you need to write code that builds tables, you can use SQL statements. For example, the following statement creates a People table. (See `http://msdn.microsoft.com/library/en-us/tsqlref/ts_create2_8g9x.asp` for the CREATE TABLE statement's syntax.)

```
CREATE TABLE People (
  LastName  VARCHAR(40) NOT NULL,
  FirstName VARCHAR(40) NOT NULL
)
```

You can do a lot with the proper SQL statements. Other commands include CREATE VIEW, CREATE INDEX, ALTER TABLE, and DROP TABLE. Consult a book on database programming or see Microsoft's online documentation for more information about these SQL statements.

If you prefer to work with objects rather than using SQL statements to build a database, you can use ADOX (ActiveX Data Objects Extensions for Data Definition Language and Security). The objects in ADOX let you define tables, fields, indexes, and all the other database paraphernalia you need. Visit Microsoft's Web page `http://msdn.microsoft.com/library/en-us/ado270/htm/pg_adox_fundamentals_1.asp` for more information on ADOX.

Summary

Access is a great product for building databases. It can also provide forms and reports that let you build reasonably complex database applications all with the Access application.

If you need to use Access data from another application, you could create an Access server and use its methods to manipulate the data. That would be rather cumbersome, however. Using a database access tool such as ADO is generally easier.

ADO provides its own object hierarchy that lets you select, create, modify, and delete records from the database. The Connection object's Execute method also lets you execute SQL statements that can alter data or even the database's structure.

ADO programming is such a big topic (whole books have been devoted to it) that this chapter cannot hope to cover a significant fraction of the possibilities. It does, however, give you an introduction to selecting and manipulating data using ADO. In many cases, this may be all you need to interact with the database from your application.

CHAPTER 12

Outlook

L<small>IKE</small> A<small>CCESS</small>, O<small>UTLOOK</small> provides a self-contained programming environment all its own. Using Outlook's tools, you can build forms for creating specific kinds of e-mail messages (trip reports, lost luggage reports, recipes), calendar entries (lunch with the boss, appointments with your bookie), tasks, folders, and so forth.

In addition to performing these personal information manager (PIM) tasks, Outlook is also a gateway for e-mail. It lets you send and receive mail, and filter incoming messages. It is also the place you are most likely to encounter e-mail viruses and other attacks on your computer.

Just as Access provides database services on which the database front end sits, so too Outlook stores and manipulates e-mail messages and other data on which its own front end lies.

Outlook's schizophrenic nature sometimes makes figuring out where to place application code confusing. You can manipulate Outlook's underlying data at least three ways. First, you can use Outlook itself. You can build forms, reply templates, and other Outlook objects to manage e-mail exchanges and Outlook folders. The advantage of this method is that the forms and templates can travel along with the e-mail, so recipients don't need any special software installed (other than Outlook). Using Outlook in this way is more about using Outlook rather than programming it using VBA, so it isn't covered in any detail here.

A second method for manipulating Outlook data is to use VBA code to control Outlook's object model. Using VBA code, you can create new messages, schedule appointments, make tasks, and so forth. You can use this type of automation within Outlook itself, from another Office application such as Word or Excel, or from applications that you write in a high-level programming language such as Visual Basic. Programming Outlook using VBA is the subject of this chapter.

A third method for interacting with Outlook is to use MAPI (Messaging Application Programming Interface). MAPI is a library of routines that lets an application work directly with the computer's mail system. Much as ADO lets you work with the data stored in an Access database, MAPI lets you work with the mail system that is also used by Outlook. CDO (Collaboration Data Objects) is a newer library layered on MAPI that also lets your applications work with e-mail. Chapter 13 provides a quick introduction to MAPI and CDO.

Although many people think of Outlook as simply a program for reading and writing e-mail, the object model spends more effort on supporting Outlook's PIM features. It has objects for examining all of the specific types of Outlook objects that can reside in a user's mailbox: folders, items, reminders, tasks, and appointments, as well as for specific windows in the Outlook application. It is probably more accurate to think of Outlook's object model as describing a PIM than a mail system.

The rest of this chapter describes some of the most important objects in Outlook's object model. If you think of these objects in terms of Outlook's PIM capabilities, they will probably make more sense than if you think of them as objects for working with an e-mail system. For more information on the object model, search the online help for Microsoft Outlook Objects or visit `http://msdn.microsoft.com/library/en-us/vbaol10/html/oltocObjectModelApplication.asp`.

Before you look at the bulk of the object model, however, you should learn a little about the MAPI namespace, and about Outlook items and the `Items` collection.

The MAPI Namespace

Another possible source of gratuitous confusion is the notion of a namespace. A namespace is an abstract location for some sort of data. For example, when you include a reference to the ADO libraries so you can use ADO in an application, the reference defines the ADODB (ActiveX Data Objects Database) namespace. Your code can explicitly refer to objects in the ADODB namespace as in the following statement that declares a `Recordset` object.

```
Dim rs As ADODB.Recordset
```

If you add other references to the project, your code may be able to refer to other namespaces.

Outlook has the notion that you might someday define other namespaces that Outlook might be able to use. The idea is that Outlook might be able to store and retrieve data from some new data store containing PIM information. However, MAPI is the only namespace that Outlook currently supports. Perhaps someday you'll need to be able to interact with messages or appointment information stored in some other namespace, but for now you can generally ignore namespaces in your Outlook code.

Outlook Items and the Items Collection

Outlook's purpose in life is to manage PIM entities such as e-mail messages, contact information, appointments, and miscellaneous notes. The Outlook design crew decided to call these entities "items." From a typical personnel manager's, casino pit boss's, or reference librarian's point of view, calling these things "items" makes sense (and sounds more dignified than dingle, thingy, or doohickey).

From a Visual Basic programmer's point of view, however, it is pretty confusing, because the word "item" already means something special. It means an object contained in a collection. In fact, many collection classes have a method named `Item` that returns a particular object in the collection.

To make matters worse, the Outlook object model doesn't define a single `Item` class to represent a general Outlook "item." Instead it defines a whole swarm of item classes: `AppointmentItem`, `ContactItem`, `DistListItem`, `DocumentItem`, `JournalItem`, `MailItem`, `MeetingItem`, `NoteItem`, `PostItem`, `RemoteItem`, `ReportItem`, `TaskItem`, `TaskRequestAcceptItem`, `TaskRequestDeclineItem`, `TaskRequestItem`, and `TaskRequestUpdateItem`.

A `MAPIFolder` object, for example, has an `Items` property that is a collection of these assorted item types. When your code digs through this collection, it should use `TypeOf`, `TypeName`, or the items' `Class` property (which returns a constant indicating the object's class) to figure out what type of item is present.

Don't look in the online help for a definition of the "`Item` object," because you won't find it. You can find only the specific Outlook item classes. To reduce confusion slightly, the rest of this chapter uses the word "item" only in the sense of an Outlook item. To refer to an object in a collection, it uses the word "object" instead.

This chapter uses the term "item object" to refer to an object representing an Outlook item. For example, an e-mail message is an "item." A `MailItem` object representing it is an "item object."

The following sections describe some of the most commonly used of the item classes in more detail. To learn more about Outlook's item objects, search the online help for "Outlook Item Objects" or visit `http://msdn.microsoft.com/library/en-us/vbaol10/html/olmscOutlookItemObjects.asp`.

MailItem

A `MailItem` represents an Outlook e-mail item. You use a `MailItem` to create, manipulate, and delete mail items. For instance, a VBA program might open an Excel workbook and an Access database, gather information, and use it in to initialize a `MailItem`. It could fill in a list of recipients and then display the item to let the user make changes before sending it.

Tables 12-1 and 12-2 describe some of the `MailItem`'s most useful properties and methods. For more information, search the online help for "MailItem Object" or visit `http://msdn.microsoft.com/library/en-us/vbaol10/html/olobjmailitem.asp`.

Table 12-1. Useful MailItem *Properties*

PROPERTY	PURPOSE
Attachments	A collection representing a message's attachments. Items other than mail messages also can have attachments, so this collection is discussed later in its own section "Attachments (C)."
BCC	Gets or sets a string listing the message's Bcc recipients. Use the Recipients collection rather than this property to change the recipients.
Body	Gets or sets the message's plain text body. If you set this property, the message's Inspector object's EditorType property automatically switches to Outlook's current default value.
BodyFormat	Gets or sets the message's body format. It can take the values olFormatHTML, olFormatPlain, olFormatRichText, and olFormatUnspecified.
CC	Gets or sets a string listing the message's Cc recipients. Use the Recipients collection rather than this property to change the recipients.
GetInspector	Returns an Inspector object representing the mail message. You can call the Inspector's Display method to show the message to the user. The Display method takes an optional Boolean parameter that indicates whether the Inspector should be displayed modally. When the Inspector closes, it asks the user whether it should save changes to a new or modified message. If the user clicks Yes, the Inspector saves the item so your code doesn't need to call the MailItem's Save method.
HTMLBody	Gets or sets the message's body as HTML code. Setting this value automatically changes the message's Inspector object's EditorType property to olEditorHTML.
Importance	Gets or sets the message's importance level. This property can take the values olImportanceLow, olImportanceNormal, and olImportanceHigh.
Recipients	A collection listing the message's recipients. Use its methods to add and remove recipients. Use the properties of the items in the collection to change the recipient types (To, Cc, or Bcc).
ReceivedTime	Returns the date and time when the message was received.

Table 12-1. Useful MailItem *Properties (continued)*

PROPERTY	PURPOSE
RecipientReassignmentProhibited	A Boolean value that indicates whether the recipient is allowed to forward the message to another user. Set this property to True on sensitive messages to discourage the recipient from sharing the information.
Saved	Returns True if the item has not been modified since it was loaded or saved.
Sensitivity	Gets or sets a value indicating how sensitive the item is. This property can take the values (in increasing order of sensitivity) olNormal, olPersonal, olPrivate, and olConfidential.
Sent	Returns True if the message has been sent.
SentOn	Returns the date the message was sent.
Size	Returns the size of the message including any attachments.
Subject	Gets or sets the message's subject text.

Table 12-2. Useful MailItem *Methods*

METHOD	PURPOSE
Close	Closes the MailItem. This method's optional parameter tells the item whether it should discard changes (olDiscard), prompt the user to save changes (olPromptForSave), or save any pending changes (olSave).
Copy	Makes a copy of the message and returns a new MailItem representing the copy.
Delete	Deletes the MailItem.
Display	Displays the MailItem in an Inspector window.
Forward	Performs the message's Forward action and returns a MailItem representing the new forwarding copy of the message.
Move	Moves the message into another Outlook folder.
PrintOut	Prints the message.
Reply	Makes a reply message and returns a MailItem representing it.
ReplyAll	Makes a "reply all" message and returns a MailItem representing it.
Save	Saves the message into its folder (usually the Drafts folder for a MailItem). When you create a new MailItem or make changes to an existing one, you must call Save, or Outlook will discard your changes.
SaveAs	Saves the message in a disk file.
Send	Sends the message.

The following example creates a mail message with To, Cc, and Bcc recipients.

FILE *Ch12\Ch12.bas*

```
' Make a mail item with To, Cc, and Bcc recipients.
Sub MakeMailRecipients()
Dim mail_item As MailItem
Dim recip As Recipient

    ' Create a new mail item.
    Set mail_item = Application.CreateItem(olMailItem)

    ' Add some recipients.
    ' This one's Type defaults to olTo.
    Set recip = mail_item.Recipients.Add("Cindy@somewhere.com")

    Set recip = mail_item.Recipients.Add("Bob@somewhere.com")
    recip.Type = olCC

    Set recip = mail_item.Recipients.Add("Sandy@somewhere.com")
    recip.Type = olCC

    Set recip = mail_item.Recipients.Add("MikeH@somewhere.com")
    recip.Type = olBCC

    mail_item.Subject = "Recipients"
    mail_item.Body = _
        "This message has To, Cc, and Bcc recipients."

    mail_item.Save
End Sub
```

ContactItem

A `ContactItem` represents an Outlook contact. Many of its properties represent data contained in the contact entry and are self-explanatory. For example, you should be able to figure out the purposes of the `BusinessAddressCity`, `CompanyName`, `Email1Address`, `HomeTelephoneNumber`, `FirstName`, and `LastName` properties with little trouble.

The ContactItem stores the contact's name in the FullName property and uses that value to parse out the FirstName, MiddleName, LastName, and Suffix properties (although you can set those properties, too).

The object provides a few convenience properties such as FullNameAndCompany (which returns the contact's full name followed by a carriage return and the contact's company name), LastNameAndFirstName (as in Stephens, Rod) and Initials (as in R.S.). Several similar properties such as LastFirstNoSpace, LastFirstAndSuffix, and LastFirstSpaceOnlyCompany work only if the related fields contain Asian double-byte character set (DBCS) characters.

The ContactItem object provides many of the same methods provided by the MailItem object and listed in Table 12-2. It provides Close, Copy, Delete, Display, Move, PrintOut, Save, and SaveAs methods. See Table 12-2 for descriptions of these methods.

For more information, search the online help for "ContactItem Object" or visit http://msdn.microsoft.com/library/en-us/vbaol10/html/olobjContactItem.asp.

AppointmentItem

An AppointmentItem object represents an appointment or meeting, or a recurring appointment or meeting in the Calendar folder.

NOTE *A* MeetingItem *object is an item in the Inbox folder that represents a change to the recipient's calendar caused by another user. For example, suppose a VBA program creates an* AppointmentItem *representing a meeting. It adds recipients, indicating those who should attend the meeting, and sends the* AppointmentItem *to them. Those recipients receive* MeetingItem *objects in their Inboxes. For more information on the* MeetingItem *object, search the online help for* "MeetingItem *Object" or go to* http://msdn.microsoft.com/library/en-us/vbaol10/html/olobjMeetingItem.asp.

If an AppointmentItem is recurring, its IsRecurring property returns True. In that case, a RecurrencePattern object defines the recurrence. See the section "RecurrencePattern" later in this chapter for more details.

Table 12-3 describes some of the AppointmentItem's other most useful properties.

Table 12-3. Useful AppointmentItem *Properties*

PROPERTY	PURPOSE
AllDayEvent	True if this is an all-day event.
Duration	The duration of the appointment in minutes.
End	The appointment's end date and time.
Location	A string describing the appointment's location.
MeetingStatus	Gets or sets the appointment's meeting status. Set this to olMeeting to make the appointment a meeting and create a MeetingItem for it. The example that follows demonstrates this property.
OptionalAttendees	Returns a list of required meeting attendees. Use the Recipients collection instead of this property to change attendees.
Organizer	Returns the name of the meeting's organizer. Use the Recipients collection instead of this property to change the organizer.
Recipients	Collection listing the appointment's recipients. Use its methods to add and remove recipients. Use the properties of the items in the collection to change the recipient types (organizer, required, optional, or resource).
RequiredAttendees	Returns a list of required meeting attendees. Use the Recipients collection instead of this property to change attendees.
ReminderMinutesBeforeStart	Gets or sets the number of minutes before the meeting at which Outlook should display a reminder.
ReminderTime	Gets or sets the time at which Outlook should display a reminder.
Resources	Returns a list of meeting resource attendees. Use the Recipients collection instead of this property to change attendees.

The following example creates a new AppointmentItem representing a meeting. It creates the object and sets the object's Subject, Location, Start, Duration, and ReminderMinutesBeforeStart properties.

It then sets the object's MeetingStatus property to olMeeting to make the appointment a meeting. It adds several recipients, setting their Type properties to indicate whether they are organizers, required attendees, optional attendees, or resource attendees. Finally, the code sends the item to the recipients.

```
' Create a meeting appointment.
Sub CreateMeeting()
Dim appt_item As AppointmentItem
Dim attendee As Recipient

    ' Create the appointment.
    Set appt_item = Application.CreateItem(olAppointmentItem)

    ' Set some descriptive properties.
    appt_item.Subject = "Project Review"
    appt_item.Location = "Rod's office"
    appt_item.Start = #8/20/2003 4:00:00 PM#
    appt_item.Duration = 45
    appt_item.ReminderMinutesBeforeStart = 15

    ' Make it a meeting.
    appt_item.MeetingStatus = olMeeting

    ' Specify attendees.
    appt_item.Recipients.Add("Rod Stephens").Type = olOrganizer
    appt_item.Recipients.Add("Alice Archer").Type = olRequired
    appt_item.Recipients.Add("Bill Blah").Type = olRequired
    appt_item.Recipients.Add("Cindy Carter").Type = olOptional
    appt_item.Recipients.Add("David Dart").Type = olResource

    ' Send the appointment to the recipients.
    appt_item.Send
End Sub
```

The AppointmentItem object provides many of the same methods provided by the MailItem object: Close, Copy, Delete, Display, Move, PrintOut, Save, SaveAs, and Send. See Table 12-2 for descriptions of these methods.

The AppointmentItem object also provides some useful appointment-related methods. The ClearRecurrencePattern method removes the appointment's recurrence pattern and makes it a single-occurrence event.

The GetRecurrencePattern method returns a RecurrencePattern object representing the appointment's recurrence. You can use this object's properties to modify the pattern.

Finally, the Respond method responds to a meeting request contained in the AppointmentItem. This method takes as a parameter a value indicating whether the responder will attend (olMeetingAccepted), will not attend (olMeetingDeclined), or will probably attend (olMeetingTentative).

For more information, search the online help for "ApplicationItem Object" or visit http://msdn.microsoft.com/library/en-us/vbaol10/html/olobjContactItem.asp.

TaskItem

A TaskItem represents a task in the Tasks folder. Table 12-4 lists some of the TaskItem's more important properties.

Table 12-4. Useful TaskItem *Properties*

PROPERTY	PURPOSE
ActualWork	Gets or sets the actual number of minutes spent on the task.
Complete	Gets or sets a Boolean value indicating whether the task is complete.
DateCompleted	Gets or sets the date the task was completed.
DelegationState	Returns a value indicating whether the task has been delegated. This property can return the values: olTaskDelegationAccepted, olTaskDelegationDeclined, olTaskDelegationUnknown, and olTaskNotDelegated.
DueDate	Gets or sets the date the task is due.
Importance	Gets or sets the task's importance level. This property can take the values olImportanceLow, olImportanceNormal, and olImportanceHigh.
Ordinal	Gets or sets the task's position in the task list.
Ownership	Returns a value indicating the task's ownership. This property can take the values olDelegatedTask, olNewTask, and olOwnTask.
PercentComplete	Gets or sets the percentage of the task that is complete.
StartDate	Gets or sets the task's start date.
Status	Gets or sets the task's status. This property can take the values olTaskComplete, olTaskDeferred, olTaskInProgress, olTaskNotStarted, and olTaskWaiting.

If a TaskItem is recurring, its IsRecurring property returns True. In that case, a RecurrencePattern object defines the recurrence. See the section RecurrencePattern later in this chapter for more details.

The TaskItem object provides many of the same methods provided by the MailItem object: Close, Copy, Delete, Display, Move, PrintOut, Save, SaveAs, and Send. See Table 12-2 for descriptions of these methods.

The TaskItem object also provides some useful task-related methods. The Assign method allows you to assign the task to someone. You create the TaskItem, calls its Assign method, define recipients, and call the item's Send method.

The ClearRecurrencePattern method removes the appointment's recurrence pattern and makes it a single-occurrence event.

The GetRecurrencePattern method returns a RecurrencePattern object representing the appointment's recurrence. You can use this object's properties to modify the pattern.

The MarkComplete method marks the task as complete. It sets the TaskItem's
PercentComplete property to 100, sets Complete to True, and sets DateCompleted to
the current date.

Finally, the Respond method responds to a task request contained in the
TaskItem. This method takes as a parameter a value indicating whether the responder will accept (olTaskAccepted) or decline (olTaskDeclined).

For more information, search the online help for "TaskItem Object" or visit
http://msdn.microsoft.com/library/en-us/vbaol10/html/olobjTaskItem.asp.

Application

Like all other Office applications, Outlook begins its object model with an
Application object. In many ways, Outlook's version of this object is simpler
than those provided by other Office applications. It provides only a few important
properties and methods, and most of those simply give you access to other objects
that control more specific parts of the Outlook application.

For example, the Explorers, Inspectors, and Reminders properties are collections that contain Explorer, Inspector, and Reminder objects, respectively. The
ActiveExplorer and ActiveInspector properties just give references to the currently
active Explorer or Inspector, if one is active. ActiveWindow returns either an Explorer
or an Inspector depending on which type of object is active, if any. Later sections
in this chapter describe these kinds of objects.

The following sections describe some of the Application object's less self-
evident properties and methods.

AdvancedSearch

This method performs an advanced search for items that meet certain criteria.
The basic syntax is:

```
Application.AdvancedSearch Scope, Filter, SearchSubfolders, Tag
```

The Scope parameter tells Outlook where to begin the search. For example, this
can be a folder name.

SearchSubfolders indicates whether Outlook should search the initial folder's
subfolders.

Tag is a name you assign to this particular search. This value is useful in the AdvancedSearchComplete event handler described shortly.

The online documentation describes the Filter parameter as similar to an SQL WHERE clause. It is SQL-like in the sense that it uses AND, =, LIKE, and other SQL operators to compare fields to desired values. However, the things that correspond to the fields in a SQL WHERE clause are unlike anything seen in a normal SQL statement.

For instance, the filter urn:schemas:mailheader:subject LIKE '%Attach%' searches for Outlook items where the subject field contains the word "attach." The value urn:schemas:mailheader:subject doesn't look much like a SQL field name.

Two namespaces are useful for defining the fields in Outlook items: urn:schemas:mailheader and urn:schemas:httpmail. Tables 12-5 and 12-6 list field names defined by these namespaces.

Table 12-5. urn:schemas:mailheader *Field Names*

approved	disposition-notification-to	received
bcc	distribution	reply-to
cc	expires	referenccs
comment	followup-to	relay-version
content-base	from	return-path
content-description	in-reply-to	return-receipt-to
content-disposition	keywords	sender
content-id	lines (number of lines)	subject
content-language	message-id	summary
content-location	mime-version	thread-index
content-transfer-encoding	newsgroups	thread-topic
content-type	organization	to
control	original-recipient	x-mailer
date	path	xref
disposition	posting-version	x-unsent

Table 12-6. urn:schemas:httpmail *Field Names*

attachmentfilename	from	sender
bcc	hasattachment	subject
cc	htmldescription	textdescription
content-disposition-type	importance	thread-topic
content-media-type	htmldescription	to
date	priority	
datereceived	reply-to	

Create a full filter name by adding the field name to the namespace, as in
`urn:schemas:mailheader:to` or `urn:schemas:mailheader:subject`.

 TIP *You can get information about the specific meanings of these fields at these URLs:* `msdn.microsoft.com/library/en-us/cdosys/html/_cdosys_schema_mailheader.asp` *and* `msdn.microsoft.com/library/en-us/cdosys/html/_cdosys_schema_httpmail.asp`.

To learn about other filter field names that are available, select a folder in Outlook. Then open the View menu and select Current View ➤ Customize Current View. In the View Summary dialog, click the Filter button. Use the Messages, More Choices, and Advanced tabs to define the folder's filter.

The Advanced tab shown in Figure 12-1 can be particularly useful. Click the Field dropdown and wander through the cascading menus to find the fields you want.

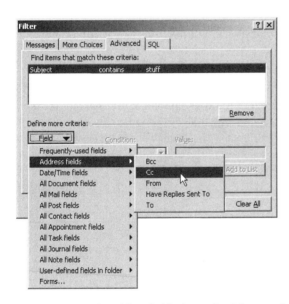

Figure 12-1. Select filter fields from the Advanced tab.

After you finish defining the filter, click on the SQL tab to see the corresponding filter statement as shown in Figure 12-2. This figure shows the SQL statement for a filter where the subject must contain the string "attach," the item has an attachment, and the item's size is more than 100KB. Who would have guessed that the field name for size was 0x0e080003?

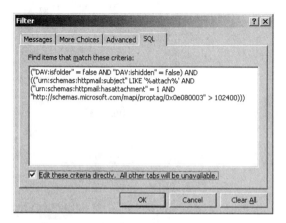

Figure 12-2. The SQL tab shows the SQL statement corresponding to the filter you have defined.

When you define a filter and call the AdvancedSearch method, the method doesn't return the results of its search. Instead it starts the search asynchronously and fires the Application object's AdvancedSearchComplete event handler when the search is finished. You can use code in that event handler to take action on whatever items the search finds.

For example, the following code starts a search in the Calendar folder for items with a subject containing the string "stuff." It sets the search's Tag property to "stuff" so the AdvancedSearchComplete event handler can check the SearchObject's Tag property to determine which search has finished.

 FILE *Ch12\Ch12.bas*

```
' Search Calendar for items
' with subjects containing "stuff".
Sub SearchForStuff()
    Application.AdvancedSearch _
        Scope:="Calendar", _
        Filter:="urn:schemas:mailheader:subject LIKE '%stuff%'", _
        Tag:="stuff"
End Sub
```

The following code runs when an advanced search finishes. It displays the search's Tag value and the number of items that matched the search criteria. It then loops through the found items and displays their subjects.

 FILE *Ch12\Ch12.bas*

```
' Display the selected items.
Private Sub Application_AdvancedSearchComplete(ByVal SearchObject As Search)
Dim rslts As Results
Dim i As Integer

    Set rslts = SearchObject.Results
    Debug.Print "Search " & SearchObject.Tag & _
        " finished, " & rslts.Count & " hits"

    ' Display the hits.
    For i = 1 To rslts.Count
        Debug.Print i & ": " & rslts.Item(i).Subject
    Next i
End Sub
```

CopyFile

The CopyFile method copies a file into an Outlook folder. The file can be just about anything, such as a text file, Word document, image file, or Web page. Outlook represents these files with appropriate icons similar to those you would see in Windows Explorer.

If you double-click one of these files, Outlook behaves much as an Internet download does. Depending on the file type, Outlook may display a warning to remind you that some files may contain harmful viruses. It gives you the option of copying the file to another location or opening it with its usual application, such as Word or Notepad. Outlook isn't terribly smart about this, so it displays the warning for some files that probably won't contain viruses, such as JPEGs and bitmap files.

When you copy a file into a folder, it becomes an Outlook item. You can then use Insert ➤ Item to insert the item into another item, such as a mail message or appointment.

The following example copies four files into the Notes and Inbox folders.

 FILE *Ch12\Ch12.bas*

```
' Copy some test files into the Notes and Inbox folders.
Sub CopyFiles()
Dim file_names As Variant
Dim i As Integer

    ' Define the file names.
    file_names = Array( _
        "C:\OfficeSmackdown\Src\Ch12\CodeFragment.txt", _
        "C:\OfficeSmackdown\Src\Ch12\TextFragment.doc", _
        "C:\OfficeSmackdown\Src\Ch12\Test.html", _
        "C:\OfficeSmackdown\Src\Ch12\dog.jpg")

    ' Copy the files.
    For i = LBound(file_names) To UBound(file_names)
        Application.CopyFile file_names(i), "Notes"
        Application.CopyFile file_names(i), "Inbox"
    Next i
End Sub
```

CreateItem *and* Items.Add

The CreateItem method creates a new standard Outlook item. The method's single parameter indicates the kind of item to create and should be one of olAppointmentItem, olContactItem, olDistributionListItem, olJournalItem, olMailItem, olNoteItem, olPostItem, or olTaskItem.

The following code makes a new appointment. It creates an AppointmentItem and sets its subject, body, start time, duration (in minutes), importance, location, and time when Outlook should display a reminder. It calls the Save method to save the new item in its default folder, Calendar.

FILE *Ch12\Ch12.bas*

```
' Make a new 90 minute appointment item
' for 1:00 PM tomorrow.
Sub MakeAppointmentTomorrow()
Dim appt As AppointmentItem

    Set appt = Application.CreateItem(olAppointmentItem)
    With appt
        .Subject = "Conference call re. Office Smackdown"
        .Body = "Editor will call."
        .Start = DateAdd("d", 1, Date) + #1:00:00 PM#
        .Duration = 90
        .Importance = olImportanceHigh
        .Location = "Office"
        .ReminderMinutesBeforeStart = 30
        .Save
    End With
End Sub
```

CreateItem makes an item in an appropriate folder. For example, if you make a new AppointmentItem, CreateItem puts it the Calendar folder.

If you want to create a different kind of item in a folder, you can get a reference to the folder's MAPIFolder object and use its Items.Add method to create a new object. For example, the following code gets the Inbox folder and uses its Items.Add method to create a new PostItem. The code fills in a few fields and saves the item.

FILE *Ch12\Ch12.bas*

```
' Make a new Post item in Inbox.
Sub MakeAppointmentTomorrowInInbox()
Dim inbox_folder As MAPIFolder
Dim post_item As PostItem
```

```
    ' Get the Inbox folder from the session's MAPI namespace.
    Set inbox_folder = Session.GetDefaultFolder(olFolderInbox)

    ' Create the new item.
    Set post_item = inbox_folder.Items.Add(olPostItem)
    With post_item
        .Subject = "Need stamps"
        .Body = "This is a simple Post item."
        .ExpiryTime = DateAdd("d", 2, Now)
        .Importance = olImportanceHigh
        .Save
    End With
End Sub
```

NOTE *Some item types resist being placed in arbitrary folders. For example, if you try to create a* ContactItem *in the Calendar folder, Outlook moves it into the Contacts folder. Similarly, if you try to create an* AppointmentItem *in the Inbox, Outlook moves it to the Calendar.*

GetNameSpace

This method returns a NameSpace object for a particular namespace. Currently, the only namespace supported is MAPI, so this may not seem very useful. However, the MAPI NameSpace object provides access to other objects in the Outlook object model.

For example, the following code fragment gets a reference to the MAPI NameSpace and uses its GetDefaultFolder method to get a reference to the MAPIFolder object representing the current user's Inbox. It can then use this object to manipulate the folder's contents.

```
' Get the MAPI NameSpace object.
Set mapi_namespace = Application.GetNameSpace("MAPI")

' Get the Inbox folder from the session's MAPI namespace.
Set inbox_folder = mapi_namespace.GetDefaultFolder(olFolderInbox)
...
```

The `Application` object's `Session` property returns the `NameSpace` object for the current Outlook session. Because MAPI is the only supported namespace, `Session` returns that `NameSpace`. The following code does the same thing as the previous fragment but uses `Session` instead of `GetNameSpace`.

```
' Get the Inbox folder from the session's MAPI namespace.
Set inbox_folder = Application.Session.GetDefaultFolder(olFolderInbox)
...
```

Quit

This method closes Outlook. Normally, Outlook asks the user whether it should save changes to any modified Outlook items. You can avoid this by looping through the `Inspectors` currently displaying items and closing each individually, telling Outlook whether to save or discard the changes for each. Then you can safely call Outlook's `Quit` method.

The following code uses this technique to close Outlook, discarding any unsaved changes.

 FILE *Ch12\Ch12.bas*

```
' Close Outlook discarding any unsaved changes.
Sub CloseOutlook()
    ' Close all open Inspectors.
    Do While Inspectors.Count > 0
        Inspectors(1).Close olDiscard
    Loop

    ' Close Outlook.
    Application.Quit
End Sub
```

Explorers *(C)* and Inspectors *(C)*

The Explorers collection contains Explorer objects that represent windows displaying the contents of Outlook folders. For instance, Figure 12-3 shows an Explorer listing the contents of the Drafts folder.

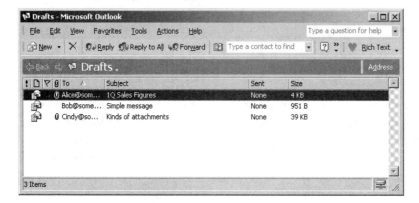

Figure 12-3. An Explorer *lists the contents of an Outlook folder.*

TIP *To open an Explorer in its own window, right-click a folder and select Open in New Window.*

The Inspectors collection holds Inspector objects representing windows displaying Outlook items. For example, when you create a new mail message, exit a contact record, or view an appointment item, Outlook displays the item in an Inspector.

You can use Explorer and Inspector objects to work with the items that the user has open. The Application object's ActiveExplorer, ActiveInspector, and ActiveWindow properties let you work with items the user is currently using. For instance, the following code adds a copyright statement at the end of the body of the currently open item.

FILE *Ch12\Ch12.bas*

```
' Add a copyright statement at the end of the current item.
Sub AddCopyright()
    ActiveInspector.CurrentItem.Body = _
        ActiveInspector.CurrentItem.Body & vbCrLf & _
        "Copyright " & Year(Date) & " S. Nob Esq."
End Sub
```

MAPIFolder

A MAPIFolder object represents an Outlook folder. A MAPIFolder can contain other nested folders. Use the Folders collection to access nested folders.

The Session NameSpace object's Folders collection gives you access to the top-level folders. Typically, this top-level may include folders named Personal Folders and Archive Folders. The actual top-level folders vary depending on the user's configuration. For example, they may include Mailbox - Rod and Public Folders.

Personal Folders (or whatever it is called on the user's system) would contain Inbox, Calendar, and all the other key folders you use on a daily basis.

The DisplayAllFolders method shown in the following code iterates through the Session NameSpace's Folders collection, calling the DisplayFolder subroutine for each top-level folder. DisplayFolder lists a folder's name and recursively calls itself to display the names of the folder's children.

FILE *Ch12\Ch12.bas*

```
' Display the top-level folders and their descendants.
Sub DisplayAllFolders()
Dim child_folder As MAPIFolder

    For Each child_folder In Session.Folders
        DisplayFolder child_folder, 0
    Next child_folder
End Sub

' Display the folder hierarchy within this folder.
Sub DisplayFolder(ByVal start_folder As MAPIFolder, ByVal level As Integer)
Dim child_folder As MAPIFolder
```

```
        Debug.Print Space$(level) & start_folder.Name
        For Each child_folder In start_folder.Folders
            DisplayFolder child_folder, level + 4
        Next child_folder
    End Sub
```

The following output shows the folders listed by subroutine `DisplayAllFolders` on one computer. Your results will depend on your Outlook configuration.

```
Personal Folders
    Deleted Items
    Inbox
    Outbox
    Sent Items
    Calendar
    Contacts
    Journal
    Notes
    Tasks
    Drafts
    New Templates
Archive Folders
    Deleted Items
    Sent Items
    Calendar
    Journal
    Tasks
```

You can use the `Folders` collection's `Add` method to create child folders. An optional parameter tells Outlook what types of items should be allowed in the folder. This parameter can take the values `olFolderCalendar`, `olFolderContacts`, `olFolderDrafts`, `olFolderInbox`, `olFolderJournal`, `olFolderNotes`, and `olFolderTasks`.

The `MakeInboxSpamFolder` subroutine shown in the following code finds the Inbox folder and uses its `Folders` collection to create a new Spam subfolder. The `DeleteInboxSpamFolder` subroutine finds the Inbox/Spam folder and calls its `Delete` method to remove it and its contents from Outlook.

 FILE *Ch12\Ch12.bas*

```
' Make a sub-folder inside Inbox named Spam.
Sub MakeInboxSpamFolder()
Dim inbox_folder As MAPIFolder

    Set inbox_folder = Session.GetDefaultFolder(olFolderInbox)
    inbox_folder.Folders.Add "Spam", olFolderInbox
End Sub

' Delete the Inbox/Spam folder.
Sub DeleteInboxSpamFolder()
Dim inbox_folder As MAPIFolder
Dim spam_folder As MAPIFolder

    Set inbox_folder = Session.GetDefaultFolder(olFolderInbox)
    Set spam_folder = inbox_folder.Folders("Spam")
    spam_folder.Delete
End Sub
```

The MAPIFolder object's Items property lets you access the items inside the folder.
See the following section for some details and examples.

Items (C)

The MAPIFolder object's Items property contains objects representing the items
inside the Outlook folder.

The following example displays the contents of the Deleted Items folder. The
DisplayDeletedFolderContents subroutine finds the folder and passes its MAPIFolder
object to the DisplayFolderContents subroutine. DisplayFolderContents displays the
folder's name, lists the items it contains, and then recursively calls itself to display
the contents of any subfolders.

FILE *Ch12\Ch12.bas*

```
' Display the Deleted Items folder's contents.
Sub DisplayDeletedFolderContents()
Dim deleted_folder As MAPIFolder
```

```
    ' Find the folder.
    Set deleted_folder = Session.GetDefaultFolder(olFolderDeletedItems)

    ' Display the folder's contents.
    DisplayFolderContents deleted_folder, 0
End Sub


' Display the folder, its items, and its subfolders.
Sub DisplayFolderContents(ByVal start_folder As MAPIFolder, _
    ByVal level As Integer)
Dim obj As Object
Dim child_folder As MAPIFolder

    ' Display the folder's name.
    Debug.Print Space$(level) & "Folder: " & start_folder.Name

    ' Display the items in this folder.
    For Each obj In start_folder.Items
        Debug.Print Space$(level + 4) & "[" & obj.Subject & "]"
    Next obj

    ' Display the subfolders.
    For Each child_folder In start_folder.Folders
        DisplayFolderContents child_folder, level + 4
    Next child_folder
End Sub
```

The objects in the Items collection have different data types depending on what they represent. For example, an object representing an appointment item has type AppointmentItem, whereas an object representing a mail message has type MailItem.

Some folders allow only one type of item. For example, the Calendar folder can contain only AppointmentItems. If you are working in such a folder, your code need only be prepared to work with the appropriate type of item.

If you must iterate through the items in a folder that allows more than one type of item, you can use a variable of generic Object type. You can then use TypeOf, TypeName, or the object's Class property (which returns a constant indicating the object's type) to determine the object's true type.

Unfortunately, when you work with variables of the generic Object data type, VBA cannot give you IntelliSense support. After you check an object's type and know you need to work with it, you can get IntelliSense support by assigning the generic object to a variable with a more specific data type.

The following code loops through the items in the ProgressReports folder. For each mail item it finds, the code assigns a MailItem object to the generic object. It then uses the MailItem's Recipients collection to add a new recipient to the message.

 FILE *Ch12\Ch12.bas*

```
' Add a recipient to every mail message in the
' ProgressReports folder.
Sub AddRecipient()
Dim pr_folder As MAPIFolder
Dim obj As Object
Dim mail_item As MailItem

    Set pr_folder = Session.Folders("Personal Folders"). _
        Folders("ProgressReports")
    For Each obj In pr_folder.Items
        ' See if this is a MailItem.
        If obj.Class = olMail Then
            Set mail_item = obj
            mail_item.Recipients.Add "121ProjectHistory@nowhere.com"
            mail_item.Save
        End If
    Next obj
End Sub
```

 NOTE *To protect against viruses, Outlook displays a warning message each time the code accesses a* MailItem's Recipients *property. It may also display other warnings depending on your Outlook version and security settings.*

Selection (C)

An Explorer object's Selection property is a collection of objects representing the items currently selected in the Explorer. The following example lists the subjects of the items selected in the active explorer.

FILE *Ch12\Ch12.bas*

```
' List the items selected in the active Explorer.
Sub ListSelectedItems()
Dim obj As Object

    For Each obj In Application.ActiveExplorer.Selection
        Debug.Print obj.Subject
    Next obj
End Sub
```

Views (C)

You can use views to make customized displays of items in an Outlook folder. For example, you might define a view that lists entries in the Inbox sorted by Subject.

A MAPIFolder object's Views property is a collection of objects representing the views defined for the folder. You can loop through the collection in the usual ways to examine the views. Use the collection's Add method to create a new view. The CreateView subroutine shown in the following code defines a new view for the Inbox folder.

FILE *Ch12\Ch12.bas*

```
' Make a new view in the Inbox.
Sub CreateView()
Dim inbox_views As Views
Dim new_view As View

    Set inbox_views = Application.Session.GetDefaultFolder(olFolderInbox).Views
    Set new_view = inbox_views.Add( _
        Name:="Sort By Subject", _
        ViewType:=olTableView, _
        SaveOption:=olViewSaveOptionThisFolderEveryone)
End Sub
```

The View object represents a view. Unfortunately, the properties that you use to define a view interactively in Outlook don't match the properties provided by the View object very well. For example, Figure 12-4 shows Outlook setting the sorting properties for the Sort By Subject view. Use View ➤ Current View ➤ Define Views to define and modify views.

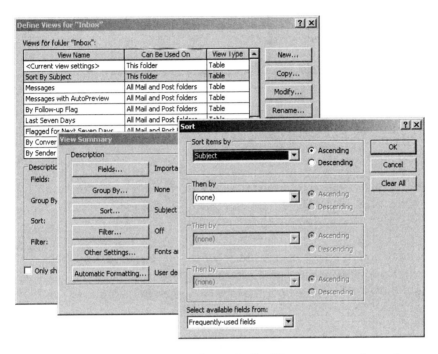

Figure 12-4. Use View ➤ Current View ➤ Define Views to customize a view.

Instead of providing properties comparable to the values you set interactively, the View object has an XML property that defines the view. The values in the XML data determine how the view is sorted. For instance, the following section of a view's definition indicates that the view sorts ascending on the string urn:schemas:httpmail:subject field and labels the field Subject.

```
<orderby>
    <order>
        <heading>Subject</heading>
        <prop>urn:schemas:httpmail:subject</prop>
        <type>string</type>
        <sort>asc</sort>
    </order>
</orderby>
```

Given enough motivation, you could probably decipher the XML format for defining views and generate your own XML data when you needed it. An easier approach is to define a view similar to the one you want and then examine its XML code to see how it works. The following code displays the XML code for the Sort By Subject view defined in the Inbox folder.

 FILE *Ch12\Ch12.bas*

```
' Display the XML code defining the Sort By Subject view.
Sub ListViewXML()
Dim inbox_views As Views

    Set inbox_views = Application.Session.GetDefaultFolder(olFolderInbox).Views
    Debug.Print inbox_views("Sort By Subject").XML
End Sub
```

Your VBA program can modify the XML code to suit your needs and then set the view's XML property to the new value or create a new view based on the value. For example, the following code finds the Inbox's "Subject and From" view and adds the To field.

```
' Add the To field to the Inbox's "Subject and From" view.
Sub FromToField()
Dim inbox_views As Views
Dim xml As String
Dim to_field As String
Dim pos As Integer

    ' Get the view's current XML.
    Set inbox_views = _
        Application.Session.GetDefaultFolder(olFolderInbox).Views
    xml = inbox_views("Subject and From").xml

    ' See if the To field is already present.
    If InStr(xml, "<prop>urn:schemas:httpmail:displayto</prop>") > 0 _
        Then Exit Sub

    ' Find the end of the last column.
    pos = InStrRev(xml, "</column>") + Len("</column>")
```

```
    ' Add the From field.
    to_field = vbCrLf & _
"    <column>" & vbCrLf & _
"        <heading>To</heading>" & vbCrLf & _
"        <prop>urn:schemas:httpmail:displayto</prop>" & vbCrLf & _
"        <type>string</type>" & vbCrLf & _
"        <width>47</width>" & vbCrLf & _
"        <style>text-align:left;padding-left:3px</style>" & vbCrLf & _
"    </column>"

    xml = Left$(xml, pos) & to_field & Mid$(xml, pos)

    ' Set the view's new XML value.
    inbox_views("Subject and From").xml = xml
End Sub
```

AddressLists (C)

The Session object's AddressLists property is a collection containing AddressList objects. Each of those objects has an AddressEntries property that is a collection containing AddressEntry objects. Those objects contain information about the actual entries in the Outlook address book.

The following code loops through the AddressLists collection. For each AddressList object, the code displays the list's name and loops through its address entries, displaying their names and addresses.

 FILE *Ch12\Ch12.bas*

```
' List available address lists and their entries.
Sub ListAddresses()
Dim address_list As AddressList
Dim address_entry As AddressEntry

    For Each address_list In Session.AddressLists
        Debug.Print "***** " & address_list.Name & " *****"
        For Each address_entry In address_list.AddressEntries
            Debug.Print address_entry.Name & _
```

```
                    " (" & address_entry.Address & ")"
        Next address_entry
    Next address_list
End Sub
```

When your code tries to access addresses in the address book, Outlook displays a warning similar to the one shown in Figure 12-5.

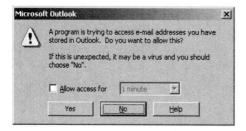

Figure 12-5. Outlook warns the user when your code accesses the address book.

TIP *You can click Yes to allow the program to access a single address book entry. In code such as the preceding example, which iterates through every address, Outlook will display the message again, and you must click Yes for each. To make things easier, check the "Allow access for" box, select "1 minute," and click Yes. Most sensible VBA macros will be able to access all the address entries they need in less than 1 minute.*

Actions `(C)` and `Action`

Outlook's various item classes have an `Actions` property that contains a collection of `Action` objects defining actions that can be applied to the item. For example, a mail item has an action that generates a reply message.

The following code loops through a mail item's `Actions` collection and lists its defined actions.

FILE *Ch12\Ch12.bas*

```
' List an item's actions.
Sub ListActions()
Dim draft_item As MailItem
Dim an_action As Action

    Set draft_item = Session.GetDefaultFolder(olFolderDrafts).Items(1)
    For Each an_action In draft_item.Actions
        Debug.Print an_action.Name
    Next an_action
End Sub
```

The following output shows the actions for a simple mail message.

```
Reply
Reply to All
Forward
Reply to Folder
```

You can apply an item's action by finding the `Action` object and invoking its `Execute` method. For instance, the following code executes a mail item's Reply to All action.

FILE *Ch12\Ch12.bas*

```
' Invoke an item's Reply to All action.
Sub ReplyToAllAction()
Dim draft_item As MailItem
Dim reply_action As Action
Dim reply_item As MailItem

    Set draft_item = _
      Session.GetDefaultFolder(olFolderDrafts).Items("1Q Sales Figures")
    Set reply_action = draft_item.Actions("Reply to All")
    reply_action.ReplyStyle = olIndentOriginalText
    Set reply_item = reply_action.Execute()
    reply_item.Subject = "Re: " & reply_item.Subject
    reply_item.Save
End Sub
```

CAUTION *Don't forget to call the new item's* Save *method, or it will not appear in Outlook's folders.*

When you call the Execute method, Outlook displays a warning similar to the one shown in Figure 12-6. Click Yes to allow the program to perform the action.

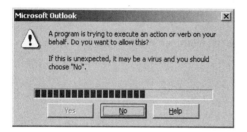

Figure 12-6. Outlook warns the user if your VBA code tries to call an Action's Execute *method.*

The progress bar wastes several seconds hoping you'll read the message and actually think about it instead of just fuming about Outlook's wasting your time and then clicking Yes.

A more important reason for this dialog's slowness is that it makes building macro viruses a bit harder. To get past the dialog, a virus would need to wait until the dialog was ready and then click the Yes button. The dialog also limits how quickly a virus can spread. Even if a virus is clever enough to respond to the dialog, it can only send out a few messages per minute. Chances are good you'll see the dialog and put a stop to things before the virus does too much damage.

Attachments (C)

An item object's Attachments collection contains documents or links to documents attached to the item. The following example creates a new mail item and adds three attachments. Chapter 5 talks more about Outlook attachments.

FILE *Ch12\Ch12.bas*

```
' Make a mail item with three different kinds
' of attachments.
Sub MakeMailWithAttachments()
Dim new_item As MailItem
Dim ns As NameSpace
Dim draft_folder As MAPIFolder
Dim attachment_item As MailItem

    ' Create a new mail item.
    Set new_item = Application.CreateItem(olMailItem)
    new_item.To = "Cindy@somewhere.com"
    new_item.Subject = "Kinds of attachments"
    new_item.Body = _
        "This message contains three kinds of Outlook attachments: " & _
        "by value, by reference, and embedded item." & vbCrLf & vbCrLf
    new_item.Attachments.Add _
        "C:\OfficeSmackdown\Src\Ch05\Colors.doc", _
        olByValue
    new_item.Attachments.Add _
        "C:\OfficeSmackdown\Src\Ch05\Food.doc", _
        olByReference

    ' Find the "Simple messaage" mail item.
    Set ns = Application.GetNamespace("MAPI")
    Set draft_folder = ns.GetDefaultFolder(olFolderDrafts)
    Set attachment_item = draft_folder.Items("Simple message")

    ' Attach this item as an embedded item.
    new_item.Attachments.Add _
        attachment_item, _
        olEmbeddeditem
    new_item.Save
End Sub
```

Recipients (C)

An item object's Recipients collection lists the item's recipients. You can use the collection's Add method to add a new recipient. The following code adds a new e-mail address to a mail message.

```
mail_item.Recipients.Add "SuperCoder@bugfree.com"
```

For another example that adds a recipient to every mail item in the ProgressReports folder, see the section "Items (C)" earlier in this chapter.

RecurrencePattern

An AppointmentItem or TaskItem object can have an associated RecurrencePattern object that determines how often the item reoccurs. For example, you can use a RecurrencePattern to make a project review appointment repeat every Tuesday afternoon at 4:00.

The following code does just that. It creates a new AppointmentItem, fills in its Subject and Body, and calls GetRecurrencePattern to get a reference to the appointment's RecurrencePattern object.

NOTE *Calling* GetRecurrencePattern *automatically sets the* IsRecurring *property to True. Similarly, calling* ClearRecurrencePattern *automatically sets* IsRecurring *to False.*

The program sets the recurrence pattern's DayOfWeek, StartTime, and Duration properties to make the appointment reappear every Tuesday at 4:00 p.m.

FILE *Ch12\Ch12.bas*

```
' Make a project review appointment that happens
' every Tuesday at 4:00 pm.
Sub MakeProjectReviewAppointment()
Dim appt As AppointmentItem
Dim recurrence_pattern As RecurrencePattern

    ' Make the new appointment.
    Set appt = Application.CreateItem(olAppointmentItem)
    appt.Subject = "Weekly project review"
    appt.Body = "Review the week's progress, outstanding issues, etc."

    ' Make the recurrence.
```

```
    Set recurrence_pattern = appt.GetRecurrencePattern()
    recurrence_pattern.DayOfWeekMask = olTuesday
    recurrence_pattern.StartTime = "4:00PM"
    recurrence_pattern.Duration = 60
    recurrence_pattern.NoEndDate = True

    ' Save the appointment.
    appt.Save
End Sub
```

Using a `RecurrencePattern` object, you can make an appointment reoccur daily, weekly, monthly, every N months, annually, or every N years. See the online help for details.

Reminders (C)

The `Application` object's `Reminders` collection contains objects representing reminders for appointments. For instance, suppose you create a meeting that gives you a reminder 15 minutes before the meeting. A `Reminder` object in this collection represents the 15-minute reminder.

The following code lists information about current reminders. It loops through the `Reminders` collection, displaying each reminder's date, the date of its appointment, the reminder's caption, and the appointment's body text.

 FILE *Ch12\Ch12.bas*

```
' List reminders.
Sub ViewReminderInfo()
Dim a_reminder As Reminder

    For Each a_reminder In Application.Reminders
        Debug.Print "*****"
        Debug.Print a_reminder.NextReminderDate & _
            " (" & a_reminder.Item.Start & ")"
        Debug.Print a_reminder.Caption
        Debug.Print a_reminder.Item.Body
    Next a_reminder
End Sub
```

The following output shows a typical entry for a reminder.

```
*****
6/17/2003 3:45:00 PM (6/17/2003 4:00:00 PM)
Weekly project review
Review the week's progress, outstanding issues, etc.
```

Use the `AppointmentItem`'s `ReminderTime` property to determine when the reminder appears.

Summary

Compared to Word and Excel, Outlook's object model is relatively simple and primitive, but it still contains plenty of complex features to keep you busy. The object model is geared toward managing Outlook folders and performing Outlook's personal information manager tasks rather than just sending and receiving e-mail. In fact, you'll probably get a better feel for the object model if you think of Outlook as a personal information manager rather than simply as an e-mail engine.

Many applications written in VBA or other programming languages such as Visual Basic send e-mail. You could use Outlook automation to do this. You could create a new Outlook `Application` object and use its properties and methods to compose and send the e-mail.

This is a rather cumbersome process, however. It is much easier to send e-mail with MAPI and CDO, which are described in Chapter 13. Chapter 13 also explains how you can send a mail command to the operating system and let the system handle the details.

Outlook, MAPI, and CDO

ACCESS IS A DATABASE ADMINISTRATION application. Although another program can use Access to manipulate a database, it is usually easier to use ADO or some other database access tool to work with the database rather than using Access itself.

Similarly, one of Outlook's functions is to manage e-mail. Another application can use Outlook to manipulate the e-mail system, but usually there are easier methods. For example, MAPI (Messaging Application Programming Interface) lets a program work directly with the e-mail system much as ADO lets a program work with an Access database.

CDO (Collaboration Data Objects) is a newer library layered on MAPI that also lets your applications work with e-mail. Since the first version of CDO, Microsoft has released several different CDO sequels, some with very different focuses and capabilities. The section "Understanding CDO Versions" later in this chapter has more to say about these versions.

In some cases, you can use an even simpler solution than CDO. If you just want to help your program's user send e-mail, you can use the ShellExecute API function. ShellExecute sends a command to the operating system. If you use ShellExecute to send the system an e-mail address link, the system automatically opens the default e-mail application and inserts the e-mail address, subject, and other fields. This solution is very simple and ideal for letting users e-mail you feedback, bug reports, and other messages to specific known addresses.

ShellExecute

Most applications have little or no e-mail requirements. Many need a simple way to help the user send a message to a specific e-mail address. They don't need to actually send the e-mail automatically, receive e-mail, or rearrange mail folders. In this case, the ShellExecute API function provides a simple solution.

ShellExecute makes the operating system perform some operation on a file. One typical use for ShellExecute is to open a file. This makes the operating system open the file using whatever application is registered as appropriate for that type of file. For instance, if you use ShellExecute to open a file with a .doc extension, your system will open the file using Microsoft Word (assuming no other application has registered as the default program for .doc files).

If you use `ShellExecute` to "open" a URL, the system opens that URL using the system's default Web browser, possibly reusing an existing instance of the browser if one is available. The following code displays the VB Helper home page. The `Declares` statement (split across four lines) defines the `ShellExecuteA` API function so Visual Basic knows to find it in the shell32.dll library. For information on this function, go to http://msdn.microsoft.com/library/en-us/shellcc/platform/shell/reference/functions/shellexecute.asp.

The code then uses `ShellExecuteA` to tell the operating system to perform the action "open" on the file http://www.vb-helper.com. That makes the system open the URL in the default Web browser.

```
Private Declare Function ShellExecute Lib "shell32.dll" _
  Alias "ShellExecuteA" (ByVal hwnd As Long, ByVal lpOperation As String, _
  ByVal lpFile As String, ByVal lpParameters As String, _
  ByVal lpDirectory As String, ByVal nShowCmd As Long) As Long
Private Const SW_SHOW = 5

Private Sub Command1_Click()
    ShellExecute hwnd, "open", _
        "http://www.vb-helper.com", _
        vbNullString, vbNullString, SW_SHOW
End Sub
```

If you open a `mailto` URL, the system opens its default mail application and begins composing a message. You can even specify the message's initial `subject`, `body`, `cc`, and `bcc` fields within the URL. Separate the basic URL from the first field with a question mark (?) and separate the other fields with ampersands (&). This is the standard query string syntax for Web URLs.

For example, the following URL starts an e-mail message to ignore_me@vb-helper.com. The `cc` field includes the users no_one@vb-helper.com and nobody@vb-helper.com, and the `bcc` field contains the name somebody@vb-helper.com. The subject is "You must buy this book" and the message body contains the text "Office XP Programming Smackdown."

```
mailto:ignore_me@vb-helper.com
?cc=no_one@ vb-helper.com;nobody@vb-helper.com
&bcc=somebody@vb-helper.com
&subject=You must buy this book
&body=Office XP Programming Smackdown
```

TIP *You cannot use this technique to send attachments, but your program may be able to use the* SendKeys *statement to coerce the mail system into attaching a file. For information that works if the mail system is Outlook Express, see* http://www.vb-helper.com/howto_send_outlook_express_attachment.html. *Unfortunately, the keys you need to use will vary by mail system, so this isn't a great solution if the code will run on a large number of customer computers.*

You can use this simple technique to help users send you feedback and other e-mail. You can fill in the to field, subject, and body, and then launch the system's mail system. The user only needs to click Send.

There is one additional detail you may need to handle, however. A mailto URL cannot contain special nonprinting characters. In particular, it cannot contain carriage returns and line feeds, which you might reasonably want to include in the message's body.

You can replace these characters with their hexadecimal codes. For instance, the carriage return character has ASCII code 13 or D in hexadecimal. You can replace carriage returns with the string %0D in the URL. Similarly, you can replace the line feed character with %0A.

The following code shows how a program can start the e-mail editor. First it creates a string named url containing the mailto URL. It starts with mailto:, the to e-mail address, and a question mark. It uses the HexifySpecialChars function to replace any nonprinting characters in the e-mail address with their hexadecimal codes.

Next the program examines the cc, bcc, subject, and body fields stored in its text boxes. If one of these fields is nonblank, the program uses HexifySpecialChars to fix any nonprinting characters in the field and adds it to the URL.

When it has finished examining the mail fields, the URL ends with a question mark or ampersand. The code removes that trailing character and uses ShellExecute to "open" the URL.

The HexifySpecialChars function loops through the characters in a string. If a character is nonprinting or &, it replaces the character with a percent sign and the character's two-digit hexadecimal code. If the character is a normal character, the function simply adds it to its result string.

NOTE *An ampersand (&) cannot appear in the URL because it's used as a delimiter for the mail fields. The question mark can appear (as long as it's not in the* to *address) because only the first question mark is a delimiter.*

FILE *Ch13\StartMail.vbp*

```
' Start the email system with the indicated values
' filled in.
Private Sub cmdStartMail_Click()
Dim url As String

    ' Compose the mailto URL.
    url = "mailto:" & HexifySpecialChars(txtTo.Text) & "?"
    If Len(txtCc.Text) > 0 Then _
        url = url & "cc=" & HexifySpecialChars(txtCc.Text) & "&"
    If Len(txtBcc.Text) > 0 Then _
        url = url & "bcc=" & HexifySpecialChars(txtBcc.Text) & "&"
    If Len(txtSubject.Text) > 0 Then _
        url = url & "subject=" & HexifySpecialChars(txtSubject.Text) & "&"
    If Len(txtBody.Text) > 0 Then _
        url = url & "body=" & HexifySpecialChars(txtBody.Text) & "&"

    ' Remove the final ? or &.
    url = Left$(url, Len(url) - 1)

    ' "Open" the URL.
    ShellExecute hwnd, "open", url, _
        vbNullString, vbNullString, SW_SHOW
End Sub

' Replace special characters with their hex codes.
Private Function HexifySpecialChars(ByVal txt As String) As String
Dim i As Integer
Dim ch As String
Dim result As String

    ' Examine each character.
    For i = 1 To Len(txt)
        ch = Mid$(txt, i, 1)
        ' See if this character could cause trouble.
        If (ch < " ") Or (ch > "~") Or (ch = "&") Then
            ' Replace the character with its hex code.
            ch = Right$("00" & Hex(Asc(ch)), 2)
            result = result & "%" & ch
```

```
    Else
        ' Leave the character alone.
        result = result & ch
    End If
Next i

' Return the result.
HexifySpecialChars = result
End Function
```

You can use ShellExecute in only a relatively limited way to launch the system's default mail editor, but that's all many applications ever need. If you just need to help the user send e-mail to a feedback address, you can use ShellExecute to help the user fill in the e-mail address and subject lines correctly.

If your application has more elaborate e-mail needs, consider using CDO.

CDO

ShellExecute is fine for simple scenarios. For more complex applications that need send, receive, delete, and otherwise manipulate mail folders in more complicated ways, you need a more powerful solution such as CDO.

Just as Microsoft has produced many different database access tools over the years (DAO, RDO, ADO, ADO.NET, and so forth), it has also produced several different messaging tools. CDO (Microsoft Collaboration Data Objects) 1.2.1 is not the latest of these tools, but it's one of the most useful to Visual Basic and VBA programs.

NOTE *CDO has also been called OLE Messaging (in versions prior to 1.1) and Active Messaging (in version 1.1). Other versions include CDO for Windows NT Server (CDONTS), CDO for Windows 2000 (also called CDO 2.0 and CDOSYS), and CDO for Exchange Server (CDOEX).*

These versions are not all compatible. For example, CDONTS is not based on MAPI, so it won't run CDO 1.2.1 code. It will coexist on a system with CDO 1.2.1 installed, however. For more information on these versions, including a list of products that install them, go to http://msdn.microsoft.com/library/ en-us/dncdsys/html/cdo_roadmap.asp.

CDO is not really a new technology; it's really a new interface for MAPI. CDO includes two libraries. The first, cdo.dll, contains the basic CDO functionality. The second library, cdohtml.dll, is a rendering library that deals with displaying CDO objects and collections in HTML on the Web.

Both of these CDO libraries sit atop the MAPI libraries. If you have installed Microsoft Office XP, chances are very good that you have all of the necessary MAPI and CDO libraries installed. If you can't find the necessary references, search Microsoft's Web site. A good place to start, and a good source of CDO information in general, is the Overview of CDO at http://msdn.microsoft.com/library/en-us/cdo/html/_olemsg_overview_of_cdo.asp.

The following section gives a brief overview of the CDO object model. Later sections explain how to perform common operations using CDO in a VBA application.

Understanding the CDO Object Model

To work with CDO, a VBA program starts by creating a Session object. This object provides access to other CDO objects much as an Application object provides access to other objects in an Office application. This section describes some of the most useful CDO objects.

The Session object's Inbox and Outbox properties are Folder objects representing the obvious mail folders.

The GetDefaultFolder method returns a Folder object representing some other mail folder. For example, the following code displays the number of messages in the deleted items folder.

```
Debug.Print _
    mapi_session.GetDefaultFolder(CdoDefaultFolderDeletedItems).Messages.Count
```

The Session object's GetFolder method returns a Folder if you know its ID.

A Folder object's Messages collection manages the messages within the folder. Its Add method creates a new message and returns a corresponding Message object. This object has properties and methods that you can use to manipulate the message. For example, you can use the Recipients and Attachments properties to manage the message's recipients and attachments. The Add methods provided by these collections return an object you can use to define the new item. For example, Recipients.Add returns a Recipient object that you can use to define the new recipient's name, address, and type (To, Cc, or Bcc).

The Message object's Delete, Forward, Reply, ReplyAll, and Send methods do exactly what their names imply.

The Session object's AddressLists collection contains AddressList objects. In turn, an AddressList has an AddressEntries property that contains AddressEntry objects. The AddressEntry objects contain address book entries holding names and e-mail addresses.

The following sections demonstrate these objects. For more information on the CDO object model, go to http://msdn.microsoft.com/library/en-us/cdo/html/_olemsg_object_model.asp.

Sending Mail

Working with CDO (or MAPI) is a two-part process. First, you create a Session object and connect it to the underlying MAPI system. Second, you use other objects to perform messaging system operations. For example, you might create a new Message object, add Recipient objects to its recipients list, and invoke the message's Send method.

To use CDO, open the VBA development environment and select Tools ➤ References. Select the box next to Microsoft CDO 1.2.1 Library and click OK. Now your code can create new API objects defined by the CDO library.

The following code shows how a VBA application might send an e-mail message. It begins by declaring the CDO objects it will need from the MAPI namespace. It declares Session, Message, and Recipient variables.

It then uses CreateObject to create a new MAPI.Session object and invokes its Logon method to connect it to the underlying MAPI system. You can specify a profile name appropriate to your system in the call to Logon. If you omit the profile name, the system displays the message shown in Figure 13-1 to let the user select a profile.

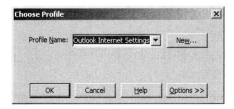

Figure 13-1. If you omit the profile name, the Logon *method lets the user select a profile.*

Next the program uses the Session's Outbox.Messages.Add method to create a new message and fills in the message's subject and body text.

The code uses the new message's `Recipients` collection's `Add` method to make a new `Recipient` object. It puts the recipient's display name in the `Name` property and sets the recipient's type to `CdoTo` to indicate that this is a primary recipient. It then sets the recipient's `Address` field to `SMTP:` followed by the e-mail address.

Alternatively, the program could have called the recipient object's `Resolve` method. At that point, the object would try to look up the recipient's name in the address book. That makes the system display the warning shown in Figure 13-2. Click Yes to let the program continue.

Figure 13-2. The system displays this message when a program tries to access the address book.

If the Resolve method finds an exact match for the recipient's name, it fills in the address and continues. If it finds an ambiguous match, it displays the message box shown in Figure 13-3. In this example, the user's name Bug is a reasonable match for two address book entries: Bug Reports and Bug Fixes. The user can pick one or click Show More Names to pick any entry in the address book.

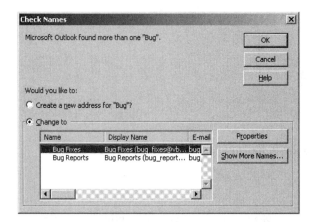

Figure 13-3. The system uses this message box to let the user pick between ambiguous recipient names.

TIP *A large company address database may contain duplicate entries for the same users. In that case, knowing the user's full name isn't enough to guarantee an unambiguous match. To avoid the Check Names dialog, your program can search the address book itself and try to figure out which name is correct. For example, it might know that the company has a new domain (rod@new_domain.com) and pick addresses at that domain rather than those at an older one (rod@old_domain.net).*

Even if it can't figure out which address to use, the program may be able to help the user pick the right name more easily than the Check Names dialog does. For instance, two addresses may look almost the same in the standard dialog. Your program may be able to determine the difference and ask the user whether the correct recipient has an office in building 8 or building 2.

Finally, you may want to log these sorts of ambiguities to a file so someone can update the address book.

After it has created the primary recipient, the program adds another recipient. It sets this one's type to CdoCc to indicate that this is a Cc address.

Next the program calls the message object's Send method to send the e-mail. That makes the system display the dialog shown in Figure 13-4. The progress bar counts off several seconds while the Yes button is disabled in the hope that you will actually read the message and think about whether you want to allow the program to send the e-mail rather than automatically clicking Yes. This message, which your code cannot turn off, is designed to prevent simple viruses from sending e-mail without your knowledge.

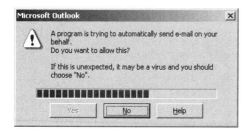

Figure 13-4. The system displays this dialog when the program tries to send e-mail.

The code sets the Send method's ShowDialog parameter to False. This doesn't prevent the warning dialog from appearing. It prevents a send mail dialog from appearing to allow the user to change the message's contents and recipients.

Finally, after the message has been sent, the program logs the session object out of the messaging system.

FILE *Ch13\SendMapiMail.doc*

```
' Send an email using MAPI/CDO.
Sub MAPISendMail()
Dim mapi_session As MAPI.Session
Dim mapi_message As MAPI.Message
Dim mapi_recipient As MAPI.Recipient

    On Error GoTo SendMailError

    ' Create the MAPI session.
    Set mapi_session = CreateObject("MAPI.Session")
    mapi_session.Logon 'ProfileName:="Microsoft Outlook Internet Settings"

    ' Create a message.
    Set mapi_message = mapi_session.Outbox.Messages.Add
    mapi_message.Subject = "Test email"
    mapi_message.Text = "This is a test email" & vbCrLf & "sent my MAPI"

    ' Add a recipient.
    Set mapi_recipient = mapi_message.Recipients.Add
    mapi_recipient.Name = "Bug Reports"
    mapi_recipient.Type = CdoTo
    mapi_recipient.Address = "SMTP:bugs@vb-helper.com"
    ' mapi_recipient.Resolve

    ' Add a CC entry.
    Set mapi_recipient = mapi_message.Recipients.Add
    mapi_recipient.Name = "Project 0216 History"
    mapi_recipient.Type = CdoCc
    mapi_recipient.Address = "SMTP:history_0216@vb-helper.com"
    ' mapi_recipient.Resolve
```

```
    ' Send the message.
    mapi_message.Send ShowDialog:=False

    mapi_session.Logoff
    Exit Sub

SendMailError:
    MsgBox "Error " & Format$(Err.Number) & " sending mail" & _
        vbCrLf & Err.Description, vbExclamation, "Error"
    mapi_session.Logoff
    Exit Sub
End Sub
```

Sending Attachments

Once you know how to send a basic e-mail message, it's relatively easy to add an attachment. The following code fragment runs before the program executes a message's Send method. It declares a MAPI Attachment variable and uses the message object's Attachments collection's Add method to create the new attachment. It sets the attachment's type to CdoFileData to indicate that the attachment is a file.

 NOTE *This is one case where CDO provides more flexibility than using the* ShellExecute *method, which cannot handle attachments.*

The code adds a space character to the end of the message text and sets the attachment's position to the location of that character. The position is given to mail viewing programs such as Outlook as a hint about where to display the attachment. The mail viewer may display the attachment as an icon, by including the attachment, or by some other method. The character in this position may be replaced by the attachment's representation, depending on how the viewer decides to display it. Putting a space character here is relatively safe because it isn't visible even if the viewer decides to leave it there.

FILE *Ch13\SendMapiMail.doc*

```
Sub MAPISendMailWithAttachment()
...
' Add an attachment.
Dim mapi_attachment As MAPI.Attachment
Set mapi_attachment = mapi_message.Attachments.Add
mapi_attachment.Type = CdoFileData
mapi_message.Text = mapi_message.Text & " "
mapi_attachment.Position = Len(mapi_message.Text)
mapi_attachment.Source = ActiveDocument.Path & "\" & ActiveDocument.Name
...
End Sub
```

Reading Mail

The Session object's Inbox property returns a Folder object representing the Inbox folder. That object's Messages property is a collection containing Message objects representing the items in the Inbox. Your program can loop through the items in the Messages collection and display their subjects, examine their text, call their Delete methods, and so forth.

The following code examines each message's Unread property. It displays the subjects of the unread messages, placing brackets around those of messages that have been read.

FILE *Ch13\SendMapiMail.doc*

```
' Read messages in the Inbox.
Sub MAPIReadInbox()
Dim mapi_session As MAPI.Session
Dim mapi_message As MAPI.Message
```

```
    On Error GoTo SendMailWithAttachmentError

    ' Create the MAPI session.
    Set mapi_session = CreateObject("MAPI.Session")
    mapi_session.Logon ProfileName:="Microsoft Outlook Internet Settings"

    ' Loop through Inbox's Messages.
    For Each mapi_message In mapi_session.Inbox.Messages
        If mapi_message.Unread Then
            Debug.Print mapi_message.Subject
        Else
            Debug.Print "[" & mapi_message.Subject & "]"
        End If
    Next mapi_message

    mapi_session.Logoff
    Exit Sub

SendMailWithAttachmentError:
    MsgBox "Error " & Format$(Err.Number) & " readin Inbox" & _
        vbCrLf & Err.Description, vbExclamation, "Error"
    mapi_session.Logoff
    Exit Sub
End Sub
```

A more elaborate example might keep track of the time it last checked for new messages and then report only those with a TimeReceived value after that time.

Deleting Mail

To delete a message, you can search a Folder object's Messages collection until you find the message you want. Then you can call the Message's Delete method to permanently delete it. Alternatively, you can move the message into the Deleted Items folder as shown in the following code.

The code begins by creating a MAPI session as usual. It uses the Session object's GetDefaultFolder method to find the Deleted Items folder. It records that object's ID property for later use.

The code then loops through the messages in the Inbox folder. If a message's subject contains the string "mortgage," the program uses the message object's MoveTo method to move the message into the Deleted Items folder.

FILE *Ch13\SendMapiMail.doc*

```
' Delete messages that have the word "mortgage" in the subject.
Sub MAPIFilterInbox()
Dim mapi_session As MAPI.Session
Dim mapi_message As MAPI.Message
Dim deleted_id As String

    On Error GoTo MAPIFilterInboxError

    ' Create the MAPI session.
    Set mapi_session = CreateObject("MAPI.Session")
    mapi_session.Logon ProfileName:="Microsoft Outlook Internet Settings"

    ' Get the Deleted Items folder's ID.
    deleted_id = mapi_session.GetDefaultFolder(CdoDefaultFolderDeletedItems).ID

    ' Loop through Inbox's Messages.
    For Each mapi_message In mapi_session.Inbox.Messages
        If InStr(LCase$(mapi_message.Subject), "mortgage") <> 0 Then
            Debug.Print "Deleting: " & mapi_message.Subject
            mapi_message.MoveTo deleted_id
        End If
    Next mapi_message

    mapi_session.Logoff
    Exit Sub

MAPIFilterInboxError:
    MsgBox "Error " & Format$(Err.Number) & " readin Inbox" & _
        vbCrLf & Err.Description, vbExclamation, "Error"
    mapi_session.Logoff
    Exit Sub
End Sub
```

NOTE *This type of filtering by looking for a single keyword is somewhat tricky. After all, your mother could send you an e-mail entitled "Good news, I finally paid off the mortgage." Many of the sneakier spammers change the subject text so it doesn't contain obviously offensive words. For example, they might write MORTGAGE where the letter O is replaced with a zero. It looks about the same to you but the filter misses it.*

A safer solution is to move suspected spam into a special spam folder that you can skim every few days for messages from mom and others. This doesn't save you from MORTGAGE ads, but it may save you a little time.

Finding Folders

The MAPI Session object provides a couple methods for locating a particular folder. The GetDefaultFolder method takes a parameter indicating the type of folder you want to find and returns the corresponding Folder object. Predefined constants for the parameter begin with CdoDefaultFolder followed by Calendar, Contacts, DeletedItems, Inbox, Journal, Notes, Outbox, SentItems, or Tasks. For example, the value CdoDefaultFolderInbox finds the Inbox folder.

The Session object's GetFolder method takes as a parameter a folder's ID and returns the corresponding Folder object. Unfortunately, a folder's ID is a very long string that's pretty meaningless to a programmer. If you find a folder in some other way, you can record its ID property for later use, but finding a folder using some more useful parameter, such as its name, is difficult.

The following code finds a folder in the Personal Folders root folder space using a specific folder name. It creates a MAPI Session object. It then loops through its InfoStores collection until it finds the Personal Folders InfoStore. That object's RootFolder property contains a Folders property that represents the folders in the Personal Folders root space. The code calls this Folders object's GetFirst method to make the variable mapi_folder refer to its first folder. Then, while mapi_folder doesn't have the value Nothing, the code examines the folder to see if it has the desired name. If it does not, the code calls the Folders object's GetNext method to move mapi_folder to the next folder.

If the function finds the target folder, it returns the folder's ID. The program can then use the Session object's GetFolder method to fetch the corresponding Folder object if necessary.

The TestMAPIFindFolderId subroutine tests the MAPIFindFolderId function by finding the Inbox folder (which should exist) and the Snarf folder (which probably doesn't exist on your system).

FILE *Ch13\SendMapiMail.doc*

```
' Search the Personal Folders folder for a specific folder.
Function MAPIFindFolderId(ByVal folder_name As String) As String
Dim mapi_session As MAPI.Session
Dim mapi_folders As MAPI.Folders
Dim mapi_folder As MAPI.Folder
Dim i As Integer

    On Error GoTo MAPIFindFolderIdError

    ' Create the MAPI session.
    Set mapi_session = CreateObject("MAPI.Session")
    mapi_session.Logon ProfileName:="Microsoft Outlook Internet Settings"

    ' Search the InfoStores for Personal Folders.
    For i = 1 To mapi_session.InfoStores.Count
        ' See if this is the Personal Folders InfoStore.
        If mapi_session.InfoStores(i).Name = "Personal Folders" Then
            ' This is it.
            ' Search the root folder's subfolders.
            Set mapi_folders = mapi_session.InfoStores(i).RootFolder.Folders
            Set mapi_folder = mapi_folders.GetFirst
            Do While Not (mapi_folder Is Nothing)
                ' See if this is the one we want.
                If mapi_folder.Name = folder_name Then
                    ' This is the target.
                    MAPIFindFolderId = mapi_folder.ID
                    mapi_session.Logoff
                    Exit Function
                End If

                ' Move to the next folder.
                Set mapi_folder = mapi_folders.GetNext
            Loop
```

```
              ' We searched Personal Folders but didn't find the target.
              Exit Function
          End If
      Next i

      mapi_session.Logoff
      Exit Function

MAPIFindFolderIdError:
      MsgBox "Error " & Format$(Err.Number) & " finding folder" & _
          vbCrLf & Err.Description, vbExclamation, "Error"
      mapi_session.Logoff
      Exit Function
End Function

' Find some folders' IDs.
Sub TestMAPIFindFolderId()
      Debug.Print "Inbox: " & MAPIFindFolderId("Inbox")
      Debug.Print "Snarf: " & MAPIFindFolderId("Snarf")
End Sub
```

The Folder object also has a Folders property that is a collection representing subfolders contained within the folder. You can loop through this collection by using GetFirst and GetNext much as the previous code loops through the Personal Folders root folder. You can use this method to find folders within another folder.

You can also recursively search the entire Personal Folders InfoStore to find a particular folder wherever it lies in the folder hierarchy. The MAPIFindSubfolderId function shown in the following code begins much as the previous function does by finding the Personal Folders InfoSpace. It then passes that object's RootFolder.Folders collection to the MAPISearchFoldersObject function.

MAPISearchFoldersObject loops through a Folders object's folders. If a folder's name matches the target name, the search is complete. If a folder's name doesn't match the target, MAPISearchFoldersObject calls itself recursively to search the folder's Folders collection.

Subroutine TestMAPIFindSubfolderId tests the MAPIFindSubfolderId function by searching for the folders Spam2, SubSpam, and Snarf. On the test system, the function finds folder Deleted Items/Spam2 and Deleted Items/Spam4/SubSpam. The folder Snarf doesn't exist.

FILE *Ch13\SendMapiMail.doc*

```
' Search the whole Personal Folders Infostore for a specific folder.
Function MAPIFindSubfolderId(ByVal folder_name As String) As String
Dim mapi_session As MAPI.Session
Dim i As Integer

    On Error GoTo MAPIFindSubfolderIdError

    ' Create the MAPI session.
    Set mapi_session = CreateObject("MAPI.Session")
    mapi_session.Logon ProfileName:="Microsoft Outlook Internet Settings"

    ' Search the InfoStores for Personal Folders.
    For i = 1 To mapi_session.InfoStores.Count
        ' See if this is the Personal Folders InfoStore.
        If mapi_session.InfoStores(i).Name = "Personal Folders" Then
            ' This is it.
            ' Search the root folder's subfolders.
            MAPIFindSubfolderId = MAPISearchFoldersObject(folder_name, _
                mapi_session.InfoStores(i).RootFolder.Folders)

            ' We either found it or not.
            Exit Function
        End If
    Next i

    mapi_session.Logoff
    Exit Function

MAPIFindSubfolderIdError:
    MsgBox "Error " & Format$(Err.Number) & " finding folder" & _
        vbCrLf & Err.Description, vbExclamation, "Error"
    mapi_session.Logoff
    Exit Function
End Function
```

```
' Search this Folders object for the target folder.
Function MAPISearchFoldersObject(ByVal folder_name As String, _
  ByVal mapi_folders As MAPI.Folders) As String
Dim mapi_folder As MAPI.Folder
Dim folder_id As String

    ' Loop through the subfolders.
    Set mapi_folder = mapi_folders.GetFirst
    Do While Not (mapi_folder Is Nothing)
        ' See if this is the one we want.
        If mapi_folder.Name = folder_name Then
            ' This is the target.
            MAPISearchFoldersObject = mapi_folder.ID
            Exit Function
        Else
            ' This is not the target.
            ' Search the subfolders.
            folder_id = MAPISearchFoldersObject(folder_name, _
                mapi_folder.Folders)

            ' See if we found the target.
            If Len(folder_id) > 0 Then
                ' We found it.
                MAPISearchFoldersObject = folder_id
                Exit Function
            End If

            ' We didn't find it. Continue looking.
        End If

        ' Move to the next folder.
        Set mapi_folder = mapi_folders.GetNext
    Loop
End Function

' Find some folders' IDs.
Sub TestMAPIFindSubfolderId()
    Debug.Print "Spam2:   " & MAPIFindSubfolderId("Spam2")
    Debug.Print "SubSpam: " & MAPIFindSubfolderId("SubSpam")
    Debug.Print "Snarf:   " & MAPIFindSubfolderId("Snarf")
End Sub
```

Summary

Just as you can access the information in an Access database without using Access, you can also work with e-mail and the system of folders used by Outlook without using Outlook. If you just need to help the user write an e-mail message, you may be able to use the ShellExecute function to launch the system's default e-mail application. For more elaborate needs, you can use CDO and the underlying MAPI tools to send, receive, and manipulate messages relatively painlessly.

This chapter provides a brief introduction to ShellExecute and CDO, and describes how to perform several useful tasks using CDO in VBA. For information on other CDO programming tasks, see the online help or go to http:// msdn.microsoft.com/library/en-us/cdo/html/_olemsg_programming_tasks.asp.

CHAPTER 14

Smart Tags

SMART TAGS WERE INTRODUCED in Office XP as a way to allow Word, Excel, and Outlook (using Word as your default editor) to react to specific content as you type. Office 2003 added PowerPoint and Access to the list.

For an example, suppose you install a smart tag that recognizes the word "Smackdown." When you type Smackdown in Word 2002, it highlights the word with a dotted purple underline. If you hover the mouse over Smackdown, Word displays a smart tag icon that looks like an "i" in a circle. If you click that icon, Word displays a list of actions it can perform for you, such as logging onto the Office Smackdown Web site or sending feedback e-mail.

NOTE *This book's working title was* Office XP Programming Smackdown, *so you'll see "Smackdown" used in the examples in this chapter.*

Figure 14-1 shows a simple smart tag in action. You can't tell in the figure because of the menu's position, but the smart tag icon is sitting above the word "Office" in the text "Office Smackdown." This computer has two smart tags installed that match the word "Office." One recognizes MSDN-related (Microsoft Developers Network) terms, and the other recognizes the term "Office Smackdown." Because two smart tags recognize this text, Word displays a cascading menu allowing the user to select either.

In this case, the user opened the Office Smackdown Terms menu. At the top of the child menu, you can see the smart tag's name (Office Smackdown Terms) followed by the term it has recognized (Office Smackdown). The tag's two actions open the book's Web site and send feedback e-mail.

Smart tags lie in an odd corner of Office programming that mixes several dissimilar programming technologies including Visual Basic, COM (Component Object Model), VB .NET, XML, and XSD. Some of the more elaborate smart tag solutions are quite complicated and involve most of these technologies. The following sections describe two of the simpler approaches.

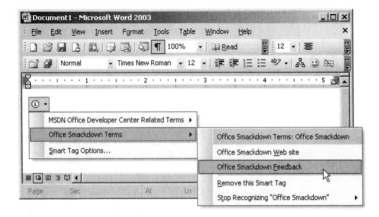

Figure 14-1. The Office Smackdown Terms smart tag can open a Web site or send feedback e-mail.

Smart Tags in Different Applications

As is the case with so many other things, different Office applications handle smart tags slightly differently. Word and PowerPoint match smart tag terms within the flow of text and mark them with a purple dotted underline.

Excel only matches smart tag terms exactly. If a smart tag recognizes the term "Office Smackdown," it will not recognize the text "Office Smackdown Rocks." To flag a cell containing recognized text, Excel places a small purple triangle in the cell's lower-right corner. If you hover the mouse over the cell, Excel displays the usual smart tag icon. Figure 14-2 shows Excel displaying the smart tag icon and the little triangle.

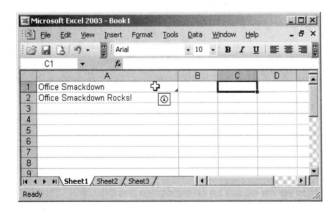

Figure 14-2. Excel marks smart tag terms with a small triangle in a cell's lower-right corner.

CAUTION *If a smart tag recognizes the cell containing the insertion point, it displays the smart tag icon. If the mouse hovers over another cell recognized by a smart tag, it displays the icon, too. That means you can see two smart tag icons at the same time, and picking the one you want can sometimes be confusing.*

In Word, Excel, and PowerPoint, you need to have smart tags enabled before any will take effect. Select Tools ➤AutoCorrect Options, click the Smart Tags tab, and check the "Label text with smart tags" box. Check the boxes next to any smart tags that you want to use and click OK. Figure 14-3 shows the dialog for Power-Point. The dialogs for Word and Excel are slightly different but not drastically.

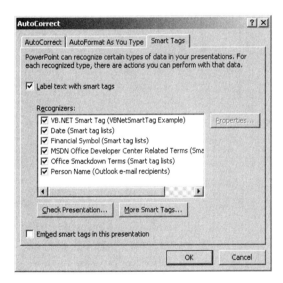

Figure 14-3. Use this dialog to enable smart tags for PowerPoint.

Click the Check Presentation button to make PowerPoint recheck the active presentation for smart tag terms. The other Office applications provide a similar button with a slightly different name on their AutoCorrect dialogs.

Access takes a different approach from Word, Excel, and PowerPoint. Rather than searching text for recognized terms, it lets the database developer attach smart tags to a particular field or control. To add a smart tag, in design view, open form, report, data access page, table, or query. Select the object you want to attach to a smart tag and look in its Properties window. In the Smart Tags property box, enter the smart tag's URI (Uniform Resource Identifier) or click the ellipsis button to select a smart tag from a list.

Figure 14-4 shows the Smart Tags dialog where you can select smart tags for the Books table's Title field. Beneath the dialog, you can see the field's Smart Tags property box displaying the URI from a previously selected smart tag.

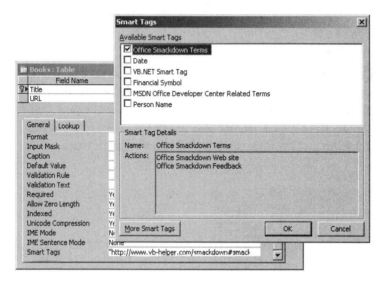

Figure 14-4. In the Properties window, enter a smart tag's URI or click the ellipsis to display the Smart Tags dialog.

Smart Tag Lists

By far the simplest way to build a smart tag is to make a MOSTL (Microsoft Office Smart Tag List). A MOSTL is simply an XML file that satisfies a smart tag schema defined by Microsoft. This file includes elements that define such values as the smart tag's name, description, and a Web site where a developer can get more information. It also defines words the smart tag should recognize and actions it should let the Office user perform.

The following code shows an XML file that defines the Office Smackdown Terms smart tag. The entire file is enclosed in a `smarttaglist` element, which indicates that the file defines a smart tag list. Top-level tags define the smart tag's name, LCID (locale ID), and Web page for obtaining more information.

NOTE *An LCID is a number that identifies a language, sort method, and other identifying information. For example, the LCID 1033 identifies United States English. For more information and a list of LCIDs, go to* http://support.microsoft.com/support/kb/articles/q221/4/35.asp.

The smarttag element defines the list's recognized words and actions. The caption tag gives the text an Office application should display at the top of the smart tag's action menu. The terms element lists the terms the smart tag should recognize separated by commas.

The actions element contains a series of action elements that define the actions the smart tag can perform. Each action contains a caption to display in the action menu and a url for the smart tag to open when the user selects that action.

TIP *Place an ampersand by using the code* & *in front of the shortcut letter you want underlined in the menu. For example, look at the definition of the OfficeSmackdownWebSite action in this code and notice that the W in the "Office Smackdown Web site" menu item is underlined in Figure 14-1.*

Notice that this code uses a mailto URL for its second action. That element is not indented in this listing so that it all will fit on one line. If the user selects this action, the smart tag launches the system's default mail system to create a message to OfficeSmackdown@vb-helper.com with subject set to Feedback. (Remember that trick from Chapter 13?)

FILE *Ch14\smackdown.xml*

```
<FL:smarttaglist xmlns:FL="urn:schemas-microsoft-com:smarttags:list">
    <FL:name>Office Smackdown Terms</FL:name>
    <FL:lcid>1033</FL:lcid>
    <FL:description>Terms related to the book Office Smackdown.</FL:description>
    <FL:moreinfourl>http://www.vb-helper.com/office.htm</FL:moreinfourl>
    <FL:smarttag type="http://www.vb-helper.com/smackdown#smackdownterms">
        <FL:caption>Office Smackdown Terms</FL:caption>
```

```
<FL:terms>
    <FL:termlist>office smackdown, office xp smackdown </FL:termlist>
</FL:terms>
<FL:actions>
    <FL:action id="OfficeSmackdownWebSite">
        <FL:caption>Office Smackdown &amp;Web site</FL:caption>
        <FL:url>http://www.vb-helper.com/office.htm</FL:url>
    </FL:action>
    <FL:action id="OfficeSmackdownFeedback">
        <FL:caption>Office Smackdown &amp;Feedback</FL:caption>
<FL:url>mailto:OfficeSmackdown@vb-helper.com?subject=Feedback</FL:url>
    </FL:action>
</FL:actions>
</FL:smarttag>
</FL:smarttaglist>
```

 TIP *If you insert the token* {TEXT} *inside the* url *element's value, the smart tag replaces this token with whatever term it is currently matching. For example, consider the tag* <FL:url>mailto:Feedback@vb-helper.com? subject={TEXT}</FL:url>. *If the smart tag is currently recognizing the term "Office Smackdown," then this action creates an e-mail message to the address* Feedback@vb-helper.com *with the subject "Office Smackdown."*

After you create the list file, place it in the directory C:\Program Files\Common Files\Microsoft Shared\Smart Tag\Lists. Now when you open Word 2002 or one of the other Office applications that recognizes smart tags, the smart tag should work. If you type "Office Smackdown," Word should flag the text with the purple underline.

Smart Tags with Visual Basic .NET

The smart tag list described in the previous section is relatively easy, but it's quite limited. It lets you define a list of terms and a series of actions, but the actions can only open a URL. With more effort, you can write a DLL (Dynamic Link Library) to recognize more elaborate strings of text and to perform much more complicated actions.

You can build a smart tag DLL in Visual Basic, Visual Basic .NET, or some other language such as C#. The following sections explain how to build and install a smart tag DLL using Visual Basic .NET.

NOTE *If you don't have Visual Studio .NET, you can get a 60-day trial copy at* http://msdn.microsoft.com/vstudio/productinfo/trial/default.aspx *for a small shipping-and-handling fee. Microsoft is slowly starting to phase out support for Visual Basic 6, so you might want to order the trial version if you want to build smart tags. This version will let you decide whether you want to move to VB .NET, and it will let you continue to follow the examples later in this book.*

NOTE *To build a smart tag DLL, you must install the Smart Tag SDK. Get more information and download it at* http://www.microsoft.com/downloads/details.aspx?FamilyId=3D8EDCEE-0246-43EF-A70F-94C0899F1E8F.

The example described here watches for the words *book, oeuvre, tome,* and *opus.* When it finds one of these, the smart tag displays a menu entitled "Office Smackdown Actions" that holds two commands. The "Change text to Office Smackdown" command replaces the matched text with the string "Office Smackdown." The "Open Office Smackdown Web site" command opens Internet Explorer and sends it to the book's Web site.

Creating a smart tag DLL is a fairly long process, although the individual steps aren't too complicated. The basic idea is to create a class library that contains a recognizer class and an action class. The recognizer class inspects text passed to it by an Office application and determines whether the smart tag recognizes some of the text. The action class performs some action when the user selects an item from the smart tag's menu. To set up communications between the Office applications and the smart tag, you must properly register the classes in the System Registry. At that point you can test the DLL and finally use the smart tag from Office applications.

The following sections explain these steps in detail.

TIP *By default the Smart Tag SDK is installed in the directory C:\Program Files\ Smart Tag SDK. The file stsdk.chm in that directory contains the SDK's help file. You will probably find it useful as you build smart tags.*

Start a New Project

Start by creating a new Visual Basic .NET project. In the New Project dialog, select Class Library. Give it the name BookSmartTag.

The next few steps involve only the project itself, not its class modules. In the Solution Explorer, right-click the project entry labeled BookSmartTag and select Properties. Open the Configuration Properties entry and select Debugging. Click the "Start external program" and enter the path to Microsoft Word as shown in Figure 14-5. This tells Visual Basic to use Word to run the smart tag when you debug it later.

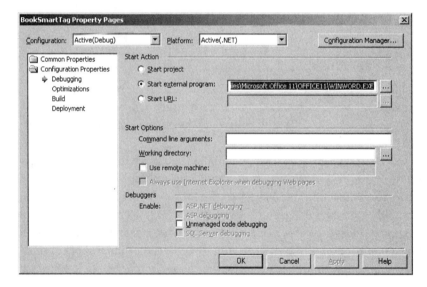

Figure 14-5. Select the "Start external program" option to allow debugging with Word.

Next select the Build entry and check the "Register for COM Interop" box, as shown in Figure 14-6, to tell Visual Basic that the project will expose COM objects needed to interact with Office applications. Click OK to save your choices and close the dialog.

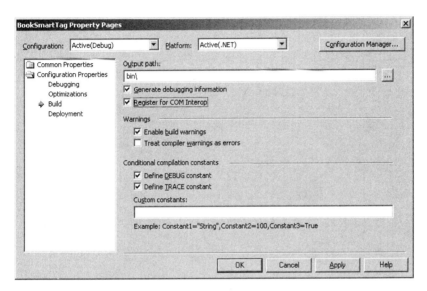

Figure 14-6. Select the "Register for COM Interop" box.

Now open the file AssemblyInfo.vb that Visual Basic created for the project. At the bottom of the file, specify a fixed version (one with no asterisks) for the project as shown in the following code. You can use any version number you want as long as it's fixed so you can use it later to register the DLL.

```
<Assembly: AssemblyVersion("1.0.2.3")>
```

The project's recognizer and action classes must implement the interfaces ISmartTagRecognizer and ISmartTagAction. To define these interfaces, you must set a reference to the Smart Tag SDK. Select Project▶Add Reference, click the COM tab, and select the Smart Tags Type Library as shown in Figure 14-7. Then click OK.

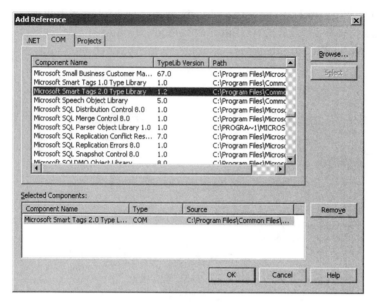

Figure 14-7. To build a smart tag DLL, you must add a reference to the Smart Tags Type Library.

At this point, the project itself is ready to go. Now you need to build the recognizer and action classes.

Build the Recognizer Class

Start by changing the default class's name from Class1 to SmartTagRecognizer. This creates the ProgID BookSmartTag.SmartTagRecognizer, which you will use later.

To make using the smart tag library's namespace easier, add the statement Imports SmartTagLib to the top of the file. The example will also use Interop services so also add the statement Imports System.Runtime.InteropServices.

Immediately inside the class's definition, add the statement Implements ISmartTagRecognizer. This tells Visual Basic that the class will provide all of the methods defined by the ISmartTagRecognizer interface. You'll see how those methods work a little later. First, you should finish defining the class itself.

The next step is to define GUIDs (Globally Unique Identifiers) for the recognizer class. Use the Tools ➤ Create GUID command to start the Create GUID application shown in Figure 14-8. Select the Registry Format and click New GUID. Then click Copy to copy the GUID to the clipboard.

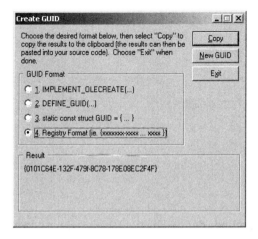

Figure 14-8. Use the Create GUID application to make GUIDs for the recognizer class.

 NOTE *If the Tools ➤ Create GUID command doesn't run or is missing, execute the program guidgen.exe, which by default is located in C:\Program Files\ Microsoft Visual Studio .NET\Common7\Tools.*

Add the following code immediately before the Class statement. Paste your GUID in place of the one shown here.

```
<ProgId("BookSmartTag.SmartTagRecognizer"), _
    GuidAttribute("1B580979-D406-4f1c-B337-D7C8A0E100F0"), _
    ComVisible(True)> _
```

Notice that this code ends with a line continuation character so it becomes part of the following Class statement.

At this point the recognizer class's code should look like the following.

 FILE *Ch14\BookSmartTag\SmartTagRecognizer.cls*

```
Imports SmartTagLib
Imports System.Runtime.InteropServices

' Class to recognize terms.
<ProgId("BookSmartTag.Recognizer"), _
    GuidAttribute("1B580979-D406-4f1c-B337-D7C8A0E100F0"), _
    ComVisible(True)> _
Public Class SmartTagRecognizer
    Implements ISmartTagRecognizer

End Class
```

The next step is to implement the methods defined by the `ISmartTagRecognizer` interface. You could type in all of these methods yourself, complete with their required parameters. It's a lot easier, however, to let Visual Basic fill in the basic templates for you. In the code window, open the left dropdown list and select the `SmartTagRecognizer` class's `ISmartTagRecognizer` entry. Then in the right dropdown, select one of these methods to make Visual Basic create an empty routine for you to fill in.

The following sections describe the methods you need to implement.

Name

The `Name` method returns the recognizer class's short name.

FILE *Ch14\BookSmartTag\SmartTagRecognizer.cls*

```
' The recognizer's short name.
Public ReadOnly Property Name(ByVal LocaleID As Integer) As String _
  Implements SmartTagLib.ISmartTagRecognizer.Name
    Get
        Return "Book Smart Tag Recognizer Class"
    End Get
End Property
```

Desc

The Desc method returns a longer description of the recognizer.

 FILE *Ch14\BookSmartTag\SmartTagRecognizer.cls*

```
Public ReadOnly Property Desc(ByVal LocaleID As Integer) As String _
  Implements SmartTagLib.ISmartTagRecognizer.Desc
    Get
        Return "Watch for select book synonyms"
    End Get
End Property
```

ProgId

The ProgId method returns the recognizer's ProgId. This string includes the name of the library containing the class (BookSmartTag) and the class's name (SmartTagRecognizer).

 FILE *Ch14\BookSmartTag\SmartTagRecognizer.cls*

```
' Return the smart tag's prog ID.
Public ReadOnly Property ProgId() As String _
  Implements SmartTagLib.ISmartTagRecognizer.ProgId
    Get
        Return "BookSmartTag.Recognizer"
    End Get
End Property
```

SmartTagCount

The SmartTagCount property returns the number of smart tag types the recognizer recognizes. This example recognizes only one type.

FILE *Ch14\BookSmartTag\SmartTagRecognizer.cls*

```
Public ReadOnly Property SmartTagCount() As Integer _
    Implements SmartTagLib.ISmartTagRecognizer.SmartTagCount
        Get
            Return 1
        End Get
End Property
```

SmartTagName

The SmartTagName property returns URIs for each smart tag type, one for each type indicated by SmartTagCount.

FILE *Ch14\BookSmartTag\SmartTagRecognizer.cls*

```
Public ReadOnly Property SmartTagName(ByVal SmartTagID As Integer) _
    As String Implements SmartTagLib.ISmartTagRecognizer.SmartTagName
        Get
            Return "http://www.vb-helper.com#BookSmartTag"
        End Get
End Property
```

SmartTagDownloadURL

The SmartTagDownloadURL property returns a URL where the user can download actions if they are not already installed for the smart tag. This example doesn't have such a URL, so it returns an empty string.

 FILE *Ch14\BookSmartTag\SmartTagRecognizer.cls*

```
Public ReadOnly Property SmartTagDownloadURL(ByVal SmartTagID As Integer) _
    As String Implements SmartTagLib.ISmartTagRecognizer.SmartTagDownloadURL
    Get
        Return ""
    End Get
End Property
```

Recognize

The Recognize method is the most interesting part of the recognizer. It examines text sent by an Office application and looks for items it should recognize. When it finds such an item, it makes a property bag. It can store arbitrary information in the bag for later use by the action class.

When it has added any data it wants to the property bag, the Recognize method calls a RecognizerSite object's ComitSmartTag method to send the information to the host application.

This example stores a list of terms in the m_Terms array. The Recognize method looks for each of these in the text it is passed and uses the RecognizerSite object's CommitSmartTag method to tell the host application when instances of the terms occur.

Notice that the Recognize routine passes the CommitSmartTag method the position of the term plus one (pos + 1) to tell it where it found the term. It adds one because the host Office application expects the term's position to be one-based, whereas Visual Basic .NET treats string positions as zero-based.

NOTE *When Visual Basic creates the empty* Recognize *method, it calls the text sent from the host application* [Text]. *In this code, this variable was renamed* examine_text *to be a bit more meaningful.*

FILE *Ch14\BookSmartTag\SmartTagRecognizer.cls*

```
' Make a list of terms we will recognize.
Private m_Terms() As String = { _
        "book", _
        "oeuvre", _
        "tome", _
        "opus" _
    }

' Check for recognized text.
Public Sub Recognize(ByVal examine_text As String, _
  ByVal DataType As SmartTagLib.IF_TYPE, ByVal LocaleID As Integer, _
  ByVal RecognizerSite As SmartTagLib.ISmartTagRecognizerSite) _
  Implements SmartTagLib.ISmartTagRecognizer.Recognize
    Dim i As Integer
    Dim pos As Integer
    Dim property_bag As ISmartTagProperties

    ' Check each term.
    examine_text = examine_text.ToLower()
    For i = 0 To m_Terms.GetUpperBound(0)
        ' See if this term is present.
        pos = examine_text.IndexOf(m_Terms(i))
        Do While pos >= 0
            ' The term appears at position pos.
            ' Get a new property bag
            property_bag = RecognizerSite.GetNewPropertyBag()

            ' Commit the term.
            ' Note that we add 1 to the position
            ' because the property bag expects a
            ' 1-based position.
            RecognizerSite.CommitSmartTag( _
```

```
                "http://www.vb-helper.com#BookSmartTag", _
                pos + 1, m_Terms(i).Length, property_bag)

            ' Look for the term's next occurrence.
            pos = examine_text.IndexOf(m_Terms(i), pos + m_Terms(i).Length)
        Loop
    Next i
End Sub
```

Build the Action Class

Use the Project➤Add Class command to add a new class named SmartTagAction to the project. This creates the ProgID BookSmartTag.SmartTagRecognizer, which you will use later.

Setting up the action class is similar to setting up the recognizer class. Add the same Imports statements as before. Add the statement Implements ISmartTagAction after the Class statement. Use Tools➤Create GUID to make a new GUID and use it to add a ProgId attribute to the class. At this point, the class should look like the following.

 FILE *Ch14\BookSmartTag\SmartTagAction.cls*

```
Imports SmartTagLib
Imports System.Runtime.InteropServices

' Class to provide actions.
<ProgId("BookSmartTag.SmartTagAction"), _
    GuidAttribute("B28B112D-38FE-427f-847D-FFC4C82B2301"), _
    ComVisible(True)> _
Public Class SmartTagAction
    Implements ISmartTagAction

End Class
```

The next step is to implement the methods defined by the ISmartTagAction interface. Again use the code window's dropdown lists to make Visual Basic generate the empty methods for you. The following sections describe these methods.

Name

The Name method should return the action class's short name.

 FILE *Ch14\BookSmartTag\SmartTagAction.cls*

```
Public ReadOnly Property Name(ByVal LocaleID As Integer) As String _
    Implements SmartTagLib.ISmartTagAction.Name
        Get
            Return "Book Smart Tag Action Class"
        End Get
End Property
```

Desc

The Desc method returns a longer description of the class.

 FILE *Ch14\BookSmartTag\SmartTagAction.cls*

```
Public ReadOnly Property Desc(ByVal LocaleID As Integer) As String _
    Implements SmartTagLib.ISmartTagAction.Desc
        Get
            Return "Offer replacements for select book synonyms"
        End Get
    End Property
```

ProgId

The ProgId method returns the program's ProgId.

FILE *Ch14\BookSmartTag\SmartTagAction.cls*

```
Public ReadOnly Property ProgId() As String _
  Implements SmartTagLib.ISmartTagAction.ProgId
    Get
        Return "BookSmartTag.SmartTagAction"
    End Get
End Property
```

SmartTagCaption

The SmartTagCaption method returns the caption the smart tag should display at the top of its action menu.

FILE *Ch14\BookSmartTag\SmartTagAction.cls*

```
Public ReadOnly Property SmartTagCaption(ByVal SmartTagID As Integer, _
  ByVal LocaleID As Integer) As String _
  Implements SmartTagLib.ISmartTagAction.SmartTagCaption
    Get
        Return "Office Smackdown Actions"
    End Get
End Property
```

SmartTagCount

The SmartTagCount property returns the number of smart tag types that this action class supports. In this example, the action class supports only one smart tag type.

FILE *Ch14\BookSmartTag\SmartTagAction.cls*

```
Public ReadOnly Property SmartTagCount() As Integer _
   Implements SmartTagLib.ISmartTagAction.SmartTagCount
      Get
         Return 1
      End Get
End Property
```

SmartTagName

The SmartTagName method returns URIs representing the smart tag types defined by the SmartTagCount method. The URIs should match the URIs returned by the corresponding smart tag recognizer classes.

FILE *Ch14\BookSmartTag\SmartTagAction.cls*

```
Public ReadOnly Property SmartTagName(ByVal SmartTagID As Integer) _
   As String Implements SmartTagLib.ISmartTagAction.SmartTagName
      Get
         Return "http://www.vb-helper.com#BookSmartTag"
      End Get
End Property
```

VerbCount

The VerbCount method returns the number of actions this class supports. This example supports two actions: changing the identified text to "Office Smackdown" and opening the Office Smackdown Web site.

FILE *Ch14\BookSmartTag\SmartTagAction.cls*

```
Public ReadOnly Property VerbCount(ByVal SmartTagName As String) _
    As Integer Implements SmartTagLib.ISmartTagAction.VerbCount
        Get
            Return 2
        End Get
End Property
```

VerbID

The VerbID property returns a numeric ID for the verbs defined by VerbCount. The VerbIndex parameter gives the number of the verb for which the system wants an ID. For instance, when VerbIndex = 1, VerbID should return the ID of verb number 1. You can use any numbers for the verb IDs, although it may be less confusing if you make the IDs match the verb indexes as shown in this code.

FILE *Ch14\BookSmartTag\SmartTagAction.cls*

```
Public ReadOnly Property VerbID(ByVal SmartTagName As String, _
    ByVal VerbIndex As Integer) As Integer _
    Implements SmartTagLib.ISmartTagAction.VerbID
        Get
            Return VerbIndex
        End Get
End Property
```

VerbCaptionFromID

The `VerbCaptionFromID` method returns the caption the verb should have in the smart tag's menu.

 FILE *Ch14\BookSmartTag\SmartTagAction.cls*

```
Public ReadOnly Property VerbCaptionFromID(ByVal VerbID As Integer, _
  ByVal ApplicationName As String, ByVal LocaleID As Integer) As String _
  Implements SmartTagLib.ISmartTagAction.VerbCaptionFromID
    Get
        Select Case VerbID
            Case 1
                Return "Change text to Office Smackdown"
            Case 2
                Return "Open Office Smackdown Web site"
        End Select
    End Get
End Property
```

VerbNameFromID

The `VerbNameFromID` property returns a verb's name given its ID.

 FILE *Ch14\BookSmartTag\SmartTagAction.cls*

```
Public ReadOnly Property VerbNameFromID(ByVal VerbID As Integer) _
  As String Implements SmartTagLib.ISmartTagAction.VerbNameFromID
    Get
        Select Case VerbID
            Case 1
                Return "changeToOfficeSmackdown"
            Case 2
```

```
            Return "openOfficeSmackdownWebSite"
        End Select
    End Get
End Property
```

InvokeVerb

The InvokeVerb method performs whatever action is appropriate for a given verb ID. This example can perform two actions.

If the parameter VerbID = 1, the program replaces the recognized text with "Office Smackdown." The Target parameter is an object that represents the recognized text for the host Office application. If the host is Word, Target is a Word Range object. If the host is Excel, Target is an Excel Range object. If the host is PowerPoint, Target is a PowerPoint TextRange object. The code determines the type of object and replaces the text using its properties.

If VerbID = 2, the code creates a new Internet Explorer application server, sends it to the book's Web site, and displays it.

 FILE *Ch14\BookSmartTag\SmartTagAction.cls*

```
Public Sub InvokeVerb(ByVal VerbID As Integer, _
  ByVal ApplicationName As String, ByVal Target As Object, _
  ByVal Properties As SmartTagLib.ISmartTagProperties, _
  ByVal txt As String, ByVal Xml As String) _
  Implements SmartTagLib.ISmartTagAction.InvokeVerb
    Select Case VerbID
        Case 1  ' Change text to "Office Smackdown."
            If ApplicationName.StartsWith("Word.Application") Then
                Target.Text = "Office Smackdown"
            ElseIf ApplicationName.StartsWith("Excel.Application") Then
                Target.Value = "Office Smackdown"
            ElseIf ApplicationName.StartsWith("PowerPoint.Application") Then
                Target.Text = "Office Smackdown"
            End If

        Case 2  ' Open Ofice Smackdown Web site.
            Dim browser As Object
            browser = CreateObject("InternetExplorer.Application")
```

```
            browser.Navigate2("http://www.vb-helper.com/office.htm")
            browser.Visible = True
      End Select
End Sub
```

> **NOTE** *When Visual Basic creates the empty* InvokeVerb *method, it calls the text that was recognized (in the second-to-last parameter)* [Text]. *In this code, this variable was renamed* txt *to avoid the unusual name* [Text].

Register the Classes

After you've built the recognizer and action classes, you must register them. Start by selecting Build➤Build Solution to compile the DLL. This automatically creates some of the System Registry entries you need. You can manually create the other entries by using the regedit tool. Click the system's Start menu, select Run, enter regedit.exe, and click OK.

> **CAUTION** *Modifying the System Registry is dangerous. If you mess up the registry, you can cause all kinds of damage that could go as far as making your system unbootable. Use care when editing the Registry. Back up the Registry before you make changes.*

Open the key HKEY_CURRENT_USER\Software\Microsoft\Office\Common\SmartTag\ Recognizers. Create a new key named after the recognizer class's GUID including the brackets ({1B580979-D406-4f1c-B337-D7C8A0E100F0} in this example).

Within that key, create new string values named Assembly and Type. Set Assembly to the string "BookSmartTag, Version=1.0.2.3, Culture=neutral, PublicKeyToken=null" replacing the version number with the value you specified in the project's file AssemblyInfo.vb. Set Type to BookSmartTag.SmartTagRecognizer.

Now make similar entries for the action class. Open the key HKEY_CURRENT_USER\ Software\Microsoft\Office\Common\Smart Tag\Actions and create a new key named after the action class's GUID ({B28B112D-38FE-427f-847D-FFC4C82B2301} in this example). Within that key, create the string values Assembly and Type. Set Assembly to the same string as before. Set Type to BookSmartTag.SmartTagAction.

Test the DLL

To test the DLL, invoke Visual Basic's Debug➤Start command or press F5. Visual Basic will launch the external program you specified in the project's properties dialog (Word). Enter some text that the smart tag should recognize. Word should highlight the text with a purple dotted underline. When you hover the mouse over the text, Word will display the smart tag icon. If you click the icon, you should see the menu shown in Figure 14-9.

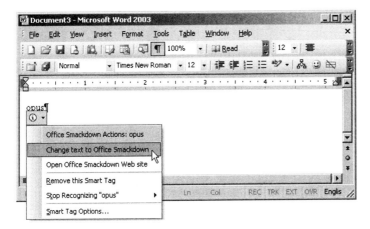

Figure 14-9. The Office Smackdown smart tag recognizes the word opus.

As you work with Word, you can set break points in the Visual Basic code to test the recognizer and action methods. When you close Word, Visual Basic automatically stops the DLL.

After you have tested the DLL, it is ready to run. Unfortunately, installing a smart tag by manually altering the Registry is time consuming and dangerous. If you wanted to provide the smart tag for dozens or even hundreds of users, using regedit would be impractical.

For a different approach to installing smart tags, see the Microsoft article "Deploying Smart Tag DLLs by Using the Visual Studio Installer" at http://msdn.microsoft.com/ library/en-us/dnsmarttag/html/odc_deployst.asp. For information on using Visual Basic .NET's reflection capabilities to make smart tag DLLs that install themselves, see the article "Building Smart Tags in Microsoft Visual Basic .NET" at http:// msdn.microsoft.com/library/en-us/dnsmarttag/html/odc_stvbnet.asp.

Summary

Building a MOSTL is relatively easy. By building a relatively simple XML file, you can tag one or more terms for action. By invoking a term's smart tags menu, the user can jump to a Web site or start composing an e-mail message.

Building a smart tag DLL, on the other hand, is relatively complicated. Individually, the steps aren't too confusing, but there are a whole lot of them. A smart tag DLL gives you much greater flexibility than a MOSTL, however.

The following list describes some URLs that provide more information on building smart tag DLLs using Visual Basic.

- Developing Simple Smart Tags: This article explains how to build and install MOSTLs. `http://msdn.microsoft.com/library/en-us/dnsmarttag/html/odc_stxml.asp`.

- XML Schema for Smart Tag Lists: This download includes the XSD schema that a MOSTL must follow. `http://www.microsoft.com/downloads/details.aspx?FamilyID=65d80f8e-a64b-4ac4-9d37-d3c9e4a25d01&DisplayLang=en`.

- Smart Tag SDK: You need this SDK to build smart tag DLLs. `http://www.microsoft.com/downloads/details.aspx?FamilyId=3D8EDCEE-0246-43EF-A70F-94C0899F1E8F&displaylang=en`.

- Developing Smart Tag DLLs: This article explains how to build a smart tag DLL by using Visual Basic 6. `http://msdn.microsoft.com/library/en-us/dnsmarttag/html/odc_smarttags.asp`.

- Deploying Smart Tag DLLs by Using the Visual Studio Installer: This article explains one method for installing smart tag DLLs. `http://msdn.microsoft.com/library/en-us/dnsmarttag/html/odc_deployst.asp`.

Chapter 15 discusses new features provided by Office 2003, including some smart tag enhancements.

It seems a bit strange that the Office development team chose not to implement smart tags by using VBA. A VBA programmer can certainly build a class that implements the ISmartTagRecognizer and ISmartTagAction interfaces. The Office developers would only need to add a few new properties and methods to the Office object models to allow a VBA developer to attach this kind of class to a document. Then you would not need to use XML (to build a MOSTL) or an external development environment (such as Visual Basic 6 or Visual Basic .NET). You would also not need to manually alter the System Registry to make the smart tag available, a somewhat dangerous process. Perhaps the Office development team will give us this capability and simplify smart tag creation in a future release.

CHAPTER 15

Office 2003

MICROSOFT OFFICE 2003 is a relatively major upgrade, including quite a few important enhancements. Some of the most important changes include:

- Enhancements for programmatically using XML content, XSD schemas, and XSL transformations

- Smart tag enhancements

- Visual Studio .NET Tools for Office, which lets you integrate Visual Studio .NET code with Office

- InfoPath (formerly XDocs), a new XML-based tool for providing fill-in-the-blank business forms

- Smart documents that interact with the task pane

That's quite a lot to absorb all at once. The good news is that you don't need to use all of these features. Although Visual Basic .NET is replacing the traditional Visual Basic language, VBA is still alive and well in Office 2003. It's likely that Visual Basic .NET will move inside the Office applications at some point, but it hasn't happened yet. (In fact, it seems probable that Microsoft will move all of Visual Studio into Office as well so you'll be able to program with C# if you prefer.) You don't have to use these new features to make Office 2003 work more or less the same way Office XP does now.

Several of these enhancements deal directly or indirectly with XML. Earlier chapters in this book avoided XML because it is a fairly complex topic in its own right. This book assumes you understand the basics of programming Visual Basic or VBA, but it doesn't assume that you know XML, XSD, XSL, SOAP, Web Services, and all of the other related topics that go along with XML.

The following section gives a brief introduction to XML so you can understand these Office 2003 enhancements. To learn more, see a book about XML, such as *Visual Basic .NET and XML* by Rod Stephens and Brian Hochgurtel (Wiley, 2002). You can also find XML information online. For example, `http://www.w3schools.com/xml` has a beginner's XML tutorial.

The rest of the chapter describes the major Office 2003 enhancements.

Introduction to XML

Several Office 2003 enhancements deal with XML. This section provides a quick introduction to XML and some of the related technologies so you can make some sense of these enhancements. To really get the most out of these new features, you will probably need to learn a lot more about XML, but at least this section can get you started. It should at least help you understand what the enhancements do so you can decide whether you care enough to learn more.

XML is a very simple data storage language. It uses a system of user-defined *tags* to delimit data. An *element* begins with an open tag consisting of a word surrounded by pointy brackets. An element ends with a corresponding close tag that has the same name as the open tag, except a slash comes before the name.

 NOTE *The starting and ending tags must have* exactly *the same name and matching capitalization.*

Elements can be nested to any depth and may define quite complex data structures. To be properly formatted, an XML document must have a single root-level element that contains all other elements. For example, the following XML text defines a Book record with elements named Author, Title, and Publisher. The Author element contains two sub-elements LastName and FirstName.

```
<Book>
    <Author>
        <LastName>Stephens<LastName>
        <FirstName>Rod<FirstName>
    </Author>
    <Title>Office Smackdown</Title>
    <Publisher>Apress</Publisher>
</Book>
```

That's about all there is to XML, at least in concept. XML defines some special tags that are used by an XML *parser*. The most important of these is an XML declaration tag that goes at the very top of the XML file. This tag defines the XML version (1.0 is the only version currently available), may include an "encoding" field that identifies the file's character set, and may include a "standalone" field that indicates whether the file is self-contained or needs external definitions. The following code shows a complete XML document defining a series of Title elements.

```
<?xml version="1.0" encoding="utf-8" standalone="yes" ?>
<Books>
    <Title>Visual Basic Graphics Programming</Title>
    <Title>Ready-to-Run Visual Basic Algorithms</Title>
    <Title>Visual Basic Code Library</Title>
</Books>
```

In the never-ending quest to save keystrokes while adding new features, developers have taken XML from this humble starting point and extended it to a level of bewildering complexity. For instance, tags can have *attributes* that define conditions on an element. The following statement defines a phone number with a "kind" attribute set to the value "work."

```
<Phone kind="work">234-456-7890</Phone>
```

Sometimes an element can define its data without actually containing any text, often by including the data in an attribute. In that case, the empty element can use a shorthand version that includes a trailing slash inside the opening tag and has no closing tag. For example, the following two lines both define the same image file.

```
<Image src="http://www.vb-helper.com/vbhelper_213_33.gif"></Image>
<Image src="http://www.vb-helper.com/vbhelper_213_33.gif" />
```

The last topic mentioned here is that of namespaces. If lots of different businesses tried to define their data in XML files, many would come up with similar elements for common items. They would probably end up using the same names for elements such as Customer, Employee, InventoryItem, Bribe, Attorney, and so forth. Different companies would probably have different definitions of these objects, however, so a program trying to work with documents from more than one company would have trouble with data mismatches.

You can use namespaces to resolve these kinds of conflicts. You declare a namespace by adding an xmlns statement to the document's root node. The following code identifies the vbhelper namespace with the URL www.vb-helper.com/smackdown.

```
<?xml version="1.0" encoding="utf-8" ?>
<Books xmlns:vbhelper="www.vb-helper.com/smackdown">
    <vbhelper:Title>Visual Basic Graphics Programming</vbhelper:Title>
    <vbhelper:Title>Ready-to-Run Visual Basic Algorithms</vbhelper:Title>
    <vbhelper:Title>Visual Basic Code Library</vbhelper:Title>
</Books>
```

Note that the URL doesn't need to exist; it just needs to be unique. As long as different developers don't use the same URL, their element names won't collide.

TIP *You can also define a default namespace for every element in the document by omitting the namespace's name in the root element. For instance, the following code makes* www.vb-helper.com/smackdown *the default namespace for the document. Whatever program parses the XML code should add that namespace to every element in the document.*

```
<?xml version="1.0" encoding="utf-8" ?>
<Books xmlns="www.vb-helper.com/smackdown">
    <Title>Visual Basic Graphics Programming</Title>
    <Title>Ready-to-Run Visual Basic Algorithms</Title>
    <Title>Visual Basic Code Library</Title>
</Books>
```

There's not a whole lot more to XML. The real complexity comes from auxiliary technologies added to XML. For example, DTD (Document Type Definition), XDR (XML Data Reduced), and XSD (XML Schema Definition) are all XML schema definition languages. Their files define the types of data that an XML file is allowed to contain. For example, an XSD file can declare that an XML file's Address element must contain Street, City, State, and Zip elements exactly once each and in that order.

By attaching a schema to an XML file, you can provide some data validation. For example, if a customer sends you an order in an XML file that has been validated against a schema, you know that it contains whatever fields it must: Name, Address, Phone, CreditCard, and so forth. Unfortunately, schema languages are relatively complex, so they're not covered in any detail here.

XSL (eXtensible Stylesheet Language) is another XML accessory technology. XSL is a data transformation language. You can use it to tell a *transformation engine* how it should convert XML data into some form of output. For example, you might use different XSL files to transform a single XML document into versions in plain text, HTML, or VoiceXML. You could even transform the XML file into a new XML file with a different structure or containing only parts of the whole dataset.

XSL consists of three parts: XSLT (XSL Transformation Language), FO (XSL Formatting Objects), and XPath (XML Path). XSLT is the language of XSL. It lets you specify how you want different elements transformed.

FO includes the objects that make up the output document. These are the element, attribute, and other entities in the document. Generally, you don't need to think about these objects or even really know they exist.

XPath is a language (yes, another one!) that specifies nodes inside an XML document. An XPath statement looks a bit like a directory specification. For example, the statement `/Books/Book/Author/LastName` means the LastName element inside an Author element inside a Book element inside the Books root element.

XPath uses two kinds of wild cards to skip intermediate values. The * symbol tells XPath to match any single intermediate element. For example, the statement `/Books/*/Author` matches any Author element that is a grandchild of the Books element. If the XML file contains Book, Article, and WebPage elements, this statement would find the Author elements of all three (assuming Author is the next level down in the hierarchy).

The `//` sequence tells XPath to skip any number of intermediate nodes. The statement `/Books//Author` matches any Author element that is a descendant of the Books data root node.

XSL is much more complex than this simple discussion indicates, but there's no room to go into any kind of depth here. For more information, see a book on XML or XSL. You can also find an introductory tutorial at `http://www.w3schools.com/xsl`.

Word Tools for Manipulating XML

In Office XP, Excel 2002 can load and save properly formatted XML files. When you save a workbook in an XML file, Excel includes document properties, worksheet styles, and worksheet options in addition to the data itself. Excel 2002 can load a file saved in this format but it cannot load an arbitrary XML file.

Word 2003 and Excel 2003 can both load arbitrary XML files intelligently. The following code shows a very simple XML file.

```
<Books>
    <Book>Visual Basic Graphics Programming</Book>
    <Book>Ready-to-Run Visual Basic Algorithms</Book>
    <Book>Visual Basic Code Library</Book>
</Books>
```

Figure 15-1 shows Word 2003 displaying this file. The file's start and end tags are outlined so they are easy to find. The pointer is hovering over a </Book> end tag, so Word is displaying a popup that says End of Book. The first Book element is selected in the XML Structure panel on the right, so that element is highlighted in the main document.

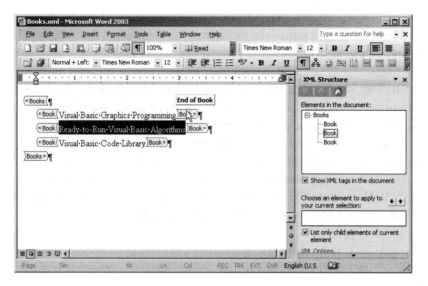

Figure 15-1. Word 2003 can load arbitrary XML files.

NOTE *To get the full benefit of Word's XML tools, you must attach a schema to the XML document.*

To transform an XML file, load the file, select File ➤ Save As, check the "Apply transform" box, click the Transform button, and select the XSL file to apply.

A Word document can also hold XML data inside a normal text document. Simply invoke the Insert menu's File command and select the file.

All this is new but it's not VBA programming. The following sections describe new objects and methods that let you examine and manipulate a document's XML content using VBA code.

The XMLNode *Object*

The new XMLNode object represents a node in an XML hierarchy. You can use these objects to navigate over and manipulate the XML data's structure. Table 15-1 lists some of the XMLNode's most important properties and methods.

Table 15-1. Useful XMLNode Properties and Methods

PROPERTIES/METHODS	PURPOSE
Attributes	A collection holding XMLNode objects representing the node's attributes. The attribute node's BaseName property gives the attribute's name, and its NodeValue property gives its value.
BaseName	The name of the node without the namespace.
ChildNodes	A collection holding XMLNode objects representing the node's child nodes.
Delete	Removes the node from its XML hierarchy. Contrary to what you might expect, this leaves the node's contents behind. If the node contained other nodes, those nodes become children of the parent node. If the node contains text, the text becomes part of the parent's text. See also the RemoveChild method.
FirstChild, LastChild	The first and last child nodes of this node. You can use these together with NextSibling and PreviousSibling to loop through the node's children.
HasChildNodes	True if the node has child nodes.
NextSibling, PreviousSibling	Return the node's next and previous sibling (brother or sister) in the parent node's child collection.
NodeType	Returns wdXMLNodeAttribute or wdXMLNodeElement to indicate whether the node is an element or another node's attribute value.
NodeValue	A string containing an attribute node's value.
ParentNode	The XMLNode that is this node's parent.
RemoveChild	Removes a specified child from the node. The specified child node must be a child of this node. This method removes the child's contents, including any text and child nodes it contains. See also the Delete method.
SelectNodes	Returns a collection of XMLNode objects satisfying an XPath query. See the following section for more information.
SelectSingleNode	Returns a single XMLNode object satisfying an XPath query. See the following section for more information.
Text	The node's text. For example, in the XML code `<Flavor>Chocolate</Flavor>` the Flavor node has Text value Chocolate. Note that this text includes the text of all nodes contained in this one.
Validate	Validates the node against any attached XML schemas.
XML	Returns the node's XML code. This method's parameter indicates whether the method should include the Word XML markup.

The following sections describe some of the ways you can use XMLNode objects to examine and manipulate XML structure.

Using SelectNodes *and* SelectSingleNode

The XMLNode object's SelectNodes and SelectSingleNode methods search the XML hierarchy below the node and return any nodes that match a given XPath expression. The section "Introduction to XML" earlier in this chapter briefly described XPath and mentioned that it allows the wildcards * and //. To see how these work, suppose a document contains the following XML data.

```
<Desserts>
    <IceCream>
        <Flavor>Chocolate</Flavor>
        <Flavor>Vanilla</Flavor>
        <Flavor>Strawberry</Flavor>
    </IceCream>
    <Cookie>
        <Flavor>Chocolate Chip</Flavor>
        <Flavor>Pecan Sandy</Flavor>
    </Cookie>
</Desserts>
```

The following statement uses the first node's (the Desserts node's) SelectSingleNode method to display the text contained in the first Flavor node. It uses the // wildcard so it would search as deeply as necessary to find a Flavor node.

```
Debug.Print ActiveDocument.XMLNodes(1).SelectSingleNode("//Flavor").Text
```

The following code displays all of the Flavor node text values whether they are contained in the IceCream node or the Cookie node. The XPath statement uses the * wildcard to skip one level in the hierarchy (both the IceCream and Cookie nodes) between the Desserts node and its Flavor grandchildren. Note that the XPath statement begins with the name of the current node, Desserts.

```
For Each node In ActiveDocument.XMLNodes(1).SelectNodes("/Desserts/*/Flavor")
    Debug.Print node.Text
Next node
```

After these methods return one or more XMLNodes, you can use the nodes' properties and methods to manipulate them.

Examining the XML Hierarchy

You can use XMLNode objects to navigate over the XML hierarchy to examine its data.

For example, the following code displays the XML structure of a Word document. Subroutine ShowDocumentXMLHierarchy searches the active document's XMLNodes collection looking for nodes with no parents. Those are the root nodes for the document's various blocks of XML data embedded in the Word document. For each of those root nodes, the code calls subroutine ShowNodeXMLHierarchy.

The ShowNodeXMLHierarchy subroutine builds a string to describe the node it received as a parameter. It begins with the node's name. If the node has attributes, the code adds them to the string. It then displays the string in the Debug window.

Next subroutine ShowNodeXMLHierarchy loops through the node's ChildNodes collection calling itself recursively to display information on each child node.

FILE *Ch15\Books.doc*

```
' Display the document's XML hierarchy.
Sub ShowDocumentXMLHierarchy()
Dim node As XMLNode

    ' Search the nodes for those with no parents.
    For Each node In ActiveDocument.XMLNodes
        If node.ParentNode Is Nothing Then
            ShowNodeXMLHierarchy node
        End If
    Next node
End Sub

' Display this node's XML hierarchy.
Sub ShowNodeXMLHierarchy(ByVal node As XMLNode, _
  Optional ByVal indent As Integer = 0)
Dim txt As String
Dim attr_node As XMLNode
Dim i As Integer

    ' Display this node.
    txt = Space$(indent) & node.BaseName
    If node.Attributes.Count > 0 Then
```

```
            txt = txt & " ("
            For Each attr_node In node.Attributes
                txt = txt & attr_node.BaseName & "=" & attr_node.NodeValue & ", "
            Next attr_node
            txt = Left$(txt, Len(txt) - 2) & ")"
        End If
        Debug.Print txt

        ' Display the hierarchy below this node.
        ' (A bug seems to make For Each not work.)
        For i = 1 To node.ChildNodes.Count
            ShowNodeXMLHierarchy node.ChildNodes(i), indent + 4
        Next i
End Sub
```

The following text shows the output produced for the file Ch14\Books.doc. This file contains two chunks of XML data with root nodes named Books and Desserts.

```
Books
    Book (Price=$49.99, Pages=395)
        Title
    Book (Price=$49.99, Pages=684)
        Title
    Book (Price=$49.99, Pages=712)
        Title
Desserts
    IceCream
        Flavor
        Flavor
        Flavor
    Cookie
        Type
        Type
```

Building XML Data

You can also use XMLNode objects to build XML data. You can use the Add method provided by the XMLNodes collection in the Document, Range, and Selection objects to create new nodes. Then you can use the Add method provided by the ChildNodes collection in those nodes to add child nodes.

An example described shortly shows how to do this. Before it can work, however, the document must have the proper XML namespace installed. The schema file Books.xsd (shown in the following code) defines the namespace for the document. This file sets its target and default namespaces to `http://www.vb-helper.com/bks`. It then defines a Books element. That element is a sequence containing a series of Book elements. Each Book element is a sequence containing Title, URL, Image, Price, and Page elements. Each of those elements is a string that can occur zero or one times.

FILE *Ch15\Books.xsd*

```
<?xml version="1.0"?>
<xsd:schema
  xmlns:xsd="http://www.w3.org/2001/XMLSchema"
  targetNamespace="http://www.vb-helper.com/bks"
  xmlns="http://www.vb-helper.com/bks"
  elementFormDefault="qualified"
>
  <xsd:element name="Books">
    <xsd:complexType>
      <xsd:sequence>
        <xsd:element name="Book">
          <xsd:complexType>
            <xsd:sequence>
              <xsd:element name="Title" type="xsd:string"
                  minOccurs="0"
                  maxOccurs="1"/>
              <xsd:element name="URL"    type="xsd:string"
                  minOccurs="0"
                  maxOccurs="1"/>
              <xsd:element name="Image" type="xsd:string"
                  minOccurs="0"
                  maxOccurs="1"/>
              <xsd:element name="Price" type="xsd:string"
                  minOccurs="0"
                  maxOccurs="1"/>
              <xsd:element name="Pages" type="xsd:string"
                  minOccurs="0"
                  maxOccurs="1"/>
```

```
        </xsd:sequence>
      </xsd:complexType>
    </xsd:element>
  </xsd:sequence>
  </xsd:complexType>
  </xsd:element>
</xsd:schema>
```

The following code builds an XML hierarchy from scratch. It begins by trying to get the necessary namespace object from the `Application` object's `XMLNamespaces` collection. If the namespace doesn't exist, the program adds it. After it has a reference to the `XMLNamespace` object, the code attaches it to the Word document.

Now the code makes a `Range` object and collapses it so it indicates the end of the document. It calls the `Range`'s `XMLNodes.Add` method to create a new Books node. The Namespace parameter specifies the value `http://www.vb-helper.com/bks` defined in the schema file. Note that the schema defines the Books element.

Next the code calls subroutine `MakeBookNode` three times to define more nodes in small XML subtrees. Subroutine `MakeBookNode` uses the Books node's `ChildNodes.Add` method to create a new Book node. The subroutine then adds Title and URL elements to the Book element. As it does so, the code sets the text values of these new elements. Notice that the schema defines all of these elements.

 FILE *Ch15\BuildXml.doc*

```
' Build some XML data from scratch.
Sub BuildXML()
Dim ns As XMLNamespace
Dim rng As Range
Dim books_node As XMLNode

    ' Get the XMLNamespace.
    On Error Resume Next
    Set ns = Application.XMLNamespaces( _
        "http://www.vb-helper.com/bks")
    On Error GoTo 0

    ' Add the namespace if necessary.
    If ns Is Nothing Then
        Set ns = Application.XMLNamespaces.Add( _
            "Books.xsd", _
            "http://www.vb-helper.com/bks")
    End If
```

```
    ' Attach the schema to the document.
    ns.AttachToDocument ActiveDocument

    ' Make a Range at the end of the document.
    Set rng = ActiveDocument.Range()
    rng.Collapse wdCollapseEnd

    ' Create a Books node.
    Set books_node = rng.XMLNodes.Add( _
        Name:="Books", Namespace:=ns.URI)

    ' Make some Book nodes.
    MakeBookNode books_node, _
        "VB .NET and XML", _
        "http://www.vb-helper.com/xml.htm"
    MakeBookNode books_node, _
        "Visual Basic Graphics Programming", _
        "http://www.vb-helper.com/vbgp.htm"
    MakeBookNode books_node, _
        "Ready-to-Run Visual Basic Algorithms", _
        "http://www.vb-helper.com/vba.htm"
End Sub


' Add a Book node as a child of this node.
Sub MakeBookNode(ByVal parent_node As XMLNode, ByVal book_title As String, _
    ByVal book_url As String)
Dim book_node As XMLNode

    ' Make the Book node.
    Set book_node = parent_node.ChildNodes.Add( _
        Name:="Book", Namespace:="http://www.vb-helper.com/bks")

    ' Add the Title node child.
    book_node.ChildNodes.Add( _
        Name:="Title", Namespace:="http://www.vb-helper.com/bks").Text = _
            book_title

    ' Add the URL node child.
    book_node.ChildNodes.Add( _
        Name:="URL", Namespace:="http://www.vb-helper.com/bks").Text = book_url
End Sub
```

CAUTION *While I was working with this code, I had a lot of trouble getting Word to refresh the schema file. It kept using old versions of the file, so the code didn't work. The solution I found was to interactively use the Schema Library (Tools* ➤*Templates and Add-Ins* ➤*Schema Library button) to delete the schema, detach the schema on the Templates and Add-Ins dialog's XML Schema tab, close the dialog, reopen it, and read the schema. You should be able to reload the schema as in* `ActiveDocument.XMLSchemaReferences(1).Reload`, *but I had trouble getting it to work properly in the beta.*

Although this code works, it's somewhat cumbersome. If you just want to create a block of XML data, you can use the `Range` object's `InsertXML` method to dump the data's XML definition right into the document.

The following code builds a string representing some XML data and inserts it into the active Word document.

FILE *Ch15\InsertXml.doc*

```
' Build some XML data from scratch.
Sub MakeXML()
Dim rng As Range

    Set rng = ActiveDocument.Range()
    rng.Collapse wdCollapseEnd

    Dim txt As String
    txt = "<?xml version=""1.0""?>"
    txt = txt & "<Desserts>"
    txt = txt & "  <IceCream>"
    txt = txt & "    <Flavor>Chocolate</Flavor>"
    txt = txt & "    <Flavor>Vanilla</Flavor>"
    txt = txt & "    <Flavor>Strawberry</Flavor>"
    txt = txt & "  </IceCream>"
    txt = txt & "  <Cookie>"
    txt = txt & "    <Type>Chocolate Chip</Type>"
    txt = txt & "    <Type>Pecan Sandy</Type>"
    txt = txt & "  </Cookie>"
    txt = txt & "</Desserts>"
    rng.InsertXML txt
End Sub
```

This method is more convenient when you want to create a whole block of data, but the BuildXML subroutine described earlier demonstrates techniques you could use to add nodes in the middle of an existing piece of XML code.

The Document *Object*

The Document object provides several new tools for working with the document's XML content. Its XMLNodes collection contains XMLNode objects that describe the content. The following section describes the XMLNode object. See the previous sections for examples that manipulate XMLNode objects.

The Document object's XMLSaveDataOnly property indicates whether Word saves the document's XML data only or whether it saves the full Word XML markup. Saving the full markup takes a bit more space in the document file.

The XMLUseXSLTWhenSaving property indicates whether Word should transform the document using XSL when you save it as XML. This only applies when you save the file as XML, not when you save it as a normal Word document.

If XMLUseXSLTWhenSaving is True, then Word applies the XSL template indicated by the Document object's XMLSaveThroughXSLT property.

When you select the XML document type in the Save As dialog, the dialog displays a "Save data only" check box. Check this to save only the data. Leave the box unchecked to save the entire document in Word XML format.

NOTE *Saving through XSLT may produce some strange results if the document is not an XML file.*

The XML *Method*

The Range, Selection, and SmartTag objects now have an XML method that returns an object's XML contents. The method's only parameter is a Boolean that indicates whether the routine should include the Word XML markup. Set this parameter to False to get just the XML data.

Note that XML data ignores carriage returns and other white space between tags, so many programs strip these off. The XML data is valid but may be hard to read. The following XML code shows the results of the XML method for one Word document. The output is broken here to fit on the page, but the actual result is all on two lines (the XML declaration gets its own line).

```
<?xml version="1.0" standalone="no"?>
<Books><Book Price="$49.99" Pages="395"><Title>Ready-to-Run Visual Basic Algor
ithms</Title></Book><Book Price="$49.99" Pages="684"><Title>Custom Controls Li
brary</Title></Book><Book Price="$49.99" Pages="712"><Title>Visual Basic Graph
ics Programming</Title></Book></Books>
```

Excel Tools for Manipulating XML

Excel uses XML mappings to transform XML data into worksheet cells. Typically, you use an XSD schema to define the mapping. Then, when you load an XML file that uses the namespace defined by the schema, Excel uses that mapping to display the data.

For example, consider the following schema. Note that the elements in this schema use the namespace http://www.vb-helper.com/bks. Later, when VBA code wants to load XML data using this schema's mapping, it must define data using the same namespace.

FILE *Ch15\Books2.xsd*

```
<?xml version="1.0"?>
<xsd:schema
  xmlns:xsd="http://www.w3.org/2001/XMLSchema"
  targetNamespace="http://www.vb-helper.com/bks"
  xmlns="http://www.vb-helper.com/bks"
  elementFormDefault="qualified"
>
  <xsd:element name="Books">
    <xsd:complexType>
      <xsd:sequence>
        <xsd:element name="Book">
          <xsd:complexType>
            <xsd:sequence>
              <xsd:element name="Title" type="xsd:string"
                  minOccurs="0"
                  maxOccurs="1"/>
              <xsd:element name="URL"    type="xsd:string"
                  minOccurs="0"
```

```
                maxOccurs="1"/>
            <xsd:element name="Image" type="xsd:string"
                minOccurs="0"
                maxOccurs="1"/>
            <xsd:element name="Price" type="xsd:string"
                minOccurs="0"
                maxOccurs="1"/>
            <xsd:element name="Pages" type="xsd:string"
                minOccurs="0"
                maxOccurs="1"/>
          </xsd:sequence>
        </xsd:complexType>
      </xsd:element>
    </xsd:sequence>
  </xsd:complexType>
  </xsd:element>
</xsd:schema>
```

The following VBA code makes an XmlMap object to represent a mapping for this schema. The code begins by using the ActiveWorkbook object's XmlMaps collection to create a new XmlMap object and changes its name to Books_Map. The code saves the object's RootElementNamespace.Prefix property. This is a namespace abbreviation that Excel created for the namespace.

The routine then uses the ActiveWorksheet object's ListObjects collection to make a new ListObject to represent a new List. A List is a new feature in Excel 2003 that defines the fields in the schema that should be mapped onto the worksheet.

When the ListObjects collection creates a new ListObject, it initially places one item in the ListObject's ListColumns collection. The ListColumns entries define the columns that should be selected from the schema. After it creates the ListObject, the code changes the name of this initial ListColumn object to Title. It then calls the object's SetValue method to tell the ListColumn what element it represents in the schema. The first parameter to this method is the XmlMap it should use.

The SetValue method's second parameter is an XPath expression describing the data that this ListColumn should represent. The program defines the expression using @ symbols as namespace placeholders and then replaces the symbols with the XmlMap object's namespace prefix. After this first call to SetValue, the first ListColumn object represents the /Books/Book/Title element in the schema.

Now the code makes a new ListColumn object, sets its name to URL, and assigns it to the /Books/Book/URL schema element.

Finally, the code makes one more ListColumn object, sets its name to Price, and assigns it to the /Books/Book/Price schema element.

FILE *Ch15\Books2.xls*

```
' Map an XSD shema.
Sub MapSchema()
Dim books_map As XmlMap
Dim books_list As ListObject
Dim books_column As ListColumn
Dim pfx As String
Dim xpath_spec As String

    ' Load the schema.
    Set books_map = ActiveWorkbook.XmlMaps.Add("Books2.xsd")
    books_map.Name = "Books_Map"

    ' Get the XmlMap's namespace prefix.
    pfx = books_map.RootElementNamespace.Prefix

    ' Create a new list.
    Set books_list = ActiveSheet.ListObjects.Add
    books_list.Name = "Books_List"

    ' Map the Title element in the initially
    ' created ListColumn.
    books_list.ListColumns(1).Name = "Title"
    xpath_spec = Replace("/@:Books/@:Book/@:Title", "@", pfx)
    books_list.ListColumns(1).XPath.SetValue _
        books_map, xpath_spec

    ' Map the URL element in a new ListColumn.
    Set books_column = books_list.ListColumns.Add
    books_column.Name = "URL"
    xpath_spec = Replace("/@:Books/@:Book/@:URL", "@", pfx)
    books_column.XPath.SetValue _
        books_map, xpath_spec

    ' Map the Price element in a new ListColumn.
    Set books_column = books_list.ListColumns.Add
    books_column.Name = "Price"
    xpath_spec = Replace("/@:Books/@:Book/@:Price", "@", pfx)
    books_column.XPath.SetValue _
        books_map, xpath_spec
End Sub
```

After it has defined an XmlMap object for a schema, the code can use that object to load an XML file. The following code shows the XML data for this example. Notice that the Books element declares itself as using the http://www.vb-helper.com/bks namespace. It's the fact that this namespace matches the one used by the elements defined in the schema that tells Excel to use the schema's mapping when loading this data.

FILE *Ch15\Books2.xml*

```xml
<?xml version="1.0"?>
<Books xmlns="http://www.vb-helper.com/bks">
    <Book>
        <Title>Visual Basic .NET and XML</Title>
        <URL>http://www.vb-helper.com/xml.htm</URL>
        <Image>http://www.vb-helper.com/xml.jpg</Image>
        <Price>$39.99</Price>
    </Book>
    <Book>
        <Title>Ready-to-Run Visual Basic Algorithms</Title>
        <URL>http://www.vb-helper.com/vba.htm</URL>
        <Image>http://www.vb-helper.com/vba.jpg</Image>
        <Price>$49.99</Price>
    </Book>
    <Book>
        <Title>Custom Controls Library</Title>
        <URL>http://www.vb-helper.com/ccl.htm</URL>
        <Image>http://www.vb-helper.com/ccl.jpg</Image>
        <Price>$49.99</Price>
    </Book>
    <Book>
        <Title>Visual Basic Graphics Programming</Title>
        <URL>http://www.vb-helper.com/vbgp.htm</URL>
        <Image>http://www.vb-helper.com/vbgp.jpg</Image>
        <Price>$49.99</Price>
    </Book>
</Books>
```

The following code loads the XML file. It retrieves a reference to the Books_Map XmlMap object and calls that object's Import method passing it the name of the XML file to load. Excel loads the data by using the defined mapping and returns a success or failure code.

FILE *Ch15\Books2.xls*

```
' Load XML data using the Books_Map map.
Sub LoadXmlData()
Dim books_map As XmlMap

    ' Get the XmlMap.
    Set books_map = ActiveWorkbook.XmlMaps("Books_Map")

    ' Import the data.
    Select Case books_map.Import("Books2.xml")
        Case xlXmlImportSuccess
            MsgBox "OK"
        Case xlXmlImportElementsTruncated
            MsgBox "Some data was truncated"
        Case xlXmlImportValidationFailed
            MsgBox "The XML file doesn't match the schema"
    End Select
End Sub
```

NOTE *In my tests, the* Import *method always returned* xlXmlImportValidationFailed *even though the XML file looked like it matched the schema. Loading the file interactively using this mapping worked perfectly. This may be a bug in the beta, and it may be fixed before Office 2003's final release.*

Figure 15-2 shows the results. The cells A1:C5 contain the imported data. The XML Source pane on the right shows the XML mapping. The Title, URL, and Price elements are bold because ListColumn objects define mappings for them.

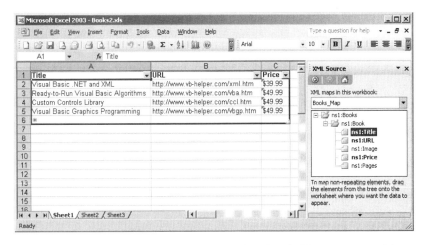

Figure 15-2. Excel 2003 can display XML data loaded by an XmlMap *object.*

Excel List Tools

The previous section explains how to use a List in Excel to display XML data. You can also use Lists to display non-XML data.

The following code makes an empty List and then fills it with data. It begins by making the variable ws refer to the active worksheet. The code could use ActiveSheet instead of a variable; however, VBA doesn't provide IntelliSense for the ActiveSheet object, but it does for a variable of type Worksheet.

Next the program uses the Worksheet object's ListObjects.Add method to make a new List. It specifies that the new List should come from the range consisting of the single cell A1.

NOTE *Two Lists cannot overlap. If you try to create a List with a range already being used by another List, VBA raises an error.*

The code then uses a With statement to work with the new ListObject. It could work directly with the result of the ListObjects.Add method as in With ws.ListObjects.Add(...), but again VBA wouldn't provide IntelliSense.

Next the program sets the List's Name property. Note that the name must be unique. If you try to give a List the same name as an existing List, Excel raises an error.

The subroutine uses the ListObject's Range method to add values to the List. It finishes by specifying some formatting for the List, fitting the List's columns to their data, making the header row bold, and making the body rows nonbold.

FILE *Ch15\Lists.xls*

```vba
' Make a List from scratch.
Sub MakeListFromScratch()
Dim ws As Worksheet
Dim books_list As ListObject

    ' Make the list starting at cell A1.
    Set ws = ActiveSheet
    Set books_list = ws.ListObjects.Add( _
        SourceType:=xlSrcRange, _
        Source:=ws.Range("A1"), _
        XlListObjectHasHeaders:=xlYes)

    ' Work with the list.
    With books_list
        ' Name the list.
        .Name = "Book_List"

        ' Make some data.
        .Range(1, 1).Value = "Title"
        .Range(1, 2).Value = "URL"
        .Range(1, 3).Value = "Price"

        .Range(2, 1).Value = "Visual Basic .NET and XML"
        .Range(2, 2).Value = "http://www.vb-helper.com/xml.htm"
        .Range(2, 3).Value = "$39.99"

        .Range(3, 1).Value = "Ready-to-Run Visual Basic Algorithms"
        .Range(3, 2).Value = "http://www.vb-helper.com/vba.htm"
        .Range(3, 3).Value = "$49.99"

        .Range(4, 1).Value = "Visual Basic Graphics Programming"
        .Range(4, 2).Value = "http://www.vb-helper.com/vbgp.htm"
        .Range(4, 3).Value = "$49.99"

        ' Format the results.
        .HeaderRowRange.Font.Bold = True    ' Bold headers.
        .DataBodyRange.Font.Bold = False    ' Non-bold data.
        .Range().Columns.AutoFit            ' Fit to the data.
    End With
End Sub
```

You can also make a List by using data in an existing range rather than creating the List first and then adding data to it. The following code creates a Range variable and uses its FormulaArray property to fill it with data. It then creates a new List object much as the previous example did, but this time it builds the new List on the data-filled range. That automatically fills the List with the range's data. The code finishes by setting the List's name and performing some formatting as before.

FILE *Ch15\Lists.xls*

```
' Make a List from an existing Range.
Sub MakeListFromRange()
Dim ws As Worksheet
Dim rng As Range
Dim books_list As ListObject

    ' Place data in the Range A7:C10.
    Set ws = ActiveSheet
    Set rng = ws.Range("A7:C10")
    rng.FormulaArray = Array( _
        Array("Title", "URL", "Price"), _
        Array("Visual Basic .NET and XML", _
            "http://www.vb-helper.com/xml.htm", "$39.99"), _
        Array("Ready-to-Run Visual Basic Algorithms", _
            "http://www.vb-helper.com/vba.htm", "$49.99"), _
        Array("Visual Basic Graphics Programming", _
            "http://www.vb-helper.com/vbgp.htm", "$49.99") _
    )

    ' Make the list on the pre-populated range E1:G4.
    Set books_list = ws.ListObjects.Add( _
        SourceType:=xlSrcRange, _
        Source:=rng, _
        XlListObjectHasHeaders:=xlYes)

    ' Format the list.
    With books_list
        .Name = "Book_List2"
        .HeaderRowRange.Font.Bold = True    ' Bold headers.
        .DataBodyRange.Font.Bold = False    ' Non-bold data.
        .Range().Columns.AutoFit            ' Fit to the data.
    End With
End Sub
```

The ListObject class provides a couple methods for working with a List. The Delete method removes the List from the workbook along with the data it contains. The Publish method publishes the List to a SharePoint server so other users can access it.

The Unlist method converts the List into a normal Excel range. The range contains the List's data but doesn't provide the List's special features. The following code converts the List named Book_List2 into a normal range.

FILE *Ch15\Lists.xls*

```vba
' Convert the list into a regular range.
Sub ListToRange()
Dim ws As Worksheet
Dim books_list As ListObject

    Set ws = ActiveSheet
    Set books_list = ws.ListObjects("Book_List2")
    books_list.Unlist
End Sub
```

The ListObject's ShowTotals property determines whether the List automatically adds a total row at the bottom. The following code creates a List using a three-column data-filled range. It adds a fourth column to the List, calculating its values by multiplying the second and third columns. It then formats the List, making the second and fourth columns display as monetary values and the third display as a whole number.

FILE *Ch15\Lists.xls*

```vba
' Make an expense List from an existing Range.
Sub MakeExpenseList()
Dim ws As Worksheet
Dim rng As Range
Dim invoice_list As ListObject
Dim i As Integer
```

```
' Place data in the Range A7:C10.
Set ws = ActiveSheet
Set rng = ws.Range("E1:G6")
rng.FormulaArray = Array( _
    Array("Item", "Unit Cost", "Quantity"), _
    Array("Floppy Discs, 50", "$25.95", "2"), _
    Array("CD RW discs, 50", "$43.50", "1"), _
    Array("Mouse Pad", "$4.95", "1"), _
    Array("Laser Printer Labels", "$1.95", "6"), _
    Array("Notebook Computer", "$1,234.00", "1") _
)

' Make the list on the pre-populated range E1:G4.
Set invoice_list = ws.ListObjects.Add( _
    SourceType:=xlSrcRange, _
    Source:=rng, _
    XlListObjectHasHeaders:=xlYes)

' Format the list.
With invoice_list
    ' Add the Total Price column.
    .HeaderRowRange(1, 4).Value = "Total"
    For i = 1 To .DataBodyRange.Rows.Count
        .DataBodyRange(i, 4).Value = _
            .DataBodyRange(i, 2).Value * _
            .DataBodyRange(i, 3).Value
    Next i

    .Name = "Invoice_List"
    .HeaderRowRange.Font.Bold = True     ' Bold headers.
    .DataBodyRange.Font.Bold = False     ' Non-bold data.

    .DataBodyRange.Columns(2).NumberFormat = "$#,##0.00"
    .DataBodyRange.Columns(3).NumberFormat = "0"
    .DataBodyRange.Columns(4).NumberFormat = "$#,##0.00"

    .ShowTotals = True                   ' Display totals.
    .Range().Columns.AutoFit             ' Fit to the data.
End With
End Sub
```

Figure 15-3 shows the resulting List. In this Figure the List is selected so it is displaying its "insert row" (with the asterisk in the leftmost column). Below that is the total row.

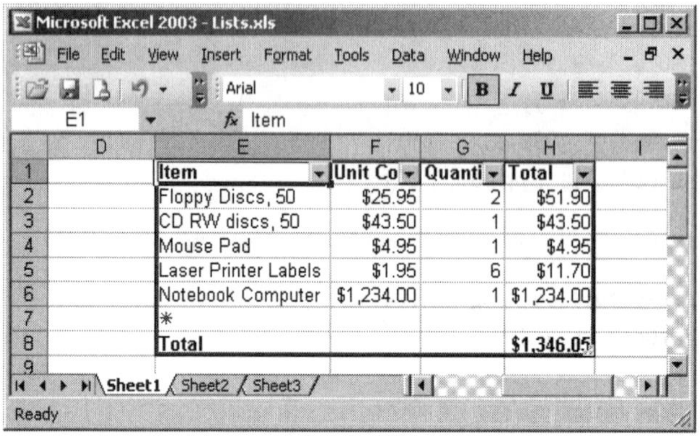

Figure 15-3. This List has ShowTotals *set to True.*

For information about other ListObject properties and methods, consult the online help.

Smart Tag Enhancements

Chapter 14 explained how to build a smart tag DLL by using Visual Basic .NET. All those techniques still work with Office 2003, but Office 2003 has also introduced a few new tools for building smart tag DLLs.

The ISmartTagRecognizer2 and ISmartTagAction2 interfaces define new methods you can define for the smart tag classes. Leave the ISmartTagRecognizer and ISmartTagAction interfaces you have already defined in the classes and just add the new ones.

NOTE *If you haven't already read Chapter 14, you may want to at least skim its material on smart tags. The example described here assumes it already implements the* ISmartTagRecognizer *and* ISmartTagAction *interfaces. If you want to follow along and add the new code yourself, but you don't want to implement these interfaces, you can start with the BookSmartTag example from Chapter 14.*

The ISmartTagRecognizer2 interface defines four new methods. The SmartTagInitialize method is called before any other recognizer method. It's ApplicationName parameter lets you learn earlier which host application is using the smart tag.

The PropertyPage method should return True if you are supplying a property page for the smart tag. If PropertyPage returns True, the DisplayPropertyPage method should display the property page.

The Recognize2 method is where the class tries to recognize text. One new feature here is the TokenList parameter. The TokenList contains a list of the text's words broken into tokens at spaces, carriage returns, punctuation, and other characters that normally separate words. Instead of examining the entire text sent by the host application, the code can look at the words in this list if that is easier for it.

The following code fragment shows the FlavorSmartTag recognizer class's Recognize2 method. This example simply looks for the string "flavor."

 FILE *Ch15\FlavorsSmartTag\SmartTagRecognizer.vb*

```vb
Public Sub Recognize2(ByVal examine_text As String, _
  ByVal DataType As SmartTagLib.IF_TYPE, ByVal LocaleID As Integer, _
  ByVal RecognizerSite2 As SmartTagLib.ISmartTagRecognizerSite2, _
  ByVal ApplicationName As String, _
  ByVal TokenList As SmartTagLib.ISmartTagTokenList) _
  Implements SmartTagLib.ISmartTagRecognizer2.Recognize2
    Dim i As Integer
    For i = 1 To TokenList.Count
        If TokenList.Item(i).Text.ToLower = "flavor" Then
            RecognizerSite2.CommitSmartTag2( _
                "http://www.vb-helper.com#FlavorsSmartTag", _
                TokenList.Item(i).Start, _
                TokenList.Item(i).Length, _
                RecognizerSite2.GetNewPropertyBag())
        End If
    Next i
End Sub
```

The ISmartTagAction2 interface defines five new methods. The SmartTagInitialize method is called before any other action method. Its ApplicationName parameter lets you learn earlier which host application is using the smart tag.

The VerbCaptionFromID2 method returns the smart tag menu's caption for a verb given its VerbID. This would be the same as the existing VerbCaptionFromID method except this method allows you to build cascading menus. Simply insert three slashes (///) in the caption where you want similar captions to match. For example, the following three captions define a menu labeled "Replace with..." that cascades to three submenu items labeled "Chocolate," "Vanilla," and "Strawberry."

```
Replace with...///Chocolate
Replace with...///Vanilla
Replace with...///Strawberry
```

The following code shows the FlavorSmartTag example's VerbCaptionFromID2 method. It provides captions for two top-level menu items labeled "Replace with..." and "Go To Web Site." The first menu has three submenus labeled "Chocolate," "Vanilla," and "Strawberry." Figure 15-4 shows the result.

FILE *Ch15\FlavorsSmartTag\SmartTagAction.vb*

```
Public ReadOnly Property VerbCaptionFromID2(ByVal VerbID As Integer, _
  ByVal ApplicationName As String, ByVal LocaleID As Integer, _
  ByVal Properties As SmartTagLib.ISmartTagProperties, _
  ByVal recognized_text As String, ByVal Xml As String, _
  ByVal Target As Object) As String _
  Implements SmartTagLib.ISmartTagAction2.VerbCaptionFromID2
    Get
        Select Case VerbID
            Case 1
                Return "Replace with...///Chocolate"
            Case 2
                Return "Replace with...///Vanilla"
            Case 3
                Return "Replace with...///Strawberry"
            Case 4
                Return "Go To Web Site"
        End Select
    End Get
End Property
```

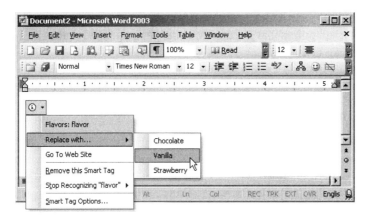

Figure 15-4. Smarts tags in Office 2003 can display cascading menus.

The IsCaptionDynamic method should return True if the caption is dynamic. If IsCaptionDynamic is True, the smart tag's SmartTagInitialize method executes every time the menu displays.

The ShowSmartTagIndicator method should return True if you want the smart tag indicator (for example, the purple dotted underline in Word) to be visible. The following code shows the FlavorSmartTag example's ShowSmartTagIndicator method.

FILE *Ch15\FlavorsSmartTag\SmartTagAction.vb*

```
Public ReadOnly Property ShowSmartTagIndicator(ByVal VerbID As Integer, _
  ByVal ApplicationName As String, ByVal LocaleID As Integer) As Boolean _
  Implements SmartTagLib.ISmartTagAction2.ShowSmartTagIndicator
    Get
        Return True
    End Get
End Property
```

Finally, the InvokeVerb2 method works much as the InvokeVerb method does except it provides an extra LocaleID parameter. The following code fragment shows the FlavorSmartTag example's InvokeVerb2 method. It examines its VerbId parameter to see which action it should perform. If the action is a replacement, the method calls subroutine PerformReplacement to make the replacement. Subroutine PerformReplacement replaces the recognized string with the word that the user selected. It does a little work to try to give the replacement word the same case as the word it is replacing.

If the user selected the Go To Web Site action, InvokeVerb2 creates an Internet Explorer application server, points it at the appropriate Web page, and makes it visible.

 FILE *Ch15\FlavorsSmartTag\SmartTagAction.vb*

```
' Perform the appropriate action.
Public Sub InvokeVerb2(ByVal VerbID As Integer, _
  ByVal ApplicationName As String, ByVal Target As Object, _
  ByVal Properties As SmartTagLib.ISmartTagProperties, _
  ByVal recognized_text As String, ByVal Xml As String, _
  ByVal LocaleID As Integer) _
  Implements SmartTagLib.ISmartTagAction2.InvokeVerb2
    If VerbID <= 3 Then
        ' Make a replacement.
        PerformReplacement(VerbID, ApplicationName, Target, recognized_text)
    Else
        ' Go to the Web site.
        Dim browser As Object
        browser = CreateObject("InternetExplorer.Application")
        browser.Navigate2("http://www.vb-helper.com/office.htm")
        browser.Visible = True
    End If
End Sub


' Replace the recognized text.
Public Sub PerformReplacement(ByVal VerbID As Integer, _
  ByVal ApplicationName As String, ByVal Target As Object, _
  ByVal recognized_text As String)
    Dim new_text As String

    ' Figure out what to replace the text with.
    Select Case VerbID
        Case 1
            new_text = "chocolate"
        Case 2
            new_text = "vanilla"
        Case 3
            new_text = "strawberry"
    End Select
```

```
    ' Set the proper case.
    If recognized_text = recognized_text.ToLower() Then
        ' Lower case.
        new_text = new_text.ToLower()
    ElseIf recognized_text = recognized_text.ToUpper() Then
        ' Upper case.
        new_text = new_text.ToUpper()
    Else
        ' Mixed case.
        new_text = StrConv(new_text, VbStrConv.ProperCase)
    End If


    ' Replace the text for different hosts.
    If ApplicationName.StartsWith("Word.Application") Then
        Target.Text = new_text
    ElseIf ApplicationName.StartsWith("Excel.Application") Then
        Target.Value = new_text
    ElseIf ApplicationName.StartsWith("PowerPoint.Application") Then
        Target.Text = new_text
    End If
End Sub
```

Visual Studio .NET Tools for Office

Visual Studio .NET Tools for Office is an SDK that helps integrate Visual Studio .NET code with Office applications. In a nutshell, it lets you use Visual Studio .NET code in more or less the same way you use VBA code.

NOTE *When this was written, the Visual Studio .NET Tools for Office beta was located at* http://www.microsoft.com/downloads/ details.aspx?FamilyID=9e0b1b7c-4ab5-40d2-b4d9-5817ab0bc1e5. *The beta SDK's documentation and samples were at* http://www.microsoft.com/ downloads/details.aspx?familyid=2fa2f8fe-a435-4cb8-9c74-0b25a2fa5ac9. *You will probably find this package extremely useful. Of course, in the final release, the help and samples may be included with the SDK.*

When it is installed, this SDK adds some new items to the Visual Studio .NET environment's New Project dialog. When you select New➤Project, the dialog shown in Figure 15-5 appears. Open the Microsoft Office 2003 Projects folder to see the new choices. Open that folder's Visual Basic Projects subfolder to see Visual Basic .NET selections.

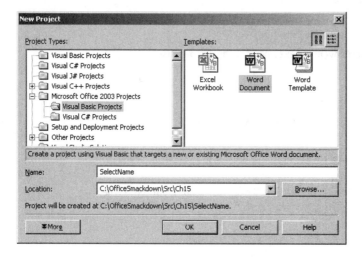

Figure 15-5. Visual Studio .NET Tools for Office adds new options to the IDE's New Project dialog.

The following sections step through an example that shows how Visual Basic .NET code can manipulate a Word document.

Start a Project

To build a simple example, select New➤Project, select the Word Document project, give it a meaningful name, and click OK. This makes Visual Studio display the dialog shown in Figure 15-6.

If you select the "Create new document" option, Visual Studio will make a new Word document for you. By default, the document has the same name as the project and is placed in the same directory.

If you select "Use existing document," you must enter the Word document's name and location manually. You can use the ellipsis (...) button to browse for it.

Click on the Security Settings link on the left to display the dialog's second tab, shown in Figure 15-7. Leave the box checked if you want Visual Studio to set your local permissions to allow the compiled project to run.

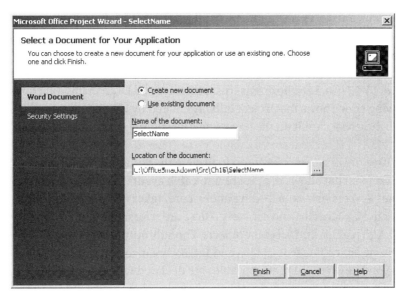

Figure 15-6. Select a Word document for the project to manipulate.

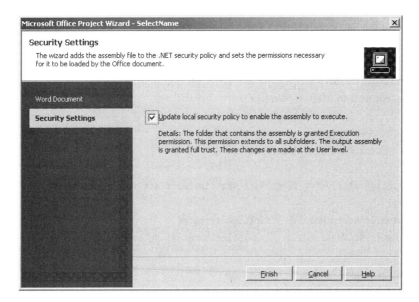

Figure 15-7. Check the box to allow the final compiled assembly to run.

NOTE *Normally, you'll want to leave this box checked. One reason you might not want Visual Studio to change the security options automatically is if you want to do this yourself, which requires more experience but gives you more options.*

When you click Finish, Visual Studio builds the new project (it may take a while, so be patient). In this case, where the project's name is SelectName, it builds a SelectName_bin directory in addition to the usual files. This directory will contain the compiled DLL file. If you left the box checked in the Security Settings page shown in Figure 15-7, Visual Studio grants trusted status to all DLLs in this directory.

The following code shows the project initially created by Visual Studio, but reformatted slightly so it can fit on the page. A few key points deserve special attention.

The code uses the `WithEvents` keyword to declare the variables `ThisDocument` and `ThisApplication`. That allows the program to catch events for those variables.

Subroutine `_Startup` (note the leading underscore) takes two parameters of type `Object` named `application` and `document`. These are references to the Word object model's `Application` and `Document` objects. The subroutine saves these objects into the variables `ThisApplication` and `ThisDocument` so you can catch their events if you like. Because these variables are declared with the detailed `Word.Application` and `Word.Document` data types, they also allow Visual Studio to provide IntelliSense.

The code includes two overloaded versions of the `FindControl` function. The first simply invokes the second to find a control on `ThisDocument`. The second version loops through a `Document` object's `InlineShapes` collection looking for the control. If it doesn't find the control, the code looks through the `Document`'s `Shapes` collection.

Finally, the code defines empty `ThisDocument_Open` and `ThisDocument_Close` event handlers for you to fill in if you like.

```
Imports System.Windows.Forms
Imports Word = Microsoft.Office.Interop.Word

' Office integration attribute. Identifies the startup class for the document. _
' Do not modify.
<Assembly: System.ComponentModel.DescriptionAttribute( _
    "OfficeStartupClass, Version=1.0, Class=SelectName.OfficeCodeBehind")>

Public Class OfficeCodeBehind

    Friend WithEvents ThisDocument As Word.Document
    Friend WithEvents ThisApplication As Word.Application

#Region "Generated initialization code"

    ' Default constructor.
    Public Sub New()
    End Sub
```

```
' Required procedure. Do not modify.
Public Sub _Startup(ByVal application As Object, ByVal document As Object)
    ThisApplication = CType(application, Word.Application)
    ThisDocument = CType(document, Word.Document)

    If (ThisDocument.FormsDesign = True) Then
        ThisDocument.ToggleFormsDesign()
        ThisDocument_Open()
    End If
End Sub


' Required procedure. Do not modify.
Public Sub _Shutdown()
    ThisApplication = Nothing
    ThisDocument = Nothing
End Sub


' Returns the control with the specified name in ThisDocument.
Overloads Function FindControl(ByVal name As String) As Object
    Return FindControl(name, ThisDocument)
End Function


' Returns the control with the specified name in the specified document.
Overloads Function FindControl(ByVal name As String, _
  ByVal document As Word.Document) As Object
    Try
        Dim inlineShape As Word.InlineShape
        For Each inlineShape In document.InlineShapes
            If (inlineShape.Type = _
              Word.WdInlineShapeType.wdInlineShapeOLEControlObject) Then
                Dim oleControl As Object = inlineShape.OLEFormat.Object
                Dim oleControlType As Type = oleControl.GetType()
                Dim oleControlName As String = _
                  CType(oleControlType.InvokeMember("Name", _
                  Reflection.BindingFlags.GetProperty, Nothing, _
                  oleControl, Nothing), String)
                If (String.Compare(oleControlName, name, True, _
                System.Globalization.CultureInfo.InvariantCulture) = 0) Then
                    Return oleControl
                End If
            End If
        Next
```

```
            Dim shape As Word.Shape
            For Each shape In document.Shapes
                If (shape.Type = _
                  Microsoft.Office.Core.MsoShapeType.msoOLEControlObject) Then
                    Dim oleControl As Object = shape.OLEFormat.Object
                    Dim oleControlType As Type = oleControl.GetType()
                    Dim oleControlName As String = _
                      CType(oleControlType.InvokeMember("Name", _
                      Reflection.BindingFlags.GetProperty, Nothing, _
                      oleControl, Nothing), String)
                    If (String.Compare(oleControlName, name, True, _
                    System.Globalization.CultureInfo.InvariantCulture) = 0) Then
                        Return oleControl
                    End If
                End If
            Next

        Catch Ex As Exception
            ' Returns Nothing if the control is not found.
        End Try
        Return Nothing
    End Function
#End Region

    ' Called when the document is opened.
    Private Sub ThisDocument_Open() Handles ThisDocument.Open

    End Sub

    ' Called when the document is closed.
    Private Sub ThisDocument_Close() Handles ThisDocument.Close

    End Sub
End Class
```

Set Additional Security

When it creates the project, Visual Studio modifies your local security settings to
allow the compiled DLL to run (if you left the box checked on the Security Settings
tab in Figure 15-7). That doesn't give the Word document permission to run the
DLL's code.

NOTE *This seems like a rather annoying feature, so it may be changed in the final release of Visual Studio .NET Tools for Office. If so, you need only read this section for more detailed information on the security settings.*

To allow Office documents to run your assemblies, open the Control Panel, open Administrative Tools, and run Microsoft .NET Framework 1.1 Configuration. This opens the application shown in Figure 15-8.

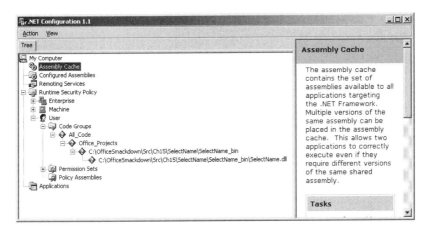

Figure 15-8. Use the .NET Configuration tool to manage assembly security.

NOTE *Depending on which versions of Visual Studio .NET you have had installed, you may have more than one version of the .NET Configuration tool installed. Be sure you select the right version for your current installation.*

Right-click on the Assembly Cache entry and select Add. Select the file msosec.dll and click open. By default, this file should be in C:\Program Files\Microsoft Office\Office11\Addins\msosec.dll.

Now in the .NET Configuration tool, open the path User/Code Groups/All_Code/Office_Projects so you see a display similar to the one in Figure 15-8. Inside that folder, you should see an entry for the project you just created. This entry ends in the name of the directory where Visual Studio will place the DLL. In this example, the directory is named SelectName_bin. This entry indicates that all DLLs inside this directory should be allowed to execute.

Inside that entry is another named after the compiled DLL. In this example, that's SelectName_bin/SelectName.dll. This entry grants full trust to that specific DLL.

To allow Office documents to run the code, right-click the outer entry and select New. Enter a name and description for the new code group in the dialog as shown in Figure 15-9. Then click Next.

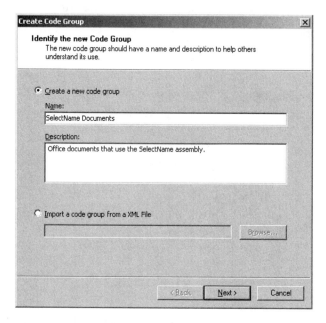

Figure 15-9. Specify the new code group's name and description.

On the next tab, shown in Figure 15-10, scroll the combo box down to the "(custom)" entry. Click Imports and select the file MSOSEC.XML. By default, this file should be in C:\Program Files\Microsoft Office\Office11\Addins\MSOSEC.XML. Click Next.

On the next tab, shown in Figure 15-11, select the "Use existing permission set" option, select the FullTrust permission, and click Next.

On the next tab, click Finish. Now the DLL has permission to run and your Office document has permission to run it. Close the .NET Configuration tool and write some code.

Note that changes to the settings do not necessarily take effect immediately. You must close all instances of Word 2003 before they take effect.

 TIP *For more information on using the .NET Configuration tool, see the help provided with the beta SDK's documentation and samples download mentioned earlier in this chapter.*

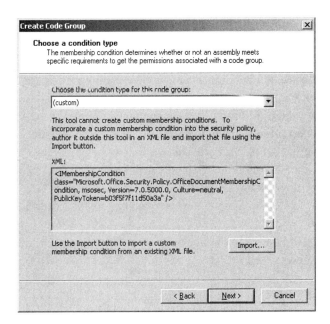

Figure 15-10. Select (custom), click Import, and select the file MSOSEC.XML.

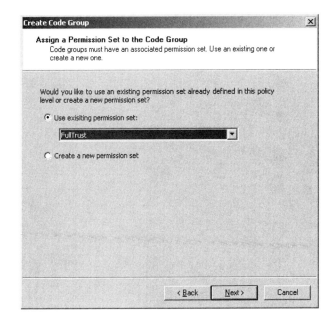

Figure 15-11. Select "Use existing permission set" and FullTrust.

Prepare the Word Document

After all this setup, writing code to manipulate the ThisApplication and ThisDocument objects is relatively straightforward. Earlier chapters in this book show how to use the Word object model to modify the document.

This example displays a combo box named cboNames that lists several names inside the Word document. When you select a name, the DLL inserts the selection in the bookmark named bmName. Before the code can work with the combo box and bookmark, however, you need to add them to the document.

Use Word 2003 to open the document that Visual Studio created for you. Ignore any error messages for now. Select View➤Toolbars and enable the Control Toolbox.

Click the ComboBox tool to add a combo box to the document. Right-click the control and select Properties. Then in the Properties window, change the control's name to cboName.

Below the control, add the following text to the Word document.

```
Dear <NAME>,

Blah, blah, blah.
```

Highlight the text <NAME>, select Insert➤Bookmark, enter the name bmName, and click Add. The result should look like Figure 15-12.

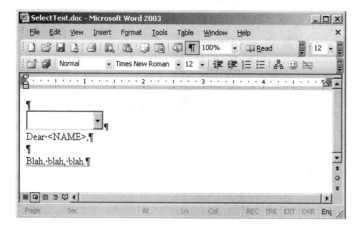

Figure 15-12. This document holds the combo box and bookmark used by the SelectName DLL.

Customize the Code

Now you're ready to write some code. Start by adding the following statement at the top of the file.

```
Imports MSForms = Microsoft.Vbe.Interop.Forms
```

Unfortunately, the project doesn't contain a reference to this namespace by default, so you must add it. Select Project▶Add Reference and click Browse. Select the file FM20.DLL. On my system, it's at C:\WINNT\SYSTEM32\FM20.DLL.

Click OK. For some strange reason, Visual Studio seems to try to add this reference twice, so it displays an error message. Ignore the error, remove the reference you just added from the Add Reference dialog, and close the dialog. Now you should see MSForms listed in the Project Explorer's References section.

Below the declarations of the ThisApplication and ThisDocument variables, add the following code to define a combo box variable.

```
Private WithEvents cboName As MSForms.ComboBox
```

Edit the ThisDocument_Open event handler as shown in the following code. This code finds the Word document's cboName control and saves a reference to it in the variable cboName. It then clears that control's list of items and adds some new ones.

```
' Called when the document is opened.
Private Sub ThisDocument_Open() Handles ThisDocument.Open
    ' Find and initialize the ComboBox.
    cboName = FindControl("cboName")
    cboName.Clear()
    Try
        cboName.AddItem(ThisDocument.BuiltInDocumentProperties("Author").Value)
    Catch ex As Exception
    End Try
    cboName.AddItem("George Bush")
    cboName.AddItem("Annie Lennox")
    cboName.AddItem("Sergio Aragonés")
End Sub
```

Finally, add the following code to the class. Because the cboName variable is declared WithEvents, this event handler executes when the user clicks the combo box. The code finds the document's bookmark named bmName and replaces its text with the user's selection. The code then recreates the bookmark using its new text so the user can change the name again later.

```
' Insert the selected name.
Private Sub cboName_Click() Handles cboName.Click
    ' Find the bmName bookmark.
    Dim bm As Word.Bookmark
    Try
        bm = ThisDocument.Bookmarks("bmName")
    Catch ex As Exception
        MsgBox("Cannot find bookmark bmName")
        Exit Sub
    End Try

    ' Replace the bookmark's text with the selection.
    Dim rng As Word.Range = bm.Range
    rng.Text = cboName.Text

    ' Make the new text the bookmark.
    ThisDocument.Bookmarks.Add("bmName", rng)
End Sub
```

Test the Code

At this point, everything's ready to run in the debugger. When you told Visual Studio to build a Word Document project, it automatically configured the project to use Word as its external program for debugging.

To verify that the program will use Word, go to the Project Explorer, right-click the project name, and select Properties. Open the Configuration Properties item and select Debugging. The "Start external program" option should be selected, and the corresponding text box should contain the path to the Word 2003 executable.

 NOTE *This may seem familiar because it's the same procedure you follow manually when testing a smart tag in Office XP. See the section "Start a New Project" in Chapter 14.*

To debug the project, set break points in the code and select Debug➤Start or press F5. At that point, Visual Studio automatically starts Word. When you open the file SelectName.doc, the `ThisDocument_Open` event handler fires and initializes the combo box. If you select an entry, the `cboName_Click` event handler runs and places your selection in the bmName bookmark.

After you debug the project, you can open the file SelectName.doc directly from Word 2003 without going through Visual Studio.

Ponder the Results

Having built this example project using Visual Basic .NET, it's worth taking a few minutes to think about what it does. This program responds to a Word document's events and uses Word objects to modify the document.

But that's exactly what VBA code does with a lot less effort. Writing VBA code that responds to document events and uses the Word object model to modify a document is relatively straightforward, and you can do it within the IDE provided by Word. It doesn't require a separate development environment (Visual Studio) and a rather cryptic security configuration tool (Microsoft .NET Framework 1.1 Configuration).

On the other hand, Visual Studio .NET Tools for Office has some advantages. It allows you to package code in a compiled DLL, which should generally give you better performance than interpreted VBA code. The system administrator can manage the DLL's security rather than relying on possibly inexperienced Word users to protect themselves against macro viruses. This technique also gives you access to all of Visual Studio .NET's tools, powerful namespaces, and framework. For example, if you want to process XML files or use functions in .NET's crypto-graphic namespaces, it may be easier to use Visual Studio .NET than trying to perform these chores in VBA.

InfoPath

InfoPath, formerly code named XDocs, is a new addition to Office that lets you build fill-in-the-blank style forms. This is nothing you cannot do using a VBA form or even a Word document that contains controls. The big difference is that InfoPath focuses strongly on XML and related technologies such as XSD, XSL, and scripting (JScript and VBScript).

For example, Figure 15-13 shows a very simple name and address entry form. Using InfoPath, I built this form in just a few minutes. The only customizations I made were to change the fields' names from their default names (field1, field2) to something meaningful (txtFirstName, txtLastName), and to make each field required.

After you design a form, you can use InfoPath to run it and fill in the blanks. If you save the results, InfoPath stores the results in a relatively simple XML document. The following code shows the results produced by the form in Figure 15-13. The data begins with the myFields element. That element contains the data in its txtFirstName, txtLastName, and other child elements.

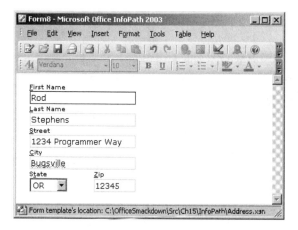

Figure 15-13. InfoPath lets you build fill-in-the-blank style forms.

 FILE *Ch15\InfoPath\AddressOut.xml*

```xml
<?xml version="1.0" encoding="UTF-8"?>
<?mso-infoPathSolution solutionVersion="1.0.0.5"
  productVersion="11.0.5329" PIVersion="1.0.0.0"
  href="file:///C:\OfficeSmackdown\Src\Ch15\InfoPath\Address.xsn" ?>
<?mso-application progid="InfoPath.Document"?>
<my:myFields xmlns:my=
  "http://schemas.microsoft.com/office/infopath/2003/myXSD/2003-08-08T15:13:41"
  xml:lang="en-us">
    <my:txtFirstName>Rod</my:txtFirstName>
    <my:txtLastName>Stephens</my:txtLastName>
    <my:txtStreet>1234 Programmer Way</my:txtStreet>
    <my:txtCity>Bugsville</my:txtCity>
    <my:cboState>OR</my:cboState>
    <my:txtZip>12345</my:txtZip>
</my:myFields>
```

This output is remarkably easy to understand. You could easily build an application to parse this data and add it to a database or Excel worksheet, use it to generate Word documents, and so forth.

TIP *You can use libraries of XML tools to easily read, write, and modify XML files. Visual Studio .NET has XML tools built in. For more information, see a book about XML programming such as my book* Visual Basic .NET and XML *by Rod Stephens and Brian Hochgurtel (Wiley, 2002).*

If you select the File menu's Extract Form Files command, InfoPath saves a series of files that define the form's structure. These files include:

- A template XML file that shows the XML file structure containing no data

- A sample data XML file showing the file's structure with default values you assigned to each field filled in

- A schema file that restricts the values allowed in the form's fields

- An XML "manifest" that describes the files that make up the form's solution

- XSL stylesheet files used to generate the form's different views

- Any VBScript or JScript code you attached to the form

InfoPath lets you use JScript or VBScript to provide code for a form much as you can add VBA to an Office document. Unfortunately, for those of us who use Visual Basic, InfoPath uses JScript by default. You can change the scripting language it uses, but not if the form has any script code. I have yet to figure out how to remove any existing script files from a form once you add them, so if you want to use VBScript you should change the scripting language right away before you write any script code.

To use VBScript, select Tools ➤ Form Options, open the Advanced tab, and select VBScript in the "Form script language" combo box.

To add an event handler to a control, right-click the control and select the Properties option at the bottom of the context menu. On the Data tab, click the Data Validation button. In the Events dropdown, select the event you want to add. For example, a text box supports the events `OnBeforeChange`, `OnValidate`, and

OnAfterChange. After you select an event handler, click the Edit button to open MSE (Microsoft Script Editor).

Initially, InfoPath generates a script file filled with dire warnings and cautions saying InfoPath created the file and that you should not change function names or their parameters. This is good advice, so leave the declarations alone and add the code you need to the event handler's body.

The following example shows how the form Address2 verifies that the value in txtZip looks like a ZIP code. It creates a RegExp object representing a regular expression. It sets the object's Pattern property to "^[0-9]{5}$" so it matches only strings that consist of exactly five digits. It calls the object's Execute method passing it the new value the txtZip field is about to have, and it examines the results. If the new value doesn't match this expression, the code displays a message and indicates failure by setting the event object's ReturnStatus property to False.

 FILE *Ch15\InfoPath\Address2.xsn*

```
Sub msoxd_my_txtZip_OnBeforeChange(eventObj)
    ' Note: eventObj is an object of type DataDOMEvent.
    ' Use a RegExp object to verify that the new value
    ' looks like a ZIP code.
    Dim reg_exp, matches
    Set reg_exp = New RegExp
    reg_exp.Pattern = "^[0-9]{5}$"
    Set matches = reg_exp.Execute(eventObj.NewValue)
    If matches.Count < 1 Then
        eventObj.ReturnMessage = "Invalid Zip code format"
        eventObj.ReturnStatus = False
    End If
End Sub
```

InfoPath is a lightweight application intended to let you quickly and easily generate forms that produce XML output that you can integrate easily into other applications. It is strongly based on XML and related technologies such as XSD, XSL, and the Web scripting languages VBScript and JScript. If you want to build a simple form to produce XML results, you may find InfoPath helpful.

On the other hand, VBScript is more cumbersome than VBA, Visual Basic, or other programming languages. Because it provides only one variable type, Variant, the MSE cannot provide IntelliSense. MSE also seems somewhat stark after using the VBA development environment provided by other Office applications.

If you want IntelliSense and the more familiar VBA or Visual Basic programming environment and you don't need XML output, you may want to stick with VBA and Visual Basic.

Web Services Support

A Web Service is basically a server that responds to remote function calls. A client application sends the service a request, and the service returns a response. The service can perform such tasks as looking up data in its local database, providing access to special purpose hardware, calculating the result of a function, providing price quotes, or storing bug reports in a database. The request and response sent between a client and a Web service are written in XML and packaged using SOAP (Simple Object Access Protocol).

You can use the Office XP Web Services Toolkit 2.0 to add Web Services to your Office XP applications. Office 2003 will provide integrated support for Web Services as an add-on. After it is installed, you can open the IDE's Tools menu, click Web Service References, and provide information identifying the Web Service. Then you can write code to interact with the service. For more information on using this add-on, see the online help. For information about Web Services, see a book on Web Services or XML.

NOTE *Currently you can download Office XP Web Services Toolkit 2.0 at* http://www.microsoft.com/downloads/ details.aspx?FamilyId=4922060F-002A-4F5B-AF74-978F2CD6C798.

Smart Documents

A smart document is a document that works with Word 2003 or Excel 2003. The document contains embedded XML tags that give the application some idea of what the user needs to do in different parts of the document. The document can control the Word or Excel task panes to provide context-sensitive help, links to relevant information, or controls such as combo boxes and text boxes to help the user enter appropriate information.

Programmatically, a smart document is similar to a smart tag. You build a DLL containing a class that implements the ISmartDocument interface. The methods provided by this interface let the application ask the class about its properties and tell the class when to perform its specialized actions.

Building a smart document is a bit more complicated than building a smart tag, however. The ISmartDocument interface requires you to implement more methods, although some can be empty depending on what you want the document to do.

Installing a smart document is also a bit more complicated than installing a smart tag. To install a smart document, you build an expansion pack. The expansion pack includes a manifest written in XML that describes the locations and purposes of the files that make up the expansion pack. It includes such items as the solution's type (smart document), the smart document's name, the DLL file's name, and CLSID values identifying the solution and class in the Registry.

A smart document provides access to the task pane and is sensitive to the user's position in the document. You can implement most of its other capabilities more easily using controls embedded in the document and VBA code.

Summary

Word's and Excel's new XML tools let your code easily create and manipulate XML data embedded in Word documents and Excel worksheets. The new classes and methods are fairly straightforward, so your main challenge in using them may be to become familiar with the structure and capabilities of XML files.

Office 2003 includes smart tag enhancements that make building smart tags a little easier. The Recognize2 method provides a TokenList parameter that breaks text into tokens for easier processing, and the VerbCaptionFromID2 method allows cascading smart tag menus, a nice feature.

Visual Studio .NET Tools for Office helps you integrate code written in Visual Studio .NET into an Office application. It seems likely that Office will support Visual Studio .NET in addition to or in place of VBA in some future release. When that happens, integration with externally compiled Visual Studio .NET code should become easier. Until then, the Visual Studio .NET Tools for Office SDK makes this kind of integration possible.

One of the new members of the Office suite, InfoPath, makes building fill-in-the-blank style forms relatively painless. It's a bit of an oddball in the Office family because it uses JScript or VBScript as a scripting language rather than VBA. It still may be useful if you want to use forms to generate XML data.

The last topic discussed in this chapter, smart documents, shows promise. A smart document lets an externally compiled DLL provide context-sensitive support for Word or Excel users. Building a smart document is rather difficult (harder than building a smart tag, for example), but this should become easier in future Office releases.

Until then, you can always stick with embedded controls, toolbar and menu items, and VBA code. These aren't as reactive to the user's position within a document, but they are intuitive, easy to build, and easy to use.

Index

forums.apress.com

JOIN THE APRESS FORUMS AND BE PART OF OUR COMMUNITY. You'll find discussions that cover topics of interest to IT professionals, programmers, and enthusiasts just like you. If you post a query to one of our forums, you can expect that some of the best minds in the business—especially Apress authors, who all write with *The Expert's Voice*™—will chime in to help you. Why not aim to become one of our most valuable participants (MVPs) and win cool stuff? Here's a sampling of what you'll find:

DATABASES
Data drives everything.

Share information, exchange ideas, and discuss any database programming or administration issues.

PROGRAMMING/BUSINESS
Unfortunately, it is.

Talk about the Apress line of books that cover software methodology, best practices, and how programmers interact with the "suits."

INTERNET TECHNOLOGIES AND NETWORKING
Try living without plumbing (and eventually IPv6).

Talk about networking topics including protocols, design, administration, wireless, wired, storage, backup, certifications, trends, and new technologies.

WEB DEVELOPMENT/DESIGN
Ugly doesn't cut it anymore, and CGI is absurd.

Help is in sight for your site. Find design solutions for your projects and get ideas for building an interactive Web site.

JAVA
We've come a long way from the old Oak tree.

Hang out and discuss Java in whatever flavor you choose: J2SE, J2EE, J2ME, Jakarta, and so on.

SECURITY
Lots of bad guys out there—the good guys need help.

Discuss computer and network security issues here. Just don't let anyone else know the answers!

MAC OS X
All about the Zen of OS X.

OS X is both the present and the future for Mac apps. Make suggestions, offer up ideas, or boast about your new hardware.

TECHNOLOGY IN ACTION
Cool things. Fun things.

It's after hours. It's time to play. Whether you're into LEGO® MINDSTORMS™ or turning an old PC into a DVR, this is where technology turns into fun.

OPEN SOURCE
Source code is good; understanding (open) source is better.

Discuss open source technologies and related topics such as PHP, MySQL, Linux, Perl, Apache, Python, and more.

WINDOWS
No defenestration here.

Ask questions about all aspects of Windows programming, get help on Microsoft technologies covered in Apress books, or provide feedback on any Apress Windows book.

HOW TO PARTICIPATE:
Go to the Apress Forums site at **http://forums.apress.com/**.
Click the New User link.